BRIEF CONTENTS

CONTENTS

PREFACE

The purpose of this book is to introduce the substantive fundamental issues of cognitive psychology. It is written with the conviction that students can be introduced to cognitive psychology so that its fundamental principles are revealed in bold relief. We want to portray cognitive psychology as an exciting, problem-solving enterprise that will engage and stimulate students. To accomplish these objectives, we have chosen to discuss basic conceptual issues in detail, believing that the reporting of data makes little sense unless the problems and issues are clear. We think this approach is very important in introductory cognitive psychology where, in many cases, the conceptual issues tend to be very abstract. Empirical work, however, is thoroughly covered. Our approach is to discuss selected experiments in depth and their implications for the conceptual issues rather than attempt an exhaustive survey of the empirical literature. Again, we have found this approach to be effective when introducing students to cognitive psychology. Detailed discussion of selected experiments allows students to appreciate the intricacies of problem-solving activity in cognitive psychology. We also think students can more readily grasp the relationship between theory and data if given extensive discussion of a few experiments rather than if overwhelmed with a large amount of data. Following such an introduction, students should have a firm foundation on which to build additional knowledge and understanding in advanced courses.

The book is also written with the belief that the principles of cognitive psychology should be introduced in such a way that students see their direct pertinence to and potential impact upon human affairs. Illustrations and practical applications are liberally provided, with the hope that students will gain a fuller and richer understanding of the principles as they relate them to their personal experiences. These illustrations cannot, of course, perfectly reflect principles derived from laboratory settings, but they can approximate them, and thus, we hope, lead students to think of other illustrations as well as of potential exceptions.

This book is aimed principally at the undergraduate who is taking a basic course in cognitive psychology, in memory and cognition, or in human memory. It would also be appropriate as a text in an introductory graduate course when the students lack a background in cognitive psychology or memory. Supplementary readings can be assigned by instructors who want more detail on specific topics. The book is written so that certain chapters can be omitted without disrupting the flow of topics. In this sense, the chapters can "stand alone"; however, interconnections among the chapters are made but can be understood by the prevailing context in each chapter. Finally, the text is written for the typical one-semester or one-quarter course.

This book can be used flexibly by instructors who wish to use certain portions of it and not others. For example, if an instructor teaches a comprehensive survey of Cognitive Psychology, all chapters would be appropriate. In contrast other combinations are possible. Here are a few of the possibilities:

	Chapters
Comprehensive cognitive survey	1–13
Memory survey	1, 3–8
Basic cognition	1–9

NEW TO THIS EDITION

- The chapter on Forgetting and False Memory provides up-to-date coverage of research on false memory.

- The chapter on Implicit Memory covers major theories of test dissociation and recent research from these theories

- The chapter on Meta-Cognition addresses theory and research on monitoring and control of cognitive processes.

- The coverage of cognitive neuroscience of perception, attention, memory, and knowledge is expanded.

- Each chapter has been thoroughly revised to provide updated research.

FEATURES RETAINED FROM THE LAST EDITION

Most chapters begin with a familiar story, example, or illustration that helps students think about their mental processes. These introductions are designed to help students understand new concepts and add interest to the material. Each chapter is prefaced with an outline that the student can use as an advance organizer to assist the student in better understanding the material. Each chapter also ends with a summary that highlights the chapter's main feature. Thought questions are placed at the end of each to be used by the student. A handy glossary also is included along with an extensive bibliography.

TEACHING PACKAGE

Instructor's Manual with Test Bank on CD–ROM has been prepared by Dr. Susan McDonald. The *Instructor's Manual* contains key terms, demonstrations, ideas for student research projects, handouts, and sources of additional reading for each chapter. The Test Bank section contains multiple-choice, true-false, and essay questions for each chapter.

ACKNOWLEDGEMENTS

We are grateful to the many people who contributed to the preparation of the 7th edition of the *Fundamentals of Cognitive Psychology*. We especially thank Jeffrey Toth who wrote the neuroscience sections for the book, John Dunlosky who wrote Chapter 8 on metacognition, and to Katherine Rawson who extensively revised Chapter 11 on language comprehension.

   We also wish to thank the reviewers for this edition, whose suggestions provided invaluable guidance for revising the text:

Jeanette Altarriba, State University of New York at Albany
Scott W. Brown, University of Southern Maine
Joshua D. Landau, York College of Pennsylvania
James R. Prather, University of Louisville
Marilyn L. Turner, Wichita State University
W. Richard Walker, Winston-Salem State University

   Continuing appreciation extends to the people who provided comments on previous editions. Many of their suggestions are retained in the new edition of the book:

Paul Amrhein, *University of New Mexico*
Janet Andrews, *Vassar College*
Bernard Barrs, *SUNY, Stony Brook*
Brian Babbitt, *Missouri Southern College*
Charles Brewer, *Furman University*
Bruce Britton, *University of Georgia*
Fergus Craik, *University of Toronto*
Robert Crowder, *Yale University*
Terry Daniel, *University of Arizona*
Harold Delaney, *University of New Mexico*

Gilles Einstein, *Furman University*
Paul Foos, *Florida International University*
Danalee Goldthwaite, *Cariboo College*
William Gordon, *Wake Forest University*
David Gorfein, *University of Texas, Arlington*
Paula Hertel, *Trinity University*
David Horton, *University of Maryland*
Marcia Johnson, *Yale University*
Peder Johnson, *University of New Mexico*
William Johnston, *University of Utah*
Stanley Klein, *University of California, Santa Barbara*
Joseph LaVoie, *University of Nebraska*
Leah Light, *Pitzer College*
Frank Logan, *University of New Mexico*
Ruth Maki, *Texas Tech University*
David Mitchell, *Loyola University*
John Mueller, *University of Calgary*
Douglas Nelson, *University of South Florida*
Jean Newman, *University of New Mexico*
Marcia Ozier, *Dalhousie University*
Frederick Parente, *Towson University*
James Pate, *Georgia State University*
Stan Parkinson, *Arizona State University*
Roddy Roediger, *Washington University*
Michael Scavio, *California State University, Fullerton*
Steven Schmidt, *Middle Tennessee State University*
Pennie Seibert, *Boise State University*
Ronald Shaffer, *Western Washington University*
Rebekah E. Smith, *University of North Carolina at Chapel Hill*
Blair Stone, *University of Utah*
Sherman Tyler, *University of Pittsburgh,*
Eugene Winograd, *Emory University*

The people at McGraw-Hill provided superb support and assistance throughout this project. We were fortunate in having the support and cooperation of a first-rate staff who were also encouraging and enthusiastic. We especially thank Ken King, our publisher, who did everything possible to make our association with McGraw-Hill an enjoyable experience and provided valuable advice on the structure of this edition. We also thank Dawn Gernhardt and Jane Acheson whose editorial assistance greatly facilitated completion of the manuscript. Roger Geissler, the Project Manager, oversaw the complex job of getting the book through production and handled all of the numerous details that arose in this job.

1

INTRODUCTION TO COGNITIVE PSYCHOLOGY

What is cognitive psychology? In part, this is a question we hope to answer throughout the book, but a preliminary discussion of the question will be helpful in gaining a perspective on what you are about to read. Perhaps the most direct answer to the question is that cognitive psychology is the study of mental processes such as perceiving, remembering, and reasoning. Several questions are begged by this answer. We shall answer some of these questions in this chapter.

Why do psychologists study mental processes? Since the beginning of recorded history, people have expressed curiosity about the operation of the mind, largely because they believed that behavior, particularly voluntary action, is the result of mental processes. For example, how are we to understand the very behavior in which you are engaged at this moment, reading this book? At one level, we are interested in explaining your ability to comprehend what you are reading, and in so doing, we are likely to appeal to processes of perception of words and computation of meaning. At another level, we might explain your motivation for reading in terms of your goal to complete this course, which in turn is motivated by your goal of obtaining a college degree in order to follow some plan that you have for a career. The point is that your behavior of reading this book is determined in part by your intent to meet some goal and fulfill some plan. Intentionality, goals, and plans are mental phenomena that affect behavior. Further, the specific behavior, in this case, reading, is understood by appeal to the specific mental processes involved in perception and comprehension of text. In short, the study of mental processes is important because these processes are responsible for much of the behavior we find interesting.

Your appreciation for cognitive psychology can be increased by consideration of a few examples of everyday experiences that are also of theoretical interest to cognitive psychologists. *How many times have you carefully proofread written work, only to be embarrassed later by an obvious error you overlooked?* Many times what we see is determined as much by the context in which it occurs as by what is actually there, an issue of pattern recognition described in chapter 2. *Have you noticed the difficulty of simultaneously taking notes in class and understanding a lecture?* You will find several explanations for this difficulty in the discussion of attention in chapter 3. *When you dial Directory Assistance for a telephone number and do not have a pencil to record the number, why do you have to repeat the number until you have dialed it? And why do you have to repeat your call to Directory Assistance if someone talks to you before you dial the number?* These are problems associated with short-term memory and will be discussed in chapter 4. *You may have heard a television commercial for aspirin claim, "You cannot buy a more effective pain reliever than our brand." Later you remember that this brand is the most effective pain reliever you can buy. Your memory of what was claimed is actually quite different from the assertion made by the commercial.* Your comprehension of what you hear involves going beyond what is actually said and includes processes such as inferences about the statement. Inferences are often remembered as having been a part of what really occurred. We shall talk about these matters in chapter 7 on memory distortions and in chapter 11 on comprehension. *Do you remember the experience of working on a problem or a puzzle that you were unable to solve, but, after taking a break from the problem, you subsequently obtained a solution?* This phenomenon, known as incubation effect, along with other commonly experienced aspects of problem solving will be described in chapter 12. These are just a few of the many examples of everyday experiences which are discussed throughout this book and which are addressed by the experiments and theory of cognitive psychology.

Two points about these examples should be considered as we attempt to gain an overview of cognitive psychology. First, all represent instances of difficulty or failure of mental processes. Interestingly, we tend to treat our mental functions or processes the same way we treat our car: we rarely think of them unless they fail to work. Failures of mental processes are immediately noticed because they can be frustrating, embarrassing, and sometimes even dangerous and, consequently, such failures become useful tools for the psychological analysis of mental phenomena. You should be alerted, however, to the fact that most of the analysis focuses upon the successful operation of the mental processes. Although we tend to appreciate the successes less than we notice a failure, the adaptive success of the human intellectual machinery far exceeds its failure.

The second point is that cognitive psychology is interested in what is generally called mental phenomena. In this sense, the examples just discussed are consistent with the dictionary definition of cognitive psychology: "the scientific study of the mind." While it is hoped that the examples help clarify the definition, questions undoubtedly remain concerning how one goes about this "scientific study of mind." To address these questions, we provide a brief discussion of the scientific method, followed by an extensive description of the important historical events leading up to modern cognitive psychology. We believe that the historical developments offer the best explanation of why cognitive psychologists do the things that will be described in this book.

THE SCIENTIFIC METHOD

All of psychology, including cognitive, is defined by the use of the scientific method. The scientific method is first and foremost a powerful way to acquire knowledge about the causes of certain kinds of phenomena. The process begins with some idea about the potential cause or causes of the phenomenon. This idea will have implications for what will happen to the phenomenon under various circumstances. The next step is to observe the phenomenon in these circumstances to see if the idea correctly predicts the behavior of the phenomenon. Finally, the observations are compared to the original predictions to see if the idea

TABLE 1.1
THE SCIENTIFIC METHOD

1. Begin with idea (theory) about cause of some phenomenon:
   a. Derive prediction from theory
   b. Prediction is specification by theory that some particular circumstance will produce some particular behavior
2. Perform controlled observation (usually an experiment) testing prediction:
   a. Manipulate circumstance in accord with theory's prediction (independent variable)
   b. Observe effect on predicted behavior (dependent variable)
3. Compare observed behavior to predicted behavior
4. Draw conclusion about validity of theory

was correct. The component steps of the scientific method are outlined in table 1.1 and can be illustrated by the example that follows.

Suppose the question is why do people sometimes have trouble remembering the names of people to whom they have just been introduced. One idea, or *theory,* about this question is that information in short-term memory does not last long if it is not used. This theory predicts that you will have trouble remembering recent information if you are prevented from rehearsing it. You could then set up circumstances, an *experiment,* that allows you to see if this is in fact true. You could expose people to a small amount of new material—for example, three unfamiliar names—and tell some of the people to repeat the names until you tell them to stop. Other people would hear the names and then do something—for example, work on math problems that prevents them from thinking about the names. After a brief period of either repeating the names or working on the math problems, you ask everyone to tell you the names. The theory specifies that the group repeating the names should remember more than the group required to do math problems. If this does not happen, we know the theory is wrong.

Several important aspects of the scientific method need to be noted. First, the method can only be applied to questions that have observable answers. Some questions, like how many angels fit on the head of a pin, do not have potentially observable answers because we cannot observe angels. Second, the observations that are made and the circumstances under which they are made are dictated by the theory. This is a useful point for you to remember as you study this book. We shall describe lots of experiments, but the only reason to do an experiment is to see if the more general idea or theory is correct. Therefore, one thing you should do as you read about experiments is to ask yourself why the experiment was done. If you can answer that question, you can be sure that you understand the more important thing, the theory. You should also always ask yourself what the results of an experiment mean. Again, if you can answer that question you understand the important matter of the relationship between the experiment and the theory.

Finally, most of the observations we describe in the book will be in the form of an experiment. The scientific method does not require the use of experiments; other forms of systematic observation can serve the purpose of testing the theory. But experiments are extremely useful means to obtain such observations because they are controlled observations. In an experiment, something is intentionally manipulated to observe its effect on behavior. In the example given earlier, the experiment manipulated whether or not the rehearsal of the names was allowed, and the behavior observed was memory for the names. The thing that is manipulated is referred to as the *independent variable,* and the behavior observed is the *dependent variable.* A controlled experiment attempts to hold constant other variables that might affect the dependent variable. In the previous example, the age of the participants could make a big difference, and unless one were asking questions about age effects, one would want the participants to all be roughly the same age. By controlling these other potential influences on the dependent variable, one can determine if the independent variable chosen for manipulation causes an effect on the dependent variable.

The scientific method is the tool used by the cognitive psychologist to study the mind. The remaining question concerns the material to which the tool is applied. Psychology is a curious and sometimes frustrating discipline because there have been disagreements about what exactly psychology studies. The best way to understand the subject matter studied by cognitive psychology is to examine the history of psychology.

A BRIEF HISTORY OF COGNITIVE PSYCHOLOGY

Psychology began as a scientific study of human knowledge and experience. The problem of what knowledge is has intrigued philosophers for centuries. One aspect of the problem of knowledge had direct bearing on the birth of psychology, and that is the relationship between the world of physical objects and your mental experiences. Here is one example. As strange as it may seem, the certainty of your sensory "knowledge" is not at all clear. For example, can you be sure that the book you are reading is really there? What a stupid question, you may think, but consider the problem. The only way you know the book is there is through your mental experiences; you may see it; you may feel it; you may even smell or taste it; you may hear someone else tell you that it is there. Regardless, in all cases it is not the book itself you know but, rather, the mental experiences. Lest you think the problem has nothing to do with the real world of psychology, consider the case of hallucinations or the more common instances of perceptual illusions as examples of dissociations between what we know through our mental experiences and what is objectively true. Sometimes what we know to be there is, in fact, not there. So again we ask you, how do you know the book is really there?

You believe the book is really there because you assume that your mental experiences are related to physical energy corresponding to objects in the environment. For example, you assume that the information you have about the book arises from the reaction of your receptors to the physical energy from the environment. The receptors then begin a process of neural transmission to the brain, where the interpretation of the physical energy culminates. But brain activity is not exactly the same thing as perception. Perception has qualitative characteristics such as color, loudness, and pain. Brain activity is electrical and biochemical; brain activity has no quality of sound or feeling in and of itself. If it were possible for you to watch a brain function in a vat, you would not see any color exuding from the brain, hear any sound of activity, or observe anything that you could interpret as a feeling of pain or anything else. You would simply see the brain. The point is that, while we might all agree that the brain is essential to our mental life, it remains the case that what you and I really are aware of is our own psychological experience, not our brain activity. We raise this point simply to keep ourselves honest about the problem of knowledge; the most difficult issue facing modern science is the old question of the relation between psychological experiences and physical processes corresponding to environmental energy and processes of the central nervous system. Nonetheless, you can be certain that cognitive psychologists believe that psychological processes are related both to physical energy from the environment and to the central nervous system, and we hope you now see why it is important to examine history for the origins of this belief. The origins lie partially in the first research programs that were conducted.

Psychophysics

As peculiar as it may seem to you, people have not always assumed that our mental experience, especially perception, is directly related to physical energy in the environment. Because much of what psychology does involves studying the effects of environmental events on our thought and behavior, psychology as you know it could not begin to develop until people accepted the belief that physical energy from the environment affects our mental experience. Some of the first research in psychology was designed to establish this simple but fundamental fact. When this research began in the middle nineteenth century, the goal was to determine if some regular and measurable relationship existed between mental experience and physical energy from the environment. Experiments were performed in which participants were asked to make judgments about the level of physical energy present, and these judgments were taken as the measure of mental experience. In this simple but elegant way, a correlation could be established between physical energy and psychological processes.

As an example of the psychophysical method, consider the research of Ernst Weber from the mid-1800s. Weber asked the subject to lift two objects and judge their relative weight. Weber discovered that the amount by which the two weights needed to differ in order for a subject to notice that they were different depended on how heavy the weights were. If one of the weights was relatively light, say an ounce, the other weight needed to be 1.3 ounces to notice the difference. If the first weight was 10 pounds, then the second weight needed to be 13 pounds to notice the difference. In general, Weber reported that the amount of physical energy necessary to produce a change in sensation is proportional to the original level of physical energy. This observation is very much a part of your common experience. If the music is very loud, you must shout to be heard over it, whereas, if the music were to cease suddenly, you would have to modulate your volume to avoid being silly or rude.

The significance of Weber's work was realized by Gustav Fechner in 1850. Fechner developed a mathematical theory of the relationship between physical energy and sensation that was based on Weber's observation. This theory specified that physical energy and psychological experience of that energy are related by a logarithmic function; very simply, as the intensity of the physical stimulus increases geometrically, the psychological experience changes arithmetically. The details of this formulation need not detain us here, *but the important historical point for cognitive psychology is that the mind now appeared open to science. Changes in mental experience were measurable; the level of mental reaction appeared to be quantitatively related to the level of physical energy, opening the door for manipulation of stimulus variables with the full expectation that these variables do affect the psychological experience.*

Consciousness and Qualities of the Mind

With the possibility of scientific study of the mind established, the emerging discipline quickly advanced to concerns about qualities of mental experience. Psychophysics focused on the quantitative relationship between physical energy and sensation; in other words, how much energy was necessary to change the intensity of the perception. The further challenge was to describe the *qualities* of the perception, to develop a theory of perception that renders colors, smell, and sounds different and distinct. Leading the way was Wilhelm Wundt, who established the first research laboratory in psychology in 1879 at the University of Leipzig.

You may have encountered descriptions of Wundt's theory, suggesting that the mind has elementary structures and each perception is a composite of these elementary structural parts. This approach came to be known as *structuralism,* and, although many historians attribute structuralism primarily to Wundt, we now know that it was Wundt's student, Titchener, who really was the primary advocate of structuralism (Blumenthal, 1975; Danziger, 1979). Furthermore, Wundt is usually portrayed as the person who pioneered the use of *analytic introspection.* Introspection is a technique by which experimental subjects are asked to analyze their current perception into its elementary parts. This technique became very controversial because of its subjectivity and the difficulty of replicating introspective data. Later, the behaviorists would use introspection as the major villain in overthrowing the structuralists' approach to psychology. Again, however, it was less Wundt than Titchener who relied on introspective analysis. Wundt's laboratory used a variety of methods and Wundt's theory was far richer than is sometimes suggested. One facet of that theory deserves our attention because Wundt advocated a position that sounds peculiar to most cognitive psychologists, yet it is easily accepted by most laypeople. The issue had to do with whether the mind is analogous to a machine.

Although you may not think of the mind as anything like a machine, psychologists have always used the analogy to describe how the mind works. The reason, which will be elaborated in the next section on mechanism, is machines are predictable. All machines are constructed of parts and each part serves a particular function, which may be to initiate the action of another part. The machine is set in motion by an external source such as dropping money in a slot or turning on the electricity, and the end result is that the machine accomplishes its designated function, whether it is to dispense a drink or to compute the most direct route to Wichita. To draw an analogy between the mind and a machine is to assume that mental processes begin with external input from the environment, which will predictably cause certain ensuing operations. With this analogy, the job of the psychologist is to discover the various parts of the processing. The reason a machine's behavior is so predictable, if it is not broken, is machines do not have plans, intentions, or emotions. We don't want machines to decide whether they will do what we ask. Wundt did not believe the mind was at all like a machine, and consequently his theory, which reflected that belief, became controversial.

The controversy can be illustrated through one of the simple experiments from Wundt's lab. The subjects were asked to listen to a metronome set at one beat per second and to pay close attention to what they heard. On the face of it, the task appears trivial, but the results contained a subtle phenomenon that is hard to explain. Even though each beat of a metronome is identical in its physical properties, people do not consciously experience a series of identical beats. Rhythm is added. The most common experience is to hear something like the tic-toc of a clock. The rhythm is an example of what we mean by a qualitative experience as opposed to a quantitative index such as loudness. Where does this rhythm come from?

Obviously, we won't find any rhythm in the environmental energy of the metronome. Perhaps the sensory nerves or even the brain somehow add the rhythm, but, to this day, no satisfactory answer has been found in neurophysiology. Thus, we have a real psychological event to be explained, but the explanation is not found in the environmental energy or in any known working of the nervous system. Wundt's own theory appealed to psychological processes that essentially created the conscious experience. He suggested that psychological processes operate on environmental input to produce the conscious experience, but the psychological reaction cannot be predicted by the environmental input because the input does not cause the processes. The processes are what cause mental experience.

For Wundt, cognitive processes were active and creative, an idea embodied in his principle of *creative synthesis*. Essentially, the idea is that mental operations produce products that are not just the sum of separate elements. Rather, the conscious mental products emerge from the psychological processes. These processes involve such things as momentary intentions, attention, even memory. In short, the psychological processes cause the conscious experience and, consequently, these processes must be studied in their own right. The controversial aspect of this theory is that one cannot predict the outcome in advance, even for simple experiences such as the rhythm of the metronome and certainly not complex experiences such as the decision about whom to marry, based on the environmental input or the nervous system.

Consider this example from Viney (1993) that illustrates how the problem goes far beyond the simple metronome experiment and into the important realm of decision making and choice. Suppose you and I encounter an ice cream vendor on the street, and you know that I like ice cream and that I like vanilla and chocolate equally well. I must make a decision about which to order. I decide that I want chocolate. What made this conscious experience of wanting chocolate come to mind? Perhaps it was the smell of the chocolate combined with the realization that I had not had chocolate for a while combined with just having seen a discarded vanilla cone. The question is, could my decision to order chocolate have been predicted? Certainly not from the individual facts just mentioned. Knowing that I had not had chocolate for a while does not predict that I want it now. A discarded cone of vanilla might remind me that vanilla is good or it might be disgusting and steer me away from vanilla. Wundt's position was that psychological experience is created out of a multitude of sensations, memories, and intentions, none of which could individually predict the experience. Explanation of conscious experience had to occur after the experience and would be based on factors that might be unknown until the experience actually occurred.

Shortly after Wundt, a great American psychologist, William James, made a similar argument in the context of attention. James used the concept of attention much the same as it is used today, as the process of selecting events that rise to consciousness. The most fundamental question about attention is what controls the selection process. What determines in a predictable way the contents of your conscious thought? James argued that we could not know the answer to this question and, thus, like Wundt, denied the possibility of predicting conscious experience in the manner prescribed by physical science. For both James and Wundt, intentionality and volition were crucial elements of cognition and, as such, should be given serious roles in cognitive theory.

Mechanism

These ideas of Wundt and James are completely foreign to modern cognitive psychology, and it is very important to understand why. Wundt's view of creative synthesis and James' idea about attention ran counter to a widely held view of science known as *mechanism*. Understanding mechanism is important because it will allow you to appreciate why contemporary cognitive psychologists, almost all of whom are mechanists, are so enamored with computers and brains. It is also important to realize that along with other social and biological sciences as well as the humanities, part of the job of psychology is to describe human nature. What does it mean to be human? The implication of mechanism is that humans are fundamentally machinelike.

BOX 1.1

FREUD, THE COGNITIVE PSYCHOLOGIST

At the same time Wundt was at work in Leipzig, Germany, another massive event, the formulation of Freudian theory, was in progress in Vienna. Sigmund Freud is among the intellectual giants of modern times, and his legacy is the founding of a discipline known as psychoanalysis. Freud's theory is rich with implications for a variety of areas in psychology, including cognitive psychology. The most well-known and far-reaching idea in the theory is that much of behavior is controlled by the unconscious influence of prior experience. You will see in later chapters that this idea is the basis for much research in cognitive psychology. The details of the more recent work on unconscious influences are very different from those contained in Freud's theory, particularly the question of repression. Freud proposed repression as an active psychological process that drives threatening thoughts and perceptions into the unconscious, where they are inaccessible to the individual's conscious memory. Repression has become the focus of the current controversy over *false memory syndrome,* a topic to which we shall return in chapter 7. The controversy about repression aside, you will see in later chapters that the idea of conscious versus unconscious influences of our prior experience is central to research ranging from attention to memory to categorization and problem solving.

You also will see the impact of Freud's theory on the techniques that are currently used in many experiments in cognitive psychology. If unconscious influences on behavior are inaccessible to the individual, how can we, as researchers or therapists, gain access to those influences? In Freud's case, this need drove the development of therapeutic techniques such as dream analysis and projective tests. The idea was that the contents of dreams or of a patient's responses to an association test contain information about the unconscious contents. The therapist interpreted these responses in search of the unconscious material, and, once the therapist believed he knew what the unconscious thoughts were, the patient was confronted with them and had to consciously resolve the conflict caused by those thoughts. Thus, memory testing is central to psychoanalytic therapy. Again, you will see in later chapters that contemporary research techniques differ in some detail from Freud's therapeutic technique, but they share the Freudian logic of eliciting prior experiences from a person without requesting intentional memory of that experience.

Indeed, Freud's ideas are sufficiently rich for cognitive psychology that they have been directly compared to the concepts of more recent theory. The interested student is referred to Matthew Erdelyi's fascinating book, *Psychoanalysis: Freud's Cognitive Psychology* (1985), to learn more about the relationship between psychoanalytic theory and current cognitive theory.

Mechanism is a *type of explanation* that has its origins in physics and, as the result of the work in psychophysics in the nineteenth century, had gained credibility as a way to explain the mind. Mechanistic explanations describe parts working together in an automatic, machinelike fashion to produce the phenomenon to be explained. For example, a car can be explained by describing its parts, how each works, and the effect of one operation on another, such as depression of the accelerator opens a throttle that allows more gas to flow.

A successful mechanical explanation is one that allows prediction before the fact. In psychology, such prediction requires a theory that specifies what effect the environmental input will have on theoretical processes that produce the phenomenon to be explained. The mechanical explanation specifies the initiating causal event and then each succeeding part of the mechanism. The prevailing mechanistic view of the mind at Wundt's time was one in which the sensory nerves were activated by environmental energy, and this activity reached the brain where it could, through the process of association, activate a representation, or memory, of a previous experience. The activated representation corresponds to the conscious experience. The mind, in this view, becomes as automatic as a vending machine into which a coin is dropped, a switch is activated, and a product is released.

Neither Wundt's nor James' ideas conformed to this view. They believed that certain psychological processes cannot be approached with this methodology. For example, because the rhythm we hear when listening to a metronome cannot be found in the metronome itself, nor so far has it been found in the physical energy produced by the metronome nor, so far, has it been found in the nervous system, the general mechanistic theory of the mind had no explanation for Wundt's simple demonstration. Nonetheless, mechanism had become so thoroughly equated with science itself that Wundt and James lost the battle. Indeed, because prediction is not possible, the ideas and approach favored by Wundt and James are even taken to be unscientific by some people. Modest reflection will convince you this is not true.

For example, evolutionary theory is usually considered scientifically respectable, but prediction of future events is inherently impossible except in the most general sense by evolutionary theory. The theory suggests that the origin of variability among individuals is random and that the environment selects among individuals. Environmental change is also largely random with respect to options among which selection occurs. Thus, to predict the adaptive value of a specific characteristic is not possible, but the theory is invaluable in explaining that success after the fact. The theory of natural selection is an example of a developmental explanation. In this case, the phenomenon of interest is explained by describing events that occurred in the past. Thus, science does use explanations other than mechanism.

The nonmechanistic theory proposed by Wundt was not unscientific, but its defeat at the turn of the twentieth century had a profound impact on the way cognitive psychology is studied at the beginning of the twenty-first century. You will see that contemporary cognitive psychology is thoroughly mechanistic, although the machine is assumed to be more complicated than a vending device.

The Origin of Memory Research

At the same time that Wundt and James were at work, Hermann Ebbinghaus published the first book describing experimental research on memory. The year was 1885 and we can mark the beginning of memory research at that time. Ebbinghaus' experiments were brutal; for example, in one experiment the subject was required to learn 420 lists of 16 nonsense syllables each (Slamecka, 1985). Learning consisted of successful recitation by heart of the 16 syllables of each of the 420 lists, and the learning phase alone required 14,280 trials in this experiment! Humanely enough, Ebbinghaus himself was the only subject.

Unlike Wundt and James, Ebbinghaus was squarely in the mechanistic tradition of physical science. The concept of association, which Ebbinghaus used to explain memory, is pure mechanism. An association is a link between things. If one member of the associated group appears, the association is automatically activated, and that leads inexorably to the appearance of the other associated member or members. If the word *grass* is associated with the word *green,* anytime you think of *grass, green* will also automatically come to mind. In this sense, the contents of conscious thought are mechanically determined. There is no Wundtian-Jamesian choice or decision.

Ebbinghaus invented the nonsense syllable because he was interested in understanding retention of newly learned material. He reasoned that nonsense syllables, unlike words, would have no associations at the outset of the experiment; thus, he would be able to study the factors that determined association formation in his experiments. Because learning was defined as memory for the correct order of the syllables (now known as serial learning), Ebbinghaus assumed that associations were being formed between and among the nonsense syllables in order for them to be successfully remembered. Over the course of his research, he verified the intuitions that repetition facilitates memory and that memory declines as a function of the time since the experience. He discovered the serial position effect and argued for a limited span of immediate memory, both phenomena that you will encounter in chapter 4. But, without question, his central importance lies in establishing the feasibility of experimental studies of memory.

Some have complained that Ebbinghaus' influence was unfortunate or at least has lasted long enough (Anderson, 1985). For example, the procedure of rote memorization encourages a view of memory as passive registration of events. This view may distort our understanding of memory. Memory does not operate in isolation but, rather, is one of the cognitive processes servicing some goal such as comprehension or problem solving. Factors such as our prior knowledge are important to both the structuring of experiences and their later use, all of which are ignored by a view of passive registration of events and later associative retrieval. Memory is affected by the conscious intent of the individual, both at the time of the original experience and certainly at the time of the memory test. As you will see in chapter 5, the influence of a prior experience on your current behavior varies, depending on whether you intend to remember the past or you intend to be doing something else. Intentionality is not a concept that is easily folded into a mechanistic explanation, and the legacy of Ebbinghaus is pure mechanism in memory explanation. On the other hand, some of the research that brought these facts to light might never have been conducted if Ebbinghaus had not shown us the feasibility of experimental studies of memory.

The Triumph of Mechanism: Behaviorism

By the turn of the twentieth century, psychology had gained a strong presence in the United States. Although a number of historically important ideas and events occurred, the most salient of these was the idea of behaviorism and its rapid acceptance by psychologists and the public. By 1919, the leading American psychologist introduced a book by warning his readers that they would find "no discussion of consciousness and no reference to such terms as sensation, perception, attention, image, and the like because frankly I do not know what they mean" (Watson, 1919, p. viii). Everyone knows what these words mean; what was Watson up to? He was up to fomenting a change in the subject matter of psychology. Psychology began as the scientific study of conscious experience because of the belief that a person's conduct would be the result of his or her knowledge, which includes his or her current perceptions. Watson attempted to undermine this structure by suggesting that one need not refer to knowledge or any other psychological concept such as attention, perception, or memory to understand behavior.

As mentioned previously, one of the major complaints raised by Watson concerned the lack of reliability of introspective data. How could you have a science if, each time you did an experiment, you obtained different results? The lack of reliability was blamed on the subjectivity inherent in introspective analysis; after all, only the subjects can "see" their own perceptions to introspect on them. The subjectivity, in turn, was blamed on the subject matter as defined by Wundt. To be a science, Watson argued, the subject matter has to be something more objective than conscious experience.

Psychology, as defined by Watson, would proceed as the study of objective behavior, not subjective mental experiences. Actually, "objective behavior" is not as objective as it sounds; for example, if you tell 10 people to observe a particular social interaction and report the behavior they observed, you are unlikely to receive 10 identical reports. In fact, behaviorism has an elaborate set of subjective assumptions that form the basis of its "objectivity." In most places, Watson described behavior in terms of stimulus-response connections. Notice that such a description is a conceptual abstraction of the actual behavior. Consider, for example, a child pleading for candy in the grocery checkout line. What you observe is a child screaming and an adult admonishing the child, not stimuli and responses. Reducing behavior to stimulus-response connections adds a layer of abstraction to the description that is not available to your immediate observation.

The abstraction used by Watson is based on the model of a reflex. A reflex is the automatic movement elicited by an environmental event. For example, a tap on the patellar tendon elicits a knee-jerk. The tap is then a stimulus, something that automatically and invariably elicits the response. The response itself is some muscle movement. The reflex is an established fact of physiology, but Watson took the reflex as the building block of behavior. It is not that all behavior is a reflex but that all behavior can be described as stimulus-response connections, where stimulus takes its meaning from the reflex model as a goading cause of the response to which it is connected.

The advantage of the reflex model is that the stimulus is a potentially observable environmental event, as is the ensuing response. One need not become ensnared in the difficulty of inferring the mental processes underlying behavior. Of course, there is the problem of agreeing on what is the stimulus and what is the response if objectivity is to be achieved; after all, the world does not come to us parsed in stimulus-response units. Leaving that matter aside, the reflex model then provided a highly mechanistic account of behavior. The mechanism lies in the stimulus-response connection. One can predict the response if one knows the stimulus and, if this is all there is to the science of psychology, all behavior is very much the same as a vending machine.

Learning

The behaviorist's program required a mechanism to introduce flexibility into the reflex model. Living organisms take advantage of their prior experiences and adapt their behavior in accord with those experiences. In short, the reflex model had to accommodate the process of learning. The discoveries of Ivan Pavlov provided such a mechanism.

Pavlov was a Russian physiologist who won a Nobel Prize for his work on the physiology of the digestive system. He never considered himself a psychologist, but, ironically, his observations yielded one of the most powerful methodological and conceptual tools available to psychology, particularly behaviorism. The discovery has come to be known as classical conditioning and its importance is that it allowed the reflex to become more flexible.

Classical conditioning essentially involves associating a previously neutral stimulus with a reflexive response. For example, consider the situation that led Pavlov to his discovery. As part of his research on digestive processes, Pavlov used a procedure to collect saliva from dogs. He noticed that, when the laboratory assistant who fed the dogs walked into their holding room, the dogs began to salivate. Salivation is a reflexive response to eating, but why would the dogs salivate to the sound of the assistant's footsteps? One could explain this behavior as anticipation based on knowledge gained from prior experience, but the stimulus-response language of the reflex model offers a more objective description. Namely, the food is a stimulus that evokes the salivation reflex and, with repeated pairings of the food and the assistant, the sight, sound, and maybe even the smell of the assistant came to be associated with food and salivation. Thus, the previously neutral stimulus gains the power to elicit the reflex.

The ability of neutral stimuli to evoke responses through association with a reflex unit gave the behaviorist a powerful tool to describe learning. The phenomenon of classical conditioning provided a potential basis for explaining cognitive and emotional reactions such as expectation, value (of money, for example), anxiety, and fear. For example, do you become just a bit uncomfortable when entering the dentist's office? And what about when you hear the whine of the drill? Certainly this anxiety is not a reflex but must have been learned. You can easily see how the classical conditioning paradigm described above can encompass this situation. Classical conditioning provided an objective language of stimuli and responses to talk about subjective phenomena. One could hope to explain all of behavior, assuming that environmental energy triggered a response and, through the mechanism of associative bonding, prior experience can influence behavior. Watson's idea that the reflex could be the building block of all behavior became more plausible with classical conditioning. One need not refer to such things as perception, memory, and attention. The objective language of stimulus-response seemed to provide the final ingredient to mechanism's triumph.

THE COGNITIVE RENAISSANCE

But something happened such that by the 1960s an increasing number of psychologists were studying the mind again. In violation of the arguments made by behaviorism, some people began to believe that human behavior could not be adequately described without including mental processes. As this idea gained momentum, there was talk of a cognitive revolution against behaviorism. What was at stake was the very subject matter of psychology. Because the subject matter of the emerging cognitive psychology is identical to what the earliest psychologists studied, the break with behaviorism was more of a renaissance than a revolution.

The success of the renaissance required two things, one negative and one positive. The negative event was that the fundamental ideas of behaviorism had to be shown to be inadequate to explain human behavior. The positive event was the development of a new way to think about the mind. We shall briefly describe both of these events in what follows.

Problems for Behaviorism

We cannot document with certainty all of the critical events that produced the cognitive renaissance, and, in retrospect, some of the contributing factors were rather amorphous and unnoticed at the time. For example, the research of the behaviorists became increasingly esoteric to others in psychology. Part of the behaviorist's program was the belief that all behavior is derived from basic principles of learning. Thus, clinical psychologists, social psychologists, and developmental psychologists, among others, were supposed to wait until these basic principles of learning were established and then we might understand clinical or social phenomena. But, as the research of the behaviorists turned inward toward continuing refinement of the theories, its relevance to other areas became suspect. For example, an important point of theoretical dispute was whether learning and motivation combined additively or multiplicatively. However important this point was for learning theory, you can imagine the growing impatience of the rest of the community as they waited for resolution of these sorts of very particular issues, invariably to be decided by studies of rats.

Behaviorism conducted almost all of its research with nonhuman species, and sometimes the results of this research then were extended to human behavior in a noncritical fashion. The eminent linguist, Noam Chomsky, outraged some psychologists when, in 1959, he accused B.F. Skinner of "playing at science." Skinner, who was the most prominent behaviorist at the time, had written a book applying his ideas to language acquisition in humans. He suggested that language is like any other response and is under the control of reinforcement. The basis of Chomsky's accusation was that Skinner had conducted no research that specifically studied language acquisition. Chomsky noted that while we might all agree that grain could be considered reinforcing to the hungry pigeon, it remained an untested assumption that parental reactions were the same sort of reinforcement to the young child. Indeed, what little actual evidence existed suggested that adults do not reinforce the language of the young child, particularly the syntax or grammar.

The credibility of the behaviorist program also came into question on some specific issues. One basic assumption of behaviorism was that all stimuli and responses functioned in the same fashion. A stimulus is a stimulus and a response is a response, no matter where they are found. This assumption justified the use of simple systems such as rats, pigeons, and primitive human motor responses to study behavior in general. Any stimulus could be associated with any arbitrary response through the mechanism of repetition. This assumption would be severely challenged by the research of John Garcia (e.g., Garcia & Koelling, 1966). Garcia conducted experiments on taste aversion in rats. The animals drank water flavored with saccharin, a sweet taste that rats normally seem to like. The point of the experiment was to teach the rats to avoid the sweet water by either giving them an electric shock after they drank or exposing them to radiation in small doses. Radiation makes a rat sick much as it would a human, including symptoms such as nausea. Even though electric shock is aversive to rats and is a sufficient punishment to affect some of their behavior, the shock had no effect on their consumption of the water. The radiation, however, resulted in almost complete avoidance of the sweet water. As an interesting side note, psychological research on this phenomenon of taste-aversion learning has contributed to managing the nutritional needs of patients receiving radiation and chemotherapy for cancer.

The most important impact of Garcia's research was to demonstrate biological contraints on learning. No longer could you assume that the processes of learning were the same for all species, an assumption made by behaviorists that justified their use of rats and pigeons. Poison is a very important event in the life of a rat, and the taste of the substance is readily associated with sickness and, hence, avoided in the future. Taste, apparently, is not readily associated with shock. The evolutionary history of a given species is an important determinant of the learning possibilities, apparently including the readiness with which some events are associated with certain behavior. The messages are that not all stimuli are equivalent and that differences among species are important. If you had not already done so, you begin to wonder whether the key pecking response of a pigeon will really tell you anything about language acquisition in humans.

Other serious questions about the basic stimulus-response analysis arose from research on human verbal learning. The study of verbal learning developed within the tradition of associative learning theory and attempted to extend the mechanistic stimulus-response view to verbal learning. However, the research soon produced anomalous data for that program. For example, serial learning, first analyzed in the associative tradition by Ebbinghaus, was viewed as a simple matter of chaining stimuli and responses. The first item of a serial list was the stimulus for the second item, and the second item was both the response to the first item and the stimulus for the third item. Learning of the list, then, was a fairly simple matter of establishing these associations.

If this analysis is accurate, a very specific prediction follows. Suppose a group of participants learns a list of words in correct serial order. After they have accomplished this, they are transferred to a paired-associate task. In the paired-associate task, the subject sees a word and must anticipate the word paired with it. After the attempt to produce the paired word, the pair is shown to the subject and the next pair is presented in the same sequence until the entire list of pairs has been presented. After sufficient repetitions of the pair, learning, as evidenced by the ability to produce the response on the appearance of the stimulus, occurs. Theoretically, learning is the result of forming an association between the stimulus and response of the pair. With this description of paired-associate learning, we can return to the experiment designed to test the prediction that serial learning occurs when associations are formed between the adjacent items in the serial list.

After the participants have successfully mastered the serial learning list, they should have formed associations among items in that list. The participants are now given a paired-associate list but are not told that the words in the paired-associate list are the same as those in the serial list. In fact, for half of the participants, the word pairs consist of items that were directly adjacent in the serial list. For example, if the serial list included the words *horse, theatre, mountain, paper,* the paired associate items would be *horse-theatre, mountain-paper.* The other half of the participants also see the same words in paired associate learning, but the pairs consist of nonadjacent words from the serial list—for example, *theatre-paper, horse-mountain*. Based on the stimulus-response associative analysis of serial learning, who should learn the paired associate list more rapidly? Clearly, the first group, who had the same pairs in serial learning and paired associate learning, should have the advantage. But, as was demonstrated by the work of Young (1959, 1961), this did not happen. No differences are found in paired-associate learning between the two groups. The straightforward prediction of a stimulus-response associative explanation of serial learning is false.

We must keep sight of our goal here; why did Watson's manifesto to expunge the mind from the science of psychology lose favor after dominating psychology for approximately 50 years? Serial learning of a list of words is not a complex task relative to most of the things we do, a fact that magnifies the impact of the predictive failure of the stimulus-response analysis. If the explanation of this simple situation is wrong, the claim that all human learning can be objectively described as stimulus-response connections becomes even more incredible.

The examples mentioned above are only a few of the many instances of conceptual difficulty encountered by stimulus-response associationism in accounting for simple human learning. Contrary to Watson's hope, a successful theory of psychology seemed to require discussion of the mind and its function. Developments outside of psychology, particularly in linguistics during the 1950s and 1960s, reinforced this conclusion.

The Contribution of Linguistics

The earliest psychologists, psychophysicists and Wundtians alike, believed and attempted to prove that mental processes are affected by environmental energy, but, at the same time, they never believed that cognitive experiences could be completely explained by appeal to the physical input. They assumed that certain psychological processes might use the environmental input but the product of these processes was not identical to the sensory information. Wundt's process of creative synthesis is an example. That is, at least part of what we know is not a direct result of a particular prior experience but, rather, is the result of thought processes and volition. Such knowledge is abstract in that it is not identical to a prior experience. The processes that produce abstract knowledge are rational processes. *Rationalism* is to be contrasted with *empiricism*, which is the belief that all of our knowledge is in the form of particular prior experiences. One way you can think about this distinction is that rational knowledge is produced by thought, whereas empirical knowledge is current perception and memory for past perceptions.

This distinction between rationalism and empiricism was at the heart of the problem of knowledge when psychology began. At the time, no one seriously doubted the reality of rational knowledge. It was the reality of empirical knowledge that had to be proven through such work as that of the psychophysicists. Ironically, as the mechanistic position took hold in the late nineteenth century and then became dominant with behaviorism, rational processes were either ignored or even denied by psychologists. With the exception of the work of the great developmental theorist, Piaget, and some theory in clinical psychology, analysis of abstract knowledge and rational thought disappeared. Given the goal of mechanism to anchor the cause of all thought in external causes and the goal of behaviorism to avoid subjectivity in the subject matter, it is not surprising that rational processes and abstract knowledge were no longer even discussed. On the other hand, their reappearance was almost guaranteed once psychologists again began to study complex human behavior. Abstract knowledge seems to be a necessary component of activities such as reasoning or problem solving or, for that matter, language use and comprehension. And, mostly as a matter of historical circumstances, it was from the domain of linguistics that psychologists were reminded of the importance of rationalism and abstraction.

The reemergence of rationalism and abstract knowledge eventually would influence all of cognitive psychology, but the instigating events occurred in the discipline of linguistics. Chomsky's attack on the Skinnerian analysis of linguistics was an attention grabber. The mechanical, stimulus-response approach to language requires some direct experience with the stimuli and responses in question. To a point, one could imagine that something like this happens: the mother says, "Cat," when the child sees a cat and then says, "Very good," when the child says, "Cat." But the stimulus-response analysis of language acquisition can't go much further because of an important feature of language; it is creative. Can you understand the sentence "Mr. Rogers' neighborhood was comfortable fantasy for children"? Of course, you can. The point is that we can understand as well as produce sentences that we have never heard before. If you have never experienced it, obviously there has been no opportunity for any stimulus-response bond to be reinforced.

George Miller, a prominent leader of the cognitive renaissance, illustrated the creative and novelty of language by calculating that an adult with a modest vocabulary is capable of creating more unique sentences than could be spoken in an average lifetime. How are we to understand this ability possessed by every competent speaker to produce novel utterances? Here is where the influence of linguistics was crucial. Chomsky developed a theory that dealt largely with the use of grammar or syntax. Every language has a set of rules for producing sentences, and by plugging words into these rules, language is generated. Combinations of words could be entered into the set of rules, producing an infinite variety of utterances, all of which would be acceptable to a native speaker.

The implication is that there are psychological processes that actively generate language. If this depiction is accurate, language is the result of psychological processes that are not simple stimulus-response association but, rather, are processes combining the rules and the vocabulary to produce an appropriate utterance in a given situation. The psychological processes generate the response; it is not mechanically determined by the stimulus. There is a hint here of the position taken by Wundt on creative synthesis. Certainly, if you are capable of an infinite number of sentences, it seems unlikely that one could predict exactly what you are going to say before you say it.

The generative component of Chomsky's theory is based on use of a rule, and here we can conclude our point about rationalism and abstract processes by simply defining a rule. A rule is a set of principles that define how something is to be done. To be of maximum use, a rule is not flexible. The rule remains the same regardless of the circumstances to which it is applied. Thus, a rule is abstract because it is independent of a particular context. Rules of a game, for example, apply no matter when or where the game is played. Therefore, even if a rule were learned through some particular prior experience, its application also requires rational processes in that the rule is known over and above that particular prior experience. The rule can be applied without remembering the specific circumstances under which it was learned. But a rule is nothing like a stimulus. It does not goad a response, and a rule is a general statement, whereas a stimulus is a specific event.

The details of Chomsky's theory were less important to the reemergence of cognitive psychology than were the theory's more general influences. As a linguist, Chomsky was trying to explain language itself, not the language user. Nonetheless, some psychologists quickly noted the power of a generative approach to explain language, and it prompted people to consider extension of the general approach to other intellectual abilities. The renewed emphasis on rationalism and abstract knowledge was incompatible with the behaviorists' insistence on empiricism and environmental determinism and encouraged a return to the study of mental processes that characterized the beginnings of psychology.

Information Processing

It is not enough to decide that mental processes are necessary for psychological theory, and no amount of anomalous data or theories of linguistics would have provoked the research programs of cognitive psychology unless there also existed some general way to talk about these mental processes. Suppose you decided you wanted to understand memory. What would you do? You, of course, could see how well people remember experiences, and you could even see what effects other things, such as the time since the experience, have on memory. But how would you describe the mental process; what terms would you use? In other words, where would you get your ideas about and explanations of the memory performance you observed? Cognitive psychology would not have reappeared without an answer to this question. The answer came from the *model* provided by computer science, perhaps the most influential development in the reappearance of cognitive psychology.

It is extremely important to understand what a model is and why it is important. A model is an analogy. Analogical reasoning, a topic we shall discuss later, is something you do frequently. If someone asks you to explain something, among the easiest ways to do so is to compare the thing he or she does not know to something he or she does know. For example, suppose you visited Stockholm over the summer and your friends ask you about the city. Also suppose your friends are familiar with Seattle. You can tell them a lot by saying that Stockholm is very much like Seattle, only much more expensive. Seattle is an analogy for Stockholm. The model allows you to think on the basis of similarity. With the model of Seattle, your friends can now ask questions about Stockholm that they could not have asked without the model. The same situation exists in science.

The model of computer science was essential to cognitive psychology in that it provided a language to talk about mental processes in very much the same way that the physiological reflex model provided the language of stimulus-response. The language system came to be known as *information processing*.

Several dimensions of similarity recommended the computer as a model. A computer is controlled by software, or a program. The program is a set of rules written in some symbolic form, usually words and numbers. Both the rule and symbolic nature of the program seem to be analogous to rational knowledge, which we described earlier as general and abstract. Notice, for example, that one could imagine Chomsky's grammatical rules existing as a program. The program could take words as an input and manipulate them in accord with the rules to generate sentences.

Programs specify operations that manipulate symbols. Symbol manipulation seemed to some people to correspond directly to thinking. The program can be written to solve problems, and that is certainly a major function of thinking. In 1957, Newell, Shaw, and Simon wrote a program, called the Logic Theorist, that could prove complicated mathematical theorems. The computer began to look like a thinking machine.

As we mentioned, the importance of a model is to allow one to think and talk about something that one previously had little way of doing. In the case of the information-processing model, one now could refer to the environmental energy as information rather than as a stimulus. The psychological processes of perception and comprehension could be thought of as coding, analogous to the coding operations necessary to transform the input to a computer into a form the machine can use. Memory could be described as storage and retrieval. Theories could be proposed based on the model and experiments designed to test those theories. For example, storage capacity was proposed to be an important feature of memory, just as it is in the machine, and experiments were designed to investigate the capacity limitations of human memory. Capacity reflected the amount of information that could be held in a particular system. All of this description was metaphorical language; the metaphor of the mind was the computer.

A somewhat more nebulous but equally important aspect of the computer model in the 1950s was the fact that the computer was a machine. The behaviorists had banned mental concepts as unscientific because, they argued, such concepts had no referents in the physical world. Science cannot address nonphysical matters. The behaviorists got away with a pretty shallow argument here (in what sense is memory not a physical phenomenon?) but, regardless, psychologists had become paranoid of concepts referring to mental processes. The computer cured the paranoia in that the concepts used were instantiated in a machine. The thing was made of metal and plastic, clearly a part of the physical world, and the internal operations were known and not mysterious. In this sense, the language of information processing provided an objective description of subjective phenomena, and the terms of information processing replaced the stimulus-response language. The computer model legitimized a focus on psychological processes in an important way that probably nothing else could have done.

Culmination of the Cognitive Renaissance

The result of the events and activities of the 1940s and 1950s was clear by the end of the 1960s. Behaviorism's attempted transformation of the discipline had failed, and the subject matter had returned to questions of mental function. A number of specific publications signaled this result. British psychologists interested in applied problems began to develop theories of human performance and attention. A leader in this movement was Broadbent (1958), who proposed a theory of how human attention works. Other psychologists such as Miller, Galanter, and Pribram (1960) sounded a clarion call for "a new theoretical approach" to psychology, which would allow for the study of plans, images, and other mental processes. In the same year, in his presidential address to the American Psychological Association, Hebb (1960) described what he called "the American Revolution," a resurgence of interest in mental processes and cognitive psychology. Renewed interest in mental processes such as imagery (Paivio, 1969), search and scan processes in short-term memory (Sternberg, 1966), and organizational processes in memory (Bower, 1970; Mandler, 1967) served to bring cognitive psychology to the forefront. Neisser (1967) published a textbook, entitled *Cognitive Psychology,* that widely disseminated the new research interests among graduate students, who became the teachers and researchers of the 1970s.

Nonetheless, the history you have just read left its impact on the current practices in the discipline. Much of the subject matter of contemporary cognitive psychology was defined at the end of the nineteenth century. The psychophysicists were studying sensory and perceptual processes. Wundt also was interested in perceptual processes, as well as topics ranging from attention to problem solving. Ebbinghaus had set a trend in memory research that remains in place today. James' 1890 book, *The Principles of Psychology,* covered every topic area you will find in this book. In this context, contemporary research truly is a renaissance of the subject matter of cognitive psychology.

Many of the people who brought about the renaissance were educated as behaviorists and brought with them the methodological rigor of behaviorism that was sometimes missing from the earlier work. Perhaps more important, behaviorism served as a conduit for the influence of the mechanistic tradition to flow smoothly into cognitive psychology, even though the subject matter was shifting from overt responses back to mental processes.

Mechanistic explanations require that theories be stated in mechanical terms, and here the computer model of information processing becomes the vehicle of mechanism in cognitive psychology. An important requirement of mechanism is that the theory states the working parts underlying a phenomenon. For example, if memory for your last boyfriend's face is the thing to be explained, one might develop a theory that suggests a representation of his face exists in memory and certain processes of retrieval act to bring that representation to mind under appropriate cuing conditions. It is here that you will see the impact of the computer model on the theories of cognitive psychology. The computer provides the model parts, such as representations, to explain the phenomena.

The mechanistic approach goes a step further. *Mechanism* literally refers to the physics of motion or the study of mechanics. The additional step is to state the explanation in the language of a more basic science, ultimately physics. Many steps separate psychological concepts such as memory from concepts in physics such as quark, but the obvious first step for many people is neuroscience. Thus, the tradition of mechanism encourages one to search for explanations of mental processes in the central nervous system. The idea is that cognitive phenomena can be explained, at least in part, by discovering their origins in the brain. We shall elaborate on this development in the concluding section of the chapter, where we describe the current state of affairs.

CURRENT STATUS: COMPUTER MODEL AND COGNITIVE NEUROSCIENCE

The computer model continues to be an important influence on cognitive psychology. The influence is exerted largely by providing a metaphorical language, as we described earlier. Neuroscience research on cognitive phenomena has surged with the development of new technologies for observing brain function. Some of these observations have led to advances in computer science as the computer scientist attempts to write new programs that mimic brain functioning. We shall briefly describe these developments here and elaborate on them in later chapters.

The Computer as an Analogy

The analogy between computer functioning and human cognitive functioning is obvious. People take in information in the form of environmental energy and store it for later use. Just as input is transformed into machine language, incoming information from the environment undergoes important transformations. We know that the brain cannot use electromagnetic energy, which is the physical energy involved in light. Electromagnetic energy is transformed into chemical energy and then into electrical energy in the course of transmission from the eye to the brain.

The storage function of the computer is analogous to the process we normally think of as memory. The stored information can later be retrieved, used to solve a problem, and then expressed as output from the computer. Again, the analogy with a search process and problem-solving activities in human beings is striking.

Using the computer as an analogy, however, is far from suggesting that the human brain works like a computer. The brain processes that correspond to such activities as perception, memory, thinking, and language are much more complex than those of any existing computer. Rather, the computer model provides a general way of thinking about human cognitive functioning. This general framework is known as information processing. The basic model is depicted in Figure 1.1. As you can see in this figure, cognition can be divided into three components: input processing, storage, and output. Although it is convenient to think of these components as sequential stages, this need not always be the case. For example, in figure 1.1 feedback from long-term memory to the perceptual processes is indicated. The three components may all contribute to ongoing activity at any point

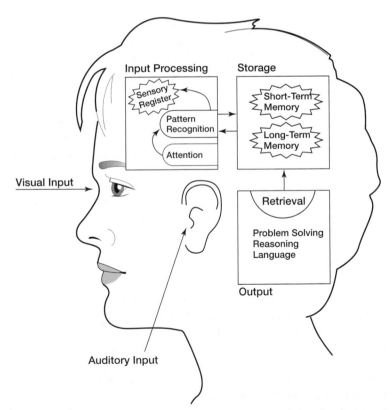

FIGURE 1.1
Defining cognitive psychology.

in time. Regardless, the information-processing analogy has been a useful tool in the analysis of human cognitive functioning.

Cognitive Neuroscience: A Brief History

The relationship between mental abilities and brain functioning has been a topic of speculation for at least 2000 years. However, it wasn't until the nineteenth century that these speculations began to be systematically examined. Two fundamental questions frame this early period in the history of neuroscience. First was the question of whether the brain is one interconnected mass of neural fibers or is instead composed of discrete nerve cells. Of course, mainly due to the development of sophisticated microscopes, we now know that the latter hypothesis was correct and that individual nerve cells or *neurons* are the fundamental unit of information processing in the brain. Note, however, that the success of the "neuron hypothesis" raised many more questions than it answered (always a sign of good science!). For example, if neurons are discrete and thus not physically connected to one another, then how do they interact or communicate? Based on advances in cellular biology, as well as a good deal of creative experimentation, the answer that has emerged is that neuron-to-neuron communication is primarily achieved by the release of chemicals (*neurotransmitters*) into the junctions (*synapses*) between neurons, a process that changes a neuron's electrical activity. The chemical composition of these neurotransmitters (of which there are many types), the specific neurons and parts of the brain to which they are applied, and the timing of their release all appear to have systematic effects on our thinking and behavior.

Another question raised by the success of the neuron hypothesis concerns how these cells work together to produce complex cognition. Although certainly a wonder of nature, neurons are relatively simple in the realm of biology. How then do they produce the forms of cognition of interest to psychologists, forms such as attention and language, as well as love and creativity? There appear to be two general answers to this question. The first is that, although neurons are indeed relatively simple, there is an enormous number of them. In fact, it is estimated that the average brain contains close to 100 *billion* neurons, with each one having connections with up to 15,000 other neurons. Such large numbers enable complex cognition by allowing your brain to achieve a staggeringly wide range of activity patterns.

A second, more specific, answer to the question of how neurons produce complex cognition concerns their ability to be modified by experience, a topic known as *neural plasticity*. Thus, when one or more neurons consistently cause another neuron to fire, the connections between them become strengthened, thereby forming a so-called *Hebbian circuit* (based on the Canadian researcher Donald Hebb, who proposed this idea). Hebbian circuits are widely agreed to be one of the primary neural mechanisms underlying the creation of memories, as well as a variety of other cognitive abilities that depend on memory. Exactly how these circuits are formed, whether by growth of new synapses, the metabolic alteration of existing ones, or both, continues to be the subject of intense research. One way to remember the concept of Hebbian circuits is via the phrase *neurons that fire together, wire together.* Keep in mind, however, that while the creation of Hebbian synapses causes the brain to act somewhat like a set of interconnected fibers or "wires" (as originally proposed by some early neuroscientists), neurons remain separate throughout their lives, never physically fusing with each other.

In addition to the question of whether neurons are physically separate or connected, a second question framing the early history of modern neuroscience—a question that in many ways is still with us today—is whether mental functions are localized to specific neural regions or are more widely distributed throughout the brain. This issue has important implications for how one understands and investigates mind/brain relations, so it is worth reviewing a little history. In the early 1800s, Franz Joseph Gall (1758–1828) and Johann Spurzheim (1776–1832) proposed that higher mental functions are associated with specific areas of the brain and that the size of the brain area devoted to particular abilities could be measured by the pattern of bumps and ridges on an individual's skull. This approach to the relation between mind and brain became known as *phrenology* and, although eventually discredited, was the first theory to hypothesize that specific cognitive functions reflect the operations of specific parts of the brain. As will be seen in subsequent chapters, much of contemporary research in the field of cognitive neuroscience has essentially the same goal as phrenology—the localization of cognitive functions in the brain—but the experimental techniques, as well as the theories that those techniques have inspired, are much more sophisticated.

Phrenology was discredited for a number of reasons. Most problematic was its assumption that the shape of a person's head could be used to infer the anatomy of her or his brain. Two other incorrect assumptions of phrenology, however, are more informative with regard to modern research in cognitive neuroscience. First, note that the particular cognitive abilities proposed by Gall and Spurzheim—which included "hope," "spirituality," and "combativeness" to name just a few—were subjective and not part of any larger, empirically based theory of cognition or behavior. This is not the case in modern cognitive neuroscience, where the processes investigated are firmly rooted in the theories and research of cognitive psychologists. The second important difference between phrenology and modern cognitive neuroscience concerns what one is trying to localize, Thus, while Gall thought that high-level cognitive abilities would be found in one specific place in the brain, we now know that complex abilities like memory, attention, and language result from the operation of a number of more *elementary operations,* or "subprocesses," and that these subprocesses may often be widely distributed throughout the brain. Note how this insight—complex cognitive processes are built up from simpler operations—parallels our discussion of how complex cognition can arise from the operation of a large number of relatively "simple" neurons. It also provides a surprising answer to the question of whether cognitive processes are localized or distributed. In particular, modern research on the brain suggests that both the localized and distributed perspectives are (partially) correct. The localized perspective is correct in the sense that, contrary to the notion that the brain is one undifferentiated mass, specific parts of the brain are indeed specialized for performing specific cognitive functions. However, the distributive perspective is correct in the sense that rather than being located in one particular place, the neural mechanisms underlying particular cognitive functions are often found in widely separated parts of the brain. Indeed, some cognitive processes such as memory are so widely distributed that, in a general sense, they may be considered a characteristic of the entire brain.

Cognitive Neuroscience: Methods and Basic Anatomy

Research on the neural basis of cognitive processes has increased dramatically in the last twenty years. Indeed, it is probably safe to say that we have learned more about the relation between mind and brain in the last two decades than we learned in the prior two millennia. What accounts for such rapid progress? Although a variety of factors could be mentioned, two stand out as especially critical for the recent successes of cognitive neuroscience—the development of sophisticated technologies for investigating what the brain is doing as it performs specific cognitive tasks, and an increasingly detailed understanding of neural anatomy. This section briefly reviews each in turn.

Perhaps the two most important questions to be asked about the brain activity associated with cognitive processing are *where* and *when.* Knowing *where* processing occurs in the brain is important because, rather than being one homogenous mass of neurons, the brain is more appropriately thought of as a collection of distinct processing areas, each of which supports only a subset (or perhaps only one) of the brain's various cognitive functions. Thus, knowing that area A (e.g., the left frontal lobe) is activated by task X (free-associating to a list of words) can provide important clues as to the cognitive operations involved in the (free-association) task. This information also informs neuropsychologists and neurosurgeons about what might happen if this area was damaged or removed. In addition to knowing *where* neural processing occurs (i.e., what brain areas are active), it is also important to know *when* they occur in relation to each other. Knowing *when* can provide cognitive psychologists with important insights into which neural areas are associated with stages of information processing for example, telling us that processing in area A must be completed before area B can do its cognitive job.

Until recently, answering the *where* question was based almost entirely on observing the effects of brain lesions, either those that occurred "naturally" in humans (as a result of car accidents, gun-shot wounds, or unavoidable brain surgery, for example), or those that were intentionally produced in nonhuman animals. In fact, this "lesion approach" continues to be a source of evidence (and curious findings) today. Thus, by examining how task performance is impaired by damage to a particular area of the brain, one can infer the cognitive functions normally performed by that area. With nonhuman animals, very precise damage can be produced in the laboratory, resulting in highly specific behavioral deficits that can be used to test cognitive theories. Brain damage in humans is generally not as precise as that produced in laboratory animals; nevertheless, many clinical populations have damage specific enough to allow localization of particular cognitive functions. For example, damage to an area of the brain known as the hippocampus has been consistently shown to produce a very specific memory deficit known as anterograde amnesia, a topic we will discuss in more detail in chapters 4-6. On the basis of such results, it is now widely agreed that this structure plays a fundamental role in memory.

Although lesion studies continue to be a useful source of evidence, especially in nonhuman animals, answering the *where* question in humans has almost entirely been given over to advances in neuroradiology and nuclear medicine. Two approaches in particular, Positron Emission Tomography (PET) and functional Magnetic Resonance Imaging (fMRI) have become indispensable techniques in cognitive neuroscience. What makes these techniques so important is that they allow scientists to measure the *function* or activity of the brain, that is, the set of processes or elementary operations that underlie cognitive performance. These techniques are thus to be distinguished from CT or MRI scans, which provide an image of the *structure* or anatomy of the brain. What also makes PET and fMRI so exciting is that they allow the neural activity associated with cognitive processing to be measured *in vivo* (literally, "within the living body") without penetrating or otherwise damaging the brain.

How do these techniques work? To function properly, neurons require glucose and oxygen, which are supplied by the blood. Increased neuronal activity (as a function of cognitive activity, for example) depletes glucose and oxygen faster than normal, resulting in a temporary increase of blood flow to the active area. PET and fMRI allow this increased blood flow to be measured, thereby providing a three-dimensional image, or "map," of the brain activity underlying performance of a particular cognitive task. PET scans create this map by introducing a small amount of radioactive tracer into the bloodstream and measuring the number of photons, or gamma rays, generated from particular locations within the brain. Gamma rays are generated when a positron (a positively changed electron) that is emitted from the radioactive tracer interacts with an electron (a positron's antiparticle), resulting in their mutual annihilation. fMRI, in contrast, creates activity maps by measuring change in the magnetic properties of the blood, taking advantage of the fact that deoxygenated (oxygen-depleted) blood provides a stronger magnetic signal than does oxygenated (oxygen-rich) blood. The key point to remember is that both of these techniques provide an image or even a series of images, like a movie, of the *activity* of the brain. Thus, both PET and fMRI scans can be done while people perform different cognitive tasks such as remembering a past event or attending to one thing while ignoring another, and the resulting activity maps, derived from changes in blood flow, can be used to infer which areas of the brain were important for performing these tasks.

As noted previously, measuring *where* neural activity occurs when performing a cognitive task is a critical step in relating mind to brain, but it is only part of the story. Another critical piece of information is *when* this activity occurs in relation to the other processes involved. There are two reasons why answering the *when* question has always been more difficult than answering the *where* question. First, although the brain processes information more slowly than do modern computers, the timescale at which neural processing occurs is still quite fast, being measured in thousandths of a second or milliseconds. Second, it is now widely agreed that the processes involved in most cognitive activities do not occur in strict *serial* fashion, with one cognitive process being completed before another begins. Rather, the brain appears to be a highly *parallel* processing device such that, for most cognitive tasks, there are multiple processes involved, all of which are overlapping in time (hence, "in parallel"). The combination of multiple fast processes overlapping in time makes answering the *when* question a difficult task.

Nevertheless, quite a good deal of progress has been made on this front by using the elctroencephalograph (EEG) to measure what are known as Event-Related Potentials (ERPs). As you probably know, the EEG is a device that can measure changes in the brain's electrical activity over time via a set of electrodes that are placed on a person's head. Although the standard EEG has provided a number of insights into the nature of brain function, especially in the domain of sleep, this technique has not been extensively used by cognitive neuroscientists because of its inability to separate the different subprocesses involved in a task. Part of the problem is that, unlike PET and fMRI, the EEG is much less able to tell one exactly *where* in the brain the electrical activity is being generated because the activity measured at the scalp represents a "mixture" of different electrical sources within the brain. Moreover, if different cognitive processes overlap in time (i.e., they are occurring in parallel), then it becomes even more difficult to know what electrical activity is associated with the different relevant subprocesses. One way to solve this problem is to have a person perform the same task over and over again—for example, free-associating to a long series of words. By averaging the EEG signal across each word trial, the "Event" in ERP, and tightly time-locking the electrical activity to the onset of each word, one can better see the time course of electrical activity, or "Potentials," associated with performing the task; hence, Event (free-association)-Related (electrical) Potentials (ERPs). ERPs have become an important tool for answering the *when* question associated with the neural basis of cognitive processing. However, there will be little discussion of this research in the subsequent chapters. This is not because the techniques are invalid but, rather, because results from this technique are too complex and provisional to be covered in this introductory text. Nevertheless, you should realize that understanding the relative timing of cognitive processes is a critical issue for both cognitive psychology and cognitive neuroscience.

As we leave our discussion of methods, we should note that although we have described some of the most popular techniques used by cognitive neuroscientists, there is a variety of other, more specialized methods that have not been described; and new techniques, as well as creative variations on existing techniques (e.g., combining ERPs with PET), are being invented all the time. One particular technique that is quite interesting—and which, in many ways, combines the *where* and *when* questions with the lesion approach—is known as Transcranial Magnetic Stimulation (TMS). TMS involves sending a brief electromagnetic pulse through the intact skull (hence, *transcranial*) and into a specific region of a person's brain while he or she is performing a cognitive task. The pulse disrupts neural function, thereby acting as a "functional" (reversible) brain lesion. By varying both the location (the *where*) and the timing (the *when*) of the pulse, one can gain insights into how cognitive tasks are performed and test specific theories about the relation between cognition and the brain. For example, as we see in chapter 5, a key question surrounding mental imagery is whether this phenomenon uses the same neural mechanisms employed in normal vision. Use of TMS has provided strong evidence that this is indeed the case, thus suggesting that there is a very real sense in which we can be said to "see" a mental image.

Before concluding this section on cognitive neuroscience, you should briefly review the major anatomical regions of the brain, regions that will be referred to in subsequent chapters. Figure 1.2 shows a side view of the brain's left hemisphere. Major anatomical features and regions are shown, along with some of the more widely agreed upon cognition functions that these regions are thought to support. You may wish to refer to these figures whenever specific regions are mentioned in subsequent chapters.

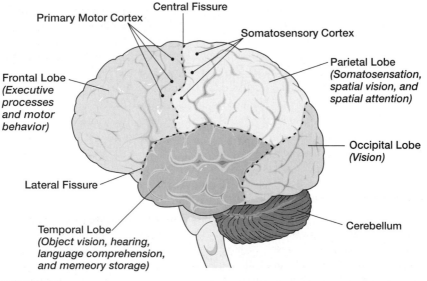

FIGURE 1.2
Sequence of information processing.

Parallel Distributed Processing

One of the themes in this chapter is that there are important similarities between how people and computers process information. Indeed, although it is widely known that cognitive psychologists often use the computer as an analogy for the mind, what is less known is that one of the inventors of the modern computer (Alan Turing) explicitly used information processing in the mind as an analogy for thinking about how to build a computer. This interplay between cognition and developments in computer science continues today except rather than using the mind as an analogy, scientist have taken inspiration from our understanding of the brain. Two ideas in particular, parallel processing and the notion of distributed representations, have resulted in the development of brain-inspired computer models of cognition that go under the general heading of Parallel Distributed Processing. Parallel processing, discussed previously (see also chapter 2), refers to the notion that, rather than having cognitive processes occur one at time in sequence (known as *serial processing*), the brain appears to "run" multiple cognitive processes at the same time, or *in parallel.* The notion of "distributed representations" also appears to be a central characteristic of the brain. That is, rather than having one neuron represent one piece of information (such as the letter *a*), information in the brain appears to be *distributed* across many neurons (such that our representation of the letter *a* may be distributed across 1000 or more neurons).

Parallel distributed processing takes these two brain-based principles and implements them as a computer program. The computer can thus be viewed as a model of the brain, which in turn, is presumed to be the basis of the mind. Parallel distributed processing simulates the distributed functioning of the neurons with simple processing elements, or units. The units are connected in a parallel fashion and when a unit receives input, it sends a signal to numerous other units. The units can represent anything—a letter, a word, a sentence, or even the features of a letter (i.e., lines, curves, etc.)—but the overall goal of the model is to decompose higher levels of information into lower levels that can be easily represented by simple units, or neurons. Once the progamming is completed, the research then proceeds by giving the program a problem to solve such as recognizing an object or remembering a prior input. Successful solution of such problems by the computer is taken as evidence that the details of the program, including its distributed representations and parallel processes, provide a faithful reflection of how the brain, and thus the mind, processes information.

The Importance of Behavioral Research

Both neuroscience and computer science are important contributors to contemporary cognitive psychology, but it is still the case that most of the research uses the standard psychology experiment conducted with human subjects and equipment no more exotic than a personal computer. Depending upon the topic, studying the effects of selected variables upon particular responses is still the most frequent type of research in cognitive psychology.

Cognitive psychology proceeds with its study of mental functioning through the scientific method, which is just a way of trying to solve problems through a combination of thinking and data gathering. Thinking is typically known as a theoretical enterprise and data gathering is accomplished by experiments. The exercise begins with an idea or theory about how a particular mental process works. The idea or theory contains certain implications, so that if the idea or theory is reasonable, then certain other events should follow. An experiment can then be set up to see whether these events actually do happen.

For example, consider one of the problems mentioned earlier: why is it so hard to simultaneously take notes and understand a lecture? One theory suggests it is because we can attend to only one thing at a time, and when we are attending to one event, the information about other events is completely ignored. One implication of this theory is that, when attending to one event, a person should have no memory of other events. As we shall see in chapter 3, experiments can be set up to approximate this situation and allow us to determine the validity of this theoretical idea.

An important aspect of the scientific process is inference; in this context, inference is perhaps best defined as educated guessing. A situation in which we know the surrounding circumstances is established, and then the behavior of the person in this situation is observed. Based on our knowledge of the circumstances plus our observations of the behavior, we infer what types of processes the person must use in order to respond in that fashion. The work of inferring the nature of mental processes based on observations of overt behavior has produced most of the theoretical advances you will study, and the credit for our progress goes not so much to technology but rather to the clever, dedicated scientists.

LIMITATIONS OF MECHANISM

Throughout this book, we shall try to give you several sides to the issues under discussion. In most cases, the question will not have been resolved and it is important for you to learn of the alternative solutions. We begin here by noting some of the criticisms of the mechanistic assumptions about the mind that are contained in the computer model and in cognitive neuroscience.

A variety of criticisms and concerns have been raised about the computer model. Perhaps the most aggressive arguments are those of Herbert Dreyfus in his book, *What Computers Can't Do* (1979). These arguments range from concerns about the relative inability of any computer program to perform general cognitive functions such as "understanding" to philosophical concerns about the relationship between levels of descriptive analysis. For example, the information-processing approach might describe a situation as beginning with "olfactory stimulus input" that is "processed" and gives rise to the perception of "chocolate chip cookies." Dreyfus' provocative argument is that this description seduces you to feel as if something has been explained when, in fact, it has not. Olfactory stimulus input literally is in the form of certain molecules that contact certain receptors in the nose. These receptors respond with electrical impulses that are transmitted in and are responded to by the central nervous system. Where and how does the very real experience of smelling chocolate chip cookies arise?

While critics such as Dreyfus argue that the computer is a bad model for the mind, a weaker criticism is that the model is not useful for some of the questions

---

BOX 1.2

MAN VERSUS MACHINE

The year 1997 will be remembered by some people as the year a computer became world champion of chess. Actually, the champion is not a particular machine but, rather, a chess-playing program named Deep Blue (the corporate colors of IBM are blue). Deep Blue defeated the reigning human champion, Gary Kasporov, in a highly publicized series of matches, sparking a wealth of speculation in the media about the relative intelligence of humans and computers. The question seems to fascinate the general public. Is it possible that a machine can be smarter than humans?

Well, it all depends on what you mean by "smart." Computers are now capable of performing some tasks more efficiently than humans, mostly tasks involving vast memory requirements. For example, the scanning techniques used by most retail stores feed information to a computer, which not only controls the cash register but keeps an inventory. This technology allows information to be processed and stored more rapidly and probably more reliably than if done by a person. On the other hand, if what you mean by "smart" is understanding and comprehending situations, the argument becomes much more interesting. Did Deep Blue beat Kasporov because the program understood chess?

John Searle (1984), another critic of the computer-as-mind, offered an interesting thought experiment that applies to our example of Deep Blue. Searle called his experiment the "Chinese Room" and it goes like this. Suppose you are locked in a room with several baskets of Chinese symbols, but you understand no Chinese. You are, however, given a rulebook written in English for manipulating the symbols, telling you which Chinese symbols to put together but nothing about the English equivalent meaning of the symbols. Now suppose that some additional Chinese symbols are passed into the room. Your rulebook also specifies which Chinese symbols you are to pass back out of the room. Finally, imagine that the person outside of the room calls the symbols passed into the room "questions" and the symbols you give back "answers to questions." You and your English rulebook are sufficiently good at manipulating the symbols that your "answers" are indistinguishable from those of a native Chinese speaker. Searle reasonably suggests that you could participate in this exercise forever and still not understand Chinese. Furthermore, Searle argues that a computer is doing exactly what the person locked in the room is doing. The program is a rulebook and symbols are passed into and out of the computer, but, according to Searle's reasoning, the computer does not understand Chinese, chess, or anything else in the sense that a human does.

of interest. For example, a central issue in psychology is the function of consciousness. You will recall that psychology began largely as an attempt to scientifically study conscious experience, but the subjective mental states comprising conscious experience are very difficult for the mechanist. Indeed, consciousness was declared unscientific as a topic largely because the mechanistic approach had no way to analyze consciousness. Now consciousness is again a serious concern of scientific psychology. But is our mechanistic model any more useful than previous attempts? Is a computer conscious? If not, it cannot provide ideas about the function of consciousness; that is, the computer would be irrelevant to the question. Since the computer is not a biological entity and humans are, many important issues about the human mind may resist computer modeling.

Essentially the same argument has been offered time and again against any attempt to explain mental processes by referring to the operation of the brain. The argument is that no piece of tissue is conscious and, thus, the explanation of conscious experience cannot be found by reducing the description to this level of analysis. This does not mean that cognitive neuroscience has no value. Quite the contrary—cognitive neuroscience is invaluable in providing information about the brain and its relation to cognitive phenomena. For example, exciting new research suggests that the frontal lobes of the brain are associated with the type of control of behavior that characterizes conscious cognition. But does this finding really offer an explanation of consciousness? Surely it tells us the corresponding brain part, but, without prior ideas from psychology about the nature of consciousness, we would not have even been able to make sense of the brain research. Indeed, the argument goes, psychological theory is necessary to accomplish meaningful research in neurocognition, but the information obtained about the brain is not an explanation of the cognitive phenomenon. The explanation will be found in psychological theory.

OVERVIEW OF HISTORY

We have traveled quite a distance since the time of Wundt, Ebbinghaus, and James. Some might think we have spent the time going in circles because the questions about mental processes are much the same as they were 100 years ago, but such an opinion belittles the importance and difficulty of these questions. Understanding of the mind is among the last frontiers to be conquered by science, and the conquest is not going to be easy. Herein lies the excitement. We have seen that attempts to divest the study of human behavior of mental concepts failed, in part because mental functioning seems to be a real cause of behavior. Powerful new weapons became available to describe mental processes in a traditional, mechanistic fashion, but, as you will see, some of the old issues (e.g., what controls attention) continue to resist a completely mechanistic analysis. Psychological theory has not been rendered obsolete by computer science or neuroscience.

THE IMPORTANCE OF MEMORY

People are sometimes surprised by the emphasis placed on memory by cognitive psychology; after all, isn't memory just the dredging up of past events? Why would memory be so important in the general study of the mind? We want to begin to remove some of that surprise at the outset. Memory is the heart of human intellectual functioning and, consequently, is involved in all processes from perception to reasoning. Memory is much more than a static storage bin of facts; indeed, the storage function, while important, is much less interesting than the dynamic functions served by memory. Ellis (1987) illustrates this point by encouraging you to imagine life without memory. Of course, without memory you would be completely incapacitated in the working world, unable to function in even the simplest situation and unable to communicate coherently with your colleagues. Much more serious, however, is the fact that your social life would be nonexistent. You would have no friends because you would not be able to recall a person or anything about that person from one encounter to the next. Most devastating would be the lack of personal identity, or self-concept. With no memory for prior personal experiences, how could continuity exist such that you could answer the question, who am I? You literally would confront a stranger in the mirror.

Ellis (1987) notes an extremely important implication of memory loss that you may not have considered but that underscores the centrality of memory to human behavior. With no memory for the past, you would have no basis for predicting the future. We are not talking about crystal balls but, rather, the commonplace phenomenon of setting goals and planning your actions toward those goals. You probably have some idea of what you are going to do when you finish reading this chapter. With no access to the past, you would not be capable of even this mundane level of planning, let alone grandiose schemes for your future. If you think about it for a moment, almost all your plans are based upon experiences you have had; with no memory of those experiences, development of plans would be impossible.

Endel Tulving (1985) reports a conversation he had with a densely amnesic patient who had suffered severe head injury. The patient was incapable of remembering information for any extensive period of time, but of interest to Ellis' point about the future is the patient's response when Tulving asked him what he planned to do after the interview. The patient replied that he did not know what he would do. Tulving asked the patient to think about it, but still no plan came to mind. When asked what his mind was like when he thought about what he was going to do, the patient replied that it was very much like an empty room, a room with no furniture. Tulving's fascinating interview confirms the importance of memory, not just as a repository of the past but as an important basis for making plans for the future, plans which are essential to guiding our behavior.

You will see in this book the central role of memory in various aspects of normal behavior. As was shown in figure 1.1, memory assists in the perception of your world and is an indispensable tool in reasoning and in solving the problems confronting you daily.

SUMMARY

Cognitive psychology is the scientific study of mental processes. Although psychology historically was established as a discipline devoted to such study, attempts were made to divert attention from this goal. Psychology has returned to the original mission armed with new techniques and models such as brain imaging and parallel distributed processing. Cognitive psychology proceeds through a combination of theory and experiment, as does all of science. Observations of performance are used to infer the psychological processes which must be necessary to produce the performance. With the help of the computer model, the cognitive psychologist develops ideas about the most important and interesting questions facing science: what are the structure and function of mental processes that account for human behavior.

TO THE STUDENT

At the end of each chapter, a set of thought questions is provided. These questions sample some of the chapter content and, thus, provide an index of your comprehension of the material. The questions are not, however, exhaustive of the content of the chapter and, hence, should not be relied upon exclusively for study and review. Some questions tap the factual information of the chapter, whereas others attempt to apply concepts and principles to new situations not directly described in the text.

THOUGHT QUESTIONS

1. Why is the concept of intentionality difficult to explain in a mechanistic fashion?
2. Describe the difference between empiricism and rationalism? Why is this distinction important in the history of cognitive psychology?
3. What was the important contribution of psychophysics to the development of psychology?
4. What were some of the reasons that behaviorism fell out of favor among some psychologists?
5. What was the importance of the computer to the development of cognitive psychology?

2

PERCEPTUAL PROCESSES

All of your experience of the world begins when physical energy from the environment contacts appropriate sensory receptors. Even though you are aware only of your perception—the smell of a pine forest, the sound of your favorite music, the sight of the Manhattan skyline, the feel of a silk shirt, the taste of smoked cheddar cheese—each experience starts when physical energy contacts nerve cells that will respond to that energy. Not everyone understands this simple point (see box 2.1), but now that you do, you are in the position of appreciating the deep mystery of your ability to perceive the world. Namely, the meaningful psychological experiences of smelling, hearing, seeing, feeling, and tasting are initiated by properties of the environment that bear no physical resemblance to what you ultimately perceive. How does this happen? Understanding the translation of physical energy into meaningful psychological experience is the goal of cognitive psychologists studying perception.

Consider the problem posed by vision. Visual recognition of an object is based upon the physical energy of light; yet the physical description of light waves is nothing like the psychological experience of the object we see. Light waves are

---

BOX 2.1

MISCONCEPTIONS ABOUT PERCEPTION

Several ancient Greek philosophers, including Plato, Euclid, Empedocles, and Ptolemy, believed that visual perception was caused by some form of ray that was emitted from the eye and then bounced back from whatever object was hit by the ray. This theory is essentially the direct opposite of the truth as we now know it. But not everyone knows the truth. In a fascinating series of experiments, Winer, Cottrell, Gregg, Fournier, and Bica (2002) have studied normal adults' belief about how visual perception works. For example, people were given several different schematic versions of the relationship between the eye, a seen object, and the transmission of energy between the two. In one version, the energy was emitted by the eye and went to the object; another version correctly depicted energy coming from the object to the eye. When asked to select the diagram that showed how perception actually occurs, over 50 percent of the people chose the version with energy coming out of the eye. The same result occurred when verbal descriptions were used instead of schematic drawings, demonstrating that the results were not due to misinterpretation of the drawings.

Perhaps the most astonishing aspect of the research was that this false belief was not changed by education. Several experiments involved participants who had completed the section on perception in their introductory psychology course. In addition, some of these participants were given a reading on visual processing and told they would be tested on that reading. In spite of these educational opportunities, the majority of the students persisted with the erroneous view that the eye emits something when we see. If you held such beliefs, obviously you were not alone, but now you can recognize that the belief is totally wrong.

actually electromagnetic energy, one of the four basic forms of energetic forces accepted by physicists. Waves of electromagnetic energy are produced by acceleration of electrons, and the electromagnetic wave carries energy from one space to another. A familiar example is the light emitted by an ordinary light bulb, which is due to electrons undergoing rapid acceleration within the hot filament. The electromagnetic energy generated by electrons accelerating in the filament is carried across space as a wave of electromagnetic energy. This wave contacts receptors of your eye and starts the process of seeing. *The point of this discussion is that the literal physical stimulus is nothing like your perceptual experience.* Electromagnetic energy contains no psychological meaning. Psychological processes must interact with this physical energy in order to add meaning to sensory experiences. The following example helps clarify this point.

Imagine that you are playing a variation of the old game twenty questions. The game is very simple: one player describes an object to another player, who must guess the object from the description. In our special version of the game, however, your description must be limited to the way the object looks. You can provide as cues only the visual attributes of the object. Does this sound simple? Try to describe an apple using only the properties that are available to vision so that another person will be able to guess that you are describing an apple. Do not use attributes that cannot be seen such as *tart, juicy, crunchy,* or *fruit.* This exercise demonstrates that just providing the visual description of a common object is difficult enough, and that a person attempting to guess what the object is will probably require several tries. When we recognize an object in the environment, the information-processing sequence begins with the same type of raw sensory information. Nonetheless, we rarely experience difficulty in moving from sensory information to full identification of a familiar object. How does this commonplace but remarkable event occur? This example illustrates the central issue of *pattern recognition,* translating patterns of sensory signals into psychological experiences of recognizable objects. Before pattern recognition is considered, however, we must discuss a prior step in processing, the *sensory register.*

Let us return to the example of the modified twenty questions game. Why is it so difficult to identify an object when cues are based solely on visual description of that object? The difficulty is due, at least in part, to the fact that visual properties do not exhaust the *meaning* of an object. Indeed, the visual properties alone have very little meaning in the sense of precisely specifying an object for someone else. Thus, we do not extract meaning from the physical energy of light, but, rather, we actually add information to what is provided by stimulation of the receptors. For example, the visual properties of an apple somehow activate other knowledge of apples, such as their taste and smell and abstract information such as apples are fruit. This constellation of information, then, constitutes the meaning of *apple,* and activation of this information allows us to identify the visual experience as apple. Notice that we have now moved far beyond the visual information initially provided to the retina of the eye.

Critical for our present purpose is the realization that the enrichment of sensory information takes time. In the twenty questions game, some amount of time is obviously required to guess the object being described. During this time, the guesser is searching for objects that meet the description. Although visual information processing rarely requires such a lengthy period of deliberation, some real time elapses between reception of visual information and recognition of the object represented by that information. If this point is understood, the function of the sensory register is easily grasped.

THE SENSORY REGISTER

The sensory register is a memory system designed to store a record of the information received by receptor cells. Receptor cells are the specialized sense organs of the eye, ear, nose, tongue, and skin which respond to physical energy from the environment. Firing of the receptor cells begins the psychological processes of sight, hearing, smell, taste, and feeling. Once these receptor cells have been activated, the record of this activation is preserved, or stored, on the sensory registers. The stored record is known as the *sensory trace.*

Perception, thus, begins with the activation of sensory receptors, and this pattern of activity is stored in a memory system, the sensory register (the terms *sensory register* and *sensory store* are used interchangeably). It seems a bit strange that the initial stages of processing include a memory system. Why do we need to store or maintain the sensory trace? Why not assume that the processing of receptor activity begins immediately, without the necessity for storage? Actually, the concept of the sensory register serves a very specific function. Figure 2.1 outlines the main reasons for postulating a sensory register, and you

FIGURE 2.1
Why do we need a sensory register?

Why do we need a sensory register? The answer to this question determines the necessary characteristics of the sensory register.

- We continuously receive large amounts of information from our environment.
  - continuously → *short duration*
  - large amounts of information → *large capacity*
- This information is received in the form of physical energy.
  - physical energy → *precategorical*
- It takes time to translate this to a meaningful form. Thus, we need a way of maintaining this information until meaning can be applied.
  - maintaining this information → *veridical*

may find this outline helpful as we now describe the functions and characterisics of the sensory register.

Function of the Sensory Register

To understand why the sensory register is assumed to be important, let us again return to the example of the twenty questions game. Guessing the identity of an object from its visual description takes time. We now assume that "guessing" an object from the receptor activity also takes time. That is, processing the sensory information for meaning, adding information to the sensory pattern, is not accomplished instantaneously. Furthermore, we assume that we are limited in our ability to process multiple patterns of sensory information. In other words, we can determine the meaning of only one sensory pattern at a time. Imagine the impossibility of *simultaneously* guessing the identity of two objects from two different visual descriptions in the twenty questions game. These two assumptions now demand that we have a sensory register.

To understand this point, suppose that you are actually looking at an apple. While you are interpreting the information corresponding to *apple,* a worm pokes its head out of the apple for a fraction of a second. The physical energy corresponding to the worm activates the sensory receptors, but the processing system is occupied interpreting the previous information corresponding to *apple.* What happens to the information about the worm? Does it simply fade away without being interpreted? Obviously, such a situation would be very maladaptive; in this example, we would never know that the worm is in the apple. Of course, other more catastrophic events than eating a worm would result if we were unable to process much of the sensory information impinging upon the receptors. What is needed is a buffer, or holding bin, for the sensory information until the interpretive processes are free. This, then, is the function of the sensory register.

The sensory register maintains sensory information until other cognitive processes are capable of interpreting or adding meaning to it. With this initial memory system, we avoid losing present information while we are processing information that has just occurred. Each sensory modality has a corresponding sensory register, but in human beings the most widely studied systems are vision and audition.

The need for a sensory memory may be more acute in audition. For example, when we comprehend conversation, the extraction of meaning lags behind the rate of speech. That is, we do not compute the meaning of each word as it is spoken but, rather, speech continues while we are determining the meaning of what was just said. Unless some means for storing the ongoing speech is available, we would lose much of what is currently being said while we determine the meaning of what was just said. The auditory sensory register then serves the purpose of briefly holding information that cannot be immediately processed. The sensory register thus functions to maintain sensory information until it can be processed, but as we shall now see, this function can be served only if the sensory register has certain characteristics.

Characteristics of the Sensory Register

Three important characteristics of the sensory register allow the system to serve its storage function optimally. First, the information is stored in a *veridical* form. This simply means that the information stored should accurately reflect what happened at the sensory receptor. The second important characteristic is that the sensory register needs to be *relatively large,* at least large enough to store all of the information impinging on the sensory receptor. Both of these characteristics are necessary because the sensory trace has no psychological meaning. Think back to our discussion of the physical description of light at the beginning of the chapter and how electromagnetic waves are nothing like your perception. The sensory trace is the pattern of responding by receptor cells to the physical stimulus. Literally, these responses are either electrical or chemical reactions to the stimulus. As such, the sensory trace has no more psychological meaning than the external stimulus energy.

Consequently, all of the potential information in the energy that contacted the receptors must be preserved in the sensory trace. The sensory trace must be *veridical,* which means a true representation of the energy received by the receptors. Otherwise, the primary function of the sensory register, holding information until it can be processed for psychological meaning, would be defeated. You can easily understand why this is true. Given the ultimate goal of perceiving what is really in the environment, the information in the original stimulus must be faithfully represented by the sensory trace because the sensory trace will be used to construct the meaningful perception.

The third important characteristic is that the information must remain on the sensory register for a *brief* time. Since the sensory register stores all information from the sensory receptors and the receptors are continually receiving information, the sensory register must be cleared quickly to avoid superimposing information from two exposures. For example, the information on the visual sensory register would be blurred if two scenes were registered in quick succession. The resulting image would be difficult to interpret, much as a photographic double exposure supplies blurred images. One conceivable means of avoiding this problem is a rapid decay time for sensory memory. A second way in which the superimposition of two discrete events can be avoided is for the second event to erase the first. Incoming information might displace the existing information on the sensory register. These two mechanisms, rapid decay time and erasure, could clear the sensory register of old information to allow vivid representation of information.

Experiments have provided evidence for each of the three characteristics listed here. Since these studies are the primary support for the existence of sensory register, it is important that these experiments be discussed.

Size and Duration of the Sensory Register   Sperling's (1960) research on the visual sensory register (the visual sensory register is also known as *iconic memory*) illustrates the technique and data used to argue for the large but brief memory system we call a sensory register. Sperling's work is important not only because it addresses the size and duration of the sensory register, but also because it provides clever solutions to several difficult methodological problems. Understanding these problems and Sperling's solutions to them will help you understand the sensory register.

The first problem was the presentation of the to-be-remembered material. Since the sensory register stores information directly from the sensory receptors, a pure test of the system would measure retention from a single activation of the receptors. But how can material be presented such that the receptors are activated only once? In vision, the eyeball tremors or moves every ¼ of a second to prevent a single receptor from receiving constant stimulation. The answer to this question is to present the to-be-remembered material at a rate more rapid than that of eye movement. Sperling presented the materials for 50 milliseconds (1 millisecond = 1/1,000 seconds), a rate you can approximate by closing your eyes and then opening and closing them again as rapidly as possible. In order to have such rapid presentation, special equipment is necessary to provide precise timing and to ensure that the subject is fixating upon the point at which the materials will appear. The stimulus materials were matrices of consonants, containing either 9 or 12 letters. As you can see in figure 2.2, the matrices were arranged in 3 rows of 3 or 4 letters each.

With the issue of how to present the material resolved, Sperling could measure what a person remembers from a single glance at a letter matrix. Now, however, a second serious problem arises which basically questions the need for such an experiment. Prior to Sperling's research, it was well known that people could remember only about 4 letters from a set of 9 or 12 letters. These data are inconsistent with expectations based on the sensory register. If all of the information from the receptors is stored on the sensory register, memory should be virtually perfect. Sperling argued, however, that the temporal characteristics of the sensory register prevent human beings from demonstrating how much information is actually available. The sensory trace is assumed to fade from memory very rapidly; consequently, the time required to report a few items is sufficient to allow

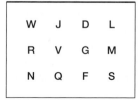

FIGURE 2.2
Example of a letter matrix used in a partial report experiment.

decay of the remainder of the sensory register. The problem now becomes one of demonstrating that subjects have perfect memory for the letter matrix without asking them to recall all of the letters.

The ingenious answer Sperling provided to this problem is based on a technique used by most teachers in assessing what students have learned. Rather than to ask for recall of all of the material—a procedure known as *whole report*—the teacher can ask the student to report only part of the material. If the student does not know which part of the material will be tested, the only sure way to do well on the tested material is to know all of the material. Thus, the teacher can assume that the student's performance on the tested part of the material reflects knowledge of all the material.

The procedure just described is known as the *partial report technique* because the subject has to report only part of the information. Sperling used the partial report technique in the following manner. The letter matrix was shown for 50 milliseconds, and immediately upon termination of the matrix, a tone sounded. The tone was either high, medium, or low frequency and served as a signal for which row to report. The high tone indicated that the top row of letters was to be reported, the middle tone signaled the middle row, and the low tone signaled the bottom row. Thus, only one row of letters was reported on any trial, but the subject didn't know which row to report until the matrix disappeared. Thus, the responses had to be based on memory for the matrix.

With this procedure, Sperling found that the participants were quite accurate, remembering almost 100 percent of a 9-letter matrix and about 75 percent of a 12-letter matrix. With both 9- and 12-letter matrices, the partial report technique suggests that the subjects have approximately 9 letters available on the sensory register. This is a marked contrast to the whole report procedure in which subjects are asked to recall the entire matrix, and they remember only 3 or 4 letters. The higher level of memory in the partial report condition suggests that all of the information in the matrix was available immediately on cessation of the stimulus, just as the reasoning about the sensory register suggests that it should be. Moreover, the difference in performance between partial and whole report performances suggests that the information in visual sensory memory decays very rapidly.

This latter point concerning the duration of visual sensory memory was examined more thoroughly by Sperling in the same experiment. On some trials the indicator tone was delayed following offset of the letter matrix. The delays ranged between 0 and 1 second. The delay conditions were added to see what happens to performance under partial report conditions when the report is not immediate. The results of the delay conditions, as well as the immediate partial report and whole report results, are shown in figure 2.3. Notice the high performance at 0 delay of the tone (immediate partial report). As the tone is delayed further, performance steadily declines to about 1 second. At this point, partial report performance is equivalent to that of whole report. The rapid drop in performance across these short intervals is indicative of a very transient *trace*. Indeed, significant trace decay

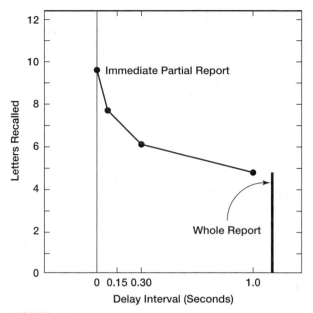

FIGURE 2.3
Number of letters recalled in Sperling's experiment as a function of delay between offset matrix and onset of partial report cue. *(From "The Information Available in Brief Visual Presentations" by G. Sperling,* Psychological Monographs, *1960, 74, Whole No. 948. Copyright 1960 by the American Psychological Association. Reprinted by permission of the publisher and author.)*

seems to have occurred following a 300-millisecond delay, which suggests that visual sensory memory has an effective life of about $^1/_3$ of a second.

Supporting evidence for this conclusion has come from studies of *backward masking,* a phenomenon discovered by Averbach and Coriell (1961). Masking refers to the technique designed to erase the information on the memory register. For example, suppose a letter matrix is presented, and immediately upon offset of the matrix, a cue is given for the partial report. Rather than a tone, however, suppose the cue is either a bar appearing under the position formerly occupied by a letter or a circle surrounding the position formerly occupied by a letter. The participant's task is to report the letter indicated by the marker, a partial report task requiring the subject to report one letter. An example of the use of bar and circle markers is given in figure 2.4. Keep in mind that the markers occur following offset of the matrix. The bar marker produces partial report performance similar to that found by Sperling. With the circle as a cue, however, performance is very poor. Why does a circle disrupt performance in the partial report situation?

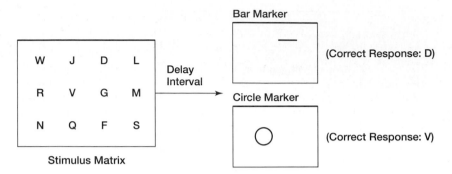

FIGURE 2.4
Example of the use of bar and circle markers, showing the input (stimulus) matrix followed by the marker.

The answer to this question appeals to the erasure of information from the sensory register. The circle appears in the same location as the letter and, consequently, may displace the letter on the sensory register. Since the bar marker is slightly removed from the location of the letter, it would not interfere with the letter's representation. The disruption produced by the circle is due to the masking or erasure of the letter. Since the circle occurs after the letter and its effect must operate backward in time, the technique is known as backward masking. We shall see this technique used to study subliminal perception in chapter 3.

Estimates of the duration of visual sensory memory have been obtained using the technique of backward masking. Since the masking stimulus has its deleterious effect by erasing the sensory representation, the mask should be effective only as long as the information is on sensory memory. Once the information has left sensory memory, either through decay or selection for higher-order processing, performance following a masking stimulus should be no worse than following a nonmasking partial report cue. Thus, the duration of sensory memory can be estimated by systematically delaying the mask following the offset of the target stimulus. Studies using this method show that the mask disrupts performance if it is imposed between 0 to 300 milliseconds after offset of the target. If the mask is delayed to 300 milliseconds after the offset of the matrix, performance is no longer affected by the mask. During the first 300 milliseconds following the offset of the target, an active sensory trace is available, and the mask interferes with this representation. After 300 milliseconds, the mask is ineffective because the sensory representation has decayed. Thus, the estimates of visual sensory memory duration using backward masking have been very similar to those proposed by Sperling, on the order of $1/3$ of a second.

Veridical Representation   The final characteristic of the sensory register is that the representation be veridical to the activation of the sensory receptors. The information on the sensory register must faithfully represent the pattern of receptor activity. Recall our earlier discussion of the lack of psychological meaning in the physical energy of the stimulus, and the receptor activity that is caused by that energy. Because of the lack of meaning, the sensory trace is said to be precategorical. *Precategorical* means that the physical energy and corresponding receptor activity have not been categorized with respect to the object they represent. These patterns do not yet specify any particular object; further processing is necessary for object identification. The primary implication of the assumption of veridical representation is that information on the sensory register will be precategorical. Can we demonstrate that the sensory information requires further processing to attain meaning?

Several studies have addressed this issue by using Sperling's partial report technique in a special way (e.g., von Wright, 1968). Suppose the stimulus matrix presented to the participant consists half of letters and half of numbers. For a partial report cue, you use letters or numbers; notice that this procedure conforms to partial report in that only part of the information must be reported. But an important difference exists between this partial report cue and the spatial cue used by Sperling. To label a visual pattern a letter or number requires categorization of the visual pattern. In other words, the sensory trace corresponding to each symbol has to be processed to decide whether it is a letter or a number before that symbol can be reported. If every symbol must be processed to use the partial report cue, the advantage of partial report is lost. Notice that sensory cues, such as spatial location, do not impose similar requirements. If the cue signals a single row to be reported, no other symbols in the matrix need be processed.

According to the previous discussion, the additional processing for categorization will take time and the sensory memory will decay during the time required for this processing. Thus, if the information in the sensory register is precategorical, any partial report cue which requires that the meaning of the information be processed to determine what is to be reported will produce very poor performance. On the other hand, if the sensory register contains meaningful information, a categorical cue, such as letters or numbers, should give the standard advantage of partial report over whole report.

The data from these studies are clear. A participant given a categorical partial report cue, such as "report all the letters," does no better than a participant given whole report instructions. Apparently, the processing time required to determine if information in the sensory register is a letter or number is great enough to allow remaining information to decay. The results of these studies strongly suggest a precategorical memory system.

Thus, the picture which emerges from research on visual sensory memory is of a brief storage system which holds all of the information received by the receptors. The information is in precategorical form, awaiting further processing to allow interpretation of the information and to bring it to our awareness. In the absence of this further processing, the information will be totally lost, particularly if the external source of stimulation has ceased. But that portion of the information selected for further processing represents what we come to know about our world.

Auditory Sensory Register

As we have seen, the function of the sensory register is to maintain information if the central processing system is otherwise engaged. The need for such a memory in audition is even more acute than in vision. Audition generally requires the integration of information over time. For example, to understand a two-syllable word, the first syllable must be integrated with the second syllable, but, obviously, the second syllable occurs later in time than the first syllable. The same point can be made more dramatically with sentences. Comprehension of a sentence requires that the subject be related to the predicate, but some amount of time separates these two parts of a sentence. If anything, the auditory system may require a longer-lasting sensory memory than vision.

Preliminary evidence for auditory sensory memory, also known as *echoic memory,* was provided by studies comparing partial and whole report performance. As in studies of visual sensory memory, more information was presented than could be processed, and recall was prompted by partial or whole report cues. For example, Darwin, Turvey, and Crowder (1972) asked participants to listen to three different messages, played simultaneously over three different speakers. In the whole report condition, the participant simply tried to recall as much as possible. Partial report required recall from only one of the three speakers. As with visual sensory memory, partial report performance was superior to that in the whole report condition. A number of other experiments have confirmed this partial report advantage in audition, suggesting that more information may be available initially than the person can report.

The Modality Effect   In an attempt to study further the characteristics of echoic memory, some researchers have taken advantage of a memory phenomenon known as the *modality effect.* The modality effect refers to the higher level of recall of the last few items of a list when presentation is auditory rather than visual. For example, participants may be given a list of nine words, presented one at a time. One group of participants sees the words and a second group of subjects hears the words. The people who hear the words recall the last two or three words at a higher level than the people who see the words. The same effect can be obtained even if both groups see the list, but one group is instructed to read the words silently and the other group reads the words aloud. The people who read aloud recall the last few words better than the people who read silently (Conrad & Hull, 1968; Murray, 1966). Since the superior recall of the last words depends upon the presence of auditory input, the modality effect has been attributed to information in echoic memory.

The Suffix Effect   Explanations of the modality effect as the operation of echoic memory have been strengthened by another discovery known as the *suffix effect.* Suppose the nine-word list is followed by another word, which the participants have been told signifies the end of the list. The word can be any nonlist word, and the participants have been told they need not remember the word. Under these circumstances, the last word of the list itself is remembered more poorly than in the case where the subject simply hears the nine-word list. This result is the suffix effect, and the redundant last word is the suffix. A depiction of the effect can be seen in figure 2.5.

The suffix effect occurs only when both the to-be-remembered words and the suffix are presented auditorily. A visual presentation of the suffix does not disrupt memory for auditorily presented words. Further, the extent of the disruption is determined by the physical similarity of the suffix to the target items. If the suffix word is read by a different voice than the target words, for example, the suffix effect is less than if the suffix and targets are read in the same voice. The semantic, or meaningful, relationship between the target and suffix has little effect upon performance (Crowder, 1976).

The relationship between the suffix effect and the modality effect is grasped easily if we assume the modality effect is due to the availability of echoic information, which aids recall of the last items. If, however, a suffix word is appended to the list, the echoic information corresponding to the last list item is masked by the suffix. That is, the suffix is assumed to cause backward masking of the list item in echoic memory and thereby interferes with memory for the last word.

On the basis of this interpretation, one can use the modality and suffix effects to estimate the duration of echoic memory. For example, Watkins and Watkins (1980) asked participants to remember a list of 12 words presented either auditorially or visually. After the list was presented, the recall test was delayed for

FIGURE 2.5
Schematic depiction of suffix effect. Note the data plotted are errors.

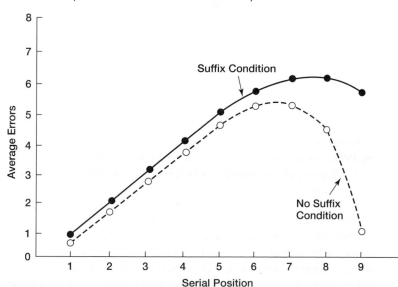

20 seconds during which time the subjects engaged in a silent verbal distractor task. Even after a 20-second delay, the last 3 list words were much better recalled following auditory than following visual presentation, indicating that the modality effect persists for at least 20 seconds. If an auditory distractor task is inserted in the delay interval, the advantage of auditory presentation is eliminated, but a visual distractor task has little effect upon the superior recall of the auditorily presented items. This last result is important in suggesting that the modality effect is modality specific. Because sensory memory is defined as a modality-specific memory, Watkins and Watkins' research corresponds nicely with interpretation of the modality effect in terms of echoic memory.

Questions about Echoic Memory   In spite of the encouraging research described above, questions have been raised about the interpretation of this work. For example, Greene and Crowder (1986) have reported a modality effect when the to-be-remembered items are silently mouthed. Such a situation does not involve auditory sensory input, and if the modality effect were due to echoic memory, the effect would not be expected in situations that do not contain auditory stimulation.

It is unclear, however, that the modality effect obtained when the stimuli are silently mouthed is caused by the same psychological processes as the modality effect obtained when the stimuli are said aloud. In a series of experiments designed to make this point, Turner, LaPointe, Cantor, Reeves, Griffeth, and Engle (1987) discovered that only certain types of stimuli were susceptible to modality effects following silent mouthing. All of the stimuli they used showed modality effects when said aloud. This difference suggests that the modality effects in the two situations may be caused by different psychological processes and leaves open the possibility that the modality effect actually is due to echoic memory processes.

Another difficulty has been establishing the precategorical status of echoic memory. Remember that the partial report superiority is attributed to the additional processing time required in the whole report condition. The additional time is required because the whole report procedure requires that more items be processed than for the partial report. Although several studies have reported the partial report advantage in auditory sensory memory, the interpretation is complicated by difficulty in demonstrating that the auditory sensory trace is precategorical. The precategorical status of visual sensory memory was established by experiments such as the one discussed, which compared partial report using letters and numbers versus spatial location as cues. Letters and numbers are categorical; hence, the additional processing required to use these cues should offset the partial report advantage. Unlike studies of visual sensory memory, categorical cues provide performance equivalent to spatial cues in auditory sensory memory (Darwin, Turvey, & Crowder, 1972; Massaro, 1975).

In summary, the research on echoic memory has produced less agreement about auditory sensory memory than there is agreement about visual sensory memory. This disagreement, however, has been an important impetus for continued research on echoic memory. Such research continues to be quite active and offers the promise of a better understanding of the initial phases of auditory information processing.

PATTERN RECOGNITION

We began this chapter with the mystery of how physical energy in the environment is transformed into perception. What are the processes governing the transformation of physical energy such as light into a meaningful psychological experience?

BOX 2.2

VISUAL SENSORY MEMORY AND SPECIFIC READING DISABILITY

Theory and research on visual sensory memory has been applied to the problem of specific reading disability. *Specific reading disability* is a syndrome which has long been of interest to educators and psychologists because of its unique characteristics. There is now a host of diagnostic categories that include poor reading as a symptom: learning disability, reading disability, dyslexia, and even attention deficit disorder. It is not at all clear, however, that all reading problems have the same cause. After all, lots of different illnesses have coughing as a symptom. In fact, it seems obvious that there are numerous potential causes of reading difficulty. Researchers in psychology have become very sensitive to this problem because if we are to help a person who has trouble reading we must know what causes the problem.

This sensitivity has led to a very precise definition of specific reading disability in research (Morrison, 1991). The definition specifies four criteria for specific reading disability. (1) The person has an IQ score in the normal to above normal range (95 or above). Research has shown that low IQ poor readers are deficient on a broad range of cognitive skills, whereas normal IQ poor readers are deficient on a more limited range of language-related tasks. (2) Poor reading skill is assessed by tests of word-decoding, not by tests of comprehension. Word decoding tests measure phonics skills, which are the ability to translate visual patterns of letters to appropriate sounds. Comprehension tests measure memory skills, reading speed, inferencing, and other general intellectual skills. Comprehension tests of reading ability, thus, will identify poor readers who potentially have a wide variety of cognitive or even social/emotional problems. Word decoding tests assess more specific reading skills. (3) At least among younger children, specific reading disability is not accompanied by deficiency in math. Low IQ poor readers, on the other hand, often show lags in their math achievements. (4) Children who are low achieving in reading and math tend to show social/emotional problems at a much higher rate than specific reading-disabled children. Thus, studies of specific reading disability must be careful to assess participants for social/emotional difficulties. All of these criteria are designed to discriminate between people who have a specific reading problem and people whose reading problem may result from more general causes.

For many years, the primary hypothesis concerning specific reading disability

(Continued)

BOX 2.2   (Continued)

VISUAL SENSORY MEMORY AND SPECIFIC READING DISABILITY

ity was the *perceptual deficit hypothesis*. In its simple form, the idea suggested that reading-disabled children do not see the same images as do normal readers. For whatever reason, the visual system of disabled readers was assumed dysfunctional such that the information available was distorted.

The data supporting the perceptual deficit hypothesis were based, by and large, upon simple perceptual tasks. For example, a child might be shown a single letter or a small set of letters and then asked to say or write the letters after they were removed. The reading-disabled child was likely to perform more poorly than the normal reader and to make mistakes such as letter reversal (mistake *b* for *d*) in these simple tasks. Since the test was administered very soon after termination of the stimuli, the task was assumed to measure the sensory information available to the child, not memory. With the advent of the information-processing framework, a new perspective on the simple perceptual task was available. Perhaps the reading-disabled children did see exactly the same images as the normal readers but memory performance between the two groups differed. In other words, the good and poor readers may register the same information on visual sensory memory but then differ in their *ability to process the information* off of the sensory register.

This idea was tested by Morrison and colleagues (Morrison, Giordani, & Nagy, 1977), using groups of good and poor readers from the sixth grade. The procedure used was a variation of Sperling's partial report in which the subjects were shown a circular array of eight symbols. Three types of stimuli were used: letters, geometrical shapes, and random shapes. The stimulus array was shown for 100 milliseconds and was replaced by a marker at the position of one of the eight symbols. The marker was presented at delays following offset of the array varying from 0 to 2 seconds. After the marker appeared, the child was shown a card containing several symbols. The child's task was to indicate which of the symbols on the card had appeared at the position of the marker on the original array. The test was, thus, recognition rather than recall. The primary questions addressed in this study were: Do poor readers differ from good readers? If they do, is this difference a function of the delay interval? The perceptual deficit hypothesis would predict superior performance by good readers at all delay intervals.

The results, which are presented in figure 2.6, were quite striking. As you can see, there was no difference in the number of trials on which correct recognition occurred until the indicator was delayed by about 300 milliseconds. Beyond this point, the good readers recognized more items than did the poor readers. This outcome was consistent across all types of stimuli.

Using the previous estimates of the duration of visual sensory memory, Morrison's data clearly indicate that poor readers perform as well as good readers when the information is in sensory memory. It is at the point of *higher-order processing* that the poor reader is disadvantaged. The deficit may be a problem of translating visual information to phonetic information, or it may be some confusion of the visual information. Regardless, Morrison's study shows that good and poor readers do register the same sensory information, contrary to the perceptual deficit hypothesis. This is important information in both the understanding and treatment of specific reading disability.

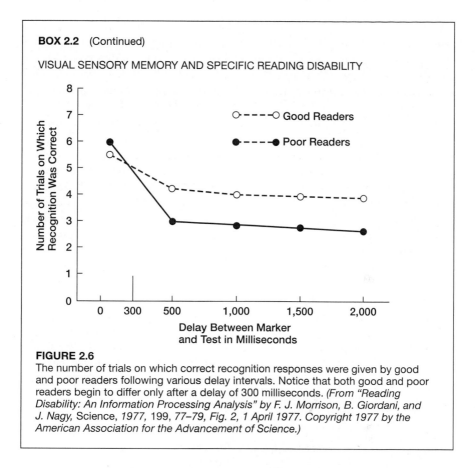

BOX 2.2   (Continued)

VISUAL SENSORY MEMORY AND SPECIFIC READING DISABILITY

FIGURE 2.6
The number of trials on which correct recognition responses were given by good and poor readers following various delay intervals. Notice that both good and poor readers begin to differ only after a delay of 300 milliseconds. *(From "Reading Disability: An Information Processing Analysis" by F. J. Morrison, B. Giordani, and J. Nagy,* Science, *1977, 199, 77–79, Fig. 2, 1 April 1977. Copyright 1977 by the American Association for the Advancement of Science.)*

Our ability to recognize patterns of physical energy is obviously an absolute necessity for survival. Perhaps not so obvious, however, is the flexibility and complexity of the pattern-recognition process. Consider first the enormous range of patterns a person can recognize. The number of people, objects, and events that are immediately and effortlessly recognized by adults is virtually uncountable. You may have difficulty recalling the name of a particular person or object, but rarely do you have trouble recognizing the pattern as a person, a tree, or an airplane. In fact, pattern recognition at this level is accomplished with such ease that the entire issue may appear trivial.

But the ability to recognize patterns of sensory information is neither simple nor trivial. The complexity of pattern recognition can be illustrated by considering some very common situations. You and a friend are standing by the ocean, and you see an object in the distance. You point out the object to your friend and remark on the danger of a swimmer being that far from shore. Your friend laughs and says that the object is not a person but is a sea turtle. You look again and still see a person. A mild argument ensues. Cases of two people disagreeing about a pattern when both are receiving approximately the same physical information are notoriously common. Indeed, you may be surprised to learn that you will frequently respond differently to exactly the same pattern of physical energy. For instance, examine the top row of figure 2.7, which is taken from an experiment of Bugelski and Alampay (1961). What is the fifth symbol in that row? Now examine the second row of figure 2.7. What is the fifth symbol? In the top row, the fifth symbol is easily recognized as a rat, but in the second row the same pattern is just as easily recognized as a face. The same auditory patterns can also give rise to different recognition responses. In normal conversation, the physical pattern of the utterance "new display" is the same as that of "nudist play." Rarely, however, would we fail to recognize the appropriate pattern in normal conversation. Our attempts to understand the apparently simple process of pattern recognition are then complicated by the ability to correctly recognize the same physical energy as different patterns.

The other side of this coin also must be considered. Different patterns of physical energy are frequently recognized as the same pattern. Think, for a simple example, of the enormous variety of ways in which the letter *A* may be written: not only is everyone's handwriting different, but also infinite variations in size and shape are possible. In spite of the incredible variability presented by physical information, the psychological mechanisms respond consistently and accurately. This flexibility in the pattern recognition process is highly adaptive and again illustrates the complexity of the interface between physical energy and psychological experience.

FIGURE 2.7
(From Bugelski, B. R., & Alampay, D. A. (1961). The role of frequency in developing perceptual sets. Canadian Journal of Psychology, 15, *205–211. Copyright 1961 by Canadian Psychological Association. Reprinted by permission.)*

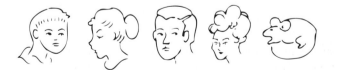

The flexibility of human pattern recognition has been extraordinarily difficult to simulate in machines. Computers can recognize patterns, but the input must be unambiguous. The bizarre numbers on credit cards are necessary for computer recognition because normal Arabic numerals are too similar for consistently accurate recognition by a computer.

Thus, the study of pattern recognition addresses a number of complex issues related to the process of extracting meaning from sensory experience. First, how are we to conceptualize the extraction of meaning from sensory information, capturing both the speed and accuracy of pattern recognition? Moreover, the conceptualization must account for the enormous flexibility of the pattern recognition process, including the influence of contextual information. The complexity of some of these issues is so great as to allow only a general understanding at present, but the discussion of the general conceptualization will lead to more specific ideas and research.

Pattern Recognition and Memory

Pattern recognition works with the information on the sensory register. Remember that information on the sensory register is assumed to be *precategorical,* or without meaning. Pattern recognition is the process by which meaning is derived. In general, pattern recognition is assumed to involve the match between sensory information and the corresponding representation stored in long-term memory. The sensory pattern is recognized as one of the patterns stored in the long-term system. Once this recognition occurs, the information associated with the pattern in long-term memory is available, and in this sense the sensory pattern acquires meaning. The sensory representation is categorized as an instance of something you experienced in the past. Pattern recognition, then, is a process that interprets sensory information by matching that information to previous experiences stored in long-term memory.

Within this general framework, more specific questions can be asked of the pattern-recognition process. For example, pattern recognition requires the interaction of two separate memory systems, sensory register and long-term memory. What is the nature of the representations that are to be matched between these systems? Moreover, how is the decision concerning the "goodness" of the match reached? In other words, the description must consider not only the nature of the codes to be matched but also the processes that are responsible for the matching. In order to give a feeling for the necessary complexity of an adequate description, we shall begin with a very simple theory of pattern recognition.

Template Theory

Perhaps the most intuitive hypothesis of pattern recognition involves a direct match between the sensory experience and the literal copy of that experience. The literal copy, known as the *template*, is stored in long-term memory. The pattern presented by the sensory experience is compared to templates stored in long-term memory until a direct match is found. The matching or decision process is made on the basis of perfect overlap between the sensory pattern and the template, and once overlap is achieved, the pattern is recognized as the template. Template theory in this simple form is essentially a lock-and-key type of hypothesis. The match process continues until a template is found that fits the sensory experience.

The simple template hypothesis is difficult to reconcile with the speed, accuracy, and flexibility of pattern recognition. For example, in day-to-day activities, most familiar patterns are recognized rapidly. Identification of familiar objects in the environment such as a face, or a type of car, seems to occur instantaneously and with no effort. Although we now know from laboratory studies that pattern recognition does require measurable amounts of time, the brief period of time required does not seem perfectly consistent with the description of pattern recognition by template theory. A potential solution to this problem is to assume that the sensory experience is matched against all templates simultaneously, a process known as parallel processing.

Serial and Parallel Processing   According to template theory, the number of templates stored in long-term memory have to equal the number of patterns a person can recognize. This would be a very large number, indeed, if you consider all of the possible variations of all of the possible patterns you can recognize. If each sensory pattern is matched against each template, the process could be quite time consuming. One solution to this dilemma is to make an assumption about the comparison process. Rather than match the sensory patterns to each template one at a time, which is known as *serial processing*, perhaps the match is made against all templates simultaneously. Matching the sensory experience against a number of templates simultaneously, known as *parallel processing*, would greatly enhance the speed of the matching process.

Although parallel processing is not intuitively plausible, probably because of the difficulty of doing two complex things simultaneously, Neisser (1964) provided some evidence in favor of parallel processing in pattern recognition. Neisser's experiment required that subjects scan a sheet of paper containing 50 lines of 4 letters each and press a button as soon as they detected a particular target letter. The target letter was randomly positioned among the letters on the sheet. In the first condition, the subjects were given only one target letter, but in the second condition, the subjects were told to respond to any of 10 different letters. If we assume that the instructions concerning the target letter activate the template for that letter, the sensory patterns are then compared to the activated template. The critical aspect of the experiment for evaluation of serial processing and parallel processing is the number of templates against which the sensory pattern must be matched. If pattern matching is serial in nature, specifying one letter should produce faster recognition than specifying 10 letters. With 10 letters, each sensory experience—that is, each letter on the sheet—would have to be matched against 10 templates, one at a time, whereas the other condition requires only one match for each letter. Parallel processing, however, should produce no difference in match time as a function of the number of potential targets. All activated templates would be matched simultaneously against the sensory pattern, such that the number of activated templates would be irrelevant to the decision time. The results of this experiment, and others since, have in fact shown no difference in the time to detect targets as a function of the number of targets. These data are consistent with ideas about parallel processing, and parallel processing offers a potential solution to one of the problems facing template theory. Unfortunately, other, more serious problems exist.

Preprocessing   Yet another and perhaps more serious difficulty arises for template theory when we try to explain the ability to recognize patterns in spite of wide variation in their physical form. The most obvious position for template theory is to argue that a template exists for every recognizable variation of every pattern. Considering again only the numerous variations in the pattern that can be recognized as *A,* the number of templates necessary is very large. If all of the potential variations of all of the patterns a person can recognize are imagined, the required number of templates is staggering. The large number of templates requires massive long-term memory capacity and the ability to resolve ambiguity concerning which of two or more possible patterns an ambiguous or unusual sensory pattern represents.

One solution to this difficulty is to assume some *preprocessing* of the sensory pattern prior to the matching decision. Preprocessing essentially functions to "clean up" the pattern—for example, to place it in proper orientation, to reduce or expand its size, and to remove extraneous information. For example, the pattern Ɐ might be rotated 180 degrees to form the pattern A prior to being matched with a template. The advantage of preprocessing is that it reduces the number of templates needed in long-term memory. A further logical problem now arises, however. In order for preprocessing to function efficiently, it seems that the pattern must already have been recognized. That is, to reorient or clean up the pattern, you may need to know what the pattern is, yet this is the very process that preprocessing serves. In other words, how does preprocessing decide to reorient Ɐ to A, as opposed to removing the extraneous horizontal line to form V?

A possible solution lies in the influence of contextual information; the context in which a pattern appears delineates the possibilities. For example, the context of Ɐ might be such that an upside-down A is more probable than a V; hence, preprocessing reorients the pattern rather than removes the horizontal line. Indeed, some evidence is available to indicate that reorientation does occur in contextually constrained situations.

If the task is to decide whether you are seeing the pattern R or its mirror image, Я and the pattern is presented in other than its normal orientation—for example, Я—the amount of time to make the decision systematically increases as the stimulus departs from its normal orientation (Cooper & Shepard, 1973). One interpretation of this finding is that the pattern is being *mentally rotated* prior to the match decision. Notice, however, that the alternative patterns have been specified in advance; the subjects *expect* particular patterns. This expectation or prior knowledge can be described theoretically as the activation of the long-term memory representation of the patterns prior to the presentation of the actual stimulus. Activation of the memory representation prior to presentation of the stimulus is under control of the instructions in this task, and these instructions serve as the contextual constraint. Preprocessing becomes possible under these circumstances because the sensory pattern, once it is presented, can be rotated or refined in other ways until it matches the activated template.

This situation is analogous to the rather common experience of looking for a particular person in a crowd, such as searching for a friend at a large party. You know for whom you are looking; that is, the template for that face is activated. If the person for whom you are searching has changed in physical appearance (grown a beard, for example), it is still possible to clean up the pattern to match your memory of the person. Remember, however, the previous criticism of preprocessing. Preprocessing requires that the pattern to be recognized already be activated in long-term memory; although contextual constraints may serve this function, we certainly are capable of recognizing patterns in the absence of knowledge of which pattern is to be recognized. We recognize a face even when a person is unexpected.

Simple template theory thus, has, proved inadequate in describing the richness and flexibility of pattern recognition. Even when supplemented with concepts such as preprocessing, template theory leaves many questions unanswered. As is often the case in science, however, the inadequate theory is invaluable in raising questions for other theories to answer. It is to one of these other theories that we now turn.

Feature Theory

The general class of theories known as feature theories were initially proposed by computer scientists (e.g., Selfridge, 1959) interested in machine pattern recognition and subsequently were brought to the attention of psychologists by Neisser (1967). Although several versions of this approach are available, certain basic ideas are common to all, and we shall discuss these ideas under the general rubric of analysis-by-synthesis. The term *analysis-by-synthesis* describes the process by which pattern recognition is assumed to occur. The initial step in the process is analysis, or breakdown, of the pattern of sensory information on the sensory register. Recognition ultimately occurs through synthesis or reconstruction of the pattern from its component parts. The synthesis process involves the comparison of the sensory information with corresponding representations in long-term memory and a decision concerning the sufficiency of the match between the two. For example, the letter *A* might be analyzed into two oblique lines and one horizontal line, /, /, –. The list of components are then *compared* to lists stored in long-term memory that represent patterns. During the comparison stage, several patterns having some of the features provided by the analysis are uncovered. For example, *M, N, R, V, W, X,* and *Y,* in addition to *A,* all have oblique lines. Horizontal lines are present in *A, E, F, H, I, J,* and *Z.* Thus, the comparison stage might generate several candidates from long-term memory, necessitating a *decision* concerning which is the best match for the sensory pattern. The decision stage determines the amount of evidence for a particular recognition response.

As can be seen from this overview, feature theory involves more complicated *processes* than the simple pattern match proposed by template theory. As will be discussed, the additional complexity adds explanatory power. It also should be clear from the outset that feature theory requires a different kind of long-term memory representation. Rather than holistic templates, patterns are represented by component *features.*

Features All patterns consist of a configuration of elements, and theoretically any pattern can be broken down into these basic elements. The basic elements, or parts, of a pattern are known as *features* of the pattern. For example, the letter *A* consists of the three features /,/, and –. Angles might also be included as features, in which case *A* also has the feature obtuse angle. Any visual pattern, thus, can be described by listing its features. Likewise, acoustic patterns, the sensory information in speech perception, can also be analyzed as combinations of features. As lines and angles seem to be important visual features, speech contains basic units of sounds, called *phonemes,* which determine meaning. The sounds of *b, c,* and *h* in the words *bat, cat,* and *hat* are phonemes in that each of the distinct sound patterns changes the meaning of the word. Much of the exciting research in speech perception is currently devoted to identifying acoustic features.

If physical patterns of light and sound can be described in terms of their components, it then seems reasonable that long-term memory be composed of lists of features describing patterns. Thus, some theorists suggest that patterns are represented in long-term memory as *feature lists.* To recognize a sensory pattern, it then becomes necessary to transform that pattern into the same code as that of long-term memory; specifically, the pattern would have to be analyzed into its component features. The features are then compared to the feature lists of long-term memory to reach a recognition decision.

The concept of features may appear to complicate unduly the process of pattern recognition, particularly compared to the rather straightforward template hypothesis. What advantage does the concept of featural representation offer that could possibly justify the complexity?

The feature hypothesis handles several problems that are difficult for the template theory. For example, template theory is forced to postulate an enormous number of templates in long-term memory corresponding to each pattern we recognize. Feature theory, on the other hand, can reduce this load on long-term memory by assuming that only the finite set of features is represented in long-term memory. That is, the number of possible lines and angles of visual stimuli is large but not as large as the total number of patterns we can recognize. By assuming that any pattern can be described as some combination of features, long-term memory need only contain one complete listing of features, and each pattern is represented by the activation of some unique subset of the features. Thus, feature theory enjoys a conceptual advantage over template theory in terms of the burden placed on long-term memory.

Further justification for a featural representation is derived from studies demonstrating the psychological reality of features. Research from both physiological and behavioral perspectives yield results highly consistent with feature theory. For example, a number of physiological studies on a variety of animals have shown that specific cells in the visual system respond differentially to simple stimuli such as line orientation or angles (Hubel & Wiesel, 1962; Lettvin, Maturana, McCulloch, & Pitts, 1959). These cells seem to be specialized in detecting the simple visual stimuli, that correspond to what have been called features of a pattern. Cells have even been identified in the frog's visual system that respond only to small, dark, moving objects. Perhaps these cells function as a lunch detector for the frog. Equally impressive are data demonstrating cortical cells in monkeys that fire only to the visual stimulus of a monkey paw! The important point here is that neural mechanisms fire to specific patterns, a fact that corresponds well with feature theory.

Behavioral data also have been offered in support of feature theory, particularly in the form of confusion matrices. Confusion matrices summarize the patterns of errors a person makes in making judgments about rapidly presented letters. For example, when the letter *A* is presented very rapidly and a mistake in judgment is made, the letter reported is likely to share visual features with *A,* such as do *H, K,* or *N.* If the process of recognizing these patterns entails the use of basic features, confusion among patterns sharing features would be expected. Feature theory thus helps us understand data from both behavioral and physiological research and therefore gains credibility. Armed with both logical and empirical justification for a feature code in memory, the analysis-by-synthesis approach describes a series of steps by which the sensory features of a pattern are matched in long-term memory.

The Process of Analysis-by-Synthesis   Essentially, three steps are involved in analysis-by-synthesis, as illustrated in figure 2.8. The *first* step is extraction of information from the sensory register. Unlike template theory, which assumes that the holistic sensory representation is lifted from the sensory register, analysis-by-

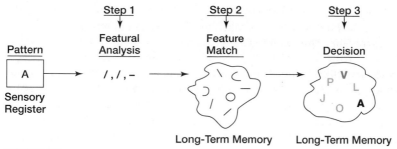

FIGURE 2.8
The three steps in pattern recognition in analysis-by-synthesis. Degree of activation is indicated by the boldness of the pattern.

synthesis assumes that the sensory representation is analyzed into component features. The first step, then, is to extract information from the sensory register through the featural analysis of the pattern. The identification of these features is the *second* step. Here, the features contained in the pattern are matched to features in long-term memory. As you can see, this stage of pattern recognition is very similar to template theory. Each sensory feature must be matched against what amounts to a template in long-term memory. In spite of this similarity, the advantage of feature theory is that the number of feature templates necessary to describe all patterns is assumed to be smaller than the total number of patterns. The *third* step is the decision process itself in which the set of features selected and identified in the first two stages are compared with feature lists in long-term memory. The feature lists in long-term memory define the patterns, and for convenience, figure 2.8 shows the third step as wholistic patterns. The best match in terms of the number of overlapping features is selected as the pattern represented by the sensory information. The pattern in long-term memory containing the most features in common with the sensory pattern is then selected as the recognition response. Notice that other patterns also receive some activation in the decision process if their features are present in the analyzed set of features. This is depicted in figure 2.8 where the letter *V* receives some amount of consideration in the decision process. The process of analysis-by-synthesis, thus, proceeds from initial analysis of the sensory pattern into component features, to identification of these features, to the final decision concerning what pattern is represented by the features. The final step represents a synthesis in that the separate features are now put together in the pattern decision.

As described thus far, analysis-by-synthesis appears to be completely *data driven.* That is, the entire process seems to be guided by the features of the sensory pattern. As we have previously seen, however, certain recognition decisions cannot be determined solely by the sensory data; the same sensory pattern may be recognized as a different pattern in a different context. Refer again to figure 2.7. Because the sensory data from the specific pattern are the same in the two situations, some other information and process must account for the recognition decision. The additional information is derived from the context in which the pattern occurs, and the context is assumed to affect recognition by activating conceptual information or *presynthesizing* the pattern.

Context and Conceptually Driven Processing   Let us illustrate the effects of context and the process of presynthesis through an experiment by Reicher (1969) on the *word superiority effect.* Suppose that the word *BOOK* is presented at a very fast exposure rate. Immediately at the offset of the word, the subject sees _ _ _ ?, and the task is to report the letter which had appeared in the space occupied by the question mark—in this example, *K.* In order to estimate the influence of the word context upon letter recognition, it is also necessary to measure recognition in a nonword context. For example, the stimulus *OBOK* could appear, followed by the same test query, _ _ _ ?. Note that in both cases *K* is the pattern to be reported, but in one instance, *K* occurs in the context of a word and, in the second instance, it occurs in nonword context. The results of such comparisons show both more accurate and more rapid recognition when the letter occurs in the context of a word.

This result, however, is not perfectly straightforward because the probability of guessing the correct letter is higher in the word context. That is, the participant may not have seen *K,* but only *BOO.* Knowing the response should be a letter that completes the word beginning in *BOO* makes *K* a fairly obvious guess. Correct guessing in the nonword context is much less likely. Thus, the advantage provided by word contexts may have little to do with true recognition but may result simply from a higher probability of guessing. It is possible, however, to control for guessing by changing the test to recognition with alternative choices, either of which would make a word. For example, the test alternatives for *BOOK* might be *K* and *T,* and the subject must choose the correct response. The same test is given following the nonword context. The important point is that any differences between the two conditions can no longer be attributed to guessing from the word context. With the guessing probability thus controlled, recognition of the final letter is still more accurate when that letter is presented in the context of a word.

How does the analysis-by-synthesis approach describe this facilitating effect of context? First, it should be apparent that context serves to narrow the possible choices among the incoming patterns. Whether we are talking about a letter, an object in the environment, or a face, the context in which a pattern occurs limits the possible choices. Another way of saying this is that the context establishes expectations concerning incoming patterns. Analysis-by-synthesis tries to capture this expectation through the concept of presynthesis. Remember that the final stage of recognition involves synthesis of the sensory features, in that the previously analyzed sensory features are compared to feature lists in long-term memory. Contextual information, however, could serve to activate the patterns in long-term memory prior to the appearance of the actual sensory representation of the pattern. In other words, the context leads us to expect a particular pattern, which may be constructed with minimal reference to the sensory information.

BOX 2.3

WHY PROOFREADING IS SO DIFFICULT

Since presynthesis amounts to constructing a pattern based on expectation of what the pattern should be rather than on sensory information, certain situations are likely to lead to embarrassing recognition failures. A prime example of such a situation involves proofreading a paper. People commonly fail to detect misspellings or typographical errors when proofreading their own written work. In terms of the analysis-by-synthesis model, you usually know what you have written or at least what you meant to write. Consequently, in proofreading, you are likely to construct patterns on the basis of your expectations, and it is sometimes difficult to force yourself to check carefully the sensory pattern, the actual writing itself. Errors may, thus, go undetected even after "careful" proofreading of the material. If you understand that pattern recognition in normal reading usually proceeds with a great deal of presynthesis, you may realize that extra effort is required to avoid presynthesis or at least to force yourself to check the presynthesized pattern against the sensory information. An effective means of doing this is to get someone to help you proofread important material. One person reads the material aloud to the other person, who follows along, using another copy of the material. By reading aloud, you can slow the normally rapid pattern recognition in reading and perhaps reduce the tendency to rely heavily on presynthesized patterns. By having a person unfamiliar with the material read along with you, you further increase the chance of detecting errors. Although this may seem to be a rather extreme measure just to correct minor errors (it certainly requires a good friend to tolerate the tedious task), you should not underestimate the impact minor errors can have upon supervisors, clients, or colleagues in whatever career you choose. You probably already know of professors' reactions to "minor" errors. The point is that the normal operation of the pattern recognition system can work to your disadvantage, and sometimes it is worth extraordinary effort to ensure that what you think you see is really there.

A competent reader, for example, certainly does not analyze each letter in each word. Indeed, reading seems to involve much in way of presynthesis or anticipation of patterns. Adult readers rarely notice the omission of articles such as *the* and *a*. Did you notice that the sentence before last omitted *the* prior to *way?* We seem to fill in the blanks with patterns that fit with the prevalent context. This process is an example of *conceptually driven* pattern recognition in which the final recognition decision is guided by long-term memory rather than by sensory information. The startling implication is that people may "recognize" patterns *without* any sensory experience with those patterns!

Structural Theory

Feature theory assumed that patterns are recognized by consulting lists of features stored in long-term memory. Some theorists consider this idea insufficient to

FIGURE 2.9
Two objects with the same constituent parts. The spatial relation between the parts differentiates the objects. *(Adapted from Biederman, 1987.)*

explain some very simple cases of object recognition. For example, look at the two objects in figure 2.9. One is obviously a cup and the other obviously a pail, but the two clearly have the same features. What is missing from feature theory is any means to represent the spatial relationship among the parts. This spatial relationship is critical even when perceiving two-dimensional objects such as words, (e.g., *on* versus *no*) and is essential when trying to understand the three-dimensional perception of objects. To remedy this shortcoming, a third type of theory has been suggested known as *structural theory.* Structural theory, like feature theory, assumes that objects are perceived on the basis of parts, but these parts are three-dimensional geometric components of the objects rather than features. For example, the components may be such things as cylinders, blocks, and wedges; geometric shapes that are primitive components of three-dimensional objects.

Perhaps the best known of the structural theories was proposed by Biederman (1987), who called his idea recognition-by-components. At the heart of the theory is the representation called a geon, geon meaning geometrical icon. *The geon is hypothesized to be the primitive long-term memory representation analogous to features in feature theory.* An object is stored in long-term memory as a set of geons in a particular spatial relation to one another. Examples of geons and objects containing those geons are presented in figure 2.10.

Pattern recognition begins with an analysis of the sensory pattern into component geons. The idea is very much like feature theory in that activation of the geons comprising an object is the basis of pattern recognition. Unlike feature theory, the process of pattern recognition also takes the spatial relations among geons into account, allowing easy discrimination between objects such as the cup and pail in figure 2.9. Another substantial difference between recognition-by-components and feature theory is that Biederman argues that 36 geons are sufficient to provide the primitive representations for all of pattern recognition. The number of features necessary has never been stated, but it is safe to assume that the number would be considerably larger than 36. Remember that one of the advantages of feature theory over template theory was the smaller number of long-term memory representations required by feature theory. If this is an important consideration, and it surely is in programming a machine to recoognize patterns, then structural theory is an advance over feature theory.

Research on structural theory has been quite promising. For example, Biederman, Ju, and Clapper (1985) studied the ability to rapidly identify objects based on line drawings. In some cases, the drawings were of a partial object constructed such that it contained the largest geons as specified by the theory but was otherwise incomplete. The number of geons in the partial objects was

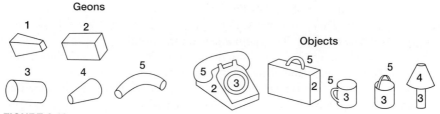

FIGURE 2.10
On the left are some geons, and on the right are objects created from these geons. The numbers correspond to particular geons. *(From Biederman, I. (1985). Recognition by components: A theory of human image understanding.* Computer Vision, Graphics, and Image Processing, 32, 29–73. *Copyright 1985 by Academic Press. Used by permission.)*

systematically manipulated in the experiment but at least two geons were represented in each drawing. The drawings were presented at a very rapid rate (50-100 msecs.) and subjects tried to identify the object. The significant result was that recognition accuracy was quite good with even a small percentage of the total component geons present and, further, that the speed of recognition was almost as fast with only a few of the largest geons present as it was with all of the geons. The point of the experiment is that specifying geons as the input does lead to successful pattern recognition, even for partial patterns.

Concerns about the adequacy of structural theory of pattern recognition are similar to some concerns about feature theory. For example, some patterns are not obviously described as geons. A puddle of water has no obvious geometric components. Another potential limitation is that some objects that can be discriminated as different patterns do not seem to have different geometric components. A Shetland pony is recognized as different from a Saint Bernard but the geonic difference is not immediately apparent. Nonetheless, structural theory is early in its development and further refinements of the theory may clarify these and other questions.

Parallel Distributed Processing

Another theory of pattern recognition is parallel distributed processing (PDP). PDP incorporates most of the ideas we have described in previous theories but also adds new assumptions that vastly increase the complexity of the framework. The PDP approach differs fundamentally from previous theories in that its model of pattern recognition is the *activity of the brain* rather than the activity of a computer. The important manifestations of this difference are that all processing is assumed to be parallel and that knowledge resides in the connections among units rather than the units themselves.

Parallel Processing   The parallel processing assumed by PDP is of two sorts. First, all of the information available to the sensory field is processed simultaneously. In the simple case of recognizing a word, the assumption is that the processing of each letter of the word begins simultaneously if all of the letters are in the visual field. This is in contrast to the possibility that each letter of the word is processed sequentially. The second sense of parallel processing is that the "parts" of the object are processed simultaneously with the "whole" object. This processing of part and whole is interactive such that, for example, the processing of a word influences the recognition of the letter. Advocates of PDP argue that massive parallel processing is required by the "neural model" of pattern recognition because neurons are so slow. Neurons operate on a time scale of milliseconds, whereas computer components operate on a time scale of nanoseconds, much faster than neurons. Given that the psychological processes to be modeled are often very complex and that the neurons are relatively slow, the assumption must be that the processes operate in parallel in order to accomplish their function in a reasonable time frame (McClelland, Rumelhart, & Hinton, 1986).

An illustration of parallel processing can be seen in figure 2.11. This illustration is taken from McClelland and Rumelhart's (1981) theory of pattern recognition.

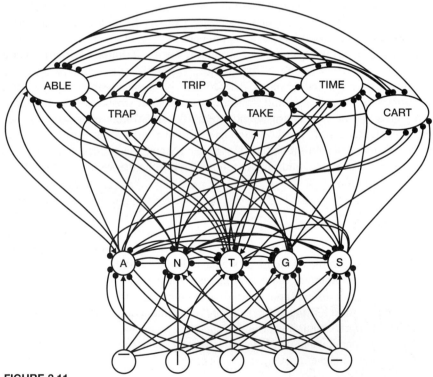

FIGURE 2.11
An illustration of the connectionist network proposed by McClelland and Rumelhart (1981). *(From "An interactive activation model of context effects in letter perception: Part 1, An account of basic findings" by J. L. McClelland and D. E. Rumelhart. Psychological Review, 1981, 88, 375–407.)*

In this illustration the presented pattern is the letter *T*. The analysis begins with feature extraction that provides input to letter activation. But notice that the connections from all features go to all letters; the letters themselves are interconnected, and the letters and words are connected so that activation can proceed in both directions. On appropriate activation, all of this interconnected network can operate simultaneously. This is massive parallel processing.

Distributed Knowledge   The second assumption that is driven by the neural model is that knowledge resides in the connections, not the units connected. We have known for some time that most brain functions operate in accord with mass action; that is, the brain function is not localized to one exclusive structure such as a single neuron. Therefore, the assumption of most theories that the knowledge required for recognition and comprehension is localized to a single representation (node or proposition) is at odds with this fact of brain functioning. PDP models assume that the knowledge is distributed across the connections and that knowledge is represented by these connections, not by the units.

Again consider the illustration in figure 2.11 from McClelland and Rumelhart (1981). The connections among the units can be excitatory or inhibitory. Excitatory connections in this example are indicated by an arrow at the terminal point and inhibitory connections by a dot. The eventual recognition of the presented pattern as a *T* is not modeled by the activation of a T-node but, rather, it is the sum of the activity, both excitatory and inhibitory, in the network that represents *T*. It is the activity of the connections that represent knowledge in the PDP framework. The connections and their valence, excitatory or inhibitory, are formed as the result of experience. Thus, the knowledge is the result of learning.

An Example of PDP and Pattern Recognition   Let us illustrate this general overview of PDP with a specific example from McClelland and Rumelhart. Suppose the word *WORK* has been presented to a subject, and the subject has extracted the features as shown in figure 2.12. All of the features of *W, O,* and *R* have been processed, but the features of the final letter are consistent with both *R* and *K*. Note that the situation is somewhat similar to the experiment by Reicher (1969) that we described previously. How does a connectionist framework lead us to recognition of the last letter as *K?*

FIGURE 2.12
A hypothetical set of features that might be extracted from the word WORK. *(From "An interactive activation model of context effects in little perception: Part 1, Basic findings" by J. L. McClelland and D. E. Rumelhart. Psychological Review, 1981, 88, 375–407.)*

At the word level of knowledge (refer to figure 2.12), a number of possibilities exist—such as *WORK, WEAR, WORD, WEAK,*—but only *WORK* is consistent with the available evidence. Therefore, *WORK* will have the highest level of activation, and this activation of *WORK* will result in inhibition to the other words from *WORK*. The excitation these other words are receiving from their feature activation is dampened by the inhibition coming from the word *WORK*. The excitation of *WORK* feeds back into *K* at the letter level but notice, again referring to figure 2.12, that the activation of the letter *K* will continue to excite the word *WEAK* as well as the word *WORK*. The excitation of *WEAK* feeds back to the letter *K*. Even though the word *WEAK* is receiving inhibition from *WORK,* the letter *K* receives the excitation from the residual activation of *WEAK*. Over a relatively short period of time, the parallel activity in this interactive set of connections strengthens *K* to a level of activation that allows recognition of the word *WORK*.

This example illustrates the use of ideas from various other theories of pattern recognition such as feature detection, associative interconnection, spreading activation, top-down processing, and bottom-up processing. Added to these notions, however, are the important ideas of parallel processing and distributed knowledge. Application of PDP has provided successful simulation of various recognition phenomena when run on computers, and although questions have been raised about its importance to psychology (e.g., Pinker & Prince, 1988), this critical inhibition is not likely to dampen the excitement of researchers in this area.

THE COGNITIVE NEUROSCIENCE OF PATTERN RECOGNITION

The world is filled with a dazzling array of different objects, each defined by a particular combination of shape, color, size, and texture, as well as by characteristic patterns of movement. Rapidly recognizing (assigning meaning to) these objects has been crucial for our survival as a species. Note, however, that the survival value of object recognition depends not only on identifying *what* kind of objects are in our environment (whether an object is predator or prey, for example), but also *where* those objects are located and which way they are moving. Indeed, this distinction between "what" and "where" appears to be so important that it is built into the very anatomy of our brains.

The "What" and "Where" Visual Pathways

Visual information processing begins when light stimulates photoreceptors (rods and cones) on the retina. Activity from the photoreceptors is then integrated in bipolar and ganglion cells (also part of the retina), the projections from which make up the optic nerve. The optic nerve transmits activity to a number of different areas in the brain, but the vast majority of its projections are to the lateral geniculate nucleus (LGN) of the thalamus, the brain's major hub for distributing incoming sensory information. From there, the activity that started in the eye is transmitted to the primary visual cortex of the occipital lobe, an area known as V1 (located at the back of the head and named V1 because it is the first cortical station for visual information processing). Area V1 (as well as V2, the second cortical visual processing area) contains a variety of cell types that are specialized for processing information related to form, color, and motion. These cells then project forward to an astonishingly large number of additional processing areas that are more specialized in their visual function. Indeed, over 30 separate visual areas have been identified in the monkey, each of which appears to perform a relatively specific task related to vision (see Felleman & Van Essen, 1991). Moreover, these areas are linked by well over 100 pathways, most of which are *reciprocal,* meaning that they involve both feed-forward and feed-back connections (see below). Figuring out the specific function performed by each area, as well as how "seeing" arises from the patterns of connectivity among these areas, has become a major goal of cognitive neuroscience.

Although the complexity of the neural areas underlying vision can be overwhelming, neuroscientists now believe that these areas are organized into two anatomically distinct pathways, each of which is functionally specialized for accomplishing one of the two major goals of pattern-recognition: the identification of "what" and "where" (see figure 2.13). One pathway starts in V1 and then projects forward into the ventral (lower) portions of the temporal lobe. Known as the *occipitotemporal pathway,* the *ventral stream,* or more heuristically, the *what system,* this pathway is specialized for the identification of objects. Consistent

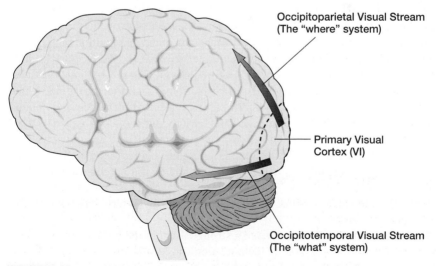

FIGURE 2.13
The anatomical locations of the "what" and "where" symptoms in vision.

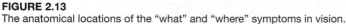

with this function, numerous areas along this pathway appear to be selectively tuned to the features, such as shape, texture, and color, making up an object. The other pathway—referred to as the *occipitoparietal pathway, dorsal stream,* or *where system*—also begins in V1 but then projects dorsally (upward) into the parietal lobe. This pathway is specialized for localizing objects in space as well as processing the spatial relations among objects (i.e., left vs. right, above vs. below, etc.). Areas along this pathway also appear to be selectively tuned to a number of different forms of motion, including direction, velocity, rotation, and expansion/contraction.

Two major sources of evidence support the distinction between these two visual pathways. First, lesion studies in both monkeys and humans have shown that damage along the ventral (occipitotemporal) pathway produces impairment in the identification of objects and the features making up these objects but little impairment on tasks that require judgments about spatial locations. In contrast, damage along the dorsal (occipitoparietal) pathway produces the opposite pattern of deficits—impairment in spatial localization but little or no impairment in the identification of objects. Taken together, these results constitute a "double dissociation" such that one kind of lesion affects performance on one task but not the other, while the other brain lesion produces the opposite pattern of spared and impaired performance. As such, these data provide strong evidence that the two visual pathways are specialized for processing very different kinds of visual information.

The second source of evidence for the what/where distinction comes from neuroimaging studies. For example, Haxby and colleagues (see Ungerleider & Haxby, 1994) used PET (see chapter 1) to examine brain activity while people performed either an object identification task or a spatial localization task. For the object identification task, subjects had to indicate which of two faces matched a target face, a task that makes heavy demands on object recognition but little demand on spatial processing. For the spatial localization task, subjects had to indicate which of two choice stimuli—each consisting of a dot above a double line—had the same spatial relation as in a spatially rotated target stimulus; thus in this task, spatial processing was critical for correct performance but the need for object recognition was minimal. Brain activity during performance of these tasks showed a clear distinction between the pathways described above, with the face-matching task showing activity predominantly along the occipitotemporal pathway and the spatial localization task showing activity predominantly along the occipitoparietal pathway. These highly selective patterns of activity have now been replicated in a number of different studies using a variety of object and spatial processing tasks.

Although the above results make a strong case that the human visual system has specialized pathways for the identification and localization of objects, a number of questions remain. One interesting question, for example, is *why* the brain evolved separate systems for object and spatial vision. A potential answer to this question concerns the computational demands of the two visual functions. Thus, one of the major goals of any object recognition system is *object constancy*—the ability to identify an object as the same regardless of changes in its size, orientation, or position in the visual field. One way to accomplish this goal is to have neurons that respond to relatively abstract ("view-invariant") features of an object (an angry bear, for example), regardless of minor variations in its distance (size), orientation, or motion. The existence of such neurons would allow for the rapid detection of important stimuli (such as angry bears), but such rapid recognition would be achieved at the expense of knowing how far away the bear is, whether it was to your left or right, and the direction of its movement. Obtaining such "view-dependent" information would require the existence of a separate system specifically devoted to the processing of spatial relations and motion, hence the need for the occipitoparietal (where system) pathway. Thus, although initially counterintuitive, the segregation of visual functions into those concerned with *what* and those concerned with *where* appears to be a highly adaptive solution for visual information processing.

A second question raised by the brain's division of labor between "what" and "where" concerns the neural basis of action. Thus, if a single object is processed in parallel by both the ventral (object-based) and dorsal (space-based) visual streams, which of the two streams is used to direct behavior toward that object? One possible answer to this question comes from the work of Goodale and Milner (e.g., 1992), who conducted detailed behavioral studies of a brain-damaged patient known as DF. DF suffered diffuse damage to the brain, concentrated in the occipital cortex, as a consequence of carbon monoxide poisoning. As a result, DF could not *consciously* identify even the most basic features of an object, such as the orientation of a slot or the size of a wooden block. Yet when asked to *act* on such objects, picking up the block or placing her straightened hand into the slot, she performed nearly as well as non-brain-damaged subjects. In addition to showing another dissociation between the dorsal and ventral streams, these results suggest that, instead of being a *where* system, the dorsal stream may be better thought of as a *how* system; that is, a system whose main job is to mediate spatially defined actions such as reaching, grasping, and even looking.

Results from DF, as well as similar patients, show that the dorsal (occipitoparietal) stream plays a key role in mediating visually guided actions. But does this mean that actions are controlled without input from the ventral (occipitotemporal) stream? To answer this question, consider how the visual system works to mediate a simple action like picking up an open pocketknife. Obviously, information processing along the occipitoparietal pathway would be most critical for grasping such an object because this pathway provides detailed information about the knife's orientation in space. However, information about the parts and features of the knife could also be critical—for example, in helping to distinguish the blade from the case, or for determining whether the blade is made of a sharp metal or only a dull plastic. This example brings out an important point: Although we know that the computation of *what* and *where* reflects relatively segregated visual pathways, the information derived from these pathways must somehow be coordinated to allow goal-directed action. Understanding the nature of this coordination is a central topic in visual neuroscience.

The existence of the occipitoparietal (where) pathway emphasizes the point that knowing the location, orientation, and motion of an object is a critical aspect of the pattern recognition process. However, it is the identification of objects that has received the most attention in visual neuroscience (as well as in this chapter), so it is to this issue that we now turn.

The Neural Basis of Object Recognition

As previously noted, neurophysiological studies have shown that individual cells in the primary visual cortex respond selectively to very simple features such as dots, lines, and angles, whereas other cells (along the ventral stream in the inferior temporal lobe) respond to more complex objects such as paws, hands, and faces (e.g., Perret, Rolls, & Caan, 1982). The fact that both kinds of cells can be found in the brain would seem to support both the feature-based analysis-by-synthesis theory as well as the more holistic template-matching theory. In fact, the balance of evidence coming from neurophysiological studies suggests that both kinds of processes (feature analysis and template matching) may be involved in the recognition of objects.

Part of the evidence for such a view is that, consistent with the single-cell activation studies (which have mainly been conducted with cats and monkeys), focal brain damage in humans can produce highly selective impairments in object recognition that span a wide range of stimulus complexity. Thus, while some brain-damaged patients show selective deficits in the perception or identification of simple features such as colors (a condition known as *achromatopsia*) and basic lines and shapes (*apperceptive agnosia*), other patients show deficits restricted to more complex stimuli such as meaningful objects (*associative agnosia*), words (*alexia*), and faces (*prosopagnosia*). This range of deficits suggests that object recognition is supported by representations at different levels of complexity, from simple features to combinations of features to complete objects. Brain imaging studies of word processing also support this interpretation. For example, in a study using PET (see chapter 1), Peterson and coworkers (1990) found that both real words (boar) and pronounceable nonwords (twip) are processed by a different, and more extensive, set of brain regions than are nonsense strings of letters (nfpt) and letter-like forms. These data are consistent with the notion that object recognition along the ventral pathway is a *hierarchical process* involving the activation of both low-level features as well as higher-level holistic representations.

Although the existence of both feature representations and more complex template-like representations certainly adds complexity to our understanding of object recognition, it might well be in accord with how quickly and easily we recognize both familiar objects (those with existing templates) and novel objects (those that have to be built up from component features). It may also help solve some of the problems noted for earlier theories of pattern recognition. For example, it was noted above that a potential problem for template theory concerns the time it would take to match incoming sensory information to the vast number of templates stored in long-term memory. One possibility is that low-level features, such as lines, angles, and geons, are used to initially narrow down the relevant templates in long-term memory (an example of a "feed-forward" process). These activated templates are then used to drive additional analysis of critical low-level stimulus features (a "feed-back" process). Both of these ideas—that the brain contains multiple levels of representations, and that pattern recognition reflects both feed-forward and feed-back mechanisms—are key assumptions of many parallel-distributed processing (PDP) models.

The idea that object recognition reflects both the extraction of low-level features as well as the activation of higher-level templates also raises the question of whether preprocessing is a part of the object recognition process. On the one hand, neuropsychological studies appear to suggest a role for preprocessing of the kind postulated in template matching theory. For example, some patients with damage along the ventral (what) pathway have been shown to have little difficulty recognizing an object when it is presented in its normal ("canonical") orientation but to be unable to identify the same object when it is presented in an unusual orientation (e.g., from directly above). These patients suggest the possibility that objects undergo some form of preprocessing in order to place them into an "object-centered" (view-invariant) orientation, prior to being matched to representations in long-term memory. On the other hand, recent psychophysical and physiological data have suggested that experience with an object results in the creation of a limited number of "view-based" templates (i.e., neurons tuned to respond to different orientations of the same object) that mediate between feature representations and more "object-centered" templates (see Riesenhuber & Poggio, 2000, 2002). For this theory, difficulties in identifying an object in an unusual orientation could result from damage to the relevant view-based templates rather than damage to any preprocessing operation. Regardless of how this debate is resolved, the view emerging from visual neuroscience is of a complex system of representations and processes that interact to produce relatively effortless identification of both familiar and novel objects.

SUMMARY

The emerging picture, then, is of a memory system in which the stimulus is available to the subject both during and immediately after cessation of the stimulus. This information decays very rapidly, however, and much of what is available will not be processed for meaning. Since the information on the sensory register is assumed to be precategorical, it must undergo additional processing to attain meaning. During the brief time required for additional processing, the remaining information decays.

The implication of this situation is quite striking: the vast majority of the information that activates the senses goes totally unnoticed because of the time and effort required to process some minuscule portion of that information. Much of the information stimulating the receptors remains unknown. The ramifications of this conclusion are quite fascinating. What is *missed?* Even more important for cognitive psychology, how is information from the sensory register (which has no meaning) *selected* such that it is consistent with the meaning of what has been processed? As we shall see, this has been a major question in the study of selective attention.

Pattern recognition is the process by which sensory information is used to construct a meaningful perception. Through contact with long-term memory, the meaning of the sensory information is derived. Adequate descriptions of pattern recognition require considerable complexity, as illustrated by the analysis-by-synthesis model. Analysis-by-synthesis assumes a featural representation of patterns in long-term memory, which in turn requires the assumption that sensory patterns are analyzed into features to match long-term memory. Moreover, context affects pattern recognition such that a pattern may be recognized with minimal reference to the sensory information. In some sense, context allows us to make a highly educated guess about a pattern, avoiding the more time-consuming analysis and synthesis of the sensory pattern. Presynthesis of the pattern may increase the speed of pattern recognition, but the potential for error is also increased because the sensory data may contribute minimally to the recognition decision.

More recently, parallel distributed processing and connectionism have entered the arena of theory in pattern recognition. This approach differs from analysis-by-synthesis in assuming explicitly that patterns are processed in parallel. That is, the recognition of letters and words is occurring simultaneously, and the processing of a letter or a word interacts with recognition of other letters and words. In this fashion, the activation of any letter or word is distributed in the form of inhibition or activation to other letters and words.

THOUGHT QUESTIONS

1. What critical function is the concept of a sensory register designed to serve?
2. What was Sperling's experiment and how did the results indicate a short-duration but large-capacity memory system.
3. How are the modality effect and the suffix effect explained by appealing to echoic memory?
4. Why is template theory inadequate to describe the pattern recognition process? How does feature theory deal with these inadequacies?
5. How do the data of cognitive neuroscience contribute to the theoretical debate on pattern recognition?

3

ATTENTION

As of June 1, 2001, 116 million people in the United States subscribed to a cellular phone service, and surveys indicate that 85% of those people use their cell phones while driving. In a study of 699 accidents involving cell phone subscribers, the phone records showed that 24% of the accidents occurred within 10 minutes of a call (Redelmeier & Tibshirani, 1997). At this rate, the increased risk of accidents accompanying cell phone use is equivalent to the increase found with blood alcohol levels above the legal limit. What is it about using the phone while driving that causes problems? An obvious factor is the use of your hands and eyes to do something other than drive, but if this is the only factor, the problem is solved easily by using a hands-free device. Unfortunately, the problem is not so simple.

In a series of experiments by Strayer and Johnston (2001), people were asked to track a moving object on a computer screen by using a joystick to control the cursor. Their job was to keep the cursor as close to the moving object as possible, a task that simulates the visual/motor demands of driving. The tracking task was done under one of three conditions. Two of the conditions involved having a phone conversation, in one case with a handheld phone and in the other with a hands-free mechanism. The third condition involved listening to a radio broadcast. Periodically, either a red light or a green light appeared on the monitor, and the participants were instructed to press the button on the joystick as soon as they saw a red light, a measure designed to model braking while driving. The results of the experiment are presented in figure 3.1. This figure shows the difference in performance when only tracking the object (single task) and when tracking the object while either talking on the phone or listening to the radio (dual task). What you see in figure 3.1 is quite striking. Both the probability of missing a red light entirely as well as the speed to respond to a red light were vastly increased by the phone conversation. It did not matter whether the conversation required a handheld or hand-free device. Listening to the radio had no effect on performance.

The experiments of Strayer and Johnston nicely illustrate the operation of central attention in a common situation. The disruption caused by phone conversation was not due to an inability to see the monitor or to using one hand. Rather, the phone conversation seemed to engage conscious thought in the familiar sense that concentration is required to listen to someone and plan your reply to what they say. Listening to the radio, even though you hear it clearly, does not require this level of concentration. Driving also can require moments of concentrated thought to maneuver through sudden, unexpected events. The fact that the conscious thought devoted to phone conversation impairs driving illustrates the point that our ability to devote conscious thought simultaneously to multiple events is severely limited. Interestingly, research has shown that conversation with a passenger does not impair driving, most likely because the passenger can anticipate demands imposed by driving circumstances and stop conversation when these demands are intense.

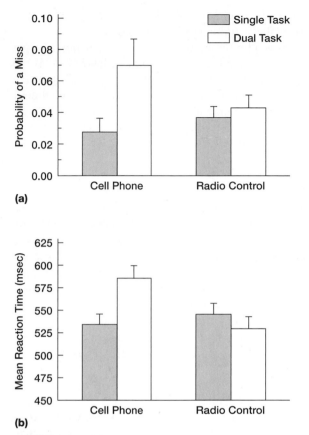

(a)

(b)

FIGURE 3.1
Probability of missing stop light and reaction time to stop at
the light when only driving (single task) or when driving and
using a cell phone or listening to the radio (dual task).

ATTENTION AND CONSCIOUSNESS

Attention and consciousness have a close relationship that developed from the
observation that conscious processing capacity is quite limited. For the moment,
consciousness will be taken to be synonymous with awareness, and to say that
conscious processing is limited is to say that we can be aware of only a few things
at any one point in time. To seriously think about two things simultaneously—for
example, your daydreams and a lecture—is virtually impossible. The psychological process of attention is assumed to select information for conscious thought,
and, since the amount of conscious capacity is limited, attention simultaneously
prohibits other information from reaching awareness. Attention can be seen as

the gatekeeper for consciousness. Attention filters information before it reaches awareness, and whatever passes the attention filter becomes conscious.

But what happens to *unattended* information? Does this information also get processed, or is it completely unavailable to affect behavior later? This is the same question as: does information of which you are unaware influence your behavior? The question is a consistent theme that we shall follow through the research on attention. Even though they may not always be explicit about it, all theories of attention take a position on this issue. However, providing convincing evidence of unconscious processing is not an easy matter.

FILTER MODELS OF ATTENTION

When we use the word *attention* in everyday language, as when we say, "Johnny, pay attention," we are referring to the selective aspect of the attentional process. A classic example of the ability to attend selectively is the well-known cocktail party phenomenon. Suppose you are at a large party, with much good conversation and music. The result is a noisy situation. Yet, you have little difficulty "paying attention" to the conversation in which you are involved. More impressively, if someone far across the room should mention your name, you hear it and may even switch your attention to that conversation. Most people have had this experience, which requires ignoring the adjacent conversation and focusing upon a discussion some distance away. How do we accomplish this rather remarkable feat?

Early-Selection Filter Theories

One of the ideas that explains our ability to selectively attend to one thing and ignore other things is called *early-selection filter theory*. The basic idea is that attention selects certain of the incoming sensory information for conscious processing and filters out the remaining sensory information from conscious processing. The theory is called early-selection filter because the selection and filtering are done on the sensory information, and if you will recall the discussion of sensory information in chapter 2, *this means that attention operates to select and filter before the sensory signal has attained meaning.*

Broadbent (1958) proposed the first version of early-selection theory by suggesting that attention operated like a simple on-off switch—for example, a light switch. Operating as a switch, attention serves to direct processing to one sensory input or channel. This input will be fully analyzed for meaning and available to consciousness. Since the switch works in an all-or-none fashion, however, any additional inputs are completely blocked or filtered from meaningful processing and consciousness. Two important implications follow from this basic assumption of early selection. First, attention must select on the basis of physical properties of the sensory signal. There is no psychological meaning in the sensory pattern; thus, attention cannot be controlled by the meaning of the input.

BOX 3.1

SUBLIMINAL PERCEPTION

Research on attention frequently is directed to the question of how much a person knows about unattended information. You will see in this chapter that, in an experiment, there is a variety of ways to ensure that the participants are not attending to certain material that is presented to them. All of these techniques share the characteristic that the person is unaware of some or all aspects of the unattended input. The interesting question then is, does the material of which you are unaware influence your behavior in any way? This question is very much the same as the issue of subliminal perception. Subliminal perception essentially means perception without awareness. The reality of subliminal perception has been controversial in psychology because of arguments about whether the participant really is unaware of the unattended information, and we examine those arguments in the chapter. Outside of psychology, many people seem to assume that subliminal perception is a reality, and this assumption has led to public controversies.

Perhaps the most sensational instance is continuing concern over subliminal advertising. If subliminal perception is a real psychological phenomenon, advertisers should have intense interest in capitalizing on the process, and consumers should have real fear of its use. The reason in both cases is that one's choices can be influenced by events of which one is unaware and, therefore, cannot scrutinize. Why do I pick a particular toothpaste rather than some other, possibly less expensive, brand? If my choice is determined by events of which I cannot be aware, I not only cannot reason about the question, I won't even ask the question. I simply will select the toothpaste. The fear is that my behavior can be influenced by someone else in ways that are outside of my conscious control.

Another, more benign instance of the same principle is subliminal learning. Can I learn a foreign language by listening to a tape while I sleep? If unattended information can influence my behavior, then perhaps I can acquire useful information without conscious effort to do so. Should I spend the money for such products? Very careful research has been conducted on this question by Greenwald, Spangenberg, Pratkanis, and Eskenazi (1991). People who were interested in improving either their memory or their self-esteem were recruited to listen to commercially available self-help tapes advertised as improving memory or self-esteem. The audible content of the tapes was either music or nature sounds, below which was claimed to be subliminal messages. The participants were given pretests on measures of what they wanted to improve, either memory or self-esteem. Then they were instructed to listen to the assigned tape each day for a month, the manufacturers' recommended procedure. The interesting manipulation was that half of the people interested in improving their memory were given the self-esteem tape, and half of the people interested in improving their memory were given the memory tape. After a month, the participants were tested again on the dimesion the desired to improve.

The results were clear: everyone showed slight gains from their first test score. The people who heard the wrong tape showed as much improvement as those who heard the tape designed to target their particular concern. The conclusion was that the subliminal tapes exerted a placebo effect but were otherwise useless.

Second, unattended input should have no effect on behavior because it is not processed beyond the sensory level. As we saw in the discussion of sensory memory in chapter 2, sensory information decays rapidly; thus, the unattended input is not available to affect behavior. Only the sensory information selected by attention—the information that is processed for meaning and becomes available to consciousness—can affect future behavior.

This second implication of Broadbent's theory quickly became the focus of research and, ultimately, the assumption was shown to be wrong. The critical test is, what does a person know about unattended information? A procedure previously developed by Cherry (1953) was ideal for answering this question. People listen to two different messages through headphones, one message played to each ear. This is a dichotic listening task. They are told to attend to one of the two messages but, to ensure that they do so, the participants were required to repeat each word in the message as it occurred, a task known as shadowing. Because each word in the message must be repeated immediately, the task is very difficult and could not be accomplished if the focus of attention were on something other than the shadowed message. Thus, if shadowing is successful, we can be sure the person is attending to the appropriate message, and if shadowing performance fails, it may indicate that attention switched to the other message. By recording the shadowing performance and time locking it to the unattended message, we can test Broadbent's theory.

FIGURE 3.2
The switch model and early selection theories in general propose that all incoming stimuli are processed for their physical description in sensory memory, but only the one attended stimulus is processed for meaning. In this depiction, S1 is the attended stimulus.

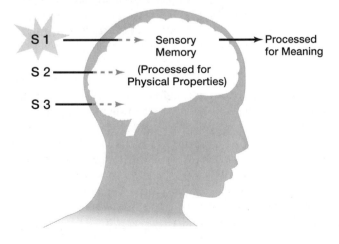

According to the theory, successful shadowing on the attended message should prohibit meaningful processing of the unattended message. Thus, the meaning of the unattended message should have no effect on behavior. The results of many experiments have shown this critical prediction to be wrong. For example, consider Anne Treisman's (1960) experiment in which subjects received dichotic presentation of sentences and were required to shadow the message in one ear. Compound sentences were used: for example, "Jordan dunked the ball, and his basket won the game," or "Marsha Ball sings marvelously, but her piano playing is incredible." The critical manipulation was that half of one sentence was presented to the shadowed ear and the other half presented to the nonshadowed ear. Simultaneously, the same thing happened to the other sentence. Thus, the subject would hear: "Jordan dunked the ball, but her piano playing is incredible" in one ear, and "Marsha Ball sings marvelously, and his basket won the game" in the other ear.

According to Broadbent's all-or-none switch model, we should have no difficulty shadowing one of these messages and ignoring the other. In fact, people find it virtually impossible to shadow consistently the appropriate message. When the meaning of the shadowed sentence switches to the nonshadowed ear, shadowing is disrupted; the subject experiences confusion and many times switches to the ear that is supposed to be nonshadowed. Instead of attending to the physical cue of location of the message, the subject follows the meaning of the message.

The critical point for Broadbent's theory is that the meaning of the nonshadowed message must be getting through to influence the participant's performance. This is a very important conclusion that is counter to subjective experience. Although you are attending to one conversation at the cocktail party or to your daydreams during a lecture, you probably are detecting some aspects of the meaning of a second conversation at the party or of the lecture in class. Usually we are completely unaware that this is happening. The question now becomes, how much of the unattended message is analyzed? One response is an alternative early-selection filter model, the attenuator model.

Treisman (1964) offered a revised early-selection filter theory that accounted for the data that challenged Broadbent's theory. Treisman's theory also treated attention as if it were a switch but, rather than a simple on-off switch, her idea was that attention operates like an attenuator. An attenuator is a switch that allows gradations in the amount of energy passing through it; the volume control on a radio or television receiver is an attenuator that can be adjusted to allow more or less of a signal through. If attention operates as an attenuator and a separate attenuator controls each input channel, then different amounts of information can come through each channel. Unlike Broadbent's all-or-none approach, however, the attenuator model allows for the processing of more than one input at a time. Attention thus becomes a matter of degree in the attenuator model.

As with the earlier switch model, the attenuator theory must specify what cues attract and hold attention. Consistent with the switch model, Treisman suggests that physical cues are used to tune the attenuator such that changes in the physical cues can serve as the basis for adjusting the attenuation on various inputs. Unlike the switch model, however, the meaning of previously analyzed material may also influence the attenuator. When the attended message switches channels, two events happen: the new information becomes incongruent with the previous information on the attended channel, and the previously unattended channel now contains information congruent with the previously attended channel, since some of the meaning of the unattended message has been processed. Thus, attenuator control is exerted by both sensory and semantic information. Notice that the attenuator model can now explain the difficulty subjects have shadowing sentences whose meaning alternates from ear to ear.

Although the attenuator model may appear more liberal on the question of unconscious processing than does the switch model, the two ideas actually are in complete agreement on this question. The attenuator model differs from the switch model only in that the attenuator allows gradations of filtering rather than all-or-none selection. The two ideas are identical, however, in that the filtering occurs at the sensory memory level. While the attenuator permits some attention to multiple messages, it does not allow for any long-term effect of unattended information. Unattended information is left to decay in sensory memory and, like the switch model, the attenuator model thus assures that behavior is influenced only by conscious content.

To summarize early-selection filter theories, the revision from the switch model to the attenuator model represents loosening of the strictures on how many activities can be done at the same time. As the example illustrates, the attenuator model allows for the processing of more than one message for meaning. This idea, however, raises a logical problem for early selection theories. The selection of information based on sensory signals seems to require recognition of information before it is processed. The decision to allocate processing capacity to one message and deny capacity to another message serves the goal of maintaining continuity in meaning. But how can we sift through various sources of information for continuity in meaning without determining the meaning of all inputs? The attenuator model attempts to deal with this issue by suggesting that partial analysis of all signals occurs. Some theorists view this solution as a half-measure. Why not assume that all incoming sensory information activates a meaningful representation? Selective attention then becomes a matter of deciding to which input to respond, which is the fundamental premise of late-selection filter models.

Late-Selection Filter Models

Certain theories, most notably those of Deutsch and Deutsch (1963) and Norman (1968), are known as *late-selection* filter models because selective attention is assumed to operate on representations in long-term memory rather than on sensory input. In contrast to the early-selection assumption that information is filtered or

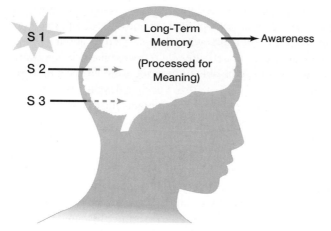

FIGURE 3.3
According to late selection theory, all stimuli are processed
for meaning, which happens in long-term memory, but only
the meaning of the attended stimulus reaches awareness.
Stimulus 1 is attended in this depiction.

blocked prior to recognition, Norman's theory is that all of the input to the sensory receptors activates the corresponding representations in long-term memory. This is the beginning step toward determining the meaning of the sensory signal. To help understand the theory, Norman suggests an analogy with looking up an unknown word in a dictionary. The word whose meaning you do not know is analogous to the sensory input and the dictionary is analogous to long-term memory. As the first step in determining the word's meaning, you match the letter pattern of the unknown word to the same pattern in the dictionary. Once the match occurs, you can go on to obtain the meaning of the word from its definition.

The idea, then, is that the sensory pattern has a matching representation in long-term memory and along with that representation is stored your knowledge of the object represented. It is this knowledge that constitutes meaning. The critical question becomes, how does attention select among the activated representations? In addition to the sensory input, the long-term memory representations differ in what Norman calls *pertinence*. Pertinence is based on the expectations established by prior processing within the channel and is very much like presynthesis in pattern recognition, described in chapter 2. For example, the sentence, "He swept the ____." establishes a strong expectation about what the final word will be. This expectation takes the form of activation of the long-term memory representation even though no sensory information corresponding to that representation has occurred. The memory representation with the highest combined activation from sensory input and pertinence will be selected to enter awareness.

The difference between early- and late-selection theories would appear easy to test. Suppose we have dichotic input with subjects shadowing one of two messages. Why not simply ask the participants what they can tell us about the nonshadowed material? If all of the input activates its representation in long-term memory, it seems that a person should be able to describe what just occurred on a nonshadowed channel. Treisman and Geffen (1967) designed what appeared to be a straightforward test of the late-selection model. Subjects heard two prose passages presented dichotically and were required to shadow one of the messages. Prior to the shadowing task, the participants had memorized a short list of words. They were then instructed to tap the table anytime that one of these words occurred in either the shadowed or the nonshadowed message. Treisman and Geffen (1967) found that the target words were detected 87 percent of the time in the shadowed message, but only 8 percent of the time in the nonshadowed message. The detection task required a response immediately upon presentation of the target word. Therefore, if all information is recognized, as the late-selection model argues, why are so few targets detected in the nonshadowed message?

The late-selection theorists argue that such results are due to the extraordinary demands of the shadowing task. Shadowing was initially devised for attention research because its very difficulty ensured that a participant focused upon one message. However, if we assume that all information is recognized and that the limitation in our processing ability is in organizing responses, the difficulty of the shadowing task makes it impossible to determine how much a participant knows about a nonshadowed message. Since only one response can be pursued, the participant cannot shadow one message and simultaneously perform *any* other response to indicate recognition of a nonshadowed message. Indeed, the late-selection theorists argue that awareness itself is a response, and, if an integrated response such as shadowing is required for one message, the subject's ability to organize a second response to a different message, even as simple a response as perceptual awareness, will be sorely limited.

In the face of this argument, shadowing experiments are inappropriate for testing late-selection theory. A proper test requires a situation in which we can detect the effect of unattended material on a participant's performance without requiring that the participant be aware of the unattended material. Such an effect, if it exists, comes very close to what we normally consider to be unconscious influences on behavior.

Marcel (1980) reported an experiment, the results of which are quite consistent with the provocative position of late-selection theory. Marcel's experiment takes advantage of an existing phenomenon known as *semantic priming*. In a simple laboratory procedure, the lexical-decision task, the participant sees a sequence of letter strings and must decide as rapidly as possible if the letter strings represent words. Semantic priming refers to the fact that, when the stimulus preceding the current stimulus is meaningfully related to the current stimulus, the response to the current stimulus is affected by the preceding stimulus. For example, if the word *doctor* is presented and was preceded by the word *nurse,* the decision on *doctor* is much faster than it would have been if it were preceded by an unrelated word such as *peach.* The assumption is that the pattern recognition of the first word, *nurse,* results in the spread of activation to semantically related words such as *doctor* and thereby makes them easier to recognize when they are presented. In terms of Norman's late-selection theory, the related word contributes to the pertinence of the following word.

Marcel made use of semantic priming in lexical decision in an experiment that strongly supports late-selection theory. The semantic relationships that caused semantic priming were among word triplets. For example, the subject might see *hand* followed by *palm* followed by *wrist.* Critical to the experiment was that the second word in the triplets was a homograph, a word that has multiple meanings. Thus, using the preceding example, a different triplet might be *tree* followed by *palm* followed by *wrist.* In the first case, the meaning of *palm* primed by *hand* is consistent with *wrist.* In the second case, the meaning of *palm* primed by *tree* is not consistent with the third word *wrist.* The final important aspect of Marcel's method was that the second word was pattern masked (refer to chapter 2 for a description of pattern masking) in one group of participants and unmasked in a second group. The question of interest is, what effect will the second word have on decision time for the third word?

The surprising result, shown in table 3.1, was that the second word primed the third word when the two were consistent in meaning, even if the second word was masked. That is, the time required to identify *wrist* as a word was faster if it was preceded by *hand-palm* than if the two preceding words were unrelated to *wrist;* but of particular importance is the observation that this priming was just as effective when *palm* was masked as when it was unmasked. As we saw in the last chapter, pattern masking seems to disrupt visual processing such that the participant is

TABLE 3.1
MARCEL'S EXPERIMENTAL DESIGN AND RESULTS

	Type of word-triplet		
	Congruent (Hand, Palm, Wrist)	Incongruent (Tree, Palm, Wrist)	Control (Clock, Race, Wrist)
No mask	487	537	522
Pattern mask	497	505	532

Time (in milliseconds) required to respond to the last word in each triplet in Marcel's experiment. Three types of triplets and examples of each head the table. The rows of the table refer to conditions in which the second word of the triplet was either unmasked or pattern masked.

unaware of the masked stimulus. This was true in Marcel's experiment in that the participants could not report the presence of the masked word. Nonetheless, the masked word produced the same level of semantic priming as the unmasked word of which the subjects were fully aware. The effect of the masked word strongly suggests *unconscious processing* of meaning in that the second word influenced responding to the third word when the participants were unaware of the presence of the second word.

Of further importance to late-selection theory was the result obtained when the meaning of the second word was not related to the third word, the case of *tree-palm-wrist*. When the second word was unmasked, allowing the subject to be aware of the word, the incongruent meaning of *palm* did not facilitate responding to *wrist*. In the condition in which the second word was masked, preventing awareness of the word's presence, response times to *wrist* were as fast as they were in the condition in which *palm's* primed meaning was congruent with *wrist*. The astonishing result is that semantic priming was equally effective for the congruent and incongruent meanings of the prime when the prime was masked!

Marcel interpreted these data entirely within the context of late-selection theory. The fact that masking the prime did not disrupt the priming effect suggests that the masked word was pattern recognized and that the activated meaning influenced semantically related words. Masking prevented awareness of the word. In this sense, Marcel argues that his data reflect unconscious processing. Information of which the participant was unaware had an effect upon later performance. Marcel goes on to argue that the function of consciousness is selectivity and thereby explains the different effects of an incongruent prime when it is masked and unmasked. Marcel argues that all meanings of a word are activated at the unconscious level, but only one meaning can enter conscious awareness. In the unmasked condition, the meaning of *palm* reaches consciousness, but the meaning is the one biased by the prime. In the incongruent case, the meaning of *palm* is not related to *wrist*. In the masked condition, however, the meaning does not reach consciousness, and, since all meanings of *palm* are activated unconsciously, the congruent meaning of *palm* is available to influence responding to *wrist*. This interpretation is a prime example of late-selection theory. Attention operates after pattern recognition so that the activation of meaning is unconscious. However, attention functions to select among the activated meanings, allowing only a limited amount of information to reach consciousness.

Our extensive discussion of Marcel's experiment was designed to clarify the sense in which late-selection theory allows for unconscious processing. We also should be careful to note that the unconscious processing allowed by most late-selection theories is quite limited in its long-term effects. The duration of the unconscious effects is determined by the duration of the activity resulting from pattern recognition. Most theorists assume that this activity decays very rapidly unless the activated meaning is selected for conscious processing. Thus, most late-selection theories are in agreement with early-selection theories in denying long-term effects of unconscious processing upon later behavior, but the two theories do disagree over the possibility of short-lived effects of unconscious processing.

Impasse between Early- and Late-Selection Theory

The critical difference between early- and late-selection theories turns on the issue of unconscious processing. Evidence on this issue derives from studies of divided attention, particularly the question of what the participant knows about the unattended input. A quandary arises, however, in that the experimental conditions demanded by early-selection theory to assure that an input is unattended are likely to be conditions that late-selection theorists will argue preclude detection of the pattern recognition of the unattended information. Early-selection theories require a stringent response to the attended message to ensure that attention is not switched to the unattended message; late-selection theories argue that all messages activate meaning, but a response to two different messages is not possible. It thus appears impossible to design an experiment that would localize attention at the sensory level or at the level of response selection. This sort of dilemma in science typically produces attempts at compromise between the competing theories. In the study of attention, the compromise begins by assuming that perhaps both early and late selections contribute to the difficulty of doing two tasks simultaneously. Rather than view attention as a selective filter located at one point in the processing sequence, a new approach considers *limitation of the entire system* in relation to the particular task requirements.

CAPACITY MODELS OF ATTENTION

As we have seen, the primary question addressed by theories of attention concerns the limitation on our ability to deal with multiple input. Capacity models of attention (Kahneman, 1973) approach this issue by assuming that our psychological resources are finite; that is, we have a certain amount of *cognitive capacity* to devote to the various tasks confronting us. Different tasks require different amounts of this capacity, and the number of activities that can be done simultaneously is determined by the capacity each requires. If a single task demands intense concentration, no capacity will remain for an additional task. Within this approach, *attention is the process of allocating the resources or capacity to various inputs.* Attention then is important in determining which tasks are accomplished and how well the tasks are performed.

Kahneman's (1973) depiction of a capacity model is shown in figure 3.4. Attention is represented in this figure as the allocation policy. Notice that the decision to allocate capacity (attention) applies to both the available capacity on the input side and to possible activities on the output side. The evaluation of demands is the governor system that causes capacity to be distributed among the activities selected by the allocation policy. Figure 3.4 illustrates Kahneman's ideas about what controls attention (allocation policy). Specifically, attention is controlled by (1) enduring dispositions, which reflect involuntary attention such as allocate capacity to the mention of your name; (2) momentary intentions such as listen to the signal in the right ear; (3) evaluation of demands with the rule that if two activities require more capacity than is available, perform one and delay the other; and (4) arousal, indicating that performance varies with the state of arousal.

Among other contrasts, notice that the capacity model is less mechanical than the previously discussed filter models. Indeed, the notion that attention is controlled by such things as momentary intentions is consistent with Wundt's volitional approach discussed in chapter 1. Of equal importance, capacity theory shifts the basic question of research away from the issue of early versus late selection to a focus on how much attention is required by certain processes and

FIGURE 3.4
Kahneman's capacity model of attention. (ATTENTION AND EFFORT, by Kahneman, Daniel, © Reprinted by permission of Pearson Education, Inc., Upper Saddle River, NJ.)

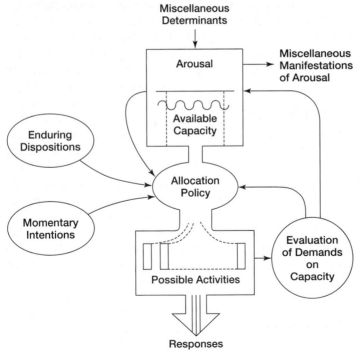

whether there are processes that require no attention. These questions required a different research method, known as the secondary task technique.

Secondary Task Technique and Cognitive Effort

The amount of capacity, or effort, required by one task will come at the expense of capacity that can be devoted to other tasks. With this assumption, measurement of the capacity demands of a task becomes possible. The technique is quite simple: the participant is instructed to perform a task and is given the impression that this primary task is the most important aspect of the experiment. Almost as an after-thought, however, instructions to perform a secondary task simultaneously with the primary task are also given. Estimates of the capacity required by the primary task are obtained on the secondary task. The harder the primary task, the poorer will be the performance on the secondary task (cf. Johnston, Greenberg, Fisher, & Martin, 1970; Britton & Tesser, 1982).

For example, consider an experiment from Ellis' laboratory. This experiment (Tyler, Hertel, McCallum, & Ellis, 1979) tested the proposition that memory for words will improve as the amount of *cognitive effort* devoted to the words in-creases. To vary the amount of effort, or capacity, exerted, the words were pre-sented as anagrams and as missing elements in sentence-completion tasks. Anagrams are words whose letters are scrambled such as *croodt*. Can you solve this anagram? How about a different anagram for the same word, *dortoc?* The second form is easier for most people than is the first. (The word, by the way, is *doctor.*) To vary effort, one group of subjects received hard anagrams and a sec-ond group received easy anagrams for the same words. To measure the capacity required by the anagrams, the participants were required to perform a second task simultaneously with the anagram task. The second task was to press a button as rapidly as possible when a tone sounded. The speed of the response to the tone was taken as a measure of capacity required by the anagram task. The more ca-pacity required by the anagram task, the less is available to tone detection and the slower is the reaction to the tone.

A similar logic prevailed in the sentence-completion task. Participants were given incomplete sentences and then were asked to select one of two words as the best completion. Some of the sentences tightly constrained the completion word; for example, "The girl was awakened by her frightening _____." The choices for this sentence were *table* and *dream,* a very easy choice. Other sen-tences contained words in which the implication was not obvious and, hence, the choices were more difficult.

Tone detection indeed was slower in the hard-anagram condition than in the easy-anagram condition and in the unconstrained sentence condition than in the constrained sentence condition. This outcome permitted an interpretation of the memory data in terms of differential capacity requirements. Hard anagrams

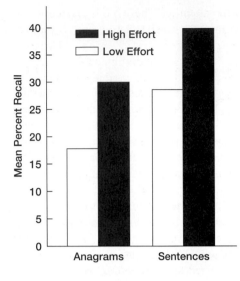

FIGURE 3.5
Recall of words in high-effort and low-effort anagrams and sentences. *(From "Cognitive Effort and Memory" by S. W. Tyler, P. T. Hertel, M. C. McCallum, and H. C. Ellis,* Journal of Experimental Psychology: Human Learning and Memory, *1979, 5, 607–617. Copyright 1979 by the American Psychological Association. Reprinted by permission of the publisher and authors.)*

produced better memory for the words than did easy anagrams, presumably due to the greater effort required by hard anagrams. Similarly, words that did not easily fit in the sentence (high-effort condition) were better recalled than those in the low-effort condition. The basic results are shown in figure 3.5, which plots recall as a function of cognitive effort.

The remaining issue is how to explain the effects of cognitive effort on recall. Two reasonable possibilities are that the allocation of capacity, or processing resources, leads to a more elaborated memory trace and/or to a more distinctive memory trace. Since this issue concerns the nature of encoding, we shall return to this topic in chapter 5. Our purpose in mentioning it here is simply to call your attention to the question of interpretation. The point of this experiment, for present purposes, is that the capacity demands of various tasks differ in measurable ways. Some tasks may require so much capacity that performing other tasks simultaneously is very difficult. Alternatively, some tasks, such as solving the easy anagrams, require little capacity. Indeed, some tasks seem to require no central processing capacity. Such tasks are said to be *automatic.*

Automatic Processing

Capacity theory leaves open the possibility that tasks can be performed without attentional control. Any task that requires no capacity obviously would not require allocation of capacity, and allocation of capacity is attention in the capacity theory. A task that requires no capacity is said to be *automatic.* Automating a task vastly increases the efficiency of performance, because other tasks can be performed simultaneously with a task that is automatic. Driving a car probably has the feel of automaticity for you. Rarely do you have to concentrate on steering or braking, leaving plenty of processing capacity for carrying on conversation, listening to the radio, and thinking about other things (but if driving could be truly automated, phone conversations would not interfere with driving performance).

Posner and Snyder (1974) offered an early characterization of automaticity that draws a clear relationship between attention and consciousness. First, automatic processes occur *without intent;* the automatic process is not something you mean to do. Second, automatic processes are *not available for conscious monitoring.* This characteristic, much like the first one, implies that automatic processes are not things you are thinking about before they occur. Consequently, it is not surprising that automatic processes do *not require any of the limited conscious capacity,* the third characteristic.

The secondary task technique is used to study automaticity in the laboratory. Again, the rationale of the secondary task method involves measuring the amount of interference between two tasks. If a particular task can be performed as well with another task as it is alone, that task is assumed to require no capacity.

A very nice demonstration of automaticity is provided in an early experiment from Posner's laboratory (Posner & Boies, 1971). The primary experimental task was letter matching; the participant had to decide as quickly as possible whether two letters were the same or different. The letters were presented successively and were preceded by a warning signal. Specifically, the warning signal occurred to alert the participant to an upcoming letter; half a second later the first letter appeared, and one-second later the second letter followed. As soon as the second letter appeared, the participant was to judge whether it was the same as the first letter. In addition to the letter-matching task, a tone-detection task was also included. The tone could occur at any stage of the letter-matching task, which allowed use of the reaction time to the tone to estimate the capacity requirements of each aspect of the letter-matching task.

Reaction times to the tone are shown in figure 3.6 as a function of the stages in letter matching. First, note that responding to the tone becomes faster after the warning signal than before the warning signal. Presumably, the participant becomes more alert and concentrates more at the onset of the warning signal. Next, you see in figure 3.6 that the reaction to the tone is not slowed by presentation of the first letter. This is the important result for our purposes. During pattern recognition of the first letter, responses to the tone are not disrupted, a clear case of two activities being done at the same time. The tone is not filtered or blocked, as early-selection theory might suppose, but, rather, both visual pattern recognition and auditory-detection tasks are performed simultaneously. We shall return to this point after a brief discussion of the remainder of the data presented in figure 3.6. Following the first letter, reaction time to the tone increases substantially. This result is reasonably interpreted as due to rehearsal of the first letter. Rehearsal does require capacity, which disrupts responding to the tone. Reaction time increases even further following the second letter, the stage at which the decision about the

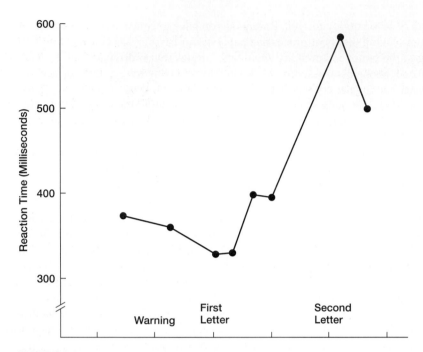

FIGURE 3.6
Reaction times to tone as a secondary task to letter matching. *(From "Components of Attention" by M. I. Posner and S. J. Boies, Psychological Review, 1971, 78, 391–408. Copyright 1971 by the American Psychological Association. Reprinted by permission of the publisher and authors.)*

letters is made. The decision process occupies even more capacity than rehearsal, which leads to this further increase in reaction time.

The major point of this experiment is that recognition of letters does not disrupt reaction time to auditory signals. Processing of the letter is automatic; little of the cognitive resources are required for this task. Of course, this result holds for college students who have had much practice in letter recognition. Imagine a young child just learning the alphabet. Letter recognition is likely to require much more effort, and only after considerable practice will it develop to an automatic skill.

Development of Automaticity

Although the precise mechanisms underlying the development of automaticity are unknown, the critical ingredient in automatization clearly is practice. Evidence for the importance of practice comes from the *memory search task*. This is a simple procedure in which the subject is asked to remember a small number of letters or numbers, usually from one to four. In the test, a series of single items is presented, and the subject must respond as rapidly as possible, indicating whether the item was among the original set to be remembered. Using this task, Shiffrin and Schneider (1977) have shown that the time to respond to the test item increases as the number of items in the original set increases, suggesting that each item in the set is compared to the test item. If, however, large amounts of practice are devoted to the original set, the amount of time required to respond to the test item does not vary as a function of either the number of items in the original set or the number of items in the test array.

Logan (1988) explains how practice leads to automaticity by suggesting that memory mediates practice effects. The idea is that a task normally will have some rule or procedure that will produce correct performance, but the use of the rule takes conscious effort and time. As the task is practiced, the correct outcome becomes part of memory and, rather than employ the rule to obtain the outcome, the task simply cues memory for the result. Consider an example from arithmetic. What is the result of 2 times 12? What is the result of 20 times 120? The same rule is used to solve the two problems, but most people solve the former problem more quickly than the latter. The case of 2 times 12 is one that has been experienced frequently and no longer requires application of the rule, although at one point you probably did use a rule to solve this problem. It now has become automated in the sense of Logan's theory that the answer does not need to be computed from the rule but can be retrieved directly from memory.

Automaticity and Reading

The concept of automaticity has been applied in interesting ways to the process of reading. At some level, reading must begin with letter recognition. But if each letter recognition required much effort before word recognition, reading would be painfully slow. Posner and Boies' (1971) demonstration that letter recognition is automatic contributes to our understanding of this problem. In addition to letter recognition, research also has suggested that access to word meaning occurs with little effort. The primary evidence for this assertion comes from studies of the *Stroop effect.*

The Stroop effect occurs in a special kind of dual-task situation. For example, suppose you are given a list of color names—*red, blue, green,* and *orange*—and each word is printed in color. Table 3.2 shows an example of such a list. Your job is to name the *ink colors* as rapidly as possible. When the word and ink color match, this task is easy, but it becomes surprisingly difficult when the word conflicts with the ink color. This difficulty is a bit of a puzzle because naming the ink color in no way requires processing the word or even noticing it. Clearly word meaning affects your ability to name the ink color, suggesting that word meaning is processed even though the task does not require word processing. Such processing meets the definition of automaticity in that it occurs without intent. Data

	Facilitation condition		Interference condition	
Ink color	Word		Ink color	Word
YELLOW	YELLOW		YELLOW	GREEN
BLUE	BLUE		BLUE	RED
ORANGE	ORANGE		BLACK	YELLOW
BLACK	BLACK		RED	BLUE
GREEN	GREEN		GREEN	ORANGE
RED	RED		ORANGE	BLACK

TABLE 3.2
Example of two types of lists used in Stroop experiments. In both cases, the subject's task is to rapidly name the ink color in which the word is printed. In the facilitation condition, the ink color and color word are the same. In the interference condition, the ink color and color word are incongruent.

from the Stroop task have led to the argument that word meaning is automatically accessed by skilled readers.

Not everyone, however, accepts this conclusion. Kahneman and Henik (1981) devised a modified Stroop task in which a square and a circle appear unpredictably on either side of a fixation point. The square and the circle always have a different word inside of them, and the words change on each new appearance of the square and circle. The words are printed in color. The participants' task is to name the ink color in the circle. An illustration of the stimulus configuration is presented in figure 3.7. Since the participant is fixating at a center point between the square and the circle, both the circle and square fall on the visual field. Thus, the word *red* within the square activates the sensory receptors, and if activation of meaning is automatic, the activation of *red* should produce the normal Stroop interference when naming the incompatible ink color in the circle. In fact, the interference produced by the color word in the square upon naming the ink color in the circle is minimal compared to the case in which the incompatible word also appears in the circle. Because the word in the square is available to the receptors, this pattern of results should not occur if word meaning were automatically accessed.

The same point has been made forcefully in a series of experiments by Besner, Stolz, and Boutilier (1997). Participants were shown words that were printed in a color (as in the standard Stroop preparation), or alternatively, only one of the letters of the word was printed a designated color while the remaining letters were gray. The participants' instructions were to indicate the color of the word or letter as quickly as possible. Besner and his colleagues discovered that the Stroop interference was greatly reduced or eliminated in the condition requiring color naming of the single letter. Because the entire word falls on the visual field, these

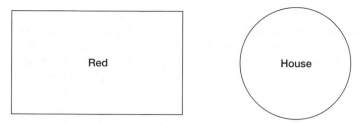

(Both Words Printed in Green Ink)

FIGURE 3.7
Example of stimuli used by Kahneman and Henik. Both the circle and
the square fall on the visual field. Significant interference occurs when
naming the ink color in the square, but no interference is present
when naming the ink color in the circle.

results agree with Kahneman and Henik's conclusion that the meaning of the word is not always processed. Indeed, Besner and his colleagues persuasively argue that the Stroop experiments do not demand the conclusion that meaningful processing of a word is automatic.

Earlier, Kahneman and Treisman (1984) proposed that results such as these contradict the notion that the Stroop effect itself and, by inference, the process of reading occur without attentional control. Their suggestion is that selective attention operates to select relevant objects, such as the circle in Kahneman and Henik's experiment, and to filter irrelevant objects, such as the square. Once an object is selected, all of its properties may be processed. That is, if the word *red* printed in green ink appears in the circle, interference in color naming would occur because once the circle is selected, the word and ink color would be processed. Thus, Kahneman and Treisman draw an important distinction between perception of different objects and perception of the properties of a given object. The former is a process under attentional control, while the latter may be automatic.

BACK TO EARLY SELECTION THEORY?

The importance of the distinction between objects and their properties is that it suggests that central attention operates to select objects for perceptual processing and that the cue for selection is the physical cue of spatial location. Attention then can be directed to a location and any object occupying that location will be processed. The subsequent processing of the attended object may include many properties of the object that are irrelevant to a task, giving the appearance of automatic processing. Contrary to the assumption of automatic processing, an object outside of the spatial location will not be processed even if it activates sensory receptors. This is very much the position of early-selection theory of attention.

Feature Integration Theory

The distinction between objects and properties is discussed in a somewhat more analytic theory known as *feature integration theory* (Treisman & Gelade, 1980; Treisman & Gormican, 1988; Treisman & Sato, 1990). This theory argues that primitive features are processed in parallel, essentially in an automatic fashion without attentional control. A simple feature such as color or shape will be easily detected regardless of the objects in which it is embedded. Detecting the one red thing in the context of a bunch of green things is easy regardless of what the things are. Treisman's feature integration idea suggests that this ability is due to the automatic, parallel processing of simple features.

On the other hand, detection of conjunctions of features may be more difficult. A feature conjunction is a combination of simple features, examples of which would be a blue square or a red circle. To convince yourself that this is the case, examine figure 3.8. On the left side of the figure are some shapes. The one circle "jumps out at you"; a circle is a simple feature whose detection is automatic. Now examine the right side of the figure and find the shaded circle. This search is based on the conjunction of shape and shading and is more difficult. Why is this the case?

Feature integration theory has a ready answer to this question. First, the task of locating a particular object embedded among other objects requires directing attention to the spatial location of the desired object. Finding the circle in the left panel of figure 3.8 is easy because a single feature, shape, differentiates the target object from other objects. Because feature processing occurs automatically, attention is quickly cued to the spatial location of the circle. Finding the shaded circle in the right panel of figure 3.8 is more difficult because now the target object is defined by a conjunction of the features, circle and shaded. The automatic

FIGURE 3.8
(a) The "pop-out" effect when searching for a single feature. (b) The conjunction of "shaded" and circle is not quite as obvious.

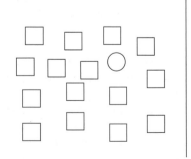 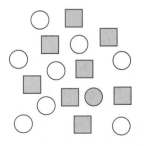

(a)   (b)

feature analysis of all of the objects yields two features, shape and shading, but the features alone are insufficient to locate the object. The target features, circle and shaded, are each shared by some of the nontarget items. Consequently, detection of the target, shaded circle, requires analysis of each object. That is, attention must be directed to each object to determine whether it has the appropriate combination of features.

Objects can be described as conjunctions of features. Consequently, the identification of an object requires that the features be combined. To combine features, attention directs processing to a particular spatial location and the feature conjunction in that location can be processed to object recognition. The processing of feature conjunctions is limited; only one conjunction can be processed at a time. Detecting the shaded circle in the right panel of figure 3.8 theoretically requires that attention be directed to the space occupied by each object and that object is then processed. If the processed object is not the target, attention is directed to another location and that object is processed. *Hence, feature integration theory is fundamentally an early-selection theory because only one object can be processed at a time, and the cue for directing processing is spatial location.*

THE SOURCE OF DUAL-TASK INTERFERENCE

As you have seen, research on attention has directed most of its energy to discovering the locus of dual-task interference. Early-selection theory says the difficulty is that only one thing can be perceptually processed at a time. For late-selection theorists, the interference is caused by the inability to select more than one of the processed things for awareness. Thus, it is not surprising that much of the research we have reviewed to this point has focused on perception; that is, what is comprehended about the unattended message in a shadowing task? Does a masked prime word facilitate responding in lexical decision? While the issue of attentional limits on perception is fundamentally important, perception is not the only psychological process that could limit our ability to perform two things at once. This is especially true for tasks that require thought and action about the perceived event. For example, if you are driving and having a conversation with a passenger, the conversation stops if the driving conditions become difficult. Difficult driving conditions entail more than just a perceptual challenge. Rapid decisions about alternative responses must be made and then executed and, once completed, a new set of circumstances immediately confronts the driver. Obviously, perceptual limitations are not the only possible cause of dual-task interference.

Capacity theory seems to provide a more satisfactory explanation because, unlike the filter theories, it does not assume that any particular psychological process is the point of the bottleneck in processing. Rather, performance is limited by the general availability of capacity. In our example, you stop the conversation because the capacity it consumed is needed for driving. Research using the secondary task technique has been offered in support of capacity theory's explanation of dual-task interference. For example, the research we described by Tyler et al. showed that solving anagrams slowed the speed of a response to a probe tone, presumably because solving anagrams took capacity from responding to the tone.

Pashler (1999) has questioned the capacity interpretation of dual-task experiments. He argues that such experiments are not good tests of capacity sharing because the experiments have used tasks that do not allow a precise time mapping of the component processes required by the tasks. For example, we do not really know what component of anagram solving was in process when the tone sounded in the Tyler et al. study. The point of Pashler's argument is that data previously taken as support for a general capacity theory of attention may well have been produced by a mechanism of attention more akin to a filter.

The Psychological Refractory Period

To support his argument, Pashler uses an experimental technique known as the psychological refractory period (PRP) paradigm. This technique has been available since the 1930s and is a simple preparation that produces an interesting result. The paradigm requires production of two different speeded responses to two different stimuli. The two stimuli are separated in time—known as stimulus-onset asynchrony (SOA) because the onset of the stimuli is asynchronous in time. The participant must respond to both stimuli as quickly as possible. A schematic depiction of the paradigm is shown in figure 3.9. For example, the two tasks could be tone detection and letter identification. The first stimulus is a tone, either high or low, and the response is to press a predetermined key on the keyboard indicating which tone occurred. The second stimulus is a letter that appears on the monitor, and the response is to name the letter. Over the course of the experiment, the SOA of the tone and letter is systematically varied from, say, 50 msecs-400msecs. Keep in mind that this manipulation of SOA is simply a variation in how soon the second stimulus follows the first stimulus.

The interesting result from this paradigm is that the speed of the second response becomes slower as the SOA becomes shorter. A typical pattern is depicted in figure 3.9. At long SOAs, responses to the second stimulus are much faster than at shorter SOAs. A converging comparison can be made between responses to the second stimulus in the dual task and responses to that same stimulus when it is presented alone. In our example, this would involve the speed of letter detection when it follows tone detection versus the speed of letter detection performed alone. The second task response is always slower in the dual task than in the single task, but the difference between dual and single tasks is much greater at short SOAs. The fact that the first task slows responding to the second task at short SOAs indicates that something in the two tasks cannot be accomplished simultaneously. What Pashler goes on to show is exactly what that "something" is.

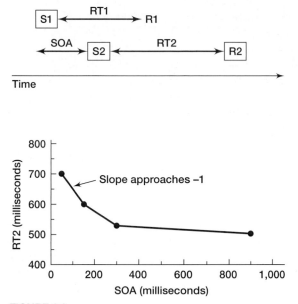

FIGURE 3.9
Top figure depicts psychological refractory period paradigm in which the S1 precedes S2 by a variable stimulus-onset asynchrony (SOA). The bottom figure shows the typical of slowing of the response to the second stimulus as the SOA decreases.

Central Bottleneck Theory

Pashler (1984) begins his analysis by suggesting that there are three general psychological components to any task that requires thought and action. The first step is *perceptual analysis,* in which the stimulus is identified. The second component is *response decision,* in which a decision is made about the appropriate response to the stimulus. Once the decision is made, the final step of *response production* can occur. If you are asked to perform two tasks, these three components of processing must occur for both tasks. The interference of the first task with performance on the second task may occur because processing is limited by one or more of these three stages or because of general capacity limitation. For example, early-selection theory maintains that perceptual analysis of the second stimulus cannot begin until perceptual analysis of the first stimulus is completed. Capacity theory argues that all aspects of second task performance suffer from a lack of capacity that has been drained away to the first task. Pashler's theory is that the response decision component is the limiting factor, a theory he calls *central bottleneck theory* (Pashler, 1999). According to the theory, response

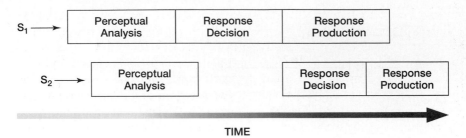

TIME

FIGURE 3.10
The three stages of processing in central bottleneck theory depicted for each of two tasks.
The bottleneck is the Response Decision stage where the decision about the response
to the second stimulus cannot occur until the decision about the reponse to the first stimulus has been made.

decisions in task 2 cannot begin until the response decision in task 1 is complete.
Figure 3.10 provides a visual depiction of central bottleneck theory.

Central bottleneck theory predicts certain outcomes in dual-task situations
that are different from the predictions of early-selection and capacity theories,
and the PRP paradigm is especially well suited to test these predictions. We shall
give you an extended discussion of an experiment by Pashler and Johnston (1989)
to illustrate the logic. They used the PRP paradigm with the simple tasks of tone
detection and letter identification. The example of the PRP paradigm described
earlier and illustrated in figure 3.9 is essentially their experiment. Each trial began
when a fixation point appeared on the monitor. One second after the onset of the
fixation point, a tone sounded. The tone was either high or low frequency, and
the participant identified the tone by pressing one of two keys as quickly as possible. Following the offset of the tone, a letter appeared on the monitor—either
A, B, or C—and the participants identified the letter by pressing one of three
keys as quickly as possible. The letter appeared either 50, 100, or 400 msec. after
the onset of the tone. These were the values of the SOA in this experiment. In addition, the physical intensity of the letters was varied such that on half of the
trials the letters were of high intensity and on the other half they were of low
intensity. High-intensity letters are easier to see than low intensity-letters. The
importance of this manipulation will be explained momentarily. Finally, on some
blocks of trials the same sequence of events occurred but participants were instructed that they need only respond to the letter and not to the tone. This condition gives us information about response speed to the letter in a single task.

The dependent measure of interest is reaction time to the second task, letter
identification, and these reaction times are shown in figure 3.11 as a function of
single-task versus dual-task intensity of the letter, and SOA. The first thing to notice in figure 3.11 is that responding is always faster in the single task than in the
dual task, indicating that performance of the first task interfered with performance
of the second task. Next, look at dual-task performance as a function of SOA,

where you see the standard PRP effect. Responses to the second task were slower at short SOAs regardless of the intensity of the letter. Finally, the intensity of the letter affected performance differently in single and dual tasks. Responses to low intensity letters were consistently slower than responses to high-intensity letters in the single task. This makes sense in that the low-intensity letters were harder to see, and perceptual analysis leading to identification of the letter would take longer. But now examine the effect of intensity in the dual-task condition. What you see is that the effect of intensity on response time decreases as the SOA becomes shorter. Even though the overall response time is longest at short SOAs, the important point is that the effect of high intensity versus low intensity is much smaller at short SOAs than at long SOAs and in the single task condition.

The intensity effects are interesting because central bottleneck theory predicts this outcome whereas capacity theory and early-selection theory predict something very different. Consider, first, capacity theory. Low-intensity letters are harder to see and thus perceptual analysis of these letters requires more capacity for low-intensity letters than for high-intensity letters. This explanation is perfectly consistent with the data from single tasks but cannot explain the dual-task results. If perceptual analysis of low-intensity letters requires more capacity, responses to low intensity letters should be uniformly slower in the dual task. This does not happen at short SOAs. Early-selection theory also is incapable of explaining the reduced effect of intensity at short SOAs. According to early-selection theory, perceptual analysis is the limiting process. Perceptual analysis of the letter cannot begin until completion of perceptual analysis of the tone in the dual task. Consequently, any variable that affects perceptual analysis should have the same effect in the dual task as in the single task.

FIGURE 3.11
The results of Pashler and Johnston's (1989) experiment. The intensity of the letter stimulus for the second response has no effect in the dual task condition at short SOAs.

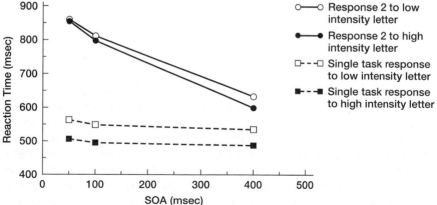

In contrast, central bottleneck theory actually predicts the intensity effect. First, the theory does not dispute that perceptual analysis will take longer for low-intensity stimuli than for high-intensity stimuli, a fact evident in the single-task data. However, performance on the second task is not limited by perceptual analysis of the first stimulus or by the overall capacity required by the tasks but, rather, is only limited by the response decision component. The decision about the response to the letter cannot be made until the decision about the response to the tone has been made. Yet perceptual analysis of the letter can occur while the response decision to the tone is being made, as depicted in figure 3.10 by the overlap of perceptual analysis of stimulus 2 with the response decision to stimulus 1. At short SOAs, the letter appears while the response to the tone is being decided. In this interval, the perceptual analysis of the letter can be completed, but the response decision about the letter must wait for the completion of the response decision to the tone. This waiting period is long enough to complete the perceptual analysis of the low-intensity letter and thus washes out the difference in response times to high- and low-intensity letters. At longer SOAs, the first response decision has already been made when the letter appears, and in the single-task condition no decision is made about the tone. In both of these situations, the response decision to the letter follows perceptual analysis, which is slower for low-intensity letters.

Using this logic and the PRP paradigm, Pashler and his colleagues have reported numerous experiments using a variety of different tasks. The summary of this research is that in almost every instance, dual-task interference is best interpreted as due to limitations in our ability to make multiple response decisions simultaneously (Pashler, 1999). This research is important in demonstrating a particular constraint on thought and action. The constraint is more central than the perceptual constraint advocated by early-selection theory. Thus, central bottleneck theory is in the class of late-selection theory, but unlike our previous discussion of late-selection theory, the constraint is not so much on selecting a processed item to bring to awareness but, rather, is on deciding what to do about the consciously perceived event. In short, central bottleneck theory suggests the limitation on processing sought by research on attention lies in connecting perception to appropriate action.

THE COGNITIVE NEUROSCIENCE OF ATTENTION

Consistent with the wide-ranging importance of attention in mental life, there is voluminous literature on the neural mechanisms underlying this complex, cognitive skill. The present section is designed to give you a quick glimpse at a few of more interesting topics that make up this exciting branch of cognitive neuroscience. We begin with neural evidence bearing on the debate between early and late selection. Next, we introduce one of the central mysteries of neural information processing—the "binding problem"—and discuss how attention may play a key role in solving this problem. Finally, we attempt to provide a more general framework for understanding the neuroscience of attention by describing one of the more popular theories of how the varied functions of attention are implemented in the brain.

Neural Evidence for Early Selection

Experiments comparing brain activity for attended versus nonattended stimuli allow for a relatively straightforward test of one of the key assumptions of the early-selection view of attention; namely, that attention can modulate early stages of perceptual processing. In fact, a number of studies using a variety of brain-based methods have examined just this issue. In general, the results provide relatively clear evidence that attention can modulate the neural activity associated with the different features of a stimulus; and that such modulation can occur at relatively early stages of neural processing. In one study of this type using PET, Corbetta and colleagues (1991) asked subjects to detect changes in multi-object displays, where the change could occur in either the shape, color, or motion of the objects. They found that, compared to a divided attention condition in which subjects were not told which of the three dimensions they should attend to, selective attention to a particular dimension increased neural activity in those areas of the cortex thought to be responsible for processing information related to that attribute. Thus, when subjects were asked to watch for (attend to) possible changes in the movement of the objects, the researchers observed increased activity in motion processing areas of the visual cortex (in the dorsal "where" stream). Alternatively, when subjects attended to the color of the objects, color-processing areas in the ventral "what" stream showed an increase in activity. These results suggest that attention acts to amplify the neural signals' coding for the features of an object to which a person is attending. Moreover, the areas exhibiting such changes are at a relatively early stage in the brain's information-processing sequence, thus providing support for early-selection views of attention.

Even more impressive evidence for the claim that attention can influence early stages of neural processing comes from single-cell recording studies performed with monkeys and from ERP studies using humans (see Luck & Vecura, 2002). These two methodologies are critical for answering questions about when attention has its effect, because they can provide precise information about the time-course of neural processing. In an ERP study looking at spatial attention, for example, it was found that the brain's response to a stimulus in an attended location was greater than when that same stimulus occurred in an unattended location, with the ERP difference emerging within 100 milliseconds of stimulus presentation. Single-cell recording studies in monkeys have produced even more impressive results, showing that attention can alter neural processing within 60 milliseconds of stimulus onset. These findings are quite impressive and show that attentional mechanisms can influence very early stages of neural processing.

Of course, while the above findings are consistent with the notion that attention can amplify neural activity early in the information-processing sequence, they do not rule out the possibility that information on nonattended channels is being deeply processed (as would be claimed by a late-selection theorist). Indeed, recent ERP experiments have shown that, under the appropriate conditions, attention does *not* alter early information processing but, rather, has its effect at a much later stage of processing (Vogel, Luck, & Shapiro, 1998). Taken together with studies showing an early modulation of perceptual processing, this result suggests that attentional selection may occur at either an early or late stage depending on the specific demands of the task.

It is important to note that studies examining the effects of attention on perceptual processing are looking at the effect or *locus* of attention selection, that is, where in the brain attention has its influence. Although certainly important, these studies do not necessarily reveal the mechanisms of attentional selection, per se. That is, most researchers believe that the neural mechanisms underlying attentional selection will be distinct from the neural sites at which these mechanisms exert their influence on processing. We will examine the putative location of these attentional selection mechanisms shortly. First, however, we discuss one of the more vexing issues in cognitive neuroscience .

The Binding Problem

In the last chapter, we learned that focal brain damage can produce *selective* deficits in the ability to perceive and recognize a number of different stimulus features, including color, shape, motion, and location. This suggests that processing of these features depends on specialized, and physically separated, areas of the brain. If this description is correct, it raises a very perplexing question: if the brain processes the different features of an object in physically separate parts of the brain, then where in the brain do all of these different features come together to form the unified perceptions that we consciously experience? The answer to this question, which sounds more like something out of Zen Buddhism than cognitive neuroscience, is "nowhere."

Consider your visual experience of a simple object such as a pencil. When you look at a pencil you see an object that has a particular shape, a particular texture, and a particular color, all of which are located in a particular region of space. Moreover, all of these characteristics (shape, texture, color, and location) appear to be "bound together" in a way that makes them seem inseparable from one another. However, when one examines what the brain is doing when we look at a pencil, one finds that each of the pencil's different features triggers activity in physically distinct neural areas; that is, shape is processed in one set of regions (area V3 in the occipital cortex, along with additional areas in the inferior temporal cortex), color in another region (area V4), and motion and location in yet another set of regions (area V5 and additional areas in the parietal cortex). Moreover, although these areas are heavily interconnected, they do not appear to feed into a central integration area that puts all of the various features together. But if there is no central integration area, then why do we perceive a pencil as a unified object, with all of its features seamlessly bound together, instead of as a collection of disconnected (unbound) features? This question is known as "the binding problem" and has emerged as one of the key mysteries of the neural basis of visual perception (see Treisman, 1996).

Although a number of different solutions to the binding problem have been proposed, part of the solution may be provided by Treisman's feature integration theory, discussed earlier. Recall that, in this theory, attention to a particular spatial location is thought to be necessary for combining (i.e., *binding*) the different features that occupy that location, thus giving rise to the perception of unified objects (such as our pencil). But binding via spatial selective attention raises another question: what neural mechanisms enable the selection of particular locations in space? Of course, we have already encountered one clue as to the neural basis of spatial selection in our earlier discussion of the "what" and "where" visual systems (see chapter 2). In particular, the occipitoparietal (dorsal, "where") visual stream appears to be critical for the perceptual processing of location-based information, making this region of the brain a prime candidate for implementing *attentional* mechanisms related to space. Consistent with this, Treisman's model proposes that attention uses a "master map" of locations based in the parietal lobes to select active features in corresponding feature maps in different parts of the visual cortex (such as V1, V2, V4, etc.).

If this theory is correct—that attention is required for binding—it leads to a very interesting and counterintuitive prediction. Specifically, if a person does not attend to an object, there should be no binding; rather, the different features of an object should be relatively "free floating" or unbound. When one first encounters this idea, it might seem ridiculous. Indeed, people's first response to this idea is to try it for themselves—attending to one object while simultaneously monitoring the features of "unattended objects" to see if they are unbound or fragmented. The problem, of course, is that it is impossible to "monitor" an object in space without also attending to it. Thus, according to Treisman's theory, when you monitor an object, you attend to it; attention, in turn, results in the features of the object being bound together, thus producing the experience of a unified object.

Does this mean that Treisman's ideas about binding cannot be tested? On the contrary, this theory can be tested in two ways. One way is to do a more controlled version of the thought experiment given above. In one paradigm of this sort (Cohen & Ivry, 1989), two white digits are briefly presented in the center of a computer screen, one of which is physically larger than the other; the subjects' task is to report the larger of the two digits, a task that requires attention to be directed at the center of the screen. Simultaneously with the digits, two colored letters are briefly presented in the periphery, one of which is always an *F* or *X* accompanied by a distractor letter (such as an *O*). Thus, after reporting on the digits, subjects are asked which of the two target letters occurred (*F* or *X*) and, most importantly, the color in which that target was presented. If attention is required for binding, one might expect to observe "illusory conjunctions" in this paradigm such that subjects miscombine the features making up the two peripheral letters.

And, in fact, that is just what is observed—when a red *O* and a yellow *X* are presented, for example, subjects often report seeing a red *X* more often than would be predicted by chance.

A second way Treisman's binding hypothesis has been tested is by examining patients who have sustained damage to the parietal lobes. If spatial attention is required to bind the separate features of an object, and the parietal lobes are critical for spatial attention, then these patients might be expected to show a large number of illusory conjunctions. In fact, using the paradigm described above, this is exactly what is found (Cohen & Rafal, 1991). An even more dramatic example of impaired binding was reported in a patient who had suffered bilateral damage to the parietal lobes (Robertson, Treisman, Friedman-Hill, & Grabowecky, 1997). When presented with multiple objects, this patient could only report the individual features making up the various objects; he was unable to correctly report which features belonged to the same object! Overall, then, spatial attention mechanisms dependent on the parietal lobes appear to be crucial for our ability to integrate the various features of an object into a unified whole.

Posner's Theory of the Neural Bases of Attention

One of the most extensive neurocognitive theories of attention has been proposed by Posner (1995), who argues that the brain contains three distinct but interrelated attention systems. The most basic of the three systems is subserved by relatively primitive, subcortical areas of the brain and is responsible both for our general level of arousal and for alerting us to significant changes in the environment. The other two, higher-level systems, are cortical. The "posterior attention system" is based in the parietal lobes and is mostly concerned with the direction of attention in space—for example, whether you are attending to the teacher's notes on the blackboard or to the squirrel that is climbing on the window sill. As you might expect, the neural circuits that comprise the posterior attention system work closely with those responsible for eye movements, as the direction of one's attention and the direction of one's gaze are often the same.

The most advanced of the three attention systems is referred to as the "anterior attention system." This system, whose neural circuitry is based predominantly in the frontal lobes, makes possible our ability to sustain attention to particular objects or events despite the existence of other stimuli in the environment that are competing for our attention (such as the squirrel mentioned above). The anterior system also provides us with the ability to switch attention among multiple tasks and, perhaps most importantly, the ability to select objects or other sources of information as a function of our long-term goals and interests.

For example, if you are studying at home but also plan to watch your favorite television program at 8 o'clock, it is largely the anterior attention system that directs you to periodically check your watch as the critical time approaches. It makes sense that such goal-directed attentional skills are based in the frontal lobes, as this area appears to house some of the most critical "executive" functions of the brain. Although the anterior attention system controls when and (in combination with the posterior system) where you direct your attention, other neurocognitive systems in the frontal lobes determine *why* you direct your attention in particular ways. Thus, it is in the frontal lobes that attention interfaces with *intention* so that attentional skills can be organized to solve problems and achieve specific goals.

Much of the evidence for Posner's neurocognitive theory of attention comes from the behavior of patients with localized damage to those areas of the brain thought to underlie the three attention systems. Perhaps the most widely investigated form of such damage involves patients who have suffered damage to the posterior attention system. Damage to this system can produce strange but informative phenomena related to the distribution of attention in space. For example, patients who have sustained damage to the right parietal lobe, often as a result of stroke, sometimes exhibit a phenomenon known as "attentional neglect," in which they fail to attend to objects and events occurring in their left visual field. In extreme cases, these patients have been known to eat only the food on the right side of their plate or to shave only the right side of their face.

In contrast to patients with parietal damage, patients with damage to the frontal lobes may exhibit abnormal behavior related to the brain's anterior attention functions. A particularly fascinating investigation of this sort was done by Lehrmitte (1986; Lehrmitte, Pillon, & Serdaru, 1986) who found that patients with frontal lobe lesions may spontaneously imitate an examiner's gestures—such as crossing their legs or combing their hair—even when explicitly instructed not to do so. Even more surprising is the behavior of these patients when placed into complex social situations. For example, when the social context implied a medical examination, one 52-year-old woman spontaneously took Dr. Lehrmitte's blood pressure, examined his throat with a tongue depressor, and attempted to give him an injection in the buttock. Lehrmitte suggests that such behaviors reflect a disorder of personal autonomy and has labeled the condition "environmental dependency syndrome."

The behavior shown by Lehrmitte's patients is related to the more common phenomenon of "action slips." Action slips, like Freudian slips of the tongue, are errors in behaviors that are nonetheless related to the general goals of the actions being performed. For example, many of us have had the experience of putting milk in the cabinet or cereal in the refrigerator or of throwing a stick of gum in the wastebasket while putting the gum wrapper in our mouth. The interesting thing about these examples is that the actions being performed are appropriate to the general situation; they are just applied to the wrong object or in the wrong order. At a cognitive level, these phenomena suggest the existence of behavioral or motoric schemas, stored routines for performing common activities. They also raise the question of where these routines are stored in the brain.

Based on patients described above, Lehrmitte has suggested that these routines are stored in the parietal lobes, an area of the brain that acts as the main "interface" between our inner cognitive life and the outside world of objects and events. These routines are triggered whenever we encounter a specific set of external conditions. The interesting question is, what keeps us from robotically acting on all the common objects and events that we encounter in a normal day? The answer, according to Lehrmitte, is that the unimpaired frontal lobes normally act to inhibit or suppress these behavioral routines unless they are appropriate to the situation and in accordance with our goals. However, when the frontal lobes are damaged, as in the patients he examined, the normally suppressed routines are "released," resulting in the unusual behavior described above.

BOX 3.2

ATTENTION DEFICIT DISORDER

Attention deficit/hyperactivity disorder (ADHD) is a familiar diagnostic label in our society. What exactly is the disorder? Research has identified two major domains of symptom expression in children classified as ADHD, attention deficit and hyperactivity. Attention deficit is evidenced by behaviors such as making careless mistakes in schoolwork, difficulty listening, failing to finish chores, disliking activities that require sustained attention, and being easily distracted by extraneous stimuli. Hyperactivity is manifested in behaviors such as fidgeting, inability to remain seated, always being "on the go," and excessive talking. Barkley (1997), a leading clinical researcher, has argued that attention deficit disorder (ADD) is different from ADHD.

According to Barkley, the attention deficiency is different in the two cases. ADD seems to be a problem in selectively attending to events in the immediate environment, which in turn leads to difficulties in information processing. ADHD, in contrast, involves a deficit in the self-control of behavior, which disrupts persistence in completing tasks. The inattentive behavior associated with ADD has a later onset than the hyperactive-impulsive behavior of ADHD. Furthermore, the hyperactive-impulsive dimension is predictive of later conduct and antisocial disorders, whereas the inattentive behavior of ADD is predictive of later learning difficulties but not of conduct disorder.

The most common medication used to treat ADHD is Ritalin, which is puzzling because Ritalin is a stimulant that has psychological effects similar to caffeine and cocaine. Why would a powerful stimulant alleviate hyperactivity? The answer to this puzzle comes from neuropsychological research that has shown that ADHD is not a problem of too much brain activity but, rather, stems from a lack of activation in the frontal lobes. The notion is that frontal lobe activity has the effect of inhibiting activation in more posterior brain areas; hence, when there is a lack of activity in the frontal lobes, as can occur in ADHD or through alcohol consumption, activity in more posterior areas is released, resulting in hyperactive or disinhibited behavior. As with most stimulants, Ritalin is known to increase brain activity, but it does so predominantly in the frontal lobes. Apparently, by increasing frontal lobe activity, Ritalin also increases the brain's ability to inhibit unwanted behavioral routines that are stored in more posterior parts of the brain, thus reducing hyperactivity and allowing those with ADHD to concentrate.

Although we are just beginning to learn about how attention is realized in the brain, the neural outlines of this important cognitive ability have already begun to emerge. Future research will no doubt fill in the details of this system, eventually providing us with a "circuit diagram" of the brain's attention system.

SUMMARY

Attention is a concept that psychologists use to explain two aspects of mental functioning, selectivity and capacity limitation. We have all experienced both of these phenomena. Selectivity refers to the fact that we consciously perceive only a portion of the stimuli that impinge on the sensory receptors. Attention is the concept that functions to select the portion of sensory activity that will become conscious perception and thought. Filter theories, both early and late selection, were written as an explanation of how the selection occurs. The two classes of filter theory differ sharply on where in the perceptual process filtering occurs and this difference leads to different implications for the possibility of unconscious influences on perception.

The second aspect of mental functioning to be explained by attention, capacity limitation, refers to our inability to perform two tasks simultaneously. Filter theories locate the limitation in perceptual analysis, but perceptual limitations are not the only possibility, particularly in tasks that require appropriate action to the perceived environment. Capacity theory assumes that all action, including mental operations, draws on a limited pool of resources that can be variously allocated to the alternative tasks. The inability to perform multiple tasks results from inadequate resources to support all of the possible activities. In contrast, central bottleneck theory argues that the limitation lies in one central process, the process of deciding what response to make to a perceived event.

The problems posed by the selectivity of perception and limitations on dual-task performance are pervasive in everyday life, from our examples of driving to the demands on pilots and air-traffic controllers. Research in psychology on attention has already contributed to alleviating some of these problems through its influence on the design and engineering of equipment more compatible with the limitations of mental functioning. The most basic limitation is the inability to maintain conscious awareness of two different things simultaneously. It is this fact that necessitates selectivity in perception and prevents simultaneous performance of multiple operations. In light of this fact, all theories, whatever else their differences, agree that attention is the gateway to conscious thought.

THOUGHT QUESTIONS

1. Describe the relationship among sensory register, pattern recognition, and attention. Be careful to include a discussion of why attention is necessary within this framework.

2. Why is unconscious influence on behavior not possible according to early selection theory?
3. Describe Marcel's experiment and its implication for early and late selection theories.
4. What is the evidence from the Stroop experiments on automaticity of word processing?
5. Compare central bottleneck theory with late selection theory.

4

SHORT-TERM, WORKING MEMORY

How many times have you been introduced to a small group of people, and as soon as the introduction is completed, you turn to the first person introduced and simply cannot remember the person's name? Equally frustrating is the experience of obtaining a telephone number from Directory Assistance and having no pencil or pen to record the number. What do you do? Usually, most of us repeat the number rapidly until we dial it, but if anyone talks to us or we even think of something other than the number before it is dialed, we must make another call to Directory Assistance. These two common examples illustrate the surprising difficulty of maintaining even small amounts of information over a short period of time. What makes this difficulty interesting is the contrast with remembering your best friend's name or your own phone number, things you are unlikely to forget even if it has been some time since you thought about them. How are we to explain the difference in these two situations?

Psychologists begin their answer to the question by making a distinction between short- and long-term memory. But these terms are just labels that describe the fact that some information is retained for a short time, while other information is retained for a long time. The real question is, what are the psychological processes that cause this difference in retention?

An early answer was offered by James (1890) with his distinction between primary (short-term) and secondary (long-term) memory. James described primary memory as the contents of consciousness; that is, short-term memory is what we are thinking about at the moment. As such, the contents of short-term memory are subject to the limitations of conscious span, and, since the content of thought is constantly changing, the contents of primary memory would be fleeting. Thus, for James, short-term memory was information in the active conscious state, subject to the capacity and duration limits of conscious thought. Secondary or long-term memory is information in an inactive state. Very simply, all of the things about which you could think, but currently are not thinking, constitute the contents of long-term memory. James' idea is one that distinguishes short- and long-term memory as active and inactive memory. We shall return to this idea later in the chapter because it has been revitalized with the renewal of interest in consciousness and awareness.

A different conceptualization of short- and long-term memory emerged with the information-processing approach in the 1960s. This view represented a much more mechanical approach to the differences between short- and long-term memory than James' position on the state of the information. Short-term and long-term memory were to be considered completely different memory systems. One manifestation of this type of distinction is that we tend to think of the two as located in different places. Although the spatial separation is not necessarily entailed by the approach, the important point is that the principles governing memory would be completely different. That is, variables affecting retention—such as the time between input and test, the meaningfulness and organization of the material, and perhaps amnesia—should exert different effects upon short-term and long-term memory. If so, the two types of memory require different theories; that is, they are different storage systems.

We shall begin by discussing a particular model of short- and long-term memory as different systems. Then we shall examine the data for and against this model and conclude the chapter by returning to the relationship between short-term memory and conscious contents.

THE MODAL MODEL OF MEMORY

Richard Atkinson and Richard Shiffrin proposed a view of the entire memory system in 1968, which subsequently became so influential that it is known as the "modal," or typical, model of memory. Their model is particularly pertinent at this point, because it concentrates heavily upon short-term memory, including the relationship among sensory register, short-term memory, and long-term memory. A schematic view of the model is presented in figure 4.1.

According to Atkinson and Shiffrin's model, incoming information flows from the sensory register to short-term memory to permanent storage in long-term memory. The transfer of information from the sensory register to short-term memory is controlled by attention. Once in short-term memory, the information is subject to *control processes,* which are operations serving a variety of memory functions. The most important control process is *rehearsal. Rote,* or *maintenance rehearsal,* functions primarily to keep information active in short-term memory. Maintenance rehearsal corresponds to simple repetition of information. *Elaborative rehearsal* involves relating the information to other known information, a process involving meaning. For example, if the words *dog, tree,* and *cat* are to be remembered, elaborative rehearsal might involve the construction of a relationship among the words, even to forming a visual image of a dog chasing a cat up a tree. Elaborative rehearsal functions to quickly transfer information to long-term memory. Rehearsal is important because the model assumes that information decays quickly from short-term memory unless it is actively used.

Other control processes include *coding,* which involves attaching appropriate information from long-term memory to the short-term information. For example, a telephone number is easier to remember if it is coded into larger units than dealt with as single digits: 1-800-555-1212 becomes 1, 800, 555, 12, 12. The smaller number of large chunks allows more frequent rehearsal of the information. The rules for transforming the single digits into larger chunks are retrieved from long-term memory and applied to the string of single digits in short-term memory. Again, you can see that the ultimate function of this control process is to combat the effects of decay.

The *strategies* for retrieving information from long-term memory are another important short-term memory control process. For example, if you are asked the question, "who is the primary author of the switch model of attention?" your strategy may be to activate long-term information concerning "names associated

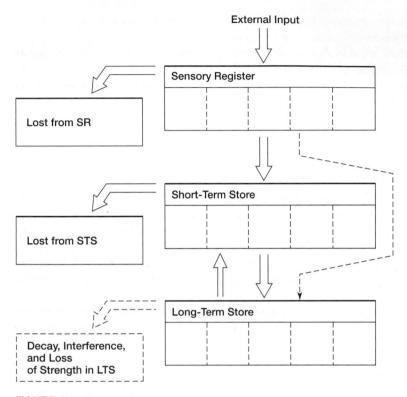

FIGURE 4.1
Atkinson and Shiffrin's stages of memory. *(From "Human Memory: A Proposed System and Its Control Processes" by R. C. Atkinson and R. M. Shiffrin, in K. W. Spence and J. T. Spence, Eds., The Psychology of Learning and Motivation: Advances in Theory and Research, Vol. 2. New York: Academic Press, 1968. Copyright 1968 by Academic Press. Used by permission.)*

with the psychology of attention." These names are then brought to short-term memory, where you decide which is the correct answer.

An important feature of the Atkinson and Shiffrin model is that the short-term memory system has a severely limited capacity. This implies not only that a small number of items can be stored, but also that the control processes require some of the limited capacity. Rehearsal, for example, may guard some information against loss from short-term memory, but this gain comes at the expense of not being able to rehearse other items. Chunking smaller units into larger units requires capacity that then cannot be devoted to storage or rehearsal of other items. In general, the control processes expedite the processing of some information, but this facilitation comes at the expense of other information. This trade-off is another instance of the assumption of limited processing capacity discussed in chapter 3.

Much of the research stimulated by Atkinson and Shiffrin's model had the ultimate goal of establishing the characteristics of short-term memory, particularly to demonstrate that these characteristics differ from those of long-term memory. Such research is essential for a distinction between short- and long-term memory systems, because elaborate theoretical descriptions of two different memory systems would be unnecessary if there were no evidence for two different types of memory.

Characteristics of Short-Term Memory

Three basic characteristics originally were proposed to distinguish short-term memory from long-term memory. These characteristics were that *forgetting is due to decay of the trace, the capacity for storage is small, and the trace is a phonetic code.* Remember from our discussion in chapter 2 that the sensory register is characterized by a rapidly decaying trace, stored in a veridical form in a large-capacity system. As the information moves on to short-term memory, the trace life increases somewhat, although it is still brief by the standards of long-term memory. The information is transformed into a phonetic code in short-term memory, and the capacity of the system is considerably smaller than either the sensory register or long-term memory. We shall now briefly consider the evidence, both positive and negative, for these characteristics.

Rapid Decay of the Trace   Among the modern classics of experimental psychology is the research claiming to demonstrate a short-term trace. Very similar experiments were reported almost simultaneously by Brown (1958) in England and Peterson and Peterson (1959) in the United States. The experimental procedure, now known as the *Brown-Peterson paradigm,* is quite simple. Participants are shown three items consisting of nonsense syllables or words for 3 seconds. Memory for these triads is then tested following a retention interval, which varies from 0 to 18 seconds. Such a task does not seem to be particularly difficult: how hard can it be to remember three simple items over a period as short as 18 seconds? Indeed, the task would be no challenge at all if the participants were allowed to repeat the items during the retention interval. This is not the case, however, because a *rehearsal prevention* task is inserted between presentation of the material and the recall test. A rehearsal prevention task is an activity that prohibits the participant from repeating the test items. For example, the participant may be required to count backward by threes from a designated number, a task which is sufficiently difficult that rehearsal becomes impossible. We are then in a position to examine memory in the absence of rehearsal.

The typical results of a Brown-Peterson experiment are shown in figure 4.2. The critical aspect of these results is the rapid forgetting that occurs over the very short retention interval. Notice that after 18 seconds, only about 10 percent of the material is remembered. Such a poor memory after such a brief period of time

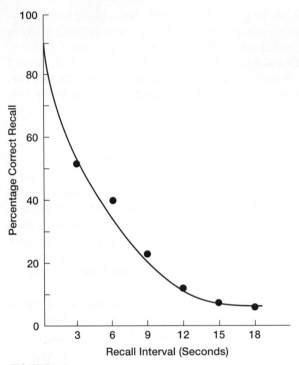

FIGURE 4.2
Percentage of items correctly recalled after various retention intervals. *(From "Short-Term Retention of Individual Verbal Items" by L. R. Peterson and M. J. Peterson,* Journal of Experimental Psychology, *1959, 58, 193–198. Copyright 1959 by the American Psychological Association. Reprinted by permission of the publisher and authors.)*

was a startling finding that served as one basis for claiming a separate, short-duration memory system.

When these data first appeared in the late 1950s, they were strikingly in contrast to what was known about forgetting, mainly from studies of long-term memory. At that time, forgetting was seen as a gradual process occurring as the result of *interference*. Interference is produced by the intervention of other material between the presentation of a to-be-remembered event and the memory test. For example, suppose you have a history class immediately after your psychology class. Your memory for the material learned about psychology is subject to interference from the material learned about history. Interference implies that memory failure results from competition among stored information. Forgotten material does not go away but, rather, loses in the momentary competition for expression.

The rapid forgetting in the Brown-Peterson paradigm challenged a unitary view of interference as the cause of forgetting. Not only did massive forgetting occur in a very short time, but also the source of interference in the Brown-Peterson task was not initially apparent. Some theorists then claimed that short-term memory is subject to *decay* of information, a position on forgetting which differs substantially from interference. Decay results from disuse, failure to rehearse in this situation, and implies that the forgotten material has disappeared from memory altogether. The important point to note here is that the Brown-Peterson data seem to imply completely different principles of forgetting in short-term memory and long-term memory.

This conclusion, however, requires the assumption that no interference is present in the Brown-Peterson paradigm. You already may have wondered if the rehearsal prevention task could be a source of interference. Counting backward, or any other activity used to prevent rehearsal, intervenes between exposure to the material and the memory test and may induce forgetting through interference. Decay theorists argued that the rehearsal prevention activities do not produce sufficient interference to account for the enormous forgetting normally found in the Brown-Peterson paradigm. This argument is based on the fact that interference increases with the similarity between target (to-be-remembered) and interfering materials, and counting backward requires the use of numbers that are not similar to the words the participants are to remember. Nonetheless, a dilemma is introduced when we try to decide between decay and interference theories. To establish a situation in which decay can occur, rehearsal must be prevented, but anything done to prevent rehearsal may actually introduce interference. Hence, it becomes extremely difficult to decide whether the forgetting is due to interference or to decay.

Keppel and Underwood (1962) identified a genuine source of interference in the Brown-Peterson paradigm. In the typical Brown-Peterson experiment, the participant faces a number of recall trials. After the first trial, each succeeding trial is subject to interference from the preceding trials. Only the first recall test is free of interference, and Keppel and Underwood found no effect of retention interval on memory for the first triad shown. Thus, it appears that interference is present in the experimental situation.

Research such as that of Keppel and Underwood seriously questions the role of decay in producing the rapid forgetting in the Brown-Peterson paradigm. If the forgetting is due to interference, then performance in the Brown-Peterson paradigm is governed by the same principle as in long-term memory studies. Consequently, the support for a distinction between short- and long-term memory provided by this paradigm is not as strong as originally thought.

Capacity of Short-Term Memory   In an influential paper, Miller (1956) argued that the capacity of short-term memory ranged from five to nine items, with the average being seven items. These estimates were obtained from Miller's study of immediate memory span performance. Immediate memory span is measured by presenting a list of items, digits, letters, or words and determining how many items can be recalled in their correct serial order immediately after presentation. Miller noticed that most people remembered between five and nine items, which suggested that short-term memory has quite limited capacity. It is no accident, by the way, that the standard telephone number is seven digits; the telephone company takes Miller's estimate quite seriously in its effort to reduce the number of calls to Directory Assistance.

Seven items may seem an unrealistically small number, especially when we consider that short-term memory must funnel vast amounts of information from the sensory register into long-term memory. Notice, however, that *item* has not yet been defined. An item is a *chunk* of information ranging from a single letter to an idea expressed by a paragraph. The previously discussed control process of coding establishes these chunks. The coding process detects relationships among individual items that allow the items to be organized, or "chunked," into a single unit. Simple examples of chunking include grouping individual letters, *c-a-t*, into a single unit, *cat*. More complex chunking involves detailed linguistic descriptions that are organized into single idea units. For example, this description, "The man, whose skin was wrinkled and leathery, had silver-white hair and supported his slow, limping walk with a cane," might be reduced to a single idea, "The man is old."

The chunking produced by the coding process can offset the extreme capacity limitations of short-term memory. This limited capacity of short-term memory contrasts sharply with the large storage capability of long-term memory. Everything we know is assumed to be stored in long-term memory, a very large amount of information, indeed. This marked difference in storage capacity is then taken as additional evidence for separate systems of short-term memory and long-term memory.

From another view, however, the capacity distinction between short- and long-term memory is not a convincing argument for the existence of two separate memory systems. Remember that the data Miller used to argue for capacity limitations were from tests of memory span. The fact that memory span is limited to correct recall of between four to seven items does not necessarily indicate small capacity. The longer lists, those in excess of seven items, may increase the possibility of interference. Studies of long-term memory consistently show that performance is worse the more one has to remember. Thus, the argument for capacity differences is not a compelling basis for a distinction between two separate systems of memory. Rather, the limitations on memory span performance may be another reflection of the limitations of conscious capacity.

The Information Stored in Short-Term Memory   Another distinction between short-term memory and long-term memory is the kind of information stored in the memory traces. Information is assumed to be stored in long-term memory in terms of its meaning, whereas sound patterns are remembered in short-term memory. Thus, long-term memory is assumed to be based on a semantic code, and short-term memory is phonetically coded. A phonetic code in short-term memory makes sense because rehearsal requires a code that is easily repeated. Sound patterns satisfy this requirement, and, therefore, a phonetic code in short-term memory becomes highly adaptive. It is much more difficult to imagine rote repetition of visual images and of meaning codes, yet these codes would be quite efficient in long-term memory where decay is no problem and rehearsal is unnecessary.

Supporting evidence for these assumptions is drawn from research demonstrating greater confusion among semantically similar words in relatively long lists and greater confusion among phonetically similar words in relatively short lists. For example, Baddeley (1966 a, b) describes an experiment in which participants were asked to remember either a five-word list or a ten-word list. A critical assumption of this experiment is that the short list is remembered from short-term memory, while the longer list reflects the operation of long-term memory because it exceeds the capacity of short-term memory. In both the five-word and ten-word lists, all of the words either sounded alike (e.g., *bat, hat, cat*), had a similar meaning (e.g., *tiny, small, little*), or were unrelated (e.g., *bat, desk, tiny*). The five-word lists were poorly recalled when all of the words sounded alike, but similarity of meaning produced recall much like that of unrelated words. With the ten-word list, however, semantic similarity produced poor recall, and phonetically similar words were recalled, as well as were the unrelated words.

This outcome can be understood by assuming that similarity among the memory codes leads to confusion about the particular words and, thus, poor performance. If what I remember is a sound pattern and all of the words share this pattern, I will experience difficulty translating that sound pattern into the words I saw. Since phonetic similarity but not semantic similarity disrupted memory for short lists, Baddeley argues that short-term memories are phonetically coded. The semantically similar words will not have similar phonetic memory codes because they do not sound alike. Semantic confusion in the longer lists suggests the existence of a meaning code in long-term memory. The phonetically similar words do not have similar semantic codes because they differ in meaning. Thus, studies such as Baddeley's are offered as further evidence that different kinds of information are stored at different stages in the retention interval. If it is valid, such a conclusion would suggest a useful distinction between short-term memory and long-term memory.

Contrary to this conclusion, however, much evidence exists indicating that no one code exclusively characterizes either short-term memory or long-term memory. In the discussion of pattern recognition in chapter 2, we mentioned the experiment on mental rotation. A letter is shown briefly, and the participant then has to decide whether the normal orientation or the mirror image of the letter is shown. Since the decision must be made rapidly, such an experiment qualifies as short-term retention. If, as the accepted interpretation implies, participants do rotate mental images to reach their decisions, the short-term code is the visual image of the target letter. In addition to other reports of visual codes in short-term memory, some investigators have even reported the existence of semantic codes in short-term memory.

Long-term memory also can be coded in less rigid ways. Abundant evidence is available to suggest the presence of visual codes in long-term memory. For example, consider this question: In your room, is the doorknob on the left or right as you exit the room? To answer this question, most people claim to retrieve "a picture" of the door. Phonetic codes also are much in evidence in long-term memory, as is clear from our ability to remember any of a range of sound patterns as well as from the evidence of experimental work.

Again, as with the distinction between the types of forgetting, short- and long-term retention cannot be neatly distinguished on the basis of codes. The ability to remember material may well depend upon whether we attend to the way it looks or sounds or to its meaning, but certainly we are not constrained to code recent experiences in one way and longer-standing memories in some other way.

Additional Evidence for Short-Term Memory

The distinction between short- and long-term memory has been used to explain other phenomena, and to the extent that these explanations are successful, we have reason to accept the reality of separate short- and long-term systems. Simply stated, if a particular phenomenon can be better understood by the assumption of a difference between short-term memory and long-term memory, we have another reason for accepting the distinction.

The Serial Position Effect   A good example of this approach is the application of the short-term–long-term distinction to the *serial position curve.* The serial position curve depicts the accuracy of recall of an ordered list as a function of the input position of an item in the list. Early items are recalled well and so are the last items, but the middle items are remembered poorly, resulting in a U-shaped function such as that depicted in figure 4.3. Examples of the serial position effect are quite common. Consider a young child learning the alphabet; *A B C* and *X Y Z* are not a problem for the child, but the middle letters are the last added to the child's knowledge. Many children in the initial stages of alphabet learning even treat *L M N O P* as a single letter.

One explanation of the serial position effect is based entirely on the distinction between short- and long-term memory systems. The early items are recalled well, which is called the *primacy effect,* because they are the first to enter short-term memory and thus can be rehearsed and transferred to long-term memory. The middle items, however, enter short-term memory while the first items are being rehearsed; hence, little capacity is available to rehearse the middle items.

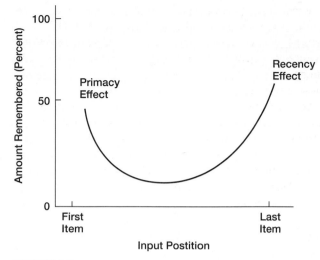

FIGURE 4.3
An idealized version of a serial position curve showing memory
as a function of the input position of the material.

Therefore, the middle items are not likely to be transferred to long-term memory. The last items in the list are also well remembered—a finding called the *recency effect,* presumably because these items are still in short-term memory at the time of recall.

Glanzer and Cunitz (1966) tested this explanation of the serial position curve in an experiment that demonstrated that the primacy and recency effects can be manipulated independently. In one condition, participants were given a list of 20 words to remember, but after the words were presented and before the memory test, the participants were required to perform a *rehearsal prevention task.* After the rehearsal prevention activity, the normal recency effect did not occur, presumably because rehearsal prevention allowed time for the last items to decay from short-term memory prior to the recall test. The primacy effect was unchanged by rehearsal prevention, as should be the case if the early list items are recalled from long-term memory. In the second part of the same research, the primacy effect was reduced by increasing the rate at which the items were presented, while the recency effect was unchanged by presentation rate. These results are consistent with the modal model for two reasons. First, faster presentation rates decrease the time available for rehearsal and, thus, should reduce the probability of items entering long-term memory. Consequently, the model predicts the effect on primacy items. Second, because the recency effect is due to immediate recall of items from short-term memory, presentation rate should not affect recency. Regardless of presentation rate, the most recently presented items are available in short-term memory. Thus, the differential effect of a variable, such as presentation rate, on the primacy and recency portions of the serial position curve is taken as strong evidence for the existence of separate memory stores.

The strength of this evidence, however, is questionable in light of further research. A particularly interesting example was offered by Bernbach (1975) who failed to replicate Glanzer and Cunitz' (1966) finding that presentation rate had no effect on recency items. The critical difference in the two experiments was that in Bernbach's case, the participants did not know how long the word lists were. In the absence of such knowledge, Bernbach suggests the primacy and recency items are processed in the same way. If the participant does know how long the list is, as in Glanzer and Cunitz' study, a strategy is adopted by which the early items are rehearsed but the last items are not. Thus, the pattern of results seems to be due to differences in strategic processing rather than to the operation of separate memory stores.

Amnesia Studies of patients suffering from amnesia have been used as another source of evidence for the distinction between short-term and long-term memory. Serious head injuries—hypoxia (a lack of oxygen to the brain), brain surgery, and conditions such as Alzheimer's disease—can produce a specific memory impairment known as anterograde amnesia, the inability to remember events that are experienced after the brain is injured.

In some cases, the patient has a normal memory span for very recent events, but cannot retain that information for long periods (e.g., Baddeley & Warrington, 1970; Milner, 1970). Such a pattern suggests that short-term memory itself is intact but the mechanisms for transferring information from short-term to long-term memory have been disrupted. In effect, these patients were thought to be incapable of learning anything new because information could not be transferred from short-term to long-term memory.

In other cases of anterograde amnesia, the immediate memory span was far below normal (e.g., Shallice & Warrington, 1970; Warrington, Logue, & Pratt, 1971). In at least one instance, the patient had an immediate memory span of one item. Performance such as this is easily interpreted as disruption of the short-term memory store. Thus, the pattern of memory loss in anterograde amnesia can also be interpreted by using the distinction between short-term and long-term memory, particularly by assuming that injury and disease can disrupt the brain processes corresponding to short-term storage and transfer from short-term to long-term memory.

An important implication of this explanation of anterograde amnesia is that the amnesiac is incapable of learning new information. If information cannot be transferred to long-term memory, it can have no lasting effect on behavior. This depressing conclusion now is known to be wrong. The evidence comes from experiments in which a person's memory for an experience is tested without the person being aware that it is a memory test. This procedure is called an *implicit memory test* and is based on the same idea underlying such techniques as free association, dream analysis, and Rorschach tests in psychotherapy.

The experiments are quite easy to follow, as illustrated by a study from Graf and Schacter (1985). Participants were shown a list of unrelated word pairs and asked to construct a sentence containing each word pair. This task was designed to induce semantic coding of the word pairs. Following the study session, an implicit memory test in which the participants were shown a long list of word stems was administered; the word stems were the first three letters of words. The participants were instructed to complete the word stem to make a word. No reference was made to the fact that some of the word stems corresponded to words in the original study list, encouraging the participant not to treat the stem-completion test as a memory test for the study words but as a test of ability to think of a word beginning with the three letters given. Following the stem-completion test, a standard cued recall test was administered in which one member of each of the original word pairs was presented and the participants were asked to recall the other member of each pair. The cue word was also present in the stem-completion test. Participants in Graf and Schacter's experiment included college students, as well as patients with anterograde amnesia caused by head injuries, strokes, and disease.

The results of the second experiment reported by Graf and Schacter (1985) for unrelated word pairs are shown in figure 4.4. The cued recall performance of amnesic patients and college students is shown in the left panel of figure 4.4. You can see that the amnesic patients recalled very few of the words, actually about 2 percent. This is not surprising; after all, amnesiacs cannot remember, or can they? The right panel of figure 4.4 shows the stem-completion performance. The amnesic patients completed about 35 percent of the stems with list words, which was about the same level of performance as college students. Considering that people who had not seen the study list completed the test stems with only 12 percent of the study words, the performance of both the amnesic patients and the college students represents a significant influence of the study session on the stem completion test. *The important point is that the amnesic patients benefited just as much as the college students from this experience.*

Results such as these indicate that anterograde amnesia is not due to the failure of information to be passed from short-term to long-term memory. In this sense, the modal model's explanation of amnesia appears to be wrong. What seems to be the case is that amnesic patients are unable to retrieve past experiences when they must exert conscious effort to memory. When circumstances allow these past experiences to be activated without conscious intent to remember, the amnesiac performs as well as anyone else.

Neurological Correlates of Short-Term Memory   Another important implication of the modal model is that short- and long-term memory are likely to occupy different locations in the brain. The most direct evidence on this issue

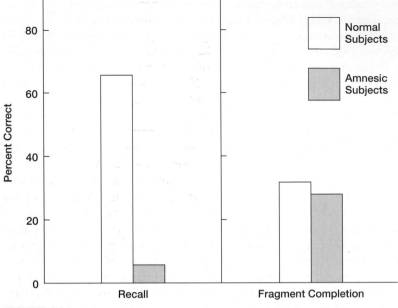

FIGURE 4.4
Performance of normal subjects and amnesic patients on a cued recall test and
a fragment completion test. *(From "Implicit and explicit memory for new
associations in normal and amnesic subjects" by P. Graf and D. L. Schacter.
Journal of Experimental Psychology: Learning, Memory, and Cognition, 1985, 11,
501–518. Copyright 1985 by the American Psychological Association. Reprinted
by permission of the publisher.)*

comes from experiments with monkeys, in which the activity of individual neurons is directly recorded while the monkeys perform simple short-term memory
tasks (Goldman-Rakic, 1987). In one kind of task, called the *spatial delayed-
response test,* a monkey looks at a central fixation point while a memory cue
(a black dot) is briefly presented in one of eight locations surrounding the point.
The monkey has been trained to continue looking at the fixation point until it dis-
appears, at which time it is to move its eyes to the position the cue had previously occupied. During the delay, which may last 6 seconds or longer, the monkey
must remember ("keep in mind") the prior location of the cue. Behaviorally,
monkeys do quite well at this task, moving their gaze to the previously cued location, thus showing good short-term memory. Of more interest, however, is the
neural activity that accompanies their performance. In particular, neurons in the
frontal lobes that are relatively "quiet" during presentation of the memory cue dramatically increase their rate of firing during the retention interval and then
abruptly stop firing once a response has been made. Such delay-specific firing—

neural activity that is time locked to the short retention interval—appears to be the direct neural correlate of short-term memory. Moreover, the neurons that fire during the delay interval appear to be selective for specific locations. That is, a particular neuron (e.g., N1) will only fire when the monkey is trying to remember a specific location (e.g., directly to the left of fixation); when a different location (e.g., right of fixation) must be remembered, N1 is silent while a different neuron that is "tuned" to that new location becomes active over the delay.

One interpretation of these findings is that the to-be-remembered locations are being "stored" in the frontal lobes during the delay period—a claim that is entirely consistent with a strong distinction between short-term and long-term memory. Alternatively, neurons in the frontal lobes may instead be acting as "pointers" to long-term memory representations stored in more posterior areas of the brain. Consistent with the interpretation, neuroanatomical investigations have shown that the short-term-memory neurons activated in the above studies are connected to neurons in the parietal lobes, which play a key role in representing our spatial environment and, as we learned in the previous chapters, are involved in both spatial perception and spatial attention. Subsequent studies have identified other neurons in the frontal lobes that, instead of being specialized for remembering spatial locations, are specialized for short-term object memory and are connected to (ventral stream) neurons in the temporal lobes (Wilson, O'Scalaidhe, & Goldman-Rakic, 1993). Furthermore, PET research has confirmed that the patterns of activation seen in monkeys can also be found in human subjects performing similar tasks (Smith et al., 1993). Thus, the emerging neurocognitive model of short-term memory is of information permanently stored in posterior areas of the brain, but temporarily activated by neurons in the frontal lobes.

Returning to our question of whether short-term and long-term memory occupy different locations in the brain, we can now see that the answer appears to be both yes and no. Information "in" short-term memory is really just information stored in long-term memory that is under active consideration by conscious processes. This conclusion is consistent with William James' view that short-term (primary) and long-term (secondary) memory do not reflect different places or systems but, rather, reflect a difference in the activation level of information in long-term memory. What neural studies have added is the finding that the brain areas responsible for initiating and maintaining this active state are located in the frontal lobes. If you recall our discussions from the last chapter, this finding should make sense because the frontal lobes are where the highest levels of attention are based, and short-term memory is basically a high-level form of attention directed at stored information. In fact, the similarity between attention and short-term memory was one of the reasons that researchers stopped thinking of short-term memory as a system separate from long-term memory (Cowan, 1988). The neurological findings support this perspective, pointing to a form of short-term memory that is more dynamic and process-oriented than that described in the original modal model. In conjunction with other research showing problems with the modal model, the neural findings suggest that, instead of acting as a place for the temporary storage of information, short-term memory is perhaps better thought of as a set of processes that *work with* information stored in long-term memory.

Summary of the Evidence for Separate Storage Systems

On the whole, the evidence we have reviewed is not favorable for the modal model's depiction of short-term memory as a discrete storage system. None of the proposed characteristics of the short-term storage, duration, capacity, or nature of the trace, definitively separate short- from long-term memory. The application of the modal model to problems such as the serial position effect and amnesia enjoyed some initial success, but the predictions of the model about some aspects of the phenomena are inconsistent with the data. Neuroscience research has shown that, rather than being a specific place in the brain, short-term memory depends on a widely dispersed network of neural areas. Thus, even though the idea of separate memory storage systems of short- and long-term memory is intuitively appealing, the scientific evidence suggests that the picture is not so simple.

As described by the modal model, the two critical factors for memory seem to be the length of time after presentation of the material and the type of processing performed on the material. For example, incoming information may be in the visual sensory register for up to 250 milliseconds after presentation but only moves on to short-term memory if it is selected by the process of attention. Information may remain in short-term memory for up to 30 seconds, but rehearsal must occur to move the information to long-term memory. If we now consider this system, we realize that the length of time after presentation is much less critical for memory than is the *activity,* or *process,* imposed on the material. Transfer from one stage to another is always determined by a process, never by mere passage of time. Moreover, memory for information within a system is also under the influence of processes. Rehearsal allows information to be maintained in and recalled from short-term memory. Recall from long-term memory requires, among other factors, the operation of the retrieval process. The point to see here is that, even from the view of the modal model, memory is primarily a function of the processes imposed upon the information. Thus, *memory is determined by what is done to the information, not by where the information is.*

Arguments of this type have convinced some researchers that the modal model is not quite as useful as once thought. Two very different ideas have been offered as substitutes. One focuses on memory processes rather than memory stores. We shall take up this idea in the next chapter. Another alternative represents a modification and extension of the concept of short-term memory known as working memory.

WORKING MEMORY

Since 1974, the British psychologist Alan Baddeley (Baddeley & Hitch, 1974) has been developing the concept of working memory (Baddeley, 1986, 1990, 1993, 1994, 2000). The principal difference between working memory and the modal model concept of short-term memory is that working memory is not a unitary storage concept. Like short-term memory, working memory is assumed to be a limited capacity system containing transient information. Unlike short-term memory, however, the function of working memory is less a matter of a storage way station to long-term memory than of holding information used for other cognitive work. The assumption is that working memory is a critical part of many important activities such as problem solving, reasoning, and comprehension.

For example, Baddeley and Hitch (1977) showed that simple reasoning problems could be performed while simultaneously maintaining a string of digits for immediate recall. As the digit string became longer, the time to perform the reasoning task increased but the errors in reasoning did not. The importance of this observation was to suggest that working memory is not a single, limited capacity store like the older short-term memory. If it were, accuracy on both tasks would be impaired. Rather, Baddeley suggests that different subsystems exist in working memory for different tasks.

Baddeley's (2000) concept of working memory includes four components. The *central executive* is the controlling, decision-making mechanism of working memory that functions to recruit and perform operations required by the current task, as well as to allocate capacity in the working memory subsystems. The three subsystems that have received some research effort are the *phonological loop, visuo-spatial sketchpad,* and *episodic buffer,* each of which is a temporary storage system. Visual-spatial material is stored and manipulated by the visuo-spatial sketchpad, whereas speech-based material is stored and manipulated by the phonological loop. These subsystems are essentially modality-specific storage/work space. The episodic buffer stores multidimensional representations, information that is integrated across modalities. Baddeley's schematic depiction of the model is shown in figure 4.5. As illustrated in the figure, each of the subsystems interfaces with both the central executive and with appropriate representations in long-term memory.

The independence of the subsystems is established by experiments showing very specific interference in dual-task situations. A good example is an experiment by Logie and Baddeley (1987) that focused on the simple but basic cognitive process of counting objects or events. Counting seems to involve subvocal articulation of the numbers in a sequence and the short-term storage of the running total. These functions would be served by the phonological loop in the scheme of working memory. If so, a secondary task requiring the use of speech-based material should interfere with simple counting, while a secondary task that does not involve speech should interfere less with counting. Logie and Baddeley (1987, Experiment 2) examined this prediction by asking subjects to count the

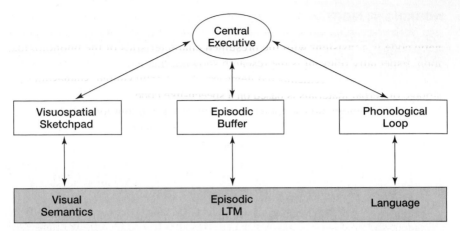

FIGURE 4.5
The components of working memory and the input to each component. (*From Baddeley, A. D. (2000). The episodic buffer: A new component of working memory.* Trends in Cognitive Science, 4, 417–423. Copyright 2000 by Elsevier Press. Used by permission of the author and publisher.)

number of times a square appeared on a computer screen. In a given trial, the square would appear between 1 and 25 times, and the subjects' task very simply was to count the number of times the square appeared. In some instances, however, the subjects also had to rapidly repeat the word *the* throughout the presentation of the sequence. In other cases, the subjects were asked to rapidly tap their fingers during the presentation sequence, a secondary task not requiring articulation. Finally, a control condition was included for which no secondary task was required.

The errors in counting are shown in figure 4.6 as a function of the type of secondary task and the length of the counting sequence. As you can see, the participants required to repeat a word while simultaneously counting performed more poorly than did the other participants. This result is evidence that counting requires the phonological loop, presumably for subvocal articulation of the consecutive numbers and for maintenance of the running total. Concurrent articulation of a word during this activity competes with counting for the capacity of the phonological loop, resulting in errors. A secondary task such as tapping your finger does not occupy the phonological loop; thus, fewer errors in counting accrue to this task. Note that tapping does produce more errors than no secondary task, suggesting that tapping occupies capacity of the central executive.

The Phonological Loop

Much of the research on working memory has focused on the phonological loop. The phonological loop consists of a store for verbal materials and a subvocal rehearsal process called articulatory control. The storage component is much like that of short-term memory and some of the evidence described earlier for a phonetic code is consistent with the presumed characteristics of the phonological loop. Especially relevant is the research showing that memory for short lists is disrupted if the to-be-remembered items are phonetically similar, suggesting that storage of verbal materials is based on a speech-like code.

Another phenomenon supporting the concept of a phonological store is the *irrelevant speech effect.* If a person is trying to remember a sequence of visually presented items, performance will be disrupted by simultaneous irrelevant spoken material. According to the theory of working memory, the effect is due to the fact that speech automatically gains access to the phonological loop, whereas visual material must be recoded into a phonetic code before it registers in the phonological loop. Recoding of the visual material is a function of the articulatory control process. Given this interpretation, two interesting predictions follow. First, if recoding of the visual material is blocked by otherwise occupying the articulatory control process, the information will not be stored in the phonological loop; hence, the irrelevant speech effect will not occur. Second, the effect requires speech sounds, but these sounds need not be complete words. Thus, the effect should occur if the irrelevant speech is in the form of the sound of a combination of letters (*ba*), but it should not occur to other nonspeech sounds. These predictions were both confirmed in experiments by Salame and Baddeley (1982).

The articulatory control process is subvocal rehearsal and functions to maintain items in the store as well as to enter items. For example, visually presented

FIGURE 4.6
The percentage of errors made in the counting task as a function of the secondary task. *(From "Cognitive processes in counting" by R. H. Logie and A. D. Baddeley.* Journal of Experimental Psychology: Learning, Memory, and Cognition, *1987, 13, 310–326. Copyright 1987 by the American Psychological Association. Reprinted by permission.)*

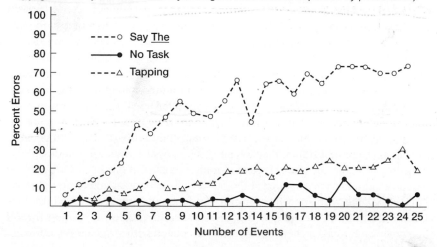

items or objects are entered into the phonological loop by articulation of the name of the item or object. The articulatory control process has been used to account for the *word length effect.* Memory span for long words such as opportunity, university, individual, etc. is smaller than for short words such as sum, harm, wit, etc. The interpretation of this effect is that long words take more time both to articulate for rehearsal and to report in recall than do short words. Thus, long words cannot be rehearsed as often in the store, and the time taken for recall allows for forgetting of other items in the store. Cowan, Day, Saults, Keller, and Flores (1992) provided strong support for this interpretation. They asked people to remember lists of six words and systematically placed longer words at the beginning or end of the list. The participants had to recall the items in the order they were seen, allowing one to determine whether the long words were more disruptive early or late in the list. When the long item occurs early in the list, rehearsal of the ensuing items will suffer because of the amount of time it takes to rehearse the long item. Furthermore, the long item presented early must also be recalled early, and the time to articulate the item in recall will be a disadvantage to the remaining items in store. The results supported the idea of a brief storage system that is sensitive to the amount of time required to pronounce the words. Memory for the list was worse when the long items had to be recalled early rather than late.

The importance of articulatory control is apparent when rehearsal is prevented by *articulatory suppression.* If a person is required to constantly utter an irrelevant sound such as the word *the* while studying a list for memory, performance will be severely disrupted. Articulatory suppression introduces irrelevant speech, but as previously described, irrelevant speech disrupts performance by occupying storage. Articulatory suppression occupies the articulatory control process such that rehearsal cannot occur. Evidence for this idea comes from studies that show suppression obliterates the word-length effect (Baddeley, Lewis, & Vallar, 1984). Additional evidence comes from the fact that suppression eliminates phonetic similarity effects on visually presented items. Visually presented items can only be stored in the phonological loop if their names are articulated, a function served by the articulatory control process. If articulation is suppressed, the visually presented items would have to be stored in a nonphonological code that would not be corrupted by phonetic similarity. Suppression does not eliminate phonetic similarity effects for auditorily presented items. Auditory presentation guarantees access to phonological storage; thus, the similarity among the sounds would be stored and cause disruption (Baddeley, et al., 1984).

Neuroimaging research has also provided strong support for the phonological loop and has begun to uncover the neural areas underlying the two components of this loop (Paulesu, Frith, & Frackowiak, 1993; see also Smith & Jonides, 1997, 1999). In particular, the phonological storage component has been traced to the left supramarginal gyrus, an area at the border of the parietal and temporal lobes that is associated with speech reception and language comprehension. In contrast, the articulatory mechanism has been traced to a region in the left frontal lobe known as Broca's area, an area that is associated with speech production.

Visuo-spatial Sketchpad

The visuo-spatial sketchpad is the component of working memory that stores and works with visual-spatial information. Much less research has been done on this component than on the phonological loop, and the evidence that is available comes from studies of visual span and from neuropsychological studies. One way to tap visual span is to show people a four-by-four matrix of cells. One of the cells is designated as the starting cell. They are then asked to remember a sequence of sentences such as *"In the starting cell put a 1; in the square to the right put a 2; in the square beneath put a 3,"* etc. Most people seem to remember this by recoding the sentences as a path through the matrix and typically show a span of about eight correct items. If nonspatial adjectives are substituted for the spatial adjectives of "up, down, left, right," visual coding does not occur. For example, the sentences to remember are changed to: *"In the starting cell put a 1; in the next square to the good put a 2; in the next square to the weak put a 3,"* etc. These sentences make no sense in relation to the matrix and, thus, are rote remembered rather than visually recoded. The span for the nonsense sentences drops to about six correct items.

Baddeley, Grant, Wight, and Thomson (1973) required participants to perform this task while simultaneously performing a visual-spatial tracking task that required they keep a stylus in contact with a moving spot of light. The tracking task severely disrupted memory for sentences containing spatial adjectives but had no effect on memory for the nonsense sentences. The same effects occur when the simultaneous task requires the participant to point to a moving sound source, a task that is spatial rather than visual. These data are consistent with the notion of an independent system that stores and manipulates visual-spatial information.

Neuroimaging research has also provided support for the claim that the neural areas responsible for the storage and manipulation of visual-spatial information are distinct from those dedicated to the storage and manipulation of verbal information. However, the "picture" emerging from neuroimaging is more complex than that proposed in Baddeley's original model (although quite consistent with the neurocognitive evidence reviewed earlier). In particular, the visuo-spatial sketchpad appears to reflect the operation of two separate working memory systems, one devoted to objects, the other devoted to spatial locations (Smith & Jonides, 1997, 1999).

Some of the best evidence for this object/spatial (what/where) distinction comes from the "N-back" task. In this task, subjects see a series of stimuli, such as different letters occurring in different positions on a computer screen, and must decide whether the current stimulus matches the stimulus presented "N" trials back (e.g., 2 or 3 trials ago). Note that this task is more demanding than the delayed-response (short-term memory) task described above because subjects must constantly update the contents of working memory in order to know what the target is. Results from experiments using variants of this procedure show that different neural networks are activated when subjects are trying to remember (store and update) objects versus spatial locations. In particular, spatial working memory activates occipital and parietal areas that are part of the dorsal (where) stream, while object working memory activates occipital and temporal areas that are part of the ventral (what) stream. Distinct areas in the frontal lobes also appear to be activated for these two stimulus types, with frontal spatial areas being more dorsal and frontal object areas being more ventral, consistent with the dorsal/ventral anatomy found in posterior visual areas (but see Cabeza & Nyberg, 2000). Thus, similar to the neural basis of the phonological loop, working memory for objects and locations appears to involve storage areas (located in the back of the brain) as well as more active rehearsal, or manipulative, areas (found in the front of the brain).

It should also be mentioned that the "N-back" task can be used to probe the neural basis of the central executive because the larger the "N" (i.e., the farther back the relevant trial) the greater the demand placed on the central executive to update the contents of working memory. Indeed, research has shown that as the "N" increases, so does the amount of activation in a critical part of the frontal lobes known as the dorsolateral prefrontal cortex or DLPFC ("dorsolateral" meaning higher-up and on the surface of the brain). These data suggest that the DLPFC, likely in combination with other areas, is the neural basis of the central executive.

The Episodic Buffer

The episodic buffer has been added to the subsystems of working memory to account for observations that cannot be explained by the other three components (Baddeley, 2000). It is well known that the memory span for words is much greater for words that comprise a meaningful sentence than for unrelated words. This is an example of the previously discussed phenomenon of chunking. The phenomenon indicates that memory span performance is influenced by long-term memory, where the information corresponding to semantic relations among words would be stored. One might expect that the chunks themselves are then briefly maintained by the phonological loop, but recent evidence argues against this possibility.

Vallar and Baddeley (1984) studied a patient whose memory span for unrelated words was 1, suggesting a severely damaged phonological loop. If the chunks formed by words that comprise a sentence were stored in the phonological loop, then the patient would be expected to show no advantage for sentential sequences. In fact, her span for sequences that formed a sentence was 5, which is far below normal but considerably higher than for the unrelated words. Because the patient's long-term memory was normal, the fact that her performance on related words was below normal suggests that the sentence effect itself is not purely a long-term memory phenomenon. Baddeley (2000) suggested that such results indicate the existence of a third storage subsystem in working memory. This system, the episodic buffer, holds information that is integrated across time and space, and, like the other subsystems, the episodic buffer is controlled by the central executive and interacts with long-term memory.

Working Memory and Long-Term Memory

As was the case with short-term memory, working memory is presumed to play some role in storing information in long-term memory. For example, the phonological loop is speculated to have evolved for the purpose of language learning (Baddeley, 1993). This speculation has produced a number of interesting studies on adult patients, language disabled children, and normal language acquisition. For example, the patient with severe deficit to the phonological loop, described in the previous section, was a native speaker of Italian. Baddeley, Papagno, and Vallar (1988) contrasted this patient's ability to learn new items from Russian with her ability to learn a list of unrelated Italian words. The patient had great difficulty acquiring new Russian vocabulary but showed close to normal performance on the Italian words. The results suggest that the damage to the phonological loop impairs the acquisition of new phonological patterns.

Evidence gathered from children has come from studies using the nonword repetition task. This task simply requires that a person hears and repeats back an unfamiliar nonword that sounds like a word, for example, *phring*. Gathercole and Baddelely (1990) studied children who were two years behind in normal language development but otherwise were of normal intelligence. They discovered that a child who was two years behind in language development, an 8-year-old with the language of a 6-year-old, was even more delayed on the nonword repetition; the 8-year-old performed like a 4-year-old. The difficulty was not due to difficulty perceiving or producing speech but was due to impaired verbal memory span. The results suggest that impaired functioning of the phonological loop caused the children's poor language development.

The rate of vocabulary acquisition in normal children also is predicted by the nonword repetition task. Gathercole and Baddeley (1989) demonstrated that differences in nonword repetition among 4-year-olds predicted differences in vocabulary one year later. Again, the evidence suggests that the phonological loop is important for learning new words, which in turn would indicate that working memory plays a crucial role in adding information to long-term memory.

Evaluation of Working Memory

The concept of working memory is intended to replace the idea of a single short-term memory store. Too much evidence weighed against the earlier characterization of the short-term store, much of which indicated that visual and semantic information was available in short-term memory. Working memory responded to this evidence by proposing multiple storage systems, each with its own particular code. Subsequent research has focused heavily on the phonological storage system, and some of this research bears a marked similarity to earlier work on short-term memory. Effects of phonetic similarity were important evidence for the original suggestion that short-term memory contained a phonetic code, and articulatory suppression clearly is a variant of rehearsal prevention tasks used in the Brown-Peterson paradigm. What has been added is considerable new information about the specificity of interfering activities. Furthermore, some of the research on the phonological loop has produced new information about important problems such language acquisition.

Even so, Nairne (2002) carefully documents data that challenge the fundamental premises of the phonological loop. For example, numerous studies have found dissociations between articulation rate and memory span. Some of these studies have shown differences in span as a function of properties of the material, (e.g., words versus nonwords) even when the articulation rate is held constant. Other studies have found that word length has no effect on span when important variables such as frequency and familiarity are controlled. These types of effects should not occur if the rate of articulation determines the activation of information in the phonological loop.

Much less is known about the other theoretical components of working memory. Especially noticeable is the lack of research on the function of the central executive. The central executive serves the same control functions as attention, and it will be useful to integrate what is known from research on attention with the concept of working memory. The visuo-spatial sketchpad and the episodic buffer were proposed to account for data that could not be explained by a system that only holds phonetic information. However, the development of these subsystems is in its early stages. As more research is accomplished, additional anomalies may well occur. A potential danger for the multiple-storage approach is the invention of a new storage system for results that challenge the existing systems. Proliferation of new systems without extensive justification would create an unwieldy theory that could explain everything but would be immune to proper testing. Because working memory is a constantly evolving theory, its ultimate value as a substitute for short-term memory awaits research that will bring the concept to greater maturity.

INDIVIDUAL DIFFERENCES IN WORKING MEMORY

An important development that emerged in the transition from short-term memory to working memory has been research on individual differences in working memory. Working memory's emphasis on both storage and processing capacity encouraged the construction of new span measures that, unlike older measures such as digit span, require processing as well as storage. Daneman and Carpenter (1980) introduced the first such measure, which they called reading span. The test requires people to read a series of sentences for comprehension and also to remember the last word of each of the sentences in order. Success at remembering the words provides the index of working memory; the more words remembered, the higher the span. This index differs from measures previously used for short-term memory span in that the working memory index requires simultaneous comprehension and memory as opposed to simply memory for a span of items.

Subsequent research has yielded additional measures such as the operations span test developed by Turner and Engle (1989). The operations span test requires that a simple arithmetic operation be read and verified as quickly as possible (e.g., "Is 6 + 9/3 = 8 (yes or no) CARROT). As in the example, a word followed each operation, and after a set of two to seven such operation-word strings, participants must recall the words in the order in which they appeared. The longer the string in which perfect recall occurs the higher the span. Another example is the counting-span task, in which two to seven displays of targets and distracters are presented with the requirement that the targets in each display be counted. For example, the targets might be light blue circles and the distracters dark blue circles. The light blue circles must be counted on each presentation and at the end of each set, the digits corresponding to the number of targets must be recalled in order of presentations of the displays. The longer the set of displays for which correct recall occurs the higher the span.

When any of these measures of working memory span are administered to a large sample of people, considerable variability will be found among the individuals. More importantly, these individual differences are highly correlated with performance on other tasks. Originally, these correlations were thought to be domain specific, such that reading span would correlate with reading comprehension but not with arithmetic ability. Subsequent research, however, has shown that the span measures predict a wide range of higher-order cognitive tasks, including ability to follow directions, vocabulary learning, note taking, writing, reasoning, bridge playing, and learning to write computer programs (Engle, 2001). Clearly, working memory span tests are measuring some fundamental aspect of cognition. What is it?

Engle (2002) and his colleagues have argued that working-memory-span scores measure a general controlled-attention capability. This capability allows people to maintain their focus on currently important goals and to avoid distraction that would denigrate performance on the current task. One might equate this with what we often call the ability to concentrate. If, in fact, span tests are measuring such a general capability, we would expect individual differences in span to predict not only higher-level cognitive performance but also performance on even simple perceptual tasks that introduce distraction. Kane and Engle (2001; Kane, Bleckley, Conway, & Engle, 2001) have shown such effects.

Kane and Engle (2001) examined performance on the Stroop task as a function of individual differences in span. The Stroop task, as you will recall from chapter 3, requires the participant to name the ink color of words as quickly as

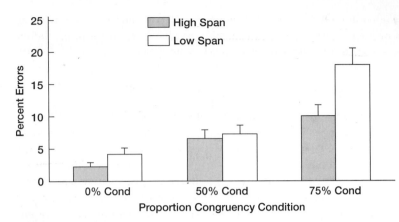

FIGURE 4.7
The results of Kane and Engle's experiment showing the effect of individual differences in working memory on the Stroop task as a function of the proportion of color-word congruent trials. (*From Engle, R. W. (2002). Working memory capacity as executive attention. Current Directions in Psychological Science, 11, 19–23. Copyright 2002 by the American Psychological Society. Used by permission of the author and the publisher.*)

possible. When the word is a color name incongruent with the color of the ink, the word can distract from the goal of the task to name ink colors. Kane and Engle reasoned that the ability to keep the goal of naming ink color in mind would be affected by the number of congruent color words presented in the task. That is, if most of the word names are the same as the ink color, one might be seduced into relying on the word name and lose the goal of naming ink color. Thus, they predicted that high-span participants would perform better on the Stroop task than low-span participants when the proportion of congruent trials was large. In their experiment, the percentage of congruent color words was 0%, 50%, or 75%. As shown in figure 4.7, the number of errors on the Stroop task was highly related to differences in span, but only for the condition in which 75% of the trial words were congruent. In the 0% and 50% congruent conditions, there are enough incongruent pairings of ink color and color word to maintain the task goal of naming ink color even for low spans. In the 75% congruent condition, however, high span participants have the capability to maintain the goal of naming the ink color in the face of distraction posed by the word.

The interpretation of span scores offered by Engle and his associates in terms of controlled-attention capability can be seen as similar to Baddeley's concept of a central executive. The central executive functions to coordinate the activity of the subsystems in Baddeley's theory and, in that regard, could serve to keep important task goals active in the appropriate subsystem. However, the research on individual differences in working memory span has not been directed to providing evidence for hypothetical memory systems, and, perhaps for that reason, this research has given us considerably more insight into potentially fundamental mechanisms of cognitive processing.

IMPROVING MEMORY FOR RECENT EVENTS

Let us now briefly consider some practical applications of what we have been describing. Many years ago, William James claimed that attention is the key to better memory. Assuming attention to be the allocation of processing capacity through rehearsal or semantic elaboration, James' suggestion has considerable merit for improving memory of recent events. Take the simple case of meeting new people and remembering their names shortly after an introduction. First, be sure you hear each name. Many times, we simply do not listen carefully when a name is mentioned. Look at the person being introduced and then use the person's name immediately when expressing your delight at meeting him or her. After that, continue to use the name frequently when addressing remarks to that person. As simple as this technique is, most of us rarely use it and all too often find ourselves in the embarrassing situation of forgetting a name immediately after an introduction. As like as not, we are thinking about something else, such as what we are going to say, rather than attending to name.

SUMMARY

Memory for recent experiences can be quite fragile. We seem to remember only a small proportion of this information, and the information is remembered for a short period of time. Observations such as these have led to the concept of short-term memory, which some researchers regarded as a system separate from long-term memory. The implication of this distinction between short-term and long-term memory systems is that different processes determine retention in the two systems. If this is the case, it should be possible to discover that the same variables will have different effects upon memory, depending upon where the information is in the system. Thus, in chapter 4 we reviewed a good deal of research designed to argue for differences in the capacity, duration, and nature of the codes in the short-term and long-term memory systems.

We also saw that the primary determinant of retention, even within the modal model of memory, is what is done to the information. A strong delineation of short-term memory and long-term memory is then necessary only if it is believed that the processes imposed on the material are different for the short-term and long-term memory systems. More recent research questioning this assumption was then reviewed, including research that examined the neurological systems involved in the short-term retention and manipulation of information.

The current view of short-term memory is that it is much less like a separate storage system, distinct from long-term memory, and more like a set of processes that enable us to work with information stored in long-term memory. This view is embodied in the concept of working memory and also can be inferred from the neurological evidence.

THOUGHT QUESTIONS

1. What is the evidence for a small capacity, short-duration memory system?
2. Why was the original version of a short-term memory store abandoned in favor of working memory
3. How does Baddeley's idea of working memory compare with Atkinson and Shiffrin's concept of short-term memory?
4. How are the word length effect and articulatory suppression explained by working memory?
5. What is the advantage of measures of operations span over measures of digit span?

5

LONG-TERM MEMORY

Long-term memory is the concept that represents the vast store of knowledge we have about the world, ranging from everyday events such as how to use a knife and fork to more esoteric information such as axioms of geometry. The power of long-term memory is truly impressive. For example, Bahrick, Bahrick, and Wittinger (1975) tested people's memory for their high school classmates by using pictures from old yearbooks. In the most extreme case, the participants in the experiment had graduated from high school 48 years earlier. These people still could recognize correctly over 60 percent of their classmates. In further studies, Bahrick and Hall (1991) showed that participants could remember surprisingly large portions of high school Spanish and algebra 50 years after they had learned them. Figure 5.1 displays results from one of Bahrick's studies showing participants' retention of Spanish over 50 years. Such demonstrations are not designed to argue that *all* of your prior experiences are available *all* of the time but, rather, that the possibility of permanent long-term memory may not be as far-fetched as our intuitions suggest. The goal of long-term memory research is to describe conditions separating successful and unsuccessful retention, as well as to offer theoretical explanation of why these conditions have their effect.

In pursuing this goal, we return to the discussion of memory processes that concluded the previous chapter. The processes underlying perception and comprehension of experiences are referred to as *encoding* processes to long-term memory. Processes occurring at the time memory is tested are *retrieval* processes. Encoding processes are discussed in the first part of this chapter, and retrieval processes are taken up in the second part of the chapter.

LEVELS OF PROCESSING

The emphasis on cognitive processes apparent in the concept of working memory was initiated by the idea of *levels of processing* (Craik & Lockhart, 1972). Levels of processing has a different goal from that of working memory. Working memory is an elaboration of the concept of short-term memory. Levels of processing was

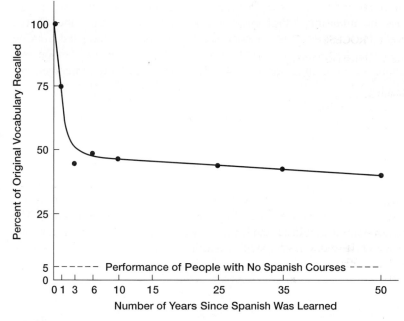

FIGURE 5.1
Memory for Spanish vocabulary as a function of years since Spanish was learned. *(Adapted by Rubin (1995) from Bahrick, H. P. (1984). Semantic memory content in permastore.* Journal of Experimental Psychology: General, 113, *1–27. Copyright by the American Psychological Association, 1984.)*

conceived as a general description of retention in both the long and short term. Levels of processing abandons the idea of discrete storage systems and concentrates on the types of processes associated with different levels of retention. Levels of processing attempts to explain the facts of retention without proposing different memory systems.

Assumptions of Levels of Processing

Levels of processing is based on two fundamental assumptions. The first is that *the memory trace is a by-product of perception and comprehension.* What you remember will be the things to which you attended. If, when introduced to a person, you devote your attention to his or her clothes, you will not remember his or her name because the perceptual processes were not allocated to the name. Another subtle but important implication of the first assumption concerns the role of *intent to remember.* The implication is that intent to remember is not crucial. We do not go through our day *trying* to remember things as they happen but, rather, we try to understand the experiences we have. For example, think of all the things you can remember from yesterday. Now, how many times yesterday did you say, "I have to remember this"? Probably not many, yet you can remember a large proportion of yesterday's events. In contrast, theories of short-term and working memory assume that conscious intent to rehearse is fundamental to retention and, surely, there is no reason to rehearse outside of an intention to remember. For levels of processing, memory results from perception and comprehension of events, not from intent to remember.

The second assumption of levels of processing is that *retention is directly related to the processing of meaning.* Semantic processing is assumed to produce better memory than nonsemantic processing. If what you notice or encode is an aspect of meaning, you will remember the event better than if what you notice is superficial aspects of the event. Semantic processing is assumed to be "deep" processing and nonsemantic processing "shallow," hence the designation "levels of processing." Why would semantic processing produce better memory? The original reason offered by Craik and Lockhart was that semantic traces last longer than nonsemantic traces. As we shall see, this assumption eventually required modification.

Experimental Tests of Levels of Processing

The two fundamental assumptions are easily captured in an experiment requiring special processing of each individual word in a list. The special processing comes in the form of an *orienting task,* which is a simple activity performed on each word. For example, the participant is asked to rate each word for its pleasantness. Alternatively, the participant might be asked to write the middle letter of each word. The first task is designed to direct attention to the meaning of the word, a semantic task. Consider making a pleasantness judgment of the word *cancer.* Most people rate this word as quite unpleasant. Why? It is not a particularly ugly-looking word, and its sound is very much like *dancer,* a word usually rated as quite pleasant. Clearly, the unpleasantness of *cancer* stems from its meaning. Thus, pleasantness ratings serve as a semantic orienting task because a pleasantness judgment requires determining the meaning of a word. Writing the middle letter of a word, however, does not require determining the word's meaning and, hence, is a nonsemantic task. Any task that can be performed without determining the meaning of a word is nonsemantic orientation. Nonsemantic tasks usually require a judgment about the letter patterns or sound patterns of a word such as estimating the number of rhymes for a word. The purpose of the orienting task is to direct the participant's attention to semantic or nonsemantic attributes.

Another characteristic of these experiments is the use of *incidental memory* instructions. Incidental instructions mean that the participants are not told to remember the words when they are studied but, rather, are led to believe that the purpose of the experiment is something other than to test memory, usually something to do with their orienting response. After the words have been seen, a surprise memory test is administered. The incidental instructions are designed to strengthen the attentional control of the orienting task by minimizing the chance that spontaneous processes of intentional memory are engaged. The sole purpose of the experiment is to determine whether more items are remembered following semantic orientation than following nonsemantic orientation.

The answer to this question is a resounding yes. Regardless of the semantic task, be it pleasantness rating, free association, sentence completion, or whatever, semantic orienting tasks produce better memory for the items than do nonsemantic tasks. Using pictures of human faces, Bower and Karlin (1974) showed that judgments of honesty produce better memory than do judgments about physical features of faces. The honesty judgment is seen as a semantic orienting task. This experiment is widely cited as evidence that levels of processing applies even to memory for faces.

Differences between semantic and nonsemantic orienting tasks have also been found at the neural level. For example, Kapur et al. (1994) used PET to examine brain activity while subjects made judgments about a series of words. In the semantic processing condition, subjects decided whether the word referred to something living or nonliving, while in the nonsemantic condition they decided whether the word contained the letter *a*. The results are presented in figure 5.2, which shows neural activity associated with the semantic judgment (left side of figure) and the nonsemantic judgment (right side of figure). Note that neural activity for each judgment task is depicted as if one were looking through a "glass

FIGURE 5.2
PET scan of brain activity induced by semantic and nonsemantic processing. *(From "The role of the left prefrontal cortex in verbal processing: semantic processing or willed action?" by Kapur et al. (1994)* Neuroreport, 5, *2193–2196.)*

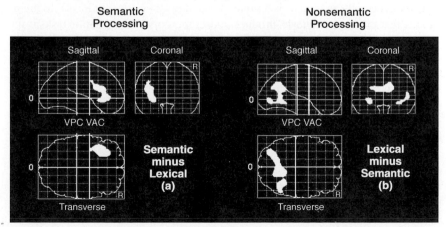

brain" from three different perspectives—from the side (*sagittal*), from the back of the head (*coronal*), and from the top (*transverse*); thus, the blobs of activity shown for semantic processing, for example, are actually the same blob, just viewed from three different angles. As can be seen in the figure, the two orienting tasks produced very different patterns of brain activity, such that semantic processing was accompanied by increased activation in the left prefrontal cortex while nonsemantic processing activated more posterior, perceptual-processing areas. Given these very patterns of activation (which can be thought of as a neural record of the judgment), it is perhaps no wonder that semantic and nonsemantic orienting tasks result in very different levels of memory performance.

Although PET data show that semantic and nonsemantic tasks activate different areas of the brain, these data do not answer the important question of *why* semantic tasks should produce better performance than nonsemantic tasks. Craik and Lockhart's original answer was that semantic information lasts longer than does nonsemantic information. Notice the similarity to the assumptions of short-term memory and working memory, where phonetic (nonsemantic) information is assumed to be stored in short-term memory and semantic information in long-term memory. In spite of many other differences between the descriptions of encoding, the previously discussed models of short-term memory agree that trace duration of nonsemantic information is briefer than that of semantic information. Unfortunately, this particular assumption appears to be incorrect.

DOUBTS ABOUT DEPTH

Research from levels of processing demonstrated that semantic orienting tasks produce better memory for items than nonsemantic orienting tasks, but the question is, why? The original notion was that semantic information lasts longer, but research quickly indicated that this assumption was wrong.

One of the nonsemantic tasks frequently used in laboratory studies is rhyming, and the fact that rhyming tasks produce poorer memory than semantic tasks is interpreted to mean that phonetic information does not last as long as semantic information. Such an interpretation appears inconsistent with some facts about real world memory. For example, can you recite the nursery rhyme "Jack and Jill"? How about the counting-out rhyme "Eenie-meenie-meini-mo"? These and other materials such as songs are remembered over long periods, in spite of the fact that in some cases it is not even clear what the meaning might be. What is salient is the rhyming character of the material.

David Rubin has made these points in his interesting research program on the oral tradition (Rubin, 1995). This research focuses on the characteristics of orally transmitted materials because people constructed the material to be easily remembered. Rubin has studied epic poems, ballads from the mountains of North Carolina, rhymes we learned as children, and memory for popular songs. In all cases, he finds that rhyming is an important aspect of the material, and this is particularly true when rhyme and meaning work together. For example, in telling the lines "she rode a dappled bay . . . one hour before day," the word *bay* may change to *gray* and back again over many tellings, but the meaning constrains the word choice such that you will not tell, "She rode a dappled Oldsmobile." It is a horse she rode and the rhyme further constrains the choice such that it will be a "dappled gray or bay" but not a "dappled palomino" (Rubin & Wallace, 1989). Rubin's careful studies of the oral tradition clearly show that rhyme information can be very useful for long-term memory.

In many respects, Rubin's research followed from the systematic experiments of Douglas Nelson of the University of South Florida. Nelson, from whose article the title of this section was drawn (Nelson, Walling, & McEvoy, 1979), has shown that memory benefits from the use of rhymes as cues under certain circumstances. Nelson's research program has been directed to understanding the relationship between conditions of encoding and types of retrieval cues and has resulted in his own recent theory of the operation of memory (Nelson, McKinney, Gee, & Janczura, 1998). This theory draws heavily on his earlier research, from which Nelson concluded that "sensory information activated by a stimulus event is not accurately described as shallow, evaporating quickly in the sunshine of semantic encoding" (Nelson, Walling & McEvoy, 1979, p. 43). In short, nonsemantic attributes are retained and used.

A good example of the persistence of nonsemantic information can be seen in an experiment by Stein (1978). In this experiment, participants were given a list of words in which one letter in each word was capitalized. After each word, the participant had to make a yes-no decision, requiring either semantic or nonsemantic information. The semantic decision was to judge whether the word fit in a sentence frame. For example, with the word *roCk,* the sentence frame was, "The _ rolled down the hill." The nonsemantic decision required a yes-no response to a statement such as "The letter *c* is capitalized." After presentation of all the words, participants were given a recognition memory test to tap their semantic or nonsemantic retention. The semantic test required that the subjects select the words on the original list from a larger group of words. The nonsemantic test required that the participants select the version of the original word that had the same letter capitalized: for example, "Among *Rock, rOck, roCk,* and *rocK,* which one was presented earlier?" Participants whose orienting task required a semantic decision performed better on the semantic recognition test, but participants who performed the nonsemantic orienting task did much better on the recognition of capital letters.

The important message of this experiment is quite clear. Nonsemantic information is retained as long as is semantic information. Consequently, the superior retention for words following semantic orientation cannot be due to more rapid decay of nonsemantic information. Again, why does semantic orientation produce better memory than does nonsemantic orientation?

Distinctiveness Hypothesis

At the time an event must be recalled, the entire event must be reconstructed from whatever subset of information was encoded. The ability to reproduce faithfully the original event will depend in large part upon how well the encoding specifies that event. A simple example clarifies this suggestion. Suppose you are asked to remember a list of words, one of which is *elephant*. If the task requires a semantic orientation, the encoded trace might contain meaningful facts such as "large, gray animal with large ears and trunk living in Africa and India." If you retrieve this information at the time of recall, *elephant* is an obvious response. However, if your task is nonsemantic orientation—for example, to check all the *es* in the word—the encoded trace might contain information that the word has two *es*. Reconstructing the word *elephant* from just that information seems to be quite unlikely. Most of us know a large number of words that contain two *es*.

This illustration is designed to introduce the distinctiveness hypothesis. *According to the distinctiveness hypothesis, memory is determined in part by how well the information encoded specifies the event being reconstructed.* Semantic information is likely to be much more specific and, thus, much more useful than nonsemantic information, as illustrated in the example of remembering *elephant*. Nonsemantic information such as letter combinations and sound patterns are considerably more redundant than semantic information. Simply put, the meanings of different words are less likely to be shared than are the letter combinations or sound patterns. Semantic orientation then produces superior performance because meaning more distinctively represents the event.

The distinctiveness hypothesis is a slight revision of the original levels of processing idea (Jacoby & Craik, 1979). It shares with levels of processing the assumption that the memory trace is a by-product of attention and pattern recognition, but the two ideas differ in their descriptions of what constitutes effective information. Rather than semantic information, the distinctiveness hypothesis emphasizes distinctive information.

This difference has interesting implications, among which is the prediction from the distinctiveness hypothesis that nonsemantic information can be useful in memory (Hunt & Elliott, 1980). If the nonsemantic information is distinctive, attention to that information should facilitate memory. Consider an experiment by Eysenck (1979). Participants were asked to attend to the sound patterns of words as an orienting task. In one condition, however, the subjects were given very unusual, atypical pronunciations of the words. Since these pronunciations are not likely to be shared by other words, the distinctiveness hypothesis predicts that they should facilitate memory. In fact, participants attending to atypical pronunciations remembered the words as well as did a group given semantic orientation. This should not happen if nonsemantic information decays more rapidly than does semantic information, as originally supposed by the depth hypothesis. The distinctiveness hypothesis, however, predicts that *unique features* aid memory for an event, regardless of whether the features are semantic or nonsemantic. Thus, Eysenck's results are more consistent with a distinctiveness explanation.

ORGANIZATION

Another important encoding process is *organization,* which is the process of grouping discrete, individual items into larger units based on a specific relationship among the items. Suppose you are given the common laboratory task of remembering a list of words. Among the words are *dog, cat, camel,* and *tiger.* You detect the relationship among the four words and *organize* them under the category *animal.* A considerable amount of research has demonstrated that such organizational processing facilitates long-term memory.

Material-Induced Organization

The majority of laboratory studies of organization and event memory use *categorized* word lists. The lists consist of words drawn from the same natural category such as *dog, cat, horse, pig,* and *cow* from the category *animal.* In most experiments, several categories are used to represent the words; for example, a list might contain 20 words having 4 words from each of five categories. Compared to uncategorized lists, participants remember categorized lists very well.

Furthermore, categorized lists are better remembered when presented in *blocked* form than when presented *randomly.* In blocked presentation, all of the items from a particular category are presented one after another before items from another category are presented. With random presentation, the items from different categories are mixed in the presentation order. The superior memory for blocked presentation again suggests the important role of organization in memory, because blocked presentation is much more organized than is random presentation.

Further indication of the importance of organization is obvious from the finding of active rearrangement of randomly presented lists. Even though items from various categories are presented in random order, participants group the items into their appropriate categories at recall. That is, the items are recalled by category in spite of having been presented randomly. This regrouping is known as *clustering in recall* (Bousfield, 1953). Clustering is an important indication of the active encoding process of organization in that the materials are rearranged from the random presentation order to an organized output order.

Subjective Organization

Organizational effects are obvious when categorized lists are compared to uncategorized lists, but careful examination of performance on uncategorized lists also reveals persuasive evidence of organizational activity. When participants are asked to remember lists of words unrelated in any obvious way, they find idiosyncratic relationships that result in consistent output groupings. Although clustering scores based on prespecified category grouping cannot be obtained from uncategorized lists, Tulving (1962) outlined a method for detecting organization of presumably unrelated lists. Tulving's measure of *subjective organization* requires multitrial recall. That is, participants receive several presentations and recall tests of a list. Subjective organization is measured by the *consistency of output order* over the recall tests. As the tests progress, the order in which the words are written on the tests becomes more consistent. The particular order differs for different individuals, since the groupings are based on idiosyncratic relationships. Nonetheless, subjective organization is an impressive indication of the prevalence of organizational activity in encoding.

Subjective organization is yet another example of using previous knowledge to interpret a current situation. Individual experiences allow us to relate the apparently unrelated words and to bring order to an otherwise chaotic event. Analogous situations exist in everyday experiences, perhaps more commonly than not. When we are confronted with actions that seem to make little sense, most of us try very hard to bring whatever information possible to bear on such situations to interpret and organize them. Consequently, the discrepancies among different persons' memory for the same event are not at all surprising. Because of differences in knowledge, an event may be organized and remembered in very different ways by different observers, just as different persons subjectively organize unrelated lists in very different ways.

THE PARADOX OF ORGANIZATION AND DISTINCTIVENESS

We now have discussed research indicating that memory benefits from distinctive processing and that memory benefits from organizational processes. These facts are well established and perfectly consistent with our intuitions, but on close inspection these facts appear paradoxical. Distinctive processing refers to the encoding of differences among events, and organization refers to the encoding of similarities among events. Distinctiveness and organization seem to be diametrically opposed prescriptions for good memory.

One resolution of this apparent dilemma is to assume that *both types of information* are important to memory (Hunt & McDaniel, 1993). Some evidence suggests that this is the case. Consider the following experiments reported by Epstein, Phillips, and Johnson (1975) and by Begg (1978). Participants were given either highly related word pairs (*beer-wine*, for example) or unrelated word pairs (*beer-dog*, for example). For each pair, the participants had to list either the similarities between the members of the pair or the differences between the members of the pair. Memory for the pairs was then tested. Related pairs were better remembered when participants oriented to the differences between the words,

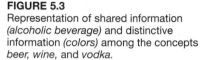

FIGURE 5.3
Representation of shared information *(alcoholic beverage)* and distinctive information *(colors)* among the concepts *beer, wine,* and *vodka.*

and unrelated pairs were better remembered when similarities were processed. Why should this be?

It appears that both similarities and differences are important. Related pairs command attention to similarity, but the similarity may produce confusion in memory. Participants may remember "alcoholic beverage," but be unable to decide whether they saw *beer, wine, vodka,* or *scotch.* Noticing the differences among similar items aids in this discrimination. The opposite problem occurs with unrelated items. The differences are obvious, but no relational structure is available to help generate the items. This relational structure or similarity among events seems to be very important in initiating the retrieval process. Remembering an event, whether it be a word in a list or what was done last Tuesday, seems to start at the general level of shared information, such as "words in the list" or "events of last Tuesday," and proceed to finer discriminations.

This interaction between similarities and differences is illustrated in figure 5.3. If each of the circles represents what is known about a word, the overlap, or intersection, of the circles represents their shared meaning and the nonoverlapping portions represent the meaning of each that is not shared. For example, *beer, wine,* and *vodka* all share *alcoholic beverage* as part of their meaning, but we also know that they have different colors. Color, then, is part of the information that does not overlap. Thus, the encoding process involves attention to certain aspects of events. Some of this information will be shared among the events and some of the information will differ. Optimal verbatim memory requires both.

MEMORY FOR PERSONALLY RELEVANT INFORMATION

In an interesting variation on the levels-of-processing paradigm, Rogers and his colleagues have shown that the personal relevance of information has a powerful effect on memory. Rogers, Kuiper, and Kirker (1977) asked participants to perform orienting tasks on lists of adjectives. In addition to the now familiar semantic and nonsemantic tasks, the participants were asked to rate how descriptive the word was of them. When later asked to recall the rated words, the words rated for personal descriptiveness were better recalled than those on which a semantic orienting task had been performed. The more *self-relevant* the event, the better the memory.

Why does self-relevance of an event enhance memory? At one level of description, Klein and Loftus (1988) have suggested that the assessment of self-relevance increases both the relational and distinctive processes at encoding. But why should self-relevance enhance relational and distinctive encoding? In all probability, events that we perceive as personally relevant attract more attention than events that are perceived as less relevant. Part of what we mean by "attract more attention" is that more processing is devoted to those events, consistent with the capacity model of attention discussed in chapter 3. It is this additional processing that influences memory, but it is the perceived personal relevance that attracts the additional processing.

SELF-GENERATION EFFECTS IN MEMORY

Folk wisdom has it that you will remember something better if you do it yourself than if you watch someone else do it. Perhaps you received this advice from your parents or teachers. Laboratory work has demonstrated conclusively that information you generate is better remembered than information you see or hear. Slamecka and Graf (1978) labeled this finding the *generation effect.*

The experiments Slamecka and Graf performed were quite straightforward. One group of people was asked to generate some words according to a specified rule. For example, each person may have been told that he or she would see a list of words, each followed by a single letter and some blank spaces. The participant's task was to generate a word that began with the letter given and contained as many letters as blank spaces. The generated word was to be an antonym of the first word. Thus, the person saw FAST-S_ _ _ and generated SLOW. A second group of participants saw a list of word pairs that were exactly the same as the words seen and generated by the first group, such as FAST-SLOW. This second group did not generate any words but, rather, simply read the list. Notice that the two groups ultimately received exactly the same words. Subsequently, when asked to remember the second word of each pair, the group that generated the words remembered many more than the group that read the words. This result was the generation effect.

We now know the generation effect occurs under a wide range of circumstances. A number of different generation rules, including rhyme, category, and associative rules, produce the effect. Different types of memory tests, such as recognition, free recall, and cued recall, all yield generation effects, and we also know the effect can be obtained with materials other than single words. The point is that memory for self-generated materials is a very general phenomenon, suggesting that the *process* of self-generation has effects on memory unlike those of perceptual processes.

The importance of the *process* of generation is apparent from a study by Slamecka and Fevreiski (1983). In this study, participants were asked to generate a word in response to a dictionary definition. For example, the participant might have heard "an astronomical instrument used in computing angular distances, especially by sailors," and the task was to generate the word defined. In the read condition, a definition was followed by presentation of the word. The interesting aspect of the experiment was those cases in the generation condition where the participant was in a tip-of-the-tongue state. Tip-of-the-tongue is the state in which you feel as if you know a word and may even be able to say things about the word such as its first letter, the number of syllables and so on, but cannot actually produce the word. Cases such as these in Slamecka's and Fevreiski study represent attempts to generate that result in failure. But what happens to these words on a subsequent memory test? Astonishingly, these "generation failures" not only are better recognized but also better recalled than read words. Keep in mind that the words in question were never successfully produced at study but, nevertheless, were better remembered. Since no "product" was produced by generation of study, this experiment strongly suggests that *the process* of generation is crucial.

BOX 5.1

PERFECT MEMORY

Research on cuing effects in memory has discovered conditions that produce nearly perfect memory for large amounts of material. Timo Mantyla (1986) asked people to produce three things that they knew about each of 600 different words. Without warning, the people were then asked to remember the 600 words, a daunting task. However, the 3 words generated at study were provided as cues in the memory test. Mantyla found that with the cues the subjects remembered on average over 90 percent of the words. Relative to most laboratory studies of recall memory, performance in Mantyla's experiment was phenomenal.

If you think about it for a moment, Mantyla's experiment seems to model the conditions of much of real-world memory. Perception and encoding always occur in the context of an individual's own idiosyncratic knowledge system. A large proportion of day-to-day memory probably is cued by self-generated cues that, according to Mantyla's data, would produce extremely accurate memory.

Hunt and Smith (1996) extended Mantyla's technique to lists of categorized words to capitalize on the combined effects of organization and distinctiveness. People were asked to study a group of words from the same category, such as *salmon, perch, bass, carp,* and *tuna.* The task was to write one thing about each of the words that was not true of the other 4. After doing this to 20 groups of 5 words (100 words), the people were given the single words they had written and were asked to recall the original words about

(Continued)

BOX 5.1 (Continued)

PERFECT MEMORY

which they had written them. Hunt and Smith found memory to average better than 95 percent correct. They suggested that the high accuracy in this situation was due to the combined memory of the category (e.g., *fish*) and the presence of the distinctive cue (e.g., *red*), which would converge precisely on a list item (e.g., *salmon*).

We can relate the idea of retrieval as a process of narrowing down the desired memory to our previous discussion of organization and levels of processing. Organization at encoding produces the general information being described in the retrieval process. Organization is the extraction of shared information from among a variety of events. Such information as "all events on Tuesday" and "all events in anthropology class" results from organizational encoding and can be a useful starting point in retrieval. Information specific to each event within the more general organization is also extracted at encoding. This specific, or distinctive, information is necessary if we are to move from general organization to specific event memory in retrieval. The combination of organization and distinctiveness provides a unique convergence on a particular event and results in nearly perfect memory.

McDaniel, Wadill, and Einstein (1988) proposed that the generation process could be explained *as enhancement of relational and distinctive processing,* which we already have discussed as important contributions to memory. Their theory assumes that generating information is analogous to problem solving, and that the participants use whatever clues are available to solve the problem, including cue words, word fragments, and even other read or generated words in the study list. In the course of solving the generation problem, the task focuses the subject on relational or distinctive aspects, or both, of the material to-be-remembered. If the memory test requires the use of the relational or distinctive processing emphasized by the generation task, memory will benefit from generation. This theory has received support from research by McDaniel, Riegler, and Waddill (1990), and the idea has additional appeal because it can explain some important cases in which generation does not facilitate memory (Begg & Snider, 1987; Slamecka & Katsaiti, 1987).

IMAGERY

Think about your room when you were 10 years old. As you left the room, was the doorknob on the left or right side of the door? In answering this question, many people report that they visualize the room including the door, which suggests an important role for imagery processes in long-term memory. Imagery is an instance of an *analogue representation.* Analogue representations directly mirror the world;

analogues contain a point-for-point correspondence with the object they represent. For example, a photograph is an analogue; a verbal description of the same object is not an analogue. Considerable debate has arisen over the existence of analogue representations in memory, particularly as they refer to visual memory.

The question at issue here is whether or not some representations in long-term memory are functionally equivalent to visual perception (Solso, 1991). Be careful to understand two things about this question. First, the controversy is not over the question of "imagination" per se but, rather, concerns the existence of images in long-term memory. That is, few cognitive psychologists would quibble with the belief that visual imagination can be an important element of intellectual functioning. For example, if you have a number of errands to run on a busy day, you may plan your schedule by visually imagining the most efficient routes for all of the stops you must make. The controversial question is was this visual information retrieved from memory or, alternatively, was the information retrieved in some nonvisual form and then converted to a subjective visual experience?

The second point to note about the question is the functional equivalence of images and visual perceptions. Since we have no way to directly determine if a representation in memory is *identical* to a visual perception, the research strategy is to establish conditions under which imagery theoretically should be a factor and then determine if performance is analogous to what would happen if the person actually were "seeing" the event. In this fashion, arguments can be made that the image functions equivalently to a visual perception. This strategy guides most of the research we shall now discuss.

Evidence for Imagery

A considerable amount of evidence indicates that we use analogue representations. Some of the strongest evidence comes from studies of mental rotation that we described in chapter 2 (Shepard & Metzler, 1971). These studies required participants to decide if two figures were identical when one of the figures was rotated to some degree. The results of interest are that the time to reach a decision about the match directly corresponded to the angle of rotation. These results, which now have been replicated many times, are interpreted by assuming that the decision is reached by mentally rotating the figure, a process that would require an analogue representation of the figure.

A different source of evidence for direct storage of visual information comes from Kosslyn's work on "mental travel" (Kosslyn, Ball, & Reiser, 1978). Participants were shown a simple map containing several important landmarks. The map was drawn so that the distance between the points differs, and these distances are labeled—for example, A to B = 5, B to F = 20, F to A = 25. An example of such a map is shown in figure 5.4. Participants were asked to remember the map, an easy task given its simplicity. With the map absent, the participants were then asked to go from one point to another, based on their memory of the

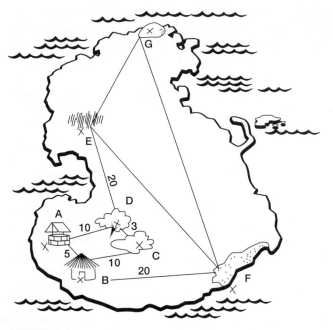

FIGURE 5.4
A map used in the studies of mental travel. *(From "Visual Images
Preserve Metric Spatial Information" by S. M. Kosslyn, T. M. Ball,
and B. J. Reiser,* Journal of Experimental Psychology: Human
Perception and Performance, *1978, 4, 47–60. Copyright 1978 by
the American Psychological Association. Reprinted by
permission of the publisher and the authors.)*

map. The request is for mental travel, and when the person reaches the destina-
tion, a button is pressed to signify the end of the journey. The button actually
stops a clock that started when "travel" began. The measure of interest in this research is the amount of time to mentally travel the map as a function of the actual
distances listed on the map. Interestingly, the times are directly correlated with
the distances. If A to B = 5 and B to F = 20, the participants take much longer to
mentally scan from B to F than from A to B. Kosslyn suggests this result indicates that subjects actually use visual representations to perform this task, much
as a person might visualize a familiar route when giving directions.

Yet another line of evidence has been drawn from studies of memory for pictures. The old saying that a picture is worth a thousand words has considerable
validity when applied to memory. Of the many experiments demonstrating this
fact, consider the work of Standing, Conezio, and Haber (1970). Participants
were shown 2,560 pictures of complex visual scenes, each picture available for
inspection for only 10 seconds. In the recognition test, the participants were able
to remember correctly 93 percent, or a total of 2,380 pictures. This remarkable

level of performance is much higher than is usually obtained with verbal materials. Moreover, the rapid rate of presentation and the complexity of the visual scenes make it unlikely that the pictures were verbally recoded. One interpretation of these data, then, is that pictures are stored in a visual form that somehow facilitates memory.

The argument for an active imaginal encoding to memory, however, is easily illustrated with materials other than pictures. For example, do we imagine an object or scene represented by words and then store the visual scene in memory? If this were so, imaginal encoding would be a very active process of converting an abstract symbol, the word, into a completely different representation. Paivio (1971; 1995) has vigorously pursued this issue with a very interesting research program. At the basis of Paivio's research is his discovery that concrete words are better remembered than are abstract words. Concrete words refer to objects such as *cigar, bicycle,* and *dog;* abstract words have less clear referents such as *belief, justice,* and *knowledge.* Paivio and his students clearly demonstrated that concrete words are better remembered than abstract words. What does this fact have to do with imagery?

To illustrate Paivio's answer to this question, close your eyes and attempt to visualize *cigar.* Most people find it rather easy to obtain a vivid image of a cigar. Now close your eyes and try to get a mental picture of *justice.* Many people report their image of justice as a statue of a blindfolded lady holding a pair of scales and a sword. Contrast this image with that of cigar. The image of cigar *is* a cigar, whereas the image of justice is not justice but a symbol for justice. Abstract words generally are more difficult to encode in an imaginal form, and when they can be coded as an image, the image is not the same thing as the actual object. Paivio has used these observations to develop an influential theory of imagery processes in memory.

Dual-Code Theory

Paivio suggests that information in memory may be stored in two forms, *verbal codes* and *imaginal codes.* Any event or object that can be described may be stored in a verbal code, and any event or object that can be visualized can be stored in an imaginal code. Thus, most events can be remembered through a verbal code, an imaginal code, or both. For example, a picture can be labeled and remembered as the verbal code implied by the label. Alternatively, the picture can be remembered through the image code, which Paivio argues will produce better memory because the visual image retains more detail than does the verbal code. Thus, superior memory for pictures is due to the ease with which they are visually stored and the amount of detail maintained in the image.

With words, a verbal code may be more probable, but words may also be transformed in encoding to a visual image code. If a word is remembered both by verbal code and image code, the probability of retrieving one of the codes is higher than if only one code is available. Very simply, two codes are better than one.

Abstract words, which are difficult if not impossible to code visually, will then be at a disadvantage compared to concrete words. Concrete words can be encoded verbally and visually, whereas abstract words can only be encoded verbally.

Kosslyn (1995) makes the same fundamental assumptions in his more complex theory of imaginal processing. According to Kosslyn's theory, the image we experience is the *surface representation* that was generated from a *deep representation* stored in long-term memory. The deep representation may be either an analogue that depicts how something looks or a proposition that is essentially a verbal description. Either type of deep representation can be used to generate the surface representation of an image. The important point is that Kosslyn's theory, like Paivio's, assumes that images are stored in memory.

Are Visual Images Stored in Memory?

The assumption that long-term memory contains representations that are functionally equivalent to visual perception is somewhat controversial. Resolving this controversy is extremely difficult, for two related reasons. First, all we can experience is the conscious representation, Kosslyn's surface representation, and everyone agrees that this experience can be in the form of an image. Second, we cannot experience directly the long-term memory representation and that representation is the source of the controversy. Experiments on mental rotation and mental travel do not require one to assume that the image is stored in long-term memory but, rather, these experiments demonstrate that the process of imagination can be useful for problem-solving. Experiments on memory for pictures and concrete words can be interpreted in terms of stored images, but alternative interpretations are also possible. Devising conclusive experimental tests of stored images is not a simple problem.

One clever attempt to provide such a test was reported by Neisser and Kerr (1973). Their reasoning was simple but very compelling. If the stored mental image is like visual perception, an object hidden in the image should not be remembered. If you are actually looking at a piano and a ball is hidden behind it, you will not see the ball. By the same token, you should not be able to "see" hidden objects in a mental image if the image is like visual perception. Neisser and Kerr instructed people to visualize scenes described by sentences such as "A harp is hidden inside the torch of the Statue of Liberty." Later the subjects were given a cue such as "torch" and asked to recall the sentence. Will they remember *harp,* which should be concealed in the torch? In fact, the subjects remembered *harp* as well in the hidden condition as they did in conditions where the harp was blatantly exposed "on top of the torch." Neisser and Kerr conclude that mental images, whatever they are, cannot be two-dimensional snapshots of the world.

Keenan and Moore (1979) criticized this conclusion on the grounds that many of the participants did not successfully hide the object in the image. Some of the people in Neisser and Kerr's experiment later reported that they could "see" the harp in the torch by mentally zooming over the top of the statue or by seeing it through the torch. In order to really test the hypothesis, the object must be truly hidden in the image. Keenan and Moore repeated Neisser and Kerr's experiment with much stronger instructions about hidden objects and found that memory for hidden objects was worse than for exposed objects. Such results, of course, suggest that the image may be like visual perception, and thus the hidden imagery experiments are unfortunately inconclusive.

In another direct attempt to determine if images stored in long-term memory are the same as visual perception, Kerr (1983) has performed imagery experiments with congenitally blind participants, people who were blind at birth. Kerr's blind participants performed exactly as sighted participants on the memory test. Instructions to imagine objects as spatially contiguous produced better memory than did imagining objects as spatially separated for both blind and sighted subjects. These results indicate that imagery effects upon memory do not depend upon prior visual experience, suggesting that the stored representation is not functionally equivalent to visual perception. Rather, the analogue component of the long-term memory representation may be spatial relationships.

Neurocognitive Studies of Imagery

As we have seen, obtaining evidence for the existence of images in long-term memory is more difficult than it might appear. Part of the problem lies in the indirect inferences from behavioral data to theoretical concepts about the mind, allowing alternative theories to explain the same behavior (Anderson, 1978). Nevertheless, our understanding of the nature of imagery has taken a quantum step forward by obtaining evidence about what the brain is doing while subjects imagine some event. If imagery and visual perception are functionally equivalent, then similar brain activity should underlie both. The advent of neuroimaging technology, coupled with extensive testing of the imagery abilities of patients with damage to perceptual-processing areas, has opened the door to this research and produced provocative data on the question of imagery.

In an early study of this type, Roland and Friberg (1985) used a variant of PET, known as SPECT (single photon emission computed tomography), to examine brain activity while subjects imagined walking through a familiar neighborhood. In comparison to relevant control tasks, results showed that this imaginary walk produced increased activity in areas of the temporal and parietal lobes known to be activated by high-level visual processing. Furthermore, these regions were different from the areas activated when the subjects did simple mental arithmetic. This study thus suggested that the brain activity associated with mental imagery can overlap with the activity produced by visual perception, both of which differ from the activity associated with nonvisual cognitive tasks.

The Roland and Friberg study has now been replicated and extended by a number of independent research groups, using different imaging techniques (SPECT,

PET, and fMRI) and a variety of different imagery tasks. In all cases, visual imagery tasks have been found to activate areas of the brain known to be involved in visual perception (for reviews, see Farah, 1995, 2000). A question that remains, however, is how early in the visual processing stream this imagery-based activation can be found; that is, does imagery only activate regions associated with late (higher-level) stages of visual perception in the temporal and parietal lobes or can it extend to the very earliest stages of visual processing? In fact, fMRI research now available indicates that visual imagery can activate area V1 in the occipital lobe, the earliest cortical station in visual processing (see Le Bihan et al., 1993; see also Klein et al., 2000). Additional support for this conclusion was provided by Kosslyn and his colleagues (1997) who showed that performance on analogous perceptual and imagery tasks can be similarly impaired when neural activity in the occipital lobe is temporarily disrupted by transcranial magnetic stimulation (TMS)—see chapter 1. Overall, then, neuroimaging and TMS studies suggest that visual perception and visual imagery engage common neural regions that extend to very early stages of visual information processing.

If the above conclusion is correct, it leads to a very interesting implication; namely, patients with damage to visual processing pathways should show impairments in imagery that parallel their perceptual impairments. An early demonstration of such parallel deficits was reported by De Renzi and Spinnler (1967) who found that achromatopsia (impaired color vision due to cortical brain damage) is often accompanied by impairments on tests that require color imagery, such as reporting the color of common objects. More recent research has pushed this perception/imagery parallel even further. For example, Levine, Warach, and Farah (1985; see also Farah et al., 1988) studied two patients, one with occipitoparietal (*where* system) damage that produced selective perceptual deficits in spatial localization, the other with occipitotemporal (*what* system) damage that produced selective perceptual deficits in object identification. Interestingly, these patients also showed imagery deficits that paralleled their perceptual deficits. For example, the patient with *what* system damage showed deficits on imagery tasks that required object visualization—tasks such as reporting the color of common objects, or whether an animal has a short or long tail. In contrast, this patient performed normally on tasks that required more spatial forms of imagery, such as letter rotation and mental scanning (mental travel). Results such as this suggests that visual imagery co-opts the same neural architecture used in visual perception. Moreover, and similar to what occurred in research on the visuo-spatial sketchpad (see chapter 4), these data also suggest that visual imagery may actually reflect two very different abilities—the ability to image objects (supported by the ventral visual stream) and the ability to image spatial relations (supported by the dorsal visual stream).

Neurocognitive experiments thus provide evidence for a very tight connection between perception and imagery. Does that mean that these studies have resolved the debate over whether images are stored in long-term memory? Unfortunately, they have not because, again, these studies are really correlating *imagination* per se (i.e., image use) with regional brain activity, whereas, as mentioned earlier, the theoretical argument in psychology is about the representation in long-term memory, not the process of imagination. That is, while visual imagination and visual perception appear to utilize many of the same brain processes, this still leaves open the possibility that the memory from which the (visual) imagination was constructed is not visual.

MNEMONIC TECHNIQUES

We conclude our discussion of encoding with a description of techniques that have been used to enhance memory. *Mnemonic* (pronounced ne-mahn'-ick) techniques typically take advantage of familiar associations to facilitate encoding of new material. A successful mnemonic device has to be easily implemented at the time of learning and, equally important, must be available at retrieval for successful decoding. For example, you may have encountered the advice to form an image that represents the name of someone you have just met. This mnemonic can be very helpful but only if the image is very precise. Imagine meeting Dr. Sands, whereupon you form an image of a beach scene. In subsequent meetings with Dr. Sands, retrieval of this image could mislead you into decoding the name as Dr. Seashore. Keep this hazard in mind as you now read about several mnemonic techniques that have been developed to enhance encoding of new material.

Method of Loci

Imagery has long been used as a mnemonic aid. For example, ancient Greek orators used a technique called the *method of loci.* In preparing an oration, they would imagine the room in which the speech would be given and associate the points of the speech with different spatial locations in the room. When delivering the talk, the orator would look to the various locations in the room to be reminded of the points. You can try the same procedure in any situation that requires you to remember some rote list—for example, a grocery list. An easy variation of the method of loci is to imagine a familiar walk and to place each item you need to remember at some landmark on that walk. Using the grocery list example, you could imagine the orange juice dangling from a tree, the cookies on some steps, the bread floating in a fountain, and so on.

These examples take advantage of another principle of imagery that can be put to mnemonic benefit. Bizarre or unusual images are better remembered than more common images. The bizarreness effect has been studied extensively in laboratory research (see Einstein & McDaniel, 1987, for a review) and the effect seems to be due to the effect of distinctiveness on retrieval (McDaniel, Einstein,

DeLosh, May, & Brady, 1995). The bizarreness effect can be incorporated into your use of method of loci in entertaining and useful ways to improve your memory for lists of items.

The Pegword Technique

The pegword technique allows you to "hang" material you are trying to remember on an easily remembered mnemonic. The first step is to develop the pegs. A widely recommended system is a series of rhyming pairs that each begins with a number, such as the following:

> One is a bun.
> Two is a shoe.
> Three is a tree.
> Four is a door.
> Five is a hive.

After learning the peg list, the items to be remembered are hung on the pegs. Suppose you have five items to buy at the grocery: milk, bread, doughnuts, shrimp, and dog food. You hang each of the items on a peg through some association such as imagery. For example, you might imagine a dog barking at a beehive with bees swarming around the dog. Retrieval of "Five is a hive" then reminds you of dog food.

Key Word Technique

The keyword technique was developed by Atkinson and Raugh (1975) to assist in the learning of a second-language vocabulary. The technique begins with thinking of an English word that sounds like some portion of the foreign word. For example, the Spanish word for sugar is *azucar,* the last syllable of which is pronounced *car.* The next step is to associate the English word with the referent of the foreign word (e.g., imagine a car filled with sugar). The idea is that upon later hearing the foreign word, the English word will come to mind along with the image. Atkinson and Raugh (1975) demonstrated that use of the keyword technique produced better memory for second-language vocabulary than just seeing the foreign word with the English translation.

Organizational Technique

A final example of mnemonic techniques is one that we suspect most people use in at least some situations. This technique involves organizing the to-be-remembered items in some familiar scheme. Grocery shopping is again a prime example. The grocery list can be organized around meals, for example, I need to buy juice, eggs, and grits—all *breakfast* items. Alternatively, the list can be organized around sections of the store, *produce, meat, dairy, frozen, etc.* Many of the things that we need to do during a day benefit from the organizational mnemonic in the simple sense that we tend to plan our day in organized segments. For example, you may think about your day as: first I have to go to class, then to the bookstore, then to the optometrist, then to Jack's party. Each of these activities in turn requires that you remember to perform more detailed actions such as remembering to take the book you wish to return to the bookstore. The broader organizational mnemonic facilitates memory for the numerous details.

When to Use Mnemonic Techniques

Most people seem to believe that their memory needs improvement, but as we discussed in the context of levels of processing, such beliefs are not really accurate among healthy people. On the other hand, rote memorization is extremely difficult and painful for most of us, a fact that probably explains why many Americans avoid acquiring additional languages. It is as though memory has not evolved to serve rote memorization and any assistance in this task is welcomed. The mnemonic techniques we described can provide such assistance, but mnemonics are not a magic potion for perfect and easy memorization. As we mentioned at the outset, the mnemonic must be available and easily decoded at retrieval to be of any use. Moreover, you can now see that most mnemonic techniques require considerable thought and effort. These are not devices that you can usually implement on the fly. Thus for things such as grocery lists, we recommend that you make a list and take it with you. For other activities such as public speaking and vocabulary acquisition, carefully developed and practiced mnemonics can be quite helpful.

SUMMARY OF ENCODING

Encoding processes are the psychological activities that determine the type of information available for later memory. Encoding generally involves the transformation of the incoming information, either through addition or deletion of information. Encoding processes are important to understand because they determine what is *potentially* remembered about an event. What is *actually* remembered, however, is determined by the ability to access or retrieve the information stored in encoding. The effect of any variable on encoding must also be explained through its impact on retrieval, which our next topic.

RETRIEVAL

Encoding processes determine the *availability* of information in memory, but to actually use the prior experience, it must also be accessible (Mandler, 1967); that is, you must be able to bring it to mind. Accessibility is the province of retrieval.

For example, what were you doing at 10:00 A.M. on November 21, 2001? At first glance, this may appear to be a difficult question, but we shall give you a clue and let you think about it. November 21 was the Wednesday before Thanksgiving Day. Now can you answer the question?

When memory is used to answer questions such as the one just posed, we generally have the sense of narrowing a set of alternatives until we arrive at the answer. Even to begin this process, however, *cues* are necessary to delineate the general set of events from which to sample. Imagine how ridiculous a question such as "What did you do?" is without context. The questioner must provide some cue as to when or where the activity occurred. Given the importance of cues to retrieval, we begin with a discussion of the effect of cues on memory.

WHAT MAKES A CUE EFFECTIVE?

If the retrieval process is critically dependent upon the use of cues, what makes for an effective cue? The obvious answer is that a good cue is any information that helps us remember. Equally obvious is that this suggestion is not very helpful. If we must wait until the time of a memory test to see what sorts of cues are useful, we have no way of predicting the level of memory performance and, even worse, no way of facilitating memory in ourselves or others. Thus, an idea about the effectiveness of cues becomes essential not only in understanding the retrieval process but also in improving memory for events. Two such ideas have dominated thinking about cue effectiveness in event memory: *associative strength* and *encoding specificity*.

Associative Strength Theory

The basic premise of associative strength theory is that a cue is effective if it has occurred frequently with the to-be-remembered event in the past. Such cues are said to be strongly associated with the event. To determine how strongly associated two words are, free-association norms are used. Free-association techniques were popularized by Freud who, interestingly enough, used free association for roughly the same purpose as does the cognitive psychologist, to study the structure of memory. In free association, a person simply responds with the first word that comes to mind when given the target word—for example, I say "grass." You say what? Associative strength is determined by the number of persons giving a particular response. The greater the number of persons who give a common response, the higher the associative strength becomes.

A substantial number of memory studies have shown that strongly associated cues produce better memory than do weakly associated cues. In these experiments, participants are typically shown pairs of words in a study or input session, some of which are strongly associated *(whistle-train)* and some of which are weakly associated *(black-train)*. At the time of the memory test, the cue *(whistle* or *black)* is provided, and the participant must produce the other member of the pair *(train)*.

Again, the strongly associated cue is more effective than is the weak cue, and this is true even when the cues are not present at study but only in the test.

Associative strength theory works on a memory structure consisting of an associative network interrelating all of the items in memory. Retrieval begins with the "activation" of the representation of the cue itself. As John Anderson (1983), a prominent associative theorist, has noted, "activation" refers to the transfer of information from long-term to short-term memory. In other words, activation is a concept describing the transformation of information from a latent state to a conscious state. An important feature of the activation of the cue's representation is that the activation then spreads through portions of the associative network. Anderson's apt analogy is of water coursing through irrigation ditches. Each memory representation is analogous to a small pool at the end of a ditch. As the pool fills, the water spills out to ditches connected with that pool. Eventually, the available water is insufficient to spill over and the spread stops.

Spreading activation is a crucial concept in the associative view of retrieval. As the activation spreads from the cue's representation, each additional representation that receives activation is a candidate to be remembered. The strength of association between a cue and another item is represented by the distance between the two in the associative network. Strongly associated items are closer together. Thus, strength of association is fundamental to retrieval because the activity spreads from the cue to associated items, and items close to the cue are most likely to receive activation before it dissipates.

How does associative strength develop? Historically, the consensual answer to this question has been the frequency of previous pairing of two events. After many pairings, the occurrence of one event quickly and automatically brings the other to mind. Thus, a fundamental premise of the associative strength theory of cue effectiveness is that the number of previous encodings of two events will determine the cue effectiveness of one for the other. This certainly sounds reasonable, but surprisingly, Tulving disagreed and proposed a competing idea.

Encoding Specificity

Tulving does not quarrel with the premise that past experience is very important to current performance. Tulving's argument, however, is the interesting suggestion that any given event occurs only once. A particular event does not occur several times, allowing frequent pairings with other events, but, rather, every event has only one episode. There is only one "last night's dinner" and now that it is over, the same event will never occur again. If this point is true, and at some level it must be, associative-strength theory, with its emphasis on frequency of past occurrence, is irrelevant to memory for particular episodes.

Tulving's alternative is to suggest that effective retrieval cues are those that were present when the event occurred. That is, *a cue will be effective if it was specifically encoded with the target event*—hence the name *encoding specificity*. Tulving and Thomson (1971) developed a simple but ingenious experiment that

TABLE 5.1
EXAMPLES OF THE STUDY CONDITION AND TEST
CONDITIONS IN THE TULVING AND THOMSON
EXPERIMENT

Study condition	Test condition
Black-TRAIN	Single item (*TRAIN, RIVER*)
Fast-RIVER	
	Weak study associate (*black-TRAIN, fast-RIVER*)
	Strong new associate (*whistle-TRAIN, lake-RIVER*)

All subjects study a weakly associated word pair and then must recognize the target member of the pair, either in its original context, or in the absence of any context, or in the context of a strongly associated item.

directly pits encoding specificity against associative strength. All participants received a study list consisting of weakly associated items such as black-TRAIN, fast-RIVER. The participants were asked to remember the capitalized word for a later memory test. On the memory test, the participant saw the original weakly associated pair, saw only the original target item without any context word, or saw the original target item paired with a strongly associated item. For each test item, the participant had to indicate whether the capitalized word was one he or she studied. Table 5.1 gives you an example of study and test items. The beauty of this experiment is that the memory target sometimes appears with a strongly associated cue that was not present at study and sometimes with a weakly associated cue that was present at study. Thus, the results will tell us which is critical, strong association between cue and target or presence of the cue with the target at encoding.

The results were unequivocal. Recognition of the target was best when it was accompanied by the weakly associated cue from study. Performance in the presence of the strongly associated cue was no better than that with no test cue at all. These data clearly favor encoding specificity over associative strength interpretations of cue effectiveness.

Episodic and Semantic Memory

The conclusion that associative strength is irrelevant to memory seems to fly in the face of what we know about our own memory. After all, why does *pepper* come to mind so quickly when you hear *salt?* Why does *George Washington* immediately come to mind when you are asked who was the first president of the

United States? Surely the answer lies in the frequent co-occurrence of the cues and targets. But notice the difference between these examples and the cases of remembering a particular word from a list or what you had for dinner two nights ago. In the latter cases, particular events are the targets; but in the former case, the target is general knowledge.

Tulving (1972) proposed that memory for specific episodes and memory for general knowledge are different and that one of the differences is the principle underlying cue effectiveness. In the case of particular episodes, which he called *episodic memory,* encoding specificity is the principle of cue effectiveness, as evidenced by the logical argument that episodes occur only once and by data such as those gathered by Tulving and Thomson. General knowledge, which he labeled *semantic* memory, represents information that recurs in various different contexts. How many times and places have you heard that George Washington was the first president? Associative strength is the principle governing cue effectiveness in semantic memory. This theoretical distinction between episodic and semantic memory has now been richly elaborated and will be important to our discussion of implicit memory in the next chapter.

RETRIEVAL PROCESSES: ONE OR TWO?

The issue we just have reviewed concerns the question of what makes a cue effective. This is an important issue, and as we have seen, it leads us to more general questions concerning the very structure of memory. On the other hand, the question of cue effectiveness does not directly address *processes* of retrieval. What are the psychological processes engaged by an effective cue? This question has a long history centering on differences between recall and recognition memory. Among those differences is the simple observation that recognition is easier than recall.

As early as 1904, McDougall proposed a single process of retrieval in which both recall and recognition decisions were based on a sense of familiarity. McDougall suggested that lower degrees of familiarity were required for a positive recognition response than for recall, and this difference explains the greater ease of recognition. While McDougall's idea is too simple to capture all that is now known about the relationship between recognition and recall, single-process theory is alive and quite well. Indeed, encoding specificity is an example of single-process theory. According to encoding specificity, the necessary condition for successful retrieval is that cues that were encoded with the target are present. Depending on other prevalent conditions, the cue will either bring the target to mind or not, and this would be true in either recognition or recall. The salient difference between most cases of recognition and recall is that the desired target is present in the recognition test to serve as a cue. Under most circumstances, the target will be a better cue for itself than whatever cue is provided for recall. Thus, recognition will appear easier than recall.

An alternative view that began with James (1890) is that retrieval in recall requires two processes. When asked to recall, we must first bring something to mind, but James suggested that whatever is brought to mind is then subjected to a recognition decision. Recognition memory requires only the recognition decision. Recall is more difficult because it involves two processes, while recognition requires only one. Because the theory proposes that responses must be generated and then recognized in recall, this theory is called *generate-recognize*. As with single-process theory, two-process generate-recognize theory continues to stimulate research (Jacoby & Hollingshead, 1991; Kintsch, 1970).

Both single-process and generate-recognize theories have garnered empirical support. Perhaps the strongest arguments for generate-recognize theory come from cases in which the same variable affects recognition and recall differently, and the most compelling of these cases is the word frequency effect. Words that appear frequently in the language, such as *house* and *people,* are better recalled than low-frequency words, such as *cider* and *loon,* but low-frequency words are better recognized than high-frequency words. More frequent exposure to a word is assumed to facilitate its accessibility; thus, the advantage to high-frequency words in recall is due to ease of generation. Low-frequency words are more distinctive because we encounter them so infrequently, and this distinctiveness facilitates the discrimination required for recognition. Consistent with this account are data from Nelson's (Nelson & McEvoy, 2000) laboratory showing better recall of low-frequency words when access is equated for high- and low-frequency words. By equating access, the generation advantage normally enjoyed by high-frequency words is eliminated, and the recognition advantage of low-frequency words can then be seen in recall. Single-process theories have difficulty accounting for the word frequency effect; if there is only one process and it is the same in recognition and recall, frequency should affect the two in the same way.

On the other hand, single-process theories have produced research that is difficult to explain by a generate-recognize process. For example, Tulving and Thomson (1973) developed a paradigm that produces the phenomenon known as *recognition failure of recallable words.* The participant is given several study-test sequences on a cue-target word pair—for example, *glue-chair.* After a few such trials, recall of *chair* in the presence of the cue *glue* is very good. Without warning, the next test is a recognition test for *chair* in the presence of a new cue—for example, *table.* Recognition of *chair,* which previously was recalled with high probability, is now very poor.

Note that the words were recalled successfully in the first part of the experiment, and for the generate-recognize theorists this means that the words were both generated and recognized in recall. If so, these same words should be correctly recognized in the recognition test. Tulving and Thomson interpret these data in terms of encoding specificity. Retrieval requires the presence of a specifically encoded cue. When the cue is changed in the recognition test, the single process of access to the encoded trace is impaired.

SUMMARY OF RETRIEVAL PROCESSES

Let us briefly return to the nature of the retrieval process. Perhaps there is less difference between the single- and two-process theories than is initially apparent. If we conceptualize retrieval as a process of narrowing down the possibilities or of making increasingly fine discriminations, we can see merit in both single-process and generate-recognize views. Consider, for example, how to answer the question of what you did in the afternoon two days ago. You may begin the search by generating fairly general information: "Let's see, two days ago was Tuesday." Then you use the general information to generate more specific information: "On Tuesday I had lunch, and then I went to anthropology class, and I had coffee with friends after class, and we discussed the exam." When generated, such information may lead to finer-grained information about what you did two days ago. This example illustrates what is meant by event retrieval being a *process of narrowing down the possibilities,* and, in this particular example, the approach appears similar to the generate-recognize model of event memory. You generate a possibility, consider it, and report it when it is correct and withhold it when it is incorrect.

Sometimes, however, possibilities do not seem to be generated and considered but, rather, the event in question is retrieved immediately. Perhaps memory for the event is quite distinctive and cues are so powerful that access is direct. For example, "Two days ago I took the worst anthropology exam ever" might come to mind immediately. The point is that some cues may be so effective that no decision is needed. For more normal, day-to-day occurrences, however, this is not likely to be the case. Usually the strategy of narrowing down the events from most general to more specific is employed. In short, some instances of retrieval seem to conform to the generate-recognize model and other instances to the single-process model.

AUTOBIOGRAPHICAL MEMORY

We conclude this chapter on long-term memory with a discussion of research on autobiographical memory, which refers to memory for personal experiences from one's life. Autobiographical memory is a subset of episodic memory in that both encompass personal experience, but autobiographical memories are those that the individual considers relevant and important to his or her life. For example, memory for what you had for breakfast two weeks ago and for your first serious romantic encounter are both episodic memories, but in recounting your life, you are much more likely to remember the second example than the first. Indeed, one could say that autobiographical memory is one's life story. In that vein, autobiographical memory is important for maintaining one's concept of self across time. The *you* of today is connected to the *you* of ten years ago by the continuity of your story, as supplied by autobiographical memory.

Given the type of questions asked by autobiographical memory research, standard laboratory procedures are ill suited for this work. Rather, techniques must be used to reveal memories for particular events that a person has experienced. For example, you could be asked to remember what you did on September 11, 2001, the day the World Trade Center was attacked. Another example is to be asked for your earliest childhood memory. Yet another example is to give people words such as *lake, ginger, bicycle* and ask them to recount a memory associated with the word. The point is that research on autobiographical memory attempts to tap memory for events in our past rather than presenting some material and then asking for memory.

A potential drawback to this approach is that we cannot always determine the accuracy of the report. That is, sometimes it is impossible to verify the relationship between the memory and the actual event. Even in these cases, however, informative data are obtained about what a person believes to be true. After all, we rarely question the veracity of our own memory, and it is those memories, whether correct or incorrect, that are our biography.

In many instances however, it is possible to verify the accuracy of the reported memory. Under these circumstances, the research reveals the extent to which our intuitions about the accuracy of our memory are correct. When the reported memory is incorrect, the contrast between the reported memory and the actual event allows inferences about the mechanisms underlying our autobiographical memory. In what follows, we describe a small sample of the research on autobiographical memory derived from three of the commonly used techniques in the area.

Flashbulb Memory

What *do* you remember about what you were doing on September 11, 2001, when you heard of the attacks on the World Trade Center? Most people, at least in the United States, can provide a detailed answer to that question, an answer they believe is based on a vivid and accurate memory. Brown and Kulik (1982) called this phenomenon *flashbulb memory*. A flashbulb memory is your personal memory for the details of a consequential event. The events may be widely shared, as was the case with September 11, 2001, John F. Kennedy's assassination, the *Challenger* explosion, and Princess Diana's death. Flashbulb memories also develop for more circumscribed events such as the death of a family member, the wedding of one's daughter, and the birth of one's child. Flashbulb memories are characterized by a sense of vividness that lends great confidence in the accuracy of the memory.

Among the interesting studies of flashbulb memory is Neisser and Harsch's (1992) discovery that flashbulb memories are not as accurate as we believe. On the day after the explosion of the space shuttle *Challenger* in 1986, Neisser and Harsch asked people to record what they were doing when they learned of the disaster. Three years later these same people were asked to remember the original event. Approximately one-third of the people confidently reported detailed memories that were demonstrably wrong. Even when confronted with their original description taken one day after the event, most were reluctant to abandon their memory, which conflicted with their own original description.

Neisser and Harsch's research illustrates several important points about flash-bulb memory. Most obvious is that the vivid details we remember often are distortions of what actually happened. These distortions probably occur because we reconstruct the details surrounding the event at the time of memory. The reconstructions are based on plausible circumstances given our knowledge of the event. For example, one person (RH) remembers seeing the explosion of the *Challenger* on live television, when in fact, he first learned of the event from the radio. The point is that some of the details vividly remembered as flashbulb memories can be reconstructions of what must have happened rather than what actually happened. Nonetheless, these reconstructions are strongly believed (RH still remembers seeing the explosion even though he knows that he is wrong). What is not forgotten, though, is the central event, and these consequential events can serve as markers in our life story.

The Cue-Word Method

If autobiographical memory serves to define our self and to connect the sense of self across time, an interesting question is the distribution of memories across the life span. That is, from what point in our life are the memories that define who we are drawn? This question has been addressed through the use of the cue-word technique. The technique involves two stages. In the first stage, volunteers are given a list of words (e.g., *street, dog, hospital, house*) and asked to associate an autobiographical memory with each word. Then the volunteers are asked how long ago each of the events occurred. From this information, we can determine the relative number of autobiographical memories from different points in one's life.

Among the many informative studies using the cue-word technique is that of Rubin, Wetzler, and Nebes (1986). In this study, people from a wide age range were administered the cue-word procedure. Four important observations emerged from the results. As with other studies, the most frequently reported memories were from the most recent time in life, essentially the preceding decade. The second observation was that the number of memories reported prior to the preceding decade shows a steep decline as a function of the time since the event. This observation is consistent with laboratory studies of forgetting. The third observation was also consistent with prior and subsequent studies in showing that very few memories are reported for events prior to age three, regardless of the participant's current age. This result is an example of childhood amnesia, which is the label for the lack of memory for early childhood events. Many explanations for childhood amnesia are available, some of which will be mentioned later in the text. For the moment, we note that no one explanation enjoys consensual acceptance.

The fourth finding from Rubin et al. was a new discovery that has come to be known as the *reminiscence bump*. The reminiscence bump occurs in people around 35 years old and above. For these people, autobiographical memories show a· steady decline as a function of the time since the event, just as they do for younger people. However, there is a positive bump in memory for events occurring when

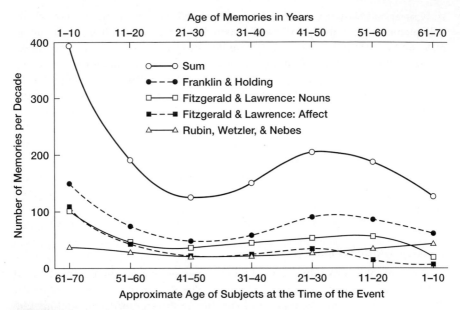

FIGURE 5.5

Results showing the "reminiscence bump." The bottom four functions are the results from four separate experiments, all using participants who were 70 years old. The top function is the sum of those four experiments. The reminiscence bump can be seen in the top function where there is a bump in the number of memories for events that occurred when the participants were between 10 and 30 years old. (*From Rubin, D. C., Wetzler, S. E., & Nebes, R. D. (1986). Autobiographical memory across the lifespan. In D. C. Rubin (Ed.),* Autobiographical memory (pp. 202–224). *New York: Cambridge University Press. Copyright 1986 by Cambridge University Press. Reprinted by permission of Cambridge University Press.*)

the person was roughly 18-24 years old. The data for 70-year-old participants in Rubin et al.'s study are shown in figure 5.5, illustrating the reminiscence bump. Although the cognitive processes responsible for the bump are not well understood (Schrauf & Rubin, 1998), Neisser (2000) notes that events occurring in this period of life tend to define one's generation. It is during this late-teen to early-adult period that most people experience what they later call their favorite music, films, and books. Political events in this period are viewed as especially important. In short, the reminiscence bump represents events that are part of the core definition of who one is.

Diary Studies

One technique that allows verification of accuracy of autobiographical memory is the diary study. Someone, usually the experimenter, keeps a diary and periodically tests his or her own memory. For example, Marigold Linton (1982, 1986) recorded at least two events that happened to her every day for six years. Once a month she tested her memory by looking at a brief description of an event and then deciding if she could date it. Over the six years of her study, Linton discovered that memory for the dates declined about 5 percent each year.

Wagenaar (1986) extended Linton's work by testing his recall not only of dates but also of the event content. He kept a diary containing one or two events from each day over a period of six years. Each event was recorded in terms of *who, what, where,* and *when.* For example, one might record *John Dunlosky, discussed research, Old Towne Tavern, Wednesday, September 12, 2002.* At the end of six years, Wagenaar began testing himself for memory of the recorded events, an exercise that extended over a year because he found it so difficult that he could attempt no more than five events a day. He used one to three of the *who, what, when, where* descriptions as cues for the event. His memory was a direct function of the number of cues used but he found that the *when* cues were the least effective of the four types. Recall decreased steadily as a function of the retention interval such that only 20 percent of the events from seven years ago could be recalled.

The diary study technique has two unfortunate methodological drawbacks of which you should be aware. The first is that only one person's memory is tested and this limits the generality of the results. The second problem is that this one person selects the events to be remembered, raising the possibility that the selected events are especially memorable for that person. If so, the diary study would have limited generality for a random selection of events. With that said, the diary study technique does offer the advantage of creating a situation where there are many memories to be tested. Moreover, the accuracy of memory can be objectively assessed against the recorded information. Thus far, these studies have rendered important information concerning retention of autobiographical memories.

Summary of Autobiographical Memory

David Rubin has been at the forefront of research on autobiographical memory since the early 1980s and has described the minimal components of what constitutes autobiographical memory (Rubin, 1996). One of the central components is imagery. Usually the imagery is visual, but other modalities also can exert powerful effects. For example, does imagining the smell of burning leaves trigger memory for any past event? The centrality of imagery may account for the detailed report of an autobiographical memory, especially flashbulb memories.

Another important component is the strong belief in the accuracy of the memory. As we saw in our discussion of flashbulb memories, people are very confident of the details of the memory even when the memory is known to be wrong. This belief in the accuracy of memory is not limited to flashbulb memory but extends to more mundane autobiographical memories. Although the belief in the accuracy of our own memory may sometimes be misplaced, it is reasonable that such a belief exists. If you are thinking of some prior experience—for example, a recent holiday—rarely would you have any reason to question the things that come to mind. Moreover, imagine how disorienting it would be if you were perpetually skeptical of what you remember. Consistent doubt in the accuracy of your memory would threaten the integrity of your self-concept and paralyze coherent thought and action.

Emotion also is a prominent component of autobiographical memory. The longevity of flashbulb memory may be due in part to the emotional impact of the event. The effect of emotion is not just that the emotion is included as part of the memory, but that emotion can influence the focus of attention. Thus, emotion can affect the perception and comprehension of an event and, in accord with levels of processing, thereby affect the content of the memory.

A crucial characteristic of autobiographical memory is its narrative structure. Autobiographical memories are always verbal and most often told as a story. Consider, for example, how you respond to a request to tell us about yourself. Most often you will provide a narrative account of events you have experienced, such as I was born in X place, went to Y schools, etc. No one has argued that the memory is necessarily stored in this narrative form, but autobiographical memories typically are told as stories, not recalled as disjointed lists of events.

A final characteristic of autobiographical memory emphasized by Rubin is that these memories are constructed. This means that the memory for an event is not encoded and retrieved as a holistic unit but, rather, is created to fit a narrative structure from the components, such as imagery and emotion. The construction of the narrative is heavily influenced by one's goals at the time of retrieval. You can imagine the difference in your narrative account—that is, the events you recall—if your goal is to impress your date versus the goal of explaining why you feel depressed. Given the constructive nature of autobiographical memory and the factors that contribute to this construction, inaccuracy, at least in the details, is to be expected.

Autobiographical memory has become an extremely active area of research within long-term memory. Exciting new information will continue to emerge from this line of work, and importantly, the issues addressed by the research have begun to encourage the study of memory in the social and linguistic context of everyday life.

SUMMARY OF LONG-TERM MEMORY

Long-term memory is a powerful biological process that carries the influences of prior experiences to current behavior. Successful long-term memory results from the coaction of psychological processes that occur at the time of the original experiences and processes that occur at the time of memory. Levels of processing taught us that successful encoding results from processes directed to comprehension of the event and that intent to remember is not necessary. Later research refined this position to include the importance of processing both similarity and difference among the elements of events. Particular processes such as imagery, self-referent encoding, and self-generation seem to enhance the encoding of similarity and difference and thereby facilitate retention. Whatever the original encoding, a prior experience will only be effective if it is accessible. Accessibility seems to be a matter of appropriate cuing, and encoding specificity says that cue effectiveness requires the presence of the cue at the time of the experience. This principle, however, appears to apply to memory for particular experiences not to retrieval of general knowledge. Our record of personal experiences not only influences our moment-to-moment behavior but also serves to define our self-concept. Research on autobiographical memory has begun to reveal the contribution of long-term memory to the development and maintenance of a coherent sense of self across time.

THOUGHT QUESTIONS

1. What are the assumptions of levels of processing?
2. Why is distinctiveness a better explanation of the effect of semantic orienting tasks than is depth?
3. What is the relationship between organization and distinctiveness.
4. What evidence favors encoding specificity over associative strength as an explanation of cue effectiveness?
5. What are the important components of a good mnemonic?

6

EXPLICIT AND IMPLICIT MEMORY

Our discussion of retrieval in the previous chapter assumed that a person intends to remember when he or she successfully relives a prior experience. That is, retrieval not only involves appropriate cues but also an intention on the part of the individual to try to remember. Memory often operates under these conditions; as the result of a request, either from someone else or from yourself, you try to remember a past event. When successful, you become aware of details of that event, and you obviously are aware that your experience is about a past event. Equally often, however, past experience influences our thoughts and behavior when we have no intent to remember and no awareness of the influence of the prior experience. In these senses, memory can be *explicit* in that we intend to remember and are aware that our experience is of a prior event, or memory can be *implicit* in that we have no intention to remember nor are we aware of the prior experience that is exerting an influence on performance. The fascinating aspect of this distinction is that the effect of a prior experience on behavior can be quite different depending on whether memory is implicit or explicit.

Consider as an example the following common situation. Suppose you park your car in the same general location when you go to the mall, but you are unable to park in that location today and must use a different spot. After you complete your shopping, your intention is to return to your car, and as you do so, you are thinking about the nice things you bought. When you arrive at the place you normally park, you realize your car is not there. At that point, you try to remember where you parked and then successfully find your car. Notice the difference in the effect of prior experience depending on whether or not you are trying to remember. When the intention was to go to your car in the absence of any intention to remember where your car was parked, your behavior was guided by the prior experiences of parking in the usual area. When the intention is to remember where your car is parked today, you go to a different location. Very different behavior resulted from intentionally remembering the past as opposed to using the past to solve a problem.

It is this dissociation of the effects of prior experience as a function of explicit and implicit memory that is interesting. Research and theory in this area have focused on explaining why the influence of past experience differs with the intent to remember. Among the reasons this question is exciting is that the dissociations seem to reflect the operation of conscious and unconscious processes. Intent and awareness are aspects of what we mean by consciousness. To the extent that the effect of prior experience differs with intent to remember, we have a difference in conscious and unconscious influence on behavior. The challenge is to explain this difference, and in this chapter we shall discuss three of the prominent attempts to do so. We begin with a discussion of the origins of the explicit-implicit memory distinction and research that brought the problem to the center of attention in cognitive psychology.

RESEARCH LEADING TO THE EXPLICIT-IMPLICIT DISTINCTION

Differences in the effects of prior experience as a function of intent to remember only became obvious when researchers began to use memory tests that were indirect with respect to conscious recollection. That is, one can assess the effect of a prior experience without asking a person to try to remember. Rather, the test can be one that requires performance on some task that we know would benefit

TABLE 6.1

EXAMPLES OF COMMONLY USED IMPLICIT MEMORY TESTS. PRIOR TO THE TEST, PARTICIPANTS WOULD HAVE SEEN MATERIALS CORRESPONDING TO THE SOLUTION TO THE TEST

Test	What the participant sees	Instructions
Fragment Completion	Fragment of a word (e.g., _ o_ us _)	Complete the fragment to make a word
Stem Completion	First few letters of a word (e.g., ele_ _ _ _ _)	Complete the stem to make a word
Perceptual Identification	Very briefly flashed words followed by mask	Identify the words that are flashed
Picture Naming	Drawings of common objects	Name each picture as quickly as possible
Category Production	Category labels (e.g., *Bird*)	Generate a specified number of category instances
Anagram Solution	Anagrams (scrambled words)	Solve the anagram to make a word
Free Association	Words	Produce the first word that comes to mind when you see this word
General Knowledge	General knowledge question (e.g., What is the most popular fruit?)	Answer each question

from the recently provided experience. This type of testing has been used in studies of learning since the time of Ebbinghaus and is known as a test of transfer. Training is provided on some materials or skill and is later tested for its effect or transfer to another task. Transfer is demonstrated when performance on the test is better following the original training than when there is no prior training. Because these tests give evidence for retention of the prior experience but do not involve instructions to remember that experience, they are classified as implicit memory tests, in contrast to the explicit memory test, which is the standard request for conscious recollection. Table 6.1 lists many of the commonly used implicit memory tests. You can see that they all have in common the lack of explicit memory instructions, and they all can be performed without a specific prior study experience. Once the importance of implicit testing was realized, research from neuropsychology and cognitive psychology converged on the discovery of dissociations of intentional and unintentional uses of memory.

Neuropsychological Studies

Neuropsychologists were the first to observe behavior that later would be attributed to implicit memory. One such early description was provided by Claparède, a French psychiatrist, at the turn of the twentieth century. Claparède (1951, for a reference in English) concealed a pin in his hand as he was introduced to an amnesic patient. As he shook hands with the patient, the pin pricked the patient's hand. On meeting Claparède at a later time, the patient had no memory of seeing Claparède previously but, nonetheless, absolutely refused to shake his hand. Even though the patient had no conscious memory of the prior event, the experience of the first meeting affected her behavior.

Although reports such as this accumulated over the first half of the twentieth century, the prevailing interpretation of amnesia was that information could not be transferred from short-term to long-term memory. In 1968, however, Warrington and Weiskrantz reported data that challenged that interpretation. Amnesic patients were shown lists of words and pictures, and then their memories were tested in various ways. When asked to try to remember the words or pictures on tests of recall or recognition, the patients performed very poorly relative to controls. This is not surprising; after all, poor memory defines amnesia. More interestingly, if the patients were given fragmented forms of the words or pictures and asked to identify them, the prior experience of seeing the items facilitated their performance. That is, if the intact form of the word or picture had recently been presented, the patients showed a greater ability to identify the fragmented form of the item, even though they showed no conscious recollection for the studied items.

Warrington and Weiskrantz' demonstration of preserved memory in amnesia opened a floodgate for neuropsychological studies of implicit memory. These studies revealed preserved memory for a variety of prior experiences among amnesic patients. Perceptual-motor skills required to perform various tracking tasks were learned and retained for weeks by amnesiacs who had no conscious recollection of previously performing the tasks (Shimamura, 1989). Amnesic patients showed normal learning of the skill required for reading mirror-image text—text that is inverted as it would be if you held this page up to a mirror—and this skill was intact on a test one month later (Cohen & Squire, 1980). Consistent with the data of Warrington and Weiskrantz, other studies showed *priming* effects of recent experience with verbal materials.

Priming refers to a facilitation or bias in performance as the result of recently encountered information. That is, the probability that the recently encountered information will be used is higher than it would have been without the recent encounter. A common example of priming occasionally occurs in conversation when an infrequently experienced word such as *exquisite* is used. Sometimes when this happens, other people in the conversation will use the word, presumably with no conscious intention to do so. Priming is studied in the laboratory by showing words and then giving a test that does not require explicit memory. For example, Graf, Squire, and Mandler (1984) showed amnesic patients a list of words and then on the test provided the first three letters of words, some of which corresponded to studied words and some of which were new. When the test instructions were to produce the first word that came to mind to complete the three-letter stem, the patients produced as many of the study words as did nonamnesic

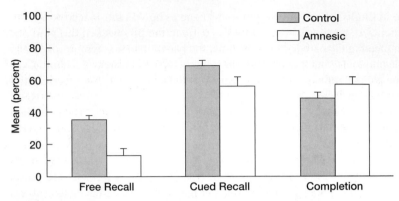

FIGURE 6.1
Results from the Graf, Squire, and Mandler experiment showing performance
on recall and fragment completion tests by amnesic and normal participants.
*(From Graf, P., Squire, L. R., & Mandler, G. (1984). The information that
amnesic patients do not forget. Journal of Experimental Psychology: Learning,
Memory, and Cognition, 10, 164–178. Copyright 1984 by the American
Psychological Association. Used by permission of the author and publisher.)*

controls. Three to four times as many of the previously seen words were produced than were words not previously seen. However, if the test instructions were
to use the word stem as a cue to recall the previous words, the performance of the
amnesic patients was much worse than that of the control participants. Figure 6.1
shows the results graphically. Thus, priming is observed with amnesic participants only if memory is assessed indirectly.

The extensive neuropsychological research on amnesia convincingly demonstrated the preservation of effects of prior experience on motor skills and cognitive processes. The important discovery was that these effects could be detected
only when the test was indirect; explicit tests for intentional, conscious recollection of the very same experience yielded little evidence for memory among amnesiacs, as had been known all along. Thus, neuropsychological research
established that the effects of prior experience were dissociated on explicit and
implicit memory tests.

Cognitive Psychology Studies

Dissociations between explicit and implicit memory also were discovered in non-
amnesic populations such as college students. For example, Jacoby and Dallas
(1981) manipulated levels of processing at study and then gave either an explicit
or implicit test. On the explicit test of recognition, participants showed the standard effect of superior memory for semantically processed study words over nonsemantically processed words. The implicit test used by Jacoby and Dallas is

known as perceptual identification in which words, both those that were studied and new words, are presented very rapidly and backward masked. The task of the participant is to simply identify the word correctly. The results of both the recognition test and the perceptual identification test are shown in figure 6.2. In perceptual identification more of the studied words were identified than nonstudied words, but the levels of processing manipulation had no effect. Nonsemantically studied words were identified just as well as semantically studied words. This result demonstrates that the variable of levels of processing is dissociated on explicit and implicit tests.

Jacoby and Dallas reported another dissociation that is quite impressive. In one of their experiments, the tests were given immediately or after a 24-hour delay. Recognition memory, the explicit test, was worse after the 24-hour delay, but perceptual identification was not affected by the delay. The same result was reported by Tulving, Schacter, and Stark (1982) who used a word-fragment completion test of implicit memory. In this test, fragments of words are presented (_le_ h_ nt), and the task is to complete the fragment to make a word. Prior study of a word that corresponds to the fragment primes completions such that more fragments of studied words are completed than nonstudied words. Fragment completion shows the same dissociation of levels of processing as described for perceptual identification; semantic study is better than nonsemantic study on the explicit test but not on the implicit test. In addition, Tulving et al. showed that priming on fragment completion did not deteriorate after a week's retention

FIGURE 6.2
Graphical depiction of data reported by Jacoby and Dallas (1981). Level of processing study materials affects recognition memory but has no effect on perceptual identification. (*Adapted from Jacoby and Dallas, 1981*)

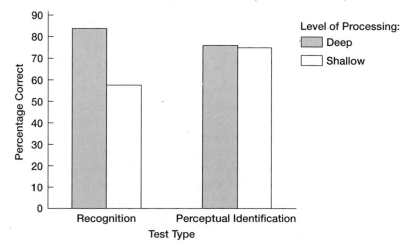

interval, whereas recognition memory showed a sharp decline when tested a week after study. This is an example of another variable, retention interval, that is dissociated on explicit and implicit memory tests.

These examples of research with normal participants are offered to show you what is meant by dissociations on explicit and implicit tests. Research with normal participants converges with that from neuropsychology in demonstrating that the effect of a particular prior experience can be very different depending on how memory is tested. We shall describe additional research that shows other dissociations as we now discuss theoretical explanations of why such effects occur.

THEORETICAL ACCOUNTS OF EXPLICIT AND IMPLICIT MEMORY

Three major ideas about the cause of test dissociations have evolved from the research on explicit/implicit memory tests. The interchange among proponents of the ideas has been an extremely productive debate, leading to discoveries about memory that would not have occurred if research had continued to focus exclusively on explicit memory. As you will see, these ideas not only offer an explanation for the dissociations between implicit and explicit tests, but in addition, each of these ideas represents a broad conceptualization of how prior experience exerts its effects in a given test environment.

Memory Systems

One prominent explanation for test dissociations begins with the assumption that memory is not a single process but, rather, consists of different systems that have evolved for particular functions. Each system is a separate structure that handles its own particular kind of information according to rules particular to that system and is subserved by different neural substrates. The origin of the systems approach is Tulving's distinction between episodic and semantic memory that was described in chapter 5. Episodic memory functions in the domain of personal experiences; thus, the information stored in episodic memory corresponds to particular prior experiences. Semantic memory has evolved to store general knowledge and is the system employed when the problem confronting us requires the use of knowledge. Thus, the two systems handle different kinds of information and, as we discussed in the last chapter, operate according to different rules. Retrieval from episodic memory follows the principle of encoding specificity whereas semantic memory operates in accord with associative strength.

The distinction between episodic and semantic memory allows us to explain certain of the test dissociations we have mentioned. Consider the results of the study by Jacoby and Dallas (1981) in which semantic orienting tasks produced better performance on a recognition memory test than did nonsemantic tasks. The effects of the study tasks did not differ on the implicit test of perceptual identification, but words in the study list were more accurately identified than nonstudied words. The systems explanation of these data begins by identifying the memory system that would serve each of the tests. Because the recognition test requires memory for a particular experience with a word—the experience of seeing the word on the study list—the episodic system would operate in recognition tests. The perceptual identification test does not require a memory judgment; it only requires that the participant read the word. Reading a word is a product of knowledge; hence, perceptual identification would rely on the semantic system.

Having identified the memory systems involved in the two tests, we can now explain the effects of the orienting tasks by appealing to the different operations of those two systems. Episodic memory operates according to encoding specificity; hence, a semantic orienting task that elaborates the encoded trace will broaden the range of effective cues at test. Thus, the semantic orienting task will lead to better recognition memory than the nonsemantic orienting task because the recognition test draws on episodic memory. The perceptual identification test is a function of semantic memory, which relies on associative strength for cue effectiveness. The word is the cue used to retrieve the semantic representation, such as the sound of the word. Years of experience have established the relationship between the visual appearance of the word and the information in semantic memory, and this associative relationship will not be altered by one preceding study trial in the experiment. Thus, the ability to read the word in the perceptual identification test will not be affected by the type of orienting task used in study. But because both the semantic and nonsemantic study tasks require that the word be identified at study, the semantic representation is activated at study. A residual of this activation is carried over to the test so that any studied word comes to mind more easily than a nonstudied word, thus explaining why studied words are better identified than nonstudied words, even though the orienting task at study has no effect.

This lengthy explanation is designed to show you how the memory systems approach explains dissociations between explicit and implicit tests. Explicit and implicit tests require the participant to do different things. Explicit tests probe for a specific memory; thus, they will always reflect the operation of episodic memory. Implicit tests require that a problem be solved. Implicit tests do not engage episodic memory but, rather, draw on some form of knowledge. Different implicit tests can demand different kinds of knowledge and to the extent that these different implicit tests show dissociations, the results would indicate the existence of additional specialized systems. Neural imaging studies become important in this research because different systems are assumed to have different neural substrates. For example, explicit/episodic memory tasks have been shown to activate a network of frontal and medial-temporal regions, including the hippocampus (see Buckner & Wheeler, 2001), while implicit memory tasks have been shown to alter activity in content-specific regions of the cortex associated with the kind of information being tested on the implicit test (e.g., word-related areas of cortex for word completion tasks, object-related processing areas for object identification tasks). Evidence that different brain areas are activated during different tests provides further evidence that the behavioral dissociations reflect the operation of separate memory systems.

Using this logic, five separate systems have now been identified (Schacter, 2000). Table 6.2 lists these five systems and the possible subsystems of each. Three of the systems are now familiar to you: working memory, episodic memory, and semantic memory. Notice that all explicit tests are identified with either episodic memory or working memory. Three different systems are identified with implicit tests, depending on the type of tests. We already have described semantic memory; the other two systems, procedural memory and the perceptual representation system, are more recent discoveries.

Procedural memory is responsible for the storage and use of skills. These skills can be motor skills, such as bicycle riding, or cognitive skills, such as the rules of addition. Notice that procedural memory does not store representations of the external world but, rather, the procedures needed for some skill. The operation of procedural memory is automatic, not consciously controlled. If you are accomplished at some motor skill (e.g., swimming or golf), conscious thought often interrupts performance. Sports psychologists label this phenomenon paralysis by analysis. In addition to being automatic, the output from procedural memory is noncognitive in the sense that it cannot be precisely verbalized. For example, try to describe only in words, no hand movement allowed, how to tie a shoe. Patients with Parkinson's or Huntington's disease show selective deficits on procedural memory tasks, implicating subcortical structures, particularly the basal ganglia, in mediating procedural memory (see Salmon & Butters, 1995).

TABLE 6.2
MAJOR MEMORY SYSTEMS, THE TYPE OF INFORMATION STORED IN EACH, AND
WHETHER RETRIEVAL FROM THE SYSTEM IS EXPLICIT OR IMPLICIT

System	Type of information	Nature of retrieval
Procedural	Cognitive and motor skills	Implicit
Perceptual Representation	Visual and auditory form of words, structural description of objects	Implicit
Semantic	Generic and factual knowledge	Implicit
Primary	Short-term visual and auditory information	Explicit
Episodic	Specific event memory	Explicit

The other system listed in table 6.2 is the *perceptual representation system.* This system stores the visual or auditory form of words and the structural form of other types of objects. The perceptual representation system was discovered largely from research showing dissociations of priming for different kinds of tests. For example, we previously mentioned that levels of processing does not affect tests of perceptual identification or fragment completion. More recent research has discovered that some kinds of implicit tests are affected by levels of processing. For example, general knowledge tests show higher priming following semantic orientation at study than following nonsemantic orientation. For example, if asked to name the capitol of Canada, you are more likely to correctly respond Ottawa if you studied it semantically than if the study was nonsemantic. General knowledge tests, perceptual identification, and fragment completion are implicit tests. The difference is that perceptual identification and fragment completion draw on your recent experience for the visual form of words, whereas the general knowledge test draws on more conceptual information. Given the dissociation of variables such as levels of processing on these tests, the perceptual representation system is now believed to be separate from semantic memory system. This example should make clear to you that the memory systems view explains test dissociations by assuming that different memory systems are used for different kinds of test demands. Many variables (e.g., amnesia, levels of processing, retention interval), have different effects on the different systems.

Priming in perceptual representation system is thought to reflect increased efficiency of neural processing in content-specific cortical processing areas (e.g., auditory-language areas for spoken words, visual-language areas for written words, object-processing areas for objects). Consistent with this interpretation, neuroimaging studies often show *decreased* neural activity for primed versus unprimed stimuli (see Schacter & Buckner, 1998). This, of course, is in contrast to the increased activity (in frontal regions, for example) that is usually seen when subjects perform explicit memory tasks.

Conceptually Driven and Perceptually Driven Processes

A fundamentally different approach to describing memory in general and the test dissociations in particular is that mental *processes,* not mental structures, are responsible for conveying the effects of prior experience. This approach generally argues that the effect of a prior experience on a subsequent test depends on the match between the mental processes engaged by the study experience and the mental processes required by the test. To the extent that the mental processes required at study overlap with those at test, test performance will be improved. This basic assumption was proposed by Morris, Bransford, and Franks (1977) and is known as *transfer appropriate processing.* Henry L. Roediger and his students have incorporated transfer appropriate processing with a distinction between

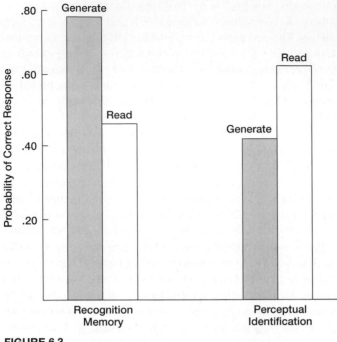

FIGURE 6.3
Dissociation of generate-read study tasks on tests of recognition
memory and perceptual identification. *(Adapted from Jacoby, 1983.)*

conceptually driven and perceptually driven processes as a major alternative to the
memory systems approach.

To see how Roediger's idea works, consider the following experiment by
Jacoby (1983). Participants were given a list of words to study for memory, but
half of the words in the study list had to be generated and half were read by the
participant. This manipulation sets the condition for the generation effect that we
described in the preceding chapter. Some of the participants were then given an
explicit test of recognition for the study words and others received the implicit
test of perceptual identification. The effect of generation versus reading at study
on the two different tests is depicted in figure 6.3. Recognition memory showed
the standard generation effect with generated items better remembered than read
items, but the perceptual identification test showed the opposite effect: more read
words than generated words were successfully identified.

The dissociation of the generation effect on recognition and perceptual identification was interpreted in terms of transfer of perceptually driven and conceptually driven processes. Reading a word at study requires perceptual processing of
the physical features of the word. These are the same processes required by the

perceptual identification test. The generation study task required participants to produce an antonym to a cue word plus the first letter of the target (e.g., *hot-c* . . .). Since the target antonym cannot be processed through the physical features of the presented information but, rather, must be retrieved from memory based on its conceptual relation to the cue, generation requires mental processing of conceptual relations. This conceptual processing is less appropriate to perceptual identification than is reading. The recognition test, on the other hand, requires a conceptual process of deciding whether the word had been seen in the study list. Generation at study is more appropriate to this test than is reading. In this fashion, the distinction between conceptually driven and perceptually driven processes explains the reversal of the standard generation effect on perceptual identification.

This explanation has been extended by Roediger and his students (Roediger & Blaxton, 1987; Roediger & Weldon, 1987) to a general account of memory. The idea is that any given task requires the use of either perceptually driven or conceptually driven processes. If past experience with the task required the same mental processes as the current version of the task, the prior experience will provide positive transfer to current performance. Importantly, variables that affect perceptual processing will have little effect on conceptual processing and vice versa. For example, variables such as type font or modality of presentation are perceptual variables and, thus, will have little effect on a conceptually driven test. Likewise, variables such as meaning will have little effect on perceptually driven tests.

The perceptually/conceptually driven distinction contrasts sharply with the memory systems approach in that explicit and implicit tests can be either perceptually or conceptually driven, whereas the systems approach assumes that all explicit tests are served by episodic memory. Teresa Blaxton (1989) designed an elegant study to test the difference between the two approaches. The study conditions in Blaxton's experiment were a read task and a generate task. Four different kinds of tests were given. As illustrated in table 6.3, these tests were selected so that the memory systems classification would predict different outcomes than the perceptually/conceptually driven classification. The graphemic cued recall test was a test in which the cue shared many letters with the target (e.g., *bushel-bashful*). Free recall was a request to recall as many words as possible. Word fragment completion was a test that required completion of fragments (e.g., *b . . sh . . u . .*). The general knowledge test required an answer to a question (e.g., "Which of the seven dwarfs comes first alphabetically?").

Graphemic cued recall and free recall are episodic tests according to the systems view; thus, both tests should yield better memory for the generate study condition. Fragment completion and general knowledge are semantic memory tests; thus, generate/read study should have no effect on performance. According to the perceptual/conceptual processing view, graphemic cued recall and word fragment completion are perceptually driven tests because the physical features of the cues in these tests drive processes similar to those of the studied target. Thus, prior

		Memory System	
		Episodic	Semantic
Type of Processing	Perceptually Driven	Graphemic Cued Recall	Word Fragment Completion
	Conceptually Driven	Free Recall Semantic Cued Recall	General Knowledge

TABLE 6.3
The design of Blaxton's (1989) experiment comparing perceptually driven/conceptually driven distinction with semantic-episodic distinction. *(From "Investigating dissociations among memory measures: Support for a transfer-appropriate processing framework" by T. A. Blaxton.* Journal of Experimental Psychology: Learning, Memory, and Cognition, *1989, 15, 657–688. Copyright 1989 by the American Psychological Association. Reprinted by permission.)*

reading of the study items should lead to better performance than generation. Free recall and general knowledge tests are conceptually driven because the physical features of the cues do not overlap with the target. Consequently, generation at study should produce better performance at study than reading.

Blaxton's results showed that performance on graphemic cued recall and word fragment completion is better following read study than generate study. Performance on free recall and general knowledge tests is better following generate study than read study. In short, the dissociations clustered as would be predicted by the conceptually driven/perceptually driven classification, but not in accord with the memory systems classification. The distinction between perceptually driven and conceptually driven processes is a broad classification of mental processes that is based on the task requirements. Notice that other classifications such as episodic versus semantic or implicit versus explicit are irrelevant. The only consideration is that the perceptual and conceptual processing test demands match the study processes so that retrieval processes required by the test benefit from the study processes.

The distinction between perceptually driven and conceptually driven processes can account for much of the data on test dissociations and has been fruitful in developing new research in general. As the research has accumulated, refinements to the theory have been made. Chief among these is the realization that not all tasks can be classified as exclusively perceptual or conceptual. For example, Weldon and Coyote (1996) asked participants to study categorized materials, and some of the items were presented as pictures and some as words. In a test of recall cued by the category labels, pictures were better recalled than words—a standard picture-superiority effect, as we discussed in the previous chapter under imagery effects. Other participants were given a category production test, which is an implicit test requiring the production of category instances in the presence of the category label. The production of study items in the category production test was not influenced by whether the item was presented as a picture or a word. Weldon and Coyote's results are interesting because both of these tests should be conceptually driven and should be affected in the same fashion by a study variable. Neil Mulligan (1996; Mulligan & Stone, 1999) has vigorously pursued the effect of dividing attention at study on different conceptual tests such as recall and category production. He, too, has discovered that the effects of this variable can differ on what should be two conceptually driven tests. Results such as these have suggested that some tests require a mixture of perceptual and conceptual processes, but these revisions are mostly a testament to the strength of the original distinction, which continues to be a dominant explanation of test dissociations.

Conscious and Unconscious Processes

A third major idea about test dissociations is a different version of the processing approach proposed by Larry Jacoby. At the heart of Jacoby's idea is a distinction between automatic and controlled retrieval processes. Unlike any of the other approaches we have discussed, this distinction is based on subjective experience. Automatic processing is the effect of prior experience in the absence of any experience of recollecting the past. Most often, the subjective experience associated with automatic processing is familiarity. A common example that we all have experienced occurs when we unexpectedly encounter someone outside of a normal context. Suppose you look up from your shopping cart and down the aisle is your professor. Often, the first reaction is a strong feeling of familiarity, which in this case would be followed by recognition of the person. Sometimes we never succeed in recognizing the person and are left with the feeling that the person is very familiar but cannot ascertain why. This automatic process is unconscious in the sense that there is no conscious experience of the past event that gave rise to the familiarity. Controlled retrieval processes are the effect of prior experience that is accompanied by a subjective experience of recollection. For example, you look up from your shopping cart and immediately think, "Oh, there is Dr. Smith, my cognitive psychology professor."

The distinction between automatic and controlled processes has obvious relevance to explaining the dissociations between explicit and implicit tests because the instructions for explicit tests are to intentionally remember a prior event, and implicit test instructions make no mention of memory for the prior event. The situation, however, is more complicated than simply suggesting that implicit tests involve automatic processes. Jacoby (1991) proposes that both controlled and automatic processes operate in both explicit and implicit tests. Unlike the systems approach and the conceptual/perceptual distinction, Jacoby's idea does not assume that a test is served by a single system or process. Therefore, an understanding of automatic and controlled retrieval processes requires a research strategy that goes beyond the simple comparison of direct and indirect tests.

Like the perceptual/conceptual processing distinction, Jacoby's approach assumes the importance of transfer appropriate processing. Prior processing increases the fluency (Jacoby's term for the positive effect of the prior processing on current processing) with which the same process operates in the future. In the case of conscious processing, one is aware that the increased fluency is due to the past experience and will attribute the fluency to memory. In the absence of conscious retrieval, however, the increased fluency still occurs but is not experienced as memory. Rather, the fluency gives rise to a subjective experience such as familiarity, which then may be mistakenly attributed to something other than the prior processing. According to this theory, test dissociations are the result of different mixtures of conscious and unconscious influences on different types of tests.

The operation of conscious and unconscious processes in both explicit and implicit tests is beautifully illustrated in an experiment by Jacoby, Woloshyn, and Kelley (1989), aptly titled "Becoming famous without being recognized." In this experiment, participants were shown a list of names and told to remember those names. Furthermore, they were told that none of the names were of famous people. The relevance of this instruction will be clear in a moment. After studying the names, the participants saw an even longer list of names, some of which were in the original list. The instructions were to indicate whether or not the person in this second list was famous. Some of the *nonstudied* names in this second list were moderately famous people (e.g., Satchel Paige, Minnie Pearl, Christopher Wren). The participants were instructed that if they recognized a name as one they had seen in the study list, they could be sure that the person was not famous. After the fame rating, the participants were shown a third list of names, again containing the names from the original study list plus an equal number of nonstudied names. The purpose of the third list was to provide a recognition memory test; that is, the participants were asked to indicate which of the names in the third list were in the original study list.

Of critical importance is that half of the participants listened to the original list of names under conditions of divided attention. While the names were being read, these participants also heard a tape recording of digits and were instructed to press a key whenever they heard three consecutive odd digits. The purpose of this manipulation was to reduce the conscious processing devoted to the study list of names. If Jacoby's ideas about conscious and unconscious processing were correct, conscious memory for the names should be impaired under divided attention, leaving the unconscious influence of study unopposed on the fame-rating test.

The results from the recognition and fame-rating tests are shown in figure 6.4. The data shown in the figure are for correct recognition and incorrect judgment of

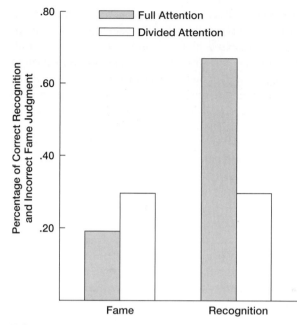

FIGURE 6.4
Probability of incorrectly calling a name famous and of
correctly recognizing a name as a study item as a function
of full and divided attention. *(Adapted from Jacoby,
Woloshyn, & Kelley, 1989.)*

fame. As you can see, dividing attention at study produces poorer recognition performance and also significantly increases the probability that a nonfamous name will be rated as famous. According to Jacoby's theory, this happens because the exposure to the names in the study list enhances the fluency of processing of those names in the subsequent test lists. Thus, the studied names are processed more fluently and, hence, will be more familiar than the nonstudied names on the fame-rating test. If the name is consciously recognized in the fame-rating test, it will be judged as nonfamous because the participants were told that the study names were nonfamous. If, however, the controlled retrieval processes fail to provide evidence leading to correct recognition, the familiarity of the name is attributed mistakenly to the person being famous. Notice that the intent induced by the test—to judge the fame of the names—has influenced the attribution of familiarity when memory fails, so the easy road to fame is to be seen but not remembered!

An important assumption of Jacoby's theory is that conscious and unconscious processes operate independently, meaning that both processes can affect any given memory test. Thus, according to the theory, we cannot study conscious and unconscious processes by simply comparing performance on different tests, as was done with the other approaches to test dissociations. We must have some method for analyzing the contributions of each type of process to a single test. To accomplish this goal, Jacoby developed a technique based on his theory that begins with placing the influences of conscious and unconscious processes in opposition to one another. In the fame study, the fluency induced by prior exposure to the name gives rise to familiarity when the name is read in the fame-rating test, but the name may also be consciously remembered in this test. Notice that the effects of conscious and unconscious processes are in direct opposition in this situation. If one consciously remembers the name, it will be rated nonfamous, but in the absence of conscious recollection, the automatic influences will lead to a rating of fame. By designing experiments that place the influences in opposition, one can gain estimates of the influences in any given situation.

Another example of such an experiment could involve study of a list of single words (e.g., *motel, horse, garage, bread,* etc.). At test, word stem cues are provided (e.g., *mot_ _*). In some test trials, a signal indicates that the cue is to be used to remember a word from the study list that completes the word stem. These trials are called inclusion tests because both conscious and unconscious influences of the study experience would lead to the correct answer. On other test trials, the signal indicates that the stem is to be completed with a word that was not on the study list. These trials are called exclusion tests because the studied experience is to be excluded as a correct answer. Notice that conscious recollection of the study experience will lead to correct exclusion, whereas unconscious influence of the study experience will lead to an error.

According to the theory, inclusion test performance can be represented by the simple formula: $C + U - CU$. (CU is subtracted because if C and U operate independently as specified by the theory, there can be no joint influence of the two). The exclusion test places conscious and nonconscious influences in opposition. If there is conscious memory for the studied word, the stem will be correctly completed with a different word, but if there is no conscious recollection of the list word, the unconscious influence of study will lead to use of the list word, resulting in an error. The theoretical probability of *making an exclusion error* can be represented: $U (1 - C)$. This formula simply represents unconscious influence minus conscious influence. Notice that if the word is consciously remembered ($C = 1$), there will be no unconscious influence and, hence, no mistake. If you expand the formula for the probability of a mistake when the list word is to be excluded ($U - CU$), you can now see that by subtracting this formula from the formula for the probability of correct completion with a list item $[(C + U - CU) - (U - UC)]$, you are left with C. Thus, we have isolated the theoretical process of conscious influences.

How do we combine these theoretical formulae with experimental data to obtain meaningful numbers as estimates of the processes? Suppose the experiment described above is performed. At the end of the experiment, we know the proportion of stems correctly completed with list words in the inclusion test and the proportion of stems incorrectly completed with list words in the exclusion test for each participant. Suppose the proportion of correct completions in inclusion for a given participant is .60 (= C + U - CU) and the proportion of errors when the list word in exclusion is .40 (= U - UC). As described in the last paragraph, the theoretical estimate for conscious influence is obtained by subtracting the proportion of exclusion errors from the proportion of correct recalls, thus C = .60 - .40. We now have three values: the correct responses, the exclusion errors, and the estimate of C. The estimate of U is easily obtained by substituting these values in either of the equations and solving for U. Given that exclusion errors = U(1 - C), .40 = U(1- .20) in our example. Thus, U = .40/(1 - .20).

But what is the point of this exercise? We are now in the position of both validating the theory and determining what effect variables have on conscious and unconscious processes. Suppose we do the experiment described above, but half of the participants study the list under divided attention. If C really is an estimate of conscious processing and U really is an estimate of unconscious processing, then dividing attention should only affect the estimate of C and leave the estimate of U unchanged. That this would happen is not obvious because the divided attention group will recall fewer of the list words correctly and also make more errors by incorrectly including list words when they should be excluded. However, experiments like the one described here (e.g., Jacoby, Toth, & Yonelinas, 1993) have shown that dividing attention reduces the estimate of conscious processing, whereas the estimate of unconscious processing is unaffected by divided attention. Results such as these imply that the theory is tapping different processes that correspond to conscious and unconscious retrieval.

We shall describe applications of this theory later in the chapter, where you will see instances in which other variables differentially affect conscious and unconscious processing, and how these effects help us understand certain phenomena of memory.

Comparison of the Theoretical Approaches

Each of the three approaches we have described provides a viable description of the dissociation of explicit and implicit memory tests. While it is true that each of the approaches is challenged by particular empirical results, which are usually generated by an opposing approach, each approach continues to attract enthusiastic proponents. The most obvious difference among the views is the reliance on structures versus processes to describe the effect of prior experience on performance. The systems view argues that separate brain structures have evolved to store different types of prior experience, and that each structure operates according to its own psychological principles. Dissociations between implicit and explicit tests are due to the fact that the two kinds of tests require different information, which must be drawn from different memory systems.

The process-based views assume that each experience is the result of the operation of particular mental processes. Dissociations between implicit and explicit tests are due to differences in the processes engaged by the tests, and dissociations within the class of either implicit or explicit tests are to be expected if the tests differ in their processing demands. For example, Blaxton's demonstration that generating versus reading items at study affects the implicit tests of fragment completion and general knowledge differently is not surprising to the process view. Generation and reading engage different processes at study, just as fragment completion and answering general knowledge questions require different processes at test. For the systems view, the dissociation found by Blaxton was unexpected at the time. Both of the implicit tests should have reflected the operation of semantic memory. The response to the unexpected dissociation is to assume the presence of a new memory system. Thus, for systems view, Blaxton's data amounted to the discovery of the perceptual representation system.

Another difference is the importance the systems view places on implicit and explicit test instructions, a factor that is much less salient for the process views. As shown in table 6.2, all explicit tests are the result of either episodic memory or working memory. For the process view, the explicit-implicit test distinction is essentially irrelevant. All that matters is the match between the processes engaged at study and test.

An important similarity between the systems view and the conceptual-perceptual process approach is that tests can be viewed as pure measures. That is, a particular test will tap a particular system according to the systems view. According to the conceptual-perceptual processing distinction, a particular test will be either conceptually or perceptually driven. Thus, the two approaches share a research strategy of inferring psychological differences based on a direct comparison of performance on different tests. The research strategy for the systems approach is to contrast two or more tests that tap two or more different systems. For the conceptual-perceptual processing approach, the strategy is to compare tests that require conceptual processing with those that require perceptual processing. Both of these approaches assume that a given test engages only one type of process. Jacoby's process view does not share this assumption. Jacoby assumes that performance on any test can involve both conscious and unconscious processes. To support this assumption, Jacoby developed his process dissociation procedure that allows for analysis of the effect of a variable on the conscious and unconscious processes within a single test.

APPLICATIONS OF THE EXPLICIT-IMPLICIT TEST DISTINCTION

Research contrasting explicit and implicit test performance has been extended to important questions in addition to issues concerning basic theoretical mechanisms of memory. Some of these questions involve performance across different populations, such as amnesic versus non-amnesic or elderly versus younger people. Other cases explore important phenomena such as prejudice. In all of these instances, new insights have been provided by employing the explicit-implicit test strategy and the theories we have just described. Equally important, this research has provided data that inform the basic theories that motivate the work.

Amnesia

As we noted at the beginning of this chapter, interest in implicit memory tests was stimulated by the observation that amnesiacs show preserved memory on implicit tests. Subsequently, an enormous amount of research has been reported on amnesic performance, much of which has been devoted to establishing the boundary conditions of preserved memory and to localizing brain areas responsible for preserved versus lost memory function in amnesia. Organic amnesia is a severe impairment of new learning capacity, which often occurs after damage to the medial temporal region (including, most notably, the hippocampus) or to regions of the diencephalic midline (i.e., the dorsomedial nucleus of the thalamus and the mammillary bodies of the hypothalamus). Damage to these structures can occur as a result of head injury, vascular accidents (e.g., stroke), surgery (to cure epilepsy, for example), hypoxia (lack of oxygen), as well as a variety of diseases (including herpes, encephalitis, and Alzheimer's). Regardless of the cause, the result is a marked deficit in the ability to recall or recognize prior experiences.

In the late 1960s, research such as that of Warrington and Weiskrantz revealed that amnesic patients do benefit from the effects of prior experience, but the benefit is evident only under conditions of implicit testing. We described these developments in an earlier part of this chapter. One of the examples of this research that we did not mention is a case study reported by Schacter (1983). In this study, Schacter observed the behavior of an amnesic patient, M. T., while playing golf with him. M. T. was a 58-year-old man who had been diagnosed with Alzheimer's disease several years earlier. His memory was grossly impaired on standard laboratory tests, showing virtually no recall for word lists if the test was delayed by as little as five minutes. However, M. T.'s behavior on the golf course clearly reflected preserved memory for some of his prior experiences. M. T. consistently selected the appropriate club for various shots and played the game according to proper rules and etiquette. These are things that he had previously learned and continued to use. What he failed to remember were specific things that happened as he played. For example, he frequently did not remember where he had just hit his ball and would go wandering off in the wrong direction searching for it. If M. T. was first to hit on a hole to be followed by Schacter's shot, he forgot that he had hit and teed up his ball again. In short, what seemed to be preserved was M. T.'s prior knowledge of golf; otherwise, M. T. was amnesic for the particular events occurring during the round.

This example is consistent with the conclusion that the preserved memory reflected on implicit memory tests is in the form of pre-existing knowledge. Poor memory on explicit tests demonstrates the amnesiac's inability to remember new events, just as Schacter's patient could not remember where he had just hit his ball. This pattern of performance is consistent with a systems view of amnesia as impairment of episodic memory while semantic memory is spared.

However, this interpretation has been challenged by the discovery that amnesiacs sometimes show priming effects for new information. The strongest evidence comes from studies using unfamiliar visual patterns where exposure to these novel patterns facilitates performance on later implicit tests (e.g., Schacter, Cooper, & Delaney, 1990). These results suggest that amnesiacs do in fact encode new information. Additional research, however, suggests that novel verbal information is not primed for amnesiacs (Shimamura & Squire, 1989). Bowers and Schacter (1993) have refined the memory systems interpretation of amnesia in light of these results. Novel visual information is handled by the perceptual representation system, whereas novel verbal information might involve the episodic system. Thus, in the systems view, amnesia attacks episodic memory, leaving the semantic and the perceptual representation systems spared.

Another interesting interpretation of amnesia has emerged from Jacoby's distinction between conscious and unconscious processes. This interpretation emphasizes the loss of conscious control of prior experience in amnesia. Cermak, Verfaellie, Butler, and Jacoby (1993) compared amnesiacs and alcoholic control patients on the false-fame test. After seeing a list of nonfamous names, the patients were asked to rate the fame of a longer list of names that included the original list. The amnesic patients made many more mistakes of falsely attributing fame to the names they had previously studied than did the alcoholic controls. Because the amnesic patients cannot consciously recollect the first list of names, the familiarity induced by having read that list is unopposed on the fame-rating test, leading the amnesiacs to mistake the familiarity for actual fame. In a second experiment, Cermak et al. incorrectly informed the participants at the time of the fame rating that the first list of names was famous. Therefore, if they remembered seeing a name from the first list, they could be sure that the name was famous. Under these instructions, the control participants endorsed many more of the first-list names as famous than did the amnesiacs. Indeed, the proportion of first-list names rated as famous by amnesiacs was the same when they were told that those names were not famous as when told that they were famous. These data suggest that whatever priming or preserved memory is demonstrated by amnesiacs results from familiarity produced by the fluency of processing generated by repetition of the process.

Aging

The general public has become very sensitive to the effects of aging on memory, a concern that is well placed in light of laboratory findings that elderly participants do perform more poorly on explicit memory tests than do younger participants. In most of the research examining aging effects, elderly participants are at least 60 years old, and the younger participants are in their late teens and early twenties. Although the effects of aging on explicit tests of recognition tend to be smaller than on explicit tests of recall, age-related deficits in performance have been consistently reported in research using explicit requests for memory.

The situation is quite different with implicit memory tests. Here, the general conclusion from a large number of studies is that age has little effect on implicit memory performance (Mitchell, 1993; Parkin, 1993; Balota, Dolan, & Duchek,

2000). This exciting development parallels the effect of amnesia in that the effect prior experience on implicit tests is unaffected by the aging process. Indeed, some have even maintained that beginning at age 3, implicit memory ability does not change across the life span (Graf, 1990). The pattern of age effects is easily interpreted by the systems approach as indicative of aging effects on episodic memory, whereas semantic memory and the perceptual representation system are unaffected by aging.

One notable phenomenon of declining memory ability with age is inappropriate repetition of stories, jokes, questions, etc. A recent analysis of this phenomenon by Jacoby (1999) points to specific processing deficits with age. In this experiment, participants were first shown a list of words, each of which occurred once, twice, or three times in the list. Following this first list, a second list was read to the participants. Each word was heard only once. A recognition memory test that contained words from both of the lists, as well as some new words, was then administered. The instructions were to recognize the words that occurred on the list that was heard, the second list. All participants were warned that some of the words on the test were from the first list and if they remembered that the word was from the first list, they could be sure that it was incorrect.

Performance of older and younger participants was compared on this task, with a particular interest in the number of times they incorrectly identified words they saw in the first list as words they heard in the second list. Recall that some words in the first list were repeated, something that should facilitate memory for those words and aid in avoiding errors. Younger participants showed this pattern; mistakes on words repeated in the first list were less likely than on words shown once in the first list. Interestingly, older participants showed the opposite effect. Mistakes on first-list words increased directly with repetition. Figure 6.5 shows the results, and the graphical presentation makes clear the opposite effect of repetition on younger and older adults' performance.

The interpretation of these data is that aging disproportionately affects processes of conscious memory. Repetition in the first list contributes to both conscious and unconscious influences from those words. For the younger participants, the increase in conscious recollection with repetition allows them to oppose the unconscious influence and avoid mistakes. For older people, however, the deficit in conscious influence of prior experience allows the unconscious influence of that experience to determine performance. Thus, repetition of first list words leads to more, not fewer, mistakes.

Jacoby characterizes the performance of the elderly participants in terms of ironic effects of repetition. The effect is ironic in that our expectation is that repetition will facilitate memory. But if memory performance is the result of the independent influences of conscious and unconscious processes, and if both processes are affected by repetition, any circumstance that requires avoiding the use of repeated material demands proper functioning of conscious processes. In the absence of conscious recollection, the effect of repetition on automatic influences

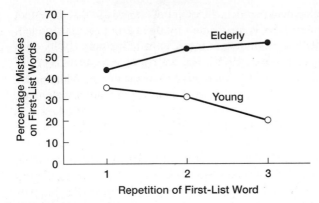

FIGURE 6.5
Graphical depiction of results reported by Jacoby (1999).
The more repetitions of first-list words, the more likely
elderly participants are to mistake first-list words as having
occurred in the second list. Younger participants show the
opposite pattern. (*Adapted from Jacoby, 1999.*)

will yield the ironic effect of increased use of the repeated material. Aging seems
to decrease the use of conscious processes; thus, you can expect that the more
times something is repeated, the more likely it is that the elderly person will say it
again. Even if you are the person to whom the joke was told or the question was
asked, chances are good that you will hear it again from your elderly friend.

Prejudice

Prejudice is the association of strong feelings, either positive or negative, toward
some object or group. As we all know, negative prejudicial attitudes toward entire groups of people are unwarranted and unconstructive. Encouragingly, racial
prejudice has shown a steady decline in the United States over the last 50 years
(Shuman, Steeh, & Bobo, 1997). In the context of our discussion of implicit and
explicit testing, however, one has to wonder if the data showing this decline are a
valid index of changing attitudes. The reason is that surveys on which such data
are based are explicit measures. People answer explicit questions about their
views, and since most people do not wish to be viewed as prejudiced, conscious
editing of responses can mask the existence of negative racial attitudes. Indeed,
recently developed implicit measures of attitude suggest that this is the case.

    One of these measures is the Implicit Attitude Test (IAT) developed by
Greenwald, McGhee, and Schwartz (1998). In this test, participants classify stimuli representing two different target concepts (e.g., Black versus White names)
and two evaluative attributes (e.g., good and bad words). Two keys are used for

the responses and one of the target concepts shares a response key with one of the evaluative attributes. For example, the target concepts could be Black versus White names (e.g., Jamal, Rassan versus Justin, Andrew). The participant is instructed to press one key (e.g., the *A* key) if they judge the name to be a Black name and another key (e.g., the *L* key) if they judge the name to be a White name. Evaluative attributes are classified as pleasant versus unpleasant words (e.g., *gentle, happy* versus *disaster, grief*) by also pressing either the *A* or *L* key. It is important to understand that the names are not being classified as good or bad, just as Black or White. Names and evaluative attributes are presented randomly, and there is little reason for the participant to explicitly notice any connection between the two judgements. The attitude measure is obtained by manipulating which concept shares a key with which attribute. In our example, Black names can share the same response key with pleasant words and White names can share the same response key with unpleasant words, or vice versa. The dependent measure is reaction time to classify the items. Notice that this measure is implicit in that the participants are never told that their attitudes are being assessed.

Figure 6.6 shows the results of an IAT, the participants for which were University of Washington students representing 20 different ethnicities (Dasgupta, McGhee, Greenwald, & Banaji, 2000). Shown in this figure are the reaction times when one key was used for White and pleasant words and the other key for Black

FIGURE 6.6
Results of the IAT to White versus Black names and to a White versus Black pictures. Prejudice is inferred from the slower responses to the Black-Pleasant; White-Unpleasant key combination than to the White-Pleasant; Black-Unpleasant combination. *(From Dasgupta, N., McGhee, D. E., Greenwald, A. G., & Banaji, M. R. (2000). Automatic preference for White Americans: Eliminating the familiarity explanation.* Journal of Experimental Social Psychology, 36, *316–328. Copyright 2000 by Academic Press. Used by permission of Elsevier.)*

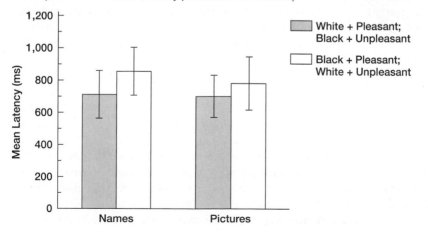

and unpleasant words versus the case in which one key was used for White and unpleasant words and the other key for Black and pleasant words. The target stimuli were either Black and White names or Black and White pictures. Regardless of whether the stimulus to be classified was a name or a picture, reaction time was faster when the White and pleasant stimuli shared the same key than when Black and pleasant shared the same key. These reaction times are taken to be the result of the activation of attitudes in which White is positively valenced and Black is negatively valenced. On this interpretation, the results of the IAT reveal negative prejudice that is not apparent on explicit questionnaires.

Dasgupta and Greenwald (2001) have gone on to show that implicit techniques can be used to modify attitudes. In two different experiments, they demonstrate reduction in racial and age prejudice by presenting admired exemplars and disliked exemplars from the groups. In the study on age bias, participants were assigned to one of three initial conditions. In the pro-young condition, participants viewed pictures accompanied by the names of admired young people and disliked older people (e.g., Ben Affleck versus Tammy Faye Bakker). In the pro-elderly condition, the pictures were of admired older people and disliked young people (e.g., Mother Teresa versus Tonya Harding). To maintain attention to these exemplars, a cover task was required in which two descriptions of each individual were presented with their pictures and names, and the participant had to choose the correct description. Twenty-four hours after exposure to the exemplars, an IAT was administered. The procedure was the same as described above for Black and White names, except the names were to be classified as young (e.g., Brittany, Kyle) or old (e.g., Agatha, Albert).

The results of the IAT are shown in figure 6.7 as a function of which exemplars were seen initially and of the response key combinations in the IAT. The important outcome is the difference in reaction times for the young-pleasant versus old-pleasant key combinations for the two-exemplar conditions. On the left side of the figure, you can see the standard, age bias effect. Reaction time when the same key is used for young and pleasant is much faster than when the same key is used for old and pleasant. This occurred following exposure to admired young and disliked elderly exemplars. On the right side of the figure are the IAT results following exposure to admired elderly and disliked young exemplars. Notice that the reaction time difference between the young-pleasant key combination and the old-pleasant key combination is considerably reduced. Thus, exposure to positive exemplars reduced negative attitudes as measured by the IAT 24 hours after the exposure. Similar results were obtained in a parallel study on racial prejudice.

The reduction in prejudice shown by Dasgupta and Greenwald is an important contribution from research on implicit memory processes. Prejudice reduction has been a central interest in social psychology for several decades, but prior research viewed prejudice reduction as a conscious relearning process. This view assumes that the influence of attitudes, as well as attitudes themselves, are within a person's awareness and can be consciously controlled. In this view, unconscious

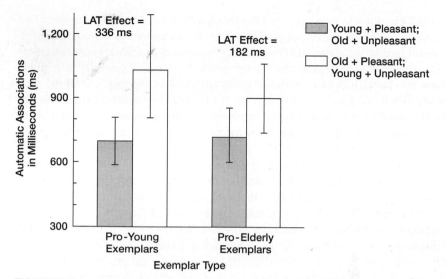

FIGURE 6.7
Data showing age bias as measured by the IAT and that the bias is reduced following prior exposure to positive examples of older people. (*From Dasgupta, N., & Greenwald, A. G. (2001). On the malleability of automatic attitudes: Combating automatic prejudice with images of admired and disliked individuals. Journal of Personality and Social Psychology, 81, 800–814. Copyright 2001 by the American Psychological Association. Used by permission of Elsevier.*)

attitudes would be inescapable habits that cannot be modified. The results from IAT tests clearly indicate that prejudicial attitudes can be implicit. That is, prior experiences, which themselves are the cause of attitudes, can exert unconscious influence on behavior such as that measured by the IAT. Modifying the unconscious influence of prior experience seems to be possible by providing additional experiences that are in opposition to the existing attitude.

SUMMARY

The research we have discussed focuses on the fact that one and the same prior experience can influence behavior differently and sometimes even have opposite effects, depending upon how memory is tested. This fact is the fundamental mystery posed by dissociations between explicit and implicit memory tests. Beginning with the dissociation of amnesia, a host of variables are now known to have different effects on explicit and implicit test performance. How is it that the same variable exerts different effects on behavior, depending upon whether one intends to remember or intends to accomplish some task for which the prior experience may be relevant? The answer to this question can only come from theories of memory and the research testing those theories.

Three prominent theories of explicit-implicit test dissociation were described. One view is that different structural systems have evolved to store and use different kinds of information. The memory systems approach argues that all explicit attempts to remember draw information from either episodic or working memory. Implicit uses of memory generally involve the application of prior knowledge to a current problem. Knowledge is the province of semantic memory. Some implicit applications of prior experience require the use of nonverbal information such as visual forms, and this type of information is stored in the separate system of perceptual representations. Other common tasks rely on a previously learned motor skill, information that is stored in the procedural memory system. Because all of these different systems store different kinds of information and operate by separate rules, tests of memory that access different systems often will be affected differently by the same variable.

In contrast, memory can be thought of as a process, rather than as a structural system that contains traces. In this view, each task we accomplish, be it a cognitive or motor task, is the result of particular psychological processes. The influence of prior experience is determined by the similarity of the processes engaged by that prior experience to the processes required by the current task. One explanation of test dissociations from the process view distinguishes between tests that demand conceptual processes and tests that demand perceptual processes. Conceptual processes are influenced by meaning, whereas perceptual processes are susceptible to manipulation of the surface features of the material. Thus, if tests differ in their demands for conceptual and perceptual processes, the effects of a prior experience that emphasized the use of either conceptual or perceptual processes will differ on the tests. The dissociations of prior experience do not depend on the explicit versus implicit nature of the test but, rather, on the conceptual and perceptual demands of the test.

A different version of the process approach relies on the distinction between conscious and unconscious processes. The effects of prior experience are manifested as either conscious recollection of a past experience, in which case the influence will be attributed to memory, or as an unconscious influence. In the case of unconscious influence, the prior experience affects current processing in accord with transfer appropriate processing, but the influence is unconscious in the sense that there is no experience of recollection. Rather the subjective experience is one of familiarity. This familiarity is attributed to a source, sometimes correctly and sometimes incorrectly. Conscious and unconscious influences can operate simultaneously but independently, which means that both types of processes can contribute to any single test. Consequently, according to this view, the strategy used by the other approaches of comparing performance on different tests is inappropriate. What is dissociated is not tests but, rather, processes. Variables may differentially affect conscious and unconscious processing, and the research strategy becomes one of separating the influences of those processes.

Research on dissociations continues to be very active in cognitive psychology because it has opened the way for exciting new discoveries. We have learned that amnesiacs are not completely amnesic. The process of aging does not affect all types of use of prior experience. Implicit processes underlying our beliefs and attitudes affect our behavior without any awareness of the effect on our part. Ongoing research in this area promises to be fruitful for both a basic understanding of the operation of memory and for how past experience manifests its effect on our daily activities.

THOUGHT QUESTIONS

1. What is the difference between explicit and implicit memory tests?
2. How does the memory systems theory account for the lack of a levels of processing effect on an implicit test of fragment completion? According to this theory, why does the study experience increase the probability of fragment completion?
3. If the modality of study presentation is different from the modality of test presentation, performance on implicit tests, such as word-stem completion, and word-fragment completion, declines. That is, if one group sees the study list and a second group hears the study list, and then both groups are shown the stems or fragments at test, performance is better in the group that saw the study list. Explain this result from each of the three different theories described in this chapter.
4. Why is the distinction between conscious and unconscious processing a useful tool in the study of attitudes?

7

MEMORY FAILURE: FORGETTING AND FALSE MEMORY

About the only time we notice our own memory is when it fails. We all have the aggravating and sometimes embarrassing experience of forgetting someone's name, what we were going to say, or what we did on a certain occasion. When is the last time that you forgot to do something, only to be reminded of it after it is too late? These examples are common instances of memory failure that we think of as forgetting. Another kind of memory failure is equally common but probably much less noticeable; that is the case in which we clearly remember something but it turns out to be wrong. You arrange to have lunch with a friend on Thursday and arrive to find your friend is not there. When you call to accuse your friend of forgetting, you learn that the lunch had been scheduled for Friday. Inaccurate or distorted memory is an interesting phenomenon because the inaccurate memory feels no different from an accurate memory. In most cases of forgetting, we know something has been forgotten without being told, but we become aware of memory distortion only through some outside agency. If I have a clear memory, I do not question its accuracy. I assume the memory is veridical with past events.

Laboratory research only recently has begun to focus vigorously on memory distortion. Historically, most research on memory failure concentrated on forgetting. Koriat, Goldsmith, and Pansky (2001) trace these trends to the fact that laboratory studies generally use quantity of remembered material as the dependent measure. For example, most of the memory studies we have described thus far have measured the proportion of the original material that is correctly remembered, and in this tradition, memory failure would be indexed by the proportion of the original material that is not remembered, which is the measure of forgetting. But as Koriat et al. point out, our concern with memory outside of the laboratory is more with accuracy than with quantity. That is, if you are describing a party you attended, I am more interested in how much of what you tell me is accurate than in how much of the party you remember. Indeed, in most settings outside of the laboratory, we have no way to measure quantity of memory because we have no way of knowing all of the things that happened—a problem that we confronted in our discussion of autobiographical memory. Often, however, we do have objective criteria for accuracy of what is reported, perhaps the most sensational example being the use of DNA tests to dispute an eyewitness account. The recent surge of interest in memory distortion was spurred largely by phenomena observed outside of laboratory settings—phenomena that have begun to receive careful study.

In this chapter we discuss both forms of memory failure. First, we describe research and theory on normal forgetting. We then move on to cases of memory distortion and discuss various instances of distorted memory in the context of their real world settings.

FORGETTING

We begin our discussion of forgetting with the caution that not everything you fail to remember has been forgotten. Sometimes, even when we think that we experienced an event, we are unable to remember because the event was not encoded and stored. In short, many instances of memory failure are due to lack of attention to the original experience. *We reserve the term* forgetting *for cases in which the material is available in memory but cannot be retrieved.*

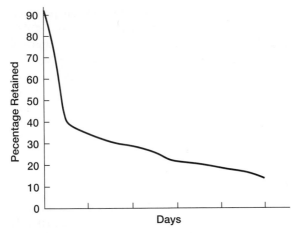

FIGURE 7.1
The forgetting function from Ebbinghaus showing very
rapid forgetting shortly after exposure and more gradual
forgetting as the retention interval increases.

The most obvious variable associated with forgetting is the length of time between the original experience and the attempt to remember. In general, the older
the memory, the more likely it is to be forgotten. This variable, known as the retention interval, has been studied extensively since the research of Ebbinghaus
(1885/1964). Ebbinghaus was the first to show that the relation between retention
interval and memory is a logarithmic function of the kind shown in figure 7.1. As
described by the logarithmic function, memory decreases rapidly in the first hour
after exposure but then levels off at longer delays. Rubin and Wenzel (1996) examined 210 different studies of retention and concluded that the decrease in memory over time is essentially that discovered by Ebbinghaus. Why should memory
become more difficult as the retention interval increases? The intuitive explanation that appeals to many people is that with time, the memory decays and is lost.

Decay Theory

Decay theory of forgetting assumes that information simply weakens or is lost
over time if it is not used. We briefly described this idea in chapter 4 in the context
of the short duration of short-term memory. However intuitively reasonable this
theory may seem, few researchers subscribe to the notion that memory decays.
This aversion to the decay theory is due in part to the fact that natural events are
influenced by factors other than the passage of time. For example, if left in a complete vacuum, iron does not rust over any period of time. As a natural phenomenon, memory should therefore not go away due only to the passage of time.

Another reason to be skeptical of decay theory is that it implies that we forgot
because a memory has been completely lost. Yet, quite often we fail to remember

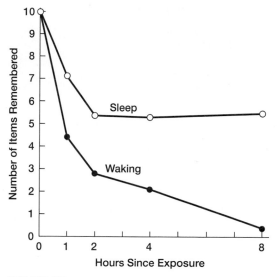

FIGURE 7.2
Data from Jenkins and Dallenbach (1924) showing
memory following various retention periods that were
filled either by sleeping or normal awake activity.

something on one occasion but successfully remember it later. The first failure
could not have been caused by a total loss of that memory. Many laboratory studies have shown that material that cannot be remembered under certain conditions
will later be remembered under different conditions. In most of these cases, the
difference in conditions is the cue environment. That is, one may fail to remember
in the presence of a given cue, but when provided with a different cue, memory
succeeds. Thus, the original memory failure could not be attributed to decay.

Finally, attacks on decay theory came very early in the form of experimental
work. For example, Jenkins and Dallenbach (1924) had people memorize a list
of nonsense syllables and then tested their memory 1, 4, or 8 hours later. During
the retention interval, half of the people went about their daily activities and the
other half slept. According to decay theory, what you do during the retention interval should not matter as long as you are not rehearsing the material. But as
you can see in figure 7.2, forgetting was much more severe when people were
doing things than when they slept. These results indicate that memory is not affected so much by passage of time as by what happens in that time.

Interference Theory

The basic assumption of interference theory is that forgetting is caused by competition among similar memories. When two or more similar memories are associated with a cue, the retrieval of one memory may block the retrieval of others.

		Retroactive Interference	Proactive Interference
Order in Which Events Occur	1	Encounter To-Be-Remembered Material	Encounter Interfering Material
	2	Encounter Interfering Material	Encounter To-Be-Remembered Material
	3	Memory Test for To-Be-Remembered Material	Memory Test for To-Be-Remembered Material

FIGURE 7.3
Sequence of events in retroactive interference and in proactive interference.

For example, when you try to remember what you had for dinner three nights ago, you can only remember what you had last night. You know that last night's dinner is not the correct answer but cannot retrieve dinner from three nights ago. Notice the important role of the similarity of the memories to the interference effect. When trying to remember what you had for dinner, it is highly unlikely that information about this morning's breakfast will interfere. By the same token, if you had an unusual dinner experience three nights ago, perhaps at the very best restaurant in town, the lack of similarity with last night's normal dinner will minimize interference.

Interference can arise from events that occurred before or after the target event. *Retroactive interference* is produced by material encountered after the target event is encoded. This would be the case in our example of last night's dinner interfering with retrieval of dinner three nights ago. *Proactive interference* is produced by material occurring prior to the target information. If you answer a question incorrectly on a multiple-choice examination and then receive correct feedback, you later may not be able to remember the correct answer because of proactive interference from the wrong answer. A schematic representation of retroactive interference and proactive interference is shown in figure 7.3.

Thus far, our use of interference has only been descriptive; that is, we have talked about the fact that forgetting happens when similar events have occurred before or after the target event. The important question is, Why does an interfering event cause forgetting? According to interference theory, there are two basic mechanisms underlying forgetting. The first is *response competition* whereby two or more responses are associated with a cue, and retrieval of the responses depends on the relative associative strength between the cue and the two targets. If the strongest associative relationship is between the cue and an incorrect response, the correct response will lose in this competition. Early evidence for response competition derives from experiments in which participants were asked to learn two different lists. The same cues were present in both lists but were associated with different responses in the two lists. Thus, if the test required the response from the first list, the association of the second-list response should compete with correct recall. In fact it does, which is a demonstration of retroactive interference. As the degree of learning on the second list increases, so should the associative strength between the cue and the second-list response, which in turn should reduce correct memory for the first list response. This, too, is the case (McGeoch, 1942).

The second mechanism of forgetting, *unlearning,* was introduced to account for an observation that cannot be explained by response competition alone. In experiments of the kind just mentioned in which the degree of second-list learning is manipulated, the association between the cue and the second-list response should become stronger with more practice on the second list. If so, one would expect the forgetting of the first-list response to be accompanied by increasing intrusions of the incorrect second-list response. In fact, with more practice on the list, incorrect recall of second-list responses decreases even as correct recall of first-list responses decreases (Melton & Irwin, 1940). Response competition is based on the notion that forgetting is due to the relative associative strengths of the cue-response pairs and, thus, cannot explain this pattern. Melton and Irwin proposed that in addition to response competition, interference weakens the association between cues and responses. This "unlearning" was attributed to learning of the association between the cue and the second-list response, during which the first-list response must be suppressed. The unlearning mechanism received support from studies by Barnes and Underwood (1959), who requested that participants recall responses from both lists in the presence of the cue. If response competition is the only mechanism underlying forgetting of first-list responses, no retroactive interference should occur because there is no competition in this situation. Yet, Barnes and Underwood continued to find forgetting of first-list responses, suggesting that learning the second list had weakened the association between the cue and the first-list response.

Cue-Dependent Forgetting

According to interference theory, response competition influences the associative relationship between single cue-response pairs, and forgetting results from the weakening of the association between the cue and the correct response. A different perspective is that forgetting is caused by the ineffectiveness of cues to access correct memories. In this view, cue ineffectiveness is due to competition among all of the items of an event, not just the single cue-response pairs. An early example of this approach is the classic paper by Hedwig von Restorff (1933). She asked participants to memorize a list of eight item pairs and varied the similarity among the pairs. Six of the pairs were digit pairs (e.g., 9–12, 3–8, 15–4) and the other two pairs were different in kind—one was a pair of nonsense syllables and the other a pair of words. After a six-minute retention interval, the first member of the pair was given as a cue for recall of the second member of the pair. Recall of items from the similar pairs was only 25 percent correct, whereas recall of the different items was 87 percent. This effect has come to be known as the *isolation effect* because items that are isolated from the primary dimension of similarity are better recalled. von Restorff's real interest was in memory for the similar items, and she attributed the poor recall to the interfering effects produced by the high degree of similarity. The interference effects in von Restorff's paradigm cannot be attributed to unlearning because no one cue was associated with more than one response. Thus, von Restorff's data are not easily explained by the mechanisms of classic interference theory.

Bower, Thompson-Schill, and Tulving (1994) extended von Restorff's preparation to a traditional two-list paradigm used in most research on interference. All participants were asked to learn two lists consisting of item pairs. The critical manipulation between the two conditions was the similarity of the pairs across the lists. Table 7.1 illustrates the manipulation of materials in the two conditions. As you can see in table 7.1, the cue member of the pairs was the same in each list for both conditions, setting the stage for response competition in the final test. In the all-same condition, all of the pairs in both lists were from the same class; for example, the cues and responses in each list were all digits. In the congruent condition, the pairs in both lists were from different classes, but within a pair the cues and responses were from the same class. For example, one cue was a digit, and its responses in both lists were also digits; another cue was the name of a famous person, and both of its responses were also names of famous people; and so on. The critical factor is that in both conditions, response competition could occur for individual pairs.

After learning both lists, a final cued recall test was given for both lists' responses. In the all-same pair condition, recall of the second-list responses was twice as great as recall for the first-list responses, a strong retroactive interference effect. In the congruent condition, however, there was no retroactive interference; recall was equally good for lists 1 and 2 responses. Importantly, these results suggest that retroactive interference is not caused by competition within single pairs,

TABLE 7.1
AN EXAMPLE OF THE MATERIALS USED IN THE TWO CONDITIONS OF THE EXPERIMENT BY BOWER, THOMPSON-SCHILL, AND TULVING (1994).

All-same condition		Congruent condition	
First list	*Second list*	*First list*	*Second list*
79 - 56	79 - 18	79 - 56	79 - 18
14 - 52	14 - 39	V - M	V - R
87 - 23	87 - 61	Picasso-Lincoln	Picasso-Marx

as is maintained by interference theory. Rather, the problem arises when the cue is not diagnostic of the response.

A cue is diagnostic to the extent that it specifies the correct response. Cue diagnosticity can be affected by the overall organization of a list, as well as by the individual pairs. As the overall similarity between cues and responses increases, the diagnosticity of the cue decreases, causing forgetting. As a simple example of this principle, suppose you saw one of your friends on Tuesday wearing a red shirt and a different friend on Wednesday, who also was wearing a red shirt. If you were asked on Thursday who you saw in a red shirt on Tuesday, you would likely have little trouble answering the question, assuming you paid attention to the shirt. But if everyone you saw on Tuesday and Wednesday wore a red shirt, the cue loses its diagnosticity for the particular friend seen on Tuesday. In this view, forgetting is dependent on cue diagnosticity, not on the associative strength between the cue and response.

Inhibition

A fourth mechanism proposed as the basis of forgetting is inhibition of the to-be-remembered information. *Inhibition* is different from the other mechanisms of forgetting that we have discussed in that it operates directly on the representation of the target item rather than on the relationship between the cue and target. This difference has an important implication. Items that are forgotten due to inhibition will be inaccessible regardless of what cue is provided. The inhibition view of forgetting is a bit like decay theory in that the item cannot be accessed through any means, but it is also unlike decay theory in a very important aspect. Inhibition does dissipate over time so that eventually the item is again accessible through appropriate cues. Inhibition does not imply permanent loss as does decay. The inhibition view, however, does suggest that forgetting is cue independent, which is contrary to the positions of classic interference theory and the cue dependent views of forgetting. Two interesting phenomena to which inhibition theory has been applied are retrieval induced forgetting and directed forgetting.

Retrieval Induced Forgetting   Remembering can cause forgetting. Under certain conditions, retrieval of some elements of an event can impair memory for the other elements of the event. This phenomenon is known as *retrieval induced forgetting.* Suppose you go to a party, and later I ask you which of my friends attended the party. Sometime later, another person asks you who was at the party. Assuming that some of the people were my friends and some were people I do not know, your memory for the people who are not my friends will be impaired by previous retrieval of my friends. You will not remember as many of the people who are not my friends as you would have if I had not asked you to remember my friends.

Anderson, Bjork, and Bjork (1994) discovered the phenomenon of retrieval induced forgetting in a three-stage experiment. In the first phase, participants

TABLE 7.2

AN ILLUSTRATION OF THE THREE-PHASE PARADIGM USED TO STUDY RETRIEVAL INDUCED FORGETTING. THE ACTUAL EXPERIMENT USED EIGHT CATEGORIES BUT ONLY TWO ARE SHOWN IN THIS ILLUSTRATION. THE MATERIAL SHOWN IS WHAT THE SUBJECT WOULD SEE IN EACH PHASE.

Study phase	Retrieval practice phase	Final test cues
Drink		Drink
Vodka	Fruit Or_____	Fruit
Rum	Fruit Le_____	
Gin	Fruit Pi_____	
Bourbon		
Ale		
Whiskey		
Fruit		
Tomato		
Strawberry		
Banana		
Orange		
Lemon		
Pineapple		

studied a categorized list of words for later memory test. The list contained 48 items, 6 items from each of eight categories. After studying the list, participants were given retrieval practice on half of the words from half of the categories. In this second phase, participants were instructed to remember list items that corresponded to the cues provided, which were the category name along with the first letters of the word (*Fruit or_ _ _ _*). Notice that for half of the categories, half of the items were tested and half were not; whereas for the other half of the categories, none of the items were tested. In the final phase of the experiment, the participants were given a cued recall test for all of the items seen in the study phase. The cues were the eight category labels. Table 7.2 illustrates the three-stage paradigm used to study retrieval induced forgetting.

The important data from this paradigm come from the final recall test. The comparison of interest is between items that were not tested in the second phase (but whose category was tested) and items from completely untested categories. In the example given in table 7. 2, the untested items from the tested category would be *tomato, strawberry,* and *banana,* and the items from the untested category would be all of the instances of *Drinks.* The untested items from tested categories represent the case in which part of the experience was recalled previously, but the untested items were not part of that recall. The question is how well those items are recalled relative to items whose categories were not tested in phase 2. In fact, the untested items from tested categories were more poorly remembered on the final test than were the items from untested categories. This result is a demonstration of retrieval induced forgetting.

The explanation of retrieval induced forgetting offered by Anderson, Bjork, and Bjork begins with response competition in the intermediate test. When the cue *Fruit or_ _ _ _* appears, fruits other than orange come to mind and must be suppressed in order to provide the correct response, *orange*. Among those fruits that would be suppressed are the untested items from the study list. Suppression is accomplished by actively inhibiting the representation of the competing items. At the time of the final test, the inhibition prevents recall of the items that were suppressed in the intermediate test.

The conditions that produce retrieval induced forgetting (i.e., an intermediate test for part of the information followed by a test for all of the information) occur frequently outside of the laboratory. For example, consider the memory of a witness to a crime. The first step in a criminal investigation is to question the witnesses, but the police do not know what happened at the crime and, thus, can only ask questions about parts of the event. Unfortunately, such questioning increases the chance that other parts of the event will not be well remembered later.

Indeed, Shaw, Bjork, and Handal (1995) have reported data that mimic this type of situation. Participants were shown a series of color slides depicting a college student's apartment. They were told to imagine that they had attended a party in the apartment and, on leaving, discovered that their wallets had been stolen from their coats, which had been in the room depicted in the slides. The participants were instructed to pay close attention to the slides of the room so they could later assist the police in their investigation of the theft. Subsequently, half of the participants were given an intermediate interrogation about some of the objects in the room, and the other half of the participants were not given this test. Later, everyone was asked to recall all of the objects in the room. Participants who had experienced an intermediate interrogation recalled fewer of the objects that were not part of the interrogation than did participants who had no intermediate interrogation. The interpretation of these results was that the items that were excluded from the original interrogation were suppressed, and the inhibition that accrued to the items impaired performance on the final recall test.

Some memories are immune to retrieval induced forgetting, and for that we can be grateful. Imagine you were mistakenly detained for shoplifting as you left a store. The store detective requests some personal information: your name, what you do, etc. The detective then asks you to wait a few minutes while she gets a form she needs from her office. On returning, she now wants to know your address and phone number. If prior retrieval of part of your personal information resulted in forgetting of untested information such as your address and phone number, considerable trouble could ensue. MaCrae and Roseveare (2002) raised this potential problem and then conducted experiments to determine if self-relevant information is subject to retrieval induced forgetting. They asked people to remember a list of items that represented gifts. In one condition, the self-relevant condition, the instructions were to imagine that the subjects themselves had bought the gift; in another condition, the participants were to imagine that their best friend had purchased the gift. After an intermediate test for half of the items, participants in the self-relevant condition showed no retrieval induced forgetting on the final test, whereas the participants who had imagined that their best friend bought the gift showed standard levels of retrieval induced forgetting. Self-relevant information is well remembered because such information is processed distinctively (Klein & Kihlstrom, 1986). (See Chapter 5 for a discussion of distinctive processing.) Furthermore, distinctive processing has been shown to protect information against retrieval induced forgetting (Smith & Hunt, 2000). Thus, distinctively processed information appears to be a boundary condition for retrieval induced forgetting.

Directed Forgetting   Inhibition also is the mechanism used to account for a voluntary form of forgetting known as directed forgetting. We usually think of forgetting as a flaw in memory, but sometimes it is adaptive not to remember. R. A. Bjork (1970) gives a nice example of such a situation in the context of a short-order cook who must prepare dozens of breakfasts during a shift. When the cook hears the order "Two over easy, potatoes, and wheat toast," it would be beneficial if the prior order "Two scrambled, sausage, and a stack" has been forgotten. Voluntary forgetting of information that is deemed to be of no further use reduces the potential for interference from that information. You probably have exercised such voluntary forgetting when you decide to "let go" of some information, a phone number or even the material from a recently completed examination.

Investigations of directed forgetting in the laboratory proceed by showing people some material and then instructing them to forget part of it. For example, participants may be instructed that they are to remember the list of words they are about to see. Halfway through the list, the directed forgetting group is told to forget all of the words they have just seen and concentrate on the remaining items. The control group also is stopped at the same halfway point, but they are just reminded to try to remember all of the words. After the entire list has been presented, a memory test is given for all of the words. The directed forgetting group remembers less of the first half of the list, the items they were instructed to forget, than does the control group. This result itself may not indicate forgetting but, rather, could be something as simple as compliance on the part of the participants. They were instructed to forget the items and, at the time of the test, may choose not to report those items even though they do remember them. Another facet of the results indicates that this is not the case. In addition to remembering fewer of the items from the first part of the list, the directed forgetting group remembers more of the second half of the list than does the control group. This outcome suggests that the first half of the list was forgotten and is not available to interfere with memory for the second half of the list.

One explanation for intentional forgetting is that the to-be-forgotten material receives shallow processing at encoding because the person knows the information does not have to be retained for a long period. For example, if you obtain a phone number that you will likely only use one time, you may do whatever you need to retain the number until it is dialed and then devote no further processing to that information. This interpretation seems unlikely in light of research by Geiselman, Bjork, and Fisher (1983). They conducted a directed forgetting experiment in which the participants were asked to rate the pleasantness of the items in the first half of the list but were not told to try to remember the items. Directed forgetting instructions were given halfway through the list, and the final test showed the standard directed forgetting results. Thus, even when a person is not trying to remember but is performing an activity that is known to produce good memory, directed forgetting occurs. These data cast doubt on an encoding deficit interpretation of intentional forgetting.

The favored interpretation of directed forgetting is that some process impairs access to items in long-term memory, a process Geiselman et al. called retrieval inhibition. One basis for this interpretation is that Basden, Basden, and Gargano (1993) found that directed forgetting instructions have no effect on a recognition memory test where all of the items are available. Thus, the effect appears to be on retrieval processes that access the item. Furthermore, reexposure to the to-be-forgotten item prior to the final test eliminates the effect of directed forgetting. Bjork (1989) discusses experiments using the standard directed forgetting paradigm, except that some of the participants were given a recognition memory test prior to the final recall test. In the recognition test, participants were asked to recognize items from the second part of the list, the part that is to be remembered. In one condition, the distracter items were taken from the first part of the list (the part that was to be forgotten) and in another condition, the distracters were not taken from the list. On the final recall test, the group that had seen to-be-forgotten items as distracters showed no directed forgetting, whereas the group that had seen nonlist distracters did show the effect. These results are taken as evidence of release from inhibition by reexposure of the item. That is, the inhibition that supposedly prevents access to the item is removed when the item is seen prior to the final test.

Summary of Forgetting

Forgetting is the inability to produce or recognize a previous experience when requested to do so. We have described four ideas about how forgetting occurs, each of which have unique implications for the fate of the forgotten information. *Decay theory* assumes that stored information is lost from memory. In this view, forgotten information cannot be recovered under any circumstances, an implication that is contrary to the fact that forgotten information is sometimes later remembered. *Interference theory* argues that forgetting results from competition among responses to a retrieval cue. This competition is based on the relative associative strength between the competing items and the cue. If an incorrect response has higher associative strength than the correct response, access to the correct response is blocked, which can lead to a reduction in the associative strength of the correct response to the cue. This latter mechanism of unlearning is similar to decay theory in that it implies that the cue no longer can access the response. Unlike decay theory, however, interference theory does not assume that the response item itself is lost from memory. Cue-dependent forgetting, like interference theory, assumes that response competition is the important setting condition for forgetting, but cue-dependent forgetting places much less emphasis on the associative relation between a cue and response. Rather, the important consideration is the diagnosticity of the cue, which can be affected by the entire context of the event in question. As with interference theory, cue-dependent forgetting assumes that forgotten information is still available in memory and could be accessed with an appropriate cue. Finally, forgetting has been attributed to the inhibition of the to-be-remembered information. Circumstances such as retrieval induced forgetting and directed forgetting instructions inhibit the desired information. The implications of inhibition are that the forgotten item is still available in memory, but for the duration of the inhibition, the item is unavailable to conscious memory. Thus like decay theory, inhibition implies that the forgotten item is totally inaccessible but, unlike decay theory, the item is not lost from memory.

FALSE MEMORY

Forgetting is not the only type of error that occurs in memory. Sometimes people remember things quite differently from the way they originally occurred, and sometimes things are remembered that never occurred at all. These types of errors are distortions of memory. Unlike forgetting, you would have no indication that a memory is distorted. When you forget, you are consciously aware of the inability to access the desired information, but you have no awareness that a memory you are experiencing is distorted unless someone convinces you of it. Consequently, we often remain unaware that our memory is actually inconsistent with the prior facts. This makes the question of how memory is distorted even more important; why would you remember something different from what you actually experienced and, especially, why would you remember something that never happened?

Answers to these questions have begun to emerge over the last 30 years of research, and the research suggests that many cases of distorted memory can be traced to the normal operation of perception and comprehension. This conclusion is simultaneously reassuring and distressing. You can be reassured that your distorted memory is not the result of some serious psychological or neurological problem (unless most of your memory is distorted), but it is distressing to learn that the normal operation of perception and comprehension frequently results in distorted memory.

As an example of what we mean by distortion of memory through the normal operation of perceptual processes, consider a study by Hastorf and Cantril (1954) entitled "They saw a game." Hastorf and Cantril asked students at Dartmouth College and Princeton University to view a recorded segment of a recent football game between the two schools. Considerable rivalry exists between the schools in football, and the previous game had been controversial. Princeton entered undefeated and eventually won the game, but only after a bitter contest that featured numerous fights and injuries. Hastorf and Cantril had students at both schools judge the number of penalties that were committed in the recorded segment of the game. The Dartmouth students saw an equal number of penalties committed by the two teams, consistent with the belief of the Dartmouth faithful that the game had been rough but fair. The Princeton students, on the other hand, judged Dartmouth to have committed twice as many penalties as did Princeton, reflecting the sentiment among Princeton followers that Dartmouth had to play dirty to be competitive. These results are consistent with our discussion in chapter 2 of the effect of prior knowledge on perception, and as we know from chapter 5, what you perceive is what you remember, apparently regardless of what was really there.

More examples of these types of distorted memory and their causes will be provided in chapter 11, where we discuss processes of comprehension that can underlie inaccurate memory. For the remainder of the present chapter, we focus on factors that seem to result in memory for events that in fact never occurred.

False Memory for Related Information

Perception and comprehension of ongoing events always brings related information to mind. For example, you briefly see your friend at a movie and, among other things, you think about her boyfriend. Unless there is some reason for you to determine if her boyfriend is at the movie with her, you later may remember seeing the boyfriend at the movie when in fact he was not there. Or perhaps someone mentions that he had a great trip to the beach over the weekend. In comprehending what he is saying, you imagine your last visit to Figure Eight Island. Later, you remember that he mentioned his trip to Figure Eight Island when, in fact, he said nothing about which beach he visited. Simple, common examples such as these illustrate how frequently we might remember information related to our ongoing perception and comprehension, even though the events represented by that information never occurred.

Laboratory observations of this phenomenon have been reported for some time (Deese, 1959; Underwood, 1965), but sustained research interest was invigorated by Roediger and McDermott's (1995) more recent work. Roediger and McDermott used materials like those developed by Deese (1959) in their studies of recognition and recall. These are lists of words, all of which are associated to a single critical item. For example, the words *pin, sew, thread, cloth, injection, serum,* and *haystack* comprise a list, and all of these words are associated with

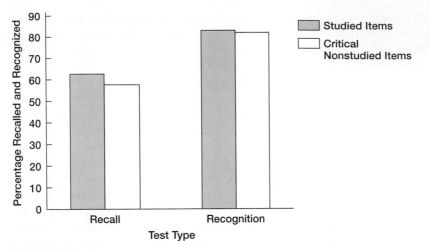

FIGURE 7.4
False recall and recognition of strongly associated, nonstudied
words compared to correct recall and recognition of studied
words. (*Adapted from Roediger and McDermott, 1995.*)

needle. Participants were presented such lists consisting of 12–15 words. The important manipulation is that the critical associated item, *needle* in our example, is not present in the list. Nonetheless, when participants were instructed to recall the words they heard, the probability of falsely recalling the critical item was just as high as correct recall of items they did hear. You can see these results in figure 7.4. Furthermore, on tests of recognition memory, which are more sensitive to stored information than recall, Roediger and McDermott discovered that the critical item was just as likely to be recognized as the items that were actually presented.

Roediger and McDermott's studies are a powerful demonstration of false memory for related information that was not presented. The false memory, like perceptual illusions, is difficult to modify even when we are aware of the possibility that the memory might be false. Gallo, Roberts, and Seamon (1997) instructed participants about the nature of false memory in this paradigm prior to asking them to remember the Deese lists. Although the prior warning did reduce the incidence of false memory for the critical item, false recall and recognition of the item still occurred at a high rate.

One explanation for why related information is often falsely remembered is that in the course of comprehending the presented material, the related information comes to mind. Basically, the related information is inferred, and in that sense, the related information is present during the original experience. Yet it is not a part of the experience that was requested by the memory test, and recollection that it was presented is false memory. Many questions remain to be answered about the phenomenon of false memory for related information, among them the issue of whether the information must come to mind consciously during the original experience (Roediger, Balota, & Watson, 2001). Nonetheless, false memory for inferences is a psychological fact, and we shall return to this matter when we discuss the process of inference in chapter 11.

Imagination and False Memory

Imagery, as we discussed in chapter 5, is a powerful aid to correct memory, but research has now shown that imagery can contribute to false memory for events that did not happen. An interesting example of the effects of imagery on false memory was reported by Garry, Manning, Loftus, and Sherman (1996). In this study, participants were first asked if they had ever experienced some rather unlikely childhood events (e.g., being chased by a bear on a camping trip). After the experimenters had this information, they selected for each participant one of the events that the participant said had not happened to him or her and asked the participant to vividly imagine this event. Two weeks later the participants were given a list of events and asked to rate the likelihood that each event had occurred in their childhood. Among the rated events was the one they previously imagined. Participants rated the imagined event as somewhat more likely than other events that had not occurred but had not been imagined. Imagination inflated the likelihood that the people would say the event happened when in fact, by their own prior admission, it had not.

The conclusions drawn from the Garry et al. experiment are limited by the use of childhood events that are not under experimental control. However unlikely, it is possible that imagining the events reminded participants of real events that did occur, in which case the final ratings would not reflect distorted memory. Goff and Roediger (1998) developed a paradigm to study imagination inflation under controlled circumstances. In the first phase of this paradigm, participants heard commands for action events (e.g., *break the toothpick* or *pick up the pencil from the floor*). Sometimes the participants actually performed the action, sometimes they only imagined performing the action, and sometimes they simply listened to the command. In the second phase of the experiment, participants were asked to imagine performing actions 0, 1, 3, or 5 times. Some of these actions had been in the first phase and some had not. Two weeks later a test was given in which a list of action statements was provided, and the participants had to recognize which of those statements had been presented in the first phase. They were also asked to judge whether the statements they recognized had been performed, imagined, or read. The critical results of the experiment were that the more times an action was imagined in the second phase, the more likely the action was to recognized as having occurred in the first phase, regardless of whether it actually had been present. Equally impressive was that the more times an action was imagined, the more likely it was to be judged as one that was performed, even if that action had only been imagined. Goff and Roediger's experiment demonstrates conclusively that imagining events that never happened can cause people to remember them as having occurred.

Retrieval Can Create False Memory

Memory tests affect later memory for tested material. This testing effect on memory has been known for a long time (Jones, 1923–24) and has been subjected to intensive investigation (Dempster, 1996). Most of the research has focused on the positive benefits of prior testing. Many studies have shown that taking a test provides greater benefit to memory for that material than does additional opportunity to study the material (Hogan & Kintsch, 1971; McDaniel & Masson, 1985). However, testing is now known to also enhance the probability of false memory.

A study by McDermott (1996) nicely illustrates the effect of testing on both veridical and false memories. She asked participants to remember Deese lists where the critical associate was not presented. Participants heard 18 of these lists. After 6 of the lists, participants took a single recall test; after a different 6 lists, three recall tests were given; and after another 6 of the lists, no recall test occurred. Following this initial presentation and testing sequence, a final recall test was administered for all 18 of the lists. The results of this final test are shown in figure 7.5, where you can see that the number of tests affected correct memory for the presented items as well as false memory for the critical items that were not presented. Items, both studied and critical nonstudied, were more likely to be recalled if tested three times than if tested once, and items tested once were more likely to be recalled than items that had not been tested. McDermott's results clearly show both the positive and negative effects of prior testing.

A place in which testing effects are of obvious concern is the classroom. A wrong answer on an exam has the potential to become a false memory that will

FIGURE 7.5
Correct recall of studied items and false recall of critical nonstudied items on a final test as a function of the number of prior tests. (*Adapted from McDermott, 1996.*)

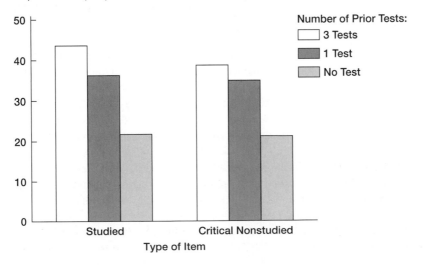

be given in answer to that same question in the future. Indeed, the perseveration of errors made on an initial exam to later tests is a well-documented phenomenon in the education literature (Aiken, 1987). The problem of perseveration errors is less severe on exams that require reproduction of material (e.g., short answer or essay questions) because people are less likely to recall incorrect answers than they are to select them in a recognition test (Koriat & Goldsmith, 1996). Even when incorrect answers are recalled, people tend to have very low confidence that they are correct, and this knowledge appears to protect against the formation of a false memory. Multiple-choice tests, on the other hand, are much more likely to lead to perseveration of errors from the first exam to later exams. Research has consistently shown that the probability of repeating errors on an initial multiple-choice test can equal or even exceed the probability of repeating a correct response (Brainerd, Reyna, & Brandse, 1995).

Of course, there is the hope that feedback following an exam will correct the error and prevent formation of a false memory. As it turns out, eliminating an original error with corrective feedback is not as easy as it may seem. The most effective technique is to provide feedback immediately after each question on an exam, a procedure that would be difficult to implement without computerized testing. But even with this immediate feedback, the errors are substantially reduced only if the second test is given immediately after the first test (Stock, Kulhavy, Pridemore, & Krug, 1992), something that does not happen in the classroom. When feedback was given immediately after each question but the second test occurred one day after the feedback, perseveration errors from the first test were above chance and nearly equaled the repetition of initially correct responses (Kulhavy, Stock, Thorton, Hancock, & Hammrich, 1990). Thus, incorrect answers to a test can lead to false memory, and at the moment, it is not clear how to eliminate the influence of a memory. Research is desperately needed on this problem.

Intervening Events, Eyewitness Accounts, and Distorted Memory

Events that intervene between an experience and memory for that experience are sometimes mistakenly attributed to the original experience. The result is a distorted memory for the original experience. It is not uncommon to have a conversation with someone and then have a similar conversation with someone else and, in remembering the first conversation later, attribute it to the first person. Such distortions can become extremely important in instances such as eyewitness accounts of a crime, where many events relevant to the crime will intervene between the original experience and courtroom testimony.

Elizabeth Loftus (1979) has pioneered laboratory research modeled on the eyewitness situation. Several interesting paradigms have been used to simulate the intervening events that occur between witnessing an event and subsequent testimony in court. For example, Loftus and Palmer (1974) showed subjects a film of an automobile accident and then questioned them about what they had seen. One of the questions was, "About how fast were the cars going when they (*hit, smashed*) each other?" Some of the participants saw the verb *hit* and others saw the verb *smashed*. The participants who were asked in the context of *hit* gave lower estimates of the speed than those asked about *smashing* cars. Furthermore, the participants who saw *smashed* remembered seeing broken glass in the scene; those who saw *hit* generally did not. No broken glass was actually depicted in the movie. The participants in this experiment were influenced by presuppositions invoked by the verbs *hit* and *smashed*. *Smashed* presupposes a more violent collision, a fact that influences both estimate of speed and amount of damage. This presupposition then appears to dramatically but subtly influence memory for the actual event.

The results of Loftus and Palmer's (1974) study are summarized in table 7.3. The table shows the speed estimates depending on the verb used in the question. There are several possible interpretations of these results, and we shall consider two of them. One is simply a response bias interpretation that says that subjects really were uncertain of the speed of the car but biased their estimates in the appropriate direction of the suggestive verb. A second possibility is that the verb actually changed the participant's memory of the scenes in the film. In this case, the participants truly remembered the severity of the accident. Both the *response bias* and *memory change* accounts have important implications for how we might regard the reliability of eyewitness testimony; however, Loftus and Palmer want to interpret the results as being due to an actual alteration in memory.

In a second phase of the experiment, Loftus and Palmer questioned their participants a week later. Here they were asked more questions about the film but were not shown the film again. With the new questions, the critical item was the query, "Did you see any broken glass?" No broken glass was shown in the film and 80 percent of the participants answered "no" correctly. However, the majority of those who answered "yes" were in the "smashed" group. Loftus and Palmer

---

TABLE 7.3
SPEED ESTIMATES FOR CRITICAL QUESTIONS
WITH VARIOUS VERBS AFTER WATCHING FILM
STRIP OF CAR ACCIDENT.

Verb	Average speed estimate (miles/hr.)
Smashed	40.8
Collided	39.3
Bumped	38.1
Hit	34.0
Contacted	31.8

(From "Reconstruction of automobile destruction: An example of the interaction between language and memory" by E. F. Loftus and J. C. Palmer, *Journal of Verbal Learning and Verbal Behavior, 1974 13*, 585–589. Reprinted by permission of the publisher and author.)

conclude that what is being remembered is the *blended* or integrated memory of two events, memory for the original film plus memory for the additional information that is inherent in the question asked later. These two memories are thought to be blended over time so that they are not distinguishable as separate memories. All we have, then, is a single blended memory that is a distortion of the original event.

Loftus, Miller, and Burns (1978) provided another example of the effect of intervening questioning on later memory. Participants saw a staged video depicting a criminal act. For example, one could stage a video depicting a plumber at work in a kitchen where there is a wallet lying on the counter. The plumber is using a pair of pliers when he notices the wallet, and after furtively glancing around, he takes the wallet and places it in his toolbox. After viewing the video, the participants are read a narrative description of the event that contains errors. For example, the narrative might say that the plumber was using a wrench when he took the wallet. Later the participants are given a memory test for the original video where one of the questions could be: *Was the plumber using pliers or a wrench?* People who heard the misleading intervening narrative are more likely to select *wrench* than are people who heard a narrative with a neutral word such as *tool*. These results, along with others we shall describe in chapter 11, demonstrate the distorting effect that intervening events can have on memory for an earlier experience.

One interpretation of this effect is that the intervening event causes the original information to be lost from memory (Loftus & Loftus, 1980). That is, the intervening event replaces the original item in subsequent memory for the event. Another possible interpretation is that the intervening event renders the original information inaccessible (Berkerian & Bowers, 1983). The paradigm is a retroactive interference paradigm in that the intervening material comes after the original experience, thus interfering with access to the original information. Zaragosa and McCloskey (1985) have offered a third possibility in terms of response bias. Zaragosa and McCloskey found no effect of intervening material when they did not use the misleading intervening information in the final test. Using our plumber example, the final test would be a choice between *pliers* and *hammer* rather than between *pliers* and *wrench*. Performance on this test was no worse following misleading intervening material than following neutral intervening material. If the intervening event displaced the original event or made it inaccessible, one would not expect these results.

Zaragosa, McCloskey, and Jamis (1987) suggest that the original studies showing distorted memory from intervening material were contaminated by two sources of response bias. One source is guessing on the final test. Suppose there is no memory for the original information; perhaps the participant did not pay attention to that aspect of the video. The participant then receives the intervening narrative. The misleading narrative says the plumber held a wrench and the neutral narrative says the plumber held a tool. On the final test, suppose the misled participant remembers hearing wrench in the narrative. Presumably, the response will be *wrench*. The participant in the neutral condition who does not remember seeing pliers in the video and who heard tool in the narrative still has a 50/50 chance of correctly guessing pliers on the final test. Thus, the difference in performance would not be due to distortion of the original memory but, rather, to a difference in the chance of correctly guessing the item on the final test.

Another source of bias is that the misled participants simply may believe the experimenter's narrative; that is, on reading the narrative, the participant may remember that pliers were shown in the video but distrust that memory because the experimenter now says it was a wrench. The neutral condition would not have this problem because a tool could be the pliers. Thus, the argument is that memory is not impaired by intervening material, but rather, the paradigm biased performance against the misled condition.

The fate of memory for an original experience following misleading information is an important question over which debate continues. What is clear, however, is that people will report intervening material as part of the original experience. When there is no memory for the requested information in the original experience, it seems highly probable that misleading information that is consistent with the original experience can be mistaken for the original experience. We shall report a case study documenting such an occurrence later in this chapter.

Social Contagion and Distorted Memory

Much of what we believe is the result of the influence from other people, including our beliefs about what occurred in the past. Memory does not occur in a social vacuum. Research concerning social influences on memory has explored both the positive and negative effects of collaboration among people attempting to remember a prior experience. Weldon (2000) discusses results on the interesting question of whether people trying to remember in a group outperform individuals tested alone. If two or three people cooperate on a memory test, their performance exceeds that of a single individual; but if the group performance is compared to the total performance of an equal number of individuals performing alone, the group does worse. This finding suggests that collaboration with others on a memory test disrupts strategies that the individual uses to optimize recall.

Roediger, Meade, and Bergman (2001) discovered that social influences can also increase the probability of false memory. In their experiment, two people participated in each session. One of the people was the real subject of the research and the other was a confederate cooperating with the experimenter. The real subject did not know that the other person was a confederate. The experiment began with participants studying pictures of six common household scenes (e.g., a kitchen). Each scene contained an average of 24 objects that would normally be found in that setting. After the study session, a cued recall test was administered for the objects depicted in each of the scenes. In this test, the subject and the confederate took turns recalling items until each person had produced 6 objects that he or she remembered. The key manipulation was that for half of the scenes, the confederate recalled 2 objects that were not present in the original scene. After this initial test, the subject and confederate were placed in separate rooms and given another cued recall test individually. The important result was that on the final test, the participant recalled a significant number of the false objects produced by the confederate on the original test.

The experiment by Roediger, Meade, and Bergman clearly shows that social contagion can create false memory. As with other instances of false memory, the source of the effect lies in a normal process—in this case the sharing of memories for a common past experience. Much of your interaction with friends and family involves conversation about shared past experience. In the course of this normal social interaction, we can update our memories based on the recollections of other people who shared the experience, but in some cases, the updated memory will be false.

Summary of False Memory

The research discussed in this section delineates circumstances under which memory for a prior experience is demonstrably wrong. Notice that none of these circumstances are out of the ordinary. They involve the normal use of prior knowledge in perception and comprehension, as well as the influence of events that intervene between the original experience and the memory test, including our reflection and imagination of the prior event and discussing the prior event with other people who shared that event. Thus, as startling as it may seem that we sometimes remember things that never happened, the facts of memory distortion can be explained without appealing to abnormal or even unusual psychological processes.

Perhaps the most important lesson we learn from research on memory distortion is that memory is not at all like a mechanical recording device. The original experience is not stored as some veridical trace of what was out there but, rather, is the result of interpretive processes of perception and comprehension. Retrieval processes construct the memory experience from a myriad of prior influences, including some that were not due to the original event. We have encountered similar situations in our previous discussion of autobiographical memory in chapter 5 and unconscious influences in chapter 6. The intriguing picture of memory that emerges is one of a powerful, adaptively important, and usually reliable psychological process that sometimes is completely wrong.

THE COGNITIVE NEUROSCIENCE OF MEMORY DISTORTION

Understanding the neural basis of memory distortion requires that one understand how the brain initially builds memories at encoding and later reconstructs those memories at retrieval. As you might expect, the specific details of these functions are quite complex, involving the interaction of numerous neural regions as well as the operation of neurochemical mechanisms that are just beginning to be understood. For detailed accounts of our current understanding of these regions and mechanisms, the reader is directed to the following sources (Buckner & Wheeler, 2001; Damasio, 1989; Eichenbaum, 2002; O'Reilly & Rudy, 2000; Squire, 1992; Squire & Kandel, 1999; Ungerleider, 1995). Here, we give a general account in order to provide a heuristic framework for understanding how and why memory distortions arise (see also Schacter et al., 1998, 1998).

Episodic experiences are composed of multiple features, the encoding of which involves neural activity that is widely distributed throughout the brain. Consider, for example, a simple event such as sitting in a classroom listening to a professor tell you a new fact. A subset of the features making up this event, along with the neural regions that process these features, might include the following: the objects in the room, such as the furniture, the clock, the professor, and other students (occipitotemporal "what" pathway); the specific identity of certain people (anterior regions of the temporal lobes, far along the "what" pathway); the locations of these people and objects (occipitoparietal pathway); what the professor is saying (speech comprehension area in the left superior temporal lobe); and what that information means (frontal lobes areas interacting with semantic regions). The event also includes psychological features such as how you feel about the information (amygdala) and how you feel in general (e.g., whether your chair is uncomfortable—somatosensory areas in the parietal lobe), along with mnemonic features concerning what the information reminds you of (such as an earlier lecture or something you heard on television—hippocampus plus other areas). Finally, the event includes any actions you are performing while listening to the lecture, such as writing the new fact in your notebook (motor areas in the frontal lobes along with subcortical motor structures).

As you can see, even a simple event is made of numerous features and associated patterns of neural activity that, together, define the event. Understanding memory encoding in the brain basically boils down to the question of how this widely distributed pattern of activity becomes integrated, or "bound" together, so that it can be reactivated at a later time, and the related question of how one bound event is made distinct from other events. As we noted in the previous chapter, the hippocampus appears to play a key role in such mnemonic binding, essentially providing a code that links all of these separate features (patterns of activity) together. Although the exact nature of this code is unknown, it can be thought of as a memory index, similar to that in a computer, that provides an address for the patterns of activity making up the original event. Of course, the binding function of the hippocampus helps explains why damage to this structure results in anterograde amnesia, the inability to form (bind together) new memories. However, even without hippocampal damage, small variations in how events are bound at encoding can still make one susceptible to memory distortions. We will describe such susceptibility in more detail in a moment. But first, let's consider how the brain retrieves (or, more accurately, reconstructs) this event at a later time.

Just as understanding neural encoding involves understanding how dispersed patterns of brain activity are initially bound together, understanding retrieval essentially boils down to how the brain is able to reactivate patterns of activity (or *partial* patterns of activity) that correspond to some earlier event (or *aspects* of that event). Such reactivation can be thought of as a process of pattern completion initiated by retrieval cues (which provide a partial pattern) and completed by the binding code stored in the hippocampus (which reactivates widely dispersed processing areas), all of which is coordinated by executive process in the frontal lobes. For example, consider a retrieval cue provided by an absent student, such as, "What did Professor Toth say about episodic memory today?" Such a cue refers to information in the original event; thus, processing this cue produces a pattern of neural activation that partially overlaps with the activation that occurred in that event—activation related to your perception and knowledge of Professor Toth, the time and location of today's lecture, and the topic of memory. Coupled with the goal of remembering a specific aspect of this (now partially activated) event, the hippocampus uses its binding code to reactivate other aspects of the event (such as what the good Professor said about memory), allowing you to help out your truant friend.

Note that this account is essentially saying that to remember is to reactivate the pattern of activity that was occurring when the earlier event was initially happening. In this sense, remembering can be thought of as less like *retrieving* the past and more like *re-living* it. Importantly, however, one's goals during remembering are almost always different from one's goals during the original event, and the contents of one's consciousness (working memory) are typically different as well. Furthermore, one usually is not trying to remember every aspect of a prior event (such as how comfortable your chair was) but, instead, only particular, goal-relevant aspects (such as what was said about episodic memory). All of these factors help to ensure that one does not get "lost in the past" when remembering. Nevertheless, our understanding of the brain suggests that remembering involves recreating patterns of neural activity that are very similar to the patterns that occurred when the event was initially experienced.

There are three other points to note about this reactivation account, each of which relates to the possibility of memory distortion. The first point is that during encoding, the hippocampus will bind together any pattern of activity that occurs during the event. Thus, you might not want to later remember that Professor Toth was wearing a particularly ugly tie this morning, but if you attend to his tie and make that (hopefully silent) observation—thereby producing corresponding patterns of neural activation—the hippocampus will bind these patterns together with the rest of the event. This example highlights another fact: not only does the hippocampus bind together external (perceived) aspects of the event, it also binds internal (mental) aspects such as thoughts and images. This fact helps to explain why sometimes we can't tell the difference between what we did and what we just thought we did (such as locking the front door). The important point is that the hippocampus appears to be a relatively "dumb" mechanism, binding together any neural activity that is ongoing during an event. Thus, to the extent that expectations, assumptions, and inferences are considered (thus producing associated patterns of neural activity), these psychological features can get bound together with the rest of the event, leading you to remember things that did not really happen.

The second point to note is that access to the appropriate binding code in the hippocampus, and thus recreation of the original pattern of activity, will depend on how well the retrieval cue specifies the prior event. If the cue is too broad, more than one code might be accessed, while if the cue is ill-formed or misleading, incorrect codes may be activated. Consider, for example, being at a party when a fellow student walks up and says, "What did Professor Toth say?" In the absence of an appropriate context to better focus the student's request, your response to such an inquiry might be something like, "what did he say *when*?" or "to *whom*?" or "about *what*?" In cognitive terms, we might say that the retrieval cue given was too broad and, thus, was nondiagnostic of the any specific prior event. In neural terms, we could say that the cue activated too many binding codes related to Professor Toth, with the result being that too many incongruent details come to mind; or, more likely, that nothing comes to mind because you resist querying your memory until an appropriately diagnostic (code-specific) retrieval cue is available.

The third point is that when trying to remember the past, people do not always just accept what comes to mind as being the truth about some earlier event. Instead, decision processes dependent on the frontal lobes act to monitor and evaluate what comes to mind in order to check whether it "makes sense". For example, if an image of your best friend comes to mind when asked about today's lecture, you might think twice about accepting this information if you also know that your friend left on a skiing trip two days ago. The point is that remembering is not only about gaining access to particular pieces of information but also involves a process of relating those pieces to each other, as well as to general information about what "could have been" or "should have been." Which is to say that remembering is as much a construction as it is a reproduction.

By now you should be getting some ideas about how memory distortion can arise from the neural mechanisms underlying both encoding and retrieval. Consider, first, encoding. Although the binding of memories at encoding is generally quite good, a variety of factors—including fatigue, stress, and lapses of attention—can produce less than perfect binding. Thus, for example, if one element of an event (e.g., the presence of pliers) was not tightly bound to the rest of the event (perhaps because of a lapse of attention), your ability to remember this detail will be compromised. Moreover, such imperfect binding could also open the door to an imagined or suggested object being more strongly bound to the original event. This might be especially likely if you experience an event that is very similar to the original but that contains a misleading feature; and if the misleading event occurs close in time to the original event, thereby taxing the ability of the hippocampus to provide distinct binding codes for the two events.

Inadequate binding at encoding can also interact with retrieval processes, depending on the specificity of the memory cue. Thus, if a retrieval cue is too broad, more than one hippocampal binding code may be accessed, resulting in information coming to mind from multiple prior events. Although we are often able to detect such "multiple activations," at times the things that come to mind may fit together so neatly that they make perfect sense, resulting in a remembered experience that actually contains elements blended from two or more prior events.

Finally, failures in decision (sense-making) processes, at retrieval may also result in false memories by biasing the nuances of what we remember. Thus, if asked how fast the cars were going when they "smashed" together, a relatively slow speed might come to mind; but such a slow speed would not be consistent with other aspects of the situation—such as the "fact" that they smashed together. Similarly, if asked if there was broken glass at the scene of the accident, the retrieval cue sent to the hippocampus might partially activate binding codes related to more than one car accident (including ones involving broken glass). If a fleeting image of broken glass comes to mind, you might believe that this image was indeed from the accident in question; this might be even more likely if the retrieval cue mentioned the cars "smashing together," as now the image of broken glass would make sense and thus more easily "slip past" your monitoring and evaluation processes. It is widely agreed that such processes are dependent on frontal lobe functions because patients with frontal damage have been known to "remember" false, and sometimes fantastic, accounts of their personal lives—a phenomenon known as *confabulation.* Generally, confabulations are a confusing mixture of fragmentary events from the patient's past, thus appearing to reflect a failure to appropriately cue memory and to evaluate the reasonableness of the information retrieved.

To summarize, episodic experiences contain multiple features (perceptions, thoughts, feelings, and actions) that activate widely dispersed regions of the brain. The hippocampus acts to integrate these features into an episodic memory by creating a binding code that links together the different patterns of neural activity associated with these features. Retrieval (reconstruction) of a memory starts with a retrieval cue that activates a subset of this earlier pattern of activity; and, coupled with the goal of remembering (directed by the frontal lobes), a binding code in the hippocampus is accessed that reactivates additional patterns of activity corresponding to other aspects of the earlier event, aspects that were not part of the retrieval cue. These reactivated patterns result in information coming to mind—information that can be thought of as candidates for what might have occurred in the original event. These candidates are subjected to evaluation by frontal lobe processes that decide whether what is coming to mind actually makes sense as being part of the event. Memory distortion occurs when fleeting or fragmentary images or thoughts get bound to the event but not strongly enough to later signal their origin as thoughts rather then real events. Memory distortion can also occur when the original event is inadequately bound, allowing different but similar events to get confused (or bound up) with the sought-after event. Finally, memory distortion also occurs when monitoring processes fail to appropriately evaluate the information that is retrieved; or when such processes are used to "fill in" details from other, similar memories, or from general knowledge—details that seem logical, but were not truly experienced.

APPLICATION OF FALSE MEMORY RESEARCH

Research on memory distortion is relevant to important social issues. In fact, much of the research on perseveration errors in repeated testing was motivated by concerns about classroom testing. Two other directly relevant situations are eyewitness testimony and therapy centered on recovering past memories. In both of these cases, the issue is the validity of the memory that the witness or patient comes to believe. The importance of this issue is that when these memories are reported, they tend to be believed by other people who have no means of determining the veracity of the memory. If these other people happen to be police, prosecutors, and juries, the consequences can be severe.

A Forensic Case Study

With the availability of DNA testing, we now have evidence that eyewitness testimony in criminal trials can be based on distorted memory. In 1996, the United States Department of Justice reported the results of an investigation of 28 cases in which persons convicted of serious crimes were subsequently exonerated on the basis of DNA evidence (Connors, Lundregan, Miller, & McEwan, 1996). In the majority of the cases, the most compelling evidence presented at trial was eyewitness testimony. Importantly, the cases selected for study were ones in which there were no trial errors or evidence that the witnesses were fabricating their testimony. In retrospect, we can see that these were all instances of distorted memory from the eyewitness.

A vivid example of such a case was provided in a broadcast by the Public Broadcasting System (1997). A woman was raped. She was subsequently shown a photo lineup of several men. The woman initially made a very tentative identification of one of the photos, saying she wasn't at all certain but that he might be the perpetrator. She subsequently was shown additional photo lineups and then one physical lineup. The critical feature of these lineups was that the person she hesitantly identified in the first lineup appeared in all subsequent lineups, while the other people changed in each lineup. With each succeeding test, the woman became more confident that he was the perpetrator and eventually identified him with certainty. Although there was no physical evidence to link the suspect to the crime, the victim's testimony at trial was sufficient for conviction, and the man received a life sentence. More than a decade later, DNA evidence positively excluded the suspect and he was released.

The events surrounding this case illustrate the powerful influence of some of the variables we have discussed. The intervening events of repeated lineups with one person as the only constant in those lineups led to a feeling of familiarity, which was eventually attributed to the person being the rapist. The victim's own account of her current memory of the original episode indicates just how powerful these effects can be. She has stated that, despite her knowledge that the man she helped convict was not her attacker, he is the man she remembers when she recalls the attack. This account of her subjective experience is particularly intriguing in light of the fact that the actual rapist was subsequently identified and confessed to committing the crime. Thus, the victim has now seen the man who attacked her but does not recognize him as her attacker. The victim knows who raped her, but as the result of the original recognition tests, she remembers someone else. False memories do not disappear after we know they are false.

The Memory Problem in Clinical Practice

The linkage between memory and psychopathology has a long history, but beginning in the 1980s, a sensational and controversial issue has arisen. The issue revolves around the possibility of memory distortion resulting from therapeutic practice. The therapy in question involves exhuming memories of childhood abuse, usually sexual in nature, so that the client can confront those memories. Such therapy is based on the claim that the memories have been repressed from consciousness and are the cause of problems such as depression, anxiety disorder, eating disorder, and substance abuse. Consequently, the appropriate therapy, it is claimed, is to bring the memories into consciousness and then to confront the perpetrators of the abuse.

The claims that motivate this therapy are loosely related to Freud's theory (Kihlstrom, 1998). Freud maintained that a variety of neurotic disorders were the result of repressed memory for childhood trauma. The affect associated with the repressed memory theoretically expressed itself in the form of various symptoms that could only be relieved by bringing the memory to consciousness and reconnecting the affect with that memory. Then, the patient could deal rationally with the feelings aroused by the previously repressed memory. All of this is easier said than done. Because the memory is actively repressed according to the theory, the patient cannot directly access it. Thus, the therapist must use indirect means to gain access to the memory. For Freud, the techniques included hypnosis and projective tools such as free association and dream analysis. The critical point is that the theory stipulates that the therapist be actively involved in suggesting the importance and reality of the repressed memory to the patient. Furthermore, in the initial stages of therapy, the therapist has to interpret the patient's thoughts and impulses as if they reflect the content of the repressed memory. Keep in mind that the repressed memory is a theoretical hypothesis, but the entire therapy is based on gathering evidence confirming that hypothesis.

Freud eventually abandoned the assumption that childhood sexual abuse was a significant factor causing adult neurosis, but the assumption has been resurrected by some clinicians. Thus, this therapy begins with the suggestion to the patient that a repressed incident of abuse may be the cause of the patient's problem and proceeds by attempting to recover the memory. The patient is encouraged to imagine scenes from childhood and to describe whatever can be remembered, and the therapist assists in interpreting the real childhood memories to reveal the repressed elements of abuse. In many instances, the patient eventually does remember horrible events.

The situation contains virtually all of the elements we have previously described from laboratory research that can produce memory distortion. Add to the suggestive nature of the therapy and the frequent use of imagination the fact that the cultural atmosphere supports the recovery of these memories through the widespread belief that large numbers of people have been sexually abused. The popular print media and television talk shows feast on lurid accounts of such memory, usually without any serious, critical analysis of the phenomenon. Thus, it would not be surprising if in some cases the recovered memory is actually false. This fact in and of itself would not be troublesome except that the therapist usually instructs the patient to confront the abuser. In cases where the accused denies the abuse, the patient's relationship with friends and family may be inappropriately disrupted, and if the matter is pursued legally, people may be unjustly accused.

There is no easy solution to this dilemma. Unfortunately, childhood abuse does occur, and people do suffer the aftermath of those events. When independent, objective evidence corroborates the accusation, the matter should be pursued in the courts. However, it is also the case that these memories can be false. Numerous instances are now available of people recanting memories recovered in therapy and subsequently suing the therapist (Pendergrast, 1995). As is the case with eyewitness testimony, it is not always possible to know whether a memory is recovered accurately or is in fact totally false. What we can do, however, is use the information from research on memory distortion to judiciously assess cases in which someone claims to have recovered a memory of a childhood event.

SUMMARY

As powerful and adaptive as human memory is, it is not perfect. You well know that we sometimes are unable to retrieve memory for events that were encoded. Four mechanisms that have been proposed to explain forgetting were discussed: decay, interference, cue-dependent forgetting, and inhibition. Although there are similarities among these theories, each has unique implications for the fate of forgotten information. Decay and inhibition suggest that forgetting is due to changes in the representation of the to-be-remembered information. According to decay theory, the information is gone, whereas the inhibitory approach suggests that the information is momentarily suppressed. Interference and cue-dependent theories emphasize the relationship between the cue and the to-be-remembered information as the cause of forgetting. For these two theories, the problem of forgetting can be surmounted with changes in the cue.

A second form of memory failure occurs when we clearly remember an event, but the memory is distorted. False memories can result from confusion among events, in which case we remember details of an event that were actually from a different event. We also remember events that never occurred. This bizarre phenomenon frequently is caused by the normal operation of perception, comprehension, and retrieval. The processes of perception and comprehension actively add information to what was available, and this added information sometimes is remembered as what really happened. The process of retrieval operates not only what is available from the to-be-remembered experience but also draws from general knowledge and other past experience. From these sources, memory is constructed. Occasionally, the constructed memory is totally false in that nothing resembling that memory ever actually happened. As research on false memory progresses, we are closer to understanding the factors that produce inaccurate memories that nonetheless are confidently expressed by the rememberer; as the result, cognitive psychology can contribute to important social issues involving false memory.

THOUGHT QUESTIONS

1. What are the similarities and differences between decay and inhibition theories of forgetting?
2. What empirical finding necessitated the concept of unlearning in interference theory?
3. Why does response competition lead to forgetting, according to interference theory and according to inhibition theory?
4. How can the normal processes of comprehension produce false memory?
5. In the course of a police investigation into a crime, what might happen in the way of intervening events and social contagion to distort the memory of an eyewitness to the crime?

8

METACOGNITION

METACOGNITION

When you read a chapter in this text in preparation for an upcoming test, a host of cognitive processes act in a coordinated fashion, many of which have already been discussed: you must direct attention to reading while selectively inhibiting irrelevant channels of information such as noise from a television program in the background; in doing so, you may direct attention toward the meaning of the content, so as to reap the benefits of a deep level of processing; and you may decide to organize the content in a meaningful way, being careful to distinguish between similar concepts so as to take advantage of organizational and distinctive processing that may help you minimize interference during retrieval. Certainly, as you become more successful at engaging these cognitive processes, you will become a more effective learner and will perform better on the class tests.

Even so, intuition suggests that more than just these cognitive processes are recruited while you are studying. While reading the previous chapter titled "Forgetting and False Memory," you may have decided to turn off the television because you have *knowledge about* the effects of divided attention, including that some signals from the TV program can grab your attention and make reading more difficult. You may have occasionally *monitored* how well you were learning a section from the chapter, such as by asking yourself, How well am I comprehending interference theory? or by using the end-of-the-chapter questions to evaluate your progress. Outcomes from such monitoring processes then may help you *control,* or regulate, your learning. For instance, you may have decided that you did not entirely understand inhibition theory and, hence, reread its description or sought advice from a classmate. Along with the other cognitive processes involved in learning, accurate knowledge about cognition and effective monitoring and control are ostensibly important for effective learning.

Although these activities are in themselves cognitive in nature, they are not considered core properties of cognition. For instance, monitoring presumably relies upon symbolic mental activities, and theories about monitoring are based on many of the same principles (and evaluated by many of the same scientific methods) as other core properties of cognition, such as memory and attention. Nevertheless, knowledge about cognition, monitoring, and control are not considered cognitive per se, but instead fall under the rubric of metacognition.

DEFINING METACOGNITION: KNOWLEDGE, MONITORING, AND CONTROL

The origin of the term *metacognition* has often been attributed to John Flavell, who has largely explored metacognition in the context of cognitive development (Flavell, 1979; for a history of metacognition, see Hacker, 1998). In general, metacognition refers to people's "cognition about cognitive phenomena" (Flavell, 1979, p. 906). The idea is that some cognitive states and processes are about (or act upon) other cognitive states and processes. "Meta" can refer to any aspect of cognition, such as metalanguage (cognitions about language) and metacomprehension (cognition about comprehension). In the present chapter, we will explore in some detail advances in our understanding of *metamemory* or cognitions about memory and learning.

Three aspects of metamemory have most often been the focus of enquiry: *knowledge, monitoring,* and *control.* As you learn about various aspects of cognition from this book, you have greatly enhanced your knowledge about memory, which pertains to *metacognitive knowledge.* Metacognitive knowledge concerns people's declarative knowledge about memory and may include implicit and sometimes inaccurate beliefs. For instance, some adults believe their learning ability has declined more dramatically in old age than it actually has (Hertzog & Hultsch, 2000). Knowledge about memory has most often been measured by having individuals answer questions that explicitly pertain to their beliefs about how memory functions (Gilewski, Zelinski, & Schaie, 1990; Hermann, 1982; Kreutzer, Leonard, & Flavell, 1975).

Monitoring involves assessing the current state or ongoing progress of any aspect of learning and retrieval. For instance, while studying for an exam, you may assess how well you are learning each section of your class notes, and while taking the exam, you may assess whether your response to each question is correct. Memory monitoring has typically been measured by having individuals make subjective judgments about memory while they are learning or retrieving information.

Control involves the regulation of ongoing learning and retrieval processes. Examples of control are when you regulate learning by deciding to stop studying a section of your notes that you believe you know well, and when you decide to keep trying to retrieve an answer to a test question even when you cannot initially recall it. Control has typically been measured by allowing individuals to regulate their learning and by exploring the products of such regulation, such as the amount of time used to study difficult versus easy materials and how long individuals persist at trying to retrieve information from memory.

Although all three concepts—knowledge, monitoring, and control—are core to metacognition, we will focus mainly on the latter two concepts, which have received growing attention in the past four decades from experimental psychologists interested in adult cognition. As eluded to above, monitoring processes and control processes may occur at any stage of learning: during encoding, during the retention interval when one needs to maintain what had been learned, and during retrieval. As depicted in figure 8.1 (adapted from Nelson & Narens, 1990), monitoring and control are tapped by different measures at each stage (which are described in detail below). During encoding, monitoring has often been measured by judgments of learning, and control has been measured by the termination of study. During retrieval, monitoring has been measured both by feeling-of-knowing judgments and by confidence judgments, and control has been measured by the initiation and termination of search. Note, too, that some

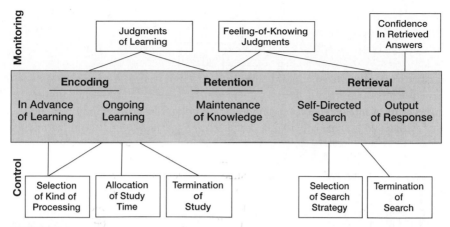

FIGURE 8.1
Encoding (learning), retention, and retrieval illustrated with some corresponding components of measures of monitoring and control. (*Adapted from Nelson and Narens (1990). Nelson, T. O., & Narens, L. (1990). Metamemory: a theoretical framework and new findings. In G. H. Bower (Ed.),* The psychology of learning and motivation, *vol. 26, (pp. 125–173). Copyright by New York: Academic Press. Used by permission of author and publisher.*)

highly investigated metacognitive judgments (such as reality-monitoring judgments and tip-of-the-tongue judgments) are not represented in this figure but are considered elsewhere in this textbook.

Because monitoring provides a central input to control processes, we turn first to memory monitoring by introducing judgments that have been used to measure it. We then move on to consider prominent hypotheses about how people make these judgments.

KINDS OF JUDGMENT ABOUT MEMORY

Consider a straightforward investigation of the monitoring of episodic memories, which is illustrated in the top panel of figure 8.2 along with some responses from a hypothetical participant. During study, participants try to learn 12 paired associates, such as vocabulary items from a French course (e.g., chien–dog, cuiller—spoon, singe—monkey). Each pair is presented individually at a fixed rate (e.g., 6 seconds per pair). Study is followed by a brief retention interval, which itself is followed by paired-associate recall in which each stimulus (e.g., chien—?) is presented and participants are asked to recall the corresponding response (i.e., dog). Finally, the recall trial may be followed by a recognition test in which each stimulus (e.g., chien) is presented once more with two alternatives—e.g., (a) monkey, (b) dog—and participants attempt to choose the correct response.

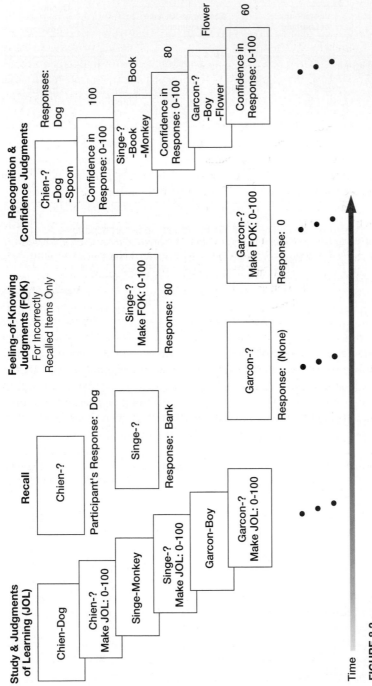

FIGURE 8.2
Stages of an investigation of monitoring judgments for episodic memories, including judgments of learning at study, feeling-of-knowing judgments for incorrectly recalled items, and confidence judgments during a test of recognition.

To assess memory monitoring during this experiment, researchers have participants make subjective judgments during each phase of the experiment. These judgments are also depicted in figure 8.2 below the corresponding phase of the experiment. Sometime after studying a particular item, participants are asked to make a *judgment of learning* (JOL), which is a rating of the likelihood of correctly recalling a given item on the criterion test (in this case, paired-associate recall). The judgments are often made on a percentage likelihood scale (i.e., 0-100 percent, where 0 means no likelihood of recalling the correct response, 20 means a 20 percent chance of recalling the correct response, and so forth to 100, which means absolute certainty in recalling the response). Other scales have been used, but the important point is that participants rate the subjective confidence in correctly recalling each response. After paired-associate recall, participants may also be asked to make *feeling-of-knowing* (FOK) judgments, which have traditionally been limited to those items that were not correctly recalled. In particular, participants rate the likelihood that they will later correctly recognize the correct response during the test of recognition. Finally, during the test of recognition, participants may make *confidence judgments* after they choose an alternative, which involves rating the likelihood that the alternative chosen is actually the correct one.

This procedure yields a rich set of data that can be used to investigate people's monitoring of learning and retrieval. A protocol from one participant is presented in the top half of table 8.1, which shows hypothetical outcomes for the judgments and performance on the criterion tests. We will refer back to this protocol when discussing typical analyses from the metacognitive literature.

As implied by Nelson and Narens' (1990) framework (figure 8.1), one reason for exploring these judgments is that they provide an indirect measure of people's

TABLE 8.1
PROTOCOL FROM A SINGLE PARTICIPANT

Item	Judgment of learning	Recall	Feeling of knowing	Recognition	Confidence judgment
chien–dog	80	1 (correct)	—	1	100
cuiller–spoon	60	1	—	1	80
livre–book	40	1	—	1	100
tapis–rug	60	1	—	1	80
banque–bank	60	0 (incorrect)	100	1	100
cheval–horse	40	0	60	1	60
plage–beach	60	0	20	0	80
singe–monkey	0	0	80	0	80
fleur–flower	40	0	0	0	60
porc–pork	80	0	80	0	60
garson–boy	60	0	0	0	60
fromage–cheese	20	0	20	0	20
Mean %	52	33	45	50	7

(continued)

TABLE 8.1   (continued)
PROTOCOL FROM A SINGLE PARTICIPANT

KINDS OF JUDGMENT ACCURACY

Relative accuracy is the correlation across items between a participant's judgments and performance on the relevant criterion test.

Absolute accuracy is often computed as the difference between mean judgements and mean performance on the relevant criterion test. Calibration curves are also used to assess absolute accuracy—see text for illustrations.

ANALYSES OF PARTICIPANT'S PROTOCOL

	Criterion test	Relative accuracy	Absolute accuracy
Judgement of learning	Recall	+.50	+19
Feeling of knowing	Recognition	+.67	−5
Confidence	Recognition	+.86	+23

monitoring of underlying states of cognition, in this case of memory and learning. That is, in order to make a given rating, an individual presumably monitors some aspect of memory and then translates this monitoring into a specific point on the rating scale. Accordingly, these judgments partly reflect an individual's introspections about his or her memory. In contrast to turn of the century introspectionism that was admonished by behaviorists (Watson, 1925), however, contemporary researchers do not assume that these judgments validly assess learning and retrieval (Nelson & Narens, 1994). For instance, if a person claims that he or she is 100% certain of remembering the pair "cuiller—spoon," his or her JOL is not *a priori* assumed to reflect that the pair has been well learned. Instead, researchers directly evaluate the validity of each kind of judgment by comparing it to an objective measure of memory performance. Such a comparison pertains to the *accuracy* of the judgments, or the degree to which the judgments accurately reflect performance on the relevant criterion test. For instance, in the example above, JOLs would be compared to performance on the test of paired-associate recall (see bottom panel of table 8.1 for a list of judgments and the corresponding criterion tests).

Another important reason for investigating judgments about memory is that their accuracy is critical for effective control. The more accurately an individual evaluates learning and retrieval, the more effective he or she will be at controlling them (Koriat & Goldsmith, 1996; Thiede, 1999). For instance, if you could perfectly judge which sections of this chapter you will versus will not remember, you could then effectively control your extra study time by focusing only on those sections that you will not remember. Thus, discovering how people make monitoring judgments and how to ensure that those judgments are highly accurate have important applied implications, especially for students who want to more efficiently achieve high grades in their classes.

In the following sections, we briefly discuss these metacognitive judgments by describing some key findings that highlight whether students are accurate at making each one. After this introduction, we then consider hypotheses about how the judgments are made that also provide insight into the loci of judgment accuracy.

Judgments of Learning (JOLs)

In the seminal research on JOLs, Arbuckle and Cuddy (1969) argued that if paired associates "differed in associative strengths immediately following presentation, people should be able to detect these differences just as they can detect differences in strength of any other input signal" (p. 126). To evaluate this claim about monitoring, they had two college students study short lists of paired associates, and as each pair was presented, the students judged whether they would successfully recall it. The accuracy of the students' JOLs was greater than chance. In other words, Arbuckle and Cuddy (1969) established that students' JOLs had some validity at predicting recall. However, their measure of accuracy did not provide an estimate of the *level* of accuracy.

Estimating the level of accuracy is possible by correlating an individual's judgments with performance on the criterion test. This correlation provides a measure of *relative* accuracy or *resolution* because the correlation indicates the degree to which the judgments accurately assess the level of test performance of one item relative to another. For instance, let's say that you were studying the chapter titled "Attention," and you predicted that you would remember the definition of late selection but would not remember the definition of early selection. If on the exam you in fact performed well on questions about late selection and poorly on questions about early selection, then your predictions—or JOLs—have good relative accuracy. To compute relative accuracy, a correlation is computed between each participants' judgments and criterion performance (for discussions of methods and measures of estimating relative accuracy, see Nelson, 1984, and Weaver, 1990). The correlation can range from -1 to $+1$. A correlation of 0 indicates that the judgments have no predictive accuracy; that is, the accuracy of the judgments is at a chance level. In this case, you might as well flip a coin to decide whether an item will be remembered. Increasing correlations—from 0 up to $+1.0$—indicate higher and higher levels of accuracy. As shown in table 8.1, the correlation between the hypothetical JOLs and recall was $+.50$, indicating above chance (i.e., greater than 0) accuracy. Contemporary reports that include correlational measures are consistent with conclusions from Arbuckle and Cuddy (1969) in that the mean across individual correlations is usually greater than 0, indicating that accuracy is above chance, but does not usually exceed $+.50$. Put differently, college students can accurately predict memory performance for simple paired-associate materials but also have plenty of room for improvement.

BOX 8.1

HOW ACCURATE ARE JURORS AT PREDICTING THEIR MEMORY OF A TRIAL?

People's confidence in their memories often influences how others react to them. For instance, an eyewitness who is extremely confident in her memory that she saw the defendant at the scene of the crime may be viewed as more credible to jurors than an eyewitness who is less confident in her memory, Of course, such beliefs in credibility may be misplaced because extreme confidence in memory can result from many factors other than good memory and hence would reflect overconfidence (for captivating, real-life examples of eyewitness overconfidence, see Loftus & Ketcham, 1991).

While deliberating the innocence of a defendant, jurors often rely upon memories for the trial, and the most confident jurors are likely to have the largest impact during the deliberation (Kassin & Wrightsman, 1988). Such reliance on others' memory would be entirely acceptable assuming each juror's memory monitoring was highly accurate. But are juror's metacognitive judgments accurate about their memory for a trial? Pritchard and Keenan (1999) evaluated the accuracy of mock jurors' memory. Participants viewed an edited video-tape of an actual murder trial. Afterward each participant made a judgment of learning in which they rated how well he or she would remember what occurred in the trial. Thus *global* JOL differed somewhat from the JOLs described in the text (which are made for every item that is studied) because the former involved making only one judgment about how well the jurors would do *overall* on a memory test of the trial. This global JOL is like telling a friend how well you think you will do on an upcoming test, such as, that you think you will get about 80 percent (or a B) correct. Finally, the mock jurors attempted to answer 30 questions about the trial and made a confidence judgment for each question.

The main measure was a correlation computed across jurors' global JOLs and performance. In two experiments, this correlation was near zero, indicating that jurors who believed they knew the most actually did not! Accordingly, Pritchard and Keenan (1999) concluded "that those jurors who are likely to participate the most and have the highest impact on the verdict may not be the most accurate" (p. 161), which is an unfortunate implication of jurors' poor predictive accuracy that certainly deserves further exploration.

Nelson and Dunlosky (1991) observed that in nearly every experiment on JOLs, each judgment was collected for an item immediately after the item had been studied. When studying vocabulary for an exam, immediately after studying "cuiller—spoon," you would judge whether you will remember it on the upcoming exam. They called these *immediate* JOLs and directly contrasted them with *delayed* JOLs. For the latter, you would first study all of the vocabulary terms on a page of the text and then return to the first one to make the JOL, so that the JOLs are delayed after study. In Nelson and Dunlosky (1991), all judgments were prompted by only the stimulus of a pair. If you had studied "cuiller—spoon," then you would view only "cuiller" to make the judgment. Accuracy was substantially less for immediate JOLs (mean across individual participant's correlations = +.38) than for delayed JOLs, which yielded close to perfect levels of accuracy (mean = +.90).

This delayed-JOL effect—in which accuracy is greater for delayed than immediate JOLs—has been replicated numerous times. Also, beyond the typical college student who is the modal participant in cognitive research, quite high levels of accuracy for delayed JOLs have also been achieved by second and fourth graders (Schneider, Vise, Lockl, & Nelson, 2001), for adults who are in their 70s (Connor, Dunlosky, & Hertzog, 1997), and even for individuals with traumatic brain injury (Kennedy & Yorkston, 2000). Obtaining such high levels of monitoring accuracy promises to support effective learning for individuals of all ages (Hertzog, 2002).

Feeling-of-Knowing (FOK) Judgments

Hart (1965) pioneered methods that provided the foundations for contemporary research on metacognitive monitoring. What made his efforts groundbreaking was the insight to validate people's judgments against relevant criterion. In particular, his method included three phases—recall, judgment, and recognition—which he referred to as the RJR method. During recall, college students attempted to answer general-knowledge questions similar to the ones used in a game like Trivial Pursuit, such as "Who wrote *The Plague*?" Can you recall the answer? If not, you may feel that you know the correct answer even though you cannot recall it. Most people have this feeling quite often, and when it is strong, we often say the answer is on the "tip of the tongue." But are these feelings accurate? To find out, for each general-knowledge question that a student did not answer, he made a FOK judgment by stating whether the correct answer would be identified on the upcoming test of recognition. After the recall and judgment phases, the students attempted to recognize the correct answer for each question from a set of three incorrect alternatives (e.g., a. Sartre, b. Camus, c. Gide, d. Genet). Hart (1965) found that the accuracy of FOK judgments was above chance at predicting performance on the recognition tests.

Contemporary research on FOK judgments has also estimated the level of relative accuracy under numerous conditions. In table 8.1, the level of relative accuracy for the participants' FOK judgment is +.67. As with Hart's (1965, 1967) research, FOK accuracy is usually above chance and typically ranges between +.35 and +.60, even for 6-year olds and adults in their 70s and 80s (Butterfield, Nelson, & Peck, 1988). That FOK judgments show any accuracy whatsoever is quite mysterious because it indicates that people are able to predict recognition of answers when in fact they are not able to recall them. How does an individual know whether he or she knows the correct response when it cannot be recalled? Such a mystery has intrigued many researchers and has made FOK judgments one of the most intensely investigated metacognitive judgments. Accordingly, we will discuss research on FOK judgments in some detail when we turn our attention to hypotheses of how people make metacognitive judgments.

Confidence Judgments

When taking a class exam, have you ever put a mark beside answers that you think may be wrong so that you could return to them to think more deeply about the alternative answers? If so, you are rating your confidence in your answers, which is another kind of metacognitive judgment that has received attention in the field. Of course, if your confidence judgments are not accurate, then you may not change answers that are incorrect, and even worse, you may change answers that you believe are wrong but that were originally correct.

How accurate are students' confidence judgments? A method often used to investigate confidence judgments is to have participants attempt to answer general-knowledge questions in a multiple-choice format: What city is the capital of North Carolina? (a) Raleigh or (b) Charlotte. A participant would choose an answer and then provide a confidence judgment, such as from 50% (I'm guessing; because if you are guessing, there is a 50% chance that you'd choose the correct answer) to 100% (I'm 100% sure I chose the correct answer). As with the relative accuracy of the hypothetical participant in table 8.1 (accuracy $= +.86$), in most cases the relative accuracy of these judgments is above chance. That is, as participants provide higher and higher confidence judgments, the likelihood that their answers are actually correct also increases.

Another measure of judgment accuracy—called *absolute* accuracy or *calibration*— is often the focus of research on confidence judgments. *Absolute* accuracy pertains to the degree to which the magnitude of the judgments accurately reflects the level of performance (for a discussion of measures of absolute accuracy, see Keren, 1991). It has generally been measured in two different ways: (a) by a difference— or bias—score between mean judgment and mean performance, which yields a positive value if participants are overconfident and a negative value if they are underconfident, and (b) by calibration curves, which plot the proportion of correct test performance as a function of the judgments. For examples of the former, take a moment to inspect table 8.1, where absolute accuracy as measured by difference scores is shown for each judgment. Both confidence judgments and JOLs show overconfidence, whereas FOK judgments for this participant show slight underconfidence.

Lichtenstein and Fischhoff (1977) had participants make confidence judgments about answers to many kinds of questions, such as whether the artist of a drawing was either a European child or Asian child and what the correct alternative is to general-information questions. Most participants would not have knowledge to do well on the former questions but would have some knowledge about the general-information questions. Regardless, overconfidence was the norm (see also Lichtenstein, Fischhoff, & Phillips, 1977), but some exceptions existed. Participants who answered more questions correctly were better calibrated, although those who performed above about 80% on the questions showed underconfidence. Moreover, whereas difficult items (ones that most participants did poorly on) produced vast overconfidence, easier items tended to produce underconfidence— a phenomenon that has been dubbed the *hard-easy* effect (for a critical review, see

Juslin, Winman, & Olsson, 2000). Lichtenstein and Fischhoff (1977) argue that "the strikingly different calibration for items of varying difficulty are a direct result of subjects' insensitivity to how much they really know" (p. 180). That is, even though the level of test performance changes dramatically across questions and across conditions, people's confidence judgments do not track these changes well.

Given that people are often not well calibrated, many researchers have investigated techniques that could potentially improve calibration (Fischhoff, 1982). For instance, Koriat, Lichtenstein, and Fischhoff (1980) argued that in making a confidence judgment, people may be more likely to consider reasons for why a choice was correct than reasons for why a choice could be incorrect. To combat such a confirmation bias, they had subjects write down reasons that either favored or opposed each of the two alternatives for a general-information question. Figure 8.3 includes calibration curves comparing this group who provided reasons for their answers to a standard control group who did not provide reasons for their answers. Perfect calibration is represented by the diagonal line, where confidence perfectly matches recognition performance. The calibration curve for the reasons group was much closer to perfect calibration (diagonal line) than was the calibration for the control group. Thus, developing reasons for one's answers can improve calibration. In a

FIGURE 8.3
Calibration curves for the reasons group and for a standard control group. Assessed probability refers to the confidence judgments. The solid diagonal line indicates perfect calibration. (*Koriat, A., Lichtenstein, S., and Fischhoff, B. (1980). Reasons for confidence.* Journal of Experimental Psychology: Human Learning and Memory, 6, *107–118. Copyright by American Psychological Association. Used by permission of author and publisher.*)

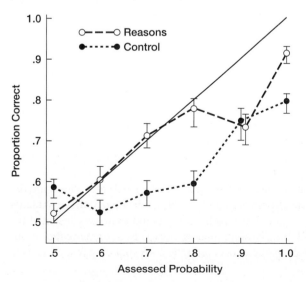

follow-up study, Koriat et al. further investigated this conclusion by contrasting three groups: participants in the supporting group who provided one reason for why they chose a given alternative, participants in the contradicting group who provided one reason why the answer they chose could be wrong, and a standard control group. Only the contradicting group achieved better calibration than a control group, indicating that when people make confidence judgments, they do not necessarily consider evidence that contradicts the potential validity of their answers. This research has straightforward implications for student scholarship. Namely, if you attempt to judge the quality of your answers on multiple choice exams, before doing so, you may first want to consider reasons why your answer could be incorrect.

Summary of Kinds of Judgments

In summary, this introduction to three kinds of judgments about memory was meant to highlight some intriguing findings relevant to each judgment as well as to describe the two most widely assessed measures of judgment accuracy: relative accuracy (i.e., resolution) and absolute accuracy (i.e., bias or calibration). Three important questions also arise from this discussion: What are the processes that underlie the monitoring judgments? What are the inputs to those processes? What underlies various levels of judgment accuracy? Next, we turn to prominent hypotheses of metacognitive monitoring that provide answers to these questions.

WHAT ARE THE PROCESSES AND INPUTS OF MONITORING JUDGMENTS?

What processes underlie the judgments? And what are the inputs to these processes? Certainly, theory of monitoring would be eloquently simplistic if the answers to these questions were the same for all of the judgments. One possibility is that all of the judgments are based on the same inferential process and involve the same kind of input. For JOLs, you may infer that you will remember the definition of "the recency effect" because the effect had been discussed repeatedly in class, and you may infer that you will not remember the definition of "geon" because the concept had not been discussed in class. For FOKs, you may also infer that you will recognize the correct definition of "the recency effect" because you remember it had been discussed so often, and so on. In this example, JOLs and FOK judgments are shown as being based on the same inferential process about the same input, which is the amount of previous experience with the definitions.

Although possible, research by Leonesio and Nelson (1990) indicates a middle ground (see also Costermans, Lories, & Ansay, 1992). They had college students study 20 paired associates in which (a) each item was individually presented for study at 7 seconds each and then (b) all items were tested by presenting the stimulus of each one and having the participants recall the corresponding response. This

---

BOX 8.2

HOW ACCURATE ARE STUDENTS AT JUDGING HOW WELL THEY HAVE
LEARNED TEXT MATERIALS?

Much of the research described in this chapter focuses on metamemory and often employs simple materials—e.g., paired associates—to explore monitoring and control processes. These processes are also being actively explored with respect to how students learn and comprehend text materials (for reviews, see Lin & Zabrucky, 1998; Otero, 1998), which arguably comprise much of student scholarship. One popular procedure to investigate monitoring of text material—or metacomprehension—parallels the procedure illustrated in figure 8.2 with an obvious change: Instead of having participants study paired associates, they study short texts, such as paragraphs from an introductory text on cognition. After reading a brief passage, a participant predicts how well he or she will do on an upcoming test over the material in the passage, which is akin to a global JOL

(see Box 8.1). A participant would read multiple passages and make a judgment for each one, and finally a test would be administered over the content from each passage.

Maki (1998) reported that the correlation between judgments and test performance across 25 studies from her laboratory was only +.27, which is relatively poor accuracy. And based on her review of the entire literature, she offered the somewhat pessimistic conclusion that " the low accuracy of text predictions may mean that students cannot predict performance well" (p. 142). Obviously, an important challenge for future research will be to better understand how individuals monitor their learning of text materials, so as to develop technologies to substantially improve the accuracy of metacomprehension judgments.

---

study-test sequence was repeated so that participants could learn items to different criteria: 10 items were studied until they were correctly recalled during the test one time, whereas 10 others were studied until they were correctly recalled four times. After an item had reached its criterion, it was dropped from the study list, and the study-test sequence was continued until all items reached criteria. Thus, some items were learned (one correct recall) and others were overlearned (four correct recalls)—a difference in learning that may impact the judgments. After the items had been studied, participants made a JOL that was functionally akin to the immediate JOLs described above. A 4-week retention interval occurred before the final phase of the experiment where participants first had a criterion recall test, made an FOK judgment for each nonrecalled item, and then had a criterion recognition test for each nonrecalled item.

This procedure allowed Leonesio and Nelson to compare the judgments on multiple dimensions because each participant made JOLs and FOK judgments. As expected, criterion recall performance was greater for overlearned items than for learned items, whereas criterion recognition performance did not differ for these subsets of items (but remember, recognition occurred only for nonrecalled items). The relative accuracy for JOLs was about $+.30$ and for FOK judgments was about $+.20$. Of most import was the correlation between JOLs and FOK judgments. If the correlation was high, that would suggest the two kinds of judgment were based on similar processes and input. By contrast, if the correlation was nil, then the two judgments may be driven by entirely unique processes and input. The mean correlation across individuals' JOLs and FOK judgments was $+.17$, a weak correlation that was not significantly greater than 0. Thus, although the judgments may have a similar basis (i.e., the correlation was above 0), they also must be based on somewhat different processes or involve different inputs (i.e., the correlation was far from $+1.0$). One difference was evident from their research because JOLs were influenced by overlearning but FOK judgments were not, suggesting that the judgments are based on different input.

Even though current research does not provide a complete picture of the similarities and differences among the judgments, many advances to our understanding have been made since Hart first demonstrated the accuracy of FOK judgments in 1965. But what are the processes and input to metacognitive judgments, and why do they often show above-chance accuracy? Some notable hypotheses and experiments are described next that provide answers to these questions.

Direct-Access Hypothesis

In making a metacognitive judgment, you may monitor the availability of the memory trace of the sought-after response as if you had a looking glass that directly magnified the representation of the response in your mind. This *direct-access* (or trace-based) hypothesis was first posed by Hart (1965, 1967) to account for the accuracy of FOK judgments, which "can serve as an indicator of what is stored in memory when the retrieval of a memory item is temporarily unsuccessful or interrupted" (1965, p. 214). If FOK judgments are based on the presence of available—albeit not accessible—memory traces, then the mystery of above-chance FOK accuracy is solved because high FOK judgments would indicate that the trace of the sought-after response was available in memory and could later be recognized, whereas low FOK judgments would indicate that a trace was not available in memory and would not be recognized. If anything, such an account calls into question the *in*accuracy of the judgments because one might expect metacognitive judgments to be perfectly accurate if people directly monitored memory traces. Do people have direct access to memory traces, which they consult when making metacognitive judgments?

Koriat (1993, 1997) has meticulously evaluated the direct-access hypothesis in his research on FOK judgments and on JOLs. Concerning the former, he argued against direct access and in favor of FOK judgments reflecting inferences about the accessibility of information elicited by the cue for the judgments, an important alternative that we will return to later. Convincing evidence against the direct-access hypothesis was reported by Koriat (1995). In Experiment 1, students answered general-knowledge questions and made FOK judgments as in Hart's recall-judge-recognition method described earlier. As usual, relative FOK accuracy was above chance (mean correlation = +.39). More important, Koriat also reported relative accuracy separately for "tricky" questions. For these questions, the answer students provide is often incorrect. For instance, many students will answer the question, "What is the capitol of California?" but not with the correct answer, "Sacramento." For these questions, FOK accuracy was -.05! If people had direct access to the underlying memory traces of the correct targets, then accuracy should always be above chance.

Similar to FOK judgments, JOLs and confidence judgments do not appear to be based on direct access to the memory trace of the item being judged (e.g., Koriat, 1997; Kelley & Lindsay, 1993). For instance, Benjamin, Bjork, and Schwartz (1998) creatively investigated the issue by employing methods originally developed by Gardiner, Craik, and Bleasdale (1973). College students first tried to answer trivia questions, which tested their *semantic* memory for the responses. After answering a question, they were then asked to predict the likelihood that they would later recall the response—without cues—in about 20 minutes. That is, they made JOLs for freely recalling the responses to the trivia questions, which tested their *episodic* memory for the responses. Although this method—having participants freely recall answers to previous questions—may seem a bit odd, it was ideal for testing a direct-access hypothesis. To understand why, consider the following counterintuitive effect: The *longer* it takes an individual to retrieve an answer to a trivia question, the *more* likely he or she will be at retrieving it during free recall. As explained by the authors, "when participants answer the question initially, they are being guided by the question on a search through semantic memory. . . . The longer they spend on such a search, the more salient or elaborated the entry they create in episodic memory for the event of having searched for that answer. The more elaborate the [episode], the more easily it can be accessed on a later free-recall task" (p. 56). In other words, answers that take longer to retrieve presumably have more elaborated memory traces immediately after study, so if JOLs directly access such traces, they should be higher for answers that take the longest time to retrieve.

What did Benjamin et al. find? Results from their first experiment are presented in figure 8.4. The initial response time quartile refers to the speed of retrieving answers for the trivia questions—the "1" pertains to the 25 percent of the answers that were most quickly retrieved, and the "4" pertains to the 25 percent that were most slowly retrieved. As expected, performance on the test of free recall, which is shown in the top panel, was greater for answers that had been retrieved more slowly than more quickly. People's JOLs are shown in the bottom panel; in contrast to free recall, JOLs were lower for answers that had been retrieved more slowly. Accordingly, the level of the participants' relative accuracy—i.e., the correlation between JOLs and free recall—tended to be somewhat negative (-.035). These outcomes are inconsistent with expectations from the direct-access hypothesis

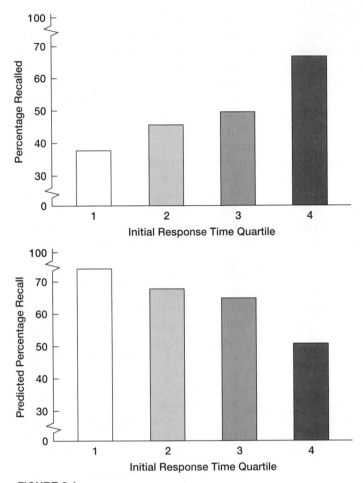

FIGURE 8.4
Mean free recall (top panel) and judgments of learning for free recall
(bottom panel) as a function of response time quartile. Benjamin, A. S.,
Bjork, R. A., & Schwartz, B. L. (1998). The mismeasure of memory:
When retrieval fluency is misleading as a metacognitive index. (Journal
of Experimental Psychology: General, 127, *55–68. Copyright by
American Psychological Association. Used by permission of author and
publisher.*)

because if people based JOLs on direct access to the underlying memory trace
after study, then JOLs should be related to recall performance.

Not only has the evidence described above cast much doubt on the assertion
that people directly monitor underlying memories, it also points toward other
processes that may drive metacognitive judgments. In the following section, we
discuss alternatives to the direct-access hypothesis.

Cue-Familiarity Hypothesis versus Accessibility Hypothesis

The cue-familiarity hypothesis is that metacognitive judgments are based on an individual's familiarity with the cue used to elicit the judgment. For instance, if you cannot recall the answer to "What is the state capital of California?" you may make a high FOK judgment because you feel familiar with the question itself (which is the cue for the judgment), partly because it occurred earlier in this chapter. Reder (1987) argued that an individual makes a preliminary FOK judgment, which is based on cue familiarity, even prior to attempting to retrieve the answer to a question. If the result of monitoring suggests the answer is available, then the individual attempts retrieval. Although it may not be obvious at first, this hypothesis can also explain the above-chance accuracy of the judgments. Because the familiarity of a cue is likely related to how often the cue (and also the target answer) has been experienced in the past, higher familiarity with the cue is likely to be linked to higher familiarity with the target answer. Initial evidence in favor of this hypothesis was reported by Reder (1987). Participants' first task was to rate a list of words; for each word, they rated how often it was encountered during reading or listening. Next, they received general-information questions and made FOK judgments. Most important, words on the first task appeared in half of the general-information questions. For instance, "California" may have been on the list of rated words, which would be in a general-information question such as "What is the state capital of California?" The rationale was that *priming* these questions would make them seem more familiar to the participants than would questions that had not been primed. If familiarity with the questions—which are the cues in this case—influences FOK judgments, then they should be greater for the primed questions than for those that had not been primed. Reder (1987) found these priming effects and concluded that cue familiarity is an important input to FOK judgments.

Often posed as a competitor of the cue-familiarity hypothesis, the accessibility hypothesis states that metacognitive judgments are based on the accessibility of information about the target (Koriat, 1993). Accessibility here pertains to the amount of information retrieved as well as to the fluency of access, such as the speed with which the information comes to mind. When asked to make a metacognitive judgment, the more information accessed and the more fluently it is accessed, the higher the metacognitive judgment. According to this hypothesis, you do not base the judgments on direct access to the trace of the target in memory but instead on the acessibility of information when making a metacognitive judgment, which at best provides an indirect indicator of the availability of the target in memory. For instance, when studying for an exam, you may ask yourself, "How well will I remember the modal model of memory and levels of processing?" When doing so, assume you quickly remember quite a bit about the modal model (e.g., short-term memory, long-term memory, transfer, and so forth), but have difficulties remembering anything about levels of processing. According to the accessibility hypothesis, you would have more confidence in your memory for the modal model than for levels of processing. Above-chance accuracy can easily be explained by the accessibility hypothesis because retrieval of target-related information will often be related to the availability of the target in memory.

Koriat's (1993) accessibility hypothesis also includes another important assumption. Namely, the quality of the information accessed is often irrelevant, so even if all the information accessed about a target is objectively false, an individual may not realize this and, hence, believe the target can be retrieved. For the example above, if you were to quickly retrieve that the modal model has an articulatory loop and a visuo-spatial sketchpad, you still may have high confidence in your memory for the modal model, even though the information accessed was wrong. Accordingly, the accessibility hypothesis also predicts that accuracy can be quite poor when the information accessed is incorrect or misleading. Consistent with this prediction, recall the experiment by Koriat (1993) described earlier: When making FOK judgments for "tricky" questions, participants presumably often accessed incorrect information about the sought-after targets, which resulted in FOK accuracy (correlation = -.05) that was not even above chance.

Metcalfe, Schwartz and Joaquim (1993) pitted the two hypotheses—cue familiarity and accessibility—against each other by using a method inspired by interference theories of forgetting. Each participant studied two lists of paired associates, and groups of participants differed with respect to the composition of each list (table 8.2). The second list was the critical one and was identical for all groups, and the first list varied across groups and was composed to interfere with memory for the second list. For the cue repetition groups (first two groups illustrated in table 8.2), the same cues were used on the first and second list. For one of these groups, the targets were also repeated, so the pairings were identical for the first and second list. This group is labeled as A-B, A-B. The first A-B pair refers to List 1 and the second one refers to List 2, and the first letter of each pair (A) refers to a cue and the second letter (B) to a target. Identical letters indicate the same words are used in both lists. For the second group, the target words differed between the first and second lists: A-D, A-B. Finally, for a control group, both cues and targets were different on the two lists: C-D, A-B. Again, note that the second and critical lists were identical (i.e., A-B) for all three groups.

During study, participants were instructed to associate the words in a pair. Also, if a cue was paired with more than one target, they were instructed to remember the last cue-target pairing. The recall-judge-recognition method was then used: paired-associate recall, followed by FOK judgments for incorrectly recalled items, followed by a recognition test of the targets. Most important, according to interference theory, accessibility will be substantially greater for the A-B, A-B group in which the pairings were repeated than either for the A-D, A-B group where proactive interference from the first list (A-D) will undermine recall of the second list (A-B) or for the control group (C-D, A-B). Consider the predictions for the accessibility hypothesis versus those for the cue-familiarity hypothesis. For the accessibility hypothesis, FOK judgments should be highest for the group that produces the most fluent access to targets, so the repetition group (A-B,

TABLE 8.2
DATA ADAPTED FROM METCALFE, SCHWARTZ, AND JOAQUIM (1993).

Group	List 1	List 2	% Target recall	FOK magnitude
A-B, A-B	pickle – lucky table – picture butter – psyche	pickle – lucky table – picture butter – psyche	39	48
A-D, A-B	pickle – carpet table – maple butter – sandal	pickle – lucky table – picture butter – psyche	17	49
C-D, A-B	single – carpet fragrant – maple marble – sandal	pickle – lucky table – picture butter – psyche	19	38

Note. FOK magnitude refers to the mean FOK judgment across pairs for a given group. FOK judgments were made on a 100-point scale, from 1 (no idea of correct response) to 100 (sure they would recognize the correct answer). The pattern of mean recognition performance was identical to recall performance.

A-B) should produce higher FOK judgments than will either of the other groups. By contrast, for the cue-familiarity group, FOK judgments should be highest for the pairs with the most familiar cues; that is, for the two groups in which the cue had been repeated across the lists (A-B, A-B and A-D, A-B). The results are presented in table 8.2. As expected, recall performance was better for the repetition group (A-B, A-B) than for the other two groups. This outcome suggests that accessibility was greatest for the repetition group. Most important, mean FOK judgments were no different for the two groups in which the cues were repeated and were greater for these two groups than for the control group in which the cues were not repeated. These outcomes support the cue-familiarity hypothesis.

Several other studies on FOK judgments also have demonstrated that metacognitive judgments can be based on cue familiarity (e.g., Reder & Ritter, 1992). As Metcalfe et al. (1993) argued, "feeling-of-knowing judgments are made by using a heuristic—specifically, by assessing the familiarity of the cue . . . [and] frequently our predictive ability is disappointing, as might well be expected given that we base these judgments on a heuristic rather than on some direct assessment of the . . . target itself" (p. 860).

At least in some cases, the influence of familiarity on FOK judgments appears stronger than the influence of accessibility. Nevertheless, accessibility also appears to influence all of the monitoring judgments at times. For instance, Koriat (1995) demonstrated that FOK judgments are higher for items in which students access more information about the nonrecalled answer, regardless of whether the information was correct or incorrect. For JOLs, Benjamin et al. (1998) demonstrated the potency of one aspect of accessibility: the fluency with which a target itself is accessed (see figure 8.4). The delayed-JOL effect—in which accuracy is greater for delayed than immediate JOLs—also owes a debt to accessibility. In particular, delayed JOLs are often cued only by the stimulus of each item; for example, if "singe—monkey" were studied, then "singe—?" would be the cue for the JOL. When people are presented with this cue (singe), they naturally try to access the correct response (monkey). Accessibility to the answer would then be a major basis of the delayed JOL (Nelson & Dunlosky, 1991). That is, if you had recalled "monkey" when cued to make your JOL, you would make a much higher judgment than if you did not recall it. Of course, if you can access the response when making a JOL, you are likely to recall it on the criterion test; whereas, if you do not access the response when making a JOL, you probably won't recall it later on. Thus, basing delayed JOLs on accessibility to the responses can contribute to their high accuracy.

Finally, Kelley and Lindsay (1993) explored whether confidence judgments are based on the fluency with which answers to general-knowledge questions come to mind, regardless of whether the answers are correct or incorrect. To do so, they used a two-phase procedure. Before answering the general-knowledge questions (e.g., What was Buffalo Bill's last name?), participants first studied a list of individually presented words: 1/3 of the words were actual answers to the general-knowledge questions (i.e., Cody), 1/3 of the words were related but incorrect answers (e.g., Hickcock), and 1/3 were unrelated fillers (e.g., Melville). For each general-knowledge question, only one of the three kinds of words (correct, related, or filler) appeared on the initial study list. After studying the list, they attempted to answer each general-knowledge question, and the speed of responding was recorded. Of course, the participants also rated confidence in the answer provided. The idea here was simply that presenting a possible answer (correct or incorrect) to an upcoming question should increase the fluency with which it was retrieved. If so, the accessibility hypothesis predicts that faster retrieval (i.e., more fluent access) will lead to higher confidence judgments, regardless of whether the response is correct or incorrect. Their results generally supported this prediction. For instance, when participants retrieved an incorrect answer (e.g., the answer "Hickcock" for the question "What was Buffalo Bill's last name?"), the latency of retrieving it was faster for questions that were initially primed with the incorrect answer (Hickcock) than by the filler word (Melville). Most important, confidence was higher when participants were primed with the incorrect answer than with the filler. Thus, confidence judgments are influenced by ease of accessing answers, even when those answer are objectively incorrect.

So, where do we stand on the cue-familiarity hypothesis versus the accessibility hypothesis? As with other hypotheses described in this textbook (e.g., organization versus distinctiveness), these two hypotheses are not mutually exclusive. In other words, people's metacognitive judgments may be influenced by both cue familiarity and accessibility. If so, a major challenge will be to understand how the two inputs are combined in making metacognitive judgments. Koriat and Levy-Sadot (2001) recently proposed how both inputs—familiarity and accessibility—could combine to influence FOK judgments. When a cue is presented for a judgment, the familiarity of the cue initially drives an FOK judgment (as per the cue familiarity hypothesis, see especially Metcalfe, 1993; Reder & Ritter, 1992). If cue familiarity is low, a low FOK judgment is made. When cue familiarity is high, however, the individual feels the response may be available and, hence, continues to search for it. During this search, new information is accessed, which then can influence the FOK judgment (as per the accessibility hypothesis). Results from multiple experiments confirmed this hypothesis (Koriat & Levy-Sadot, 2001) and, hence, showcase the importance of both cue familiarity and accessibility as bases for people's judgments about memory.

Preliminary Conclusions about Theory of Monitoring

A summary of over three decades of research on metacognitive judgments to date suggests two preliminary conclusions, which are illustrated in figure 8.5. First, research across the various judgments is echoing a similar conclusion. Namely, each of the judgments is apparently based on the same inferential, heuristic-based process (Schwartz, Benjamin, & Bjork, 1997). In particular, when making a metacognitive judgment, instead of obtaining direct access to an underlying memory, an individual infers whether a particular response will be (or has been) remembered based upon the relevant cues, or inputs, available when making the judgment. Such inferential, heuristic-based processes apparently also influence many other kinds of human judgments, as we shall see in chapter 12, and are core to the attributional approach to memory performance espoused by Jacoby and his colleagues (e.g., Jacoby, Kelley, & Dwyan, 1989; Kelley & Jacoby, 1996). Second, the inputs available as potential bases for the judgments are not identical. For instance, available inputs for immediate JOLs will often include ease of processing an item during study (Begg, Duft, Lalonde, Melnick, & Sanvito, 1989; Hertzog, Dunlosky, Robinson, & Kidder, 2003) and the degree to which the words in a pair are related to one another (Koriat, 1997). Whereas for FOK judgments, available inputs may include cue familiarity and accessibility of partial information (see also, Schreiber & Nelson, 1998). Consider these conclusions in the context of the results from Leonesio and Nelson that began this section on monitoring judgments. JOLs and FOK judgments were not highly related because one input that was readily available to JOLs (whether an item had been overlearned during study) would be less available to FOK judgments that were made 4 weeks after study.

In conclusion, let us return to a mystery that has stimulated interest in metacognitive monitoring since Hart's seminal work. Why do people's metacognitive judgments—in particular, FOK judgments—often show above-chance accuracy? The research presented above demystifies such accuracy. In particular, accuracy appears to reflect merely the degree to which inputs to the judgments are related to performance on the criterion test. Those inputs that are highly valid predictors will support the highest levels of accuracy, and those that are not valid

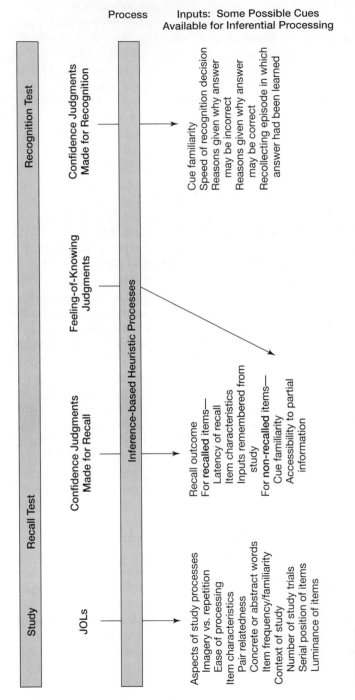

FIGURE 8.5
Kinds of judgment illustrated with some possible inputs that may be available as bases for each one.

will substantially diminish accuracy. This view presents a challenge for future researchers to discover inputs for each judgment that will routinely produce high levels of judgment accuracy.

CONTROL OF LEARNING

As you prepare for an upcoming exam or even when you attempt to master information for a new job, you can take quite a bit of control over your learning and

---

BOX 8.3

DOES AMNESIA DISRUPT THE PROCESSES UNDERLYING MONITORING JUDGMENTS?

The bulk of research on metacognition has involved participants who have relatively normal memory. This reliance on highly functioning participants begs many questions, such as: Is normal memory necessary for normal metacognition? Can someone who has had memory disrupted—e.g., through accidents, disease, or abuse—still have accurate metamemory? In general, memory and metamemory do not necessarily depend upon one another, because individuals with memory deficits can be aware of them (although lack of awareness is common, e.g., see McGlynn, 1998). But what about memory *monitoring*? Would a memory deficit undermine an individual's ability to make fine discriminations in knowledge, such as required by FOK judgments?

Answers to such questions were offered by Shimamura and his colleagues, who have explored the effects of several forms of brain dysfunction on metacognitive monitoring (e.g., Janowsky, Shimamura, & Squire, 1989; Shimamura & Squire, 1986). For instance, Shimamura and Squire (1986) investigated metacognitive monitoring for individuals with amnesia. They speculated that if metamemory deficits contribute to amnesia, then amnesic patients would not perform well on tasks that tap metamemory. Using Hart's recall-judge-recognition method, four groups were examined: amnesiac patients with Korsakoff's Syndrome, which results from chronic alcohol abuse and concomitant nutritional deficiencies; patients receiving electroconvulsive therapy (ECT), which can temporarily cause amnesia (these participants were tested 2 to 3 hours after ECT); four patients with amnesia due to unconsciousness; and a group of alcoholic participants, who acted as a control. Not surprisingly, patients with Korsakoff's syndrome showed an impairment in recalling answers to general-knowledge questions.

Most important, FOK accuracy was also significantly lower for patients with Korsakoff's syndrome than for the other three groups. In a follow-up experiment, FOK accuracy for patients with Korsakoff's syndrome was again greatly impaired and was not even reliably above chance. These results suggest that some forms of amnesia disrupt the processes underlying monitoring judgments and that memory ability and monitoring ability may rely on partly different brain systems, with frontal lobe functioning in particular being implicated for monitoring judgments (Janowsky et al., 1989).

retrieval. For instance, you often make decisions about when to stop studying and how long to persist in retrieving an important fact. In contrast to the large literature on memory described in previous chapters of this text, much less research has focused on control processes involved in learning and retrieval. One reason for this disparity is that to evaluate hypotheses of memory, such as those posed by the modal model or levels of processing, researchers have often used methods that largely undermine control processes (Nelson & Narens, 1994). For instance, in a typical *memory* experiment, a participant may be asked to learn a series of stimuli. Experimenters would pace the rate of presenting items for study and often have participants follow explicit orienting instructions. Although such methods may be critical for evaluating hypotheses of memory, they also run counter to understanding control processes because they will suppress the participants' ability to control learning. Fortunately, many researchers have become fascinated by how people control learning and retrieval; hence, methods to investigate these control processes have been developed and refined. In the next sections, we consider some key hypotheses about the control of learning that have been the focus of this new wave of research.

Function of Monitoring in the Control of Learning

A major function of monitoring is in guiding control processes. As illustrated in figure 8.1, each monitoring judgment is presumed to be involved in a particular control process. For instance, a function of JOLs presumably is in guiding the allocation of study time, and a function of confidence judgments is in guiding retrieval.

Given that the function of monitoring is in part to control cognition, the accuracy of monitoring will be critical in effective control (Bisanz, Vesonder, & Voss, 1978; Thiede, 1999). For example, consider two students who are learning French-English translation equivalents for an upcoming test. Each student makes JOLs and paces study. One student uses delayed JOLs to monitor progress, which are almost perfectly accurate; the other student uses immediate JOLs and has relatively poor accuracy. The more accurate student can use study time effectively because he or she will be able to focus only on those items (with low JOLs) that actually have not been well learned. By contrast, the less accurate student who made immediate JOLs would be less able to effectively control learning; that is, because of poor accuracy, the student may spend too much time studying items that he or she believes have not been learned (but in fact have been), and even worse, may not spend enough time studying items that he or she believes already have been learned (but in fact have not been). Such illustrations are based on the assumption that metacognitive monitoring functions to control learning. But does monitoring serve this function, and if so, exactly how is it used in the control of study and in the control of retrieval?

Hypotheses about the Control of Study Time

To investigate how people control study, researchers generally have used standard methods (figure 8.2), with a few critical twists. First, each item is briefly presented at a fixed rate so that a monitoring judgment can be obtained, such as a JOL. Second, another study trial occurs, but instead of presenting items at a fixed rate, each participant is allowed to spend as much time as he or she wants studying a particular item. When finished with an item, a participant merely signals (e.g., through a computer key press) that he or she is done, and then the next item is presented.

A key question for early research was, Are JOLs related to study time? In other words, Does monitoring play a functional role in the allocation of study time? The answer to this question is a resounding Yes. In particular, JOLs are often negatively related to subsequent study time (e.g., Nelson & Leonesio, 1988; Mazzoni & Cornoldi, 1993; and for an exhaustive review, see Son & Metcalfe, 2000). That is, students usually spend more time studying items that had been judged as poorly learned than items that had been judged as relatively well learned. This outcome certainly resonates with intuition, but why do students often allocate the most study time to the more difficult materials? And do they always prefer to study the more difficult materials? Let's consider two hypotheses that offer alternative answers to these questions.

Discrepancy-Reduction Hypothesis.   The discrepancy-reduction hypothesis provides an intuitive account of how learners allocate study time across items. *Discrepancy* here is the difference between how well you have currently learned something and how well you want to learn it—that is, the discrepancy between your current state of learning and your goal state. According to this hypothesis, a learner will continue to study a given item until this discrepancy is minimized; that is, study will continue until the learner's goal has been met. This discrepancy will typically be larger for items judged as less well learned than those judged as well learned. For instance, if your goal was to master the chapter on attention, you may judge that you have almost mastered the switch model but have not even come close to mastering the material on the late selection model. Thus, the discrepancy is larger for the late-selection model than for the switch model. Accordingly, when studying, it seems intuitive that you would spend more time studying the material on the late-selection model because you would need more time to reach your goal; or rather, you would need more time to reduce the initial discrepancy between your current learning and goal. This example jibes with the modal findings described above—namely, a negative relation between JOLs and study time.

Thiede and Dunlosky (1999) and Son and Metcalfe (2000) surmised, however, that learners are more sophisticated than is entailed by the mechanistic view instantiated by the discrepancy-reduction hypothesis, because students do not seek to reduce discrepancy in all situations. For instance, in the example above, if you began studying shortly before your exam, you may actually decide to spend *more* time studying the switch model and not study the late selection model at all. The reason for such seemingly counterintuitive behavior is simply that in realizing you cannot master all the material, you plan to study just the material that you can learn in a short bit of time—in this case, that would include the easier material. To evaluate this possibility, these researchers had participants allocate study time under conditions in which mastering all items was not viable. For instance, Thiede and Dunlosky (1999) had students pace their study of paired associates using standard methods. Some students were given unlimited time for study, whereas others were given an extremely limited time to learn all the items. Students who had unlimited time for study spent more time studying difficult items than easy items—as per the modal outcome described above and as the discrepancy-reduction model predicts. By contrast, those who were given limited time for study did just the opposite. That is, these students focused on the easiest materials, a strategy that seems like an effective one to use when under time pressure.

Region of Proximal Learning.   Metcalfe (2002) argued that discrepancy reduction may rarely—if ever—operate in the control of study. Instead, she proposed that students allocate the most study time to items within their region of proximal learning. That is, students will study materials that they believe they can learn and will devote little attention to materials outside this region of proximal learning, (i.e., items that are already well learned or too difficult to learn). Accordingly, in some cases they will spend very little time studying the most difficult items, which are outside their region of proximal learning, even though the discrepancy between current learning and the goal for these items would be extreme. For example, imagine you were preparing for an exam over three chapters, and you planned only one evening for study. You may decide to focus most of your time on sections of intermediate difficulty because you believe that the easiest sections would be readily mastered and the most difficult sections could never be mastered in time (i.e., they are out of your region of proximal learning). This hypothesis can easily account for the fact that students will often spend more time studying harder items than easier ones, because in most experimental contexts (a) students are instructed to master the to-be-learned materials and (b) even the most difficult materials are within their region of proximal learning.

In a series of experiments using Spanish-English translation equivalents, Metcalfe (2002) demonstrated that students of differing ages allocate study time as predicted by the region of proximal learning. For instance, students who already had experience with the Spanish language spent more time studying the more difficult items than did students who were novices, who spent more time studying the easier items. Thus, the students did not merely use the majority of their time in studying the most difficult items (as predicted by the discrepancy-reduction hypothesis) but instead focused on items that were in their region of proximal learning.

In this brief section, we considered how monitoring of learning is used to control study. Of course, many other factors besides monitoring of learning influence how long an individual will study for a test. For instance, you may decide to stop studying because you are not interested in the materials or become too tired to continue, not because you feel you have learned the material well. Moreover, in preparing for an upcoming exam, students control their learning in many other ways, such as in choosing where to study (library, dorm room, etc.) or in choosing the kinds of strategy to use for study (Zimmerman & Schunk, 2001; Winne & Hadwin, 1998). A major research agenda is to discover how these and other factors—monitoring of learning, interest, self efficacy, personality, social interactions, and so on—shape a learner's choice of study strategies, allocation of study time, and overall success in learning. Advances are being made, but much research is needed before we will adequately understand how people control study and how they should do so to most efficiently achieve their goals.

Control of Retrieval

Imagine that during a class lecture, the instructor asks the class, "What is the definition of metacognition?" Even in attempting to come up with the answer to such a simple question, you may control several aspects of retrieval. Let's consider some of them.

First, when the instructor poses the question, you may immediately decide whether or not you know the answer. If you decide that you do, you then may try to retrieve it. If you decide that you do not know the answer, then you may try to make one up, or even better, quickly look up the answer in the textbook. The idea is that when people are asked a question, they may often first make a rapid, preliminary FOK judgment that is based on familiarity with the question (as per the cue-familiarity hypothesis). If the FOK is positive—that is, you feel that you know the answer—then you will attempt to retrieve it. If the FOK is negative, then you will use some other strategy (e.g., looking the definition up in the text) to form an answer. Using a variety of experimental protocols, Reder and her colleagues have demonstrated that individuals use such a preretrieval decision to decide whether to initiate retrieval of the answer itself (e.g., Reder, 1987; Reder & Ritter, 1992).

Second, other control processes may come into play after an individual decides to attempt to retrieve an answer to a question or problem. Koriat and Goldsmith (1996; Goldsmith, Koriat, & Weinberg-Eliezer, 2002) have developed and tested a model of retrieval that explains when individuals will *output* a response to a question. One major assumption of their model is that the quality of an individual's retrieval performance—that is, whether the individual responds with the correct answer—is largely controlled. How control is achieved is straightforward: When a candidate answer is retrieved, an individual makes a judgment of whether it is correct; that is, he or she makes what is akin to a covert confidence judgment. If confidence in the judgment is above the individual's response criterion, he or she will output it. An individual sets the response criterion based on his or her desire to be accurate. For instance, on some tests, points may be subtracted from your score if you answer incorrectly, so you would set this criterion quite high. That is, you would only output responses that you were quite confident were correct. In other settings, you may not be penalized for responding incorrectly; hence you may set a lower response criterion and even output responses that you are not highly confident in. One implication of the model highlights the importance of accurate monitoring. That is, if your confidence judgments are inaccurate, you may often output incorrect answers and withhold correct ones. For instance, when the instructor poses the question, you may eventually retrieve the correct definition of metacognition. However, if you are not confident that the candidate definition is correct, you may withhold it. Data from multiple experiments confirmed major predictions from the model (Koriat & Goldsmith, 1996), indicating that individuals do have control over the quality of answers they will output.

Finally, you may use a variety of heuristics to decide to output a response (for a recall test) or to choose an alternative (for a recognition test). One heuristic owes its origins to distinctive processing at study and has been recently described by Schacter and his colleagues (e.g., Dodson & Schacter, 2002; Schacter, Israel, & Racine, 1999). Dodson and Schacter (2002) explain that this *distinctiveness* heuristic "is a retrieval mechanism, based on individuals' beliefs about what they expect to remember. . . . Distinctive processing during encoding sets the stage for the use of the distinctive heuristic at retrieval" (p. 406). To demonstrate the use of this heuristic, Schacter et al. (2002) used the Deese/Roediger-McDermott method described in chapter 7. Recall that the to-be-remembered list is composed of words that are semantically related to a critical lure, which itself is not presented at study but is often mistakenly retrieved at test and, hence, results in a "false" memory. In their investigation, one group merely studied the words on each list. An experimental group also studied the words, but each word was also presented with a picture that corresponded to it. The pictures were expected to enhance the distinctive processing of each word on the list. At test, participants had to recognize which words were originally presented, and of course, they should reject the critical lures as having been studied. Most important, false recognition occurred less often for participants who had initially studied the words along with the pictures. Schacter et al. argued that this reduction in false memory was due to the use of a distinctiveness heuristic: During the test, when individuals who had originally viewed pictures decided whether a given word had been studied, they would expect to retrieve distinctive pictorial information about that word if in fact it had been studied. Because they would be less likely to retrieve distinctive pictorial information when the critical lure (which had not been studied) was presented during the test, they are more likely to reject it.

SUMMARY

In an often cited passage, Tulving and Madigan (1970) heralded the importance of metacognition: "What is the solution to the problem of lack of genuine progress in understanding memory? It is not for us to say because we do not know. But one possibility does suggest itself: Why not start looking for ways of experimentally studying, and incorporating into theories and models of memory, one of the truly unique characteristics of human memory: its knowledge of its own knowledge" (p. 477). Since Tulving and Madigan's call for investigation of knowledge about knowledge, much progress has been made. Methods have been developed to assess the accuracy of people's monitoring of learning and retrieval, and outcomes from the extant literature are encouraging. Researchers have devoted much energy to understanding how people make monitoring judgments, and current accounts converge on the conclusion that the judgments are inferential in nature. When asked to judge learning of an item, instead of directly accessing the trace of the item in memory, an individual makes his or her best guess based on inputs (e.g., cue familiarity and accessibility) that are readily available. The accuracy of people's monitoring judgments are typically above chance, suggesting that the inputs to these judgments are often valid indicators of test performance.

Monitoring itself plays a functional role in human memory, such as by guiding the allocation of study time and decisions about retrieval. Therefore, the efficiency of these control processes will be in part based on monitoring accuracy. That is, students who are more accurate at monitoring their learning and retrieval will also be more efficient learners and test takers. Fortunately, as advances are made in our understanding of how people monitor memory and retrieval, techniques are also discovered that can help them improve their monitoring accuracy.

Research on metacognition is having an undeniable influence on our understanding of human consciousness and memory. Discoveries in this area have also had major impacts on other areas as well—such as developmental theories of cognition, neuropsychology, social psychology, clinical psychology and many other applied domains. Perhaps most germane, throughout this chapter we have emphasized how improving metacognitive skills can enhance student scholarship. Certainly, the overall contribution of metacognitive research to the field will be in part measured by its continued relevance to such real-world applications.

THOUGHT QUESTIONS

1. What is metacognition and how are metacognitive processes related to cognitive process?
2. What is metamemory and what are its three major components?
3. Researchers investigate monitoring by having experimental participants judge various aspects of memory and retrieval. How do people make these judgments— e.g., JOLs and FOK judgments? Are they all based on the identical set of processes and input?

4. What are the functions of monitoring? As tapped by JOLs? Confidence judgments?
5. What is the relation between measures of monitoring processes and control processes?
6. Why is accurate monitoring important for the effective control of learning and retrieval?
7. What are three ways that metacognition can potentially help you improve your learning and retrieval of classroom materials?

KNOWLEDGE: THE STRUCTURE OF CONCEPTS

Long-term memory encompasses not only specific past events but also general knowledge of the world. In fact, memory and knowledge typically are treated as different things. Why, for example, when you took algebra did the teacher not give exactly the same problems on a test as were given for homework? The standard answer is that the purpose of the test is to assess knowledge, not memory. What is this putative difference between memory and knowledge? The assumption is that knowledge is abstract. Unlike memory, knowledge is not constrained by a particular context; knowledge is not bounded by a particular time and place of prior occurrence. Thus, if you really know the principles of algebra, you will be able to apply them to new problems. As another example of the abstract nature of knowledge, you know the meaning of the symbol ●. You know what to do when confronted by the event, regardless of whether you encounter it driving a Mercedes in New York City or a Blazer in Atlanta. Notice that the knowledge you have about even this simple event reaches far beyond just "stop." It includes the action to be taken as well as the consequences of failing to take that action. In short, even a simple concept consists of a wide range of information.

The mental representations of knowledge are concepts, and as such, concepts are fundamental aspects of intelligent behavior. Research in cognitive psychology has pursued the difficult question of what constitutes knowledge by focusing on the structure of concepts. The question posed by this research is, what exactly do we know when we exhibit knowledge in some domain? In addition to the question of what a concept contains, considerable effort has been devoted to discovering how concepts are organized. We all have concepts of *dog, pet,* and *banana,* but clearly the concepts of *dog* and *pet* are more closely related than are *banana* and *pet.* Research on the structure and organization of concepts has direct bearing on questions of the acquisition and utilization of knowledge, and we shall discuss all of these matters in this chapter. By way of introduction to these topics, we begin with a description of the function of knowledge.

THE FUNCTION OF CONCEPTS

What can a person who has knowledge in a particular domain do that a less knowledgeable person cannot? This question goes to the issue of the function of concepts, and Wisniewski (2000) provides a description of four general functions of knowledge that impact important aspects of our behavior. The first and most widely studied function of concepts is that a concept provides the ability to classify equivalent things as a category. The ability to classify objects allows one to identify new objects and behave appropriately in their presence. For example, your concept of *snake* allows you to recognize that thing you encounter on the trail even though you have never seen that particular thing before and, importantly, allows you to behave in an appropriate fashion. In other words, the ability to classify new objects as an instance of a known concept guides behavior without the necessity of learning what to do in each new situation.

The classification function of concepts provides stability to the world in that nonidentical things can be treated as identical. A coiled snake presents a different appearance as it uncoils and crawls, but because you have a concept of *snake,* you know it is the same snake. Your behavior in the presence of this snake you have never seen before stems from the inferences you make based on the classification. If the crawly thing has a triangular head, you classify it as a poisonous snake and take appropriate measures to avoid it.

A second important function of concepts listed by Wisniewski involves communication with other people. Concepts allow more efficient communication in that we assume other people share similar concepts and can make the same inferences as we would. For example, if you explain to someone that you were late because of a flat tire, the person with a concept of *flat tire* will not require an explicit explanation of why a flat tire would have made you late. If, on the other hand, you say you were late because of the milkshake, the person with a concept of *milkshake* will require further explanation of why a milkshake would make you late.

Another important communicative function of concepts is to allow for indirect learning. For example, if someone tells you not to make eye contact with a growling dog, your concepts of *eye contact* and *growling dog* allow you to follow this advice the first time you encounter a growling dog. You do not have to have the direct experience with a growling dog to obtain important knowledge.

A third important use of concepts is to learn other concepts. For example, we learn something about the unfamiliar concept of *electricity* when we are told it is like water flow. In the same vein, we begin to learn about the structure of an atom by being told it is like the solar system. Both of these examples illustrate how an existing concept can guide the learning of a new concept. The existing concept provides an analogy to the new concept. We can use what we know about the existing concept to reason by analogy to the new concept.

A fourth function of concepts is to create new knowledge. We can combine existing concepts to create a new concept. For example, we all now know that a *red light camera* is a camera that photographs cars that run red lights. The concept was created from the existing concepts of *red light* and of *camera*, but notice the interesting property of the new concept; *red light camera* conveys knowledge that is different from red light and from camera. It is in this sense that existing concepts can be combined to create new knowledge. The ways in which concepts can be combined appears limitless, and you can think of lots of examples of relatively new conceptual combinations such as *doorway smoker*. Thus, the process of creating new concepts from existing concepts is a powerful way of expanding knowledge.

Wisniewski discusses other functions of concepts, but the four we have described illustrate why we said earlier that concepts are fundamental aspects of intelligent behavior. Concepts allow us to classify objects that we have not experienced previously, which is important to our ability to behave appropriately in a new situation. Concepts serve a critical role in effective communication with other people and can be used to learn new concepts, which in turn can then be communicated to others. Finally, known concepts can be combined to create new concepts, which is an efficient way to increase our knowledge. Given the importance of concepts to intellectual performance, it is not surprising that cognitive psychologists have expended considerable research effort on the topic. A fundamental issue in this research is the specification of what constitutes a concept. What is the structure of the knowledge that we call concepts?

CONCEPTS AS ABSTRACT KNOWLEDGE

Knowledge traditionally has been defined as an abstraction of information from prior experiences. Basically, the idea is that a concept represents the common properties of the variable instances of a category. For example, your abstract concept of *bird* has been formed from the properties common to the different birds you have experienced. Notice that in this view of concepts, the knowledge representing *bird* is different from any particular bird. The concept contains the information common to all birds in your experience. Any particular bird that you experience will have properties that are not part of the concept of *bird*. For example, the size of an ostrich is not usually what we think of as birdlike. However, the information contained in the abstract concept must be shared by all of the instances of the category in order for the instances to be classified as members of the category. We shall describe two ideas about the structure of concepts that are both based on the assumption that the concepts are abstract. Opposing these ideas is the notion that concepts are not abstractions but, rather, are a collection of the particular instances previously experienced.

The Classical Theory of Conceptual Structure

The earliest view of concepts assumes that our knowledge consists of the properties that are necessary and sufficient for category membership. In order to belong to the category of things defined by the concept, something must have the properties represented in the concept. Furthermore, if something does have those properties, it must be a member of the category. A common example of the classical view uses the concept of *triangle*. Three properties of a triangle are that it is (1) a closed geometric form (2) with three sides and (3) interior angles that add up to 180 degrees. These are the necessary and sufficient properties. The properties are necessary because in order to be classified as a triangle, an object necessarily must possess these properties. The properties are sufficient in that having the three properties is all it takes to make something a triangle. In short, the classical view maintains that concepts contain the information that uniquely specifies an object or event as a member of the category.

We shall now describe two theories that conform to the classical view. Both of these theories assume that classification of an item as a member of a category requires that the item's properties match those of the concept; that is, both theories assume that concepts are represented as necessary and sufficient properties. The two theories differ, however, in their assumptions about the organization of concepts.

Teachable Language Comprehender (TLC)   The first major theory of knowledge structure from cognitive psychology was actually a computer program to understand language. This program, proposed by Quillian (1968, 1969), was called the Teachable Language Comprehender (TLC). Quillian's strategy was to develop a knowledge structure for a computer that would allow the computer to answer questions. If the structure was successful for the computer, the next step would be to test the implications of the theory with humans. The first challenge was to devise a method of representing knowledge so that even a machine could demonstrate some of the flexibility inherent in human knowledge. For example, questions that seem to be based on inferences rather than on directly known information are easily answered. Does a canary have skin? Assuming that you can answer this question, how do you know? Have you ever had direct experience with canary skin? Have you ever been taught explicitly that canaries have skin? Probably not. The answer to this question is inferred, based on other things known about canaries, and part of the task confronting Quillian was to capture this inferential ability.

The structure proposed by Quillian is quite simple. It is a hierarchically organized system in which related concepts are connected by associations. *Hierarchical conceptual organization* means that concepts are organized in superordinate-subordinate relationship. Figure 9.1 provides an example of a limited portion of the structure. Notice that the superordinate *animal* subsumes subordinates *fish* and *bird*. This, then, represents the knowledge that both mammals and birds are animals. Similarly, *bird* is superordinate to *canary* and *ostrich,* as well as to all of the other facts known about birds. Concepts are abstract knowledge according to the theory because, as illustrated in this structure, knowledge of *animal* is different from knowledge of particular animals such as *bird*. Moreover, although not shown in figure 9.1, knowledge of *canary* would be different from knowledge of a particular canary. If you had a pet canary named Peetie, a separate node would represent your concept of Peetie, and this node would be associated to canary.

Notice that each node or concept has associated with it certain properties characteristic of that concept. Animals have skin and they eat and breathe. Birds have feathers and wings and they fly. Canaries are yellow. At this point, the question of why the properties are not listed at each node might be raised. After all, canaries have feathers and birds breathe. This question brings us to the assumption of *cognitive economy.*

The properties of any concept are stored at the highest possible node. For example, if all animals have skin, then *skin* is not stored with the concept of each animal but is stored with the concept of *animal.* This assumption provides obvious economy of storage in that information is not duplicated unnecessarily within the structure. The assumption also is the reason that TLC is an example of the classical view of concepts. All subordinates to the superordinate concept share the properties stored with the superordinate. That is, the properties listed at the level of the superordinate are necessary for membership in the category defined by the superordinate, and collectively, those properties are sufficient for membership in the category.

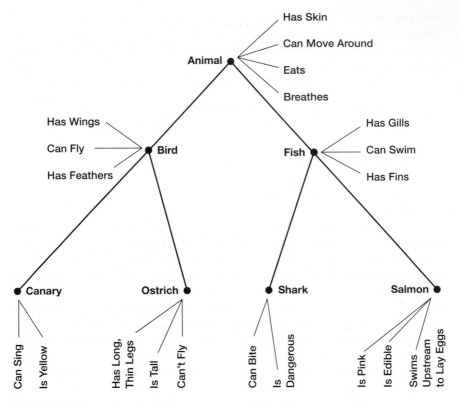

FIGURE 9.1
A portion of the teachable language comprehender (TLC) model of semantic memory.
(From "Retrieval Time from Semantic Memory" by A. M. Collins and M. R. Quillian,
Journal of Memory and Language, *1969, 8, 240247. Copyright 1969 by Academic Press.*
Used by permission.)

The process of retrieving knowledge is quite straightforward. The concept for which knowledge is to be accessed is activated by presentation of a question. The information linked to that concept is also activated by tracing the associative network. For example, the question "Is a canary a bird?" activates the concept *canary* and the association is traced to *bird.* Once the concept *bird* is found in association with *canary,* a yes response can be given to the question. The question "Does a *canary* have skin?" activates the canary node, and the network is traced directly to *animal* where the property "has skin" is found. Since *canary* is a subordinate of *animal,* it is now possible to respond, "Yes, canaries have skin." We can now see that TLC allows us to generate or infer facts not directly stored with a concept. Furthermore, it is evident that knowledge of a concept is represented both by the concept node and by the relationships or associations between nodes. Thus, TLC describes the knowledge of a concept in terms of the representative node and concepts and properties associated with the node.

The importance of Quillian's computer program for psychology lies in its ability to generate interesting predictions about human performance. One such prediction is called the *category size effect:* that is, larger categories should require more time for search than do smaller categories. *Animal* is a larger category than *bird;* very simply, *animal* includes *bird* as well as a number of other concepts. Within TLC, the superordinate of a large category is farther from an instance in the associative network than is the superordinate of a small category. As you can see in figure 9.1, *canary* is farther removed from the larger category superordinate *animal* than it is from the smaller category superordinate *bird.* From the premise that traversing the network requires time, it should follow that verifying canary as a bird would require less time than verifying canary as an animal. This is known as the category size effect.

Notice that the measure of performance is not accuracy (as in many memory experiments) but, rather, is reaction time. The reason is fairly obvious. The questions posed to the subject are designed to tap the knowledge base. In order to examine the structure of knowledge, we must ask questions for which a subject knows answers. Because accuracy will be near perfect, another measure of performance is needed. Let us see how reaction time serves as that measure.

In a series of experiments, Collins and Quillian (1969) asked participants to respond yes or no as quickly as they could to a series of statements such as, "A canary is a canary," "A canary is a bird," and "A canary is an animal." Based on the TLC model's prediction of a category size effect, reaction time should increase in the order that the statements are listed here. Collins and Quillian's results, which are presented in figure 9.2, were consistent with this prediction. The smaller the category was, the less time was required to verify an instance as a member of the category.

More impressive were the results on sentences stating property relations. For example, the TLC model predicts a regular increase in reaction time to verify the sentences "A canary can sing," "A canary can fly," and "A canary has skin." Again, the information required is stored at different levels of the hierarchy, and on the assumption of cognitive economy, reaction time should be faster to "sings" than to "flies" and faster to "flies" than to "has skin." Figure 9.2 shows that the results of Collins and Quillian's experiment were again consistent with the predictions from TLC.

The fundamental difficulty with the TLC is in the relationships between various concepts and between concepts and their properties. That is, a strictly hierarchical relationship between concepts is inconsistent with information now available, and the assumption of cognitive economy in the representation of concepts does not seem to be completely accurate.

Conrad (1972) questioned Collins and Quillian's original interpretation of the reaction times to property judgments. Rather than assume that the times to verify

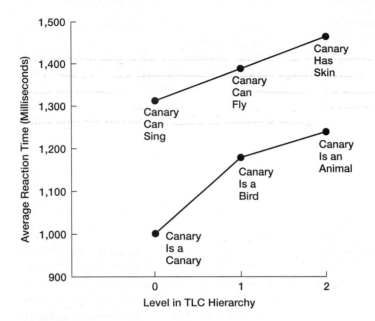

FIGURE 9.2
Reaction time to verify statements from different levels of TLC
hierarchy. *(From "Retrieval Time from Semantic Memory" by
A. M. Collins and M. R. Quillian,* Journal of Memory and
Language, *1969, 8, 240–247. Copyright 1969 by Academic
Press. Used by permission.)*

"A canary sings" and "A canary has skin" reflect differences in hierarchical storage, Conrad argued that these properties are experienced with different frequency.
That is, it is quite common to experience *singing* and *canary* together, so that
when we think of *canary,* we then think of *singing.* But very few of us have any
direct experience with canary skin and are unlikely to think *skin* when we think
canary. To explore these ideas, Conrad collected production frequency norms;
she gave participants a concept such as *canary* and asked them to write all of the
facts which came to mind when they thought of *canary.* She was then able to
arrange the properties of various concepts in order of how many participants
listed each property. For example, a large number of participants gave the response "moves" to *animal* but very few responded "has ears." It is important to
note, however, that in the hierarchical model of Quillian both properties are listed
at the *animal* node and should produce the same reaction time.

By pitting the frequency of responses against their position in the TLC hierarchy, Conrad performed an experiment whose results seriously questioned the
strict view of cognitive economy. That is, the speed with which properties are
verified was determined by the *frequency* with which they are listed rather than

by their location in the hierarchy. Conrad then suggested that the properties are stored directly at the level of the concepts, regardless of the duplication involved.

Although Conrad's data raise serious problems for the cognitive economy of TLC, the idea of direct storage seems a bit implausible. Can it be that "has a backbone" is among the information most of us store for every person we know? This certainly seems unlikely. The problem is that Conrad also seems to be assuming a rigid hierarchical representation, in which all concepts are represented in some strictly logical fashion. In fact, these data may be as critical of this type of hierarchical model as they are of the assumption of cognitive economy.

A related, and perhaps more serious, problem for a strict hierarchical network such as TLC is the relationship of various subordinates to a common superordinate. The hierarchical model treats all subordinates of a superordinate as equal; that is, all of the subordinates are directly related to the superordinate. But we know that all subordinates are not equally related to the superordinate. Not all birds are equally good examples of the concept of *bird*, nor are all dogs equally good instances of the knowledge of *dog*. Again, this fact is known from the production norms described previously. When asked to provide instances of the concept *bird*, people are most likely to respond with *robin, wren,* and *sparrow* and much less likely to say *ostrich* or *egret*, even though they know these animals are birds. In short, some subordinates seem to be more closely related to the superordinate than do others. This phenomenon is known as the *typicality effect*. The assumption that concepts are organized in a strict superordinate-subordinate relationship fails to capture the typicality effect.

Another particularly troublesome matter is research showing clear violations of the category size effect. Smith, Shoben, and Rips (1974) reported that people verify sentences such as "A cow is an animal" more rapidly than sentences such as "A cow is a mammal." Likewise, the response to "Scotch is a drink" is more rapid than the response to "Scotch is an alcoholic beverage." In both examples, the first sentences require search of a larger category than do the second sentences; nonetheless, reaction times for the first sentences are faster. This outcome is in clear violation of category size predictions, which prescribe faster reaction time for smaller categories. Any theory proposing a strict superordinate-subordinate relationship will be unable to explain violations of the category size effect.

Feature Set Theory   Another instance of the classical view of concepts is *feature set theory*. This theory avoids the problems of a strict superordinate-subordinate structure by suggesting that concepts are collections of features. Features can be viewed as component parts of the objects, much the same as were the physical features described in chapter 2 on pattern recognition; more precisely, features are values on a dimension. The dimensions may be perceptual—such as shape, size, and color—in which case the features will be particular colors (e.g., red), shapes (e.g., round), or sizes (e.g., small). Dimensions can also be functional characteristics and abstractions: mode of locomotion, a feature of which might be "flying"; eating habits, a feature of which might be "worms"; or even abstractions such as honesty and beauty, features of which might be "deceitful" and "gorgeous." Knowledge then consists of all of the features comprising that concept. This view is considerably different from the assumption that knowledge of a concept is represented by a set of interconnected nodes. The most obvious difference is that the relationships among concepts are determined by the number of shared attributes rather than distance in a network.

Smith, Shoben, and Rips' (1974) research, which caused so much difficulty for the original TLC theory, also was the springboard for feature set theory. The theory proposes a distinction between two kinds of features, *defining features* and *characteristic features*. Defining features are the necessary and sufficient features of a concept. They are the core meaning of the concept. To be classified as a member of the category defined by a concept, the instance must share the defining features of the concept. For example, to be classified a *bird,* the object must have certain features shared by all of those objects known as *birds.* Regardless of what those features are, the theory assumes that some set of the features defines an object as a member of a particular class, be it *bird, automobile, house plants,* or *college professor.* All objects in the class share the defining features.

The second type of feature is characteristic of the concept but not necessary to its definition. For example, we characteristically associate flying with *bird,* but flying cannot be a defining feature of *bird.* Flying is neither necessary nor sufficient for something to be a bird. Very simply, some of the creatures we know as *birds*—ostriches and chickens, for example—do not fly, and some of the things that fly are known not to be birds—bees and airplanes, for example. So while we may think of *fly* when we think of *bird* (most birds do fly), *fly* is not an attribute that defines an object as a bird.

Concepts consist of the entire bundle of features, both defining and characteristic. When we think of the concept, all of the information contained in these features is activated. If we must call on knowledge to answer a question such as "Is a robin a bird?" the features of both robin and bird are activated, and the decision process begins. The decision is a two-stage process of matching the features of the two concepts. In the first stage, all of the features, both characteristic and defining, are matched. If there are a large number of features in common, the question can quickly be answered yes. If there are very few features in common, the question can quickly be answered no. For example, "Is a robin a bird?" receives a quick yes response, and "Is a turnip a bird?" receives a quick no response. Some concepts, however, share an intermediate number of features—"Is an ostrich a bird?"—and then the second phase of the decision process occurs. In the *second phase,* only the *defining features* are matched. The second phase, then, requires more time in order to produce an answer.

This two-stage process allows the feature set model to describe the category size effect, as well as the anomalies associated with that effect. Furthermore, the model also accounts nicely for semantic distance effects. Understanding how this works begins with the realization that the degree of relationship is determined largely by the total amount of feature overlap. Using this basic premise, let us briefly describe how the model applies to the various empirical findings.

Beginning with the category size effect, it takes more time to verify that a *robin* is an *animal* than that it is a *bird,* the assumption being that *robin* shares more total features with *bird* than with *animal.* The retrieval and comparison processes for *robin* and *bird* can thus be completed in one stage, but the lack of overlap between *robin* and *animal* necessitates the second stage of comparing defining features.

Precisely the same analysis is applied to the typicality effect. *Robin* as *bird* is verified more quickly than *chicken* as *bird,* because *robin* shares more features with *bird* than does *chicken.* To verify *chicken* as *bird* requires matching defining features. Furthermore, the same mechanism is applied to anomalies from the category size effect, cases in which instances are more rapidly verified as members of large categories than of small categories. *Scotch* is more quickly classified as a *drink* than as an *alcoholic beverage,* and *dog* is more readily verified as an *animal* than as a *mammal,* because the instance shares more features with the large category superordinate than with the small category superordinate.

Although the feature set model seems to explain semantic distance effects and category size effects, the immediate reaction may be skepticism because it appears that the explanation is provided after the fact. To counter this criticism, Smith, Shoben, and Rips (1974) suggest that the number of features shared by an instance and its superordinate can be determined by *typicality* ratings. *Typicality* refers to how well a particular instance represents knowledge of the concept, and ratings of typicality are easily obtained by simply asking people questions such as, "On a scale of 1 to 10, how typical is *robin* of *bird*?" and "How typical is *ostrich* of *bird*?" In their theory, two concepts, such as *robin* and *bird,* share defining features when people classify one as an instance of the other. The typicality ratings, then, provide an estimate of the number of characteristic features shared by an instance and a superordinate.

According to the feature set theory, the time required to verify an instance as a member of a category should be inversely related to its typicality. That is, highly typical instances should be verified quickly because they share a large number of characteristic features with the superordinate. Atypical instances are verified less rapidly because they share fewer characteristic features and require the second phase of the decision process, matching defining features. In a test of this idea, Smith, Shoben, and Rips (1974) found that typicality ratings nicely predicted relative reaction time. Consistent with their idea, typical instances were verified more rapidly than were atypical instances.

In spite of these successes, the feature model has its troublesome side. The major problem results from the assumption that concepts contain necessary and sufficient features in the form of defining features. Specifically, what constitutes a defining feature? Take any concept—*dog* for example—and try to think of one feature or even a set of features which can be removed from an instance so that it no longer is recognizable as a member of the concept. If you see a dog with no tail or no legs, or for that matter no head, is it still a dog? The problem is the inability to identify defining features.

As Medin (1989) notes, "The classical view assumes that mental representations of categories consist of summary lists of features or properties that individually are necessary for category membership and collectively are sufficient to determine category membership" (p. 1470). The example of *dog* in the previous paragraph illustrates the lack of necessity and sufficiency in that, no matter what you remove, the thing is still identified as *dog*. Thus, whatever is removed must not be necessary to identify *dog,* and whatever remains must be sufficient to identify *dog*. Since we cannot think of things that when removed would obscure the identity of *dog,* serious questions arise concerning the existence of features that are necessary to identify a concept and that, when present, are sufficient to identify a concept.

Prototype Theory

The classical view of concepts that we have just described assumes that the core meaning of concepts is absolute in that concepts consist of necessary features. Superficially, our intuitions agree with this view to the extent that we believe some set of features uniquely specifies a particular concept, but as we have also seen, research does not support this view.

One response has been the development of *prototype theory.* The common assumption of prototype theory is that a concept is represented as the abstraction of characteristic features (Posner & Keele, 1970; Rosch, 1978). That is, as a person experiences various instances of a category, he or she abstracts the common attributes, and the abstracted representation is the concept. Like the classical theory, prototype theory assumes that concepts are abstract because the representation of the concept is different from any particular instance. On the other hand, prototype theory does not assume that the abstracted features are necessary or defining features. This approach is more probabilistic than is the classical view. In order to be classified as a member of the category defined by the concept, the instance does not have to share the defining features but, rather, only has to overlap sufficiently with the prototype.

A prototype is the best representation of a category in the sense that it consists of the features most commonly presented by the instances. For example, a prototypical fish might be about the size of a trout (12 to 15 inches), have scales and fins, and swim in an ocean, a lake, or a river. We have a general or abstract conception of fish, which somehow is typical or representative of the variety of examples with which we are familiar. When given a particular example, we compare it to this abstract prototype of the category. If it is sufficiently similar to the prototype, we then judge it to be an instance of the category. If not, then we reject it as an instance of the category. Research exists supporting the idea of prototypes for both perceptual and conceptual categories.

An example of the application of prototype theory to perceptual categories comes from research on color concepts. One question asked in this research is, are some colors better examples of color categories than are others? For example, are some reds more representative of the category *red* than others? Rosch argued that there are some colors that are best examples of a particular color category. These best examples are the prototypes.

In the case of color, Rosch hypothesized that prototypicality might be based on certain properties of the nervous system. A best blue might be best, among all the blues, because the visual system is more sensitive to that particular blue. One can then speculate that, if this is the case, people from different cultures might respond to the same color prototypes. Rosch was able to test this possibility by doing a series of color experiments with the Dani, a fairly primitive people in New Guinea. The Dani have no color-naming system as such; they differentiate colors only as dark and light. Since they have the same nervous system as people of western cultures, Rosch argued that they should respond to the same prototypical values of color.

In one experiment, she found that the Dani participants learned to associate names with color chips more rapidly when the colors were prototypical. For example, participants learned to respond to a pure green more rapidly than to a color peripheral to the category, such as yellow-green, even though they did not initially possess names for the colors. When the color chips were arranged in groups of three—for example, blue-green, pure green, and yellow-green,—participants learned the prototype more rapidly if it was made central in the category than when one of the other chips was made central. Similar findings were reported in studies of form categories. That is, there are prototypical squares and triangles as well as prototypical colors. The importance of Rosch's studies is that they establish the point that color concepts are internally structured, with some colors being more representative of a color category than others.

Rosch (1975) also contributed important research on the structure of semantic concepts. In this research, she asked participants to rate words that were members of categories—such as furniture and vehicles—as to how representative they were of the category. The results were strikingly clear; semantic-category prototypes do exist. For example, participants agreed that *chair* is very representative of the category *furniture,* whereas *desk* and *chest of drawers* are less representative. Participants also show a high degree of agreement in this task. Examples of norms for two categories, *furniture* and *vehicles,* are shown in table 9.1.

Rosch also showed that the time required to judge whether an item belongs to a given semantic category depends on the degree of category membership. Participants were presented with statements of the form "A doll is a toy." In some cases, the example was a good one—that is, very representative of the category— and in other cases, the example was a poor one. Where the statement was *true,* participants took longer to respond yes when the example was a poor member of the category.

TABLE 9.1
NORMS FOR GOODNESS-OF-EXAMPLE RATING FOR TWO SEMANTIC CATEGORIES

Furniture category member	Goodness-of-example rank	Vehicle category member	Goodness-of-example rank
Chair	1.5	Automobile	1
Sofa	1.5	Station wagon	2
Couch	3.5	Car	4
Easy chair	5	Bus	5.5
Dresser	6.5	Taxi	5.5
Rocking chair	6.5	Jeep	7
Coffee table	8	Ambulance	8
Rocker	9	Motorcycle	9
Love seat	10	Streetcar	10
Chest of drawers	11	Van	11
Desk	12	Honda	12
Bed	13	Cable car	13

From "Cognitive Representations of Semantic Categories," by E. Rosch, *Journal of Experimental Psychology: General,* 1975, *104,* 192–233. Copyright 1975 by the American Psychological Association. Reprinted by permission.

The ranking of goodness is essentially the same thing as typicality ratings, but Rosch's explanation of these data does not rely on assumptions of defining features. Rather, the rankings are presumed to reflect the similarity between the instance being ranked and the abstract representation of knowledge in the form of the prototype. The internal structure of categories also relies on the similarity among the instances in a fashion that Rosch labels family resemblance.

Family resemblance refers to how well a concept is represented by members of a category defined by the concept (Rosch & Mervis, 1975). Returning to table 9.1, we can see that people are in agreement that chairs, sofas, and tables are good examples of furniture. These concepts have been called *basic level categories.* The basic level can be contrasted with more general superordinate level such as *furniture* and with more specific subordinate concepts such as *recliner, sleeper sofa,* and *card table.* Rosch and Mervis (1975) propose that basic level concepts share many attributes with other members of the category and few attributes with members of other categories. Category members at the basic level share a larger quantity of information, which makes the basic level concept most informative.

Prototype theory can explain most of the results of classification experiments while avoiding the difficulty posed by defining features. Prototype theory claims that there are no defining features; rather, knowledge is the representation of attributes that tend to be true of the concept. Thus, prototype theory suggests objects are classified more loosely than does feature set theory. Even so, evidence exists to suggest that not even prototype theory is flexible enough to account for our use of knowledge. The evidence is in the form of context effects on performance that should be based on abstract representations.

BOX 9.1

NEURAL ORGANIZATION OF KNOWLEDGE

The study of brain-damaged subjects has recently provided a novel perspective on the organization of knowledge. It has long been known that damage to the occipital-temporal region of the brain can produce impairments in the ability to recognize objects, a condition known as "agnosia," which literally means "lack of knowledge." Agnosia is informative to the cognitive study of knowledge because it appears to reflect a basic semantic knowledge deficit, rather than a deficit in perceptual abilities. Thus, as shown in figure 9.3, an agnosic patient may be able to accurately copy an object such as a key but be unable to identify what he or she has drawn. Such dissociations between the perceptual and meaningful aspects of an object suggest that brain damage can selectively affect the knowledge system and, thus, tell us about its neural organization. Important in this regard are reports that patients with agnosia may exhibit category-specific knowledge deficits—for example, being unable to recognize plants and animals—while showing relatively intact recognition of inanimate objects. Examples of object definitions provided by one such patient (S.B.Y.) are given below (from Warrington & Shallice, 1984):

Living things:

Giraffe: "bird, not sure what it is used for"
Frog: "bird with no arms"
Poppy: "plant/tree of some sort"

Non-living things:

Umbrella: "object used to protect you from water that comes"
Scales: "measuring weight of things"
Submarine: "ship that goes underneath the sea"

The converse dissociation—impaired recognition of inanimate object despite intact recognition of plants and animals—has also been observed, suggesting that the living/nonliving distinction is a major taxonomic division of human knowledge.

Interestingly, although agnosic patients may have severe deficits in recognizing objects, they may still be able to understand scenes in which the objects play a central role. One patient (C.A.V.), for example, could not recognize a carrot but described the picture in figure 9.4(a) as depicting "enticement." Similarly, patient F.R.A., while unable to recognize a cup, could describe the action depicted in figure 9.4(b) as "drinking" (from McCarthy & Warrington, 1990).

Other studies have shown that agnosia can be restricted to particular modalities. For example, McCarthy and Warrington (1988) reported a patient (T.O.B.) who had great difficulties defining animals, but only when the animal names were presented verbally. For example, when asked to define *"dolphin"* the patient responded "A fish or a bird" but, when shown a picture of a dolphin, he stated, "Dolphin lives in water . . . they are trained to jump up and come out . . . In America during the war years they started to get this particular animal to go through to look into ships." Patients such as T.O.B. suggest the possibility that semantic knowledge is organized, not only in terms of specific taxonomic categories (such as living/nonliving) but also in terms of specific modalities (e.g., visual and auditory).

A particularly interesting form of agnosia is prosopagnosia ("lack of face knowledge"). Patients with prosopagnosia cannot identify the faces of their friends and family, the faces of famous people such as John Wayne or Madonna, and even have difficulty recognizing their

(continued)

BOX 9.1   (continued)

NEURAL ORGANIZATION OF KNOWLEDGE

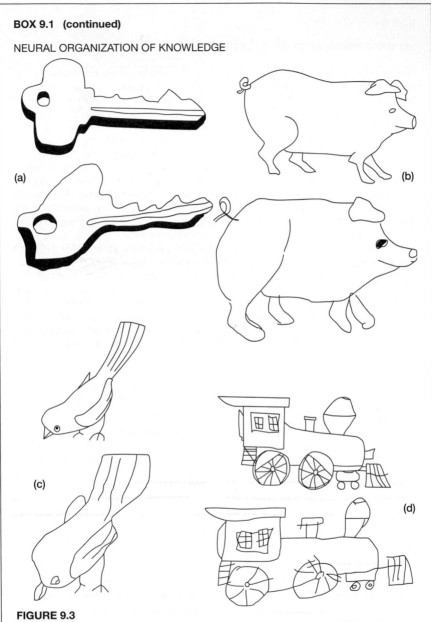

FIGURE 9.3
Copies of line drawings by a patient with associative visual agnosia. After copies
were made, the patient still misidentified drawings as follows: (a) "I still don't know."
(b) "Could be a dog or any other animal." (c) "Could be a beach stump." (d) "A wagon
or a car of some kind. The larger vehicle is being pulled by the smaller one." *(From
Rubens, A. B., & Benson, D. F. (1971.) Associative visual agnosia. Archives of
Neurology, 24, 305–317. Copyright 1971 by the American Medical Association)*

BOX 9.1   (continued)

NEURAL ORGANIZATION OF KNOWLEDGE

FIGURE 9.4
Agnostic patient could identify the actions depicted but could not identify the objects in the pictures. *(From* Cognitive Neuropsychology: A clinical introduction *by R. A. McCarthy & E. K. Warrington. 1990, San Diego: Academic Press. Copyright 1990 by Academic Press.)*

own face in photographs or when seen in the mirror. This is despite the fact that they have little or no difficulty recognizing objects, living or nonliving. Moreover, despite the prosopagnosic's failure of conscious recognition, there is evidence that some of these patients can unconsciously recognize the faces of people they had known before their brain damage. Thus, these patients may show elevated skin conductance responses to previously known faces but not to unfamiliar faces (Tranel & Damasio, 1985) or may learn correct name-face pairings of familiar people faster than incorrect face-name pairings, despite a failure to

recognize the familiar face (Bruyer et al., 1983; see also DeHaan, Young, & Newcombe, 1987).

These studies suggest both that faces are a special category of knowledge (at least for humans) and that access to knowledge may occur both consciously and unconsciously.

Although various forms of agnosia have been reported during the last 100 years, it is only recently that these patients have been studied with modern cognitive and neuroscientific techniques. It seems certain that such patients will transform our understanding of how knowledge is represented.

CONTEXT EFFECTS ON CLASSIFICATION

The way an object is classified very much depends on how it is perceived and encoded. This fact was demonstrated in experiments by Labov (1973), who showed how the verbal context associated with an object can influence the way participants classify the object. In these experiments, Labov used cuplike objects, examples of which are shown in figure 9.5. All these drawings resemble cups, although some are a bit unusual. The cups along the left side of the figure (cups 5 through 9) show increasing elongation. The cups across the top (1 through 4) show an increase in the ratio of width to depth; as they become wider they begin to look more like bowls. Other differences are obvious. Cups 10 through 12 are cylindrical, cups 13 through 15 are conical, and cups 16 and 17 have stems. In Labov's experiments, these drawings were presented one at a time, and participants were simply asked to name them. This defined a *neutral* instructional condition. In other conditions, participants were asked to name the objects under different instructional sets. For example, participants were asked to imagine the object sitting on a dinner table or filled with mashed potatoes or that someone was drinking coffee from it. After the various instructions, subjects were asked to identify the objects, one at a time, using a label or phrase.

The results are presented in figure 9.6, which shows the percentage of participants giving a particular name as a function of width of the object and instructional set. The figure shows two important points. First, the frequency of *cup* responses decreases while the frequency of *bowl* responses increases as the width

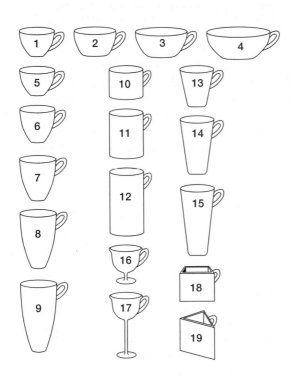

FIGURE 9.5
Series of cuplike objects for classification. *(From "The Boundaries of Words and Their Meanings." by W. Labov, in C. J. N. Bailey and R. W. Shuy, Eds., New Ways of Analyzing Variations in English. Washington, D.C.: Georgetown University Press, 1973.)*

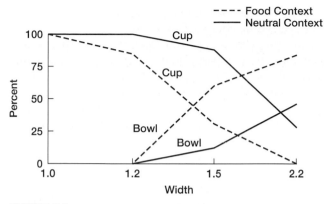

FIGURE 9.6
Percent of different name types applied to objects as the width
increases and as a function of the verbal set. *(From "The
Boundaries of Words and Their Meanings" by W. Labov, in
C. J. N. Bailey and R. W. Shuy, Eds.,* New Ways of Analyzing
Variations in English. *Washington, D.C.: Georgetown University
Press, 1973.)*

of the objects increases. The change is gradual, indicating that the boundary between *cup* and *bowl* is fuzzy. This, of course, is not particularly surprising. The
second point is that the frequency distributions of the *cup* label and the *bowl* label
are influenced markedly by the verbal instructions or context. For example, an object is more likely to be called a bowl if it is thought of as filled with mashed potatoes, as compared to the neutral context. These results show convincingly that a
category is defined *both* by the *perceptual features* of the object (width) and by
the prevailing *verbal-instructional context* under which the judgments are made.

The role of linguistic context has been further demonstrated in a study by Roth
and Shoben (1983). They presented participants with the name of an exemplar
embedded in a linguistic context; this was, in turn, followed by the names of exemplars. Specifically, the participants were presented a category in different linguistic contexts and then were asked to judge each example as to how well it fit
the category. For instance, when *animal* was presented in a sentence about *milk-
ing, cow* and *goat* were judged as typical by the participants. In contrast, when
animal was presented in a sentence about *riding, horse* and *mule* were judged as
more typical.

As Barsalou and Medin (1986) observed, these results demonstrate that the
linguistic context in which people encounter a category can have an important
impact on how they judge the category. Similarly, the point of view that a person
adopts can readily influence how examples are placed, or ordered, in a category.
Barsalou and Sewell (1984) had American undergraduate students adopt different perspectives or points of view while judging the typicality of instances.

Participants were instructed, for example, to take various international viewpoints such as those of the average American, Chinese, or French citizen, or they were asked to take the viewpoint of an average U.S. housewife or businessman. As a general rule, the point of view that participants adopted very much influenced how they classified exemplars as being typical.

Finally, people cannot only alter the representations of an existing category, as described above, but they can also develop completely new categories with new knowledge and experiences. Barsalou (1983) has observed that people frequently construct new ad hoc categories as necessary to achieve some goal. For example, if someone is going camping for the first time, the person may construct ad hoc categories for places to go camping, things to take camping, times to go camping, and so forth. But with camping experience, new categories are formed and old ones altered. Taken together, these observations are not easily explained by the theories we have considered, each of which assumes that concepts are abstract and, hence, should not be influenced by the particular context in which they occur.

EPISODIC INFLUENCE ON CLASSIFICATION

The abstract nature of knowledge is central to most ideas about the structure of concepts. Research demonstrating dissociations of memory tests has been offered as strong evidence of the existence of a separate system containing abstract knowledge. We discussed this research in chapter 6 but shall return to it here to make some additional points. Research on dissociations, as you will remember, demonstrates that certain variables have different effects on different kinds of memory tests. You also will recall that these effects are relevant to the distinction between memory and knowledge because many of the *implicit* memory tests can be completed with responses that are context independent, the very criteria presumed to define the abstract knowledge stored as concepts. Most *explicit* memory tests correspond to episodic memory because the test requires production of a particular prior event.

Not all of the research on dissociation is consistent with the use of abstract knowledge. One example is a study by Jacoby and Witherspoon (1982) that simply required participants to spell words. Spelling of a word is presumably a product of abstract knowledge. That is, spelling does not appear to require access to a specific prior episode but, rather, access to general knowledge abstracted over a number of episodes. If so, a single specific prior episode should have little influence on the simple task of spelling a word. If, for example, you have to spell the word *sale,* the fact that you had just encountered an advertisement for discounts at your favorite haberdashery or had seen the famous Arthur Miller play should make little difference to your performance.

However, in the vein of this example, what if someone *said* to you, "Spell the word *sale,*" just as you were watching a yacht race? The point, of course, is that *sale* and *sail* are homophones, words which sound alike but are spelled differently. Most homophones have a dominant sense; that is, one meaning and spelling of a homophone will have a higher probability of occurring when the word is presented out of context. Taking advantage of this situation, Jacoby and Witherspoon (1982) examined the influence of a single prior exposure upon the spelling of homophones.

The pertinent portion of Jacoby and Witherspoon's experiment is simple but ingenious. First, homophones were presented in a biased context by asking participants to respond to some simple statements such as, "Name a musical instrument that employs a *reed*." *Reed* is the low-probability interpretation of the homophone *read/reed*. After responding, the participants then were asked to spell a list of words that included the homophones from the statements. No instructions mentioned the relationship between the statements and spelling. Interest here was primarily in the spelling of a homophone, given a low-probability bias at input. In fact, the biased, low-probability spelling (*reed*) was more than twice as likely as the dominant spelling (*read*) to be given by subjects who had answered the initial statements. The point is that following a single experience (response to statement), the preferred spelling of a homophone was drastically altered. How could this happen if these preferred spellings resulted from knowledge that is abstracted from hundreds of episodes?

As with the research on verbal context effects and categories, particular aspects of context appear to influence our use of concepts to solve problems and make judgements. The theories of knowledge we have described in this chapter assume that concepts are abstracted from previous experience. It is abstract in that the information represented as knowledge does not include the contextual particulars of the previous experience. Your concept of "the first president of the United States" was acquired through numerous experiences, but the abstract representation of this knowledge does not include information about the particular episodes from which the knowledge was abstracted. The surprising aspect of Jacoby and Witherspoon's data is that a single experience could alter radically the preferred spelling of a homophone that had been acquired over numerous prior experiences. Observations such as these have led to the exemplar theory of knowledge structure.

EXEMPLAR THEORY

The final theory of the structure of concepts we shall consider actually denies the existence of abstract representations by claiming that all knowledge is episodic. This position, which is known as *exemplar* theory, does not deny the existence of knowledge but, rather, attempts to explain the use of knowledge without reference to abstracted representations of general information. Knowledge is *specific* past experience. For example, comprehension of *dog* is not a matter of activating the concept of *dog* abstracted from your numerous previous encounters with dogs. Rather, *dog,* is comprehended by retrieving a particular episode involving a dog. In other words, when you think of *dog,* you do not think of some generic canine but of a specific dog. Prominent advocates of this idea have been Lee Brooks (1978) and Jacoby and Brooks (1984).

The notion is that concepts are represented by particular instances from our previous experiences. When a problem requiring classification—for example, is that person friendly or not?—is presented, the instance is matched against some list of prior episodes that are similar to the new one. Thus, in a real sense, memory is knowledge.

Discrete prior episodes actually do affect performance that could be guided solely by an abstract rule. Allen and Brooks (1991) asked participants to learn to categorize two fictitious creatures, one called Builder and one called Digger. The animals could be classified on the basis of a simple rule. The Builders (shown in the upper left panel of figure 9.7) always had at least two of the following three characteristics, long legs, angular bodies, and spots. Anything else was a Digger. The participants in the experiment learned this rule and practiced applying it with training examples such as those shown in the left panel of figure 9.7. The training session was 40 trials of classifying the examples as either a Builder or a Digger. By the end of training, the participants possessed a simple, well-practiced rule. The situation was designed to be as lifelike as possible. For example, you probably behave in accord with rules such as the following: if it is cloudy and the forecast is for rain, take an umbrella. The point is that the rule appears to be abstract in that its application is not influenced by the prior episodes under which it was learned. In the Allen and Brooks experiment, the simple, well-practiced rule for defining Diggers and Builders should have been applied to new examples without any influence from the specific training examples.

In a clever test of this intuitively plausible hypothesis, Allen and Brooks gave a classification test of new examples that had not been seen in the training session. Examples of these test items are shown in the right column of figure 9.7. Notice that the test examples are not identical to a training example, but all test items can be correctly classified by applying the simple rule. Some of the test items, however, looked like a particular training example, and that training example was from the incorrect category. The animal in the lower right panel of figure 9.7 is clearly a Builder because it has spots and long legs; it conforms to the rule defining a Builder and should be classified as a Builder. Yet, this Builder has irrelevant features that are identical to one of the training examples of a Digger. This one training example is analogous to a single prior experience in the course of learning an abstract rule. The important result of the experiment was that performance on these negative match test items was less accurate and less rapid than on positive match test items. The only way this could happen was because a particular instance in training influenced the classification of the test items. Behavior that appears to be guided by an abstract rule actually is influenced by a very specific prior event. The general point is that knowledge may correspond to specific prior events rather than to abstract representations.

Rule: At Least Two of (Long Legs,
Angular Body, Spots) ⟶ Builder

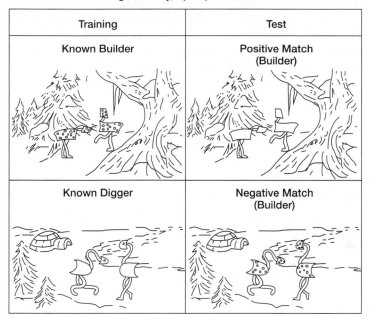

FIGURE 9.7
An example of the study and test, figures from Allen and Brooks' (1991)
study of concept acquisition. *(From "Specializing the operation of an
explicit rule" by S. W. Allen and L. Brooks.* Journal of Experimental
Psychology; General, *1991, 20 3–19. Copyright 1991 by the American
Psychological Association. Reprinted by permission.)*

Brooks, Norman, and Allen (1991) demonstrated essentially the same result
in the case of medical diagnosis. Medical diagnosis is a problem of classification
in which the particular set of symptoms presented by a patient must be classified
as a particular disease. The knowledge that supports the diagnosis is the concept
of the disease. In the Allen et al. experiment, physicians were shown pictures of
skin disorders and asked to diagnose the problem. Even though the physicians
were capable of correct diagnosis of each of the disorders, the presentation of
the slides depicting the problems affected the diagnosis. In particular, if a disorder from a particular diagnostic category was visually similar to a previous slide
from a different diagnostic category, the chance of misdiagnosis increased.
Again, a particular prior instance is influencing performance that should be governed by abstract rules.

As a final interesting example, Ste-Marie and Lee (1991) and Ste-Marie and
Valiquette (1996) have studied the performance of gymnastic judges. The task of
the judge can be viewed as matching the particular routine of a competitor against
the concept of that routine. The closer the match, the higher the score. Gymnastic

judges watch not only the competitive performance but also usually watch the warm-ups of the competitors. Competitors use the warm-up to practice the routine they will perform in the competition. Ste-Marie and her associates have demonstrated that the warm-up influences judging of the actual competition. Mistakes in the warm-up led to lower scores than were warranted by the actual performance.

Exemplar theory is consistent with all of the foregoing observations in that knowledge is particular prior experience. Situations requiring the use of concepts, be they medical diagnosis or gymnastics judging, will be determined by specific prior events rather than by an abstract representation such as a prototype. Exemplar theory is provocative in its challenge to our normal assumptions about what we mean by knowledge, but in spite of or perhaps because of its radical assumptions, the theory is enjoying considerable success. We shall have occasion to revisit this approach when we discuss the use of knowledge in reasoning and problem solving in chapter 12.

SUMMARY

Concepts are the fundamental representation of knowledge that function to group similar things into categories. The ability to classify superficially different things as the same thing facilitates numerous important aspects of behavior. Most important is that concepts allow us to recognize novel objects or events as an instance of a known category, which in turn allows us to respond appropriately to the novel event. Without the concept that is used to classify the novel object, the only guide to behavior in the presence of the novel object would be trial and error. Concepts also facilitate communication with others in that two speakers who share the same concepts can converse more efficiently. One of the reasons for the increased efficiency is that concepts are the basis for inferences, and when two speakers share concepts, much of the communication is in the form of inferences rather than more extensive verbatim accounts. For example, if you tell me that you are frustrated because you spent three hours typing a paper and the computer crashed before you saved the work, our shared concept of computer allows me to understand why you are frustrated, with no further explanation on your part. Concepts also facilitate learning. We often use a known concept as an analogy for something we are trying to understand, (e.g., water is like electricity). Another important use of concepts is to create new knowledge. Existing concepts are frequently combined to create a new concept such as tofu dog. The new concept expresses knowledge not contained in either of the other concepts.

Research on concepts has focused on the fundamental question of what is the nature of knowledge that constitutes a concept. One dimension on which theories of conceptual structure differ markedly is whether the knowledge is absolute or probabilistic. This difference was illustrated in the contrast between classical theory and prototype theory. The classical view is that concepts consist of necessary and sufficient features; that is, the concept represents the essence of a class of things. All things belonging to this class will have these features and if a thing has the features, it must be a member of the class. In contrast, prototype theory suggests that the concept consists of features that characterize members of the class. In this view, classification is probabilistic in that something can be included as a member of the class if its features overlap sufficiently with the prototype. Unlike the classical view, the feature match does not have to be exact.

Both the classic theory and the prototype theory assume that concepts are abstract. The concept represents the invariant features in the case of the classical view and the modal or common features in the case of prototype theory that have been abstracted from experienced instances. In both cases, the knowledge expressed by the concept is different from knowledge of the instances. To say that knowledge is abstract is to say that its application is not dependent on the context in which it was learned, and that variations in context should not affect the application of a concept. Research, however, has shown that manipulation of context does influence the use of context, and this finding has encouraged the development of a different view of conceptual structure. The exemplar theory proposes that concepts are lists of experienced instances, and that the classification of new instances relies on a comparison not with an abstract concept but with prior instances. For this reason, the knowledge represented by concepts in exemplar theory is not abstract but is particular. With exemplar theory, we begin to lose the distinction between knowledge and memory.

THOUGHT QUESTIONS

1. What is the meaning of abstract knowledge?
2. Why are concepts abstract in the classical theory?
3. Why did data on cognitive economy and typicality effects pose such general difficulty for hierarchically organized models?
4. What is the retrieval process a person would likely use to verify "a robin is a bird" and "an ostrich is a bird," according to the Smith, Shoben, and Rips feature model?
5. How does exemplar theory explain the results of Brooks, Norman, and Allen's (1991) experiments on medical diagnosis?

10

LANGUAGE: BASIC CONCEPTS

One form of knowledge shared by all human societies is knowledge of language. Although knowledge in the form of particular concepts differs across societies and even individuals within a society, all people, except those who have suffered severe brain injury, possess knowledge of language. Language is the principal means by which we acquire and express knowledge; thus, the study of how language is used is a central concern of cognitive psychology. In this chapter, we provide a broad overview of research on language, to be followed in the next chapter by a more detailed discussion of the processes underlying language comprehension.

Language is our principal means of communication with other people, yet we frequently take this complex ability for granted. Perhaps this is because, as adults, we have little memory of the long process of language acquisition. For many of us, language is a natural and simple process until, as adults, we attempt to learn a second language. This is not to say that learning a foreign language is the same as learning a first language. Indeed, early language learning appears relatively effortless, compared with learning a foreign language as a college student.

One theory of the relation between language and thought is that language is "the tool of thought." Jean Piaget, a distinguished Swiss psychologist, made an interesting analogy in pointing out that language is to thought as mathematics is to physics. Just as mathematics is used as the language of physics, ordinary language bears a similar relationship to thought.

Language is composed of linguistic units combined according to rules operating at several levels. For example, words are composed of basic vowel and consonant sounds, or *phonemes;* phrases are composed of words; sentences of phrases; and so on. The characteristic, or *design feature,* of language whereby units can be rearranged and combined at successively higher levels (e.g., *a, t,* and *p* into *pat* or *tap*) is referred to as *duality of patterning* and accounts for the infinite *productivity,* or creativity, of language (Hockett, 1963). The phoneme is often considered the basic linguistic unit of language, but as we shall see, it appears more likely that either syllables or words are the basic psychological units involved in the perception and comprehension of language (Johnson, 1986; Paivio & Begg, 1981).

At a general level, spoken language represents the major system available to the human being for communication, although *signs* can also be used to communicate. Technically, *sign* is a broad term including any conventionally agreed upon symbol (or string of symbols) that designates some referent. Beyond the linguistic signs of words, there are road signs that convey information relevant to motorists; mathematical formulas that convey abstract relationships and operations; bodily signs that convey emotional feelings; and *manual signs* that convey information using the hands either *iconically* or *arbitrarily,* the way that letter patterns arbitrarily stand for their referents. Manual signs include the several distinct forms of sign language used by deaf individuals (e.g., American Sign Language, signed English) as well as conventional symbolic gestures (like the "Shhh!" gesture), novel gestures, and pantomime (McNeill, 1985; see Marschark, Everhart, Martin, & West, 1987, for descriptions and related research). All of these signs are symbols in the sense that they convey meaning. They provide some kind of information, which in turn allows some kind of response by other human beings.

In this chapter, we examine some of the basic features of language. In particular, we discuss the functions of language, the structure of language, the processes in language, and a range of selected issues in language.

FUNCTIONS OF LANGUAGE

Language serves several functions, which are all related to the fundamental process of communication. Perhaps most important is that language conveys meaning and is part of almost all kinds of social interaction. Language conveys intentions, motives, feelings, and beliefs. Language is used to issue requests and commands such as "Get me a glass of water." Language is also used to teach and to convey information. Indeed, due to duality of patterning and productivity, an infinite range of knowledge and beliefs can be conveyed via language.

Language is useful because it can represent ideas and events that are not tied to the present. Hockett (1963) identified this as another of the design features of language and referred to it as *displacement*. He pointed out that through language, unlike other forms of animal communication, we can communicate about the past as well as convey plans for the future. You can describe abstract ideas, such as beauty and justice, as well as concrete objects of everyday experience. Thus, language is *symbolic,* in that speech sounds and utterances stand for or represent various objects, ideas, and events.

In any language communication system, there is a speaker (or producer), a listener (or receiver), and a system for communication, such as the English language of American Sign Language (Ameslan). Communication begins with "speakers," who decide to convey information. They select a medium of communication, such as English, and produce sentences (or approximations to them). "Listeners" receive the signals being presented (speech sounds or signs) and represent them in memory. Regardless of whether we are considering spoken language, written language, or sign language, there are three elements of human communication that have been identified as operating in this speaker-listener situation: *speech acts* (Searle, 1969, 1975), *propositional content,* and *thematic structure.* We will examine these elements in the following section, and the description follows the analysis outlined by Clark and Clark (1977).

Speech Acts

Speakers normally intend to have some influence on their listeners. To do so, speakers get the listeners to recognize the speakers' intentions. Indeed, failure to recognize these intentions can result in awkward situations. For example, consider the following short-circuited phone exchange:

Person A: "Hello, is John home?"
Person B: "Yes."

(Lengthy pause)
Person A: "May I speak with him, please?"
Person B: "Oh, you want to talk to him? I'll get him."

Person A had two intentions that needed to be recognized by Person B: to find out John's whereabouts and to talk to John. Person B recognized the former but clearly missed the latter. Utterances such as "Hello, is John home?" are called *speech acts.* Speech-act theory holds that all utterances can be classified as to the type of speech act they represent. For example, speech acts may make assertions, make verbal commitments, convey thanks, give a warning, or issue a command. Typical examples of speech acts including the following: "I insist that you turn down the volume on the stereo" (a command); "What are your plans for Saturday night?" (a question); "I promise to pay you tomorrow" (a verbal commitment); and "I know that Professor Jones is the best instructor in the Psychology Department"(an assertion). In these examples, we see the acts of ordering, questioning, committing, and telling, which are common *direct* speech acts.

Searle (1969) pointed out that some speech acts are *indirect.* When your mother asks if you live in a barn, a guest in your house asks if you are chilly, or someone in a bar asks if you would like to see his or her etchings, they are conveying information about their desires, but in a rather indirect, nonliteral way. Some indirect speech acts have gained well-recognized meanings through their repeated use. For example, consider the utterance "Can you pass the salt?" The intended meaning involves a request to pass the salt rather than an inquiry into one's ability to do so. However, the meaning of any particular speech act, including whether it is direct or indirect, will depend on the *context* in which it is uttered (Gibbs, 1986), as well as its content.

Research has uncovered how systematic the effects of context can be in certain types of conversations. For example, indirect requests appear to be tailored to assure that the speaker does not overly offend or impose upon the listener. Rather, the form of the request is devised to overcome speaker perceived obstacles to the listener's carrying out the request (Franck & Clark, 1985; Gibbs, 1985, 1986). For example, Gibbs (1986) found that when a speaker perceives that the listener is not *able* to carry out the request, the speaker is more likely to frame the request as "Can you . . . ?" than "Would you mind . . . ?" or "Will you . . . ?"

Propositional Content

The second element of communication concerns the *propositional content* of a sentence. In communication, speakers want to convey certain ideas, and to do this, they must be sure that they are understood. Thus, the content around a speech act is very important. As a general rule, the propositional content of a sentence is used to describe certain states or events; it can be part of other propositions. For example, the sentence "The bright student received an *A* in calculus" expresses two separate propositions: "the student is bright" and "the student received an *A* in calculus."

Combined into a single sentence, the propositions convey what the speaker intends to convey. Note that the statement "You weren't raised in a barn!" contains propositional content at two different levels: the superficial, literal statement of fact concerning the residence of your childhood and the nonliteral, intended reference in your having left a door open. There is experimental evidence that we represent sentences as propositions. For example, the more propositions contained in a sentence, the longer the time required to read the sentence (see van Dijk & Kintsch, 1983).

Thematic Structure

The third component in communication is *thematic structure*. To communicate effectively, good speakers pay careful attention to their listeners. Good speakers have to judge what listeners do and do not know, keep track of where they are leading their listeners, and regularly examine any assumptions about the listeners' knowledge of the topic being discussed. In short, the speaker must be able to make reasonably accurate judgments of the listener's current level of understanding.

All of these features are present in good teachers, entertaining and effective storytellers, and interesting conversationalists. Unfortunately, all of us at one time have probably experienced a talk, lecture, or presentation in which the speaker droned on without any apparent interest in our level of understanding. Sometimes we are victims of eager monologists who are so anxious to relay their views of the world that they forget to check our understanding of what is being said. Similarly, there is the occasional teacher who lectures "in a trance," following a rigid format and without pausing to check on audience comprehension. Indeed, this inability to be sensitive to the listener is a major problem in communication.

One function of thematic consideration is to convey both given (understood) and new information. Good speakers attempt to tailor their sentences to fit what they think their listeners already know. For example, the sentence "It was your *son* who scored the touchdown" assumes that the listeners (parents) know that a touchdown was scored, but not that their son scored the touchdown. Thus, the given information in the sentence is that a touchdown was made, and the new information is that their son made the touchdown. The emphasis or stress in the sentence is on *son,* not on the fact that a touchdown was made. Similarly, semantic (conceptual) and syntactic (grammatical) structures can signal differences between given and new information across as well as within sentences (Conrad & Rips, 1986).

Sometimes a speaker emphasizes a particular phrase in a sentence by placing it at the beginning. In this fashion, the speaker focuses attention on the particular context in which the event occurred. For example, "At her cocktail party, Mrs. Jones was very gracious" makes it clear that Mrs. Jones was gracious in a particular context. The reader, thus, is implicitly cautioned that Mrs. Jones may or may not be gracious in other settings, without this specially being mentioned.

To summarize, the functions of language are seen in speech acts, propositional content, and thematic structure. Speakers signal their intent by the choice of a speech act, which includes telling, asking, or commanding someone. The propositional content of a sentence is the particular information that is conveyed. The thematic structure involves making judgments about the listener's knowledge, often by stressing new information in the context of known or given information We now turn our attention to certain structural properties of language.

STRUCTURE OF LANGUAGE

As should be evident by now, language can be divided into three basic parts, each with its own structure and rules: phonology, syntax (grammar), and semantics. The first of these, *phonology,* concerns the rules for pronunciation of speech sounds. The second aspect of language, *syntax,* deals with the way words combine to form sentences. And *semantics* focuses on the meaning of words and sentences. In this section, we examine certain aspects of the structure of language.

Basic Units of Language: Phonemes and Morphemes

All languages are made of basic sounds called *phonemes.* Adult human beings can produce approximately 100 phonemes, and the English language is made up of about 45 phonemes. Languages vary in the number of phonemes, ranging from as few as 15 to as many as 85. One reason why it is difficult for many Americans to learn foreign languages is that different phonemes are used. For instance, Germanic and Slavic languages contain phonemes never used in the English language.

Phonemes, in turn, are composed of about 12 *distinctive features.* The linguist Roman Jakobson (Jakobson & Halle, 1956) constructed a classification of distinctive features by which phonemes differ. For example, a given phoneme (speech sound) may be sounded either nasally or orally. Another feature is the explosive, or tense, character of some sounds, as seen when /p/ or /f/ (phonemes for the letters *p* and *f*) are pronounced.

A *phoneme* can be defined as any single change in the sound of a word that also makes a difference in meaning: *pin* versus *bin,* for example. Furthermore, contrasts that make a meaningful difference in one language may not make a difference in another language. English speakers, for example, do not distinguish between the aspirated and unaspirated forms of /p/: *pin* (aspirated /p/) versus *spin* (unaspirated /p/). To demonstrate that the /p/ in *pin* is aspirated, hold a match in front of your mouth while saying the word and note that the flame flickers. However, this does not happen when *spin* is said.

Another unit of language is the *morpheme,* which is the smallest meaningful unit in a language. Morphemes usually consist of combinations of two or more phonemes and roughly correspond to the most elementary words. The words *good, put,* and *go* are single morphemes. *Goodness, putting,* and *going* consist of two morphemes. Thus, single morphemes may be root words of a language; they may also consist of prefixes or suffixes.

Higher Levels of Linguistic Analysis

We have just considered the most basic analyses possible of language. The study of the speech sounds which make up a language is called phonology, and the study of how these sounds combine to produce morphemes is called *morphology*. However, psychologists are frequently interested in a more global analysis of language than is provided by phonology and morphology. Psychological investigations of language typically adopt words, phrases, sentences, or prose, rather than more elementary speech sounds, as the most fundamental unit of analysis.

There are several levels at which these higher-order analyses can be made. First, one could analyze the *lexical content* of a sentence or of some other unit of language production. When a lexical analysis is performed, the question is simply, what words are used in this sample of language? This was the basic approach of Thorndike and Lorge, who tabulated the frequency with which different English words occurred in large samples of printed material. For example, these investigators reported the average frequency of occurrence per million words of text for each of a large number of common words such as *kitchen* (over 100 times per million) and of rare words such as *rostrum* (only 1 time per million). Information gained from lexical analyses of language, such as that by Thorndike and Lorge, has proved to be very useful in predicting the ease with which different words can be learned in laboratory situations.

At another level of linguistic analysis, the *syntactic content* of language text may be investigated. In the study of syntax, interest is focused on the arrangement or ordering of words to form phrases and sentences. The question asked in this type of analysis is, how is this phrase (or sentence) structured? Psychologists and linguists interested in syntactic theory have attempted to specify rules that will generate an infinite number of grammatically correct sentences and no incorrect sentences—that is, the rules that account for the productivity of language, its most important characteristic (Chomsky, 1985). The set of rules indicating how the elements of the language may be combined to make intelligible sentences is referred to as a *grammar*. Although a large number of different grammars have been proposed, linguists have not been able to write down the extremely complex system of rules that generates all the syntactically correct sentences of the English language, or of any other natural language. At present, there is little agreement about the necessary features of an adequate grammar. However, an important part of many of the proposed grammars is the rules for phrase structure, which we consider in the next section.

Perhaps the most important level of analysis of language is the one that considers the *semantic content* or meaning of a passage. This perspective on language results in the asking of questions such as the following: What does the passage communicate? What is the meaning of this particular sentence? Unfortunately, psychologists and linguists know less about the rules for determining the meanings of words and combinations of words than they do about the rules of syntax or morphology. For example, for many years it was thought that word meanings were represented as a set of fixed properties or features (see Bierwisch, 1970;

Clark & Clark, 1977; Katz, 1972). These features were "semantic primitives," from which the meanings of all words were composed. For example, the word *short* was considered to represent in our "mental dictionary" as NOT (TALL) and the verb *kill* was represented as CAUSE (TO DIE). However, it has since been found that it is difficult to specify what this set of features should be (see Lakoff, 1987; Medin, 1989). Furthermore, there is also evidence that people do not always need to use these features to understand words (Fodor, Garrett, Walker, & Parkes, 1980; van Dijk & Kintsch, 1983). Lastly, words exhibit different meanings (i.e., are polysemous) in different contexts, something that should not happen if a set number and collection of features are always conveyed by their use (Lakoff, 1987). A current, alternative, view of word meaning is based on the *categorization theories* discussed in chapter 9, where instances belong to categories that are represented as a collection of features having "fuzzy boundaries" (see Medin, 1989). In this view, word meaning is a function of the interaction between word features and the extent to which they match those belonging to certain prototypical and nonprototypical contexts (Lakoff, 1987). Here, both feature theory and prototype theory are seen as important.

The critical role of semantics is not under question and has been clearly demonstrated in a number of psychological investigations. For example, when people listen to passages of connected discourse, their recognition memory for sentences after a short delay is much more sensitive to changes in semantic content (e.g., subject-object reversal) than to changes in syntactic content (e.g., switching from active to passive voice) (Sachs, 1967). In general, current views of semantics and comprehension view the listener (or reader) as an *active participant* who formulates hypotheses about subsequent input based on context (both verbal and situational), on knowledge of constraints in the language, and on knowledge of the world. This is in contrast to the more passive view of the comprehender as someone who waits for the input before acting upon it.

Although theories of semantics cannot be considered in further detail here, it is appropriate to point out the dramatic differences in approaches to theorizing in this area. Associationistic theories have been proposed in which meaning is viewed simply as a conditioned response. Thus, the responses made to a word are thought to be modifications of the unconditioned response once made to the object referred to by that word. In contrast to this approach, more recent theories have suggested possible structures of the semantic memory necessary for the use of language. This newer approach has considered the human being as an information-processing system rather than as an association learner and has resulted in a number of computer programs that attempt to model human ability to deal with semantics. Some of these computer programs provide persuasive demonstrations of their understanding of portions of the English language. For example, computer programs have been written that can respond in ordinary English to questions concerning the properties of objects or events, which the computer has stored in its memory after being presented with a series of sentences describing those objects or events. These issues were discussed in chapter 9. The collaboration among computer scientists, psychologists, and linguists offers one of the most promising approaches to the study of how human beings acquire knowledge of semantics.

Phrase Structure of Sentences

In order to understand language in the adult, it is necessary to examine the structure of sentences. At one level of analysis, a sentence can be regarded simply as a string of phonemes. The single phoneme, however, is not a particularly useful way of analyzing sentences, since this would be looking at a sentence as a series of isolated speech sounds. At another level, a sentence can be regarded as a series of morphemes, which are groupings of phonemes. From this viewpoint, however, the sentence is viewed as a string of words. Linguists have found it more useful to describe a sentence in terms of *phrases,* which are groupings of words.

Analysis of a sentence into its various phrases describes the *phrase structure* of a sentence. A sentence is viewed as composed of two basic phrases, a *noun phrase* and a *verb phrase,* which in turn are composed of subcomponents. Figure 10.1 shows the phrase structure of a simple sentence, "The boy rode the bicycle." The noun phrase is composed of a *determiner* and a *noun,* and the verb phrase is composed of a *verb* and *noun phrase;* the latter noun phrase is also composed of a determiner and a noun. Pauses in speech usually reflect underlying phrase structure (see e.g., Gee & Grosjean, 1983). For example, we are most likely to say, "The boy . . . rode . . . the bicycle," pausing ever so briefly after *boy* and *rode.* We are not likely to say, "The . . . boy rode . . . the bicycle," grouping *boy* and *rode,* or "The . . . boy rode the . . . bicycle," grouping *boy, rode,* and *the.* While in normal speech a speaker may search and grope for a particular word and, thus, alter the pauses, the listener still tends to understand the message.

Surface and Deep Structure in Sentences

Linguists distinguish between surface structure and deep structure of sentences. The *surface structure* is the organization that describes the sequences of phrases in a sentence as it is actually spoken (or read) and reflects the phonological realization of the complex, underlying linguistic structure.

Deep structure, in contrast, refers to the underlying structure that includes the relevant string of linguistic units, the grammatical requirements for lexical (word) selection, and the grammatical relations between words in sentences. The deep structure of a sentence, thus, specifies the derivations of both its surface structure and its meaning.

Consider the sentences, "John threw the ball" and "The ball was thrown by John." Both sentences convey the same meaning despite the fact that they sound different. Hence, their deep structure is the same. But consider the sentence "The lamb is ready to eat," which can have two meanings. The lamb may serve as food

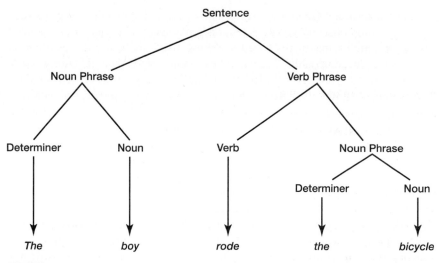

FIGURE 10.1
Phrase structure in a sentence, "The boy rode the bicycle," represented by a tree diagram. *(From* Fundamentals of Human Learning, Memory, and Cognition, *2nd ed., by H. C. Ellis. Dubuque, Iowa: Wm. C. Brown Company, 1978.)*

to be eaten, or as an animal, the lamb is prepared to eat food. Thus, the deep structure can vary within the same sentence, depending on what meaning the speaker swishes to convey. Evaluate the meanings of the following ambiguous sentences: "Visiting relatives can be a nuisance," "Bill shot the man with a gun," and "The corrupt police can't stop drinking."

These illustrations indicate the necessity of distinguishing between surface and deep structures. Sentences with essentially a single deep structure and two or more surface structures are *synonymous.* Sentences with different deep structures and the same surface structure are *ambiguous.* Thus, important problem remaining concerns the theoretical rules by which the deep structure of a sentence comes to be realized in a particular surface structure. Rules for the specification of this linkage process, called *transformational rules,* have been developed by Noam Chomsky (Chomsky, 1965, 1975) and other linguists.

Transformational rules have clear implications about what features of sentences human beings do store in memory. If the sentence is very simple, so that its deep structure approximates its surface structure, then features of the surface structure may be stored. As sentences become more complex, what is thought to be stored is some underlying base structure, or *schema,* plus one or more "footnotes" that serve as rules necessary to regenerate the sentence in its original surface form. This is simply to say that what is stored is some coded representation of the complex sentence.

Transformational Grammar   Information contained in a linguistic message tends to be comprehended, and sometimes is remembered, in syntactically defined chunks, although semantically based chunking also may be used, depending on the demands placed upon the listener and the nature of the material (Aaronson & Scarborough, 1976; Marschark, 1979). Thus, the phrase structure of a sentence appears to play an important organizational role in language processing at a very basic level (Ferreira & Clifton, 1986). Some linguists such as Chomsky point out that the phrase structure analysis of language is nevertheless incomplete, and the complete analysis of language must have a transformational component. By making a distinction between the underlying structure of a sentence and the surface form of the sentence, transformational grammar provides a way to represent relationships among sentences which on the surface take quite different forms. Transformations are based upon rules that apply to sentences, and the transformation allows the same idea to be expressed in, say, either an active or a passive sentence. For example, "The dog chased the cat" and "The cat was chased by the dog" have quite different phrase structures as sentences, but they share a common underlying or deep structure.

The surface structure of a sentence is produced by the application of various transformational rules to the deep structure. For instance, the sentence "The dog chased the cat" is an active-declarative transformation of the deep structure, and the second sentence "The cat was chased by the dog" is a passive-declarative transformation. Thus, a variety of different surface structures may be derived from essentially the same deep structure. The basic relationships expressed by a simple sentence are those among the subject, verb, and object; these are contained in the *base string,* which then undergoes transformation. The base string having to do with the description of the dog chasing the cat can be transformed into various forms (such as "The cat was chased by the dog" and "Did the dog chase the cat?"). While the surface structures may be different, they all relate to a common base string.

PROCESSES IN LANGUAGE

In this section, we will examine some basic processes in language. The focus is on three processes: production of language, speech perception and comprehension, and language development.

Production of Language

The beginning of a dialogue is usually the production of speech by one of the participants, although a gesture or other sign may initiate such an interaction and have its origins in a similar verbal plan (McNeill, 1985). But, before uttering a sentence or manually expressing any information, the speaker must do some planning based on the intended effect the utterance is to have on the listener; based on the speaker's knowledge of the listener's scope of understanding (e.g., is the listener familiar with the topic?); and based on the syntactic, semantic, and *pragmatic* (or social) form that the production and its desired effect requires. Thus, speaking is very much an *instrumental act,* which is to say that speakers talk in order to produce an effect of some kind.

The process of speaking is basically concerned with planning and execution. But just how is speech planned and executed? Clark and Clark (1977) described a rough outline of this process, which involves five steps. The first step for speakers is to decide on the kind of discourse to be initiated, which is the issue of *discourse plans.* Do they want to engage in a conversation, to describe an event, to give instructions, or to regale a friend with a humorous story? Each type of discourse has a particular structure, and speakers must plan their utterances to fit that structure. For example, if you are telling a joke, you first describe the setting or context, then describe the sequence of events, and end with the punch line. If you fail to follow this structure, you obviously will not be an effective joke teller. For example, if you give away the joke by accidentally telling the punch line before the appropriate time, you will defeat your purpose. Similarly, instructions and conversations have an orderly structure.

One set of guidelines that speakers and listeners seem to follow to foster good communication during a conversation has been described by Grice (1975) and others (e.g., Levelt, 1989). These "Gricean Maxims" are:

(1)   *Quantity:* Avoid running off at the mouth.
(2)   *Quality:* Don't lie or stretch the truth.
(3)   *Relation:* Avoid making statements irrelevant to the topic of conversation.
(4)   *Manner:* Avoid vague or ambiguous statements.

Failure to follow these maxims often results in a *conversational implicature.* For example, imagine that you are reviewing an applicant's letter of recommendation for a highly technical job, and the letter reads as follows:

> I am writing a letter on behalf of John Smith. John dresses very well and has a charming wife. He also drives a nice automobile and sings in his church's choir. Thank you.

Would you hire John based on this letter? Probably not. Clearly, the content of this letter violates the Relation Maxim. Because of this, the letter writer has conversationally implied that John is not the person for the job. Speakers (and letter writers) usually adhere to these Gricean Maxims; but, as this example demonstrates, it is quite informative when they don't.

Planning discourse is planning at the global level. The second stage of speech production involves *planning of sentences,* the components of discourse. Once the nature of the discourse is decided, specific sentences that will accomplish the objective must then be selected. The speech act, the propositional content, and the thematic structure need to be determined. The order in which sentences are produced and the type of information to be conveyed must be thought about. For example, suppose you are describing your new house. You might first describe the location: "We're 10 miles outside of town near the mountains—in South Sandia Heights." Next, you might describe the overall type of house: "It's a two-story, contemporary house made of redwood, stucco, and stone." Then you might proceed to describe the floor plan and arrangement of rooms and, finally, give specifics of each room. Notice that there is a structure that involves going from global, or general information, to progressively more specific details.

The third phase of speech production deals with *constituent plans* of the sentence. Once a sentence is decided on, its components must then be planned. The appropriate words, phrases, and so forth must be picked out and put in the right order. These first three phases describe three levels of planning. At the most general level, planning is directed toward the type of discourse. At the next level, planning concerns the type of sentence to be uttered. At the third level, planning deals with specific components of the sentence.

An interesting feature of slips of the tongue is that they point out regularities in the planning stages of productions. For example, slips are seldom "illegal" combinations of sounds for the language; morphemes tend to slip as entire units (Clark & Clark, 1977). Some classic slips are known as "bloopers" in the world of radio and television. Some bloopers are fairly obvious. For example, an announcer for the *Friendly Homemaker Program* said, "And now we present our homely friend-maker." Another example is a remark of the commentator covering a visit of the king and queen of England: "When they arrive, you will hear a 21 son galute."

The fourth phase of speech production deals with what is called the *articulatory program.* This concerns the plans for the execution of speech, which is a coordinated sequence of muscular contractions in and about the mouth. And the final phase of speech production is *articulation* itself. This is the actual output of speech. Interested readers are referred to Clark and Clark (1977) and Levelt (1989) for a detailed discussion of planning and execution of speech.

Speech Perception and Comprehension

The comprehension of speech begins with the perception of raw speech sounds. Comprehension starts where speech production ends. Speakers produce a stream of sounds that arrive at the listeners' ears; then, listeners are able to analyze the sound patterns and to comprehend them. Speech perception is not, however, the simple identification of sounds. It involves the complex processes of encoding and comprehension discussed in earlier chapters. In other words, interpretative processes, meaning, contextual influences, and the like play important roles in speech perception. Thus, the transformation from raw speech sounds to propositions in memory is a complex process. The physical signal that reaches the ear consists of rapid vibrations of air. While the sounds of speech correlate with particular component frequencies, there is no direct one-to-one correspondence between the sounds of speech and the perceptions of listeners.

Recognition of words is very much dependent on context, expectations, and knowledge. For example, a hungry child can interpret the question "Have you washed your hands for dinner?" as a call to come directly to dinner (i.e., as an indirect speech act rather than a direct question). The role of context also can be easily seen in incomplete sentences in which context allows words to be inferred quite easily. For example, the sentence "The young girl was awakened by her frightening d . . ." allows listeners to infer *dream.* There is no need to think about what the word might be; it just seems to pop out automatically. A similar context effect was studied in the laboratory by Warren (Warren & Obusek, 1971) using phonemes. Subjects were read sentences that had a single speech sound obscured. For example, the sentence "The state governors met with the respective legislatures convening in the capital city" had the first *s* in *legislatures* masked by a coughing sound. The experimenter then asked the subjects to identify where the cough had occurred. [The results indicated that subjects somehow "restored" the missing *s* sound and were unable to locate the interjected cough.] This phenomenon, appropriately called *phonemic restoration,* has been shown to be even more likely when more than a single word can result from the restoration (e.g., "_egion" can become either "legion" or "region"), indicating an active word-searching process in speech perception (Samuel, 1987).

Many people have the impression that the words they hear are distinct, separate combinations of sounds, but this impression is not correct. Cole (1979, 1980) and other speech researchers have demonstrated that words usually run together as sound patterns. This is seen by use of a spectrograph, an electronic device for measuring the variations in energy expended when a person talks. Moreover, it is often the case that a single word cannot be recognized correctly when it is taken out of its sentence context. This was shown some years ago by Pollack and Pickett (1963), who played different segments of a normal conversation for subjects. When the subjects heard just one word from the conversation, it was often incomprehensible. Without the context of the meaningful sentence, the single word could not be understood.

More generally, an important feature of speech perception is that speech is not comprehended simply on the basis of the sounds per se. Rather, speech is comprehended on the basis of many additional factors (e.g., intentions, context, and expectations) from which an interpretation of what the speaker says is constructed. (Tyler & Marslen-Wilson, 1986; see Paivio & Begg, 1981, for a review.)

Language Development

Language development follows a fairly orderly course. The beginning of language is evidenced in babbling, which is an elementary type of vocalization. Children do produce sounds earlier than six months of age, but babbling, which is the repetition of speech sounds, is most clearly evident beginning around six months. By the time children are seven or eight months of age, most parents can correctly identify different cries by an infant as hunger cries, request cries, or cries of surprise (Ricks, 1975). Between six and nine months of age, infants are able to produce all of the basic speech sounds (phonemes) that make up a language.

The emission of speech sounds, even at this early age, can be controlled to some extent by an adult. For example, the rate at which infants emit speech sounds can be increased by having an adult repeat the sounds after the infant. These responses, called *echoic responses,* can be trained or shaped in the sense of increasing their rate just like other instrumental responses. Language learning is not, however, the simple result of reinforcement of particular speech sounds and sequences. Language involves learning to use complex rules of grammar.

One of the striking features of language acquisition is that children of various cultures learn their unique languages in similar ways. For example, children of different cultures acquire speech sounds at about the same time. These regularities in language development suggest that some features of language learning are *universal* (Slobin, 1973) and, thus, perhaps innate. In fact, several studies have shown similar patterns of language development in hearing and deaf children, even though the learning of sign language by the latter is delayed due to the lack of early exposure to language (e.g., Marschark, West, Nall, & Everhart, 1986). For convenience, we henceforth will refer to "speech" and "sounds" in discussing language development, but our points generally extend to "sign language" and "signs" as well.

Making speech sounds is only the first step in acquiring language. The sounds must come to represent objects, symbols, and events in the child's environment. This is simply to say that the sounds must acquire *meaning* for the child. Moreover, children must learn to associate particular sound symbols with particular aspects of their environment. Children are familiar with many aspects of their environment before they learn to speak. Their parents, toys, pets, siblings, and household objects are familiar stimuli. At this early stage of language development, their task is one of learning to associate particular environmental stimuli with particular responses. For example, they must learn to associate the sight of mother with the sound of *Mama.* Similarly, the sight, feel, and taste of a cookie must become associated with the sound of *cookie.* Only when such associations are acquired can the speech sound come to represent or symbolize a specific object or event for the child. Thus, the development of meaning begins with the acquisition of associations between objects/events and speech sounds.

One popular view of the acquisition of word meaning is that children learn semantic features and then attempt to apply an original word that includes the features to objects that share those features. For example, a child may learn the word *ball* and then overgeneralize it to other round objects such as moon and grapefruit.

The association of speech sounds with environmental stimuli is, of course, only a part of language development. Once children acquire a rudimentary vocabulary, they must then begin to form sentences. At first, young children form quite simple sentences, usually consisting of two or three words such as "Want drink." These sentences are quite systematic, are usually understood by the parent, and are similar to adult English sentences with the unessential words omitted (cf. Brown, 1973). For these reasons, they are usually referred to as *telegraphic speech,* likening such productions to the concise, economical language of telegrams. Even as the vocabulary expands, short sentences continue to be used. The very first words that children produce often combine saying a word with a gesture such as "bye-bye" accompanied by a hand wave. Similarly, the speech act of asserting something is often accompanied by a pointing gesture such as saying "Mama" and pointing toward the mother (Greenfield & Smith, 1976).

Gradually, the child begins to construct more complex sentences that take on the characteristics of adult language. This is an enormously challenging task (Brown, 1973). Children must learn to construct increasingly complex sentences, most of which they have never heard. Thus, any type of imitation theory of language learning seems quite inadequate. Another possibility is that children might learn language by way of reinforcement principles. According to this view, children learn new utterances by being encouraged by their parents or other adults. But there is little support for the reinforcement view. Indeed, Brown reports that there is almost no evidence that parents make approval contingent upon the grammaticalness of what their children say. In addition, there is an almost infinite number of possibilities in constructing sentences, so we cannot regard the process of sentence construction as resulting from reinforcement of grammatically correct sentences.

What the child learns are sets of *grammatical, semantic,* and *pragmatic* rules for constructing sentences. Usually, children are unable to verbalize the rules, but their linguistic *performance* indicates that they do possess linguistic *competence,* the knowledge necessary to produce all and only those sentences of a given language. Indeed, many adults who speak grammatically acceptable English are unable to specify the rules they use. But these rules allow us to generate the almost infinite number of different sentences. One of the best pieces of evidence for learning syntactic rules is the phenomenon of overgeneralization. For example, children learn to say *went* correctly, apparently by rote, then learn the rule of forming the past tense by adding *ed,* and then incorrectly say *goed.* They later learn the exception to the rule and go back to saying *went.* Similar overgeneralizations occur in the deaf child's acquisition of sign language.

This brief description only begins to sketch some of the complexities of language development. What is clear is that young children have an enormously complex task in learning to speak, read, and use language in a meaningful fashion. The fact that human beings can acquire and use language emerges as a remarkable achievement.

Finally, relating language development to this chapter's earlier discussion on speech acts, there have also been some interesting findings. For example, it

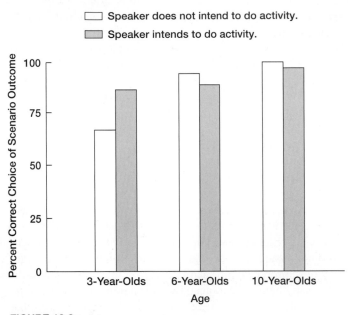

FIGURE 10.2
Percent correct choice response by children considering the
outcome of a committing scenario plotted according to age group
and whether the speaker actually intended to carry out the promised
activity. *(Adapted from Bernicot, J., & Laval, V. (1996). Promises in
French children: Comprehension and metapragmatic knowledge.*
Journal of Pragmatics, 25, *101–122.)*

appears that younger children view the meaning of "I promise" differently than
do older children and adults. According to the philosopher Sourly (1969), certain
conditions must be present for a sincere promise to be made. One condition is
that the person making the commitment actually intends to carry out the promised
action. A second condition is that it is apparent that the person to whom the
promise is directed desires the action to be carried out. In a recent study, Bernicot and Laval (1996) report that 3-year-olds have difficulty understanding both
conditions, whereas 6-year-olds have trouble understanding only the second condition. But, by age 10, children evaluate both conditions equivalently well in determining the outcome of a scenario (concerning the occurrence of the promised
activity), where these conditions were manipulated. The results of their study are
shown in figures 10.2 and 10.3. Figure 10.2 concerns whether the first condition
(speaker intention to carry out the action) is met or violated; figure 10.3 concerns
whether the second condition (apparent listener desire) is met or violated.

These findings—of little surprise to many parents and siblings of younger
children—indicate that the meaning of "I promise" is quite different, depending on

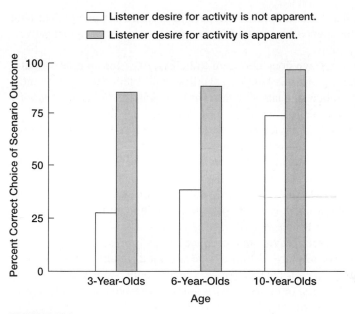

☐ Listener desire for activity is not apparent.
▨ Listener desire for activity is apparent.

FIGURE 10.3
Percent correct choice response by children considering the
outcome of a committing scenario plotted according to age group
and whether the listener actually needed the promised activity
carried out. *(Adapted from Bernicot, J., & Laval, V. (1996). Promises
in French children: Comprehension and metapragmatic knowledge.
Journal of Pragmatics, 25, 101–122.)*

the age of the child to whom it is said. Specifically, the understanding of the contextual circumstances underlying the making of a verbal commitment increments
with age. Initially, children are primarily concerned with whether the promised activity simply occurred; as they grow older, they begin to grasp the intentions of the
speaker in evaluating the likely outcome of that activity (Astington, 1988a, 1988b).

SOME ISSUES IN LANGUAGE

In this section, a few issues in language are examined. Included are the topics of
language and thought, language in animals, cultural differences in language, and
language and the brain.

Language and Thought

Language and thought are related events. The ability of children to handle concepts is related to their language development. Indeed, children who can verbalize

relationships such as "nearer than" or "larger than" are better able to deal with problems involving relationships among stimuli than children who cannot yet verbalize such relationships.

Nevertheless, language does not seem to be *essential* for complex mental processes, despite the fact that language facilitates problem solving. The most explicit attempt to relate language and thought is seen in the *linguistic relativity hypothesis,* sometimes called the *Whorfian hypothesis,* developed by Benjamin Lee Whorf (1956). Whorf argued that the structure of one's language leads one to perceive and conceive of the world in particular ways—ways that differ from those of another individual using a different language. This is simply to say that a person's language imposes a particular view of the world. Presumably, cognitive processes are in some way inevitably affected by the structure of language. The notion of *linguistic relativity* is emphasized because thought is presumed to be relative to the particular language used.

Vocabulary differences provide one instance of how language is presumably related to thought. For instance, Eskimos have several different words for labeling snow, depending upon its characteristics, whereas only one is widely used in English. Downhill skiers, of course, do distinguish between several different kinds of snow, using words that describe its consistency (e.g., "cornstarch" or "powder"). Cross-country skiers distinguish even more kinds of snow, using color words that refer to the kind of wax applied to the bottom of a ski under different conditions (e.g., "green" to "violet" snow). Does this mean that nonskiers, downhill skiers, and cross-country skiers have different *perceptions* of snow? Some cultures have many words for the colors of the spectrum; other cultures have only a few. According to Whorf, the range of words, or labels, available influences the range of cognitive activities in which human beings may engage. People having a number of different descriptive labels that they can apply to a range of events presumably are able to think about these events in more ways than are people having only a few labels.

There are two versions of Whorf's hypothesis. The *strong version* emphasizes that language *invariably* influences thought. The *weak version* emphasizes that language affects thought when the particular task directly depends upon properties of the language system. There is little support for the strong version of the hypothesis. For example, if the strong version of the Whorf hypothesis is true, we would expect that people who have many different words for different colors (parts of the visual spectrum) would perceive more distinctions among colors than people who have only a few words. But this is not the case. Rosch (1973) compared the performance of the Dani, a primitive people of New Guinea, who use only two words for colors, with English-speaking subjects who use many different color terms. Despite differences in color terms, the two groups appear to perceive colors in much the same way. In short, just because a language lacks a range of terms for various stimuli does not mean that the user of the language

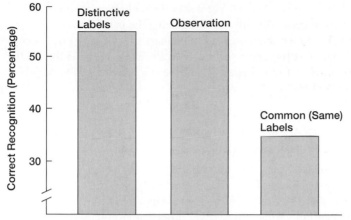

FIGURE 10.4
Shape recognition following practice in labeling and observation of
shapes. *(Adapted from "Stimulus Encoding Processes in Human
Learning and Memory" by H. C. Ellis, in G. H. Bower, Ed.,* The
Psychology of Learning and Motivation, *Vol. 7. New York; Academic
Press, 1973.)*

cannot perceive the various features of the stimuli. The lack of particular adjectives in a language may indicate the relative unimportance of those dimensions in
the culture; thus, speakers of the language may simply ignore those features or
fail to report them as significant, even when noticed.

The evidence consistent with the weak version of Whorf's hypothesis comes
from research on the effects of verbal labels on perception and recognition memory of visual patterns. In his summary of this research, Ellis (1973) noted that verbal labeling of visual patterns can affect the ease with which they are subsequently
perceived and remembered. For example, if different visual patterns are all labeled with the same term, the patterns then become more difficult to recognize.
Conversely, if the patterns are given different and meaningful verbal labels, they
become more recognizable compared with control tests.

An example of the typical results of Ellis' studies in which subjects label visual (or tactual) shapes with verbal labels and then are tested for recognition of
the shapes is shown in figure 10.4. The figure shows that subjects who are instructed to label shapes with unique, *distinctive* labels do better in subsequently
recognizing the shapes than do subjects who attach *common* verbal labels. Subjects who simply observe the shapes but are allowed to covertly label them do as
well as those who give them distinctive labels. Ellis contends that the common
verbal labels lead the subject to attend to the more common, or similar, features

of the pattern. Hence, the subjects achieve a *less* distinctive encoding for each pattern and, thus, have greater difficulty in recognizing the patterns.

Not all studies have shown that observation of shapes leads to as good recognition as does uniquely labeling them. Ellis (1968, 1973) also reports that, if the labels are *representative* of the shapes, then labeling itself leads to superior recognition.

Language in Nonhuman Animals

Psychologists have made a number of attempts to teach language to chimpanzees. Early attempts by language researchers were largely unsuccessful, with only limited evidence for language being learned. In one of the most famous studies, the Kelloggs raised their son with a chimpanzee named Gua. The chimpanzee learned to understand a number of commands but never produced a single word. In a similar study, a chimpanzee raised by the Hayeses learned to speak only three identifiable words, *mama, papa,* and *cup,* and only after great difficulty and extended training. As a result of these failures, many psychologists conclude that chimpanzees lack the vocal cord structures necessary for humanlike speech and that such efforts are doomed to failure.

The vocal inability of chimpanzees was recognized in more recent attempts to teach chimpanzees language by Gardner and Gardner (1969, 1975) and Premack (1971), who took a different approach to the problem. Their approach was to teach chimpanzees a *nonverbal* version of language. The Gardners attempted to teach their subject, Washoe, the sign language used by the deaf, which consists of making signs for different words. Using her hands, Washoe eventually learned over 150 signs. Of even greater importance was that Washoe learned to string signs together to make up primitive sentences. The fact that Washoe was able to produce simple strings is suggestive of a very primitive form of language. Premack's approach was to teach another chimpanzee, Sarah, a form of sign language using colored plastic chips displayed on a board, where each chip stood for a word. For example, a red square stood for *banana.* Sarah learned to "write" by placing chips on a magnetized board and, with practice, learned to construct simple sentences. But does this mean that Sarah uses language like human beings do? Probably not. Indeed, the language that is learned may be restricted to skills in word substitution—that is, transforming a phrase such as "Mary eat banana" to "Mary wash banana."

More recently, Terrace and colleagues continued this research in animal language with a chimp named Nim Chimpsky (Terrace, 1979). Nim was raised in a very rich social environment, something like that of a young child. For example, he was bottle-fed, praised, and given affection. Like Washoe, Nim was taught the American Sign Language and gradually learned a total of 125 signs. But, after almost four years of research, Terrace came to doubt that Nim was learning language in the same sense that a child does. For instance, the average length of Nim's utterances showed little growth. Moreover, Nim gave no indication of an expanding grasp of syntax.

Do these studies allow the conclusion that chimpanzees possess language? What we can say is that chimpanzees do show the ability to produce simple sentences, which is *one* criterion of language. But they have not shown other features characteristic of human language. For example, when these animals produce strings of three or four signs, the strings are repetitive rather than sentencelike, according to Terrace and colleagues (Terrace, Pettito, & Bever, 1976). Some linguists contend that the uniquely human aspect of language is its *reflective* quality (another of Hockett's design features), the fact that it can refer to itself in language about language. Thus far, chimpanzees have not used language to discuss the language system itself, even though they have created new lexical units (*water-bird* for a duck, *juicefruit* for a watermelon), satisfying Hockett's (1963) productivity requirement for language.

Two more recent findings from research with language-trained chimpanzees are even more significant for those researchers who think that these ape productions approach human language. One is that chimpanzees who have not been specifically trained in language nonetheless pick up signs spontaneously from other chimps who were trained and appear to use them instrumentally (Fouts, Fouts, & Schoenfield, 1984). Incidentally, this finding satisfies Hockett"s (1963) requirement that a true language have *traditional transmission*—the experienced teach the inexperienced. The second important discovery is that, as with humans, language-trained chimpanzees appear to have a variety of problem-solving abilities not possessed by chimps who are not language trained. (Premack, 1983). The implications of these findings are not yet clear, but while we attempt to determine the limits of nonhuman primates' abilities in using symbolic communication systems, the debates on whether chimpanzees truly have language and the precise definition of "language" will continue.

Bilingualism

Bilingualism is a particularly timely issue concerning language competence. In many parts of the United States, children are exposed to two (or more) languages as they grow up. Some children learn one language at home and another in a school setting. Other children learn both languages at home, where, for example, the grandparents speak one language to the child but the parents and siblings speak another. Still other children immigrate to this country speaking one language and then learn a second language in school once they are settled in their new environment. Regardless of how a child actually learns his or her languages, the result is an individual who has a greatly enhanced ability to think and communicate. In terms of language processing, bilingualism offers a rich source of

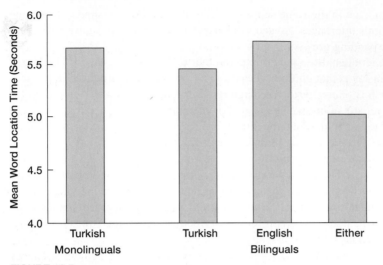

FIGURE 10.5
Mean word location time as a function of subject group (monolinguals or bilinguals) and language of word location task. *(Adapted from Peynircioglu, Z., & Tekcan, A. I. (1993). Word perception in two languages.* Journal of Memory and Language, 32, *390–401.)*

information about the organization and use of the structures and processes of language already discussed in this chapter—not only concerning bilinguals, but monolinguals as well.

Three recent issues will be briefly explored here. The first concerns "code-switching," the ability of bilinguals to select words from either of their languages during the course of uttering a sentence. Code-switching maximizes the bilingual's ability to convey his or her intended message to another bilingual and to understand another bilingual's intended message. What is fascinating is that code-switching often requires no additional time (and may, in fact, use less time) than when words from only one language are selected or perceived.

One interesting study of this ability is seen in a study by Peynircioglu and Tekcan (1993). In this study, monolinguals and bilinguals searched a completed crossword puzzle for words in their language (Turkish) or languages (Turkish and English). As figure 10.5 shows, bilinguals were equivalent to the monolinguals in the time they took to locate words in only one of their languages. But bilinguals were faster than monolinguals when they collectively located words in either of their languages. This finding indicates an advantage for bilinguals over monolinguals in word recognition, which can be demonstrated when bilinguals are allowed to use a strategy of identifying all of the words they know (from both languages).

The second important issue concerns the treatment of lexical (grammatical) and semantic knowledge by bilinguals. One theoretical view places lexical knowledge in language-specific memory stores but semantic knowledge in a common conceptual memory store (Kroll & Sholl, 1992), whereas the other theoretical view places both types of knowledge in language-specific memory stores (Paivio, 1986). The first theory would predict, for example, that semantic processing of a word in one language (e.g., translating a word presented in a categorized list into another language) should facilitate memory for that word (relative to translating that word when it is presented in a random list), whereas the second theory predicts that no such facilitation would take place (because contacting the meaning of a word in one language should not involve contacting the meaning of the word in the other language). To date, the evidence supports the first theory, known as the "Concept Mediation" account, especially in fluent bilinguals (De Groot, Dannenburg, & Van Hell, 1994; Kroll & Sholl, 1992).

The third issue concerns how language familiarity influences a person's ability to correctly identify another person's voice. In a study conducted by Goggin, Thompson, Strube, and Simental (1991), English monolinguals and Spanish-English bilinguals heard texts read by the same person in either English, Spanish, or Spanish-accented English. A short time later, these subjects then heard a voice "lineup" of individuals reading a different text, again in either English, Spanish, or Spanish-accented English. The task was to determine which voice in the voice lineup matched the original voice. Subjects could respond by specifying which voice in the lineup matched the remembered initial voice, state that none of the voices in the lineup matched the remembered voice, or state that they were not sure if one of the voices in the lineup matched the remembered voice. The subjects also rated their confidence that a lineup voice matched the voice committed in memory.

Goggin et al. (1991) found a distinctly different pattern in the responses for monolinguals and bilinguals. As can be seen in figure 10.6, for monolinguals, confidence ratings were highest for voices in English and lowest for voices in Spanish, with ratings for the Spanish-accented English voice falling in between. However, for bilinguals, these ratings were slightly higher for Spanish over English lineup voices, with the Spanish-accented English voice falling substantially lower than either. Curiously, as can be seen in figure 10.7, for the monolinguals, actual correct identifications were consistent with their confidence ratings; English voices were matched better than Spanish voices, with Spanish-accented English voices again falling in between. However, for bilinguals, correct identifications were generally the same across the three voice types.

Collectively, these findings indicate that bilinguals' knowledge of two languages aids in their identification of the voice source of the messages they encounter and represents an interesting interaction between speech perception and higher levels of language analysis. This finding also represents an advantage bilinguals have over their monolingual counterparts. An interesting complication of this advantage for bilinguals, however, is their responses to the Spanish-accented English messages. Because these messages represent aspects of two languages

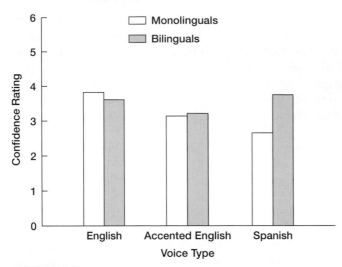

FIGURE 10.6
Mean confidence rating of match between lineup and remembered
voice plotted according to group and voice type. *(Adapted from
Goggin, J. P., Thompson, C. P., Strube, G., & Simental, L. R. (1991).
The role of language familiarity in voice identification.* Memory &
Cognition, 19, *448–458.)*

(speech sounds of one, but the grammar and words of the other), bilinguals feel
less confident in discerning the voice source of the message, although, curiously,
they are actually as good in identifying that voice source as they are for the other
two voice types.

Language and the Brain

Language is clearly dependent upon brain functioning. In this section, we will
consider two issues: hemispheric specialization and brain disorders.

Hemispheric Specialization   The human brain is divided into two hemispheres, which are not functionally equivalent. Each hemisphere receives information from the senses, but the two hemispheres generally receive separate information.
Information from the visual environment is usually divided, with information from
the right visual field being projected to the left hemisphere and information from
the left visual field being projected to the right hemisphere. Nevertheless, information that reaches each half of the brain is usually coordinated or integrated in
some fashion.

The fact that the human brain is asymmetrical is especially important for language. For most human adults, the left cerebral hemisphere controls the functions
of language, which include production of both spoken and written language and

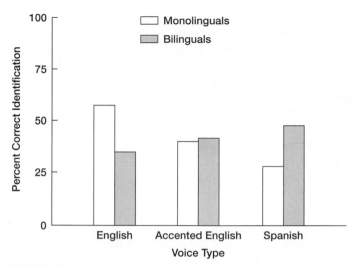

FIGURE 10.7
Mean percent correct voice identification according to group and voice type. *Adapted from Goggin, J. P., Thompson, C. P., Strube, G., & Simental, L. R. (1991). The role of language familiarity in voice identification.* Memory & Cognition, 19, 448–458.)

comprehension of verbal information. In contrast, the right cerebral hemisphere is frequently unable to produce language or to comprehend abstract words. In turn, the right hemisphere is concerned with perceptual processes such as picture recognition and comprehension and learning of visual forms. This physiological distinction has been taken as an important source of support for the dual-coding theory of memory, discussed in chapter 5 (see Paivio, 1986, for discussion). Recently, however, this picture has been clouded by evidence suggesting that image generation, unlike imaginal manipulation (e.g., mental rotation), may have its locus in the occipital region of the left hemisphere (used in visual perception) rather than, or in addition to, the temporal region of the right hemisphere (Farah, Peronnet, & Weisberg, 1987).

The knowledge of this dual functioning of the brain stems from what is called the *split-brain* experiment. A split brain usually results from surgery that severs the corpus callosum, fibers connecting the two hemispheres, in order to alleviate symptoms of certain rare forms of epilepsy. Since the normal interaction between the two hemispheres is eliminated by this operation, it is possible to observe the function of each largely independent hemisphere. Important differences in how the two hemispheres are involved in language behaviors have been discovered. For example, when a split-brain patient held an object in the right hand, allowing sensory information to be sent to the left cerebral hemisphere, the patient was able to name and describe the object. In contrast, when the patient held the object in the left hand, allowing sensory information to go primarily to the right hemi-sphere, he was unable to describe the object verbally, although he could match the object to an identical one in a recognition task. Similarly, when a split-brain patient was shown a picture of an object so that sensory information went to the right hemisphere, he was unable to label the object in the picture; however, he was able to pick out the object in a recognition test when it was presented with others (Gazzaniga, 1970, 1977).

Brain Disorders: Aphasia   Two diseases involving language function loss caused by damage to the left hemisphere of the brain are *Broca's aphasia* and *Wernicke's aphasia.* Broca's aphasia is caused by damage to the brain's premotor area, responsible, in part, for controlling motor commands used in speech pro-duction. A person suffering from Broca's aphasia exhibits speech containing excess pauses and slips of the tongue, and he or she has trouble finding words when talking. The person also fails to make use of function words such as *a, the,* and *of.* For this reason, Broca's aphasics also produce ungrammatical sentences (Tartter, 1987). Furthermore, they also have trouble using syntactic information when understanding sentences (Just & Carpenter, 1987). For example, while a Broca's aphasic has no trouble understanding a sentence such as "The bicycle that the man is holding is blue," he or she has trouble comprehending a sentence such as "The dog that the woman is biting is grey." This difference is due to the fact that while the first sentence can be understood using real-world knowledge (e.g., bicy-cles, not people, are blue), the second sentence cannot (because it is unlikely that a woman would bite a dog). Because understanding the second sentence requires correctly using syntactic information, which Broca's aphasics have difficulty doing, the sentence poses problems for them (Berndt & Caramazza, 1980).

People with Wernicke's aphasia suffer from damage to the left temporal lobe of the brain. They have generally fluent phonetic and syntactic but semantically in-coherent speech. This incoherence is exhibited through the creation of nonsense words for real-world concepts and improper substitutions of function words for content words (e.g., nouns, verbs). In contrast with Broca's aphasics, Wernicke's aphasics also exhibit problems using semantic structure in categorization and picture-word processing tasks (see Tartter, 1987). Diseases like Broca's and Wer-nicke's aphasia, while tragic, tell us much about the critical functions of certain regions of the brain. Notably, their symptoms suggest that (at least certain) phono-logical, syntactic, and semantic, language information is stored and processed separately in the brain.

Alzheimer's Disease   One other brain disorder which leads to a decrement in language processing ability is Alzheimer's disease. This disease primarily afflicts elderly persons and causes progressive, diffused, and irreversible damage to the cortical regions of the brain, impacting markedly on memory functions.

Comparison between the language decrements due to the dementing effects of Alzheimer's disease and those noted for the aphasias is useful because the average age of onset of Alzheimer's disease overlaps that of aphasias (around 50 to 60 years of age).

The language of an Alzheimer's patient is marked by a striking simplification process wherein words that once precisely described some event are now lost and are replaced by more general terms because of a fundamental loss of categorical organization in semantic memory (Chan, Butters, Salmon, & McGuire, 1993; Martin & Fedio, 1983). It appears, however, that in patients suffering from Alzheimer's disease, phonological and syntactic knowledge and use is minimally affected. Finally, a deficit in pragmatic knowledge, concerning the correct recognition of the intention of a speech act (e.g., that an utterance is meant to be taken as a request), turntaking in a conversation, and so on also occurs. Interestingly, this pattern of deficits and nondeficits again argues for the distinctiveness of the various levels of language information similar to what was seen for Broca's and Wernicke's aphasias (Bayles & Kaszniak, 1987).

Behaviorally, what distinguishes Alzheimer's disease from Broca's aphasia is speech fluency. Broca's aphasics are nonfluent, and their speech is ungrammatical. However, Alzheimer's patients (except in the advanced cases) maintain their grammatical speaking capability. In contrast, what distinguishes Alzheimer's disease from Wernicke's aphasia is the verbal and visual memory deficit in the Alzheimer's patients; here, both groups exhibit acceptable grammatical structure (again, unless the Alzheimer's patients are in the advanced stages of the disease), so it is a more basic deficit (memory in language and spatial domains) that distinguishes the two (see Bayles & Kaszniak, 1987).

SUMMARY

In chapter 10, some of the main features of language were described. As was seen, language is the principal means of human communication. The three functions of language discussed were speech acts, propositional content, and thematic structure. Speech acts involve ordering, questioning, promising, and telling others; propositional content refers to the actual content embedded in the speech act; and thematic structure involves keeping track of what listeners understand.

The basic units of language are phonemes. In order to understand adult language, the structure of sentences must be examined. Sentences possess both a surface structure and a deep structure, which can be related by transformational grammar.

The important processes of language production, speech perception, and language development were examined. Language production involves five phases: discourse plans, sentence plans, constituent plans, articulatory programs, and, finally, articulation. Speech perception begins with the production of speech sounds and ends with their interpretation in memory. Speech perception is not a matter of a one-to-one correspondence between the sounds of speech and perceptions of listeners. Rather, speech perception is heavily dependent upon content, intentions, and knowledge. Language development is a progressive and orderly process in which children learn general rules of language so that they can communicate successfully.

Language and thought are related processes; however, the evidence does not support a strong version of the Whorf hypotheses. Bilingualism is the ability to communicate in two languages. Bilinguals exhibit the ability to produce and understand words or phrases in either of their languages, even when they occur in the same utterance; this ability is know as "code-switching." The prevailing evidence is that fluent bilinguals store their word and syntactic knowledge of their two languages separately from the conceptual knowledge. One example of an advantage that bilinguals have over monolinguals is their ability to identify individuals by their voice across their two languages.

Language is heavily dependent on the left cerebral hemisphere, whereas perception is predominantly dependent on the right cerebral hemisphere. Broca's and Wernicke's aphasias are language disorders caused by left hemispheric damage to the premotor and temporal lobe regions of the brain, respectively. Broca's aphasia affects syntactic information processing, whereas Wernicke's aphasia affects semantic information processing. Alzheimer's disease affects language processing, but differently than do the aphasias. Except in advanced cases of Alzheimer's, these patients exhibit fluent speech (unlike Broca's aphasia) but demonstrate profound verbal and spatial memory deficits (unlike Wernicke's aphasics).

THOUGHT QUESTIONS

1. What are several major features of language development?
2. What is the role of context and expectations in the interpretation of speech?
3. Suppose that you had language for only four colors of the visual spectrum—say, red, yellow, green, and blue. How might this affect the way you think about colored objects in the environment?
4. What are the basic issues and findings regarding language in chimpanzees.
5. What can bilingualism tell us about language structures and processes? What are the advantages of being bilingual? Can you think of any disadvantages?
6. What do brain disorders like Broca's and Wernicke's aphasias tell us about how a healthy brain processes phonological, syntactic, and semantic information?

11

LANGUAGE
COMPREHENSION

In chapter 10, we learned that language is composed of basic units called phonemes and morphemes, and indeed, some cognitive processes are responsible for analyzing the phonological and morphological content of language. But the psychological processing of language goes well beyond these elemental processes. Ultimately, language is used to *convey meaning;* thus, some cognitive processes must be responsible for deriving meaning from surface-level linguistic information. These processes are collectively referred to as *comprehension processes,* the focus of the present chapter.

To understand what is involved in comprehension, consider the following story:

> Papa, as he was affectionately known to his close family, took his usual morning walk through the sleepy, southern town, dressed in his typical white suit, which somehow always looked rumpled. As October began to settle into the Shennandoah Valley, he increasingly found his thoughts turning to his beloved Mississippi and the old farm. The chill in the air revived memories of warm, early autumn evenings on the veranda with his wife and children. This mountain town in which he now found himself was so different, the pace of life so incongruously rapid, compared to his earlier days in Mississippi. These thoughts continued with him as he turned the block toward his large white clapboard house, where he would spend the rest of the day in essential solitude.

Reading, understanding, and remembering passages such as the preceding paragraph are such routine activities that they may appear trivially simple. But for the cognitive psychologist, an adequate description of these processes is a major challenge.

To illustrate the complexity of this challenge, reflect for a moment on your comprehension of the paragraph. In order to understand the paragraph, you obviously had to process the specific words contained in the paragraph—the idea of comprehending a passage without reading any of the words is simply nonsensical. Furthermore, you had to process the particular way in which those words combined to form sentences—you would not have been able to derive the meaning of the passage if the words had been presented randomly ordered in a list instead of in sentences. Thus, comprehending the meaning of a passage necessarily involves the processing of the particular words and sentences—the explicit content—used to convey that meaning.

Now, without referring back to the paragraph, what do you remember from it? If your response is typical, you may have remembered some of the particular words or phrases that were contained in the paragraph, but you almost certainly did not repeat the paragraph exactly, word for word. This exercise reveals one of the important characteristics of memory for prose and discourse—material is not normally recalled verbatim. Rather, you probably summarized the material, describing the essential *meaning,* or *gist,* of the paragraph. Furthermore, your summarization likely included some information that was never explicitly stated in the paragraph, information that you inferred based on what you read. The process of inferring information is essential to comprehension in order to connect or organize the various ideas expressed in a passage. The inferences can be as simple as assuming that the "he" mentioned throughout the passage refers to "Papa." Such inferences serve to connect various sentences in the passage and are essential to establishing the coherence of the text. Other types of inferences are less directly tied to the text and consist of information derived from assertions in the text. For example, you probably inferred that the character in the passage was old, but reexamination of the material will show no direct reference to the man's age. You may also have reasonably assumed that the last phrase about his returning home to solitude implies lack of opportunity to interact with other persons and that the man is rather old-fashioned and unsophisticated. Actually, the passage is a semifictional account of the latter days of William Faulkner, who held a prestigious appointment at the University of Virginia. Of course, Faulkner was anything but unsophisticated, and it was his celebrity status that forced him to seek solitude in order to work.

This simple example is meant to illustrate two important points about comprehension. First, processing the explicit content of a passage is a necessary part of comprehension (although seldom an end in itself, given that much of it is not retained after processing). In the next two sections, we will examine two of the cognitive processes involved in analyzing the explicit content of discourse, lexical analysis and syntactic parsing. Second, processing explicit content is not sufficient—deriving the meaning of a sample of language usually involves the addition of a great deal of information that is only implied by the text. In the last two sections of the chapter, we will explore the kinds of information that are typically added to explicit content during comprehension, and we will consider the important role of memory in this process.

LEXICAL ANALYSIS

As highlighted in the discussion above, the explicit content of a passage includes the specific words it contains, and comprehension arguably begins with the processing of these words.

Remember that the goal of comprehension is to go from the surface-level linguistic information discussed in chapter 10 to the meaning conveyed by that information. Thus, the processing of words must go beyond merely identifying each word based on its phonology or morphology to representing the meaning conveyed by that word. The process of representing the meaning of the words in text is referred to here as *lexical analysis.*

Deriving the meanings of words would be relatively straightforward if there existed a perfect, one-to-one mapping between words and meanings (that is, if each word had only one meaning). However, many of the words we encounter when reading are *homonyms,* or words that have multiple meanings. For example, the word *run* means something different when we read about a horse running a race than when we read about a politician running for office or a color running in the wash. Similarly, the word *bank* clearly refers to something different when we read about depositing money in a bank than when we read about a romantic picnic along the bank of a river. One needs only to skim the pages of a standard English dictionary to see how many words have many different meanings. One may also notice that words with multiple meanings are most likely to be among the most common words, those we encounter most frequently.

Given the proliferation of homonyms in everyday discourse, the ultimate accomplishment of lexical analysis is not just activating the meanings associated with a word but arriving at the *right* meaning, given the context in which the word appears. How does lexical analysis determine the contextually appropriate meanings of words? Consider how this might be accomplished. For instance, lexical analysis could proceed by initially accessing all of the meanings of a word to ensure that the contextually appropriate meaning gets activated. However, additional decision processes would be necessary to select the appropriate meaning from among those activated, and inappropriate meanings would need to be suppressed. Alternatively, to avoid the need for this additional processing, lexical analysis could be accomplished by only activating one of the word's meanings. In this case, the need for additional selection or suppression processes would be avoided. But if the activated meaning turned out to be incorrect, subsequent reanalysis would be required.

These are just two of several possible ways in which lexical analysis could be carried out, and they are described here to illustrate how particular modes of operation will have attendant costs and benefits. We will consider two key issues concerning the way in which lexical analysis operates. The first issue concerns what information can influence the activation of word meanings. The second issue concerns how many word meanings are activated.

Modular Theories of Lexical Analysis

Some theories propose that lexical analysis is *modular,* which is a term used to refer to a process that does not consider input from other processes during initial interpretation of stimuli. In this case, to say that lexical analysis is modular is to propose that the initial stage of processing—activation of word meanings—is not influenced by information computed by other comprehension processes. Meaning activation for a word would not be influenced by information about the particular syntactic role the word plays in a sentence—for example, whether *bank* was used as a noun ("I went to the bank") or as a verb ("I tried to bank a shot off the backboard"). Likewise, meaning activation would not be influenced by information about the thematic context in which the word appears—for example, whether *bank* appeared in a story about high finance or about fishing. Rather, modular theories propose that initial activation is based only on lexical information, which is information about the word and its meanings regardless of the context in which it appears. Of course, modular theories do not claim that information from other processes does not influence lexical analysis at any point. To the contrary, modular theories typically assume that these other sources of information may be used subsequently to evaluate the appropriateness of activated word meanings. The critical claim is that these other sources of information do not influence the initial stage of meaning activation.

Selectivity or Promiscuity?   Although all modular theories assume that only lexical information influences initial meaning activation, modular theories differ from one another with respect to the second of the two key issues mentioned above. Is lexical information used to activate only one word meaning; in other words, is lexical analysis *selective*? Or are multiple word meanings initially activated; in other words, is lexical analysis *promiscuous*?

One of the early modular theories of lexical analysis was the *ordered search theory* proposed by Hogaboam and Perfetti (1975). According to this theory, meaning activation was solely determined by the relative frequency of a word's meanings (lexical information) and was thus modular. In addition, lexical analysis was selective in that only the most frequent meaning of a word was activated initially. This meaning was then passed on to be evaluated for appropriateness given the current context. If this meaning is inappropriate, only then would the next most frequent meaning be activated. The important point is that initial activation would only involve the activation of one meaning.

To test the ordered search theory, Hogaboam and Perfetti had participants listen to sentences, and after each sentence, participants were to decide as quickly as possible whether the final word had more than one meaning. In half of the sentences, the final word was in fact a homonym (for example, *feet*). The content that preceded the homonym required either the more frequent meaning of the word ("The tired hiker rested his feet") or the less frequent meaning ("The building's dimensions was measured in feet"). Consider what would happen when the less frequent meaning was required. According to the ordered search model, the more frequent meaning would first be activated and evaluated in the context of the sentence. When the more frequent meaning was found to be inappropriate, the less frequent meaning would then be activated. When prompted to decide whether the final word had more than one meaning, Hogaboam and Perfetti reasoned that participants would quickly and accurately say yes, given that both the more frequent and less frequent meanings had already been considered at that point. But what about the case when sentence content favored the more frequent meaning? According to the theory, only the more frequent meaning would be activated. In this case, when prompted to decide whether the final word had more than one meaning, Hogaboam and Perfetti predicted that participants would be slower and less likely to say yes, because only the more frequent meaning would have been activated in this case. In support of the theory, they did find that responses to homonyms were slower and less accurate when the content required the more frequent meaning.

However, subsequent research called into question this evidence for selectivity (e.g., Onifer & Swinney, 1981; Till, Mross, & Kintsch, 1988). Onifer and Swinney (1981) raised the concern that the experimental task used by Hogaboam and Perfetti may not have been sensitive enough to detect initial activation of more than one meaning. Additionally, the fact that the task explicitly required participants to attend to the homonymous nature of words may have evoked task-specific, strategic processes that may have influenced the results.

Although Onifer and Swinney did not dispute the claim that lexical analysis is modular, they proposed that the lexical-analysis module is also promiscuous, rather than selective (as proposed by Hogaboam and Perfetti). To evaluate this claim empirically, they used a different experimental task to avoid the concerns raised with the homonym judgment task. Specifically, Onifer and Swinney had participants listen to sentences, some of which contained a homonym. As in Hogaboam and Perfetti's study, the homonyms appeared in sentence contexts that favored either the more frequent meaning or the less frequent meaning of the homonym. For example, the word *coach* appeared either in (1) or (2) below:

> (1) The team came out of the locker room with fire in their eyes after the coach de-livered his best speech ever. [sentence favoring more frequent meaning of *coach*]
>
> (2) A perfectly matched pair of black stallions pulled the Queen's coach up to the base of the marble stairway. [sentence favoring less frequent meaning of *coach*]

Immediately after the homonym was spoken in the sentence, a string of letters was presented on a computer screen, and the participant was to decide as quickly as possible whether the letters formed an English word. You may recognize this task as the lexical decision task introduced in chapter 3 when we discussed the study by Marcel (1980). You may also remember that faster response times to a target word than to a comparable control word is taken as evidence that the target concept had been activated, or primed. Onifer and Swinney employed the same logic in their study. Specifically, the letter string presented immediately after the homonym either named a word that was related to the more frequent meaning of the homonym (for example, *football*) or a word that was related to the less frequent meaning of the homonym (for example, *carriage*). Response times to the target words were compared to response times for unrelated control words that were matched to the targets along important dimensions, such as the number of letters in the word and word frequency. Results showed that response times were faster for both of the target probe words than for the control words, suggesting that both meanings had been activated. Particularly problematic for the ordered search theory is the finding that the less frequent meaning was activated even when the sentence context favored the more frequent meaning; according to the theory, meaning activation should have terminated after the more frequent mean-ing had been activated. Thus, Onifer and Swinney concluded that lexical analysis must be promiscuous rather than selective.

Note that Onifer and Swinney's results also provide further evidence for the modularity of lexical analysis. In each sentence, only one of the two meanings of the homonym was the "right" meaning; that is, one meaning was appropriate for the context in which the word appeared and the other meaning was not. However, given the evidence that both meanings had been activated, Onifer and Swinney argued that in addition to being promiscuous, lexical analysis must also be modular; otherwise, only the contextually appropriate meaning would have been activated.

Interactive Theories of Lexical Analysis

Although agreeing with the claim of Onifer and Swinney that lexical analysis is promiscuous, Duffy, Morris, and Rayner (1988) argued that lexical analysis is not necessarily modular. Instead, they proposed that lexical analysis is *interactive,* which is a term used to refer to a process that considers input from other processes during initial interpretation of stimuli. In this case, to say that lexical analysis is interactive is to propose that the initial stage of processing—activation of word meanings—can be influenced by information from other comprehension processes, such as syntactic and thematic information. According to Duffy et al.'s *reordered access theory* of lexical analysis, all meanings of a word are initially activated (i.e., lexical analysis is promiscuous), but nonlexical sources of information can influence the speed or strength with which the various meanings are activated (i.e., lexical analysis is interactive). They proposed that nonlexical contextual information influenced activation specifically "by increasing the availability of the appropriate meaning without influencing the alternative meaning" (p. 431).

To test their theory, Duffy et al. had participants read sentences that consisted of two clauses. One clause included a homonym, and the other clause included contextual information that favored one of the homonym's meanings. For example, the homonym *pitcher* appeared in the following sentence:

(3) Because it was kept on the back of a high shelf, the *pitcher* was often forgotten.

The information in the first clause of the sentence suggests that *pitcher* in this context refers to a container for dispensing liquid, given that a baseball player is extremely unlikely to be placed on a high shelf.

The two important manipulations in their study concerned the order of the clauses and the relative frequencies of the two meanings of the homonyms. In one condition, the clause with the contextual information came before the clause containing the homonym (as in sentence 3 above), whereas in another condition, the clauses were presented in the opposite order. In each condition, half of the homonyms had two meanings with similar frequencies of usage in the English language. We shall refer to these homonyms as *balanced* (*pitcher* is an example of a balanced homonym). The other half of the homonyms also had two meanings, but one meaning was much more frequently used than the other. We shall refer to these homonyms as *unbalanced* (for example, *port* is unbalanced because the word is much more frequently used to refer to a place for docking ships than to an after-dinner drink). When a sentence contained an unbalanced homonym, the contextual information in the other clause always indicated that the less frequent meaning was the contextually appropriate meaning. To help you keep track of the experimental conditions and the important comparisons, a sample sentence used in each condition is shown in table 11.1. You should take a moment to familiarize yourself with the information in this table, as it will help you understand the results discussed below.

Instead of using a response task as in earlier studies, Duffy et al. examined reading times as their dependent variable. They used eye-tracking equipment that recorded the eye movements of participants as they read each sentence, which allowed measures of how long participants spent reading each word. Specifically, Duffy et al. examined a measure called gaze duration. As the eye moves left to right when reading a sentence, gaze duration is the time between when the eye first moves to a word in a sentence until the eye moves rightward to the next word in the sentence. For present purposes, gaze duration is important because it is assumed to reflect primarily the very earliest stages of processing (Rayner & Sereno, 1994). Duffy et al. compared gaze durations on the homonyms with gaze durations in a control condition. Namely, in the control condition, the same sentences were used except each homonym was replaced with a matched control word that was not a homonym (see table 11.1).

TABLE 11.1
SAMPLE SENTENCES USED IN THE STUDY BY DUFFY ET AL. (1988), ALONG WITH READING TIMES IN EACH EXPERIMENTAL CONDITION. IN EACH SENTENCE, THE UNDERLINED WORD WAS PRESENTED IN THE HOMONYM CONDITION, AND THE WORD IN PARENTHESES WAS SUBSTITUTED FOR THE HOMONYM IN THE CONTROL CONDITION.

	Gaze durations on target word (in msec)	
	Homonym	Control
Context after balanced homograph: Of course the <u>pitcher</u> (whiskey) was often forgotten because it was kept on the back of a high shelf.	279	261
Context before balanced homograph: Because it was kept on the back of a high shelf, the <u>pitcher</u> (whiskey) was often forgotten.	264	264
Context after unbalanced homograph: Last night the <u>port</u> (soup) was a great success when she finally served it to her guests.	261	259
Context before unbalanced homograph: When she finally served it to her guests, the <u>port</u> (soup) was a great success.	276	255

(S. A. Duffy, R. K. Morris, and K. Rayner, "Lexical Ambiguity and Fixation Times in Reading," *Journal of Memory and Language*, 1988, *27*, 429–446.)

Let us now consider the predictions of the reordered access theory and compare them to the results in each condition. First, consider the situation when contextual information comes after a balanced homonym. No contextual information is available when the homonym is encountered, and the two meanings are equally likely, so both meanings should be activated with equivalent speed and strength. In the first row of table 11.1, we see that gaze durations are longer for homonyms than for control words in this condition, which presumably reflects the two meanings competing with one another for selection. What about the case in which contextual information came before the balanced homonym? According to modular theories, the pattern of gaze durations should not change, because these theories state that lexical analysis does not consider contextual information when activating meanings. In contrast, the reordered access theory states that the contextual information will influence the speed or strength of meaning activation, such that the appropriate meaning will be activated more quickly or strongly than the inappropriate meaning, minimizing the competition between them. Consistent with the prediction of the reordered access theory, we see in the second row of table 11.1 that gaze durations now did not differ for target and control words.

Further support for the reordered access theory is obtained in the conditions involving unbalanced homonyms. When contextual information comes after an unbalanced homonym, the only information available when the homonym is encountered is the frequency of the meanings. The reordered access theory says that both meanings will be activated, but the more frequent meaning will be activated more quickly or strongly; thus, competition between the activated meanings will be minimized. Indeed, in the third row of table 11.1, we see that gaze durations did not differ for target and control words. What about the case in which contextual information came before the unbalanced homonym? Remember that the contextual information always favored the less frequent meaning, so according to the reordered access theory, the speed or strength with which the less frequent meaning will be enhanced will be enough to compete with the more frequent meaning. Consistent with this prediction, we see in the fourth row of table 11.1 that gaze durations now were longer on homonyms than on control words.

In sum, these results provide support for the interactivity assumption of the reordered access theory because if lexical analysis does not consider contextual information when activating word meanings, then the location of the contextual information should have no bearing on meaning activation (as indicated by gaze durations).

Selectivity Revisited   But what about the promiscuity assumption of this and other theories? Note that Duffy et al. argued that both meanings of a homonym were activated in all cases, but that competition was avoided when one of the meanings was activated more slowly or weakly than the other. However, in those cases where no evidence for competition among meanings was observed, one could argue that there was no competition *because only one meaning had been activated*—that is, because lexical analysis was selective. The question suggested by this alternative interpretation is whether selective activation of meaning can be observed when the constraints of lexical and nonlexical information are strong enough.

Indeed, several researchers have recently reported evidence that lexical access can be selective in some circumstances (e.g., Lucas, 1999; Tabossi & Zardon, 1993; Vu, Kellas, & Paul, 1998). Vu et al. (1998) had participants read sentences each of which contained a homonym. The homonyms in all cases were unbalanced. In one condition, the sentences in which they appeared were neutral, in that the content of the sentence preceding the homonym did not favor either meaning of the word (for example, "The man located the *bat*"). In a second condition, the content preceding the homonym favored the more frequent meaning of the word ("The slugger splintered the *bat*"). In a third condition, the content favored the less frequent meaning of the word ("The biologist wounded the *bat*").

Vu et al. used a speeded response task (called the *naming task*) to assess the activation of the meanings of the homonyms. Immediately (0 msec) after the homonym disappeared from the screen, a word appeared that was either associated with the more frequent meaning of the homonym or the less frequent meaning. For example, after the homonym *bat,* participants would either see the word *wooden* or the word *fly.* Participants were simply required to pronounce the word out loud as quickly as possible, and the time to begin pronunciation was recorded (referred to as "naming time"). As a control condition, the same words were presented for speeded naming after unrelated sentences.

When the homonym appeared in a neutral sentence, naming times for both words associated with a meaning of the homonym were faster than in the control condition, suggesting that both meanings had been activated. In contrast, when the homonym appeared in a sentence that favored the more frequent meaning, only the naming times for the word associated with the more frequent meaning were faster than in the control condition. Likewise, when the homonym appeared in a sentence that favored the infrequent meaning, only the naming times for the word associated with that meaning were faster than in the control condition. These results suggest that in the latter two conditions, only one meaning—the contextually appropriate meaning—had been activated. They found the same pattern even when the probe words were presented 80 msec after the homonym appeared (rather than immediately after it disappeared), ruling out the concern that both meanings had initially been activated, but one had been selected so quickly that the other was no longer active when the word appeared in the first experiment.

Summary of Lexical Analysis

Lexical analysis is an early and important contributor to text comprehension, in that it identifies the appropriate meanings of words. The bulk of available evidence strongly suggests that lexical access is interactive rather than modular, in that it uses nonlexical information in addition to lexical information, even at the earliest stages of its operation.

What about the issue of selectivity? Why does evidence obtain for promiscuity in some situations but for selectivity in others? Taken together, the results suggest that the selectivity of meaning activation is best considered as a continuum. To the extent that lexical and nonlexical information strongly constrain the set of plausible meanings, lexical analysis appears to arrive at the word's meaning by limiting activation to only the contextually appropriate meaning. As the constraints weaken, however, activation is increasingly distributed to multiple meanings followed by competitive selection.

SYNTACTIC PARSING

Lexical analysis plays an important role in text comprehension, but certainly, lexical analysis is not enough. Comprehension is more than just knowing the meaning of the words in a text. Another important part of comprehension is identifying the relationships between the words in a sentence, and this is where parsing processes come in. Ultimately, the goal of parsing processes is to identify the semantic relationships between words in order to extract the propositional content of a sentence. Recall from chapter 10 that the propositional content of a sentence is the idea or set of ideas that the sentence conveys. For example, the sentences "The dog bit the man" and "The man bit the dog" contain identical words denoting identical concepts, but those words have different semantic relationships to one another depending upon the structure in which they appear; that is, they express two different propositions.

How do we determine the semantic relationships between words within a sentence? Although several different processes and sources of information are likely involved, the syntactic structure of a sentence is thought to be an important contributor. Recall from chapter 10 that syntactic structure is the grammatical arrangement of words that form phrases and the arrangement of phrases that form sentences. These kinds of syntactic relationships are thought to play an important part in determining the semantic relationships between words. For example, consider the sentence, "The troops that dropped from the plane landed on the target." Did the plane land on the target, or did the troops land on the target? These are clearly different ideas, and the syntactic structure guides us to the correct one (the troops landed on the target).

In this section, we shall explore *syntactic parsing,* which refers to the set of cognitive processes that interpret the syntactic structure of sentences. As with lexical analysis, parsing a sentence syntactically is not as straightforward as it may initially appear. Just as a word may have multiple meanings, many words can also play different syntactic roles in different sentences (for example, *bank* may be either a noun or a verb). In fact, parsing most sentences syntactically usually involves one or more choice points along the way. Given that the appropriate syntactic role for words in a sentence may be ambiguous, how does syntactic parsing arrive at the contextually appropriate syntactic interpretation of these words? We will consider the most widely researched issue concerning syntactic parsing: Is syntactic parsing modular or interactive? That is, are initial interpretation decisions only based on syntactic information, or can lexical and semantic information influence initial interpretation?

Modular Theories of Syntactic Parsing

As mentioned above, the goal of syntactic parsing is to assign the appropriate syntactic role to each word in a sentence. But as a reader moves through a sentence, the appropriate syntactic role of a word may be temporarily ambiguous. For example, consider a sentence that begins "The troops dropped . . ." The sentence could continue with "dropped" serving as a main verb, as in:

(4) The troops dropped from the plane and landed on the target.

Alternatively, the sentence could continue with "dropped" participating in a relative clause, as in:

(5) The troops dropped from the plane landed on the target.

(If you have trouble understanding this sentence, reading an unambiguous version may help: "The troops *who were* dropped from the plane landed on the target.") Upon encountering a syntactically ambiguous word, what information does syntactic parsing consider when deciding which syntactic role to assign to the word?

According to modular theories of syntactic parsing, initial interpretation decisions are based only on syntactic information. Modular accounts assume that syntactic parsing initially does not consider information from other processes, such as information about the meaning of the particular words being used or the thematic context in which they appear. Instead, initial interpretation decisions are assumed to be based only on syntactic information about those words (what part of speech they are) and about syntactic structures in general.

Modular theories may differ from one another with respect to the kind of syntactic information assumed to be used by syntactic parsing. Some theorists propose that syntactic parsing makes initial interpretation decisions based on syntactic rules (Frazier, 1987) that result in the parser selecting the interpretation with the simplest syntactic structure. For example, in the case of the main verb/relative clause ambiguity illustrated above, a syntactic rule would require a main verb interpretation of "dropped" (as in sentence 4) because that interpretation has a simpler syntactic structure than one with a relative clause (as in sentence 5). Other modular accounts propose that rather than using rules, syntactic parsing makes initial interpretation decisions based on probabilistic data about the frequency with which various syntactic structures are encountered in the language (Mitchell, 1994). According to this kind of modular theory, the main verb interpretation of "dropped" would be adopted because in the English language, main verb structures occur much more frequently than relative clause structures.

In either case, the important point is that modular theories predict that the main verb interpretation should be adopted initially. To evaluate this prediction, the standard methodology involves having participants read sentences that contain ambiguous verbs, such as "dropped." In one condition, the correct interpretation of the verb is a main verb interpretation (sentence 4). In a second condition, the correct interpretation is a relative clause interpretation (sentence 5). The primary measure of interest is reading times in the *disambiguating region* of each sentence. The disambiguating region of a sentence contains the content that indicates which interpretation of an earlier syntactic ambiguity is correct. For example, in sentence 4, the disambiguating region is "and landed," because it makes clear that "dropped" is a main verb. In sentence 5, the disambiguating region is "landed," because it makes clear that "dropped" belongs in a relative clause.

To revisit, modular theories predict that the ambiguous verb "dropped" will initially be interpreted as a main verb. In the main verb condition, the sentence continuation (" . . . *and landed* on the target") indicates that the main verb interpretation is correct and, thus, no reanalysis would be necessary. However, in the relative clause condition, the sentence continuation (" . . . *landed* on the target") indicates that the main verb interpretation is incorrect, and reanalysis thus would be necessary to reassign "dropped" to a relative clause instead of as a main verb. Since reanalysis involves additional processing, reading times in the disambiguating region would be expected to increase in this condition.

In fact, many studies have demonstrated that reading times in disambiguating regions are markedly longer in the relative clause condition than in the main verb condition. An elevation in reading time due to reanalysis of an initial misinterpretation is commonly referred to as a *garden path effect,* based on the metaphor that readers initially are led down the wrong path. We have focused on the main verb/relative clause ambiguity here, but garden path effects predicted by modular accounts of syntactic parsing have also been observed with many other kinds of syntactic ambiguities.

Interactive Theories of Syntactic Parsing

At this point, let us consider further the key prediction of modular theories. Modular theories not only predict which interpretation should be favored over another (e.g., the simplest, or the most frequent), they predict *that the favored interpretation of a structural ambiguity should be adopted every time that form of ambiguity occurs, regardless of the particular words used or the particular context in which it appears.* In other words, according to modular accounts, "there cannot exist sentences which do not cause a garden path in one context, but which do cause a garden path in another" (Altmann & Steedman, 1988, p. 210).

In contrast to this critical prediction of modular theories, interactive theories predict that garden path effects will depend upon nonsyntactic contextual information. Interactive theories postulate that in addition to syntactic information, nonsyntactic sources of information can also influence initial interpretation (e.g., MacDonald, Pearlmutter, & Seidenberg 1994; McClelland, 1987). These additional sources of information could include lexical information about the particular words in the sentence or semantic text-level information. Of course, specific interactive theories may differ from one another in the kinds of nonsyntactic information they assume can influence interpretation decisions and in the kinds of syntactic decisions they assume can be influenced. But the important point is that all interactive theories predict that garden path effects can be influenced by nonsyntactic information.

To see how one might evaluate this prediction of interactive theories, let us examine another case of syntactic ambiguity. Consider a sentence that begins, "The fireman told the woman that he had risked his life for . . . ". Here, not just a word but an entire phrase is ambiguous with respect to the syntactic role it plays in the sentence. The phrase "that he had risked his life for" could be part of a complement clause indicating what the fireman told the woman, as in:

> **(6)** The fireman told the woman [that he had risked his life for many people in similar situations]. (The complement clause is in brackets.)

Alternatively, the phrase could be part of a relative clause that was used to indicate which woman he was telling, as in:

> **(7)** The fireman told the woman [that he had risked his life for] to install a smoke detector. (The relative clause is in brackets.)

Of course, this relative clause interpretation would only seem sensible if, in fact, more than one woman had been mentioned at some point prior to the encounter of this sentence. Otherwise, there would be no need to explain which woman he was talking to. More generally, the reason that relative clauses are typically used in language is to discriminate between different entities or sets of entities. Thus, a relative clause interpretation of an ambiguous phrase would be highly plausible in a discourse that contained similar entities.

To evaluate this idea, Altmann, Garnham, and Dennis (1992) examined reading times for relative clause sentences (like sentence 7) either when those sentences were presented in isolation (as in earlier research on syntactic parsing of relative clause sentences), or when they were embedded in a story context that contained similar entities. For example, sentence 7 would either appear in a list of unrelated sentences, or it would appear in the following text:

> An off-duty fireman was talking to two women. He was telling them how serious the situation had been when their house had caught fire. The fireman had risked his life to rescue one of the women while the other had waited outside. He told the woman that he had risked his life for to install a smoke detector. (G. T. M. Altmann, A. Garnham, and Y. Dennis, "Avoiding the Garden Path: Eye Movements in Context," *Journal of Memory and Language* 31 (1992): 685–712.)

As in previous research, the measure of interest concerned reading times for the disambiguating region of the target sentence. In sentence 7, the disambiguating region is "to install," because the ambiguous phrase now makes sense as a relative clause but not as a complement clause. Reading times in the disambiguating region of the target sentences were compared to reading times for the same content in control versions of the sentences. In the control version of each sentence, the main verb was replaced with another verb that would only permit a relative clause to follow. For example, "told" was changed to "asked," because a complement clause cannot follow "asked" (to illustrate, "The fireman asked the woman that he had risked his life for many people in similar situations" is not sensible in contrast to "The fireman asked the woman that he had risked his life for to install a smoke detector"). Thus, in the control condition, the initial interpretation of each sentence would be the relative clause interpretation.

Let us first discuss the results in the case where the sentences appeared in isolation. In this condition, Altmann et al. found a significant garden path effect, in that reading times in the disambiguating region were longer for the target sentences than for the control sentences. In this case, the effect indicates that the ambiguous phrase in the target sentence was initially interpreted as part of a complement clause, which had to be reanalyzed when the disambiguating content was encountered. Initial interpretation of the ambiguous phrase as part of a complement clause is reasonable, given that similar entities have not been mentioned, and thus, there would presumably be no need for a relative clause.

In contrast, when the sentences were presented in the texts instead of in isolation, no garden path effect was observed. Reading times in the disambiguating region did not differ for target and control sentences. This result suggests that in this condition, the ambiguous phrase was initially interpreted as a relative clause. This interpretation would be reasonable, given that similar entities had previously been mentioned and would need to be discriminated from one another at that point. The most important point here is that *the initial interpretation of a syntactic ambiguity was influenced by nonsyntactic information*—in this case, conceptual information from the preceding text. In other words, contrary to the prediction of modular theories but consistent with the prediction of interactive theories, Altmann et al. demonstrated a case in which a sentence did not cause a garden path in one context but did in another. In fact, an increasing number of studies have shown that various forms of nonsyntactic information can influence the initial interpretation decisions of the syntactic parser (e.g., Garnsey, Pearlmutter, Myers, & Lotocky, 1997).

Immediacy of Initial Interpretation

When syntactic parsing makes an incorrect initial interpretation, subsequent reanalysis can often be quite costly with respect to the additional processing time required. Furthermore, initial misinterpretations may result in misunderstandings. For example, Christianson, Hollingworth, Halliwell, and Ferreira (2001) presented readers with sentences containing a syntactic ambiguity (e.g., "While Anna dressed the baby that was small and cute spit up on the bed") or unambiguous control versions (e.g., "The baby that was small and cute spit up on the bed while Anna dressed"). After reading each sentence, readers were asked a comprehension question to assess whether they had understood the sentence correctly (e.g., "Did Anna dress the baby?"). The startling result was that readers incorrectly responded 66 percent of the time after ambiguous sentences, compared to 13 percent after unambiguous sentences.

Given the potential costs involved, minimizing the occurrence of initial misinterpretations would be desirable. One way in which misinterpretations could be avoided is if syntactic parsing operated according to a *wait-and-see strategy,* that is, by postponing the interpretation of syntactically ambiguous words or phrases until subsequent content indicating the correct interpretation was encountered. Although the wait-and-see strategy would minimize misinterpretations, the demands of maintaining unanalyzed information while at the same time processing subsequent content would quickly swamp the limited capacity working memory system thought to support these operations.

But might interpretation decisions be postponed even briefly? An overwhelming amount of research suggests that the answer to this question is no. Most of this support derives from examination of the time course of garden path effects. Note that a garden path effect will only obtain if an interpretation of the ambiguous word has already been made when the disambiguating region is encountered. Perhaps surprisingly, studies have shown that garden path effects obtain even when disambiguating information immediately follows the syntactically ambiguous word (e.g., Altmann & Steedman, 1988; Ferreira & Henderson, 1990; Trueswell, 1996).

Summary of Syntactic Parsing

Syntactic parsing plays an important role in text comprehension. Determining the meaning of a sentence requires identifying the semantic relationships among words in that sentence, and these semantic relationships are constrained, in part, by the syntactic structure of the sentence. Thus, by analyzing the syntactic structure of sentences, syntactic parsing provides important information for deriving the meaning of a text.

Syntactic parsing is made more difficult by the fact that words or phrases within a sentence are often ambiguous with respect to the syntactic role they play. Research suggests that at such points of ambiguity, syntactic parsing makes immediate interpretation decisions. When an initial interpretation decision turns out to be incorrect, costly reanalysis processes are necessary. Thus, minimizing misinterpretations would be optimal. Fortunately, research also suggests that syntactic parsing is interactive, in that it considers nonsyntactic contextual information when making initial interpretation decisions. In many cases, contextual information will direct syntactic parsing to the appropriate initial interpretation, avoiding the need for subsequent reanalysis.

INTEGRATION, PRESUPPOSITIONS, AND INFERENCES

Up to this point, we have been examining some of the key processes involved in analyzing explicit text content (the particular words and the particular sentence structures in which they appear). But remember that the ultimate goal of comprehension is to arrive at the meaning of the discourse, not just the meaning of individual words or the ideas they explicitly express. Representing the meaning of a discourse requires integration of the various ideas expressed in the text. Without integration processes, comprehension would result in seemingly disassociated bits of information rather than a useful and coherent representation. Integration—and more generally, the representation of the meaning of a discourse—usually involves the addition of a great deal of information not explicitly stated in the text; that is, comprehension also involves forming the presuppositions and inferences implied by the explicit content. We shall consider each of these critical processes in turn.

Integration and the Loss of Verbatim Information

The phenomenon of integration can be demonstrated in a number of ways. The game of whispering a story to a person who, in turn, whispers it to another person until several persons have heard it, can produce amusing results at final recall because of successive integration of the ideas. Indeed, the final version of the story as told to the last person can be dramatically different from the original version.

Controlled observations of the integration effect are possible in the laboratory, as illustrated by a classic experiment of Bransford and Franks (1971). They presented participants with sentences that were derived from a complex sentence such as "The girl who lives next door broke the large window on the porch." This complex sentence expresses four propositions or ideas: (1) The girl lives next door, (2) The girl broke the window, (3) The window was large, and (4) The window was on the porch. The complex, four-idea sentence itself was not presented for study, but rather various combinations of one-, two-, and three-idea sentences were provided at input. For example, a participant might see the following sentences: "The girl who lives next door broke the window" (two-idea unit), "The window was on the porch" (one-idea unit), and "The girl broke the large window on the porch" (three-idea unit). When the ideas expressed by these separate sentences are integrated into a single, higher-order idea unit, the representation becomes a complex, four-idea sentence. To explore whether their participants were actually integrating the input sentences, Bransford and Franks gave a recognition test for the input sentences.

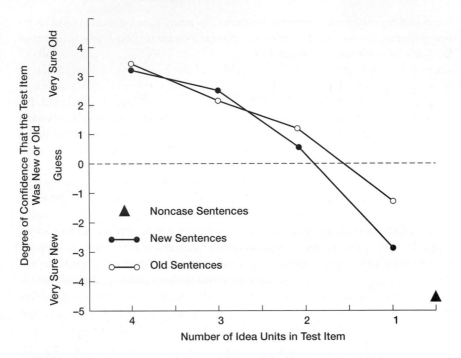

FIGURE 11.1
Degree of confidence recognition judgment for *new* and *old* test sentences, depending upon the number of idea units in the sentence. Note that all four-idea unit tests were new items. *(From "The Abstraction of Linguistic Ideas" by J. D. Bransford and J. J. Franks,* Cognitive Psychology, *1971, 2, 331–350. Copyright 1971 by Academic Press. Used by permission.)*

Several types of sentences were available in the recognition test. Some of the sentences were *old;* these sentences were actually presented during study and, from this example, included, "The girl who lives next door broke the window." Some test sentences were *new;* these sentences were not presented at study but could be derived from a complex sentence such as, "The girl who lives next door broke the large window." Although this sentence sounds familiar, a look back shows that it was not one of the sample input sentences. Finally, a third type of sentence, *noncase,* was included in the recognition test. The *noncase* sentences were quite dissimilar in meaning from the input sentences—for example, "The boy broke a window in the house next door."

The results of the study are presented in figure 11.1. As shown in the figure, the outcome of interest was how confident the subjects were that a given test sentence was actually presented during study. Figure 11.1 illustrates three essential points bearing on the integration phenomenon. First, the subjects were incapable of discriminating *old* and *new* sentences. Since the *new* sentences were derived from the complex, four-idea sentences, this result suggests that the recognition judgments were made from memory of the complex sentences. If this assumption is true, integration must have occurred because the complex sentences were never presented. Consistent with this interpretation is the second major point of the results: namely, as the number of idea units in the *old* and *new* sentences increased, participants became more confident that all sentences were actually presented. Indeed, the subjects were most confident of the four-idea sentences, the ones which were never actually presented. If the participants' memories were based on the complex sentences, the test sentences with more idea units would be most like their representation. Finally, the third point is that *noncase* sentences were well recognized as *not* being among the study sentences. Thus, if the meaning of a test sentence is quite discrepant from the study sentences, participants can easily reject the sentence.

The conclusion from this experiment is that people store different statements related to the same idea as a unit. Individual sentences are not always maintained in memory, but the *ideas expressed by the sentences are integrated into a single representation of the general idea expressed by a group of sentences.* The implication of this conclusion is that memory for individual sentences is quite poor, but memory for a general idea is good. *In other words, integration produces the gist of the message, and it is the gist, not the details, which is well remembered.*

Themes: The Central Idea

Memory of information heard or read is rarely just a verbatim account of the information. Rather, the tendency is to summarize the content and integrate the discrete details into higher-order idea units. Integration of details involves combining related information, and this, of course, requires detecting one or more relationships. One of the important cues to detecting relationships is the theme, or general idea, of the passage or discourse. The theme may be introduced in the title of a passage or in the lead sentence of a paragraph, or the theme may be abstracted as the recurring, dominant idea of a passage or discussion. Regardless of the form in which it appears, the theme anchors the information in knowledge. Once the central idea is known, the various statements can be organized around that central idea. A good deal of evidence indicates the importance of themes in comprehension and memory.

The importance of themes to both comprehension and memory has been illustrated dramatically by Bransford and Johnson (1973). Consider the following passage:

> The procedure is quite simple. First, you arrange things into different groups. Of course, one pile may be sufficient, depending upon how much there is to do. If you have to go somewhere else due to lack of facilities, that is the next step; otherwise, you are pretty well set. It is important not to overdo things. That is, it is better to do too few things at once than too many. At first the whole procedure will seem complicated.

Soon, however, it will become just another facet of life. After the procedure is completed, one arranges the materials into different groups again. Then they can be put into their appropriate places. Eventually they will be used once more, and the whole cycle will have to be repeated. (J. D. Bransford and M. K. Johnson, "Considerations of Some Problems of Comprehension," in *Visual Information Processing,* edited by W. G. Chase. New York: Academic Press, 1973.)

Although you can understand the individual sentences in this passage, the relationship among the sentences is unclear; consequently, integration of idea units is virtually impossible. The passage is difficult to understand because it is written such that the theme is quite obscure. Subjects in the Bransford and Johnson experiment had a very difficult time remembering this passage. However, if the title "Washing Clothes" is supplied, the passage becomes both more comprehensible and memorable.

The theme of a passage not only influences comprehension during the processing of a text, it can also influence subsequent retrieval. Memory for a passage will generally begin with the theme of the passage. Once the theme is retrieved, it can then aid further reconstruction of the material. For example, a friend might say, "Do you remember the conversation we had this morning?" and you respond, "Oh, yes, we were talking about your party last night." From this theme you can then go on to reconstruct some of the details of the conversation. The influence of themes on the reconstruction of passages is illustrated in an experiment by Sulin and Dooling (1974). Participants in this experiment read the following passage:

Carol Harris's Need for Professional Help. Carol Harris was a problem child from birth. She was wild, stubborn, and violent. By the time Carol turned eight, she was still unmanageable. Her parents were very concerned about her mental health. There was no good institution for her problem in her state. Her parents finally decided to take some action. They hired a private teacher for Carol. (R. A. Sulin and D. J. Dooling, "Intrusions of a Thematic Idea in Retention of Prose," *Journal of Experimental Psychology,* 103 (1974): 255–262.)

A second group of participants read the same passage except *Helen Keller* was substituted for *Carol Harris.* A week later the participants were given a recognition test that included the sentence "She was deaf, dumb, and blind." Only 5 percent of the participants who read the *Carol Harris* passage claimed to have seen this sentence. Of the participants reading the *Helen Keller* passage, over 50 percent of the subjects thought they had seen the sentence. These kinds of data encourage the generalization that the theme is the focus of the memory representation, and much of what is remembered is reconstructed from the theme.

In sum, the guidance provided by the theme facilitates integration of information during comprehension but at the risk of distorting understanding and memory of the material. Just as with the perceptual processes discussed in earlier chapters, an increase in cognitive efficiency sometimes comes at the expense of complete accuracy. This discussion also illuminates how the memory distortions discussed in chapter 7 may arise.

In many cases, however, the influence of themes on comprehension will have beneficial effects. For example, given that themes are central to comprehension and serve as the focus for organizing memory for discourse, good use of this observation can be made in class by always extracting and understanding the theme of each subsection of the material. In brief, the first thing to do when trying to understand a lecture or reading assignment is to know what it is about. Actively construct a hierarchy of themes, relating each topic to its superordinate. For example, the general topic of memory was discussed, with the subordinate topic of encoding processes and its subtopics, organization and individual item processing. By setting up such a hierarchy of themes and understanding the relationship among them, you are in a much better position to appreciate details such as individual experiments and their implications. Indeed, as simple as this activity sounds, it is at the heart of what is called understanding. If you actively construct a hierarchy of themes, you can easily increase both comprehension and memory for all kinds of materials.

Presuppositions

When a communication is understood, the directly asserted information is usually elaborated such that what is understood goes far beyond what was explicitly said. For example, to understand most statements requires that other factors are *assumed* or *presupposed* to be true. The question "Have you finally stopped smoking?" obviously presupposes that you once smoked. Although the presupposition is not expressed explicitly, memory for some event is likely to include presupposed information. Furthermore, each assertion or statement implies additional information, and given those implications, inferences are made that subsequently may be remembered. With both presuppositions and inferences, *more* is remembered than was actually said.

Many statements can be understood only if other things are presupposed to be true. For example, when a professor says, "Congratulations, Smith. You have made the highest grade again," the professor is asserting that Smith made the highest grade this time, and the presupposition is that Smith had made the highest grade in the past. A presupposition must be made in order for an assertion to be understood fully. Either or both can be remembered, and either or both may be true or false. Smith may or may not have made the highest grade this time, and Smith may or may not have made the highest grade in the past. Professors have been known to make these kinds of mistakes. In other situations, false presuppositions can have more serious consequences.

Consider the effect of eyewitness testimony upon a jury. If the jury must make a presupposition to comprehend the testimony of a witness, that presupposition may be remembered and later influence the decision. Thus, a clever attorney may try to discredit a witness by asking, "Do you still drink heavily?" The witness must deny not only the assertion, but also the presupposition. The study by Loftus and Palmer (1974) discussed in chapter 7 provides an indication of the subtlety and power of presuppositions on eyewitness accounts.

Inferences

Understanding a statement usually leads to certain conclusions or implications. If you say, "Jim does not own one single shirt with a polo pony on it," I may infer from this statement that it is important to you that a person own such a shirt and then go on to attribute to you a number of personality characteristics common to people who have such beliefs. Clearly, I have then gone far beyond your simple and rather straightforward statement. In fact, my inference may be totally wrong. You actually may have been expressing admiration for Jim, in which case a completely different set of inferences would be appropriate. In either case, this simple example illustrates the prevalence of inferences in comprehension. Virtually every statement anyone utters or writes leads the listener or reader to certain inferences.

Notice the distinction between an inference and a presupposition. A presupposition is knowledge activated by an assertion in order to understand it. An inference is knowledge that is activated once the assertion is understood. A wealth of research has indicated that comprehension may involve many different kinds of inferences.

Logical Inferences   Certain kinds of inferences, known as *logical inferences,* must follow from what was said. Logical inferences are, in a sense, demanded by the assertion. For example, the assertion that "John's actions forced Mr. Pettigrew to fire him" logically implies that John was fired. Unlike a presupposition, you do not have to think "John was fired" in order to understand the assertion, but the assertion does demand the inference because it would make little sense to conclude the assertion with "but Mr. Pettigrew did not fire John."

As an example of the effect of logical inference, consider the following experiment by Bransford, Barclay, and Franks (1972). Participants saw sentences such as, "Three turtles rested on a floating log and a fish swam beneath it." They were then given recognition memory tests for new, logically implied sentences such as, "Three turtles rested on a floating log and a fish swam beneath them." A large number of the subjects consistently claimed that they had seen the new sentences, which suggests that the logical inferences had been constructed and stored when the original sentences were presented.

Pragmatic Inferences   Not all inferences, however, are logically demanded. Some, perhaps the majority, of the inferences are invited by the assertion. This second kind of inference is known as *pragmatic inference*. A pragmatic inference does not have to follow from an assertion but, rather, is reasonable based on world knowledge. For example, to say, "Bill and Mary were looking at engagement rings" in no way demands the inference that Bill and Mary are to be engaged; however, that inference is certainly reasonable given what is known about the world.

Given that the entities, states, and events described in a text may be related to one another in many different ways, many different kinds of pragmatic inference are possible. Indeed, a substantial amount of research has established that comprehension involves referential inferences (i.e., inferences about whether two words or phrases refer to the same conceptual entity or event), causal inferences (i.e., inferences about whether one state or event caused another state or event), spatial inferences (i.e., inferences about whether two entities were present at the same location, or about whether two events took place at the same location), and temporal inferences (i.e., inferences about whether two events took place at the same time), among others (Zwaan & Radvansky, 1998).

Much of the research that has been done to explore the promiscuity of inferencing during comprehension has examined performance measures on subsequent memory tests, as in the Bransford and Franks (1971) example described previously. Another commonly used method to explore inferencing involves examination of reading times during processing of the text. For example, Klin, Murray, Levine, and Guzmán (1999) presented readers with texts that each described a situation with a likely outcome (e.g., ". . . Brad had no money but he just had to have the beautiful ruby ring for his wife. Seeing no salespeople around, he quietly made his way closer to the counter," strongly implying that Brad was going to steal the ring). When a subsequent sentence described an outcome different from the implied outcome (e.g., "Staring intensely at the ring, he promised he would buy it someday"), reading times were significantly longer than in a control condition. Interestingly, on a subsequent recall test, the predicted (but incorrect) outcome was frequently recalled. Thus, this study not only illustrates the methods by which a great deal of research has provided evidence for inference processes but also demonstrates once again that memory may be distorted by incorrect inferences.

Recognition of the prevalence and power of inferential processing is extremely important in understanding communication. Much of what is communicated is, in fact, left unsaid. Speakers rely on listeners to draw appropriate inferences, and listeners generally trust the inferences drawn from speakers' statements. The ability to communicate without explicitly saying everything we are trying to convey enormously enhances efficiency in communication. As with other cognitive processes, increased efficiency comes at the cost of increased error. Again, the error and the efficiency result from the diametrically opposed processes of abstraction and integration on the one hand and elaboration through inference on the other.

The most important point for you to take away from this section is that to understand a text, representing the explicit content of a text is not enough—the

BOX 11.1

MISCOMMUNICATION IN ADVERTISING: INFERENCES IN ACTION

Surely, all of us occasionally say things in such a way that the listener is in a position of inferring information that may not be entirely accurate. Interestingly, we do not consider this a case of blatant lying but simply claim that the listener is misled. To establish whether a speaker was indeed dishonest, the speaker's intentions must be discovered, a very hard thing to do if the actual assertion is, in fact, accurate. Consequently, it is easy to mislead either when sufficient information to evaluate an assertion is intentionally withheld or when vigilance about drawing inferences is not observed. Good advertising copy provides an interesting case in point.

Among our favorites is a classic running television commercial for a pain reliever. The script asserts, "This product contains more of the pain reliever that doctors recommend. You can't buy a more effective pain reliever without a prescription." The last sentence encourages the inference that this product is the most effective pain reliever to be bought without a prescription, but this clearly is not what the sentence asserts. Furthermore, the pain reliever that doctors recommend most is aspirin, and beyond some maximum dosage, which can be obtained from two or three tablets of any brand, additional aspirin has little effect. By not mentioning that the pain reliever in question is aspirin, the advertisement sets us up to infer that the product contains some esoteric drug and lots of it. Successfully competing in the aspirin business is difficult because all of the brands are very much alike; thus, any competitive edge provided by advertising is helpful, including misleading information. Are we really susceptible to such techniques?

Harris (1977) reported an experiment that indicates that people are quite susceptible to the inferences created by advertising assertions. Harris used the following text from a Listerine commercial:

"Wouldn't it be great," asks the mother, "if you could make him cold proof? Well, you can't. Nothing can do that. [Boy sneezes.] But there is something that you can do that may help. Have him gargle with Listerine Antiseptic. Listerine can't promise to keep him cold free, but it may help him fight off colds. During the cold-catching season, have him gargle twice a day with full-strength Listerine. Watch his diet, see he gets plenty of sleep, and there's a good chance he'll have fewer colds, milder colds this year."

Harris substituted "Gargoil" for "Listerine" in the text, but otherwise the advertisement was heard verbatim. Although the advertisement never asserts that "Gargoil" prevents colds, every subject in the experiment responded yes to the question "Does gargling with Gargoil prevent colds?" Does this commercial perpetuate a falsehood?

Regardless of the source of the information, the point of this discussion is that the elaborative nature of comprehension can be and is used to imply potentially inaccurate information. Based on what you now know about comprehension and memory, you are in the position of protecting yourself against this possibility by directly questioning assertions and carefully analyzing your own inferences.

semantic relationships between the ideas expressed by that content must be represented. That is, the ideas must be integrated. Additionally, understanding the meaning of a text will almost always require the addition of information from prior knowledge, in the form of presuppositions and inferences. In sum, integration, presupposition, and inference each play a critical role in comprehension.

THE ROLE OF RETRIEVAL IN COMPREHENSION

Much of the research on text comprehension focuses on what is remembered from a text after comprehension processes have been completed. The studies by Bransford et al. (1972) and Sulin and Dooling (1971) described previously provide examples of this kind of research on text comprehension. This body of research strongly suggests that comprehension is critical for memory—people remember what they understand. But the opposite is true as well—memory is critical for comprehension. In other words, retrieval processes are heavily involved *during* the processing of text.

Fully comprehending a text often requires integration of ideas that are separated by several sentences, paragraphs, or even pages of text. By the time one idea is encountered, other related ideas presented earlier in the text may no longer be active in working memory, given the limited capacity of the system. For integration to occur, earlier ideas must often be retrieved from long-term memory. Similarly, retrieval is also necessary for presuppositions and inferences to be formed, as they rely upon prior knowledge stored in long-term memory. Thus, retrieval processes are critical to comprehension.

As mentioned in chapter 7, perception and comprehension of everyday events often brings related information to mind. The same is true of discourse comprehension—during the processing of any given segment of a text, the content currently being processed serves as a cue that can activate related information. As an example of how text content can cue the retrieval of related information, consider the following story:

> Mary was driving in the country one day when she smelled a terrific odor. Suddenly a small black cat with a white stripe down its back ran in front of the car. Mary knew she couldn't stop in time. However, she hoped she had missed the animal and continued on her way. After a while, she noticed she was low on gas. While at the gas station, the attendant asked her what had run in front of her car. (E. J. O'Brien and J. E. Albrecht, "The Role of Context in Accessing Antecedents in Text," *Journal of Experimental Psychology: Learning, Memory, and Cognition,* 1991, *17,* 94–102.)

Note that the story explicitly mentions one entity, "cat," in the context of information that is consistent with another entity, "skunk," which is not mentioned. Also note, in the last sentence, that the attendant asking Mary what ran in front of the car invites retrieval of the entity mentioned earlier in the text. O'Brien and

Albrecht (1991) had participants read several short stories of this nature. Immediately after the last sentence, a word appeared on the screen and participants were to pronounce the word as quickly as possible (i.e., the naming task described earlier). The probe word was either the entity that had been explicitly mentioned in the text or the related but unmentioned entity. In the case of the sample text above, the last sentence would be followed by either "cat" or "skunk." O'Brien and Albrecht found that response times to both probe words were faster than response times in a control condition, suggesting that the "skunk" concept had been activated by the earlier contextual information.

The Nature of Retrieval in Text Processing

In the example above, note that although "skunk" was related to the information used to describe the cat, "skunk" was not appropriate in the context because it was a cat, not a skunk, that ran in front of Mary's car. This situation highlights an important issue about the nature of the retrieval process involved in comprehension. Earlier theories assumed that retrieval during text processing was a "smart" process that directed activation only to that information that was contextually appropriate (e.g., Sanford & Garrod, 1981). However, more recent theories assume that retrieval during text processing is promiscuous and "dumb."

Specifically, *resonance theory* states that retrieval is a fast, passive process that sends signals simultaneously to any information in long-term memory related to the cues in working memory (e.g., Myers & O'Brien, 1998). Importantly, any information that is related to the cue will receive some activation, regardless of its context relevance. Thus, retrieval is thought to involve activation of any and all information that is sufficiently related to the cues in working memory (i.e., retrieval is promiscuous), regardless of the relevance of that information to the context (i.e., retrieval is "dumb").

As further evidence for such resonance-based retrieval during text processing, consider a study conducted by O'Brien, Rizzella, Albrecht, and Halleran (1998). Each of their narratives included an introduction of a main character, a description of that character, and then an action performed by that character. For example, in the first text in table 11.2, Mary is introduced as the main character; described as loving junk food; and then, in the final sentence, described as ordering a cheeseburger and fries. Note that in this case, her action (ordering a cheeseburger) is consistent with her description (a junk-food junkie). In a second condition, the description of the character was *inconsistent* with the subsequent action, as illustrated by the description in the second segment in table 11.2. In this case, ordering a cheeseburger would be inconsistent with the description of Mary as being a health nut. O'Brien et al. found that readers took longer to read the action sentence ("Mary ordered a cheeseburger and fries") when the earlier description of Mary was inconsistent with that action than when it was consistent. This finding suggests that the content in the action sentence served as a cue to retrieve the related descriptive information presented earlier, and in the inconsistent condition, this information would make it difficult to understand why Mary would order a cheeseburger.

TABLE 11.2
SAMPLE TEXT MATERIALS USED IN THE STUDY BY O'BRIEN ET AL. (1998). THE FIRST SEGMENT CONTAINS A FULL TEXT WITH THE DESCRIPTIVE INFORMATION INCLUDED IN ONE OF THE EXPERIMENTAL CONDITIONS. EACH SUBSEQUENT SEGMENT CONTAINS THE DESCRIPTION SUBSTITUTED FOR THE ITALICIZED INFORMATION IN THE FIRST SEGMENT (ITALICS WERE NOT PRESENTED TO PARTICIPANTS).

Description consistent with action:
   Today, Mary was meeting a friend for lunch. She arrived early at the restaurant and decided to get a table. After she sat down, she started looking at the menu. *This was Mary's favorite restaurant because it had fantastic junk food. Mary enjoyed eating anything that was quick and easy to fix. In fact, she ate at McDonald's at least three times a week. Mary never worried about her diet and saw no reason to eat nutritious foods.* After about ten minutes, Mary's friend arrived. It had been a few months since they had seen each other. Because of this, they had a lot to talk about and chatted for over an half hour. Finally, Mary signaled the waiter to come take their orders. Mary checked the menu one more time. She had a hard time deciding what to have for lunch. Mary ordered a cheeseburger and fries.

Description inconsistent with action:
   This was Mary's favorite restaurant because it had fantastic health food. Mary, a health nut, had been a strict vegetarian for ten years. Her favorite food was cauliflower. Mary was so serious about her diet that she refused to eat anything which was fried or cooked in grease.

Inconsistent description negated before action:
   This was Mary's favorite restaurant because it had fantastic health food. Mary, a health nut, had been a strict vegetarian for ten years. Her favorite food was cauliflower. Mary was so serious about her diet that she refused to eat anything which was fried or cooked in grease. Nevertheless, Mary never stuck to her diet when she dined out with friends, because she enjoyed eating meat occasionally.

Inconsistent description no longer operative:
   As she was waiting, Mary recalled that this had been her favorite restaurant because it had fantastic health food. Mary recalled that she had been a health nut and a strict vegetarian for about ten years but she wasn't anymore. Back then, her favorite food had been cauliflower. At that time, Mary had been so serious about her diet that she had refused to eat anything which was fried or cooked in grease.

Inconsistent description is completely false:
   Mary remembered that at a recent party, her friend Joan played a joke by telling people that Mary had been a strict vegetarian for ten years. Joan told everyone that Mary's favorite restaurant had fantastic health food. She said that Mary was a health nut and wouldn't eat anything which was fried or cooked in grease. She also claimed that Mary's favorite food was cauliflower.

(E. J. O'Brien, M. L. Rizzella, J. E. Albrecht, and J. G. Halleran, "Updating a Situation Model: A Memory-Based Text Processing View," *Journal of Experimental Psychology: Learning, Memory, and Cognition* 24, (1998): 1200–1210.)

Even more interesting are those conditions in which O'Brien et al. wrote the texts in such a way that the inconsistent description was no longer relevant to the character in the context of the action. Consider the description in the third segment of table 11.2. Here, Mary is described as a health nut except when she goes out to eat (as in the context in which the action occurs). In this condition, O'Brien et al. still found that reading times for the action sentence were elevated, even though the description was no longer relevant. Thinking that perhaps the negation was not strong enough to indicate that the description was no longer relevant, O'Brien et al. ran a follow-up experiment using text in which the description was clearly no longer true, as in the fourth segment of table 11.2. The elevation in reading times still manifested in this condition. Finally, O'Brien et al. used text in which the description had never been true of Mary. Reading times were still longer in this condition than when the earlier description was consistent with the action. Thus, O'Brien et al. concluded that resonance-based retrieval during text processing was insensitive to the contextual relevance of the information it activated.

SUMMARY

Comprehension is the process of deriving meaning from surface-level linguistic information. Comprehension involves several different cognitive processes. Some of these processes are responsible for analyzing the explicit content of the text, or the particular words and sentences contained in the text. Two of the processes that analyze explicit content are lexical analysis and syntactic parsing.

Lexical analysis is responsible for representing the contextually appropriate meanings of words. Research suggests that lexical analysis is interactive rather than modular, in that it considers both lexical and nonlexical sources of information at all stages of processing. When these sources of information strongly converge on one meaning, lexical analysis is selective and only activates that meaning. As constraints weaken, lexical analysis becomes more promiscuous, activating multiple word meanings and then selecting from among them.

Syntactic parsing is responsible for representing the grammatical structure of words and phrases in a sentence—an important piece of information for determining the semantic ideas expressed by the sentence. Like lexical analysis, syntactic parsing is interactive, in that nonsyntactic sources of information can influence all stages of processing. Syntactic parsing is also immediate, in that initial interpretations are made at the point of a syntactic ambiguity rather than postponed until disambiguating information is encountered.

In addition to the processes that analyze explicit text content, comprehension involves other processes that represent the relationships between text ideas (integration), as well as the relationships between those ideas and prior knowledge (presupposition and inference), to arrive at the meaning of the text. Integration usually involves the combination of ideas and the loss of verbatim information and is heavily influenced by the theme of the text. Presuppositions involve adding information from prior knowledge in order to understand what is said. Inferences involve adding information from prior knowledge once what was said is understood. Inferences can follow logically from what was said (logical inferences), or they can be plausible given what was said (pragmatic inferences). While in many cases, presuppositions and inferences serve to connect ideas within a text and thus support the meaning of a text, they can sometimes be wrong and result in misunderstanding.

The processes of integration, presupposition, and inference are heavily dependent upon retrieval processes. Retrieval during comprehension appears to be "promiscuous" and "dumb," in that any information related to the cues in working memory will be retrieved regardless of its relevance to the context.

THOUGHT QUESTIONS

1. What does the process of lexical analysis do and why is this job challenging?
2. What is the difference between modular and interactive theories of lexical analysis.
3. What is the evidence on the role of context in syntactic parsing?
4. What is the "garden path effect," and what does this effect tell us about syntactic parsing?
5. What function do presuppositions play in comprehension, and what is their effect on memory?
6. What are two ways in which retrieval from memory occurs in the course of comprehension.

12

REASONING AND PROBLEM SOLVING

Reasoning and problem solving are fundamentally important areas of research in cognitive psychology because the goal of this research is to describe the process of thinking. Experimental work in this area usually involves presenting someone with a problem, the solution to which does not exist in the person's prior experience. Thus, the person cannot solve the problem by remembering the solution but, rather, must think his or her way through the problem. Thinking is notoriously difficult to define, but, whatever else we may mean, thinking is assumed to be an abstract psychological process that manipulates knowledge.

As described in chapter 9, abstract processes are unconstrained by the particulars of prior experience. Thus, unlike memory, an abstract process of thinking would be unconstrained by particular prior events, although the knowledge or content of thought may itself be a particular prior experience. For example, suppose you took an unusual route home yesterday and, on the way, had an accident. Today, you sit around thinking that you would not have had the accident if you had taken your usual route. This is an example of counter-factual thinking. The object of thought is yesterday's accident, a particular prior event, but the processes of thought that lead to the counter-factual conclusion are unconstrained by the particulars of what happened. In fact, the conclusion of the thought process is something that did not happen. Thus, the thought process is not constrained by the particular prior experience but, rather, is abstract.

The characterization of thinking as abstract is the fundamental basis of the claim for human rationality. In chapter 1, we discussed the difference between rational and empirical bases of knowledge, and we noted that empiricism is knowledge derived from experiences and memory for those experiences, whereas rationalism is knowledge acquired outside of sensory experience. People are rational to the extent that they are capable of going beyond what is given in their direct sensory experience and memory.

As an example, the culmination of cognitive development according to Piaget's influential theory is the ability to think abstractly. Tests of abstract thinking from the Piagetian framework illustrate what we mean by going beyond direct sensory experience—for example, tests of the ability to conserve volume. One test of this ability begins by showing a child a long, slender beaker filled with water. The water is then poured into a short, squat beaker as the child watches, as illustrated in figure 12.1. The child is asked if one beaker contains more water than the other. Very young children will often respond that the long, slender beaker has more water, apparently responding to the higher level of water in the beaker. Older children will say that both have the same amount, demonstrating their ability to "conserve" volume. The important point is that younger children apparently base their judgment on the visual appearance of the water level in the two beakers, whereas the older children are making their judgment outside of the constraints of the appearance of the situation. Their thought processes go beyond what is given in their sensory experience.

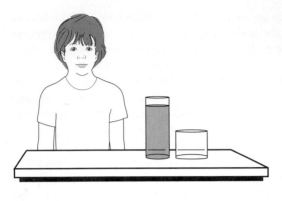

FIGURE 12.1
Piagetian task for volume conservation. Child watches as the contents of the tall, slender beaker are poured into the short, squat beaker. The child judges whether the amount of water in the short beaker is the same as in the tall beaker.

NORMATIVE AND DESCRIPTIVE MODELS OF THOUGHT

An important manifestation of the belief in human rationality is the attempt to discover normative models of thought. A *normative model* is essentially a rule system by which the thinking process might operate. As we mentioned in chapter 9, rules are abstract in that a rule applies regardless of the particular circumstances of its application. Thus, known rule systems are attractive models of thought because both are presumed to be abstract. A variety of different normative models have been suggested, chief among which are formal logic for deductive reasoning and inferential statistics and probability theory for inductive reasoning, which is the basis for most day-to-day decision making.

To ascertain the validity of a normative model, research focuses on the actual performance in reasoning tasks to determine if the normative model predicts decisions and judgments. If performance does not conform to the rules of the normative model, the goal of research becomes the development of a *descriptive model* of performance. Unlike normative models, descriptive models are psychological theories that may include such nonrational concepts as beliefs, attitudes, and memories.

As you will see, an important question is embedded in the contrast between normative and descriptive models: the question of human rationality. To the extent that thought processes do not obey a rule system—particularly if the deviation can be attributed to prior experiences and beliefs—one wonders about the abstract, rational characterization of the thought process. The extreme conclusion, to which no modern psychologist has yet come, would be that there is no such thing as abstract thought.

Nonetheless, you can organize your reading of this chapter around the question, does a particular rule system adequately describe reasoning performance? You will see that the research on reasoning is guided by normative models and that the outcomes of most interest and controversy have been the errors people make relative to a particular normative model. Most of these errors are due to prior experience or belief, a result that is inconsistent with the assumption of rationality.

REASONING

Reasoning research focuses on how a person reaches and evaluates the validity of a conclusion from either explicit or implicit premises. It is very important to understand the difference between the validity of a conclusion and its empirical truth because this distinction has implications for the question of rationality. Validity refers only to whether a conclusion can be logically deduced from the premises. The validity of a conclusion is independent of whether that conclusion is true of the real word. For example, the following deductive argument is valid but not true:

> If the earth is flat, you eventually would sail off the end.
> The earth is flat.
> Therefore, you would sail off the end if you traveled too far.

The conclusion is valid even though neither the premises nor the conclusion is true. Correctly judging the validity of logical arguments requires that the form of the argument be separated from the content. The importance of this separation is that the abstract process of reasoning should be independent of the particular prior experiences that you have had with the content of the problem. That is, if people reason logically, they should have little difficulty separating validity from truth, a prediction that will be tested in the research we describe.

Logic is the most extensively studied normative model of thinking. Logic is a formal system for deriving valid conclusions; that is, logic is the set of rules by which we can reach a valid conclusion about events or things. For instance, if you are informed that "All BMWs are German cars" and that "All German cars are reliable," then it follows that "A BMW is reliable." This same argument can be expressed with abstract terms in the premises and conclusion: All *As* are *Bs;* All *Bs* are *Cs;* Therefore any *A* is a *C*. It follows from formal logic that all *As* are *Cs,* given the first two premises. The empirical truth of Any *A* is a *C* is not an issue for logic but is an issue of fact to be determined by means other than formal logic.

The important point for our purposes is that formal logic specifies a prescription for correct reasoning. In that sense, formal logic is a normative model for thinking. As you will see, the question asked in research is, do people reason in accord with the rules of logic?

Deductive Reasoning

The rule system of formal logic applies to what is known as deductive reasoning. In deductive reasoning, a specific conclusion is drawn from a set of more general premises. The example about the reliability of German cars given above illustrates the point in that the premises are general—All German cars are reliable and All BMWs are German cars—and the conclusion—A BMW will be reliable—is specific. If the rules of logic are followed, then the deduction *must* be valid. Logic thus serves as the normative model of deductive reasoning.

Psychologists have studied several types of deductive reasoning problems, but we shall focus our discussion on two of these, syllogistic reasoning and conditional reasoning. Both types of problems can be argued to exist in day-to-day affairs.

In the case of syllogistic reasoning, consider the following argument to deny welfare assistance to homeless people:

All homeless people are poor.
Some poor people are lazy.
Therefore, some homeless people are lazy

However seductive this argument may be, it is invalid. The conclusion does not logically follow from the premises. The homeless people who are poor may not be the same poor people who are lazy; thus, the argument is not valid.

Conditional reasoning differs from syllogistic reasoning in form. Conditional reasoning takes the form of *if-then* propositions. For example, "If I win the next three cases for my law firm, I will receive a salary raise." In fact, "I win the next three cases for my law firm," then by the rules of logic we can draw the conclusion: "Therefore, I will receive a salary raise." This type of argument is called, from Latin, *modus ponens,* which is a rule of inference that states: if we are given *p* implies *q* and *p,* then we can infer *q.* We are familiar with conditional reasoning because we use it frequently in daily affairs. Here is an example that may be familiar:

Unless the dealer lowers the price of the car by $2,000, I won't be able to buy it.
The dealer will lower the price by only $600.
Therefore, I won't be able to buy the car.

We shall now turn our attention to research on syllogistic and conditional reasoning. As we do so, keep in mind that the goal is to determine to what extent performance conforms to the normative model provided by the rules of logic. In other words, how competent are people at correctly assessing the validity of arguments?

Syllogistic Reasoning   Is the following syllogism valid?

No *A*s are *B*s.
No *B*s are *C*s.
Therefore, No *A*s are *C*s.

If you have trouble deciding, substitute *hamburgers* for *A*s, *cigars* for *B*s, and *food* for *C*s. Everyone can see the invalidity of the argument when the concrete terms are substituted for the abstract symbols, and this simple illustration is an example of the fundamental issue at stake in this research. Namely, if thinking can proceed abstractly according to rules prescribed by logic, why should it matter whether the terms in the problem are concrete objects or abstract symbols?

We have known for a long time that a person's judgment of the validity of a syllogism is influenced by his or her experiences. For example, Morgan and Morton (1944) examined the influence of personal attitudes on syllogistic reasoning by varying the extent to which the conclusions to a syllogism were consistent with a prevailing attitude. The study was conducted during the Second World War, a time when people in this country not only thought of Germans as warlike but also thought of India as a pacifist nation. Consider the following syllogism:

All Germans are warlike.
No citizens of India are Germans.
Citizens of India may not be warlike

The correct response is that the validity is indeterminate from the premises, but many participants in Morton and Morton's study judged the syllogism to be valid. Such a judgment does not reflect rational processes in that the rules of logic do not lead to this conclusion; rather, it appears that the judgment is driven by beliefs about the truth of the conclusion, a distinctly nonrational process.

More recently, the same question has been asked about the effect of belief bias on syllogistic reasoning in the context of syllogisms whose conclusions are valid but unbelievable versus conclusions that are invalid but believable. Again, the point is that if reasoning follows the rules of logic, believability of the conclusions should not affect the judgments of validity. For example, Evans, Barston, and Pollard (1983) used *valid* but *unbelievable* syllogisms such as:

No addictive things are inexpensive.
Some cigarettes are inexpensive.
Therefore, some cigarettes are not addictive.

They also used *invalid* but *believable* syllogisms such as:

No addictive things are inexpensive.
Some cigarettes are inexpensive.
Therefore, some addictive things are not cigarettes.

In addition, both *valid, believable* and *invalid, unbelievable* syllogisms were included, allowing the researchers to analyze the effects of logic versus believability on performance.

The results of the experiment are shown in figure 12.2. Notice two important points about these results. An *invalid* syllogism with a *believable* conclusion is incorrectly accepted over 90 percent of the time, whereas a *valid* syllogism with an *unbelievable* conclusion is correctly accepted about 50 percent of the time. These results suggest that believability of the conclusion has a large effect on judgments,

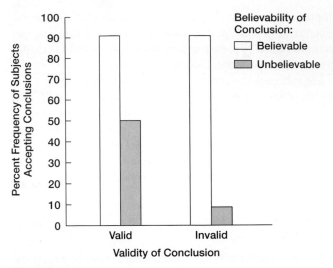

FIGURE 12.2
Acceptance of syllogistic conclusion as a function of the
conclusion's validity and believability. *(Adapted from Evans,
J. S. B. T., Barston, J. L., & Pollard, P. (1983). On the conflict
between logic and belief in syllogistic reasoning.* Memory &
Cognition, 11, *295–306.)*

but the effect is much larger for invalid than for valid syllogisms. That is, logic
does seem to govern about half the judgments for valid arguments, but logic plays
almost no role for invalid arguments.

The conclusions reached from the Evans et al. (1983) study are characteristic
of the literature on syllogistic reasoning. That is, one cannot say that people are
incapable of using logic nor that people never follow the rules of logic. Much
earlier, Mary Henle (Henle & Michael, 1956) defended the rationality of thinking by showing that the results of Morgan and Morton's study on attitudes varied
as a function of the materials. That is, Henle demonstrated that people do not always base their judgments on their attitudes but, in fact, actually perform in accord with the rules of logic on some occasions. On the other hand, the research is
clear on the point that people's attitudes, beliefs, and prior experiences sometimes assume priority over logic. In short, the research on syllogistic reasoning
indicates that people are not always rational and many times will base their judgment of an argument on the empirical truth of the conclusions rather than on the
logic of the argument. Thus, the data raise serious questions about the adequacy
of the rules of logic as a descriptive theory of human reasoning.

Conditional Reasoning   There are four basic types of arguments in conditional reasoning, which are shown in table 12.1. The first two arguments are

TABLE 12.1
ARGUMENTS IN CONDITIONAL REASONING

Example	Name	Validity
1. If John is intelligent, then he is rich. John is intelligent. Therefore, John is rich	Modus ponens	Valid
2. If John is intelligent, then he is rich. John is not rich. Therefore, John is not intelligent.	Modus tollens	Valid
3. If John is intelligent, then he is rich. John is rich. Therefore, John is intelligent	Affirming the consequent	Invalid
4. If John is intelligent, then he is rich. John is not intelligent. Therefore, John is not rich.	Denying the antecedent	Invalid

examples of valid inferences and the second two are examples of invalid inferences. The third argument is a particularly interesting case because it is a common logical fallacy that is made both in everyday reasoning and in scientific affairs (Johnson-Laird & Steedman, 1978).

Consider how the fallacy in the third argument appears in scientific reasoning. Much of scientific reasoning involves deriving predictions from a theory, testing the predictions, and determining if the results support the theory. This sequence of events readily allows for invalid reasoning of the form outlined in the third argument, as illustrated in the following example:

If theory X is true, then behavior Y will occur.
Behavior Y occurs.

Therefore, theory X is true.

The fallacy in this argument is that the occurrence of behavior Y does not prove that theory X is true. The behavior, Y, could have occurred for any number of reasons and does not necessarily mean that theory X is the explanation for that behavior. All that can be said is that the observed behavior is *consistent* with the theory, but does not prove that the theory is correct.

As with syllogistic reasoning, research on conditional reasoning is focused on the relative contributions of logic and prior experience. Consider what has come to be known as the Wason card selection task (Wason & Johnson-Laird, 1972). You see four cards:

You are told that each card has a number on one side and a letter on the other, and you are given the following rule: if a card has a vowel on one side, it has an even number on the other side. Your task is to select the minimum number of cards you need to turn over in order to determine if the rule is true. The correct responses are A and 9. You select A because, in accord with modus ponens, a vowel on one side must have an even number on the other. You select 9 because, in accord with modus tollens, an odd number on one side cannot have a vowel on the other. When asked to perform this task, however, many people select 2 as one of the cards, committing the error of affirming the consequent as listed in table 12.1.

Why do people make this logical error with such frequency? One idea is that attention is drawn to the even number by the statement of the rule (Evans, 1982). That is, they expect the information stated in the rule to be relevant to the problem. One test of this idea is to change the rule to read: if there is a vowel on one side, there will not be an even number on the other side. In this form, the correct selections would be A and 2. Evans (1982) has shown that people now select, correctly, A and 2 on this form of the task, suggesting that people match the hypothesis (rule) with the data (cards).

The card selection task, like the syllogistic reasoning problems, is heavily influenced by the contents of the problem. For example, Griggs and Cox (1982) gave college students the following rule: if a person is drinking beer, then the person must be over 21 years of age. Four cards were provided, with the instructions that each card had a beverage on one side and an age on the other. The cards facing the subject were:

If the rule is being followed, the cards reading Beer and 16 years old should be selected. Performance on this concrete version of the task was much better than on the abstract version with letters and numbers. The correct selection was made by 73 percent of the people on the drinking age problem, whereas none of the people in the Griggs and Cox experiment made the correct selection on the abstract version of letters and numbers. Several other experiments have been reported that also demonstrate the influence of prior experience on conditional reasoning (Wason & Johnson-Laird, 1972; Evans, 1982).

The implication of this research is that the psychological processes underlying conditional reasoning are not always rational. The particulars of prior experience influence judgment and affect our decision. Thus, as was the case with syllogisms, the research suggests that the rules of logic as an abstract normative model are not sufficient descriptions of thought.

A Descriptive Model of Deductive Reasoning: Mental Models Philip Johnson-Laird (1988) has offered a descriptive model of deductive reasoning that is called the mental model theory. Mental model theory assumes that reasoning begins with comprehension of the premises in syllogistic and conditional problems. This comprehension results in a representation of the problem, which is the mental model. The form of the representation could range from an image to a proposition, but, whatever the quality of the representation, its function is to mentally create and analyze the premises. An example of a problem and associated models is presented in box 12.1.

The notation used in box 12.1 is that of Johnson-Laird, and here is what it means. The idea is that given the premise, "No cats are dogs," a representation is established such that the set of cats contains no dogs. The horizontal line between cats and dogs symbolizes this disjoint representation of the two sets. The premise that "All dogs are friendly" is captured by dogs = friendly. Comprehension of the second premise also may include that there are friendly things that are not dogs, designated in the mental model by (friendly). Thus, comprehension as depicted in Mental Model 1 in box 12.1 essentially is that none of the cats are dogs, all of the dogs are friendly, and some things other than dogs are friendly. If this mental model is fully processed, it is apparent that cats may be among the friendly things. However, research suggests that the majority of people given a problem of this form endorse the conclusion "No cats are friendly" as valid. Since

---

BOX 12.1.

THREE MENTAL MODELS FOR FRIENDLY DOG SYLLOGISM

The syllogism	**Mental model 2**
Given the premises:	cat
No cats are dogs	cat = friendly
All dogs are friendly	dog = friendly
	dog = friendly
What conclusions are valid?	(friendly)

Mental model 1	**Mental model 3**
cat	cat = friendly
cat	cat = friendly
dog = friendly	dog = friendly
dog = friendly	dog = friendly
(friendly)	(friendly)

Adapted from Mayer (1992)

this conclusion is not valid, the descriptive approach of mental models suggests that people are incompletely processing Model 1. Presumably, the disjoint representation of cats and dogs discourages the thought that cats may be among the friendly things.

An alternative model is Model 2 in box 12.1. Model 2 differs from Model 1 in that the comprehension of the first premise includes "Some cats may be friendly." This slight difference is important, however, in that it allows you to avoid the error from Model 1. One might conclude from this model that "Some cats are not friendly," but again, such a conclusion does not necessarily follow. Finally, consider Model 3 in which comprehension of the first premise includes "All cats are friendly." If you combine Model 3 and Model 1, you have all of the cats as friendly and all of the dogs as friendly but none of the cats are dogs. From this combination, one might conclude that there is no conclusion from this syllogism. Wrong again.

One conclusion does logically follow from the premises and is consistent with all three models: "Some friendly things are not cats." Thus, on the approach advocated by Johnson-Laird, different mental models can result from comprehension of the premises and, in the case of our example, a correct conclusion may require comparison among alternative representations. The successful reasoner will establish several models of a situation and process each of those in comparison to others.

We can see that the mental model approach characterizes reasoning as something other than a purely rational process. For example, the comprehension of the premises results in part from the individual's prior experience and attitudes. If your experience with cats is such that you never think of cats as friendly, Models 2 and 3 will not be established. In this sense, reasoning from mental models is limited by one's experiences and attitudes.

Criticism of the mental model approach has been forthcoming from the rationalist corner. For example, Lance Rips (1994) has suggested that mental models actually presuppose the logical rules of reasoning. In order to set up the mental model described above, one must interpret the premises and draw conclusions in accord with rules of reasoning. According to this argument, mental models are less an alternative to the rational, abstract approach than an instance of such an approach.

Inductive Reasoning

The decisions that we make in day-to-day life are rarely based on deductive reasoning because the events about which these decisions are made rarely are presented in the form of a syllogism. The syllogism begins with general premises, but our day-to-day decisions often are based on particular premises. From that particular thing we reach a conclusion, which is a decision about how to respond. For example, I may notice that it is cloudy today and try to decide whether to take an umbrella when I leave. The particular premise is "It is cloudy today" from which

I move to the secondary premise "Some cloudy days in the past it has rained." Based on these premises, I conclude that "It may rain today" and decide to take my umbrella. This form of reasoning is known as inductive reasoning.

Unlike deductive reasoning, the rules of logic do not apply to inductive reasoning. No formal logical rules allow you to move from the premise of "It is cloudy today" to necessarily conclude that "It will rain today." On any given cloudy day, there is some probability that it will rain, but on many cloudy days, no rain occurs. The conclusion to an inductive argument does not have the certainty or necessity of the deductive argument; consequently, inductive reasoning cannot be evaluated in terms of the logical validity of the conclusion. An induction is something that is likely to be true on the basis of past experience, but there is no guarantee that it will be absolutely true (Pellegrino, 1985).

At best, we can apply some probability to the correctness of the induced conclusion. Most everyday problems are of this type. One essentially makes a judgment under conditions of uncertainty. Given the probabilistic character of the conclusion, it is understandable that the most widely studied normative model of inductive reasoning is probability theory.

Probability Theory as a Normative Model of Induction   Suppose you met someone named Tom W. and learned the following things about him:

> Tom W. is of high intelligence although lacking in true creativity. He has a need for order and clarity, and for neat and tidy systems in which every detail finds its appropriate place. His writing is rather dull and mechanical, occasionally enlivened by somewhat corny puns and by flashes of imagination of the sci-fi type. He has a strong drive for competence. He seems to have little feel and sympathy for other people and does not enjoy interacting with others. Self-centered, he nonetheless has a deep moral sense (Kahneman & Tversky, 1973, p. 238).

Now suppose that you were asked to judge whether Tom is majoring in computer science or humanities. Most people will say computer science. But think about the number of people majoring in computer science versus the number majoring in humanities—for example, history and English. Far more people major in humanities than computer science. The odds are heavily in favor of Tom being a humanities major and that is where you should place your bet. Why don't people do this? The example is taken from the research of Kahneman and Tversky (1973) who pioneered research on decision making from inductive reasoning. As Kahneman and Tversky point out, a normative theory of induction based on probability theory predicts that people will consider base-rates of occurrence in making their decisions, but that is not always the case, as illustrated by the example.

Consideration of base-rates can be crucial for extremely important decisions such as how to act on medical diagnosis. Eddy (1982) provides the example of a young woman who is concerned about breast cancer. She has a mammogram that returns a positive result. Eddy points out that mammogram tests correctly identify 85 percent of the cases in which cancer is present, but also incorrectly diagnose cancer in 10 percent of the cases when it is not present. Thus, given a positive mammogram, the probability of cancer is 85 percent if, in fact, cancer is present. But we must also take base-rates of the incidence of breast cancer into account because these are the numbers that provide the best estimate of the possibility that cancer is present. Suppose we know that for a woman of our patient's age, family history, and so forth, the base-rate is 1 percent. What this means is that for every 100,000 women in this group, 1000 will develop breast cancer and 99,000 will not. If we use these base-rates in conjunction with the diagnostic reliability of the mammogram, we see that out of 100,000 women with this patient's profile, the positive mammogram will correctly identify 850 cases among the 1000 women who actually have the disease. Out of these same 100,000 women, 99,000 will not develop breast cancer, but the 10 percent false-positive rate for the mammogram will lead to an incorrect cancer diagnosis in 9900 cases. By considering base-rates, a physician knows that the number of women with this profile who receive a false-positive mammogram far exceeds the number for whom cancer is present. Consequently, taking base-rates into account in this situation is critically important in deciding whether to do immediate surgery or conduct further diagnostic tests.

Perhaps not too surprisingly, research has shown that people, including experts such as physicians, frequently ignore base-rates in their decision making. This is just one of several instances in which the way people reason violates probability theory. As a result of this research, Kahneman and Tversky have suggested a descriptive model of inductive judgment in which people use heuristic devices rather than the rules of probability to make inductive judgments. Two of the important judgment heuristics are *representativeness* and *availability.*

Representativeness The representativeness heuristic is a hypothetical process of making decisions based on the similarity of a current situation to past situations. That is, the description of Tom W. in the previous example is similar to a computer scientist, and this similarity serves as the basis of judgment in lieu of consideration of such things as base-rates. The interesting aspect of this performance is that with no more information than was provided, the more reasonable solution to the problem comes from the rules of probability theory; yet, those rules are essentially ignored.

Another such example from Tversky and Kahneman's (1983, p. 299) research is the following problem:

Linda is 31 years old, single, outspoken, and very bright. She majored in philosophy. As a student, she was deeply concerned with the issues of discrimination and social justice and also participated in anti-nuclear demonstrations.

Based on this information, which of the following two alternatives is more probable?

(a) Linda is a bank teller.
(b) Linda is a bank teller and is active in the feminist movement.

Tversky and Kahneman (1983) found that people chose (b) more often than (a). From the normative model of probability theory, this is not a reasonable decision. The probability of a single event, Linda is a bank teller, would at worst be equal to the probability of the joint event of bank teller and feminist, and this would only happen if all bank tellers were feminists. Thus, it is quite likely that the probability of (a) will vastly exceed the probability of (b). The belief that the probability of two concurrent events exceeds the probability of one of the events alone is known as the *conjunction fallacy.*

Here, we have another example of the use of the representativeness heuristic rather than probability theory to reach a decision. The description of Linda is representative of someone who would be active in the feminist movement, and the rational rules of probability are overridden by this heuristic.

Availability   A slightly different heuristic strategy used in decision making is known as the availability heuristic. Whereas representativeness is based on the similarity between events, a judgment based on availability is influenced by the ease with which something is brought to mind.

Suppose we do the following experiment. One group of participants is asked to judge how many English words end in the pattern _n_. A second group is asked to judge how many words end with the pattern *ing*. People judge the *ing* pattern to be more frequent, but if you notice carefully, you will see that we have here another case of the conjunction fallacy. The _n_ pattern includes *ing* but also includes other words that have the _n_ ending. In this example, it is easier for people to think of more words with the *ing* ending than with the _n_ ending. One is more available than the other and, hence, receives a higher frequency estimate. This example shows you what is meant by basing a judgment on the availability heuristic.

Our thinking is frequently influenced by availabilty rather than the more rational facts of probability. For many people, flying is very anxiety provoking, perhaps because stepping on an airplane brings to mind crashes. This is even more likely to happen following a major accident. Statistically, however, the safest time to fly is in the wake of a major crash. Furthermore, your chances of meeting mishap in an automobile far exceed those of flying. Yet most of us do not experience anxiety in a car, unless, of course, we have just come on a bad accident.

You can see that availability is a powerful influence on our thinking, and you can imagine that it could enter into crucial decision processes in a negative way. Suppose a bad stomach virus is going around and you acquire what appear to be the appropriate symptoms. Nonetheless, you visit a physician. She has seen hundreds of cases of stomach virus in the last week and decides that is your problem without further examination. Unfortunately, pneumonia sometimes produces similar symptoms—fever, aches, nausea. The diagnosis of stomach virus based on availability could have disastrous consequences if the pneumonia is left untreated. This final example illustrates the potential importance of using a rule-based process in our thinking, but the psychology of reasoning once again demonstrates that such is not always the case.

Summary of Reasoning Research

We have discussed only a small sample of the research on reasoning, but the work described was chosen for its relevance to the central question: are people rational? To be rational is to be able to think outside the constraints of our own experiences and beliefs and to reach conclusions on the basis of abstract rules rather than particular prior experiences. Whereas the research on both deductive and inductive reasoning suggests that people sometimes behave in such a rational fashion, the research is striking in its demonstration of the powerful effects of nonrational, experiential factors on human judgment.

Performance on deductive reasoning problems is heavily determined by the content of the problem. If the content leads to a conclusion consistent with prior experiences, people endorse that conclusion; if the content leads to a logically valid conclusion that is empirically untrue in prior experience, the conclusion is not endorsed. Inductive reasoning performance can be similarly characterized. When faced with a judgment about an uncertain outcome, people tend to base their decisions on past experience, as exemplified by representativeness and availability heuristics, rather than on rules specified by probability theory. Thus, the search for normative theories of reasoning has yet to meet with unqualified success.

Much of human reasoning can be characterized by the use of heuristics, which are strategies that are efficient but do allow for error to occur. More rational, rule-based systems would eliminate the errors but would come at a great cost in efficiency. Imagine attempting to cast all of your decisions in the form of a syllogism or computing base-rates before you make any decision. Thus, while the rational mode of thought may be optimal, Simon (1957) has made the now classic argument that not every decision needs to be optimal. In many instances, perfectly satisfactory decisions can be reached through heuristic strategies.

The tentative conclusion about reasoning has enormous practical implications, particularly for education in any domain. One assumption of formal education is that the student acquires knowledge that will be used in the future to solve problems. Knowledge is presumed to be abstract and general, and the application of the knowledge to problems is presumed to occur through the abstract process of thinking. The question is, are these assumptions warranted? Research on problem solving offers some suggestions.

PROBLEM SOLVING

Research on problem solving has a rich history, but until recently, this work has remained on the periphery of mainstream psychology, a rather peculiar status given the obvious importance of problem solving activities to both theoretical questions of mental processes and to applied questions. Some explanation for this relative isolation goes back to the very definition of a problem. Generally, we might say that a person has a problem when he or she wants something he or she does not have. But this general description covers a lot of ground. Would we consider your ability to tie your shoe an instance of problem solving? Probably not. On the other hand, suppose you wanted to go to the islands over spring break, but you have no money. How can you get to the islands? Most of us would consider this a serious problem.

The crucial difference between these two examples is the role of prior experience. Tying your shoe is not a problem because you have performed that activity numerous times. Getting to the islands under the described conditions is not something you have done before. The distinction between situations for which you have prior experience and those for which you do not looms large because the former can be classified as problems of learning and memory. If, however, the goal you wish to attain and the means to attain it are not represented in your prior experience, performance on these problems could be ascribed to thought processes beyond learning and memory. Thus, defining a problem as reaching some desired goal without the benefit of specific prior experience distinguishes problem solving from learning and memory and identifies problem-solving research with the study of abstract thought. The emphasis on abstract thought ties research on problem solving to research on reasoning.

At the same time, the definition of problem solving isolated the research from the concepts of learning and memory. Consequently, many psychologists did not know what to do with research from problem solving. A concrete example of this historical circumstance is provided by the early work in Gestalt psychology.

Gestalt Approach to Problem Solving

Gestalt psychology is a school of thought that originated in Germany and subsequently immigrated to the United States. The Gestalt perspective on all psychological processes was one that emphasized organizational factors. In the case of problem solving, this approach focused on how problems were viewed and attributed successful problem solving to a reorganization of the elements of the problem. Essentially, successful problem solving resulted from a new perception of the relations among the elements of a problem, and this new perception was described as *insight,* a topic to which we shall return.

A fundamental aspect of the Gestalt approach was a distinction between *productive* and *reproductive* thinking. *Reproductive thinking* refers to situations in which old behaviors or habits are used to solve problems. This type of "rote memory" was not relevant to the Gestalt theorists' analysis of problem solving because, as previously mentioned, problem solving was to be distinguished from learning. *Productive thinking,* on the other hand, produced "structural under-standing" of the relations between components of the problem and led to insight into the problem solution. Productive thinking, then, represented problem solution resulting from abstract thought processes and was believed to yield general principles that would then transfer to future problems.

The contrast between productive and reproductive approaches to problem solv-ing can be seen in a study of solving geometry problems (Wertheimer, 1959). Stu-dents were taught how to find the area of a parallelogram by being encouraged to use either productive or reproductive thinking. In the case of productive thinking, the method emphasized the structural relations within the parallelogram—the triangle on one end of the parallelogram could be placed on the other end to form a rectangle. The reproductive means of instruction focused on the steps needed to calculate the area by dropping the perpendicular and multiplying its height times the length of the base. The two approaches are illustrated in figure 12.3.

Both methods were effective for the parallelograms that were used in the ini-tial instruction phase, but when new problems involving unusual figures were given, the students given productive instruction performed much better. They were able to transfer what they had learned to new situations more effectively than students trained with the reproductive method. The important point to notice in this discussion is the contrast between methods that produce abstract princi-ples and methods producing a set of particular steps to be followed. The distinc-tion between the two types of thinking captures the presumed difference between learning/memory and abstract thought.

Insight   The key step in thinking that produces solutions to problems was referred to as "illumination." The solution appears as a flash of insight, the "aha" experience you may have had in your problem-solving activities. Insight is the result of productive thinking that has successfully arranged the parts of the problem in a new way, representing the solution to the problem, and was studied by provid-ing subjects with novel problems or puzzles.

An example of an insight problem is the candle problem used by Duncker (1945). A participant is presented a box of tacks, some matches, and a candle, all placed on a table. The task is to mount the candle on a wall in such a way that it will burn without dripping wax on the table. The solution requires that the participant empty the box of tacks, tack the empty box to the wall, and place the candle on the box. The problem requires that the person see new structural relations among the components of the problem task. This is essentially what is meant by insight.

Notice that prior experience is not interesting to this analysis; a participant who had just been told the solution to the problem and then given the problem to solve would tell us nothing about insight. Ironically, however, the most informative re-sults of Gestalt work on problem solving centered on the effects of prior experience and insight problems. The effects on productive thought were all seen as negative.

Understanding Method (Productive Thinking)

The understanding method encouraged students to see the structural relations in the parallelogram—for example, that the parallelogram could be rearranged into a rectangle by moving a triangle from one side to the other. Since the students knew how to find the area of a rectangle, finding the area of a parallelogram was easy once they discovered the appropriate structural relations.

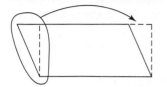

Rote Method (Reproductive Thinking)

In the rote method, students were taught to drop a perpendicular and then apply the memorized solution formula.

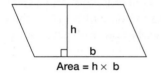

Area = h × b

Transfer

Both groups performed well on typical problems asking for the area of parallelograms; however, only the understanding group could transfer to novel problems such as finding the area of the figure below

or distinguishing between solvable and unsolvable problems such as

The response of the "rote" group to novel problems was "We haven't had that yet."

FIGURE 12.3
Wertheimer's two methods for finding area of parallelogram. *(From Mayer, R. E. (1992) Thinking, Problem-Solving, and Cognition, 2d ed. New York: W. H. Freeman and Company. Copyright 1992 by W. H. Freeman and Company).*

Functional Fixedness Duncker found that many participants could not solve the candle problem. A large part of the difficulty is that the box is seen as a container for tacks, not as a support for the candle. For example, the probability that the participant would solve the problem increased if the tacks were not in the box when the problem was introduced. *Functional fixedness* is the label used to describe this type of interference in problem solving; functional fixedness refers to the tendency to think of objects as functioning in one certain way and to ignore other ways in which they might be used.

Functional fixedness is one example from Gestalt research of how prior experience, the habitual way of doing things, actually impedes productive thinking. Thus, prior experience appears to impair our ability to solve novel problems. Another example is provided by the phenomenon known as set effects.

Set Effects   When a person repeats a mental activity, there is some tendency for it to persist in a new situation. But the persistence of an old strategy, or mode of attack, in a new situation may be inappropriate. This type of process was extensively studied by Luchins (1942) in what is called "the water-jar problem" and it provides a clear demonstration of the *set effects* in problem solving. The task requires a person to determine how to fill a jar of water in order to obtain a specified amount. All problems follow this general form: "You will be given three empty containers, A, B, and C, and your task is to describe how to obtain a specific quantity of water, Y."

Table 12.2 illustrates a typical problem sequence. Problem 1 is an illustrative problem. Here the solution is to fill jar A, then remove 9 quarts from it by filling jar B three times. Problems 2 through 6 are training problems, in which the solution is always to fill jar B first, then from that jar fill jar A once and jar C twice, which leaves the exact quantity specified. All problems, therefore, have the general solution of the form Y (the quantity specified) $= B - A - 2C$. Problems 7 and 8 can also be solved this way. However, for problem 7, there is a much simpler and direct solution in which jar A is filled first, then poured into jar C once, leaving the exact amount required for problem 7. For problem 8, the amounts in A and C are added. Problem 9 requires a simple solution. Go through the sequence of problems in table 12.2 and actually solve the problems so that you experience the task.

If people receive no instructions about the change in problems 7 and 8, they tend to persist in solving these problems like problem sequences 2 through 6. It is as if the repeated use of one successful strategy makes it difficult to discover alternative approaches. This simply illustrates the more general principle—namely, that most human beings have a strong tendency toward persistence of set. Once you have learned a rule that works, you may tend to continue applying that rule even when a simpler solution is possible. Old strategies continue to be used, even when they are less efficient, if we fail to perceive that the situation has changed.

Functional fixedness and set effects are important examples of how prior experiences can impair our ability to solve a new problem, but certainly prior experience can be beneficial for some types of problem solving. Yet, the definition of problem solving as productive thinking basically discourages investigation of the beneficial effects of prior experience on problem solving. Furthermore, the basic

TABLE 12.2
AN EXAMPLE OF THE WATER JAR PROBLEM

Problem		Size of jars (in quarts)			Quarts of water desired
		A	B	C	Y
[Example	1	29	3	—	20
	2	21	127	3	100
	3	14	163	25	99
Training problems	4	18	43	10	5
	5	9	42	6	21
	6	20	59	4	31
	7	23	49	3	20
Test problems	8	15	39	3	18
	9	28	76	3	25

From *Fundamentals of Human Learning, Memory, and Cognition,* 2nd ed., by Henry C. Ellis. Dubuque, Iowa: Wm. C. Brown Company Publishers, 1978.

product of productive thought, insight, is a concept that defies analysis; it either happens or it doesn't. Consequently, the direction for research is not exactly clear.

Information-Processing Approach

The birth of the information processing approach signaled a marked change in the study of problem solving. Whereas the Gestalt view insisted upon a distinction between learning and problem solving, between productive and reproductive thinking, the information-processing approach eventually focused on what amounts to reproductive thinking. One important consequence is a renewed interest in the effects of prior experience on problem-solving behavior, and that renewed interest has brought problem-solving research into the mainstream of theoretical psychology.

The Thinking Computer   Pioneering work on problem solving from the information processing approach employed the tool of computer simulation. The goal was to write programs that allowed the computer to solve a specified problem. The discipline of Artificial Intelligence is interested in this activity for an applied reason—namely, to allow tasks to be automated. For psychologists, the program represents a potential theory of problem solving. Thus, by examining successful problem solving programs, we may be able to uncover necessary psychological processes for problem solving.

Allan Newell and Herbert Simon (1972), two of the more influential scientists in the field, described three general characteristics of problem solving from the information-processing perspective: aspects of the task environment, mental representation of the problem as a problem space, and selection of an appropriate operator.

Task environment refers to the description of the problem as presented to the subject and includes the information, assumptions, and constraints given, as well as the context in which the problem is set. We saw earlier, for example, that whether the tacks are in the box or not can influence the person's ease of solving the candle problem. *Problem space* refers to a subject's mental representation of the problem, as well as the various solutions that may be attempted. Problem spaces are the various ideas, or hypotheses, that a person might develop about a problem. The mental representation of the problem is a central feature of effective problem solving, and this mental representation is assumed to change with progress toward solution. Finally, to get from one problem state to another an *operator* must be selected and applied to the problem. An *operator* refers to a sequence of operations that takes the problem solver from the initial state to the goal state.

Production Systems   When one talks of computer models of problem solving, the model actually lies in the program that carries out operations. Numerous programs have been put forward as theories of problem solving, but one of the commonly agreed upon concepts across these theories is the idea of production system. A production is essentially a condition-action pair in the form of an IF __ THEN __ statement. The conditions following IF specify some situation, and the action following THEN describes something to do. For example, IF THE CAR WON'T START AND THE RADIO DOESN'T WORK, THEN CHECK THE BATTERY. The production is the basic building block of goal-directed thinking in the computer program. The idea is that if the conditions represented in the problem space match the IF __ conditions, the action specified by the THEN __ will fire.

A production system is a collection of productions, all related to a class of problems. Thus, each production essentially is an operator, and as one moves toward the goal of a particular problem, the conditions change and bring different productions into play. For example, if the goal is to start the car and the previous production has run off, another production may be activated: IF THE CAR WON'T START AND THE BATTERY IS FINE, THEN CHECK THE GAS. The productions continue until the problem is solved: THEN CALL THE TOW TRUCK.

One of the most detailed theories employing production systems is ACT (Adaptive Control of Thought) by John Anderson (1990). According to Anderson, efficient problem solving results from learning a cognitive skill. Within his theory, learning a cognitive skill is a matter of converting declarative knowledge into procedural knowledge. Declarative knowledge is knowledge of facts, whereas procedural knowledge is knowledge of how to do things. For example, one may have declarative knowledge that a car that won't start and whose radio doesn't work probably has a dead battery. To solve the problem, however, requires that one know how to do something about the battery, and this is procedural knowledge represented by a production system.

A simple example is solving the following problem: $5 + 7 = 4X$. Initially, one might have declarative knowledge that 5, 7, and 4 are numbers and that X is a variable. One might also have declarative knowledge that you can always divide both sides of an equation by the same number. Using this declarative knowledge to guide problem solving, one can think about the facts and decide to divide both sides of the equation by 4. However, this thinking requires a great deal of conscious capacity. More advanced learning proceduralizes the declarative knowledge in the form of productions. In this simple example, a production may be represented: IF THE VARIABLE IS MULTIPLED BY SOME NUMBER, THEN DIVIDE BOTH SIDES OF THE EQUATION BY THAT NUMBER. Thus, when the IF conditions are met by the problem representation, the action specified by the THEN will fire. Proceduralization of knowledge makes problem solving more efficient by reducing the conscious capacity demands.

To return to the general theme of this section, you can see that the move from the Gestalt emphasis on productive thinking to the information processing view has shifted the focus. From the information processing view, efficient problem solving is very much a product of prior experience. Production systems are assumed to be learned. The emphasis on prior experience also is evident in the close attention now paid to expert performance.

Expert Problem Solving

Would you prefer to have your heart surgery performed by a new surgical resident or by a cardiologist with 20 years' experience? The question makes clear the important relation between experience and problem-solving ability. An important point to keep in mind is that experts do not excel because of superior native intelligence; the difference between the two physicians is not one of general cognitive capability. Rather, as Glaser and Chi (1988, p. xvii) put it, "the experts excel mainly in their own domain," and research shows that expert performance is directly tied to experience in the domain of problems.

Mayer (1992), in his excellent discussion of reasoning and problem solving, identifies four major aspects of problem solving that separate the expert from the novice. First, the expert seems to store factual knowledge relevant to the problem in larger units and can access those units more quickly. For example, Chase and Simon (1973) showed a chessboard with a game in progress to chess masters and to novices. They were allowed to look at the board for 5 seconds. The performance of interest was the memory for board positions, which is depicted in figure 12.4, as a function of expertise. The masters remembered the positions much better than the novices, but only if the original positions were from a real game rather than just random positions. The latter result indicates that the memory difference is specific to chess and is due to the ability of the master to see the pattern of many pieces as one meaningful unit.

Experts also show a difference on what Mayer calls semantic knowledge. By this, he means the expert is more capable of relating a particular problem to general underlying concepts. For example, if your mechanic is an expert and your

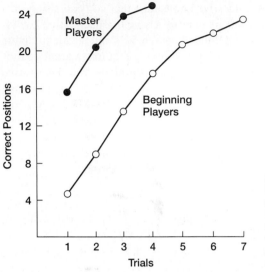

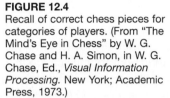

FIGURE 12.4
Recall of correct chess pieces for categories of players. (From "The Mind's Eye in Chess" by W. G. Chase and H. A. Simon, in W. G. Chase, Ed., *Visual Information Processing.* New York; Academic Press, 1973.)

car is making a funny noise, the mechanic is likely to consider the general concepts of automotive functioning in diagnosing the problem.

Expert performance is guided by superior schematic knowledge, which Mayer defines by as an ability to discriminate between types of problems. That is, when confronted by a problem the expert is capable of categorizing problems on the basis of solution strategy. Finally, the expert differs from the nonexpert with respect to strategic knowledge. The expert develops a global strategy for solving the problem but works forward by considering alternatives to the global strategy as progress is made toward the solution.

Once again, the important point in this discussion is the emphasis on prior experience in problem solving. Experienced researchers in problem solving have even proposed the 10-year rule: expertise in any domain requires at least 10 years of experience (Chase & Simon, 1973; Hayes, 1981). Combined with the information-processing emphasis on automatization of problem solving in the form of production systems, we have a very different view of thinking from the Gestalt version of productive thought. In essence, the knowledge gained through experience is a form of memory; thus, the current view of expertise is much more like Gestalt reproductive thought.

This turn of events has encouraged research into situations in which an individual has experienced the actual solution to a problem, a rather dramatic change from earlier definitions of problem solving as situations for which one has no prior experience. The question asked by current research is, how spontaneous is transfer of the prior experience to a new situation? If thinking is as mechanical as portrayed by a production system, one might expect automatic transfer to be routine in problem situations. Recent research has discovered startling exceptions to this expectation.

Analogical Reasoning in Problem Solving

Much of our thinking is analogical. When explaining something to someone, when trying to understand something ourselves, and when attempting to solve a problem, we search for similarity between the current circumstance and a previous experience. In the case of problem solving, analogical reasoning involves applying a solution strategy abstracted from a previous problem to a new problem. What could be more important about our prior experience than applying successful previous solutions to new but similar problems? The astonishing result, however, from research on analogical problem solving is how infrequently people spontaneously use analogous prior experience.

This surprising fact is illustrated by research from the laboratory of Keith Holyoak. The target task is solving the "tumor problem" posed by Duncker (1945):

> A person has an inoperable stomach tumor, but there are rays that can destroy the tumor. However, if the rays are of sufficient intensity to destroy the tumor, they will also destroy the healthy tissue they pass through. At lower levels of intensity, the rays will not harm healthy tissue but also will not destroy the tumor. How can one destroy the tumor with these rays and at the same time avoid harming the healthy tissue that surrounds the tumor?

The preferred solution to this problem is to disperse the rays such that low-level rays are applied from several different directions so that they simultaneously converge on the tumor. Gick and Holyoak (1980) report that none of the people who were asked to solve the problem were able to do so.

What would happen if you had recently experienced a problem with a solution analogous to the dispersion of the rays? Gick and Holyoak investigated this question by providing participants with the fortress problem and its solution, as depicted in box 12.2. Notice that the solution the general uses is to disperse the troops so that they simultaneously converge on the fortress, a solution analogous to the dispersion of the rays to solve the tumor problem. After receiving the fortress problem and its solution, all of the subjects successfully solved the tumor problem, a clear demonstration of the value of analogical reasoning in problem solving.

However, the participants in the Gick and Holyoak (1980) experiment were told explicitly to use the prior problem to aid their solution of the tumor problem. Usually we do not have the advantage of a reminder when we are confronted with a problem; for example, when a civil engineer is trying to solve a problem

---

BOX 12.2

THE FORTRESS PROBLEM: AN ANALOGY TO THE TUMOR PROBLEM

A general wished to capture a strong fortress occupied by a cruel dictator of a small country. Many roads led into the fortress, but the general knew that he needed his entire army for the attack to succeed. He gathered the army at the head of one of the roads but, before the attack was launched, the general learned that the roads were mined. The mines were set so that small bodies of men could safely pass over them, which allowed workers to enter and leave the fortress. However, a body as large as his army would certainly detonate the mines, destroying the army as well as the neighboring village. The attack appeared to be doomed.

The general, however, devised a simple plan. He divided his army into small groups and dispatched each group to the head of a different road. Then he gave a signal and each group marched down its road to the fortress so that the entire army arrived at the fortress at the same time. In this way, the general was able to capture the fortress.

---

in designing a highway bridge, no one reminds the engineer to think about the calculus problems he or she has previously solved, just as no one reminds you about analogous problems when you are taking an examination. What happens to analogical transfer when no reminder is given?

Gick and Holyoak (1983) addressed this question by asking participants first to memorize the fortress problem and its solution and then to solve the tumor problem. Before receiving the tumor problem, half of the participants were told to use the fortress problem to help in their solution and the other half were given no reminder. Of the people reminded about the fortress problem, 92 percent solved the tumor problem, but only 20 percent of the people who were not reminded were able to solve the problem. Almost all of the people not given a reminder reported that they had not even considered using the fortress problem as an analogous solution.

You can see what we mean by the surprising lack of spontaneous transfer. This discovery is important for both theoretical and applied reasons. The mechanistic view of thinking offered by the information-processing approach, such as the production systems theory, does not emphasize the need for conscious memory, nor do we build this assumption into most of our instructional settings. Thus, the search for conditions that favor spontaneous transfer takes on real significance. In the domain of analogical problem solving, the critical factor seems to be the similarity between the analogy and the test problem. Holyoak and Koh (1987) demonstrated that the amount of spontaneous transfer from an analogy to a test problem is directly related to the similarity of the two. Spontaneous transfer can be obtained, but the two problems must be very similar. Just *how* similar can be seen in some almost unbelievable work with insight problems.

Proceduralism in Problem Solving

Suppose that you not only have experienced an analogous problem but also have memorized the actual solution to a new problem. Now will spontaneous transfer occur? In a series of two papers from the laboratory of John Bransford and Jeffrey Franks, experiments using insight problems provided the surprising answer to this question (Adams, Kasserman, Yearwood, Perfetto, Bransford, & Franks, 1988; Perfetto, Bransford, & Franks, 1983).

The criterion task was to solve a series of insight problems such as the following:

> The Reverend Sol Loony announced that, on a certain day, at a certain time, he would perform a great miracle. He would walk for 20 minutes on the surface of the Hudson River without sinking into the water. A big crowd gathered to witness the event. The Reverend Loony did exactly what he said he would do. How did he manage to walk on the surface of the river without sinking?

In the experiments reported in 1983, participants were assigned to one of three conditions. The baseline group simply tried to solve the problems. In the other two groups, participants were asked to rate the truthfulness of the 12 sentences prior to attempting to solve the problems. Unbeknownst to the participants, these sentences were the solutions to the problems they would see—for example, "A person can walk on frozen water." One of these groups was informed of the relationship between the sentences and problems prior to problem solving and the other was uninformed of that relationship. The critical index of spontaneous transfer lies in the comparison between the uninformed group and the baseline group.

The informed group solved many more of the problems than the other two groups, demonstrating that the subjects could remember the sentences. On the other hand, the uninformed group solved no more of the problems than the baseline group, indicating a complete lack of spontaneous transfer. People who had not seen the solutions were just as proficient at solving as were people who had just read the solutions, unless they were told to use the sentences as solutions. These results are similar to the outcome of research on analogical problem solving.

The experiments reported in 1988 (Adams, et al.) used the same procedure but added a critical condition. In the new condition, the sentences were phrased in a problem-orientation form. For example, a problem orientation sentence would be phrased, "A person can walk on water if it is frozen," in contrast to the fact-orientation form, "A person can walk on frozen water." The reasoning is that comprehension of the problem-oriented sentence requires processes similar to the subsequent problem. Thus, a sentence beginning "A person can walk on water" poses a problem that is resolved with the words "if it is frozen." In this sense, comprehension of the sentence engages the same mental processes that are engaged by the problem, how can someone walk on water?

The important result was that problem-oriented sentences led to substantially greater spontaneous transfer than did fact-oriented sentences. The subtle difference in fact-oriented and problem-oriented sentences yields a marked difference in the use of the prior experience in solving the problem. These data can be interpreted in the context of a production system by assuming that the problem-oriented sentence sets up a condition-action sequence in a way that the fact-oriented sentence does not. More generally, these findings emphasize the importance of transfer-appropriate processing and the conceptualization of the effects of prior experience on mental processes as discussed in chapter 6.

This later emphasis has been exploited by Needham and Begg (1991) in research on more complicated insight problems. Essentially, Needham and Begg demonstrate that attempts to solve a problem, even when unsuccessful, provide greater spontaneous transfer than does memorization of a problem and its solution. An extremely important point for both teachers and students is embedded in this research. Successful spontaneous transfer of knowledge is facilitated by establishing conditions of acquisition that mimic later conditions of utilization. In other words, the ultimate effectiveness of instruction and study is increased by a problem-oriented rather than fact-oriented approach to learning.

Tips on Problem Solving

What can be summarized about problem solving that can be useful in everyday situations? Ellis (1978) identified five rules of thumb that are useful in virtually all problem-solving situations. They include the following: understand the problem, remember the problem, identify alternative hypotheses, acquire coping strategies, and evaluate the final hypothesis. These rules are reviewed in the following discussion. Additional suggestions are outlined in several texts such as Davis (1973), Wickelgren (1974), and Hayes (1981).

1 *Understand the problem.* Before you can solve a problem, you must first be sure you understand it. Perhaps this suggestion appears so obvious as to sound trite, yet all too frequently the basic difficulty in solving a problem is the failure to have a clear conception of its components. One of the frequent reasons that students do poorly on examinations is that in their haste to answer a question, they fail to analyze and reexamine the question itself. An all-too-familiar experience of students is to discover that they have written an answer to a question other than the one asked. Thus, not until you understand a problem can you attempt to solve it effectively. Moreover, once you have clarified a problem, it is good practice to check again to see whether your initial understanding is still correct.

2 *Remember the problem.* Another source of difficulty arises when you fail to remember the problem accurately. On occasion, students produce incorrect answers on an essay examination because they fail to remember the problem as it is formulated. In the course of writing an answer, students may veer away from the central issue and deal with irrelevant issues. They may, so to speak, shift in midstream from the main thesis to trivial, secondary, or

utterly unrelated topics if they fail to keep the problem in mind. Therefore, periodically recheck your memory of the problem to ensure that you stay with the issue.

3 *Identify alternative hypotheses.* Problem solving requires, of course, that you produce hypotheses. Rather than fixate on one or two hypotheses, try to identify and classify several hypotheses that appear reasonable. It is generally advantageous to try the easier or simpler hypotheses first and, if these fail, then shift to more complex hypotheses. Finally, avoid the premature selection of a particular hypothesis until you have had opportunity to evaluate reasonable alternatives—that is, generate a list of hypotheses.

4 *Acquire coping strategies.* Coping strategies refer to ways of dealing with the difficulty, failure, and frustration encountered in problem situations. Frustration and difficulty are inevitable accompaniments of problem solving. Since frustration cannot in the long run be avoided under all circumstances, a major task is to learn how to *cope* with such difficulty. Blind persistence in using old rules and excessive motivation, particularly in the form of frustration, are seen as barriers to successful problem solving. Therefore, you should attempt to recognize rigidity in yourself and to avoid inflexibility when solving problems. One way of doing this is to cultivate a general plan of using variable modes of attack as the situation demands. The colloquial expression "hang loose" captures much of the meaning of what is required for effective problem solving. Thus, it is important to remain open for new options, alternatives, and approaches.

5 *Evaluate the final hypothesis.* Once you have decided on a final hypothesis, reevaluate your choice. Consider the issue of implementing your choice. Even though it may be a good one on rational and logical grounds, is it practical and feasible? In summary, take one final look before you commit yourself to a particular sequence of action.

Two additional tips noted by Moates and Schumacher (1980) are relevant.

6 *Explain the problem to someone.* Talking about the problem to someone else may help you gain a better perspective.

7 *Put the problem aside.* Incubation appears to work for some people some of the time, at least according to anecdotal reports. But do not use the waiting period regularly as a way of avoiding problems.

Summary of Problem Solving

Problem solving has been defined as overcoming obstacles to reach desired goals. Historically, this definition was thought to be important in distinguishing problem solving from learning and memory in that problem solving was viewed as the study of applying abstract thought rather than applying learning. While this definition successfully delineates reason from habit, the research produced was isolated from many of the mainstream concerns of psychology. With the advent of information-processing approaches to the mind, problem solving came increasingly under the umbrella of prior experience, and many theories of problem solving such as production systems can easily be viewed as theories of learning.

With this shift in emphasis, the powerful influence of prior experience on problem solving became obvious but had an interesting complication. Prior experience with a problem and its solution does not automatically transfer to similar, new problems. The lack of transfer is not a failure of memory for the problem but reflects a lack of recognition of the relationship between the problem and the prior experience. Explicit instruction to use the prior experience facilitates performance in problem solving, but the more natural case is one in which such instruction is not provided. Under these circumstances, spontaneous use of prior experience on a new problem appears to be dictated by a very tight similarity relationship between the two.

Indeed, research suggests that the relationship in question is between the mental processes engaged by the prior experience and the problem situation. Thus, experience is crucial for successful problem solving, but the importation of the experience requires either a very close match between previous thought processes and the thought processes required by the problem or conscious recollection of the prior experience.

SUMMARY

Rationalism is the acquisition of knowledge through means other than sensory experience; generally, we assume that these other means are abstract thought processes. The abstract quality of thought differentiates it from the psychological processes of perception, learning, and memory, all of which are tied to particular experiences. This quality of abstractness means that thought processes can be applied to any situation, including new circumstances for which we have no relevant prior experience. The flexibility allows manipulation of ideas and, in the extreme, is capable of novel creation.

Initially, at least, the goal of research on reasoning and problem solving was to study these abstract thought processes. An essential feature of abstract processes is that they should operate independently of particular prior experiences, but research on both reasoning and problem solving has clearly demonstrated the powerful effects of experience. Indeed, one could argue that psychological research has had little success in even establishing the existence of abstract thought, just as the existence of abstract knowledge was questioned in chapter 9.

Does this mean that people are not rational? An objection that might be raised against our discussion is that rationality should not be defined as rationalism, that rationalism is too extreme to capture what we mean by rational behavior. Some have suggested that rational behavior is behavior consistent with all of the evidence available to the individual, including memory. Others have argued that rational behavior is behavior consistent with the beliefs and experiences of the individual. These connotations of *rational* are certainly used in our casual description of a person's behavior, but for our stricter purpose of distinguishing thought from learning and memory, these descriptions that include reference to prior experience and belief rob rationality of any distinct meaning. Thus, the rigorous equation of *rational* with *rationalism* is necessary if abstract thought is to be taken as a distinct aspect of cognition.

We have seen that psychological research has had little success analyzing abstract thought; indeed, the research seems to always wind its way back to the particulars of learning and memory. Why has this happened? Short of concluding that abstract thought and knowledge have no psychological reality, we must entertain the possibility that rational thought is inaccessible to empirical research, particularly as guided by the mechanistic tradition of controlled experiments. Abstract processes are by definition independent of sensory experience, but controlled experiments entail manipulating the sensory experience of the subject. Thus, it may be that, by definition, abstract thought will not yield to controlled experimentation but, rather, must be approached with different analytic tools.

This is exactly the conclusion Wundt reached 100 years ago, as we described in chapter 1. Wundt recommended the use of historical and developmental approaches to complex thought. More recently, Daniel Robinson (1986) has also argued that abstract thought processes will not yield to controlled experiments of the kind favored by psychology and adds the suggestion that the discipline of logic already has disclosed the laws of thought. Robinson has recommended that the question of rationality be distinguished from perception; whereas perception, learning, and memory may yield to laboratory experimentation, work on abstract thought is probably best conducted from an armchair.

THOUGHT QUESTIONS

1. What is the difference between abstract thought and memory? How do studies of reasoning that vary the content of syllogisms relate to this distinction?
2. What are the important differences between deductive and inductive reasoning?
3. What is the difference between the validity and the truth of a logical argument? How does this difference bear on the question of abstract thought?
4. Why did problem-solving research ask people to solve problems they had never previously experienced?
5. What is spontaneous transfer in problem solving? Discuss the research on spontaneous transfer and its conclusions. What does this research imply for training people to perform specific tasks?

13

COGNITION, EMOTION, AND MEMORY

Up to this point, we have described the important characteristics of memory and cognition. We have discussed the basic processes as they operate in normal people, as usually studied under typical laboratory or other conditions. We have, however, said very little about how these processes depend upon emotional states, including stress, depression, temporary moods, and similar conditions. Even without research evidence, there are impressive reasons to suspect that prevailing emotional states can influence memory and other cognitive processes.

Most of us are aware that under certain emotional states such as feeling sad or depressed we are less attentive to our environment and are less likely to process information effectively. Similarly, newspaper reports of air accidents have noted that pilot error can be a factor when a pilot is operating under stress. Likewise, air traffic controllers have been observed to make mistakes such as briefly forgetting to attend to two closely flying aircraft when under high levels of stress or tension, a characteristic of the job. In another context, clinical observations of depressed patients reveal that they frequently show memory deficits, and severe stress or trauma can lead to temporary or even prolonged amnesia. Thus, personal experiences, everyday observations of events, and clinical reports all attest to the idea that emotional states can affect cognitive processes. In this chapter, we shall examine some of the recent research on the effects of emotional states on cognitive processes and some of the theoretical accounts of emotion-cognition relationships. This area of research is sometimes referred to as "hot" cognition because emotional variables are seen as determinants of performance.

Research on the relation between emotional states and cognitive processes has burgeoned since about 1975. Ellis and Ashbrook (1988) and Ellis and Moore (1999) have noted that, although this area of research had a much earlier history of activity, it lay dormant for many years. One reason for this was a lack of interest on the part of many cognitive psychologists. For a long period, researchers in memory and cognition were preoccupied with understanding how basic processes in memory operate, with little regard for the role of emotional variables. Another reason for this lack of activity was the absence of acceptable experimental procedures for producing or manipulating emotional states in the laboratory. It was not until appropriate research procedures were available that cognitive psychologists became more interested in this area. A third reason for delay in research progress was the fact that concepts, theories, and methods in the two areas—cognition and emotion—developed to a large extent independently of each other, despite occasional efforts to describe their interrelations (e.g., Antrobus, 1970; Mandler, 1975). In recent years, this area has accelerated and has developed to the stage where it has now become a prominent domain of research activity (e.g., Blaney, 1986; Bower, 1981, 1992; Bower & Forgas, 2001; Dalgleish & Power, 1999; Ellis, 1986; Ellis & Ashbrook, 1991; Ellis & Moore, 1999; Eich, 2001; Fiedler & Forgas, 1988; Hertel & Rude, 1991; Ingram, 1986; Isen, 1984; Kihlstrom, 1991; Kuiken, 1989, 1991; Mathews, 1996; Mathews & Macleod, 1994; Riskind, 1991; Varner & Ellis, 1998).

IMPORTANCE OF COGNITION AND EMOTION

Ellis (1986) has outlined several reasons this area has become increasingly significant to cognitive psychologists, as well as to clinical, developmental, educational, and social psychologists. One straightforward reason is that it is apparent that emotional, or affective, states can very much influence cognitive processes in important ways. It is therefore essential that psychologists understand what these influences are and how they come about. A second reason is that useful ways for inducing temporary emotional states have been developed, thus allowing the experimental manipulation of emotional states as a class of independent variables. For example, subjects in an experiment can be induced, by way of hypnosis or verbal-induction procedures, into a particular mood state such as happiness or sadness. Thus, increased methodological sophistication has permitted the expansion of emotion-cognition research. A third factor has been the recognition of the limitations of clinical studies, valuable as they are. Until about 20 years ago, most of the studies of the effects of depressed mood states on memory and other cognitive processes used clinical patient populations. Leight and Ellis (1981) have noted an issue in this research:

> Although it is important to understand memory processes of clinically diagnosed depressives, there is an inherent limitation in this endeavor; it does not involve the explicit manipulation of mood state. And without a direct manipulation of mood state, there is no clear way of separating these effects from any confounding related to the general syndrome associated with the clinical entity of depression. Moreover, we believe that it is equally important to investigate how learning and memory are affected by the relatively common occurrence of more transient fluctuations in mood (p. 251).

Finally, there is a growing belief that theoretical accounts of memory and cognition must explain the influences of affective states such as stress, anxiety, depression, values, and arousal. A complete theory of cognition must ultimately account for the role of these factors. In summary, for these as well as other reasons, the area of cognition, memory, and emotion had developed into an exciting and active research enterprise.

EXPERIMENTAL FINDINGS: MOOD AND MEMORY

In this section, we shall examine some important representative experimental findings relating emotion and cognition. The majority of studies reviewed deal with mood effects on memory, and we will focus on studies that experimentally manipulated mood states. We will describe the following effects: mood-congruent effects; mood-state dependency; general effects of mood on encoding; mood and elaborative encoding; mood and effortful processing; mood effects on organization; retrieval and mood; and moods, thoughts, and memory; moods and text comprehension, and mood and false memory.

Mood-Congruent Effects

The idea of mood congruence refers to the finding that people are more likely to remember information that is congruent with the mood state they were in when they learned the material. Simply put, mood congruence means that a happy person is more likely to remember happy than sad material, and conversely, a sad person is more likely to remember sad than happy material.

A good demonstration of mood-congruent effects is seen in a study by Bower, Gilligan, and Monteiro (1981). In one experiment, subjects were made either happy or sad by hypnotic suggestion as they read a short story about two college men, Jack and Andre, who get together to play a friendly game of tennis. Andre is happy because everything is going well with him; things are great in school and with his girlfriend, and he is good at tennis. In contrast, Jack is sad because he has problems with school, with his girlfriend, and with his tennis game. The events of the two men's lives and their emotional reactions (happiness or sadness) are vividly portrayed in the stories. When the subjects had completed reading the story they were assigned, they were first asked to tell who they thought was the central character and with whom they identified. Bower, Gilligan, and Monteiro (1981) found that the subjects who were happy identified with the happy character, thought the story was about him, and thought the story contained more statements about him. In contrast, subjects who were sad identified with the sad character and thought the stories contained more statements about him. These findings pertain to mood-identification effects.

On the following day, the subjects were required to recall the stories while in a neutral mood. The subjects, recalled more facts about the character with whom they identified. Specifically, subjects who were originally in a sad mood recalled 80 percent of the facts about the sad character, Jack, and only 20 percent of the facts about the happy character, Andre. The effect of mood congruence was very pronounced. The effect was still present but less prominent with the subjects who were in a happy mood during hypnosis. The subjects originally in a happy mood recalled 55 percent of the facts about the happy character and 45 percent of the facts about the sad character. Thus, mood congruence was demonstrated because there was selectivity in recall produced by the mood state during learning.

How is mood congruity to be explained? Bower (1981) proposed two possible explanations, and we shall consider the one that is best supported: the selective reminding interpretation, which contends that, when one is sad, a sad incident in a story is more likely than a happy incident to remind one of a related incident in one's own life. Similarly, when one is happy, a happy aspect of a story is likely to remind one of a similar incident in one's personal life. In addition, the process of reminding is an event that strengthens one's memory of the material that was read. One way this can occur is that the old memory allows one to enrich or elaborate upon the emotional content of the story.

As a general rule, mood-congruent effects appear reliably under most mood states as well as in clinical and induced depressive moods (Matt, Vasquez, & Campbell, 1992). However, mood-congruent memory with clinical anxiety is less clear (Dalgleish & Watts, 1990). Ellis and Moore (1999) have summarized three factors that influenced the strength of the effect. First, mood-congruent memory is likely to occur when individuals are aware that the material they are learning is consistent with their current mood (Rothkopf & Blaney, 1991). Second, it helps if the to-be-remembered information is self-referential, that is, refers to the person who is learning the material (Bradley & Mathews, 1983; Nasby, 1994). Finally, both the mood experienced and the to-be-remembered material have to be of sufficient affective strength for mood-congruent effects to be shown (Rinck, Glowalia, & Schneider, 1992).

The mood-congruent effect has been investigated by many researchers and has received considerable support (Blaney, 1986; Ellis & Moore, 1999). However, a number of issues still remain, and many aspects need to be worked out in detail. It is a robust finding of mood-memory research, which stands in contrast to the less robust mood-state-dependent effects in memory.

Mood-State-Dependent Effects

Mood-state-dependent effects occur when material learned in a particular mood is recalled or recognized best when a person is tested under that same mood state (Eich, 1989; Eich & Metcalf, 1989). For example, if you learned a prose passage while in a happy mood, mood-state dependency would occur if you recalled the material better in a happy mood than in a neutral or sad mood. It is assumed that the mood at encoding will subsequently serve as an effective retrieval cue for the information during recall (Bower & Mayer, 1989; Mayer & Bower, 1986).

Although there is considerable evidence for mood-state-dependent effects in memory involving drug-induced states (e.g., Eich, 1980; Peters & McGee, 1982), a review of the mood-state-dependent research involving elation and depression observed that the evidence for this effect was neither strong nor consistent (Blaney, 1986) and Mayer and Bower (1985) reached similar conclusions.

The typical study of mood-state dependency is outlined below. The following table shows the simplest conditions under which mood-state-dependent effects are studied. An experimental group of subjects learns and then recalls material in the same mood, while a control group learns material in one mood, then recalls the material in a different mood. If recall is superior in the experimental (same mood) group, then it is inferred that a mood-state-dependent effect has been produced. Of course, such an experiment must demonstrate that the control group is not showing a decrement in recall simply because there has been a change in context.

	Learning	Recall
Experimental group	Mood A	Mood A
Control group	Mood B	Mood A

In an early study, Bower, Monteiro, and Gilligan (1978) studied mood-state dependency in three experiments. Hypnotized subjects were asked to produce a happy or sad mood by imagining a scene from their lives in which they had experienced a happy or sad emotion. Subjects were required to learn a list of meaningful words and were given either an immediate recall (experiment 1) or a one-day delayed recall (experiment 2). In neither case did they obtain mood-state-dependent memory for the recall of word lists. In a third experiment, the researchers made the task more difficult by having the subjects learn two lists, with interference involved. They learned one list while happy and the other while sad. Moreover, when the subjects were asked to reinstate the appropriate mood at recall, they were asked to imagine a different happy or sad scene from the one they used while learning the material. With this procedure, Bower et al. (1978) were able to obtain mood-state-dependent effects.

Unfortunately, additional studies have failed to replicate this result. Most important, Mayer and Bower (1985) have failed to replicate the results of the third experiment, just described. In addition, in a series of four experiments, Mayer and Bower (1986) found no support for mood-state-dependent effects, except in one study.

Leight and Ellis (1981, experiment 2) conducted a study in which mood-state dependency was examined, using both recognition and recall measures. Subjects were presented a task requiring them to learn a list of consonant-vowel-consonant sequences such as CAMREP. One day later, they were tested for recall of recognition while in the same mood or in a different mood. Subjects were given a mood induction using the Velten (1968) procedure, in which they read a list of statements designed to induce either a neutral or a sad mood. The experiment was designed so that mood-state-dependent effects could appear under eight possible conditions. However, in only one condition that involved recognition for the items was a mood-state-dependent effect found. Again, this experiment demonstrated that the effect appears to be fragile and not easily obtained.

Mood-state-dependent effects in memory have appeared in isolated clinical studies (e.g., Weingartner, Miller, & Murphy, 1977), in studies with children (Bartlett, Burleson, & Santrock, 1982), and in right-hemisphere studies of face recognition (Gage & Safer, 1985). Overall, however, there have been substantially more failures to produce mood-state-dependent effects.

Given the difficulty in obtaining mood-state-dependent effects, it is important to try to specify the conditions under which the effect is most likely to occur. At least four conditions have been noted as possible contributors to this effect, when it does appear:

1 Mayer and Bower (1986) have suggested that mood-state dependency is most likely to occur when the mood state is perceived as "casually belonging" to the material being remembered. The idea is that somehow, during learning, the mood state and the material being learned must become connected in the sense of belonging to each other. This position argues that, if

the mood state is to be an important retrieval cue for the target material, it must become integrated in some fashion at the time of learning. The proposal is quite similar to Tulving's idea of encoding specificity, discussed earlier in this book.

2 Leight and Ellis (1981) have proposed that mood-state-dependent effects are likely to depend on the nature of the material being learned. They have suggested that meaningful materials, because of their organized structure and more ready accessibility in memory are less likely to show mood-state-dependent effects. They proposed that such effects are more likely to be pronounced with poorly structured, unorganized, or less meaningful materials because mood is more likely to become an effective cue with these materials.

3 Eich (1980) has suggested that mood-state dependency is more likely to occur when there are relatively few other cues available to the person. Thus, mood-state dependency would be less likely to occur with cued recall, where explicit retrieval cues are presented, than, say, in free recall.

4 Finally, Isen (1984) has suggested that mood-state-dependent effects are more likely to occur when the material to be remembered is ambiguous or equivocal, as in interference-learning paradigms.

Recently, Eich (1995) has presented a more positive picture regarding mood state dependent memory. In a summary of this research, Eich concluded that the difficulty in obtaining reliable effects appears to be the result of insensitive methods used. He further argues that robust and reliable effects can be shown but *only* within a restricted range of conditions. In his summary Eich (1995) concludes that "under conditions in which subjects (a) experience strong, stable sincere moods; (b) play an active role in generating the target events; and (c) take responsibility for producing the cues required to retrieve these events, evidence for mood-dependent memory seems clear and consistent" (p. 74).

In the same vein, Beck and McBee (1995) have also obtained robust evidence for mood-dependent memory for the recall of generated words. Importantly, they found results similar to those of Eich and Metcalf (1989). In addition, their study is one of the strongest pieces of evidence for mood-dependent memory

In summary, the mood-state-dependent effect in memory does occur but is not always easy to obtain in laboratory studies. We do have some ideas as to the conditions important for this effect, and our understanding of this effect will increase as researchers develop better control of these experimental conditions.

Mood Effects on Encoding

In this section, we will turn our attention to the effects of mood states on the encoding of information. At one level, we can ask what effects mood states have on the encoding of information. At another level, we can delineate the memory processes that are importantly affected by mood states. And, at a third level, we can develop theoretical accounts of mood's effects on memory.

As an example of the first level of experiments, Leight and Ellis (1981, experiment 1) examined the effects of experimentally induced mood states on the learning of lists of consonant-vowel-consonant pairs. College students served as subjects and were given a mood induction using the Velten (1968) procedure. The subjects were placed in one of three mood states—happy, sad, or a neutral mood—by having them read a list of 60 self-referent statements from Velten's procedure. Subjects who were placed in a happy mood read a series of happy self-referent statements that dealt with feeling good and being competent, to being extremely happy. Sad subjects read a series of sad self-referent statements, and neutral subjects read statements designed to induce or maintain a neutral state. After mood induction was given, subjects were administered a questionnaire to be sure that the induction procedure was effective, which it was. Subjects were then given five trials on the list-learning task, and the results are shown in figure 13.1

As the figure clearly shows, subjects in the neutral mood induction showed the best performance, whereas subjects in the sad mood showed the poorest performance. Moreover, subjects in the sad mood failed to show any improvement in recall after the second trial, indicating the pronounced impairment of these subjects. The happy subjects were intermediate, and they continued to show improvement over trials but were always below the neutral group. This latter finding indicates that being happy, at the level induced by the Velten procedure, has a slightly interfering effect on learning the list. This does not mean that being mildly happy is undesirable but indicates that the high level of emotion induced by the elation procedure does produce some lowering of performance.

These results indicated that mood states can affect the encoding of neutral information, that sadness interferes with encoding, and that even high levels of elation have some interfering effects. Now let us examine some experiments that looked at the effects of mood states on important memory processes.

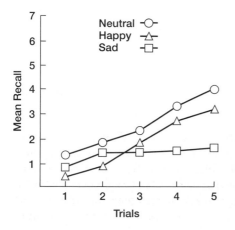

FIGURE 13.1
Recall of letter sequences following a neutral, happy, or sad mood-induction procedure. *(From "Emotional Mood States, Strategies, and State-dependency in Memory" by K. A. Leight and H. C. Ellis, Journal of Verbal Learning and Verbal Behavior, 1981, 20, 251–256. Copyright 1981 by Academic Press. Reprinted by permission of Academic Press.)*

Mood and Elaborative Encoding

In this section, we shall examine the effects of an experimentally induced depressed mood state on elaborative encoding. Elaboration is an important process in memory; therefore, it is important to understand how depression affects this process.

Ellis, Thomas, and Rodriguez (1984) addressed this issue in the first of a series of experiments. They asked the question, how would a sad mood state affect the performance of subjects in a memory task that encourages elaborative encoding? The task required that subjects read a set of 10 sentences and rate each sentence as to its comprehensibility. The sentences were either simple, base sentences or elaborated sentences containing information that enriched and elaborated upon a target adjective in the sentence. For example, the sentence "The hungry child opened the door" is a base sentence. There is nothing in the sentence that relates to or elaborates upon the adjective "hungry." In contrast, "The hungry child opened the door of the refrigerator" contains the phrase "of the refrigerator," which precisely elaborates upon the to-be-targeted word for testing in the sentence—"hungry." Previous experiments (e.g., Stein & Bransford, 1979) have shown that, if subjects are then presented the sentences without the target word "hungry" and are asked to recall the word, they do substantially better if they had seen the word embedded in the elaborated sentence than if they had seen the word in the base sentence. This occurs because of the information presented during study and is not dependent upon having a more elaborated sentence during recall testing.

Given that elaboration of information in a sentence aids recall, Ellis, Thomas, and Rodriguez (1984) were primarily interested in how a depressed mood state would affect memory for this type of material. They reasoned that, since elaboration activates a greater level of encoding, depression should have a greater impact on the processing of material in elaborative rather than base, simple sentences.

Subjects were given either a sad mood or neutral mood induction as well as a set of either base or elaborated sentences which they were to judge on comprehensibility. This was an *incidental* memory procedure; thus, subjects did not know that they would be asked to recall target words in the sentences after they had judged them. Subjects were presented the sentences for either a 7- or 10-second rate so researchers could examine the role of time in processing the information. Immediately following the sentence-rating procedure, subjects were presented the sentences with the target word removed—for example, "The ___ child opened the door"—and were asked to recall the missing word.

The results are shown in figure 13.2, which is broken down into two panels. The top panel shows recall of the target words under the sad or neutral mood state and for elaborated or base sentences for the 7-second presentation. The striking finding, and the most important one, was that subjects who were sad showed a clear reduction in recall of words in the elaborated condition, but being sad had no effect whatsoever on the recall of words in the base sentence conditions. Figure 13.2

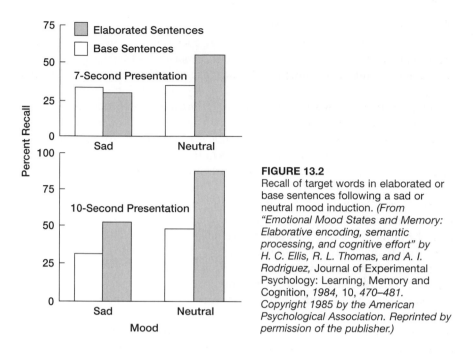

FIGURE 13.2
Recall of target words in elaborated or base sentences following a sad or neutral mood induction. *(From "Emotional Mood States and Memory: Elaborative encoding, semantic processing, and cognitive effort" by H. C. Ellis, R. L. Thomas, and A. I. Rodriguez, Journal of Experimental Psychology: Learning, Memory and Cognition, 1984, 10, 470–481. Copyright 1985 by the American Psychological Association. Reprinted by permission of the publisher.)*

presents a clear interaction between mood states and sentence conditions; that is, the effect of a sad mood induction is greatest when the task is more demanding, in the sense of requiring more elaborative encoding.

The bottom panel of figure 13.2 shows, as expected, that recall is much higher when subjects have longer to process the sentences. This is not surprising and is not of particular interest. What is of interest is that, while there is some suggestion of a mood-state interaction with the sentence conditions, the effect is much less pronounced at the 10-second presentation level.

What these findings show is that the induction of a sad mood state has a somewhat complex effect on memory. *First,* being sad will impair memory but not in all conditions. The sad and neutral mood subjects performed equally well when recalling words from the base sentences under the fast (7-second) presentation rate. However, the sad mood subjects did poorer in the remaining three comparisons. *Second,* as previously noted, there is clear evidence that elaborative processing is more impaired by depression than is base sentence processing.

Mood and Effortful Processing

The second finding of the Ellis et al. research supported more generally the idea that depression is most likely to affect the processing of more difficult, demanding materials. *Ellis, Thomas, and Rodriguez (1984) proposed that as the encoding demands of a task become greater, the interfering effects of disruptive mood states increase.* With simple tasks that require fewer encoding demands, or less effort, being sad may have little or no effect on performance. However, as the task becomes more complex, difficult, or demanding, the effects of sadness become greater. Ellis et al. (1984, experiment 3) directly examined this hypothesis in a study in which variations were made in the effortful demands on subjects. This was accomplished by presenting subjects with sentences in which a single word (the object noun) was omitted. Each incomplete sentence was followed by a pair of nouns from which the subject was to select the word that correctly completed the sentence. In each sentence, only one word (the target) fit meaningfully into the sentence. The amount of effort required in making the decision was varied. For a low-effort word, the missing item was quite obvious and virtually self-evident such as "The girl was awakened by her frightening ___." In the high-effort condition, the missing word was not obvious but was one of several possible solutions: "The man was alarmed by the frightening ___." For both sentences, the appropriate target word was *dream,* which easily fit into the low-effort sentence but required some deliberation for selection in the high-effort sentence.

It was known that in such a task subjects recall more of the high-effort items in an incidental memory task. The experimenters were interested in the effects of sadness on recall of high- and low-effort items, with the prediction that depressed subjects would show greater impairment of the high-effort items. Following the task of selecting an appropriate word for each sentence, subjects were given a surprise free-recall test for the words, and the results are shown in figure 13.3. The figure shows two important findings. First, as indicated by the neutral mood conditions, subjects show better recall for high-effort items. Second, the effect of being sad on recall is to reduce performance only on the high-effort items. In contrast, being sad has no effect on the recall of low-effort items. Again, this study supports the idea that being sad has its greatest impairment on more effortful tasks.

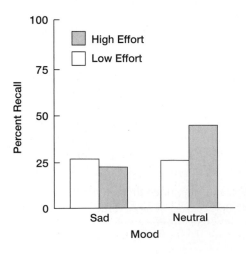

FIGURE 13.3
Recall of words in an incidental memory task involving high- and low-effort tasks following a sad or neutral mood induction. *(From "Emotional Mood States and Memory: Elaborative Encoding, Semantic Processing, and Cognitive Effort" by H. C. Ellis, R. L. Thomas, and A. I. Rodriguez, Journal of Experimental Psychology; Learning, Memory, and Cognition, 1984, 10, 470–481. Copyright 1985 by the American Psychological Association. Reprinted by permission of the publisher.)*

There is also clinical study evidence that is consistent with the idea that depression has its greatest effects on more demanding tasks. For example, Weingartner, Cohen, Murphy, Martello, and Gerdt (1981) found a decrement in the recall of depressed patients—compared with nonpatient control subjects—in three experiments that required the processing of words. They asked subjects to process concrete nouns, either semantically or acoustically, by generating either semantic associates or rhymes for the to-be-remembered words. Free recall of the target words was measured a day later. Making the assumption that the semantic-processing task requires more cognitive effort, or capacity, than does the acoustic task, then a decrease in recall of semantically processed items should be greater than that of the rhymes for the depressed patients when compared with the nonpatient controls. The depressed patients recalled fewer of the semantically processed items than did the control subjects, whereas free recall for the rhymes was essentially identical for the two groups.

In another study by Weingartner and colleagues (1981, experiment 3), they examined the effects of depression on the recall of highly organized versus unorganized word lists. Depressed patients and control subjects did not differ in their recall of the highly organized word lists. In contrast, depressed patients were much poorer in recall of the unorganized lists. Making the assumption that unorganized lists require more effort to process than do highly structured lists, these results are consistent with the interactions between mood and task demands in the Ellis, Thomas, and Rodriguez (1984) experiments examining elaboration and effort. Similarly, Cohen, Weingartner, Smallberg, Pickar, and Murphy (1982) have proposed that depressed patients' greatest impairment on cognitive tasks is found in the tasks that require *sustained effort*.

Why is it that depressed mood states have greater effects on the processing of more difficult or demanding tasks? An explanation developed by Ellis and Ashbrook (1988), which depends upon the allocation of processing capacity, can account for these findings and will be described in detail later, after our review of general theories and models.

Mood Effects on Organization

It is certainly reasonable to assume that emotional states such as depression and anxiety interfere with organizational processes in memory. Certainly, common experience suggests that when we are stressed or in a poor mood, we find ourselves forgetful, and our ability to think clearly and in an organized fashion seems impaired. Our personal impressions are borne out in both laboratory and clinical studies; however, the results again depend upon the characteristics of the task.

We noted in the previous section that depressed patients show difficulty in remembering word lists that are unorganized (Weingartner, Cohen, Murphy, Martello, & Gerdt, 1981, experiment 3). Depression impairs the ability to organize material that is poorly structured, although no impairment was found with highly organized materials. More specifically, it was found that depressed subjects use less subjective organization of randomly organized materials than do normal control subjects. Other clinical studies of depressed subjects have found deficits in the ability to organize information. For example, Russell and Beekhuis (1976) found that depressed patients show poorer free recall and reduced clustering in free recall, a measure of organization.

Experimental studies have also found deficits in organizational processes due to depression. For example, Leight and Ellis (1981, experiment 2) found a marked reduction in both recall and organizational measures for college students given the Velten depressed mood induction. In their study, subjects learned lists of eight consonant-vowel-consonant pairs (e.g., *CAMREP, BONKID, GAMLUX*). The letter sequences were broken up into grouping structures (e.g., *CA, MR, EP*) that masked the pronounceable units (e.g., *CAM, REP*). In one case, the grouping structures were the same on each presentation, a *constant* presentation condition. In the second case, the structures were *varied* on each presentation, which encouraged subjects to look for pronounceable (organized) units (see Ellis, Parente, Grah, & Spiering, 1975). Subjects were given either a depressed or neutral mood induction and either a varied or constant presentation of the letter sequences.

The results were quite striking and are shown in figure 13.4. The figure shows recall of the letter sequences as integrated units, a measure of organization, over five successive trials. The important results were that the depressed subjects showed no improvement whatsoever over five learning trials when the material was presented in constant fashion. In contrast, with varied presentation, the depressed groups did show some improvement and performed virtually identically to neutral mood subjects who learned constant sequences. The figure also shows that subjects in the varied/neutral condition performed best and showed the most rapid improvement in performance.

What was most striking was the inability of the constant/depressed group to show any gain in performance over five trials. Given a task that is difficult to organize, the induction of a depressed mood severely impairs performance in this perceptual grouping task, an organizational task that depends upon the subject's being able to chunk, or group, the letter sequences. Note that these findings parallel those of Weingartner, Cohen, Murphy, Martello, and Gerdt (1981), who found that depressed patients show reduced recall and organizational ability when required to learn poorly structured materials. Thus, it appears that depression has its greatest negative impact on organizational processes when the materials are inherently difficult to organize.

Retrieval and Mood

Another issue that has been examined is the role of mood on retrieval as distinct from the encoding of information. Studies of mood effects on retrieval require the induction of a mood state *after* subjects have processed some information. The basic sequence involves first having subjects process some materials, then placing

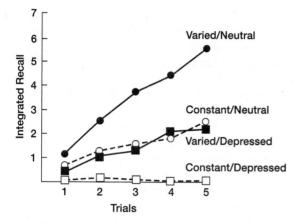

FIGURE 13.4
Integrated recall (chunking) or letter sequences under
conditions of varied versus constant presentation of letter
sequences following depressed or neutral mood
induction. *(From "Emotional Mood States, Strategies, and
State-dependency in Memory" by K. A. Leight and H. C.
Ellis,* Journal of Verbal Learning and Verbal Behavior,
*1981, 20, 251–256. Copyright 1981 by Academic Press.
Reprinted by permission of Academic Press.)*

them in a mood state, and finally testing for their recall of the information. As you
can see, this differs from studies of mood on encoding, in which subjects are given
a mood induction *prior* to performing a cognitive task. Thus, studies of the effects
of mood on retrieval examine the effects of mood on the *output* of information.

Experimental studies of mood effects on retrieval show basically two sets of
results. One group of studies has failed to find effects of mood on retrieval, but
the other group has reported that mood states do have an effect on retrieval. This
difference is not a matter of unreliable findings but is likely due to the use of different experimental conditions.

Two studies have reported no effects of mood on retrieval. First, Bower, Gilligan, and Monteiro (1981, experiment 2) failed to obtain retrieval effects when a
hypnotic mood induction was administered five hours after the subject read a
story. The delayed retention interval, as well as delay of mood induction, may be
one factor that precluded the researchers from finding an effect of mood on retrieval. As Ellis, Thomas, McFarland, and Lane (1985) suggest, it is possible that
any potential mood effects on retrieval will be attenuated after a five-hour retention interval and that any mood state will have its major effect when induced immediately or soon after a study session, rather than when it is delayed.

Similarly, Goldstein (1983) found no retrieval effects of a depressed mood
state on the recall of personal memories. He had subjects attempt to recall early

childhood memories after being given either a neutral or a depressed mood induction. His procedure was to take subjects to the laboratory and have them recall their earliest (or one of their earliest) childhood memories. Two days later, they returned to the laboratory and were given a mood induction; then they were required to recall the early memory. His null effects may have been because early childhood memories are quite likely part of a highly integrated memory system relatively impervious to a depressed mood state.

In contrast, clear effects of a depressed mood induction on the retrieval of target words in sentences have been reported by Ellis, Thomas, McFarland, and Lane (1985). In this study, they used the base and elaborated sentences used by Ellis et al. (1984). As described in the section on mood and elaborative encoding, subjects processed sentences and were later tested with an incomplete sentence, with the target adjective removed. Again using this procedure, Ellis et al. (1985) required subjects first to process the list of 10 sentences, then to undergo a neutral or depressed mood induction, and finally to be tested for recall of the target words. Subjects were given either a full Velten mood induction requiring 25 minutes or a partial induction procedure requiring 15 minutes.

The basic results are shown in figure 13.5. Regardless of the type of sentence processed or the duration of the mood induction, the depressed mood subjects recalled fewer target words than did the neutral control subjects. These results establish the general point that a depressed mood can impair the retrieval of

FIGURE 13.5
Percentage of target words recalled as a function of mood conditions, elaborated and base sentences, and retention interval. *(From "Emotional Mood States and Retrieval in Episodic Memory" by H. C. Ellis, R. L. Thomas, A. D. McFarland, and J. W. Lane, Journal of Experimental Psychology: Learning, Memory, and Cognition, 1985, 11, 363–370. Copyright 1985 by the American Psychological Association. Reprinted by permission of the publisher.)*

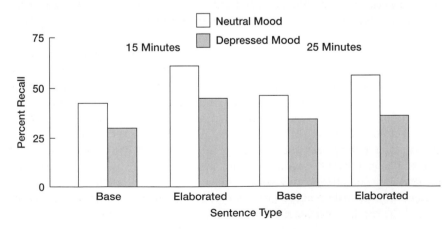

information. Much is yet to be understood about retrieval effects, including how they depend on the type of material, the instructions to subjects, the mood induction itself, and other factors.

How does the induction of a depressed mood state interfere with retrieval? Ellis, Thomas, McFarland, and Lane (1985) and Ellis and Ashbrook (1988) propose a model to account for these results. They propose that emotional states can be viewed as conditions that regulate the allocation of capacity or attentional resources in cognitive tasks. A depressive or, more generally, a disruptive mood state interferes with the retrieval of information because it preempts some capacity that would normally be allocated to retrieving information. Ellis, Thomas, McFarland, and Lane (1985) also note that an additional account is possible in that the cognitive activities associated with retrieval may interfere in a more direct sense, in that the negative cognitions (thoughts) of the depressed subject compete directly with the cognitive activities necessary for successful retrieval. In this account, emphasis is placed upon the potential competition of cognitive activities in working memory. These two accounts are complementary, and both sets of processes may occur during retrieval.

Moods and Text Comprehension

Not only does mood affect memory but it also affects the comprehension of stories. In a series of experiments, Ellis, Ottaway, Varner, Becker, and Moore (1997) studied the detection of contradictions that were built into short descriptive passages about various topics. College students who were placed in a temporary sad mood were poorer in detecting contradictions than neutral mood students. Moreover, they made more false identifications; that is, they identified more sentences as contradictory that were not actually contradictory. However, if they were informed that contradictions might be present in the passage, they were better able to identify contradictions. The ability to detect contradictions or inconsistencies in stories is only one aspect of text comprehension; however, these experiments indicate that depressed moods may play a similar role in impairing both comprehension and memory.

Being in a sad mood also affects the ability of college studies to activate and use prior knowledge. Ellis, Varner, Becker, and Ottaway (1995) had college students read ambiguous passages that they could understand if they were given the title of the passage. Even when given the title of the passage, which was designed to activate knowledge about the passage topic, students who were in a sad mood comprehended and recalled less information in the passage than students in a neutral mood. In addition, sad students were poorer in predicting how much of the passage they could recall than neutral mood students. Importantly, these studies show that being in a sad mood not only affected comprehension but also affected the ability of college students to judge how much they know about some topic as a result of studying it.

Mood and False Memory

You might suspect that if individuals are sad or depressed, they might show a greater tendency for making false recognitions. Indeed, this is precisely the case. Recall that false recognition refers to "recognizing" some item or event that you did not actually experience. Using a procedure developed by Roediger and McDermott (1995), Ellis (2000) presented lists of words to college students who were either sad or were in a normal mood. In the test, students were shown these words again plus words they had not seen (but were associates of the word shown) and asked whether or not they recognized the word. For example, if shown the word *chair* in a list, then in the test they would see *chair* and also an associate not shown, such as *table*. College students who were sad showed a stronger tendency to falsely recognize the associates, that is, to "recognize" words they had not actually seen.

These results have clear implication for eyewitness identification and for any situation in which accurate recognition is important. If people are stressed or are in a strong mood or emotional state, they are more likely to be inaccurate, in the sense of being more likely to falsely recognize some stimulus event.

Moods, Thoughts, and Memory

Several theoretical accounts of the effects of emotional states on memory have led to the idea that mood states produce a prevailing pattern of thoughts that influences performance in a variety of cognitive tasks (e.g., Beck, Rush, Shaw, & Emery, 1979; Ellis & Ashbrook, 1988; Ingram, 1984). An important assumption in these theories is that a depressed mood state produces its effect on memory and cognition via negative or unfavorable self-thoughts that interfere with performance. For example, two assumptions of the Ellis-Ashbrook (1988) model deal with the role of irrelevant, distracting thoughts. The model proposes that the production of irrelevant thoughts increases under emotional duress and that these irrelevant, distracting thoughts interfere with a person's ability to encode and organize information in memory, thus explaining poorer recall. What is particularly important about these assumptions is the contention that disruptive emotional states produce their effects on memory and other cognitive processes not directly by emotion per se but by way of intrusive, distracting, irrelevant thoughts that compete with thoughts relevant to encoding the pertinent information in the memory task.

Seibert and Ellis (1991) have directly tested this idea. College students were tested in two mood-memory experiments in which they were asked to produce all their thoughts, which were tape recorded, while they were studying a set of items. They were subsequently asked to judge their reported thoughts as being relevant or irrelevant, on a five-point scale, to the criterion memory task. Subjects were given a sad, happy, or neutral mood induction. In a second experiment, subjects were asked to list and judge their thoughts at the end of the study session. Both experiments required students to recall the study items, providing a measure of

BOX 13.1

FOCUSED ATTENTION, DEPRESSION, AND MEMORY

The cognitive disruption associated with depression is intuitively understandable as a problem of competing thoughts. Essentially, by definition a depressed individual is absorbed by negative thoughts. This intuition translates into theory as a reduction in cognitive capacity that can be allocated to concurrent experiences. Paula Hertel has offered another version of this idea to explain memory deficits in depression. Her idea is that the deficit lies in sustaining and directing attention to appropriate events, which differs from the general capacity deficit model in that depressed individuals can perform capacity-demanding tasks if attention is held to the task.

Hertel and Rude (1991) provided support for this idea in an experiment whose subjects were given a surprise recall test after they had read incomplete sentence frames in which they determined if a word properly completed a sentence. In one condition, subjects simply read each sentence and decided if the word fit; in the other condition, subjects were required to read aloud the word, at both the beginning and end of the presentation, forcing the subjects to attend to the task. Figure 13.6 shows total recall for both attention conditions (focused and unfocused) and depressed versus neutral mood states. The figure shows that having to pay attention eliminated the deficits in memory that are typically found.

Hertel has gone on to demonstrate that, when deficits are found, they are the result of failures in conscious recollection of prior experience. Using Jacoby's logic of opposition, described in chapter 6, Hertel and Milan (1994) discovered that dysphoric subjects (those who experi-

(continued)

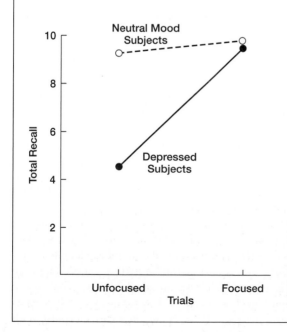

FIGURE 13.6
Recall as a function of depression and focused versus unfocused attention on the memory task. *(From "Depressive deficits in memory: Focusing attention improves subsequent recall" by P. T. Hertel and S. S. Rude.* Journal of Experimental Psychology: General, *1991, 120, 301–309. Copyright 1991 by the American Psychological Association. Reprinted by permission of the publisher and author.)*

BOX 13.1 (continued)

FOCUSED ATTENTION, DEPRESSION, AND MEMORY

ence a mild, nonclinical level of depres- sion) differ from nondysphoric subjects on their conscious recollection of prior events, but the two groups show compa- rable influences of unconscious recollec- tion of prior experience. Hertel and Milan point out that the deficit in conscious control could be either at encoding the original experience (e.g., the negative thoughts distract from the attention given

a current event) or at the time of retrieval (e.g., the negative thoughts disrupt the ability to control access to prior experi- ence). In either case, Hertel's ideas and experiments are important indicants that cognitive deficits in depression are due to deficits in controlling attention. Further discussion of Hertel's views are pre- sented in the section on Cognitive Initia- tive Theory.

---

recall for each student and a measure of judged relevance of thoughts. Using ei- ther the first procedure, concurrent verbalization, or the second procedure, thought listing, the production of irrelevant thoughts was strongly negatively correlated with recall. Similar, negative correlations were found by Ellis, Moore, Varner, Ott- away, and Becker (1997) between irrelevant thoughts and recall, but note that ir- relevant thoughts may not *necessarily* be the cause of poorer recall because both irrelevant thoughts and the level of recall may be mediated by some third factor, such as the difficulty in comprehending the material. In summary, these results, while correlations, provide support for the view that mood effects on memory may be the result of thoughts—that is, the cognitive activity, which intervenes be- tween the subjects' mood state and performance on the memory task.

THEORETICAL APPROACHES

Several somewhat independent theoretical frameworks account for the effects of emotional states on memory and cognition, and we shall examine five of them. The first is *network theory,* developed largely by Gordon Bower and his colleagues (Bower, 1981; Bower & Cohen, 1982; Gilligan & Bower, 1984). The second ap- proach is *schema theory,* which contends that a person's mood state functions like a schema (conceptual framework) for processing and organizing incoming in- formation, as well as for guiding the retrieval process (e.g., Beck, 1967; Kuiper, MacDonald, & Derry, 1983). The third approach is the *resource allocation model,* developed largely by Henry Ellis and his colleagues (e.g., Ellis & Ashbrook, 1988; Ellis, Thomas, & Rodriguez, 1984; Ellis, Thomas, McFarland, & Lane, 1985). This model is based on the idea of allocating attentional capacity to an ap- propriate task and will be discussed in more detail shortly. A fourth approach is that of *cognitive initiative* developed by Hertel and Rude (1991). These theo- retical approaches are not to be regarded as competing but are properly seen as complementary. A more general theory will likely encompass aspects from all these approaches. A fifth approach, the *Affect-Infusion Model* (Bower & Forgas, 2001) provides a good comprehensive integration of several theories.

Network Theory

Network theory is an elaborately developed approach based upon the general idea that emotional states are represented as nodes, or components, of semantic memory. There are several alternative models of network theory (e.g., Bower, 1981; Clark & Isen, 1982; Isen, 1984; Teasdale, 1983), and Bower's (1981) theory is currently the most comprehensive. His description of the semantic network captures the most essential features of his theory, as follows:

> The semantic-network approach supposes that each distinct emotion such as joy, depression, or fear has a specific node or unit in memory that collects together many other aspects of the emotion that are connected to it by associative pointers. . . . [Around each] emotion node are its associated autonomic reactions, standard role and expressive behaviors . . . , and descriptions of standard evocative situations which when appraised lead to sadness. . . . [Each] emotion unit is also linked with propositions describing events from one's life during which that emotion was aroused. . . . These emotion nodes can be activated by many stimuli—by physiological or symbolic verbal means. When activated above a threshold, the emotion unit transmits excitation to those nodes that produce the pattern of autonomic arousal and expressive behavior commonly assigned to that emotion. . . . Activation of an emotion node also spreads activation through the memory structures to which it is connected, creating subthreshold excitation at those event nodes. Thus, a weak cue that partially describes an event, such as "kindergarten days," may combine with activation from an emotion unit to raise the total activation of a relevant memory above a threshold of consciousness. . . . This recall constitutes reactivation of a sad memory and sends feedback excitation to the sadness node, which will maintain activation of that emotion and thus influence later memories retrieved (p. 135).

The network model has been applied to an understanding of a variety of mood effects, including mood-congruent effects, memory of personal episodes, similarity of emotions, mood-state-dependent effects, and general emotional effects on cognitive processes. For instance, mood-congruent effects in memory are the result of activation of emotion nodes by an emotional event that is consistent with one's network of emotional memories. If one is in a happy mood, then the semantic network system is activated and is therefore more receptive to materials that have a happy tone.

Schema Theory

The second approach, schema theory, is somewhat similar to network theory, and it accounts for the effects of emotional states on memory and cognitive processes. Schema theory proposes that people in a typical, prevailing mood have a generalized framework, or schema, that is congruent with that mood state. Thus, a sad person has a prevailing sad or depressive schema for organizing information. For instance, a sad person characteristically perceives and remembers negative experiences, sad episodes, and tends to interpret the world from a negative perspective. Not only does a sad schema predispose a person to encode unhappy, negative events more readily than happy events, but the schema also directs his or her retrieval to specific memories that have a sad content.

The idea of a negative schema is part of general cognitive theories of depression. A leading developer of cognitive theories of depression is Aaron Beck, who proposes that depression is produced by specific stressful situations that activate a prevailing schema. The activated schema selectively encodes negative information and thereby maintains the depressive state of the individual. Support for this approach is seen in a recent study by Hedlund and Rude (1995) who found evidence for latent depressive schemas in remitted depressed patients who recalled a greater number of negative words and showed more negative interpretative biases than nondepressed controls.

Schema and network theories are conceptually very similar in that they both propose that knowledge structures (semantic networks or schemas) predispose a person to selectively encode and retrieve information that is consistent with the person's knowledge structure. There are, however, two important distinctions that have been noted (Ingram, 1984). First, network theories typically adopt the assumption of spreading activation (Collins & Loftus, 1975), whereas schema theories have not typically adopted this assumption. Second, some have noted that the schema concept is less well developed than the network concept. Nevertheless, the status of the schema concept has become better developed in recent years, and it is clearly a useful and important concept (Mandler, 1984).

Resource Allocation Model

The third general approach to accounting for the effects of emotional states on cognitive processes is called the resource allocation, or capacity, model. In general, the resource allocation model is designated to explain the effects of emotional states on memory and cognition and has considered two issues: the role of emotional states in regulating the amount of capacity allocated to a cognitive task, and the demands on processing capacity made by the cognitive task itself. The resource allocation model is based upon two important concepts: *attention* and *cognitive interference*. The basic idea is that mood-related deficits in memory are the result of two processes: the failure to pay sufficient attention to the memory task, and the production of intrusive, irrelevant thoughts which compete with appropriate task-oriented thoughts (cognitive interference). This approach has been most fully developed by Ellis and Ashbrook (1988), who characterize their model as follows:

> The model adopts the concept of capacity or resource allocation which is part of general capacity models of attention. . . . [These models] have assumed that there is a limited, momentary pool of capacity (attentional resources) which can be allocated to any given task. . . . From this perspective, it is our position that emotional states can affect

the amount of attentional capacity that can be allocated to a given cognitive or motor task. Thus we are considering the effect of emotion on attention but from the view of capacity (resource) models of attention as distinct from other conceptions of attention. The essence of the resource allocation model, in accounting for the effects of generally disruptive mood states on memory, is to assume that emotional states regulate the amount of capacity that can be allocated to some criterion task. Most tasks involving memory of information require some allocation of capacity and thus the effect of a disruptive mood state is to reduce the amount of capacity available for processing the criterion task (p. 26).

This model makes five principal assumptions in order to account for the effects of emotional states on memory and cognitive tasks: (1) emotional states produce their effects on cognitive activities by regulating the amount of capacity available to be allocated to a given task; (2) the encoding of information usually requires some allocation of cognitive capacity, or effort; (3) memory performance is frequently correlated with the amount of capacity allocated to the cognitive task, an assumption based on the empirical findings regarding cognitive effort (e.g., O'Brien & Myers, 1985; Swanson, 1984; Tyler, Hertel, McCallum, & Ellis, 1979). Assumptions 4 and 5 deal with mood effects on irrelevant-task processing and extra-task processing and propose that emotional states increase the production of irrelevant thought, which in turn impairs memory for criterion tasks. These last two assumptions have been found valid by Seibert and Ellis (1991), as noted earlier in this chapter.

A wide range of research findings support the Ellis-Ashbrook (1988) model. These include the results from studies on overall decrements in recall due to depression; the effects of depression on the encoding of easy versus demanding tasks; and the effects of depression on retrieval, personal memories, organization, and schema recall.

One of the most important predictions of the model is that depression will have its greatest impairment in the recall of difficult tasks. As noted earlier, this finding has appeared in a number of experiments. The model explains this outcome by assuming that a depressed mood state or, more generally, any disruptive mood state can interfere with the encoding of material because it takes away some resources that might otherwise be allocated to the memory task. When a task is very demanding, there are fewer resources available to process the task and, if a person is already depressed, then insufficient resources are available. In contrast, if a person is processing an easy task, then adequate resources are available to process the task and little or no decrements in recall should occur (Ellis & Ashbrook, 1988; Ellis, Thomas, and Rodriguez, 1984). Thus, the model does not assume that mood states will uniformly impair memory.

Cognitive Initiative Theory

Another view of how moods and emotions can impair memory is that of *cognitive initiative* proposed by Paula Hertel and colleagues (Hertel, 1994; Hertel &

Rude, 1991). She contends that depressed individuals may lack sufficient cognitive initiative to carry out memory tasks. This means depressed individuals may fail to activate strategies necessary for remembering material. However, if they are encouraged to use cognitive strategies, they may remediate memory deficits. We saw earlier how this might operate in the study by Hertel and Rude (1991) in which depressed patients who are encouraged to focus their attention on a memory task were able to eliminate the memory deficits that are typically found (See box 13.1). Hertel (1994) has summarized the results of several studies to show that depression does not always impair memory if subjects are required to pay attention to the task.

The importance of cognitive initiative theory is that it emphasizes the role of cognitive strategies as a factor in mood-memory deficits and that these deficits can be remediated. In addition, this theory is important because it focuses on attentional control as an important process in remediating memory. Finally, just as we saw that attention was an important component of the resource allocation model, its importance is again emphasized in cognitive initiative therapy.

Interestingly, the preferred treatment for clinical depression is now cognitive therapy. One aspect of cognitive therapy is to encourage patients to monitor their thoughts and to consciously test their intrusive, negative thoughts against the reality they confront. Research on treatment outcomes has shown this therapeutic approach to be very successful. The techniques used in cognitive therapy are consistent with three of the theories just discussed: schema theory, resource allocation theory (attention and cognitive interference), and cognitive initiative. All three theories point to the importance of *thought processes* in depressive states or sad moods. The resource allocation theory and cognitive initiative theory point to the importance of *attentional processes.*

The four general approaches we have described are seen as complementary and not competing. Network and schema theories approach the issue of mood effects on memory from the perspective of how organized knowledge structures such as network models or schemas influence the encoding and retrieval of information. In turn, the resource allocation model approaches this from the viewpoint of how mood affects attentional resources and intrusive thoughts, which ultimately are correlated with memory. A complete model of how mood affects memory will see an integration of these conceptual approaches, and Ingram (1984) has similarly argued for such integration.

Affect-Infusion Model

The affect-infusion model goes beyond the previous models and theories. It places the network theory, described earlier, within a broader theoretical context regarding the links between affect and cognition (Bower & Forgas, 2001; Forgas, 1995; Forgas, 1999). The model recognizes that affective states have a wide variety of effects on memory, attention, associations, and evaluations that people make, and that these effects are not invariable. Furthermore, Forgas (1999) argues that these effects are context sensitive; that is, they depend on characteristics of the task.

The affect-infusion model places great importance on the *processing strategies* used by people. It contends that "the nature and extent of mood effects on cognition should depend on the particular kind of processing strategy used to deal with a given task" (Forgas, 1999, p. 599). In addition, another assumption is that people will tend to minimize cognitive effort; that is, they will tend to adopt the easiest or least effortful strategy. This assumption differs from the earlier network model that assumes a more-or-less universal, robust processing strategy. Forgas's position is consistent with the resource allocation model which makes the important assumption that mood effects on memory do depend very much on the effortful demands of the task (Ellis & Ashbrook, 1988).

The affect-infusion model adopts a multiprocess approach, which assumes that the role of affect or mood depends on the type of processing strategy most likely to be used. The power of this approach is that it does not assume that affect or moods will universally influence cognition, but, instead, will depend upon processing strategy.

Four strategies are described: *direct access, motivated processing, heuristic processing,* and *substantive processing.* Forgas (1999) contends that the first two types involve search processes that tend to limit the role of affect, whereas the latter two strategies require more constructive and flexible thinking, allowing for greater opportunities for the role of affect, that is, affect infusion.

This distinction can be made clear by the following example. For example, if you are asked to give your opinion about a familiar object such as a car or to deal with routine information such as giving your phone number on a job application form, these tasks (direct access) do not warrant extensive processing. Accordingly, the role of affect is likely to be minimal. Similarly, if you are working on a task involving a strong, pre-existing objective such as the simple task of taking out the garbage, the role of affect is again likely not to be very important.

Heuristic processing occurs when you do not have a ready response nor a strong motivational goal. You develop a strategy to deal with the particular task. Here the role of affect may enter because more open-ended thinking may occur.

The role of affect is *greatest* when substantive processing is involved. This is the most complex type of processing in which "people need to select, learn, interpret, and process information about a task, and relate this information to pre-existing knowledge structures using memory processes" (Forgas, 1999, p. 602). In general, the more extensive the processing required, the greater the likelihood of affect-infusion, that is, of affect influencing cognition. This assumption is quite similar to that made by Ellis and Ashbrook (1988), which notes that as the encoding demands (effort) of a task increase, memory decrements due to a depressed-mood state will increase.

The affect-infusion model incorporates the network model but does not deny or refute the network model. The network model is most applicable when substantive processing is required. For example, substantive processing is likely to enhance mood congruity and, thus, provides support for the network model.

In summary, the affect-infusion model provides a valuable way of integrating research in cognition and emotion. It does so by indicating that the role of affect in cognition depends on the type of processing employed.

SPECIFIC ISSUES IN EMOTION AND COGNITION

In the final section of this chapter, we shall consider six special issues that go beyond the usual research on mood and memory: mood states and judgments of contingency, emotion and eyewitness testimony, flashbulb memory, anxiety and performance, anxiety and processing bias, and arousal and memory.

Mood States and Contingency Judgments

A person's mood not only affects memory, but it also influences other cognitive processes such as judgment. Since depression has been shown to interfere with memory in a variety of settings, we might suspect that depression similarly impairs the accuracy of judgments a person makes. However, in a surprising series of experiments by Alloy and Abramson (1979), students who were depressed were actually more accurate in contingency (relationship) judgments than were nondepressed students.

In their studies, Alloy and Abramson examined the ability of depressed and nondepressed college students to detect the degree of contingency between their responses and environmental outcomes. Each student was presented with a contingency problem in which the subject made one of two responses (pressing a button or not pressing it) and received one of two outcomes (a green light or no green light). At the end of a series of trials, the subject was asked to judge the degree of contingency that existed between pressing a button and the onset of the green light.

In one study (Alloy & Abramson, 1979, experiment 2), students were presented with one of two problems in which responses and outcomes were *non-contingently* related (unrelated) but differed in the overall frequency with which the green light came on. If people use the rule of percentage of reinforcement (percentage of time the green light comes on), then they will believe they have more control in the problem in which the green light occurs more frequently than in the situation in which the green light occurs less frequently. In one problem, designated 25-25, the subjects had no control over the green light, but the green light was presented 25 percent of the time. In the second problem, called 75-75, the subjects also had no control, but the green light was presented 75 percent of the time.

The basis results are shown in figure 13.7, which shows judged control for the two problems for depressed and nondepressed subjects, as well as separate results for male and female subjects. Any judgment of perceived control is in error in a noncontingent situation, because pressing a button did not cause the green

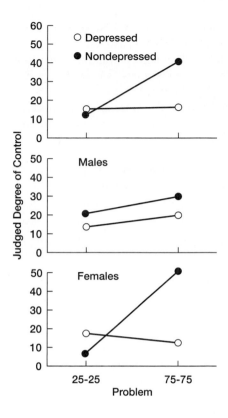

FIGURE 13.7
Judged degree of control for depressed and nondepressed students as a function of problem type. *(From "Judgment of Contingency in Depressed and Nondepressed Students: Sadder but Wiser?" by L. B. Alloy and L. Y. Abramson,* Journal of Experimental Psychology: General, *1979,* 108, *441–485. Copyright 1979 by the American Psychological Association. Reprinted by permission of the publisher.)*

light to appear, so the greater the degree of judged control, the greater the actual error in judgment. As you can see from the top panel of the figure, the nondepressed subjects thought they had little control in the 25-25 problem, but they considerably overestimated their degree of control in the 75-75 problem. In contrast, the depressed subjects made relatively accurate judgments for both problems. Looking at male-female results, it is clear that the nondepressed females overestimated the 75-75 problem—that is, they thought they had greater control than did the males.

The most important issue is why depressed subjects should be more accurate in judging contingencies. Or the alternative issue is why nondepressives are less accurate in making contingency judgments. Alloy and Abramson (1979) suggest several alternative hypotheses. They favor a generalized motivational account in which it is assumed that nondepressed people have a more self-enhancing attributional style—that is, they tend to attribute success or good outcomes to themselves and, therefore, are more likely to develop the illusion of control in a situation when none actually exists. In contrast, depressives do not have this self-enhancing attributional style and, hence, suffer fewer illusions. As Alloy and Abramson suggest, depressives may be "sadder but wiser" in these judgmental tasks.

This issue of the illusion of control was subsequently examined by Alloy, Abramson, and Viscusi (1981). They selected nondepressed and depressed subjects, according to a depression inventory, and then induced a mood of depression or elation. Naturally nondepressed subjects who were made temporarily depressed by a Velten (1968) mood induction gave accurate judgments of control, whereas naturally depressed subjects who were made temporarily elated showed an illusion of control and made overestimates in judgments.

More generally, these studies reveal the important effects of mood states on judgments and the illusion of control over events. They further indicate the importance of emotional factors in influencing cognitive processes and yield findings that were surprising and unexpected in the initial Alloy and Abramson (1979) studies.

Emotion and Eyewitness Testimony

Since about 1970, there has been a renewed interest in eyewitness testimony, both with respect to basic questions about memory and perception and practical issues concerning the application of knowledge about eyewitness testimony to the courtroom situation (e.g., Kassin, Ellsworth, & Smith, 1989; Loftus, 1986; McCloskey, Egeth, & McKenna, 1986). A fairly large body of information about eyewitness testimony has developed, much of it associated with the issue of unreliability of eyewitness testimony. Some of the important findings include the lack of any substantive correlation between the accuracy of an eyewitness and the degree of confidence expressed by the witness (Wells & Murray, 1984), the role of postevent misleading information in producing distortions of memory or perception (Loftus, Miller, & Burns, 1978), the role of bias in cross-racial identification (Brigham & Malpass, 1985), and the limited amount of information that jurors have about eyewitness perception and memory (Deffenbacher & Loftus, 1982).

In this section, we shall briefly comment on the role of emotional states in eyewitness testimony. A frequent claim has been that emotional stress produces an impairment in memory such that witnesses to a traumatic emotional event will be less accurate in recall. Indeed, experts in the field tend to believe that very high levels of stress impair the accuracy of eyewitness testimony (Kassin, Ellsworth, & Smith, 1989).

In a review of this literature, Christianson (1991) indicates that the results are somewhat complex. For instance, some studies have shown that unpleasant emotional events are poorly remembered, compared with neutral events (e.g., Loftus & Burns, 1982; Neisser & Harsch, 1993). Neisser and Harsch found that, in studies of college students' memories of the *Challenger* space shuttle disaster, poorer recall was associated with stronger negative emotions, as remembered. Other studies, however, have shown that unpleasant events can be remembered fairly well (e.g., Heuer & Reisberg, 1990).

It is not possible to resolve the divergence in findings in any brief or simple fashion. The results seem to depend upon the type of task used, the kind of information required in memory, and a variety of other features. One resolution of these differences may lie in Easterbrook's (1959) cue-utilization hypothesis. According to this position, as emotional arousal increases, there is a progressive restriction in the range of cues used or attended to. At a moderate level of arousal, a restriction in attention to environmental cues can benefit performance because relevant cues will still be attended to, whereas irrelevant or unimportant cues will receive little attention. However, at high arousal levels, as seen in high stress or anxiety, even fewer cues would receive attention, including relevant ones, thus degrading performance. Thus, according to Easterbrook's hypothesis, whether emotion helps or hinders ultimately depends upon the level of arousal. These findings can also be accounted for by Ellis and Ashbrook's (1988) model, in which it is proposed that moderate levels of emotional arousal are unlikely to impair memory, especially with easy tasks. In contrast, strong levels of emotion are likely to impair memory, especially if the task is more difficult.

In an excellent review of the research on eyewitness identification, Bekerian and Goodrich (1999) also point out some of the complications regarding the role of emotion on eyewitness memory. What is known is that available research indicates that memory can be unstable, changing over time, particularly when the event is emotionally salient (Reyna & Titcomb, 1997). And, as noted earlier in this chapter, a sad or depressed mood state increases the likelihood of false memory (Ellis, 2000). Finally, Bekerian and Goodrich point out that the accuracy of reported information may be questioned if an eyewitness has been exposed to misleading information.

Flashbulb Memory: Personal Memories Revisited

Flashbulb memory is the recall of very important, vivid, and often emotionally arousing events. The term *flashbulb memory* was used by Brown and Kulik (1977), who asked their subjects if they could recall how they had heard the news about President John Kennedy's assassination, as well as other striking events. Many subjects reported a very vivid and personal recollection of these events, with a lot of attendant details. The focus of flashbulb memory is on memory for one's personal circumstances such as where one was, what one was doing, and how one felt about the shocking news of Kennedy's death, as distinct from memory about the event itself (Pillemer, 1993). Much of the research concerns memory for shocking public events such as the attempted assassination of President Reagan (Pillemer, 1984), the *Challenger* space shuttle disaster (Bohannon, 1988), and President Nixon's resignation (Winograd & Killinger, 1983).

An initial interpretation of flashbulb memory, proposed by Brown and Kulik (1977), was that a surprising and important event produces an initial registration in memory that is automatic. However, the subsequent recollections that people produce are constructed from their imagery of the events and their covert rehearsal and overt retelling of the events. Brown and Kulik further assumed that automatic encoding of shocking events would have survival value for people in that the memories contain information about how to act when having similar shocking, presumably threatening experiences in the future. Subsequently, Neisser (1982) argued that one value of flashbulb memories is that the ability to convey rich memorial detail to others is important in facilitating social communication. For example, answering questions on the basis of personal memories by citing anecdotes enables the speaker and listener to relate in a more empathetic manner. Moreover, by retelling an event in a personal manner, the speaker becomes more interesting and may be more convincing in his or her recollection.

Descriptions of personal details that are usually contained in flashbulb memories can have a very persuasive effect in communication. This point has been illustrated by David Pillemer (1993) and reveals how the personal activities and feelings of a person in recalling an event increase the listener's acceptance of the recollection. Pillemer (1993) describes the testimony of George Schulz, who was secretary of state in 1988, before the Senate and House committees concerning covert military assistance to Iran. Schulz' testimony contained frequent references to personal details:

> So I picked up the phone Sunday morning, and I called the President. I said "Mr. President, I have something I should bring over here and tell you about now." So he said "Fine, come over." . . . I went up to the family quarters, and Al Keel, who was then Acting National Security Advisor, went with me at my request. And I told the President the items on this agenda, including such things as doing something about the Dawa prisoners, which made me sick to my stomach that anybody would talk about that as something we would consider doing. And the President was astonished, and I have never seen him so mad. He is a very genial, pleasant man and doesn't—very easy going. But his jaws set and his eyes flashed, and both of us, I think, felt the same way about it, and I think that in that meeting I finally felt that the President deeply understands that something is radically wrong here! (From Pillemer, 1993, p. 130, quoting the Select Committees on the Iran-Contra Investigation, 1988).

As you can see, this type of testimony helps communicate the sense of things as George Schulz remembered them and adds face validity to his recollection. Moreover, Pillemer (1993) points out that the sharing of detailed memories of personal circumstances sets an intimate stage for communication. A personal recollection can draw in the listener and evoke a more empathetic response than do abstract, generalized recollections.

What about the accuracy of flashbulb memories? Here the evidence is complex, with some reports showing low accuracy and others showing high accuracy. Even though a memory may be very vivid, it may also contain many errors

(Neisser, 1982). Neisser and Harsch (1993) interviewed subjects one day after the *Challenger* space shuttle explosion and then again three years later. They found relatively little agreement between the initial and delayed recollections, even with respect to who delivered the news and other details. Nevertheless, the subjects were highly confident of their delayed recollections. In another study of the space shuttle disaster, McCloskey, Wible, and Cohen (1988) also reported many errors in their subjects' recollections; nevertheless, they recalled a good deal of information. After a nine-month delay, 67 percent of the subjects' reports matched their reports given immediately after the disaster.

Is there a special mechanism underlying flashbulb memory? Brown and Kulik (1982) have proposed that there is a neural mechanism that is activated by striking and vivid events. This neural mechanism causes the whole scene or event to be "printed" on the memory, making it a different kind of memory. Moreover, such memories have a particular structure, in that people remember such details as location (where they were), activity (what they were doing), affect (how they felt), and aftermath (what happened next).

As you might suspect, another view of flashbulb memories has been proposed. Although agreeing that a flashbulb memory is a subjectively compelling account of an important event, Neisser (1982) contends that there is no need for a special interpretation of flashbulb memories; the vividness and persistence of such memories is the result of rehearsal and frequent retelling after the event, rather than any special neural mechanism activated at the time of the event. Similarly, Rubin and Kozin (1984) suggest that flashbulb memories are not necessarily different from other vivid memories. In both cases, Neisser and Rubin argue that flashbulb memories do not require special mechanisms and are to be explained by the usual memory processes involving rehearsal, elaboration, and organization. At present, the evidence seems to support the views of Neisser, Rubin, and others who share this position.

Anxiety and Performance

Anxiety and depression are somewhat related in that depressed individuals are frequently anxious (cf. Ellis & Hertel, 1993; Eysenck, 1982). In the studies described so far, depression tended to impair memory performance by reducing the appropriate processing of the information—that is, by reducing the attentional resources allocated to a task—and by increasing the number of distracting, irrelevant thoughts, which are usually negative self-referent thoughts (Ellis & Ashbrook, 1988; Seibert & Ellis, 1991). Anxiety can also increase the number of distracting, irrelevant thoughts, but it can also produce distortions in people's perceptions of events (cf. Eysenck, 1991; Williams, Watts, MacLeod, & Mathews, 1988, 1997). The research on anxiety and performance provides strong evidence that anxiety, as well as stress in general, produces performance decrements in a variety of situations, especially so with tasks that make high demands on resources (e.g., Darke, 1988).

One feature of anxious people is that they tend to expect unpleasant outcomes. Butler and Mathews (1983) investigated this issue by having nonanxious people and anxious or depressed patients rate the likelihood of occurrence of a number of pleasant and unpleasant events. The subjects were asked to estimate the likelihood that each event would happen to themselves and to other people. The three groups were similar in their estimates of positive events but differed in their estimates of negative events. Both the anxious and depressed subjects thought that the unpleasant events were more likely to happen to themselves, but not to other people.

Classical studies of anxiety and learning proposed that anxiety can either interfere with or facilitate learning, depending upon the complexity of the task. If the task was complex, meaning that many alternative responses were available to the person in learning the task, then anxiety usually interfered with learning. In contrast, if the task was relatively simple, allowing few alternative responses such as in eyelid conditioning, then anxiety could facilitate learning. For practical purposes, anxiety is more likely to impair our important everyday activities because they do allow for multiple response alternatives.

In an important review of the research on anxiety and performance, Eysenck (1983) reported that anxiety generally impairs performance, but he also found exceptions; sometimes it has no effect and sometimes it can actually facilitate performance. He attributes this divergence in findings to two processes: worry and arousal. First, he notes that anxiety tends to increase worry, which leads to an increase in distracting thoughts, which interfere, or compete, with relevant thoughts. Recall that Seibert and Ellis (1991) have reported direct confirmation of this idea. Second, Eysenck proposed that anxiety increases the overall arousal level of people, thus inducing them to allocate more effort to the task. Additional effort, however, may or may not enable anxious individuals to overcome the negative effects of worry and the associated distracting thoughts. Hertel and Rude (1991) have provided some evidence in support of this second process, in that individuals can be assisted in overcoming performance deficits by allocating more effort to the task; however, their subjects were depressed rather than anxious.

Eysenck's (1983) two-process idea may help to explain the divergent effects of anxiety on performance. For example, many people report that *a little* anxiety is actually helpful in preparing for a test, giving a speech, or undertaking some other important task, whereas excessive anxiety impairs performance. What is reported is that a little anxiety is motivating in that it arouses us to do our best, which is the arousal aspect of anxiety. In turn, too much anxiety can overwhelm us so that performance is poorer.

Finally, another approach toward studying the effects of stress and anxiety on performance attempts to produce the emotional state under highly realistic conditions or examines performance in work settings. In an unusual experiment, Keinen, Friedland, and Arad (1991) simulated stress, and the attendant anxiety, in a realistic and convincing manner. Subjects were assigned to a high- or low-stress condition and then were given a classification task. In the high-stress condition, subjects were trainees in a parachuting course, just learning to jump. They were sitting on a runway, harnessed into their parachutes, waiting to board an airplane for their first night parachute jump. Parachute jumping, at least for novices, is a stressful experience, and the prospect of parachuting in the night would add to the subject's anxiety. Under the low-stress situation, subjects simply performed the criterion task during a break in training. The criterion task was a classification procedure in which subjects categorized a list of objects. The high-stress subjects categorized the objects more rapidly but used fewer groups to categorize the objects than did the low-stress people. The results suggested that high-stress people pay less attention to distinctive features and/or that they tend to show greater overgeneralization due to stress.

Anxiety and Processing Bias

As shown in the previous section, anxiety can clearly affect performance. Let us now turn to processing bias. Experimental studies of the effect of anxiety on processing information have found evidence for a *processing bias* for threat-related information. People who are clinically anxious or high in trait anxiety more readily detect and process information that is somehow personally threatening to them (Williams, Watts, MacLeod, & Mathews, 1997). In one experiment (Williams, Mathews, & MacLeod, 1996), people were shown colored words in which threat-related words were shown. They were asked to name the color of the words, and anxious individuals showed increased interference in naming the color in which threat-related words were presented.

A similar kind of effect is found when people are asked to interpret ambiguous information. Most of us have probably observed that people who are anxious while walking on a dark street are more likely to interpret shadows and movements as potentially threatening. Indeed, this effect has been demonstrated in several experiments (e.g., Calvo, Eysenck, & Castillo, 1997).

In other studies, a processing bias has been shown in a visual-probe task. Individuals are shown both neutral and threat-related items and are faster at detecting a visual probe when it is projected in the same location as a threat-related item (Mogg, Bradley, & Hallowell, 1994). What this indicates is a heightened sensitivity to threatening material as the result of anxiety.

From an evolutionary perspective, the function of emotions such as anxiety and fear is to facilitate the detection of environmental danger and, accordingly, help people to respond effectively to threatening situations (Mogg & Bradley, 1999). But it is also the case that excessive anxiety or fear can disrupt performance. Indeed, people who show a fairly consistent tendency to be hypervigilant to threat stimuli appear to be more prone to anxiety disorders when stressed.

A variety of explanations have been proposed to account for anxiety on processing bias. We shall consider a model proposed by Williams, Watts, MacLeod, and Mathews (1988). According to their model, two processes are responsible for the attentional bias effects just described. First, an *affective decision mechanism* assesses the threat value of environmental stimuli. Then, once the threat value is determined, it is fed into a *resource allocation mechanism* which determines how much processing resources should be allocated to the threatening task. High-anxious individuals allocate more resources to the threatening situation, whereas low-anxious individuals allow few, if any, resources. In summary, high-anxious individuals become more vigilant, especially when under stress.

Arousal and Memory

Arousal has been proposed as an important process in mediating cognition-emotion effects. The role of arousal, however, has been controversial for many years. Researchers in the field have proposed divergent views ranging from Zajonc's (1984) primacy-of-affect theory, emphasizing arousal, to Lazarus' (1991) theory which argues that cognitive (thought) processes underlie the effects of emotion on cognition.

We shall examine two experiments (one pro and one con) which evaluate the role of arousal in memory. In an experiment by Clark, Milberg, and Ross (1983), evidence for arousal was obtained. Individuals learned two lists for free recall, one while relaxing and one while exercising (presumably aroused). Later, they attempted to recall both lists after watching a relaxing nature film or a sexually arousing erotic film. Individuals better recalled the list learned while relaxed after watching the relaxing film. In contrast, individuals better recalled the list after exercising and while aroused from watching the erotic film. These results support the view that arousal may prime memory for arousing events.

Alternatively, Varner and Ellis (1998) found no support for arousal in their study. They compared the relative effects of cognitive priming versus arousal, which was induced by having individuals exercise by stepping up and down on a cinder block. Individuals were given either a sad mood induction or read a paper on how to plan and write an essay (two types of priming). Varner and Ellis found that free recall of the categorized word list (half the words were mood related and half were related to writing a paper) was better for those words primed either by a sad-mood or by reading an explanation of how to plan and write an essay. Specifically, individuals in a sad mood recalled more of the negative words in the list; in turn, individuals in the essay-reading condition recalled more of the essay-related words in the list. Arousal produced no effect on recall; individuals in the exercise condition (arousal) showed no difference in recall for the two types of words in the list.

In a review of the literature on arousal, Riskind (1989) concludes that cognitive priming, not arousal, is the important mechanism in mood-memory studies. In a recent summary of the research on affect, memory, and social cognition, Bower and Forgas (2001) reach a similar conclusion regarding the importance of cognitive priming.

SUMMARY

This chapter indicated that emotional states can play an important role in memory and cognition. This research area has become very active since about 1975, with several factors contributing to its development. There is strong evidence for mood-congruent effects in memory, in which memory for effectively toned material is best when one is in a mood like that of the material to be learned. In contrast, the evidence for mood-state-dependent memory is more limited and the effect is not robust.

Mood influences a range of encoding effects as well as retrieval. Subjects in a sad mood show learning decrements. Subjects who are given a sad mood induction show greater impairment in tasks that require elaborative encoding and enhanced cognitive effort. The induction of a sad mood interferes with organizational processes in perceptual grouping and free-recall tasks. Finally, depressed subjects make more accurate judgments of contingency; that is, they have fewer illusions of control in contingency judgments.

Network and schema theories represent two approaches to accounting for the effects of emotional states on memory, approaches based upon knowledge structures. The third major approach is that of a resource allocation model, which assumes that emotional states regulate the amount of capacity that can be allocated to a cognitive task. Finally, we examined six special issues: mood states and judgments of contingency, emotion and eyewitness testimony, flashbulb memory, anxiety and performance, anxiety and processing bias, and arousal and memory.

THOUGHT QUESTIONS

1. How does selective reminding explain mood-congruent effects in memory?
2. Why is it that depressed subjects are more accurate in judgments of contingency?
3. How does the resource allocation model account for greater decrements in tasks that are more effortful?
4. Why are mood-state-dependent effects difficult to obtain in laboratory studies?
5. What role does the organized structure of material to be learned play in deficits due to depressed moods?
6. How can we account for flashbulb memories?
7. What does the Easterbrook hypothesis predict about the role of emotion in eyewitness testimony?
8. How might Eysenck's two-process idea explain the effects of both the facilitating and the interfering aspects of anxiety on human performance?

GLOSSARY

absolute accuracy   The match between the overall magnitude of metacognitive judgments and the overall magnitude of criterion test performance.

action slips   Inadvertent mistakes in action whereby one performs an unintended action rather than the intended action.

algorithm   A solution rule or procedure which ensures a solution.

analogue representation   A representation stored in memory that is similar in storage format to the perceptual experience; used particularly in regard to visual images stored in memory.

analysis-by-synthesis   A theory of pattern recognition which advocates the decomposition of the sensory pattern into component features prior to matching with long-term memory.

anterior attention system   The most advanced of the known neural systems underlying attention. The system is located in the frontal lobes and is presumed to be responsible for sustaining attention.

anterograde amnesia   Inability to remember events that occur after injury due to accident or disease.

aphasia   Disorder involving loss of language function.

articulatory loop   The verbal storage system of working memory.

associative strength theory   Theory of the effectiveness of retrieval cues; that a cue is effective depending on how strongly associated it is with the to-be-remembered item of information.

attention   Process of focusing selectively on part of the environment while ignoring other aspects.

autobiographical memory   Memory for events in one's own past.

automatic processing   Processing of information that appears to occur without involvement of resources or central capacity requirements.

backward masking   Process in which previously presented information is erased from sensory memory.

basic-level category   The level of a category which has the clearest perceptual features and is most readily distinguished from other categories.

Brown-Peterson paradigm   Famous distractor paradigm for measuring short-term retention.

calibration   See absolute accuracy.

capacity model   Model of attention which assumes that attention is the process of allocating resources, or capacity, to various sensory inputs.

category size effect   Prediction from semantic memory models that larger categories require more search time than do smaller categories.

central bottleneck theory   Theory of attention that says processing is limited at the stage of response decision.

central executive   Controlling, decision-making mechanism such as that in working memory.

clustering in recall   The tendency of human beings to organize items in free recall so that they are recalled according to conceptual or other categories. Items from a particular category tend to be recalled adjacently.

coding   Process by which external stimulation is transformed into a representation for purposes of memory.

cognition   A class of symbolic mental activities such as thinking, reasoning, problem solving, memory search, and so forth.

cognitive effort   Amount of capacity allocated to a given task. Concept is typically measured in the secondary-task paradigm used in attention.

conceptually driven processes   Psychological processes initiated by meaning.

confidence judgment   A metacognitive judgment indicating one's certainty that an answer on a criterion test is correct.

congruity effect   A result from levels-of-processing research, indicating that orienting tasks that require a positive response lead to better memory than orienting tasks that require a negative response.

connectionism   Memory structure in which elements are connected by associations differing in strength. Combined with parallel distributed processing in theories of pattern recognition and memory.

constructive processes   The tendency of human beings to construct or reconstruct information in memory, altering the information to make it more consistent with a schema.

control processes   Terms that refer to all regulatory processes in memory models such as attention, search, organization, coding, retrieval, and so forth.

convergent thinking   Thinking that moves in a direct fashion toward a specific answer.

creative synthesis   A concept from Wundt's theory that suggests that conscious experiences are created through the process of apperception.

cue-dependent forgetting   A failure in retrieval due to ineffectiveness of the cue.

data-driven processing   Psychological processes corresponding to the physical features of the stimulus.

decay theory   Theory of forgetting which says that forgetting is due to an autonomous weakening or decay of the memory trace.

deductive reasoning   Drawing a logical, specific conclusion from a set of general premises.

dependent variable   The variable, usually behavior, measured in an experiment.

descriptive model of thinking   A theory of thought processes based on hypotheses developed following empirical work.

dichotic listening   A laboratory procedure used primarily for the study of attention, in which two different messages are played simultaneously.

directed forgetting   Purposive forgetting.

distinctiveness hypothesis   Hypothesis which emphasizes that information is better retained in memory when the memory traces, or representations, are more distinctive.

divergent thinking   Thinking that moves outward from a problem in a variety of directions.

dual-code theory   Theory which says that information stored in memory may be in two forms: verbal codes and imaginal codes.

early selection theory   A theory of central attention which presumes that attentional filtering occurs prior to pattern recognition.

echoic memory   The sensory register for audition.

elaboration   Process by which information to be remembered is linked or related to information already known.

empiricism   Knowledge acquired from sensory experience.

encoding   Process by which the to-be-remembered information is transformed into a form suitable for storage in memory.

encoding specificity theory   Theory which says that a cue is effective only if it was specifically encoded with the to-be-remembered item of information.

episodic buffer   Component of working memory that stores both visual and auditory information.

episodic memory   Memory for specific events that happened at a particular time or place.

exemplar theory   Theory of knowledge that specifies particular prior instances as the unit of representation.

explicit memory   Memory resulting from intentional retrieval.

family resemblance   Degree to which an instance of a category resembles the prototype of that category.

feature set theory   Model of semantic memory which emphasizes that semantic memory can be described in terms of bundles, or sets, of features.

feeling-of-knowing (FOK) judgment   A metacognitive judgment in which one predicts for a nonrecalled answer the likelihood of recognizing it on a recognition test.

filter model   Model of attention that assumes that some or all of the information presented to one sensory channel is filtered or blocked.

flashbulb memory   Recall of especially important, vivid events that are often emotionally arousing.

forgetting   Failure to access information stored in memory.

free recall   Task requiring a person to recall items of information in any order.

functional fixedness   Tendency to think of objects as functioning in a particular way and failing to perceive other ways the object might be useful.

generate-test method   A problem-solving strategy in which a possible solution is first generated and then tested to see if it works.

generation effect   The empirical finding that self-generated material is better remembered than externally provided material.

generation-recognition model of retrieval   Model which involves two stages in retrieval: first, the generation of candidates for retrieval and, second, the decision process in which the candidates are evaluated.

geon   Basic unit of representation on Biederman's structural theory of pattern recognition.

Grice's Maxims   Guidelines that speakers and listeners follow in order to foster good communication during a conversation.

heuristic   A rule of thumb or approximation which helps in solving a problem but does not ensure its solution.

iconic memory   Visual sensory memory.

ill-defined problems   Problems in which the original state, the objectives, or the rules to be used are poorly defined.

implicit memory   Use of prior experience without intent to remember.

incidental memory   Memory for an event that one did not intend to remember at the time of the original experience.

independent variable   The manipulated variable(s) in an experiment.

inductive reasoning   Drawing a probabilistic conclusion from a set of specific premises.

inference   Drawing conclusions that may or may not be valid.

inhibition   Active suppression of a mental process or mental structure.

interference theory   Theory of forgetting which contends that events are forgotten because other learning interferes with those events or prevents them from being remembered.

irrelevant speech effect   Disruption of working memory by human vocalization irrelevant to the material to be remembered.

isolation effect   Enhanced memory for information that is incongruent with the prevailing context.

judgment of learning (JOL)   A metacognitive judgment in which one predicts the likelihood of remembering an item on a subsequent criterion test.

late selection theory   A theory of attention which presumes that attentional filtering occurs following pattern recognition.

levels of processing   Principle which proposes that the depth at which information is processed determines its accessibility in memory.

lexical analysis   The process of representing the meaning of words in text.

lexical decision task   A method, used to study access to various levels of representation in which the subject must decide as quickly as possible whether he or she is viewing a word or a nonword.

linguistic relativity hypothesis   Idea that a people's language structure affects the way they perceive the world and represent information.

mechanism   A type of explanation of natural phenomena that derives from the physics of mechanics.

memory   The process by which past experience influences present thought and behavior.

memory code   The stored representation of an event in memory.

mental model   A descriptive model of thought usually applied to reasoning.

mental rotation   The process of rotating mental images so that they are imaged in a new orientation.

metacognition   A person's cognitions about his or her cognition, which includes knowledge about cognition, monitoring of cognitive process and states, and control of cognitive processes.

method of loci   A mnemonic technique in which different to-be-remembered items are imagined in different locations of a familiar scene.

mnemonic   Technique designed to assist memory.

modality effect in free recall   Better recall of the last few items of a list with auditory presentation as opposed to visual presentation.

modality effect in implicit memory   Superior memory for items presented in the same modality at study and test with an implicit test.

modal model of memory   General or typical memory model which assumes several stages in memory.

monitoring   Assessing the ongoing process or state of some aspect of cognition, such as learning.

mood congruence   Tendency to remember information that is consistent with the prevailing mood state during the encoding of that information.

mood-state dependency   Memory is facilitated when mood is the same during learning and recall.

network theory of mood   Theory explaining the effects of mood states on memory based upon the assumption that emotions are stored as nodes in semantic memory.

normative model of thinking   Any rule-based system that serves as an a priori analogue to the thought process.

organization   Process by which information to be placed in memory is grouped or rearranged in a new and more optimal manner.

orienting tasks Tasks used in human memory experiments which orient the subject to a particular task.

parallel distributed processing A model of pattern recognition and memory that assumes simultaneous processing of input and nonlocalized representations.

parallel processing Model of information processing which assumes that events are processed at the same time.

partial report technique Technique used in studies of sensory memory in which subjects produce only part of the information presented.

pattern recognition Process in which patterns of sensory signals are translated into psychological experience; that is, the process by which meaning is derived.

perceptual grouping Type of organization in which human beings chunk or organize spatially or temporally grouped information into a higher-order or more meaningful structure.

perceptual identification test A laboratory procedure that requires identification of perceptually degraded items following prior exposure to those items.

perceptual representation system A theoretical storage device in long-term memory that stores the auditory and visual forms of words as well as the structural description of objects.

phonemic restoration Tendency to perceive speech patterns correctly even when part of the pattern is masked.

phonological loop Component of working memory that stores verbal material.

precategorical Of or relating to information in the sensory register that is assumed to be stored without meaning.

preconscious processing Information that is processed below the level of awareness but that can become available to awareness.

preprocessing A process of "cleaning up" or reorienting a sensory pattern prior to matching with long-term memory in pattern recognition.

presupposition An assumption that is made in order to understand an assertion.

primacy effect Enhanced memory for the first items in a series of items.

priming Facilitation of responding to an item due to prior presentation of the item or of a related item.

prior knowledge Refers to the body of knowledge a person has prior to engaging in some specific task.

proactive interference The forgetting of currently learned material, produced by interference from previously learned material.

problem space The way a person mentally represents a problem.

procedural memory The component of semantic memory that stores knowledge of skills.

process dissociation procedure A methodology to separate conscious and unconscious influences of prior experience.

productive thought   A gestalt concept for the use of abstract thought processes in problem-solving.

propositional code   Abstract representation of both verbal and pictorial materials considered by some theorists to be the language of thought.

propositional memory   The component of semantic memory that stores factual knowledge.

propositional reasoning   Type of reasoning that involves reasoning from if . . . then . . . statements. The four basic arguments in propositional reasoning are modus ponens, modus tollens, affirming the consequent, and denying the antecedent.

prototype   The best example of a concept.

rationalism   Knowledge acquired outside of sensory experience, usually through abstract thought.

reality monitoring   Discrimination between thought and perception.

recency effect   Enhanced memory for more recently experienced events.

rehearsal, elaborative   The repeating of information aloud or to oneself in the attempt to relate the information to already known events or to other information.

relative accuracy   The degree to which judgments accurately assess performance on a criterion test for one item relative to another.

reminiscence bump   Enhanced memory for events that occurred in one's life in late teenage to mid-twenties.

reproductive thought   A gestalt concept for the use of particular prior experience in problem solving.

resource allocation model   Model explaining the effects of mood states on memory based upon the allocation of cognitive resources.

response competition   Process in forgetting in which different responses made to the same stimuli compete with each other at the time of recall.

retrieval   Process of accessing information in memory.

retrieval induced forgetting   Forgetting part of an event resulting from prior retrieval of different parts of the same event.

retroactive interference   Process in which an event learned during a retention interval leads to forgetting a previously learned event.

retrograde amnesia   Inability to remember events that occurred prior to injury.

rote rehearsal   Repetition of to-be-remembered material in a fashion that does not involve consideration of meaning.

schema   An organized body of knowledge about a class of events, ideas, objects, and so forth.

schema theory   Class of theories designed to explain how people acquire, develop, and use schematic representations.

semantic memory   General knowledge of the world.

semantic priming   Facilitation of word recognition in lexical decision provided by a prior word meaningfully related to the target.

sensory register   Memory system designed to store information received by the sensory receptors.

serial position curve   Finding that in the free recall of serially presented items, items at the beginning and end of a list are best retained and items in the middle of a list are poorly retained.

serial processing   Model of information processing which assumes that events are processed serially in time.

shadowing   Procedure in which a listener in an attention study is required to repeat aloud a message presented to one ear.

spreading activation   The idea that activity in an associative network will spread to related concepts.

state-dependent memory   Idea that memory may be dependent upon reinstatement of the original state in which information was encoded.

storage   The process by which memory representation is held in memory.

strategy   The cognitive approach used in dealing with a task involving memory, reasoning, problem solving, and so forth.

subjective organization   Tendency of human beings to organize unrelated items in accord with a self-developed mode of organization.

suffix effect   Poor recall of the last word of an auditorially presented list when followed by another speech sound.

syntactic parsing   The process of identifying the relationship among words in a sentence.

Teachable Language Comprehender (TLC)   The earliest of the major modern models of semantic memory.

template theory   Class of pattern recognition theories which assumes that a literal copy of experience is stored in memory.

theme   The central or general topic of a passage.

transfer appropriate processing   Principle that states performance will be best when the processes demanded by a task match the processes engaged by prior experience.

unlearning   Loss or weakening of first-list associations during the learning of a second list.

visuo-spatial sketchpad   The visual storage system of working memory.

whole report technique   Technique used in studies of sensory information in which subjects are asked to produce all of the to-be-remembered material.

word length effect   Short-term memory for words is inversely related to the time required to pronounce the words.

working memory   An active system of memory in which information is assembled and organized prior to recall.

REFERENCES

Aaronson, D., & Scarborough, H. (1976). Performance theories for sentence coding: Some quantitative evidence. *Journal of Experimental Psychology: Human Perception and Performance, 2,* 56–70.

Adams, L. T., Kasserman, J. E., Yearwood, A. A., Perfetto, G. A., Bransford, J. D., & Franks, J. J. (1988). Memory access: The effects of fact oriented versus problem oriented acquisition. *Memory & Cognition, 16,* 167–175.

Aiken, L. R. (1987). Testing with multiple choice test items. *Journal of Research and Development in Education, 20,* Summer, 44–58.

Allen, S. W., & Brooks, L. R. (1991). Specializing the operation of an explicit rule. *Journal of Experimental Psychology: General, 120,* 3–19.

Alloy, L. B., & Abramson, L. Y. (1979). Judgment of contingency in depressed and nondepressed students: Sadder but wiser? *Journal of Experimental Psychology: General, 108,* 441–485.

Alloy, L. B., Abramson, L. Y., & Viscusi, D. (1981). Induced mood and the illusion of control. *Journal of Personality and Social Psychology, 41,* 1129–1140.

Altmann, G. T. M., Garnham, A., & Dennis, Y. (1992). Avoiding the garden path: Eye movements in context. *Journal of Memory and Language, 31,* 685–712.

Altmann, G., & Steedman, M. (1988). Interaction with context during human sentence processing. *Cognition, 30,* 191–238.

Anderson, J. R. (1976). *Language, memory, and thought.* Hillsdale, NJ: Lawrence Erlbaum Associates.

Anderson, J. R. (1978). Arguments concerning representations for mental imagery. *Psychological Review, 85,* 249–277.

Anderson, J. R. (1985). Ebbinghaus's century. *Journal of Experimental Psychology: Learning, Memory, and Cognition, 11,* 436–438.

Anderson, J. R., & Bower, G. H. (1973). *Human associative memory.* Washington, DC: Winston.

Anderson, M. C., Bjork, R. A., & Bjork, E. L. (1994). Remembering can cause forgetting: Retrieval dynamics in long-term memory. *Journal of Experimental Psychology: Learning, Memory, and Cognition, 20,* 1063–1087.

Andrade, J. (1995). Learning during anesthesia: A review. *British Journal of Psychology, 86,* 479–506.

Antrobus, J. S. (1970). *Cognition and affect.* Boston: Little, Brown.

Arbuckle, T. Y., & Cuddy, L. L. (1969). Discrimination of item strength at time of presentation. *Journal of Experimental Psychology, 81,* 126–131.

Ashcraft, M. H. (1989). *Human memory and cognition.* Glenview, IL: Scott, Foresman.

Astington, J. W. (1988a). Children's understanding of the speech act of promising. *Journal of Child Language, 15,* 157–173.

Astington, J. W. (1988b). Children's production of permissive speech acts. *Journal of Child Language, 15,* 411–423.

Atkinson, R, C., & Raugh, M. R. (1975). An application of the mnemonic keyword method to the acquisition of a Russian vocabulary. *Journal of Experimental Psychology: Human Learning and Memory, 1,* 126–133

Atkinson, R. C., & Shiffrin, R. M. (1968). Human memory: A proposed system and its control processes. In K. W. Spence & J. T. Spence (Eds.), *The psychology of learning and motivation: Advances in theory and research* (Vol. 2). New York: Academic Press.

Averbach, E., & Coriell, A. S. (1961). Short-term memory in vision. *Bell System Technical Journal, 40,* 309–328.

Baddeley, A. D. (1966a). The influence of acoustic and semantic similarity on long-term memory for word sequences. *Quarterly Journal of Experimental Psychology, 18,* 302–309.

Baddeley, A. D. (1966b). Short-term memory for word sequences as a function of acoustic, semantic, and formal similarity. *Quarterly Journal of Experimental Psychology, 18,* 362–365.

Baddeley, A. D. (1986). *Working memory.* Oxford: Oxford University Press.

Baddeley, A. D. (1990). *Human memory: Theory and practice.* Needham Heights, MA: Allyn and Bacon.

Baddeley, A. D. (1993). Working memory or working attention? In A. Baddeley & L. Weiskrantz (Eds.), *Attention: Selection, awareness and control. A tribute to Donald Broadbent.* Oxford: Oxford University Press.

Baddeley, A. D. (1994). Working memory: The interface between memory and cognition. In D. Schacter & E. Tulving (Eds.), *Memory Systems 1994.* Cambridge, MA: MIT press.

Baddeley, A. D. (2000). The episodic buffer: A new component of working memory. *Trends in Cognitive Science, 4,* 417–423.

Baddeley, A. D., Grant, S., Wight, E., & Thomson, N. (1973). Imagery and visual working memory. In P. M. A. Rabbitt & S. Dornic (Eds.), *Attention and performance V.* London: Academic Press.

Baddeley, A. D., & Hitch, G. (1974). Working memory. In G. H. Bower (Ed.), *The psychology of learning and motivation* (Vol. 8). New York: Academic Press.

Baddeley, A. D., & Hitch, G. J. (1977). Recency reexamined. In S. Dornic (Ed.), *Attention and Performance, 6,* 647–667. Hillsdale, NJ: Lawrence Erlbaum Associates.

Boddely, A. D., Lewis, V. J., & Vallar, G. (1984). Exploring the articulatory loop. *Quarterly Journal of Experimental Psychology, 36,* 233–252.

Baddeley, A. D., Papagno, C., & Vallar, G. (1988). When long-term learning depends on short-term storage. *Journal of Memory and Language, 27,* 586–595.

Baddeley, A. D., & Warrington, E. K. (1970). Amnesia and the distinction between long- and short-term memory. *Journal of Verbal Learning and Verbal Behavior, 9,* 176–189.

Bahrick, H. P. (1984). Semantic memory content in permastore: Fifty years of learning and memory. *Journal of Experimental Psychology: General, 113,* 1–127.

Bahrick, H. P., Bahrick, P. O., & Wittlinger, R. P. (1975). Fifty years of memory for names and faces: A cross-sectional approach. *Journal of Experimental Psychology: General, 104,* 54–75.

Bahrick, H. P., & Hall, L. K. (1991). Lifetime maintenance of high school mathematics content. *Journal of Experimental Psychology: General, 120,* 20–33.

Balota, D. A., Dolan, P. O., & Duchek, J. M. (2000). Memory changes in healthy older adults. In E. Tulving and F. I. M. Craik (Eds.), *The Oxford Encyclopedia of Memory.* New York: Oxford University Press.

Barkley, R. A. (1997). *ADHD and the nature of self-control.* New York: Guilford Press.

Barnes, J. M., & Underwood, B. J. (1959). "Fate" of first-list associates in transfer theory. *Journal of Experimental Psychology, 58,* 97–105.

Barsalou, L. W. (1982). Context-independent and context-dependent information in concepts. *Memory and Cognition, 10,* 82–93.

Barsalou, L. W. (1983). Ad hoc categories. *Memory and Cognition, 11,* 211–227.

Barsalou, L. W., & Medin, D. L. (1986). Concepts: Static definitions or context-dependent representations? *Cahiers de Psychologie Cognitive, 6*(2), 187–202.

Barsalou, L. W., & Sewell, D. R. (1984). Constructing representations of categories from different points of view. In *Emory Cognition Project Report No. 2.* Atlanta, GA: Emory University.

Bartlett, F. C. (1932). *Remembering: An experimental and social study.* Cambridge: Cambridge University Press.

Bartlett, J. C., Burleson, G., & Santrock, J. W. (1982). Emotional mood and memory in young children. *Journal of Experimental Child Psychology, 34.* 59–76.

Basden, B. H., Basden, D. R., & Gargano, G. J. (1993). Directed forgetting in implicit and explicit memory tests: A comparison of methods. *Journal of Experimental Psychology: Learning, Memory, and Cognition, 19,* 603–616.

Bauer, R. M. (1993). Agnosia. In K. M. Heilman & E. Valenstein (Eds.), *Clinical neuropsychology* (3rd ed., pp. 215–278). New York: Oxford University Press.

Bayles, K. A., & Kaszniak, A. W. (1987). *Communication and cognition in normal aging and dementia.* Austin, TX: Pro-Ed Press.

Beck, A. T. (1967). *Depression: Clinical, experimental, and theoretical aspects.* New York: Harper & Row.

Beck, A. T., Rush, A. J., Shaw, B. S., & Emery, G. (1979). *Cognitive therapy of depression.* New York: Guilford.

Beck, R. C., & McBee, W. (1995). Mood-dependent memory for generated and repeated words: Replication and extension. *Cognition and Emotion, 9,* 289–307.

Begg, I. (1978). Similarity and contrast in memory for relations. *Memory and Cognition, 6,* 509–517.

Begg, I., Duft, S., Lalonde, P., Melnick, R., & Sanvito, J. (1989). Memory predictions are based on ease of processing. *Journal of Memory and Language, 28,* 610–632.

Begg, I., & Snider, A. (1987). The generation effect: Evidence for generalized inhibition. *Journal of Experimental Psychology: Learning, Memory, & Cognition, 13,* 553–563.

Benjamin, A. S., Bjork, R. A., & Schwartz, B. L. (1998). The mismeasure of memory: When retrieval fluency is misleading as a metacognitive index. *Journal of Experimental Psychology: General, 127,* 55–68.

Berkerian, D. A., & Bowers, J. M. (1983). Eyewitness testimony: Were we misled? *Journal of Experimental Psychology: Human Learning and Memory, 9,* 139–145.

Berkerian, D. A., & Goodrich, S. J. (1999). Forensic applications of theories of cognition and emotion. In T. Dagleish & M. J. Power (Eds.), *Handbook of cognition and emotion.* Chichester: John Wiley and Sons.

Bernbach, H. A. (1975). Rate of presentation in free recall: A problem for two-stage memory theory. *Journal of Experimental Psychology: Human Learning and Memory, 1,* 18–22.

Berndt, R. S., & Caramazza, A. (1980). A redefinition of the syndrome of Broca's aphasia: Implications for neuropsychological models of language. *Applied Psycholinguistics, 1,* 225–278.

Bernicot, J., & Laval, V. (1996). Promises in French children: Comprehension and metapragmatic knowledge. *Journal of Pragmatics, 25,* 101–122.

Besner, D., Stolz, J. A., & Boutilier, C. (1997). The Stroop effect and the myth of automaticity. *Psychonomic Bulletin & Review, 4,* 221–225.

Biederman, I. (1987). Recognition by components: A theory of human image understanding. *Psychological Review, 94,* 115–147.

Biederman, I. (1990). Higher-level vision. In D. N. Osherson, S. M. Kosslyn, & J. M. Hollerback (Eds.), *Visual cognition and action: An invitation to cognitive science.* Cambridge, MA: MIT Press.

Biederman, I., Ju, G., & Clapper, J. (1985). *The perception of partial objects.* Unpublished manuscript (as referenced in Biederman, 1987).

Bierwisch, M. (1970). Semantics. In J. Lyons (Ed.), *New horizons in linguistics.* Baltimore: Penguin Books.

Bisanz, G. L., Vesonder, G. T., & Voss, J. F. (1978). Knowledge of one's own responding and the relation of such knowledge to learning. *Journal of Experimental Child Psychology, 25,* 116–128.

Bjork, R. A. (1970). Positive forgetting: The noninterference of items intentionally forgotten. *Journal of Verbal Learning and Verbal Behavior, 9,* 255–268.

Bjork, R. A. (1989). Retrieval inhibition as an adaptive mechanism in human memory. In H. L. Roediger & F. I. M. Craik (Eds.), *Varieties of human memory and consciousness: Essays in honor of Endel Tulving.* Hillsdale, NJ: Lawrence Erlbaum Associates.

Bjork, R. A., & Richardson-Klavehn, A. (1989). On the puzzling relationship between environmental context and human memory. In C. Izawa (Ed.), *Current issues in cognitive processes.* Hillsdale, NJ: Lawrence Erlbaum Associates.

Blaney, P. (1986). Affect and memory: A review. *Psychological Bulletin, 99,* 229–246.

Blaxton, T. A. (1989). Investigating dissociations among memory measures: Support for a transfer-appropriate processing framework. *Journal of Experimental Psychology: Learning, Memory, & Cognition, 15,* 657–668.

Blaxton, T. A., Bookheimer, S. Y., Zeffiro, T. A., Figlozzi, C. M., Gaillard, W. D., & Theodore, W. H. (1996). Functional mapping of human memory using PET: Comparisons of conceptual and perceptual tasks. *Canadian Journal of Experimental Psychology, 50,* 42–56.

Blumenthal, A. L. (1975). A reappraisal of Wilhelm Wundt. *American Psychologist, 30,* 1081–1088.

Bohannon, J. N. (1988). Flashbulb memories for the space shuttle disaster: A tale of two stories. *Cognition, 29,* 179–196.

Bousfield, W. A. (1953). The occurrence of clustering in recall of randomly arranged associates. *Journal of General Psychology, 49,* 229–273.

Bower, G. H. (1970). Organizational factors in memory. *Cognitive Psychology, 1,* 18–46.

Bower, G. H. (1981). Mood and memory. *American Psychologist, 36,* 129–148.

Bower, G. H., & Cohen, P. R. (1982). Emotional influences in memory and thinking: Data and theory. In S. Fiske & M. Clark (Eds.), *Affect and social cognition.* Hillsdale, NJ: Lawrence Erlbaum Associates.

Bower, G. H., & Forgas, J. P. (2001). Mood and social memory. In J. P. Forgas (Ed.), *Handbook of affect and social cognition.* Mahwah, NJ: Erlbaum.

Bower, G. H., Gilligan, S. G., & Monteiro, K. P. (1981). Selectivity of learning caused by affective states. *Journal of Experimental Psychology, 110,* 451–473.

Bower, G. H., & Karlin, M. B. (1974). Depth of processing pictures of faces and recognition memory. *Journal of Experimental Psychology, 103,* 751–757.

Bower, G. H., & Mayer, J. D. (1989). In search of mood-dependent memory. In D. Kuiken (Ed.), Mood and memory: Theory, research, and applications [Special Issue]. *Journal of Social Behavior and Personality, 4*(2), 121–156.

Bower, G. H., Monteiro, K. P., & Gilligan, S. G. (1978). Emotional mood as a context of learning and recall. *Journal of Verbal Learning and Verbal Behavior, 17,* 573–585.

Bower, G. H., Thompson-Schill, S., & Tulving, E. (1994). Reducing retroactive interference: An interference analysis. *Journal of Experimental Psychology: Learning, Memory, and Cognition, 20,* 51–66.

Bowers, J., & Schacter, D. L. (1993). Priming of novel in amnesic patients: Issues and data. In P. Graf & M. M. Masson (Eds.), *Implicit memory: New directions in cognition, development, and neuropsychology.* Hillsdale, NJ: Lawrence Erlbaum Associates.

Brainerd, C. J., Reyna, V. F., & Brandse, E. (1995). Are children's false memories more persistent than their true memories? *Psychological Science, 6,* 359–364.

Bradley, B., & Mathews, A. (1983). Negative self-schemata in clinical depression. British *Journal of Clinical Psychology, 22,* 173–181.

Bransford, J. D., & Franks, J. J. (1971). The abstraction of linguistic ideas. *Cognitive Psychology, 2,* 331–350.

Bransford, J. D., & Johnson, M. K. (1973). Consideration of some problems of comprehension. In W. G. Chase (Ed.), *Visual information processing.* New York: Academic Press.

Bransford, J. D., Barclay, J. R., & Franks, J. J. (1972). Sentence memory: A constructive versus interpretative approach. *Cognitive Psychology, 3,* 193–209.

Brewer, W. F., & Nakamura, G. V. (1984). The nature and function of schemas. In R. S. Wyer & T. K. Srull (Eds.), *Handbook of social cognition* (Vol. I). Hillsdale, NJ: Lawrence Erlbaum Associates.

Brigham, J. C., & Malpass, R. S. (1985). The role of experience and contact in the recognition of faces of own- and other-race persons. *Journal of Social Issues, 41,* 139–155.

Britton, B. K., & Tesser, A. (1982). Effects of prior knowledge on use of cognitive capacity in three complex cognitive tasks. *Journal of Verbal Learning and Verbal Behavior, 21,* 421-436.

Broadbent, D. E. (1958). *Perception and communication.* London: Pergamon Press.

Brooks, L. R. (1978). Non-analytic concept formation and memory for instances. In E. Rosch & B. Lloyd (Eds.), *Cognition and categorization.* Hillsdale, NJ: Lawrence Erlbaum Associates.

Brooks, L. R., Norman, G. R., & Allen, S. W. (1991). Role of specific similarity in medical diagnosis task. *Journal of Experimental Psychology: General, 120,* 278–287.

Brown, J. A. (1958). Some tests of the decay theory of immediate memory. *Quarterly Journal of Experimental Psychology, 10,* 12–21.

Brown, R. (1973). *A first language: The early stages.* Cambridge, MA: Harvard University Press.

Brown, R., & Kulik, J. (1977). Flashbulb memories. *Cognition, 5,* 73–99.

Brown, R., & Kulik,, J. (1982). Flashbulb memories. In U. Neisser (Ed.), *Memory observed: Remembering in natural contexts* (23–40). San Francisco: Freeman.

Bruyer, R., Laterre, C., Seron, X., Feyereisen, P., Strypstein, E., Pierrard, E., & Rectem, D. (1983). A case of prosopagnosia with some preserved covert remembrance of familiar faces. *Brain and Cognition, 2,* 257–284.

Buckner, R. L., Petersen, S. E., Ojeman, J. G., Miesin, F. M., Squire, L. R., & Raichle, M. E. (1995). Functional anatomical studies of explicit and implicit memory retrieval tasks. *Journal of Neuroscience, 15,* 12–29.

Buckner, R. L., & Wheeler, M. E. (2001). The cognitive neuroscience of remembering. *Nature Reviews Neuroscience, 2,* 624–634.

Bugelski, B. R., & Alampay, D. A. (1961). The role of frequency in developing perceptual sets. *Canadian Journal of Psychology, 15,* 205–211.

Butler, G., & Mathews, A. (1983). Cognitive processes in anxiety. *Advances in Behavior Therapy, 5,* 51–62.

Butterfield, E. C., Nelson, T. O., & Peck, V. (1988). Developmental aspects of the feeling of knowing. *Developmental Psychology, 24,* 654–663.

Cabeza, R., & Nyberg, L. (2000). Imaging cognition II: An empirical review of 275 PET and fMRI studies. *Journal of Cognitive Neuroscience, 12,*1–47.

Calvo, M. G., Eysenck, M. W. & Castillo, M. D. (1997). Interpretation bias in test anxiety: The time course of predictive inferences. *Cognition and Emotion, 11,* 43–63.

Calvo, M. G., Eysenck, M. W., & Estevez, A. (1994). Ego-threat interpretative bias in test anxiety: On-line inferences. *Cognition and Emotion, 8,* 127–146.

Cermak, L. S., Verfaellie, M., Butler, T., & Jacoby, L. L. (1993). Fluency versus conscious recollection in the word completion performance of amnesic patients. *Brain and Cognition, 20,* 367–377.

Chan, A. S., Butters, N., Salmon, D. P., & McGuire, K. A. (1993). Dimensionality and clustering in the semantic network of patients with Alzheimer's disease. *Psychology and Aging, 8,* 411–419.

Chase, W. G., & Simon, H. A. (1973). The mind's eye in chess. In W. G. Chase (Ed.), *Visual information processing.* New York: Academic Press.

Cherry, C. (1953). Some experiments on the recognition of speech with one and two ears. *Journal of the Acoustical Society of America, 23,* 915–919.

Chi, M. T. H., & Glaser, R. (1985). Problem solving ability. In R. J. Sternberg (Ed.), *Human abilities: An information processing approach.* New York: Freeman.

Chi, M. T. H., Glaser, R., & Rees, E. (1982). Expertise in problem solving. In R. J. Sternberg (Ed.), *Advances in the psychology of human intelligence* (Vol. 1). Hillsdale, NJ: Lawrence Erlbaum Associates.

Chiesi, H. L., Spilich, G. J., & Voss, J. F. (1979). Acquisition of domain-related information in relation to high- and low-domain knowledge. *Journal of Verbal Learning and Verbal Behavior, 18,* 257–273.

Chomsky, N. (1965). *Aspects of the theory of syntax.* Cambridge, MA: MIT Press.

Chomsky, N. (1975). *Reflections on language.* New York: Pantheon Books.

Chomsky, N. (1985). *Knowledge of language: Its nature, origin, and use.* New York: Praeger.

Christianson, K., Hollingworth, A., Halliwell, J. F., & Ferreira, F. (2001). Thematic roles assigned along the garden path linger. *Cognitive Psychology, 42,* 368–407.

Christianson, S. A. (1991). Emotional stress and eyewitness memory: A critical review. *Psychological Bulletin, 112,* 284–309.

Claparede, E. (1951). Recognitive and "me-ness." Translation in D. Rappaport (Ed.), *Organization and pathology of thought.* New York: Columbia University Press.

Clark, H. H., & Clark, E. V. (1977). *Psychology and language.* New York: Harcourt Brace Jovanovich.

Clark, M. S., & Isen, A. M. (1982). Toward understanding the relationship between affect and social behavior. In A. Hastorf & A. M. Isen (Eds.), *Cognitive social psychology.* New York: Elsevier/North Holland.

Clark, M. S., Milberg, S., & Ross, J. (1983). Arousal cues arousal-related material in memory: Implications for understanding effects of mood on memory. *Journal of Verbal Learning and Verbal Behavior, 22,* 633–649.

Cohen, A., & Ivry, R. (1989). Illusory conjunctions inside and outside the focus of attention. *Journal of Experimental Psychology: Human Perception and Performance, 15,* 650–663.

Cohen, A., & Rafal, R. D. (1991). Attention and feature integration: Illusory conjunctions in a patient with a parietal lobe lesion. *Psychological Science, 2,* 106–110.

Cohen, N. J., & Squire, L. R. (1980). Preserved learning and retention of pattern analyzing skill in amnesia: Association of knowing how and knowing that. *Science, 210,* 207–209.

Cohen, R. M., Weingartner, H., Smallberg, S. A., Pickar, D., & Murphy, D. L. (1982). Effort and cognition in depression. *Archives of General Psychiatry, 39,* 593–597.

Cole, R. A. (1979). Navigating the slippery stream of speech. *Psychology Today,* 77–87.

Cole, R. A. (1980). *Perception and production of fluent speech.* Hillsdale, NJ: Lawrence Erlbaum Associates.

Collins, A. M., & Loftus, E. F. (1975). A spreading activation theory of semantic processing. *Psychological Review, 82,* 407-428.

Collins, A. M., & Quillian, M. R. (1969). Retrieval time from semantic memory. *Journal of Verbal Learning and Verbal Behavior, 8,* 240–247.

Connor, L. T., Dunlosky, J., & Hertzog, C. (1997). Age-related differences in absolute but not relative metamemory accuracy. *Psychology and Aging, 12,* 50–71.

Connors, E. T., Lundregan, N. M., Miller, J. M., & McEwan, T. (1996). *Convicted by jurors, exonerated by science: Case studies in the use of DNA evidence to establish innocence after trial.* Washington, DC: U.S. Department of Justice, NCJ 161258.

Conrad, C. (1972). Cognitive economy in semantic memory. *Journal of Experimental Psychology, 92,* 149–154.

Conrad, F. G., & Rips, L. J. (1986). Conceptual combination and the given/new distinction. *Journal of Memory and Language, 25,* 255–278.

Conrad, R., & Hull, A. J. (1968). Input modality and the serial position curve in short-term memory. *Psychonomic Science, 10,* 135–136.

Conway, A. R. A., & Engle, R. W. (1994). Working memory and retrieval: A resource-dependent model. *Journal of Experimental Psychology: General, 123,* 354–374.

Corbetta, M., Miezen, F. M., Dobmey, S., Shulman., G. L., & Peterson, S. E. (1991). Selective and divided attention during visual discrimination of shape, color, and speed: Functional anatomy by positron emission tomography. *Journal of Neuroscience, 11,* 2383–2402.

Cooper, L. A., & Shepard, R. N. (1973). Chronometric studies of the rotation of mental images. In W. G. Chase (Ed.), *Visual information processing.* New York: Academic Press.

Costermans, J., Lories, G., & Ansay, C. (1992). Confidence level and feeling of knowing in question answering: The weight of inferential processes. *Journal of Experimental Psychology: Learning, Memory, & Cognition, 18,* 142–150.

Cowan, N. (1988). Evolving conceptions of memory storage, selective attention, and their mutual constraints within the human information processing system. *Psychological Bulletin, 104,* 163–191.

Cowan, N., Day, L., Saults, J. S., Keller, T. A., Johnson, T., & Flores, L. (1992). The role of verbal output time in the effects of word length on immediate memory. *Journal of Memory and Language, 31,* 1–17.

Craik, F. I. M., & Jacoby, L. L. (1979). Elaboration and distinctiveness in episodic memory. In L. Nilsson (Ed.), *Perspectives on memory research: Essays in honor of Uppsala University's 500th anniversary.* Hillsdale, NJ: Lawrence Erlbaum Associates.

Craik, F. I. M., & Lockhart, R. S. (1972). Levels of processing: A framework for memory research. *Journal of Verbal Learning and Verbal Behavior, 11,* 671–684.

Crowder, R. G. (1976). *Principles of learning and memory.* Hillsdale, NJ: Lawrence Erlbaum Associates.

Dalgleish, T., & Power, M. J. (1999). *Handbook of cognition and emotion.* Chichester: John Wiley and Sons.

Dalgleish, T., & Watts, F. N. (1990). Biases in attention and memory in disorders of anxiety and depression. *Clinical Psychology Review, 10,* 589–604

Damasio, A. R. (1989). Time-locked multi-regional retroactivation: A systems-level proposal for the neural substrates of recall and recognition. *Cognition, 33,* 25–62.

Daneman, M., & Carpenter, P. A. (1980). Individual differences in working memory and reading. *Journal of Verbal Learning and Verbal Behavior, 19,* 450–466.

Daniel, T. C. (1972). The nature of the effect of verbal labels on recognition memory for form. *Journal of Experimental Psychology, 96,* 152–157.

Danziger, K. (1979). The positivist repudiation of Wundt. *Journal of the History of the Behavioral Sciences, 15,* 205–230.

Darke, S. (1988). Anxiety and working memory capacity. *Cognition and Emotion, 2,* 145–154.

Darwin, C. T., Turvey, M. T., & Crowder, R. G. (1972). An auditory analogue of the Sperling partial report procedure: Evidence for brief auditory storage. *Cognitive Psychology, 3,* 255–267.

Dasgupta, N., & Greenwald, A. G. (2001). On the malleability of automatic attitudes: Combating automatic prejudice with images of admired and disliked individuals. *Journal of Personality and Social Psychology, 81,* 800–814.

Dasgupta, N., McGhee, D. E., Greenwald, A. G., & Banaji, M. R. (2000). Automatic preference for White Americans: Eliminating the familiarity explanation. *Journal of Experimental Social Psychology, 36,* 316–328.

Davis, G. A. (1973). *Psychology of problem solving: Theory and practice.* New York: Basic Books.

Deese, J. (1959). On the prediction of occurrence of particular verbal intrusions on immediate recall. *Journal of Experimental Psychology, 58,* 17–22.

Deffenbacher, K. A., & Loftus, E. F. (1982). Do jurors share a common understanding concerning eyewitness behavior? *Law and Human Behavior, 6,* 15–30.

DeGroot, A. M. B., Dannenburg, L., & Van Hell, J. G. (1994). Forward and backward translation by bilinguals. *Journal of Memory and Language, 33,* 600–629.

DeHaan, E. H. F., Young, A., & Newcombe, F. (1987). Face recognition without awareness. *Cognitive Neuropsychology, 4,* 385–415.

Dempster, F. N. (1996). Distributing and managing the conditions of encoding and practice. In E. L. Bjork & R. A. Bjork (Eds.), *Memory.* San Diego: Academic Press.

De Renzi, E., & Spinnler, H. (1967). Impaired performance on color tasks in patients with hemispheric lesions. *Cortex, 3,* 194–217.

Deutsch, J. A., & Deutsch, D. (1963). Attention: Some theoretical considerations. *Psychological Review, 70,* 80–90.

Devitt, M., & Sterely, K. (1989). *Language and reality.* Cambridge, MA: MIT Press.

Dodson, C. S., & Schacter, D. L. (2002). Aging and strategic retrieval processes: Reducing false memories with a distinctiveness heuristic. *Psychology and Aging, 17,* 405–415.

Dreyfus, H. L. (1979). *What computers can't do: The limits of artificial intelligence.* New York: Harper & Row.

Duffy, S. A., Morris, R. K., & Rayner, K. (1988). Lexical ambiguity and fixation times in reading. *Journal of Memory and Language, 27,* 429–446.

Duncker, K. (1945). On problem solving. *Psychological Monographs,* No. 270, *58.*

Dunlosky, J., & Connor, L. T. (1997). Age differences in the allocation of study time account for age differences in memory performance. *Memory & Cognition, 52,* 178–186.

Easterbrook, J. A. (1959). The effect of emotion on cue utilization and the organization of behavior. *Psychological Review, 66,* 183–201.

Ebbinghaus, H. (1885). On memory. (H. A. Ruger and C. E. Bussenius, Trans.). New York: Teachers' College, 1913. Paperback edition, New York: Dover, 1964.

Eddy, D. M. (1982). Probabilistic reasoning in clinical medicine: Problems and opportunities. In D. Kahneman, P. Slovic, & A. Tversky (Eds.), *Judgment under uncertainty: Heuristics and biases.* Cambridge: Cambridge University Press.

Eich, E. (2001). *Counter-points: Cognition and emotion.* New York: Oxford University Press.

Eich, J. E. (1980). The cue-dependent nature of state-dependent retention. *Memory and Cognition, 8,* 157–173.

Eich, J. E. (1989). Theoretical issues in state-dependent memory. In H. L. Roediger & F. I. M. Craik (Eds.), *Varieties of memory and consciousness* (pp. 331–354). Hillsdale, NJ: Lawrence Erlbaum Associates.

Eich, J. E., & Metcalf, J. (1989). Mood dependent memory for internal versus external events. *Journal of Experimental Psychology: Learning, Memory, and Cognition, 15,* 443–455.

Eichenbaum, H. (2002). *The cognitive neuroscience of memory: An introduction.* London: Oxford University Press

Einstein, G. O., & Hunt, R. R. (1980). Levels of processing and organization: Additive effects of individual item and relational processing. *Journal of Experimental Psychology: Human Learning and Memory, 6,* 588–598.

Einstein, G. O., & McDaniel, M. A. (1987). Distinctiveness and the benefits of bizarre imagery. In M.A. McDaniel & M. Pressley (Eds.), *Imagery and related mnemonic processes: Theories, individual differences, and applications* (pp. 78–102). New York: Springer-Verlag.

Ellis, H. C. (1968). Transfer of stimulus predifferentiation to shape recognition and identification learning: Role of properties of verbal labels. *Journal of Experimental Psychology, 78,* 401–409.

Ellis, H. C. (1973). Stimulus encoding processes in human learning and memory. In G. H. Bower (Ed.), *The psychology of learning and motivation* (Vol. 7). New York: Academic Press.

Ellis, H. C. (1978). *Fundamentals of human learning, memory, and cognition.* Dubuque, IA: Wm. C. Brown.

Ellis, H. C. (1986). *Emotional mood states and memory.* Presidential Address to the Division of Experimental Psychology, APA, Washington, DC.

Ellis, H. C. (1987). Recent developments in human memory. In V. P. Makosky (Ed.), *The G. Stanley Hall Lecture Series* (Vol. 7, pp. 159–206). Washington, DC: American Psychological Association.

Ellis, H. C. (2000, August). *Emotion, motivation, false memory, and false comprehension.* Paper presented at the C. Spielberger Symposium on Emotion, Motivation, and Personality, American Psychological Association, 2000, Washington, DC.

Ellis, H. C., & Ashbrook, P. W. (1988). Resource allocation model of the effects of depressed mood states on memory. In K. Fiedler & J. Forgas (Eds.), *Affect, cognition and social behavior.* Toronto: Hogrefe.

Ellis, H. C., & Ashbrook, P. W. (1991). The "state" of mood and memory research: A selective review. In D. Kuiken (Ed.), *Mood and memory: Theory, research, and applications.* Newbury Park, CA: Sage.

Ellis, H. C., Bennett, T. L., Daniel, T. C., & Rickert, E. J. (1979). *Psychology of learning and memory.* Monterey, CA: Brooks/Cole.

Ellis, H. C., & Daniel, T. C. (1971). Verbal processes in long-term stimulus recognition memory. *Journal of Experimental Psychology, 90,* 18–26.

Ellis, H. C., & Hertel, P. T. (1993). Cognition, emotion and memory: Some applications and issues. In C. Izawa (Ed.), *Cognitive psychology applied.* Hillsdale, NJ: Lawrence Erlbaum Associates.

Ellis, H. C., & Moore, B. A. (1999). Mood and memory. In T. Dalgleish & M. J. Power (Eds.), *Handbook of cognition and emotion.* Chichester: John Wiley and Sons.

Ellis, H. C., Moore, B. A. Varner, L. J., Ottaway, S. A., & Becker, A. S. (1997). Depressed mood, task organization, cognitive interference, and memory: Irrelevant thoughts predict memory. *Journal of Social Behavior and Personality, 9,* 363–382.

Ellis, H. C., Ottaway, S. C., Varner, L. J., Becker, A. S., & Moore, B. A. (1997). Emotion, motivation, and text comprehension: The detection of contradictions in passages. *Journal of Experimental Psychology: General, 126,* 131–136.

Ellis, H. C., Parente, F. J., Grah, C. R., & Spiering, K. (1975). Coding strategies, perceptual grouping, and the "variability effect" in free recall. *Memory and Cognition, 3,* 226–232.

Ellis, H. C., Thomas, R. L., McFarland, A. D., & Lane, J. W. (1985). Emotional mood states and retrieval in episodic memory. *Journal of Experimental Psychology: Learning, Memory, and Cognition, 11,* 363–370.

Ellis, H. C., Thomas, R. L., & Rodriguez, I. A. (1984). Emotional mood states and memory: Elaborative encoding, semantic processing, and cognitive effort. *Journal of Experimental Psychology: Learning, Memory, and Cognition, 10,* 470–482.

Ellis, H. C., Varner, L. J., Becker, A. S., & Ottaway, S. A. (1995). Emotion and prior knowledge in memory and comprehension of ambiguous stories. *Cognition and Emotion, 9,* 363–382.

Engle, R. W. (1995). Individual differences in memory and their implications for learning. In R. Sternberg (Ed.), *Encyclopedia of intelligence.* New York: MacMillan.

Engle, R. W. (2002). Working memory capacity as executive attention. *Current Directions in Psychological Science, 11,* 19–23.

Engle, R. W., Cantor, J., & Carullo, J. J. (1992). Individual differences in working memory and comprehension: A test of four hypotheses. *Journal of Experimental Psychology: Learning, Memory, and Cognition, 18,* 972–992.

Epstein, M. L., Phillips, W. D., & Johnson, S. J. (1975). Recall of related and unrelated word pairs as a function of processing level. *Journal of Experimental Psychology: Human Learning and Memory, 1,* 149–152.

Erdelyi, M. H. (1985). *Psychoanalysis: Freud's cognitive psychology.* New York: W. H. Freeman.

Evans, J. St. B. T. (1982). *The psychology of deductive reasoning.* London: Routledge and Kegan Paul.

Evans, J. St. B. T., Barston, J., & Pollard, P. (1983). On the conflict between logic and belief in syllogistic reasoning. *Memory & Cognition, 11,* 295–306.

Eysenck, M. W. (1979). Depth, distinctiveness, and elaboration. In L. Cermak & F. I. M. Craik (Eds.), *Levels of processing: An approach to memory.* Hillsdale, NJ: Lawrence Erlbaum Associates.

Eysenck, M. W. (1982). *Attention and arousal: Cognition and performance.* Berlin: Springer.

Eysenck, M. W. (1983). Anxiety and individual differences. In G. R. J. Hockey (Ed.), *Stress and fatigue in human performance.* Chichester: John Wiley & Sons.

Farah, M. J. (1995). The neural bases of mental imagery. In M. S. Gazzaniga (Ed.), *The cognitive neurosciences* (pp. 963–975). Cambridge, MA: MIT Press.

Farah, M. J. (2000). *The cognitive neuroscience of vision.* Malden, MA: Blackwell Publishers.

Farah, M. J., Hammond, K. L., Levine, D. N., & Calvanio, R. (1988). Visual and spatial mental imagery: Dissociable systems of representation. *Cognitive Psychology, 20,* 439–462.

Farah, M. J., Peronnet, F., & Weisberg, L. (1987, November 6–8). *Brain activity underlying mental imagery: An ERP study.* Paper presented at the annual meetings of the Psychonomic Society, Seattle, Washington.

Ferreira, F., & Clifton, C. (1986). The independence of syntactic processing. *Journal of Memory and Language, 25,* 348–368.

Ferreira, F., & Henderson, J. M. (1990). Use of verb information in syntactic parsing: Evidence from eye movements and word-by-word self-paced reading. *Journal of Experimental Psychology: Learning, Memory, and Cognition, 16,* 555–568.

Fiedler, K., & Forgas, J. (1988). *Affect, cognition, and social behavior.* Toronto: Hogrefe.

Fischhoff, B. (1982). Debiasing. In D. Kahneman, P. Slovic, & A. Tversky (Eds.), *Judgment under uncertainty: Heuristics and biases* (pp. 422–444). Cambridge: Cambridge University Press.

Flavell, J. H. (1979). Metacognition and cognitive monitoring: A new area of cognitive-developmental inquiry. *American Psychologist, 34,* 906–911.

Fodor, J. A., Garrett, M. F., Walker, E. C. T., & Parkes, C. H. (1980). Against defi-nitions. *Cognition, 8,* 263–367.

Foley, M. A., & Johnson, M. K. (1985). Confusions between memories for performed and imagined actions: A developmental comparison. *Child Development, 56,* 1145–1155.

Forgas, J. P. (1995). Mood and judgment: The affect-infusion model (AIM). *Psychological Bulletin, 117,* 1–28.

Forgas, J. P. (1999). Network theories and beyond. In T. Dalgleish & M. J. Power (Eds.), *Handbook of cognition and emotion.* Chichester: John Wiley and Sons.

Fouts, R., Fouts, D. & Schoenfield, D. (1984). Sign language conversational interaction between chimpanzees. *Sign Language Studies, 42,* 1–12.

Francik, E. P., & Clark, H. H. (1985). How to make requests that overcome obstacles to compliance. *Journal of Memory and Language, 24,* 560–568.

Frazier, L. (1987). Sentence processing: A tutorial review. In M. Coltheart (Ed.), *Attention and performance XII: The psychology of reading* (pp. 601–681). Hillsdale, NJ: Lawrence Erlbaum Associates.

Gage, D. F., & Safer, M. A. (1985). Hemispheric differences in the mood state-dependent effect for recognition of emotional faces. *Journal of Experimental Psychology: Learning, Memory, and Cognition, 11,* 752–763.

Gallo, D. A., Roberts, M. J., & Seamon, J. G. (1997). Remembering words not presented in lists: Can we avoid creating false memories? *Psychonomic Bulletin and Review, 3,* 208–214.

Garcia, J., & Koelling, R. A. (1966). Relation of cue to consequence in avoidance learning. *Psychonomic Science, 4,* 123–124.

Gardiner, J. M., Craik, F. I. M., & Bleasdale, F. A. (1973). Retrieval difficulty and subsequent recall. *Memory and Cognition, 1,* 213–216.

Gardner, B. T., & Gardner, R. A. (1969). Teaching sign language to a chimpanzee. *Science, 165,* 664–672

Gardner, R. A., & Gardner, B. T. (1975). Evidence for sentence constituents in the early utterances of child and chimpanzee. *Journal of Experimental Psychology: General, 104,* 244–267.

Garnsey, S. M., Pearlmutter, N. J., Myers, E., & Lotocky, M. A. (1997). The contributions of verb bias and plausibility to the comprehension of temporarily ambiguous sentences. *Journal of Memory and Language, 37,* 58–93.

Garry, M., Manning, G. C., Loftus, E. F., & Sherman, S. J. (1996). Imagination inflation: Imagining childhood event inflates confidence that it occurred. *Psychonomic Bulletin and Review, 3,* 208–214.

Gathercole, S., & Baddeley, A. D. (1990). Phonological deficits in language-disordered children: Is there a causal connection? *Journal of Memory and Language, 29,* 336–360.

Gazzaniga, M. S. (1970). *The bisected brain.* New York: Appleton-Century-Crofts.

Gazzaniga, M. S. (1977). Consistency and diversity in brain organization. *Annals of the New York Academy of Sciences, 299,* 415–423.

Gee, J. P., & Grosjean, F. (1983). Performance structures: A psycholinguistic and linguistic appraisal. *Cognitive Psychology, 15,* 411–458.

Geiselman, R. E., Bjork, R. A., & Fishman, D. L. (1983). Disrupted retrieval in directed forgetting: A link with posthypnotic amnesia. *Journal of Experimental Psychology: General, 112,* 58–72.

Gibbs, R. W. (1985). Situational conventions and requests. In J. P. Forgas (Ed.), *Language and social situations.* New York: Springer-Verlag.

Gibbs, R. W. (1986). What makes some indirect speech acts conventional? *Journal of Memory and Language, 25,* 181–196.

Gick, M. L., & Holyoak, K. J. (1980). Analogical problem solving. *Cognitive Psychology, 12,* 306–355.

Gick, M. L., & Holyoak, K. J. (1983). Schema induction and analogical transfer. *Cognitive Psychology, 15,* 1–38.

Gilewski, M. J., Zelinski, E. M., & Schaie, K. W. (1990). The memory functioning questionnaire for assessment of memory complaints in adulthood and old age. *Psychology and Aging, 5,* 482–490.

Gilligan, S. G., & Bower, G. H. (1984). Cognitive consequences of emotional arousal. In C. Izard, J. Kagan, & R. Zajonc (Eds.), *Emotions, cognitions, and behavior.* New York: Cambridge University Press.

Glanzer, M., & Cunitz, A. R. (1966). Two storage mechanisms in free recall. *Journal of Verbal Learning and Verbal Behavior, 5,* 351–360.

Glaser, R., & Chi, M. T. H. (1988). Overview. In M. T. H. Chi, R. Glaser, & M. J. Farr (Eds.), *The nature of expertise.* Hillsdale, NJ: Lawrence Erlbaum Associates.

Glisky, E. J., & Rabinowitz, J. C. (1985). Enhancing the generation effect through repetition of operations. *Journal of Experimental Psychology: Learning, Memory & Cognition, 11,* 193–205.

Goff, L. M., & Roediger, H. L. (1998). Imagination inflation for action events: Repeated imaginings lead to illusory recollections. *Memory & Cognition, 26,* 20–33.

Goggin, J. P., Thompson, C. P., Strube, G., & Simental, L. R. (1991). The role of language familiarity in voice identification. *Memory & Cognition, 19,* 448–458.

Goldman-Rakic, P. S. (1987). Circuitry of primate prefrontal cortex and regulation of behavior by representational memory. In F. Plum (Ed.), *Handbook of physiology, Section 1: The nervous system, Vol. V: Higher functions of the brain, Part 1* (pp. 373–417). Bethesda, MD: American Physiological Society.

Goldsmith, M., Koriat, A., & Weinberg-Eliezer, A. (2002). Strategic regulation of grain size memory reporting. *Journal of Experimental Psychology: General, 131,* 73–95.

Goldstein, D. B. (1983*). Changes in early memory content and verbal productivity after a depressed mood induction.* M. A. thesis, University of New Mexico.

Goodale, M. A., & Milner, A. D. (1992). Separate visual pathways for perception and action. *Trends in Neurosciences, 15,* 20–25.

Graesser, A. C., & Riha, J. R. (1984). An application of multiple regression techniques to sentence reading times. In D. Kieras & M. A. Just (Eds.), *New methods in reading comprehension research* (pp. 183–218). Hillsdale, NJ: Lawrence Erlbaum Associates.

Graf, P. (1980). Two consequences of generating: Increased inter- and intraword organization of sentences. *Journal of Verbal Learning and Verbal Behavior, 19,* 316–327.

Graf, P. (1990). Life-span changes in implicit and explicit memory. *Bulletin of the Psychonomic Society, 27,* 417–420.

Graf, P., Mandler, G., & Haden, P. E. (1982). Simulating amnesic symptoms in normal subjects. *Science, 218,* 1243–1244.

Graf, P., & Schacter, D. L. (1985). Implicit and explicit memory for new associations in normal and amnesic subjects. *Journal of Experimental Psychology: Learning, Memory, and Cognition, 11,* 501–518.

Graf, P., Squire, L. R., & Mandler, G. (1984). The information that amnesic patients do not forget. *Journal of Experimental Psychology: Learning, Memory, and Cognition, 10,* 164–178.

Greene, R. L., & Crowder, R. G. (1986). Recency effects in delayed recall of mouthed stimuli. *Memory and Cognition, 14,* 355–360.

Greenfield, P. M., & Smith, J. H. (1976). *The structure of communication in early language development.* New York: Academic Press.

Greeno, J. G. (1978). A study of problem solving. In R. Glaser (Ed.), *Advances in instructional psychology* (Vol. 1). Hillsdale, NJ: Lawrence Erlbaum Associates.

Greenwald, A. G., McGhee, D. E., & Schwartz, J. L. K. (1998). Measuring individual differences in implicit cognition: The implicit association task. *Journal of Personality and Social Psychology, 74,* 1464–1480.

Greenwald, A. G., Spangenberg, E. R., Pratkanis, A. R., & Eskenazi, J. (1991). Double-blind tests of subliminal self-help audiotapes. *Psychological Science, 2,* 119–122.

Grice, H. P. (1975). Logic and conversation. In P. Cole & J. L. Morgan (Eds.), *Syntax and semantics: 3. Speech acts.* New York: Academic Press.

Griggs, R. A., & Cox, J. R. (1982). The elusive thematic materials effect in Wasson's selection task. *British Journal of Psychology, 73,* 407–420.

Hacker, D. (1998). Definitions and empirical foundations. In D. J. Hacker, J. Dunlosky, & A. C. Graesser (Eds.), *Metacognition in educational theory and practice* (pp. 1–24). Hillsdale, NJ: Lawrence Erlbaum Associates.

Harris, R. J. (1977). Comprehension of pragmatic implications in advertising. *Journal of Applied Psychology, 62,* 603–608.

Hart, J. T. (1965). Memory and the feeling-of-knowing experience. *Journal of Educational Psychology, 56,* 208–216.

Hart, J. T. (1967). Memory and the memory-monitoring process. *The Journal of Verbal Learning and Verbal Behavior, 6,* 685–691.

Hasher, L., & Zacks, R. T. (1979). Automatic and effortful processes in memory. *Journal of Experimental Psychology: General, 108,* 356–388.

Hastorf, A. H., & Cantril, H. (1954). They saw a game: A case study. *Journal of Abnormal and Social Psychology, 49,* 129–134.

Hayes, J. R. (1981). *The complete problem solver.* Philadelphia: Franklin Institute Press.

Hebb, D. O. (1960). The American Revolution. *American Psychologist, 15,* 735–745.

Hedlund, S., & Rude, S. S. (1995). Evidence of latent depressive schemas in formerly depressed individuals. *Journal of Abnormal Psychology, 104,* 517–525.

Henle, M., & Michael, M. (1956). The influence of attitudes on syllogistic reasoning. *The Journal of Social Psychology, 44,* 115–127.

Herrmann, D. J. (1982). Know thy memory: The use of questionnaires to assess and study memory. *Psychological Bulletin, 92,* 434–452.

Hertel, P. T., & Hardin, T. S. (1990). Remembering with and without awareness in a depressed mood: Evidence of deficits in initiative. *Journal of Experimental Psychology: General, 119,* 45–59.

Hertel, P. T., & Milan, S. (1994). Depressive deficits in recognition: Dissociation of recollection and familiarity. *Journal of Abnormal Psychology, 103,* 736–742.

Hertel, P. T., & Narvaez, A. (1986). Confusing memories for verbal and nonverbal communication. *Journal of Personality and Social Psychology, 50,* 478–481.

Hertel, P. T., & Rude, S. S. (1991). Depressive deficits in memory: Focusing attention improves subsequent recall. *Journal of Experimental Psychology: General, 120,* 301–309.

Hertzog, C. (2002). Metacognition in older adults: Implications for application. In T. J. Perfect & B. L. Schwartz (Eds.), *Applied metacognition.* Cambridge: Cambridge University Press.

Hertzog, C., Dunlosky, J., Robinson, A. E., & Kidder, D. P. (2003). Encoding fluency is a cue used for judgments about learning. *Journal of Experimental Psychology: Learning, Memory, & Cognition, 29,* 22–34.

Hertzog, C., & Hultsch, D. F. (2000). Metacognition in adulthood and aging. In T. A. Salthouse & F. I. M. Craik (Eds.), *Handbook of aging and cognition II.* Mahwah, NY: Erlbaum.

Heuer, F., & Reisberg, D. (1990). Vivid memories of emotional events: The accuracy of remembered minutiae. *Memory & Cognition, 18,* 496–506.

Hockett, C. F. (1963). The problem of universals in language. In J. H. Greenberg (Ed.), *Universals of language.* Cambridge, MA: MIT Press.

Hogaboam, T. W., & Perfetti, C. A. (1975). Lexical ambiguity and sentence comprehension. *Journal of Verbal Learning and Verbal Behavior, 14,* 265–274.

Hogan, R. M., & Kintsch, W. (1971). Differential effects of study and test trials on long-term recognition and recall. *Journal of Verbal Learning and Verbal Behavior, 10,* 562–567.

Holyoak, K. J. (1985). The pragmatics of analogical transfer. In G. H. Bower (Ed.), *The psychology of learning and motivation* (Vol. 19, pp. 59–87). Orlando: Academic Press.

Holyoak, K. J., & Koh, K. (1987). Surface and structural similarity in analogical transfer. *Memory and Cognition, 15,* 332–340.

Hubel, D. H., & Wiesel, T. N. (1962). Receptive fields, binocular interaction, and functional architecture in the cat's visual cortex. *Journal of Physiology, 160,* 106–154.

Hunt, E. B. (1962). *Concept learning: An information-processing problem.* New York: Wiley.

Hunt, R. R. (1975). How similar are context effects in recognition and recall? *Journal of Experimental Psychology: Human Learning and Memory, 1,* 530–537.

Hunt, R. R. (1976). List context effects: Inaccessibility or indecision? *Journal of Experimental Psychology: Human Learning and Memory, 2,* 423–430.

Hunt, R. R., & Einstein, G. O. (1981). Relational and item-specific information in memory. *Journal of Verbal Learning and Verbal Behavior, 20,* 497–514.

Hunt, R. R., & Elliott, J. M. (1980). The role of nonsemantic information in memory: Orthographic distinctiveness effects upon retention. *Journal of Experimental Psychology: General, 109,* 49–74.

Hunt, R. R., Elliott, J. M., & Spence, M. J. (1979). Independent effects of process and structure on encoding. *Journal of Experimental Psychology: Human Learning and Memory, 5.* 339–347.

Hunt, R. R., & Ellis, H. C. (1974). Recognition memory and degree of semantic contextual change. *Journal of Experimental Psychology, 103,* 1153–1159.

Hunt, R. R., & McDaniel, M. A. (1993). The enigma of organization and distinctiveness. *Journal of Memory and Language, 32,* 421–445.

Hunt, R. R., & Mitchell, D. B. (1978). Specificity in nonsemantic orienting tasks and item specific information in memory. *Journal of Experimental Psychology: Human Learning and Memory, 4,* 121–135.

Hunt, R. R., & Mitchell, D. B. (1982). Independent effects of semantic and non-semantic distinctiveness. *Journal of Experimental Psychology: Learning, Memory, and Cognition, 8,* 81–87.

Hunt, R. R., & Smith, R. E. (1996). Accessing the particular from the general: The power of distinctiveness in the context of organization. *Memory & Cognition, 24,* 217–225.

Ingram, R. E. (1984). Toward an information-processing analysis of depression. *Cognitive Therapy and Research, 8,* 443–478.

Ingram, R. E. (1986). Processing of depressive and anxious information by depressive and anxious individuals. In P. H. Blaney (chair), *Mood and memory: Current research issues.* Symposium conducted at the meeting of the American Psychological Association, Washington, DC.

Isen, A. M. (1984). Toward understanding the role of affect in cognition. In R. S. Wyer & T. K. Srull (Eds.), *Handbook of social cognition.* Hillsdale, NJ: Lawrence Erlbaum Associates.

Izawa, C. (1989). *Current issues in cognitive processes.* Hillsdale, NJ: Lawrence Erlbaum Associates.

Izawa, C. (1993). *Cognitive psychology applied.* Hillsdale, NJ: Lawrence Erlbaum Associates.

Jacoby, L. L. (1983). Remembering the data: Analyzing interactive processes in reading. *Journal of Verbal Learning and Verbal Behavior, 22,* 485–508.

Jacoby, L. L. (1991). A process dissociation framework: Separating automatic from intentional uses of memory. *Journal of Memory and Language, 30,* 513–541.

Jacoby, L. L. (1999). Ironic effects of repetition: Measuring age-related differences on memory. *Journal of Experimental Psychology: Learning, Memory, Cognition, 25,* 3–22.

Jacoby, L. L., & Brooks, L. R. (1984). Nonanalytic cognition: Memory, perception and concept learning. In G. H. Bower (Ed.), *The psychology of learning and motivation: Advances in research and theory* (Vol. 18). New York: Academic Press.

Jacoby, L. L., & Craik, F. I. M. (1979). Effects of elaboration of processing at encoding and retrieval: Trace distinctiveness and recovery of initial context. In L. S. Cermak & F. I. M. Craik (Eds.), *Levels of processing in human memory* (pp. 1–22). Hillsdale, NJ: Lawrence Erlbaum Associates.

Jacoby, L. L., & Dallas, M. (1981). On the relationship between autobiographical memory and perceptual learning. *Journal of Experimental Psychology: General, 3,* 306–340.

Jacoby, L. L., & Hollingshead, A. (1990). Toward a generate/recognize model of performance on direct and indirect tests of memory. *Journal of Memory and Language, 29,* 433–454.

Jacoby, L. L., Kelley, C. M., & Dywan, J. (1989). Memory attributions. In H. L. Roediger & F. I. M. Craik (Eds.), *Varieties of memory and consciousness: Essays in honour of Endel Tulving* (pp. 391–422). Hillsdale, NJ: Lawrence Erlbaum Associates.

Jacoby, L. L., Toth, J. P., & Yonelinas, A. P. (1993). Separating conscious and unconscious influences of memory: Measuring recollection. *Journal of Experimental Psychology: General, 122,* 139–154.

Jacoby, L. L., & Witherspoon, D. (1982). Remembering without awareness. *Canadian Journal of Psychology, 32,* 300–324.

Jacoby, L. L., Woloshyn, V., & Kelley, C. M. (1989). Becoming famous without being recognized: Unconscious influences of memory produced by dividing attention. *Journal of Experimental Psychology: General, 118,* 115–125.

Jakobson, R., & Halle, M. (1956). *Fundamentals of language.* The Hague: Mouton.

James, W. (1890). *The principles of psychology.* Boston: Henry Holt.

Janowsky, J. S., Shimamura, A. P., & Squire, L. R. (1989). Memory and metamemory: Comparison between frontal lobe lesions and amnesic patients. *Psychobiology, 17,* 3–11.

Jenkins. J. G., & Dallenbach, K. M. (1924). Oblivescence during sleep and waking. *American Journal of Psychology, 35,* 605–612.

Johnson, M. K. (1988). Discriminating the origin of information. In T. F. Oltmans & B. A. Maher (Eds.), *Delusional beliefs: Interdisciplinary perspectives* (pp. 34–65). New York: John Wiley & Sons.

Johnson, N. F. (1986). On looking at letters within words: Do we "see" them in memory? *Journal of Memory and Language, 25,* 558–570.

Johnson-Laird, P. M. (1988). *The computer and the mind: An introduction to cognitive science.* Cambridge, MA: Harvard University Press.

Johnson-Laird, P. N., & Steedman, M. (1978). The psychology of syllogisms. *Cognitive Psychology, 10,* 64–99.

Johnston, W. A., Greenberg, S., Fisher, R., & Martin, D. (1970). Divided attention: A vehicle for monitoring memory processes. *Journal of Experimental Psychology, 83,* 164–171.

Jones, H. E. (1923–1924). The effects of examination on the permanence of learning. *Archives of Psychology, 10,* 21–70.

Juslin, P., Winman, A., & Olsson, H. (2000). Naive empiricism and dogmatism in confidence research: A critical examination of the hard-easy effect. *Psychological Review, 107,* 384–396.

Just, M. A., & Carpenter, P. A. (1984). Using eye fixations to study reading comprehension. In D. Kieras & M. A. Just (Eds.), *New methods in reading comprehension research* (pp. 151–182). Hillsdale, NJ: Lawrence Erlbaum Associates.

Just, M. A., & Carpenter, P. A. (1987). *The psychology of reading and language comprehension.* Boston: Allyn and Bacon.

Kahneman, D. (1973). *Attention and effort.* Englewood Cliffs, NJ: Prentice-Hall.

Kahneman, D., & Henik, A. (1981). Perceptual organization and attention. In M. Kubovy & J. R. Pomerantz (Eds.), *Perceptual organization.* Hillsdale, NJ: Lawrence Erlbaum Associates.

Kahneman, D., & Triesman, A. (1984). Changing views of attention and automaticity. In R. Parasuraman & D. R. Davies (Eds.), *Varieties of attention.* New York: Academic Press.

Kahneman, D., & Tversky, A. (1973). On the psychology of prediction. *Psychological Review, 80,* 237–251.

Kane, M. J., Bleckley, M. K., Conway, A. R. A., & Engle, R. W. (2001). A controlled-attention view of working-memory capacity. *Journal of Experimental Psychology: General, 130,* 169–183.

Kane, M. J., & Engle, R. W. (2003). Individual differences in executive attention and the Stroop. *Journal of Experimental Psychology: General, 132,* 47–70.

Kapur, S., Craik, F. I. M., Jones, C., Brown, G. M., Houle, S., & Tulving, E. (1995). Functional role of prefrontal cortex in memory retrieval: A PET study. *Neuroreport, 6,* 1880–1884.

Kapur, S., Craik, F. I. M., Tulving, E., Wilson, A., Houle, S., & Brown, G. M. (1994). Neuroanatomical correlates of encoding in episodic memory: Levels of processing effect. *Procedures of the National Academy of Science, USA, 91,* 2008–2011.

Kapur, S., Rose, R., Liddle, P. F., Zipursky, R. B., Brown, G. M., Stuss, D., Houle, S., & Tulving, E. (1994). The role of the left prefrontal cortex in verbal processing: Semantic processing or willed action? *Neuroreport, 5,* 2193–2196.

Kassin, S. M., Ellsworth, P. C., & Smith, V. L. (1989). The "General Acceptance" of psychological research on eyewitness testimony. *American Psychologist, 44,* 1089–1098.

Kassin, S. M., & Wrightsman, L. S. (1988). *The American jury on trial: Psychological perspectives.* New York: Hemisphere Publishing Corp/Harper and Row Publishers, Inc.

Katz, J. (1972). *Semantic theory.* New York: Harper & Row.

Keenan, J. M., & Moore, R. E. (1979). Memory for images of concealed objects: A reexamination of Neisser and Kerr. *Journal of Experimental Psychology: Human Learning and Memory, 5,* 374–385.

Keinan, G., Friedland, N., & Arad, L. (1991). Categorization and integration: Effects of stress on the structuring of information. *Cognition and Emotion, 5,* 133–145.

Kelley, C. M., & Jacoby, L. L. (1996b). Memory attributions: Remembering, knowing, and feeling of knowing. In Reder L. M. (Ed.), *Implicit memory and metacognition* (pp. 287–307). Hillsdale, NJ: Lawrence Erlbaum Associates.

Kelley, C. M., & Lindsay, D. S. (1993). Remembering mistaken for knowing: Ease of retrieval as a basis for confidence in answers to general knowledge questions. *Journal of Memory and Language, 32,* 1–24.

Kennedy, M. R. T., & Yorkston, K. M. (2000). Accuracy of metamemory after traumatic brain injury: Predictions during verbal learning. *Journal of Speech, Language, & Hearing Research, 43,* 1072–1086.

Keppel, G., & Underwood, B. J. (1962). Proactive inhibition in short-term retention of single items. *Journal of Verbal Learning and Verbal Behavior, 1,* 153–161.

Keren, G. (1991). Calibration and probability judgments: Conceptual and methodological issues. *Acta Psychologica, 77,* 217–273.

Kerr, B. (1973). Processing demands during mental operations. *Memory and Cognition, 1,* 401–412.

Kerr, N. H. (1983). The role of vision in "visual imagery" experiments: Evidence from the congenitally blind. *Journal of Experimental Psychology: General, 112,* 265–277.

Kihlstrom, J. F. (1991). On what does mood-dependent memory depend? In D. Kuiken (Ed.), *Mood and memory.* Newbury Park, CA: Sage.

Kihlstrom, J. F. (1998). Exhumed memory. In S. J. Lynn & K. M. McConkey (Eds.), *Truth in memory.* New York: Guilford Press.

Kintsch, W. (1970). Models for free recall and recognition. In D. A. Norman (Ed.), *Models of human memory* (pp 333–370). New York: Academic Press.

Klein, I., Paradis, A. L., Poline, J. B., Kosslyn, S. M., & Le Bihan, D. (2000). Transient activity in the human calcarine cortex during visual-mental imagery: An event-related fMRI study. *Journal of Cognitive Neuroscience, 12* (Supplement 2), 15–23.

Klein, S. B., & Kihlstrom, J. F. (1986). Elaboration, organization, and the self-reference effect in memory. *Journal of Experimental Psychology: General, 115,* 26–38.

Klein, S. B., & Loftus, J. (1988). The nature of self-referent encoding: The contributions of elaborative and organizational processes. *Journal of Personality and Social Psychology, 55,* 5–11.

Klin, C. M., Murray, J. D., Levine, W. H., & Guzmán, A. E. (1999). Forward inferences: From activation to long-term memory. *Discourse Processes, 27,* 241–260.

Koriat, A. (1993). How do we know that we know? The accessibility model of the feeling of knowing. *Psychological Review, 100,* 609–639.

Koriat, A. (1995). Dissociating knowing and the feeling of knowing: Further evidence for the accessibility model. *Journal of Experimental Psychology: General, 124,* 311–333.

Koriat, A. (1997). Monitoring one's own knowledge during study: A cue-utilization approach to judgments of learning. *Journal of Experimental Psychology: General, 126,* 349–370.

Koriat, A., & Goldsmith, M. (1996). Monitoring and control processes in the strategic regulation of memory accuracy. *Psychological Review, 103,* 490–517.

Koriat, A., Goldsmith, M., & Pansky, A. (2001). Toward a psychology of memory accuracy. *Annual Review of Psychology, 51,* 481–537.

Koriat, A., & Levy-Sadot, R. (2001). The combined contributions of the cue-familiarity and accessibility heuristics to feelings of knowing. *Journal of Experimental Psychology: Learning, Memory, & Cognition, 27,* 34–53.

Koriat, A., Lichtenstein, S., & Fischhoff, B. (1980). Reasons for confidence. *Journal of Experimental Psychology: Human Learning and Memory, 6,* 107–118.

Kosslyn, S. M. (1995). Mental imagery. In S. M. Kosslyn & D. N. Osherson (Eds.), An invitation to cognitive science (Vol 2). Cambridge, MA: MIT Press.

Kosslyn, S. M., Ball, T. M., & Reiser, B. J. (1978). Visual images preserve spatial metric information: Evidence from studies of image scanning. *Journal of Experimental Psychology: Human Perception and Performance, 4,* 47–60.

Kosslyn, S. M., Pascual-Leone, A., Felician, O., Camposano, S., Keenan, J. P., Thompson, W. L., Ganis, W. L., Sukel, K. E., & Alpert, N. M. (1997). The role of area 17 in visual imagery: Convergent evidence from PET and rTMS. *Science, 284,* 167–170.

Kroll, J. F., & Sholl, A. (1992). Lexical and conceptual memory in fluent and nonfluent bilinguals. In R. J. Harris (Ed.), *Cognitive processes in bilinguals.* (pp. 191–204). Amsterdam: North-Holland.

Kuiken, D. (Ed.). (1989). Mood and memory: Theory, research, and applications [Special Issue]. *Journal of Social Behavior and Personality, 4*(2), 1–192.

Kuiken, D. (Ed.). (1991). *Mood and memory.* Newbury Park, CA: Sage.

Kuiper, N. A., MacDonald, M. R., & Derry, P. A. (1983). Parameters of a depressive self-schema. In J. Suls & A. G. Greenwald (Eds.), *Psychological perspectives on the self* (Vol. 2, pp. 191–217). Hillsdale, NJ: Lawrence Erlbaum Associates.

Kulhavy, R. W., Stock, W. A., Thorton, J. B., Hancock, T. E., & Hammrich, P. L. (1990). Written feedback: Response certitude and durability. *Contemporary Educational Psychology, 15,* 319–332.

Labov, W. (1973). The boundaries of words and their meanings. In C. J. N. Bailey & R. W. Shuy (Eds.), *New ways of analyzing variations in English.* Washington, DC: Georgetown University Press.

Lachman, R., Lachman, J. L., & Butterfield, E. C. (1979). *Cognitive psychology and information processing.* Hillsdale, NJ: Lawrence Erlbaum Associates.

Lakoff, G. (1987). *Women, fire, and dangerous things: What categories tell us about the nature of thought.* Chicago: University of Chicago Press.

Lazarus, R. S. (1991). Progress on a cognitive-motivational-relational theory of emotion. *American Psychologist, 46,* 819–834.

Le Bihan, D., Turner, R., Zeffiro, T. A., Cuenod, C. A., Jezzard, P., & Bonnerot, V. (1993). Activation of human primary visual cortex during visual recall: A magnetic resonance imaging study. *Proceedings of the National Academy of Sciences, 90,* 11802–11805.

Leight, K. A., & Ellis, H. C. (1981). Emotional mood states, strategies, and state-dependency in memory. *Journal of Verbal Learning and Verbal Behavior, 20,* 251–266.

Leonesio, R. J., & Nelson, T. O. (1990). Do different metamemory judgments tap the same underlying aspects of memory? *Journal of Experimental Psychology: Learning, Memory, and Cognition, 16,* 464–470.

Lesgold, A. M., Roth, S., & Curtis, M. B. (1979). Foregrounding effects in discourse comprehension. *Journal of Verbal Learning and Verbal Behavior, 18,* 291–308.

Lettvin, J. Y., Maturana, H. R., McCulloch, W. S., & Pitts, W. H. (1959). What the frog's eye tells the frog's brain. *Proceedings of the IRE, 47,* 1940–1951.

Levelt, W. J. M. (1989). *Speaking.* Cambridge, MA: MIT Press.

Levine, D. N., Warach, J., & Farah, M. J. (1985). Two visual systems in mental imagery: Dissociation of "what" and "where" in imagery disorders due to bilateral posterior lesions. *Neurology, 35,* 1010–1018.

Lhermitte, F. (1986). Human autonomy and the frontal lobes. Part II: Patient behavior in complex and social situations: The "Environmental Dependency Syndrome." *Annals of Neurology, 19,* 335–343.

Lhermitte, F., Pillon, B., & Serdaru, M. (1986). Human autonomy and the frontal lobes. Part I: Imitation and utilization behavior: A neuropsychological study of 75 patients. *Annals of Neurology, 19,* 326–334.

Lichtenstein, S., & Fischhoff, B. (1977). Do those who know more also know more of how much they know? The calibration of probability judgments. *Journal of Experimental Psychology: Learning, Memory, and Cognition, 16,* 464–470.

Lichtenstein, S., Fischhoff, B., & Phillips, L. D. (1977). Calibration of probabilities: The state of the art. In H. Jungermann & G. deZeeuw (Eds.), *Decision making and change in human affairs.* Amsterdam: D. Reidel.

Light, L., & Carter-Sobell, L. (1970). Effects of changed semantic context on recognition memory. *Journal of Verbal Learning and Verbal Behavior, 9,* 1–12.

Lin, L. M., & Zabrucky, K. M. (1998). Calibration of comprehension: Research and implications for education and instruction. *Contemporary Educational Psychology, 23,* 345–391.

Loeterman, B. (Producer). (1997). What Jennifer saw. In *Frontline.* New York and Washington, DC: Public Broadcasting Service.

Loftus, E. F. (1986). Experimental psychologist as an advocate or impartial educator. *Law and Human Behavior, 10,* 63–78.

Loftus, E. F. (1997). Creating false memories. *Scientific American, 277,* 71–75.

Loftus, E. F., & Burns, T. (1982). Mental shock can produce retrograde amnesia. *Memory & Cognition, 10,* 318–323.

Loftus, E. E., & Ketcham, K. (1991). *Witness for the defense.* New York: St. Martin's Press.

Loftus, E. F., & Loftus, G. R. (1980). On the permanence of stored information in the human brain. *American Psychologist, 35,* 409–420.

Loftus, E. F., Miller, D. G., & Burns, H. J. (1978). Semantic integration of verbal information into a visual memory. *Journal of Experimental Psychology: Human Learning and Memory, 4,* 19–31.

Loftus, E. F., & Palmer, J. C. (1974). Reconstruction of automobile destruction: An example of the interaction between language and memory. *Journal of Verbal Learning and Verbal Behavior, 13,* 585–589.

Logan, G. D. (1988). Toward an instance theory of automatization. *Psychological Review, 95,* 492–527.

Logie, R. H., & Baddeley, H. D. (1987). Cognitive processes in counting. *Journal of Experimental Psychology: Learning, Memory, & Cognition, 13,* 310–326.

Lucas, M. (1999). Context effects in lexical access: A meta-analysis. *Memory & Cognition, 27,* 385–398.

Luchins, A. S. (1942). Mechanization in problem solving. *Psychological Monographs, 54* (6, Whole No. 248).

Luck, S. J., & Vecura, S. P. (2002). Attention. In H. Pashler & S. Yantis (Eds.), *Steven's handbook of experimental psychology, Vol. 1: Sensation and perception* (pp. 235–286). New York: John Wiley & Sons.

MacDonald, M. C., Pearlmutter, N. J., & Seidenberg, M. S. (1994). Lexical nature of syntactic ambiguity resolution. *Psychological Review, 101,* 676–703.

Macrae, C. N., & Rosevare, T. A. (2002). I was always on my mind: The self and temporary forgetting. *Psychonomic Bulletin and Review, 9,* 611–614.

Maki, R. (1998). Test predictions over text material. In D. J. Hacker, J. Dunlosky, & A. C. Graesser (Eds.), *Metacognition in educational theory and practice* (pp. 117–145). Hillsdale, NJ: Lawrence Erlbaum Associates.

Mandler, G. (1967). Organization and memory. In K. W. Spence & J. T. Spence (Eds.), *The psychology of learning and motivation* (Vol. 1). New York: Academic Press.

Mandler, G. (1975). *Mind and emotion.* New York: Wiley.

Mantyla, T. (1986). Optimizing cue effectiveness: Recall of 500 and 600 incidentally learned words. *Journal of Experimental Psychology: Learning, Memory, and Cognition, 12,* 66–71.

Marcel, A. J. (1980). Conscious and preconscious recognition of polysemous words: Locating the selective effects of prior verbal context. In R. S. Nickerson (Ed.), *Attention and performance VIII.* Hillsdale, NJ: Lawrence Erlbaum Associates.

Marcus, S. L., & Rips, L. J. (1979). Conditional reasoning. *Journal of Verbal Learning and Verbal Behavior, 18,* 199–223.

Marschark, M. (1979). The syntax and semantics of comprehension. In G. Prideaux (Ed.), *Perspectives on experimental linguistics.* Amsterdam: John Benjamins.

Marschark, M., Everhart, V. S., Martin, J., & West, S. A. (1987). Identifying linguistic creativity in deaf and hearing children. *Metaphor and Symbolic Activity, 2,* 281–306.

Marschark, M., West, S. A., Nall, L., & Everhart, V. S. (1986). Development of creative linguistic devices in signed and oral production. *Journal of Experimental Child Psychology, 41,* 534–550.

Martin, A., & Fedio, P. (1983). Word production and comprehension in Alzheimer's disease: The breakdown of semantic knowledge. *Brain and Language, 19,* 124–141.

Massaro, D. W. (1975). *Experimental psychology and information processing.* Chicago: Rand McNally.

Mathews, A. (1996). Selective encoding of emotional information. In D. Herrmann, C. McEvoy, P. Hertel, & M. K. Johnson (Eds.), *Basic and applied memory research: Practical applications,* Vol. 2, Mahwah. NJ: Lawrence Erlbaum Associates.

Mathews, A., & MacLeod, C. (1994) Cognitive approaches to emotion and emotional disorder. *Annual Review of Psychology, 45,* 25–50.

Matt, G. E., Vasquez, C., & Campbell, W. K. (1992). Mood congruent recall of affectively toned stimuli: A meta-analytic review. *Clinical Psychology Review, 12,* 227–255.

Mayer, J. D., & Bower, G. H. (1985). Naturally occurring mood and learning: Comment on Hasher, Rose, Zachs, Sanft, and Doren. *Journal of Experimental Psychology: General, 14,* 396–403.

Mayer, J. D., & Bower, G. H. (1986). Detecting mood-dependent retrieval. In P. H. Blaney (chair), *Mood and memory: Current research issues.* Symposium conducted at the meeting of the American Psychological Association, Washington, DC.

Mayer, R. E. (1992). *Thinking, problem solving, cognition* (2nd ed.). New York: Freeman.

Mazzoni, G., & Cornoldi, C. (1993). Strategies in study time allocation: Why is study time sometimes not effective? *Journal of Experimental Psychology: General, 122,* 47–60.

McCarthy, R. A., & Warrington, E. K. (1988). Evidence for modality specific meaning systems in the brain. *Nature, 334,* 428–430.

McCarthy, R. A., & Warrington, E. K. (1990). *Cognitive neuropsychology: A clinical introduction.* San Diego: Academic Press.

McClelland, J. L. (1987). The case for interactionism in language processing. In M. Coltheart (Ed.), *Attention and performance XII: The psychology of reading* (pp. 3–36). Hillsdale, NJ: Lawrence Erlbaum Associates.

McClelland, J. L., & Rumelhart, D. E. (1981). An interactive activation model of context effects in letter perception: Part 1. An account of basic findings. *Psychological Review, 88,* 375–407.

McClelland, J. L., Rumelhart, D. E., & Hinton, G. E. (1986). The appeal of parallel distributed processing. In D. E. Rumelhart & J. L. McClelland (Eds.), *Parallel distributed processing.* Cambridge, MA: MIT Press.

McCloskey, M., Egeth, H., & McKenna, J. (1986). The experimental psychologist in court: The ethics of expert testimony. *Law and Human Behavior, 10,* 1–13.

McCloskey, M., Wible, C. G., & Cohen, N. J. (1988). Is there a special flashbulb-memory mechanism? *Journal of Experimental Psychology: General, 117,* 171–181.

McCloskey, M., & Zaragoza, M. S. (1985). Misleading postevent information and memory for events: Arguments and evidence against memory impairment hypotheses. *Journal of Experimental Psychology: General, 114,* 1–16.

McDaniel, M. A., Einstein, G. O., DeLosh, E. L., May, C. P., & Brady, P. (1995). The bizarreness effect: It's not surprising, it's complex. *Journal of Experimental Psychology: Learning, Memory, and Cognition, 21,* 422–435.

McDaniel, M. A., & Masson, M. E. (1985). Altering memory representations through retrieval. *Journal of Experimental Psychology: Learning, Memory, and Cognition, 11,* 371–385.

McDaniel, M. A., Riegler, G. L., & Wadill, P. J. (1990). Generation effects in free recall: Further support for a three-factor theory. *Journal of Experimental Psychology: Learning, Memory, and Cognition, 16,* 789–798.

McDaniel, M. A., Waddill, P. J., & Einstein, G. O. (1988). A contextual account of the generation effect: A three-factor theory. *Journal of Memory and Language, 27,* 521–536.

McDermott, K. B. (1996). The persistence of false memories in list recall. *Journal of Memory and Language, 35,* 212–230.

McDougall, R. (1904). Recognition and recall. *Journal of Philosophical Psychology and Scientific Methods, 1,* 229–233.

McElroy, L. A., & Slamecka, H. J. (1982). Memorial consequences of generating nonwords: Implications for semantic memory interpretations of the generation effect. *Journal of Verbal Learning and Verbal Behavior, 21,* 249–259.

McGeoch, J. A. (1942). *The psychology of human learning.* New York: McKay.

McGlynn, S. M. (1998). Impaired awareness of deficits in a psychiatric context: Implications for rehabilitation. In D. J. Hacker, J. Dunlosky, & A. C. Graesser (Eds.), *Metacognition in educational theory and practice* (pp. 221–248). Hillsdale, NJ: Lawrence Erlbaum Associates.

McNeill, D. (1985). So you think gestures are nonverbal? *Psychological Review, 92,* 350–371.

Medin, D. L. (1989). Concepts and conceptual structure. *American Psychologist, 44,* 1469–1481.

Medin, D. L., & Schaffer, M. M. (1978). Context theory of classification learning. *Psychological Review, 85,* 207–238.

Medin, D. L., & Shoben, E. J. (1988). Context and structure in conceptual combination. *Cognitive Psychology, 20,* 158–190.

Melton, A. W., & Irwin, J. M. (1940). The influence of degree of interpolated learning on the retroactive inhibition and the overt transfer of specific responses. *American Journal of Psychology, 3,* 173–203.

Metcalfe, J. (1993). Novelty monitoring, metacognition, and control in a composite holographic associative recall model: Implications for Korsakoff amnesia. *Psychological Review, 100,* 3–22.

Metcalfe, J. (2002). Is study time allocated selectively to a region of proximal learning? *Journal of Experimental Psychology: General, 131,* 349–363.

Metcalfe, J., Schwartz, B. L., & Joaquim, S. G. (1993). The cue-familiarity heuristic in metacognition. *Journal of Experimental Psychology: Learning, Memory, and Cognition, 19,* 851–861.

Miller, G. A. (1956). The magical number seven, plus or minus two: Some limits on our capacity for processing information. *Psychological Review, 63,* 81–97.

Miller, G. A., Galanter, E., & Pribram, K. H. (1960). *Plans and the structure of behavior.* New York: Holt.

Miller, J. R., & Kintsch, W. (1980). Readability and recall of short prose passages: A theoretical analysis. *Journal of Experimental Psychology: Human Learning and Memory, 6,* 335–354.

Milner, B. (1970). Memory and the medial temporal regions of the brain. In K. H. Pribram D. E. Broadbent (Eds.), *Biology of memory.* New York: Academic Press.

Mitchell, D. B. (1993). Implicit and explicit memory for pictures: Multiple views across the life-span. In P. Graf & M. M. Masson (Eds.), *Implicit memory: New directions in cognition, development, and neuropsychology.* Hillsdale, NJ: Lawrence Erlbaum Associates.

Mitchell, D. B., & Brown, A. S. (1988). Persistent repetition priming in picture naming and its dissociation from recognition memory. *Journal of Experimental Psychology: Learning, Memory, & Cognition, 14,* 213–222.

Mitchell, D. B., Brown, A. S., & Murphy, D. R. (1990). Dissociations between procedural and episodic memory: Effects of time and aging. *Psychology and Aging, 5,* 264–276.

Mitchell, D. B., & Richman, C. L. (1980). Confirmed reservations: Mental travel. *Journal of Experimental Psychology: Human Perception and Performance, 6,* 58–66.

Mitchell, D. B., Hunt, R. R., & Schmitt, F. A. (1986). The generation effect and reality monitoring: Evidence from dementia and normal aging. *Journal of Gerontology, 41,* 79–84.

Mitchell, D. C. (1994). Sentence parsing. In M. A. Gernsbacher (Ed.), *Handbook of psycholinguistics* (pp. 375–409). San Diego: Academic Press.

Moates, D. R., & Schumacher, G. M. (1980). *An introduction to cognitive psychology.* Belmont, CA: Wadsworth.

Mogg, K., & Bradley, B. P. (1999). Selective attention and anxiety: A cognitive-motivational perspective. In T. Dalgleish & M. J. Power (Eds.), *Handbook of cognition and emotion.* Chichester: John Wiley and Sons.

Mogg, K., Bradley, B. P., & Hallowell, N. (1994). Attentional bias to threat: Roles of trait anxiety, stressful events. and awareness. *Quarterly Journal of Experimental Psychology, 47A,* 841–864.

Morgan, J. J. B., & Morton, J. T. (1944). The distortion of syllogistic reasoning produced by personal convictions. *Journal of Social Psychology, 20,* 39–59.

Morrell, R. W., Park, D. C., & Poon, L. W. (1989). Quality of instructions on prescription drug labels: Effects on memory and comprehension in young and old adults. *Gerontologist, 29,* 345–354.

Morris, C. D., Bransford, J. D., & Franks, J. J. (1977). Levels of processing versus test-appropriate strategies. *Journal of Verbal Learning and Verbal Behavior, 16,* 519–533.

Morrison, F. J., Giordani, B., & Nagy, J. (1977). Reading disability: An information processing analysis. *Science, 199,* 77–79.

Morrison, F. J. (1991). Learning (and not learning) to read. In L. Rieben & C. A. Perfetti (Eds.), *Learning to read: Basic research and its implications.* Hillsdale, N. J.: Lawrence Erlbaum Associates.

Moscovitch, M., Vriezen, E., & Goshen-Gottstein, G. (1993). Implicit tests of memory in patients with focal lesions or degenerative brain disorders. In F. Boller & J. Grafman (Eds.), *Handbook of neuropsychology* (pp. 133–173). Amsterdam: Elsevier.

Mountcastle, V. B. (1979). An organizing principle for cerebral function: The unit module and the distributed system. In F. O. Schmitt (Ed.), *The neurosciences: Fourth study program.* Cambridge, MA: MIT Press.

Mulligan, N. W. (1996). The effects of perceptual interference at encoding on implicit memory, explicit memory, and memory for source. *Journal of Experimental Psychology: Learning, Memory, and Cognition, 22,* 1067–1087.

Mulligan, N. W., & Stone, M. (1999). Attention and conceptual priming: Limits on the effects of divided attention in the category exemplar production task. *Journal of Memory and Language, 41,* 253–280.

Murphy, G. L., & Medin, D. L. (1985). The role of theories in conceptual coherence. *Psychological Review, 92,* 289–316.

Murray, D. J. (1966). Vocalization at presentation and immediate recall, with varying recall methods. *Quarterly Journal of Experimental Psychology, 18,* 9–18.

Myers, J. L., & O'Brien, E. J. (1998). Accessing the discourse representation during reading. *Discourse Processes, 26,* 131–157.

Nairne, J. S. (2002). Remembering over the short-term: The case against the activation model. *Annual Review of Psychology, 53,* 53–81.

Nasby, W. (1994). Moderators of mood congruent encoding: Self-/other reference and affirmative/non-affirmative judgment. *Cognition and Emotion, 8,* 259–278.

Needham, D. R., & Begg, I. M. (1991). Problem oriented training promotes spontaneous analogical transfer: Memory oriented training promotes memory for memory. *Memory & Cognition, 19,* 543–557.

Neisser, U. (1964). Visual search. *Scientific American, 210,* 94–107.

Neisser, U. (1967). *Cognitive psychology.* New York: Appleton-Century-Crofts.

Neisser, U. (1982). Snapshots or benchmarks? In U. Neisser (Ed.), *Memory observed* (pp. 43–48). San Francisco: Freeman.

Neisser, U. (2000). Remembering life experiences. In E. Tulving & F. I. M. Craik (Eds.), *The Oxford Handbook of Memory* (pp. 315–332). New York: Oxford University Press.

Neisser, U., & Harsch, N. (1992). Phantom flashbulbs: False recollections of hearing the news about the Challenger. In M. A. Conway, S. E. Gathercole, & C. Cornoldi (Eds.), *Theories of memory* (Vol. 2, pp. 9–31). New York: Cambridge University Press.

Neisser, U., & Harsch, N. (1993). False recollections on hearing news about the Challenger. In E. Winograd & U. Neisser (Eds.), *Affect and flashbulb memories*. New York: Cambridge University Press.

Neisser, U., & Kerr, N. (1973). Spatial and mnemonic properties of visual images. *Cognitive Psychology, 5,* 138–150.

Nelson, D. L., & McEvoy, C. L. (2000). What is this thing called frequency? *Memory & Cognition, 28,* 509–522

Nelson, D. L., McKinney, V. M., Gee, N. R., & Janczura, G. A. (1998). Interpreting the influence of implicitly activated memories on recall and recognition. *Psychological Review, 105,* 299–324.

Nelson, D. L., Walling, J. R., & McEvoy, C. L. (1979). Doubts about depth. *Journal of Experimental Psychology, Human Learning and Memory, 5,* 24–44.

Nelson, T. O. (1984). A comparison of current measures of the accuracy of feeling-of-knowing predictions. *Psychological Bulletin, 95,* 109–133.

Nelson, T. O., & Dunlosky, J. (1991). When people's judgments of learning (JOLs) are extremely accurate at predicting subsequent recall: The "Delayed-JOL Effect." *Psychological Science, 2,* 267–270.

Nelson, T. O., & Leonesio, R. J. (1988). Allocation of self-paced study time and the "labor-in-vain effect." *Journal of Experimental Psychology: Learning, Memory, and Cognition, 14,* 676–686.

Nelson, T. O., & Narens, L. (1990). Metamemory: A theoretical framework and new findings. In G. H. Bower (Ed.), *The psychology of learning and motivation* (Vol. 26, pp. 125–173). New York: Academic Press.

Nelson, T. O., & Narens, L. (1994). Why investigate metacognition? In J. Metcalfe, & A. J. Shimamura (Eds.), *Metacognition: Knowing about knowing* (pp. 1–26). Cambridge, MA: MIT Press.

Newell, A., & Simon, H. (1972). *Human problem solving.* Englewood Cliffs, NJ: Prentice-Hall.

Nickerson, R. S., Perkins, D. N., & Smith, E. E. (1985). *The teaching of thinking.* Hillsdale, NJ: Lawrence Erlbaum Associates.

Norman, D. A. (1968). Toward a theory of memory and attention. *Psychological Review, 75,* 522–536.

Norman, D. A., & Bobrow, D. G. (1975). On data-limited and resource-limited processes. *Cognitive Psychology, 7,* 44–64.

Norman, D. A., & Rumelhart, D. E. (1975). *Explorations in cognition.* San Francisco: Freeman.

Nosofsky, R. M. (1989). Further tests of an exemplar-similarity approach to relating identification and categorization. *Cognition and Psychophysics, 45,* 279–290.

Nyberg, L., Cabeza, R., & Tulving, E. (1996). PET studies of encoding and retrieval: The HERA model. *Psychonomic Bulletin & Review, 3,* 135–148.

O'Brien, E. J., & Albrecht, J. E. (1991). The role of context in accessing antecedents in text. *Journal of Experimental Psychology: Learning, Memory, and Cognition, 17,* 94–102.

O'Brien, E. J., Rizzella, M. L., Albrecht, J. E., & Halleran, J. G. (1998). Updating a situation model: A memory-based text processing view. *Journal of Experimental Psychology: Learning, Memory, and Cognition, 24,* 1200–1210.

O'Brien, E. J., & Myers, J. L. (1985). When comprehension difficulty improves memory for text. *Journal of Experimental Psychology: Learning, Memory, and Cognition, 11,* 12–21.

Onifer, W., & Swinney, D. A. (1981). Accessing lexical ambiguities during sentence comprehension: Effects of frequency of meaning and contextual bias. *Memory & Cognition, 9,* 225–236.

O'Reilly, R. C., & Rudy, J. W. (2000). Computational principles of learning in the neocortex and hippocampus. *Hippocampus, 10,* 389–397.

Otero, J. (1998). Influence of knowledge activation and context on comprehension monitoring of science texts. In D. J. Hacker, J. Dunlosky, & A. C. Graesser (Eds.), *Metacognition in educational theory and practice.* Hillsdale, NJ: Lawrence Erlbaum Associates.

Paivio, A. (1969). Mental imagery in associative learning and memory. *Psychological Review, 76,* 241–263.

Paivio, A. (1971). *Imagery and verbal processes.* New York: Holt.

Paivio, A. (1986). *Mental representations.* Oxford: Oxford University Press.

Paivio, A. (1995). Imagery and memory. *The cognitive neurosciences* (pp. 977–986). Cambridge, MA: MIT Press.

Paivio, A., & Begg, I. (1981). *Psychology of language.* Englewood Cliffs, NJ: Prentice-Hall.

Parkin, A. J. (1993). Implicit memory across the lifespan. In P. Graf & M. M. Masson (Eds.), *Implicit memory: New directions in cognition, development, and neuropsychology.* Hillsdale, NJ: Lawrence Erlbaum Associates.

Pashler, H. E. (1984). Processing stages in overlapping tasks: Evidence for a central bottleneck. *Journal of Experimental Psychology: Human Perception and Performance, 10,* 358–377.

Pashler, H. E. (1999). *The psychology of attention.* Cambridge, MA: MIT Press.

Pashler, H. E., & Johnston, J. C. (1989). Interference between temporally overlapping tasks: Chronometric evidence for central postponement with or without response grouping. *Quarterly Journal of Experimental Psychology, 41A,* 19–45.

Paulesu, E., Frith, C. D., & Frackowiak, R. S. J. (1993). The neural correlates of the verbal component of working memory. *Nature, 362,* 342–345.

Pellegrino, J. W. (1985). Inductive reasoning ability. In R. J. Sternberg (Ed.), *Human abilities: An information processing approach.* San Francisco: Freeman.

Pendergast, M. (1995). *Victims of memory: Incest accusations and shattered lives.* Hinesburg, VT: Upper Access Inc.

Penfield, W. (1959). Consciousness, memory, and man's conditioned reflexes. In K. Pribram (Ed.), *On the biology of learning.* New York: Harcourt, Brace, & World.

Perfetto, G. A., Bransford, J. D., & Franks, J. J. (1983). Constraints on access in a problem solving context. *Memory & Cognition, 19,* 24–31.

Perret, D. I., Rolls, E. T., & Caan, W. (1982). Visual neurons responsive to faces in the monkey temporal cortex. *Experimental Brain Reseach, 47,* 329–342.

Peters, R., & McGee, R. (1982). Cigarette smoking and state-dependent memory. *Psychopharmacology, 76,* 232–235.

Peterson, L. R., & Peterson, M. J. (1959). Short-term retention of individual verbal items. *Journal of Experimental Psychology, 58,* 193–198.

Peterson, S. E., Fox, P. T., Snyder, A. Z., & Raichle, M. E. (1990). Activation of extrastriate and frontal cortical areas by visual words and word-like stimuli. *Science, 249,* 1041–1044.

Peynircioglu, Z., & Tekcan, A. I. (1993). Word perception in two languages. *Journal of Memory and Language, 32,* 390–401.

Pillemer, D. (1993). Remembering personal circumstances: A functional analysis. In. E. Winograd & U. Neisser (Eds.), *Affect and accuracy in recall: The case of flashbulb memories.* New York: Cambridge University Press.

Pinker, F., & Prince, A. (1988). On language and connectionism: Analysis of a parallel distributed processing model of language acquisition. *Cognition, 28,* 73–193.

Pollack, I., & Pickett, J. M. (1963). The intelligibility of language from conversations. *Language and Speech, 6,* 165–171.

Posner, M. I., & Boies, S. J. (1971). Components of attention. *Psychological Review, 78,* 391–408.

Posner, M. I., & Keele, S. W. (1970). Retention of abstract ideas. Journal of Experimental Psychology, 83, 304–308.

Posner, M. I., & Snyder, C. R. R. (1975). Facilitation and inhibition in the processing of signals. In P. M. A. Rabbitt & S. Dornic (Eds.), *Attention and performance V* (pp. 669–682). New York: Academic Press.

Postman, L., & Underwood, B. J. (1973), Critical issues in interference theory. *Memory and Cognition, 1,* 19–40.

Premack, D. (1983). Animal cognition. *Annual Review of Psychology, 34,* 351–362.

Premack, D. (1971). Language in chimpanzee? *Science,172,* 808–822.

Pritchard, M. E., & Keenan, J. M. (1999). Memory monitoring in mock jurors. *Journal of Experimental Psychology: Applied. 5,* 152–168

Quillian, M. R. (1968). Semantic memory. In M. Minsky (Ed.), *Semantic information processing.* Cambridge, MA: MIT Press.

Quillian, M. R. (1969). The teachable language comprehender: A simulation program and theory of language. *Communications of the Association for Computing Machinery, 12,* 459–476.

Rayner, K., & Sereno, S. C. (1994). Eye movements in reading psycholinguistic studies. In M. A. Gernsbacher (Ed.), *Handbook of psycholinguistics* (pp. 57–81). San Diego: Academic Press.

Redelmeier, D. A., & Tibshirani, R. J. (1997). Association between cellular-telephone calls and motor vehicle collisions. *The New England Journal of Medicine, 336,* 453–458.

Reder, L. (1987). Strategy selection in question answering. *Cognitive Psychology, 19,* 90–138.

Reder, L. M., & Ritter, F. E. (1992). What determines initial feeling of knowing? Familiarity with question terms, not with the answer. *Journal of Experimental Psychology: Learning, Memory, and Cognition, 18,* 435–451.

Reed, S. K. (1972). Pattern recognition and categorization. *Cognitive Psychology, 3,* 382–407.

Reicher, G. M. (1969). Perceptual recognition as a function of meaningfulness of stimulus material. *Journal of Experimental Psychology, 81,* 275–280.

Reisberg, D., & Heuer, F. (in press). Remembering the details of emotional events. In G. Winograd & U. Neisser (Eds.), *Affect and accuracy in recall: The case of flashbulb memories.* New York: Cambridge University Press.

Reitman, J. S. (1971). Mechanisms of forgetting in short-term memory. *Cognitive Psychology, 2,* 185–195.

Reitman, J. S. (1974). Without surreptitious rehearsal, information in short-term memory decays. *Journal of Verbal Learning and Verbal Behavior, 13,* 365–377.

Reyna, V., & Titcomb, A. (1997). Constraints on the suggestibility of eyewitness testimony: A fuzzy-trace theory analysis. In D. Payne & F. Conrad (Eds.), *Intersections in basic and applied memory research.* Mahwah, NJ: Erlbaum.

Richman, C. L., Mitchell, D. B., & Reznick, J. S. (1979). Mental travel: Some reservations. *Journal of Experimental Psychology: Human Perception and Performance, 5,* 13–18.

Ricks, D. M. (1975). Vocal communication in preverbal normal and autistic children. In N. O'Connor (Ed.), *Language, cognitive deficits, and retardation.* London: Butterworth.

Riesenhuber, M., & Poggio, T. (2002). Neural mechanisms of object recognition. *Current Opinion in Neurobiology,12,*162–168.

Riesenhuber, M., & Poggio, T. (2000). Models of object recognition. *Nature Neuroscience, 3,*1199–1204.

Rinck, M., Glowalia, U., & Schneider, K. (1992). Mood-congruent and mood incongruent learning. *Memory and Cognition, 20,* 29–39.

Rips, L. J. (1983). Cognitive processes in propositional reasoning. *Psychological Review, 90,* 38–71.

Rips, L. J. (1994). *The psychology of proof.* Cambridge, MA: MIT Press.

Riskind, J. H. (1989). The mediating mechanisms in mood and memory: A cognitive-priming formulation. In D. Kuiken (Ed.), Mood and memory: Theory, research, and application. Special issue of *Journal of Social Behavior and Personality, 4,* 39–43.

Riskind, J. H. (1991). Will the field ultimately need a more detailed analysis of mood-memory? In D. Kuiken (Ed.), *Mood and memory,* Newbury Park, CA: Sage.

Robertson, L., Treisman, A., Friedman-Hill, S., & Grabowecky, M. (1997). The interaction of spatial and object pathways: Evidence from Balint's syndrome. *Journal of Cognitive Neuroscience, 9,* 295–317.

Robinson, D. N. (1986). Cognitive psychology and philosophy of mind. In T. J. Knapp & L. C. Robertson (Eds.), *Approaches to cognition: Contrasts and controversies* (pp. 1–12). Hillsdale, NJ: Lawrence Erlbaum Associates.

Roediger, H. L. (1990). Implicit memory: Retention without remembering. *American Psychologist, 45,* 1043–1056.

Roediger, H. L., Balota, D. A., & Watson, J. M. (2001). Spreading activation and the arousal of false memories. In H. L. Roediger, J. S. Nairne, I. Neath, & A. M. Suprenant (Eds.), *The nature of remembering: Essays in honor of Robert G. Crowder.* Washington, DC: American Psychological Association.

Roediger, H. L., & Blaxton, T. A. (1987). Retrieval modes produce dissociations in memory for surface information. In D. S. Gorfein & R. R. Hoffman (Eds.), *Memory, and learning: The Ebinghaus centennial conference* (pp. 349–379). Hillsdale, NJ: Lawrence Erlbaum Associates.

Roediger, H. L., & Craik, F. I. M. (Eds.). (1989). *Varieties of memory and consciousness.* Hillsdale, NJ: Lawrence Erlbaum Associates.

Roediger, H. L., & McDermott, K. B. (1995). Creating false memories: Remembering words not presented in lists. *Journal of Experimental Psychology: Learning, Memory, & Cognition, 21,* 803–814.

Roediger, H. L., Meade, M. M., & Bergman, E. T. (2001). Social contagion in memory. *Psychonomic Bulletin and Review, 8,* 365–371.

Roediger, H. L., & Weldon, M. S. (1987). Reversing the picture superiority effect. In M. A. McDaniel & M. Pressley (Eds.), *Imagery and related mnemonic processes: Theories, individual differences, and applications.* New York: Springer-Verlag.

Roediger, H. L., Weldon, M. S., & Challis, B. A. (1989). Explaining dissociations between implicit and explicit measures of retention: A processing account. In H. L. Roediger III & F. I. M. Craik (Eds.), *Varieties of memory and consciousness: Essays in honor of Endel Tulving* (pp. 3–41). Hillsdale, NJ: Lawrence Erlbaum Associates.

Rogers, T. B., Kuiper, N. A., & Kirker, W. S. (1977). Self-reference and the encoding of personal information. *Journal of Personality and Social Psychology, 35,* 677–688.

Roland, P. E., & Friberg, L. (1985). Location of cortical areas activated by thinking. *Journal of Neurophysiology, 53,* 1219–1243.

Rosch, E. (1975). Cognitive representations of semantic categories. *Journal of Experimental Psychology: General, 104,* 192–233.

Rosch, E., & Mervis, C. B. (1975). Family resemblances: Studies in the internal structure of categories. *Cognitive Psychology, 7,* 573–605.

Rosch, E. H., Mervis, C. B., Gray, W. D., Johnson, D. M., & Boyers-Braem, P. (1976). Basic objects in natural categories. *Cognitive Psychology, 8,* 382–439.

Ross, B. H., & Spalding, T. L. (1994). Concepts and categories. In R. Sternberg (Ed.), *Handbook of perception and cognition, Vol. 12. Thinking and problem solving* (pp. 119–148). San Diego: Academic Press.

Roth, E. M., & Shoben, E. J. (1983). The effect of context on the structure of categories. *Cognitive Psychology, 15,* 346–378.

Rothkopf, J. S., & Blaney, P. H. (1991). Mood-congruent memory: The role of affective focus and gender. *Cognition and Emotion, 5,* 53–64.

Rubens, A. B., & Benson, D. F. (1971). Associative visual agnosia. *Archives of Neurology, 24,* 305–317.

Rubin, D. C. (1977). Very long-term memory for prose and verse. *Journal of Verbal Learning and Verbal Behavior, 16,* 611–621.

Rubin, D. C. (1995). *Memory in oral traditions.* New York: Oxford University Press.

Rubin, D. C. (1996). Introduction. In D. C. Rubin (Ed.), *Autobiographical memory* (pp. 1–18). New York: Cambridge University Press.

Rubin, D. C., & Kozin, M. (1984). Vivid memories. *Cognition, 16,* 81–95.

Rubin, D. C., & Wallace, W. T. (1989). Rhyme and reason: Analyses of dual retrieval cues. *Journal of Experimental Psychology: Learning, Memory, & Cognition, 15,* 698–709.

Rubin, D. C., & Wenzel, A. (1996). One hundred years of forgetting: A quantitative description of retention. *Psychological Review, 103,* 734–760.

Rubin, D. C., Wetzler, S. E., & Nebes, R. D. (1986). Autobiographical memory across the lifespan. In D. C. Rubin (Ed.), *Autobiographical memory* (pp. 202–224). New York: Cambridge University Press.

Russell, P. N., & Beekhuis, M. E. (1976). Organization in memory: A comparison of psychotics and normals. *Journal of Abnormal Psychology, 85,* 527–534.

Sachs, J. (1967). Recognition memory for syntactic and semantic aspects of connected discourse. *Perception and Psychophysics, 2,* 437–442.

Salmon, D. P., & Butters, N. (1995). Neurobiology of skill and habit learning. *Current Opinion in Neurobiology, 5,* 184–190.

Samuel, A. G. (1987). Lexical uniqueness effects on phonemic restoration. *Journal of Memory and Language, 26,* 36–56.

Salame, P., & Baddeley, A. D. (1882). Disruption of short-term memory by unattended speech: Implications for the structure of working memory. *Journal of Verbal Learning and Verbal Behavior, 21,* 150–164.

Salmon, D. P., & Butters, N. (1995). Neurobiology of skill and habit learning. *Current Opinion in Neurobiology, 5,* 184–190.

Sanford, A. J., & Garrod, S. C. (1981). *Understanding written language: Explorations of comprehension beyond the sentence.* Chichester, England: Wiley.

Schacter, D. L. (1992). Understanding implicit memory: A cognitive neuroscience approach. *American Psychologist, 47,* 559–569.

Schacter, D. L. (1993). Amnesia observed: Remembering and forgetting in a natural environment. *Journal of Abnormal Psychology, 92,* 236–242.

Schacter, D. L., & Buckner, R. L. (1998). Priming and the brain. *Neuron, 20,* 185–195.

Schacter, D. L., Cooper, L. A., & Delaney, S. M. (1990). Implicit memory for unfamiliar objects depends on access to structural descriptions. *Journal of Experimental Psychology: General, 119,* 5–24.

Schacter, D. L., Coyle, J. T., Fischbach, G. D., Mesulam, M. M., & Sullivan, L. E. (1998). *Memory distortion: How minds, brains, and societies reconstruct the past.* Cambridge, MA: Harvard University Press.

Schacter, D. L., Harbluk, J. L., & McLachlan, D. R. (1984). Retrieval without recollection: An experimental analysis of source amnesia. *Journal of Verbal Learning and Verbal Behavior, 23,* 593–611.

Schacter, D. L., Israel, L., & Racine, C. A. (1999). Suppressing false recognition in younger and older adults: The distinctiveness heuristic. *Journal of Memory and Language, 40,* 1–24.

Schacter, D. L., Norman, K. A., & Koutstaal, W. (1998). The cognitive neuroscience of constructive memory. *Annual Review of Psychology, 49,* 289–318.

Schacter, D. L., Wagner, A. D., & Buckner, R. L. (2000). Memory systems of 1999. In E. Tulving & F. I. M. Craik (Eds.), *The Oxford handbook of memory.* New York: Oxford University Press.

Schneider, W., Visé, M., Lockl, K., & Nelson, T. O. (2000). Developmental trends in children's memory monitoring: Evidence from a judgment-of-learning (JOL) task. *Cognitive Development, 65,* 1546–1563.

Schrauf, R. W., & Rubin, D. C. (1998). Bilingual autobiographical memories in older adult immigrants: A test of cognitive explanations of the reminiscence bump and the linguistic encoding of memories. *Journal of Memory and Language, 39,* 1–21.

Schreiber, T. A., & Nelson, D. L. (1998). The relation between feelings of knowing and the number of neighboring concepts linked to the test cue. *Memory and Cognition, 26,* 869–883.

Schuman, H., Steeh, C., & Bobo, L. (1997). *Racial attitudes in America: Trends and interpretations.* Cambridge, MA: Harvard University Press.

Schwartz, B. L., Benjamin, A. S., & Bjork, R. A. (1997). The inferential and experiential bases of metamemory. *Current Directions in Psychological Science, 6,* 132–137.

Searle, J. (1984). *Minds, brains, and science.* Cambridge, MA: Harvard University Press.

Searle, J. R. (1969). *Speech acts.* Cambridge: Cambridge University Press.

Searle, J. R. (1975). Indirect speech acts. In P. Cole & J. L. Morgan (Eds.), *Syntax and semantics* (Vol. 3). New York: Seminar Press.

Seibert, P. S., & Ellis, H. C. (1991). Irrelevant thoughts, emotional mood states and cognitive task performances. *Memory and Cognition, 19,* 507–513.

Selfridge, O. G. (1959). Pandemonium: A paradigm for learning. In *The mechanization of thought processes.* London: H. M. Stationery Office.

Shallice, T., & Warrington, E. K. (1970). Independent functioning of verbal memory stores: A neuropsychological study. *Quarterly Journal of Experimental Psychology, 22,* 261–273.

Shaw, J. S., Bjork, R. A., & Handal, A. (1995) Retrieval induced forgetting in an eyewitness-memory paradigm. *Psychonomic Bulletin & Review, 2,* 249–253.

Shepard, R. N., & Metzler, J. (1971). Mental rotation of three-dimensional objects. *Science, 171,* 701–703.

Shiffrin, R. M., & Schneider, W. (1977). Controlled and automatic human information processing: 2. Perceptual learning, automatic attending, and a general theory. *Psychological Review, 84,* 127–190.

Shimamura, A. P. (1989). Disorders of memory: The cognitive science perspective. I. F. Boller & J. Grafman (Eds.), *Handbook of neuropsychology.* Amsterdam: Elsevier Press.

Shimamura, A. P., & Squire, L. R. (1986). Memory and metamemory: A study of the feeling-of-knowing phenomenon in amnesic patients. *Journal of Experimental Psychology: Learning, Memory, and Cognition, 12,* 452–460.

Shimamura, A. P., & Squire, L. R. (1989). Impaired priming of new associations in amnesia. *Journal of Experimental Psychology: Learning, Memory and Cognition, 15,* 721–728.

Simon, H. A. (1957). *Models of man.* New York: Wiley.

Simon, H. A. (1973). The structure of ill-structured problems. *Artificial Intelligence, 4,* 181–201.

Simon, H. A. (1978). Information-processing theory of human problem solving. In W. K. Estes (Ed.), *Handbook of learning and cognitive processes.* Hillsdale, NJ: Lawrence Erlbaum Associates.

Simon, H. A., & Kotovsky, K. (1963). Human acquisition of concepts for sequential patterns. *Psychological Review, 70,* 534–546.

Slamecka, N. J. (1985). Ebbinghaus: Some associations. *Journal of Experimental Psychology: Learning, Memory, and Cognition, 11,* 414–435.

Slamecka, N. J., & Fevreiski, J. (1983). The generation effect when generation fails. *Journal of Verbal Learning and Verbal Behavior, 22,* 153–163.

Slamecka, N. J., & Graf, P. (1978). The generation effect: Delineation of a phenomenon. *Journal of Experimental Psychology: Human Learning and Memory, 4,* 592–604.

Slamecka, N. J., & Katsaiti, L. T. (1987). The generation effect as an artifact of selective displaced rehearsal. *Journal of Memory and Language, 26,* 589–607.

Slobin, D. I. (1973). Cognitive prerequisites for the acquisition of grammar. In C. A. Ferguson & D. J. Slobin (Eds.), *Studies of child language development.* New York: Holt.

Sloman, S. A., Hayman, C. A. G., Ohta, N., Law, J., & Tulving, E. (1988). Forgetting in primed fragment completion. *Journal of Experimental Psychology: Learning, Memory, and Cognition, 14,* 223–239.

Smith, E. E., & Jonides, J. (1997). Working memory: A view from neuroimaging. *Cognitive Psychology, 33,* 5–42.

Smith, E. E., & Jonides, J. (1999). Storage and executive processes in the frontal lobes. *Science, 283,* 1657–1661.

Smith, E. E., Shoben, E. J., & Rips, L. J. (1974). Structure and process in semantic memory: A featural model for semantic decision. *Psychological Review, 81,* 214–241.

Smith, R. E., & Hunt, R. R. (2000). The influence of distinctive processing on retrieval induced forgetting. *Memory & Cognition, 28,* 503–508.

Smith, S. M. (1988). Environmental context-dependent memory. In D. M. Thomson & G. M. Davies (Eds.), *Memory in context: Context in memory.* New York: Wiley.

Solso, R. L. (1991). *Cognitive Psychology,* Boston: Allyn and Bacon.

Son, L. K., & Metcalfe, J. (2000). Metacognitive and control strategies in study-time allocation. *Journal of Experimental Psychology: Learning, Memory, and Cognition., 26,* 1–19.

Sourly, E. (1969). *Philosophy of language.* New York: The Free Press.

Sperling, G. (1960). The information available in brief visual presentations. *Psychological Monographs, 74* (Whole No. 498).

Spilich, G. J., Vesonder, G. T., Chiesi, H. L., & Voss, J. F. (1979). Text processing of domain-related information for individuals with high- and low-domain knowledge. *Journal of Verbal Learning and Verbal Behavior, 18,* 275–290.

Squire, L. R. (1992). Memory and the hippocampus: A synthesis from findings with rats, monkeys, and humans. *Psychological Review, 99,* 195–231.

Squire, L. R., & Kandel, E. R. (1999). *Memory: From mind and molecules.* New York: Scientific American.

Standing, L., Conezio, J., & Haber R. N. (1970). Perception and memory for pictures: Single trial learning of 2560 visual stimuli. *Psychonomic Science, 19,* 73–74.

Ste.-Marie, D. M., & Lee, T. D. (1991). Prior processing effects on gymnastic judging. *Journal of Experimental Psychology: Learning, Memory, & Cognition, 17,* 126–136.

Ste.-Marie, D. M., & Valiquette, S. M. (1996). Enduring memory-influenced biases in gymnastic judging. *Journal of Experimental Psychology: Learning, Memory, & Cognition, 22,* 1498–1502.

Stein, B. S. (1978). Depth of processing reexamined: The effects of the precision of encoding and test appropriateness. *Journal of Verbal Learning and Verbal Behavior, 17,* 165–174.

Stein, B. S., & Bransford, J. D. (1979). Constraints on effective elaboration: Effects of precision and subject generation. *Journal of Verbal Learning and Verbal Behavior, 18,* 769–777.

Sternberg, S. (1966). High-speed scanning in human memory. *Science, 153,* 652–654.

Strayer, D. L., & Johnston, W. A. (2001). Driven to distraction: Dual-task studies of simulated driving and conversing on a cellular phone. *Psychonomic Science, 12,* 462–466.

Stock, W. A., Kulhavy, R. W., Pridemore, D. R., & Krug, D. (1992). Responding to feedback after multiple choice answers: The influence of response confidence. *Quarterly Journal of Experimental Psychology: Human Experimental Psychology, 45A,* 649–667.

Sulin, R. A., & Dooling, D. J. (1974). Intrusions of a thematic idea in retention of prose. *Journal of Experimental Psychology, 103,* 255–262.

Swanson, H. L. (1984). Effects of cognitive effort and word distinctiveness on learning disabled and nondisabled reader's recall. *Journal of Educational Psychology, 76,* 894–908.

Tabossi, P., & Zardon, F. (1993). Processing ambiguous words in context. *Journal of Memory and Language, 32,* 359–372.

Tartter, V. C. (1987). *Language processes.* New York: Holt, Rinehart & Winston.

Teasdale, J. D. (1983). Negative thinking in depression: Cause, effect, or reciprocal relationship? *Advances in Behavioral Research and Therapy, 5,* 3–25.

Terrace, H. S. (1979). How Nim Chimpsky changed my mind. *Psychology Today,* November, 1979.

Terrace, H. S., Pettito, L. A., & Bever, T. G. (1976). *Project Nim: Progress Report I.* New York: Columbia University Press.

Thiede, K. W. (1999). The importance of monitoring and self-regulation during multi-trial learning. *Psychonomic Bulletin & Review, 6,* 662–667.

Thiede, K. W., & Dunlosky, J. (1999). Toward a general model of self-regulated study: An analysis of selection items for study and self-paced study time. *Journal of Experimental Psychology: Learning, Memory, and Cognition, 25,* 1024–1037.

Till, R. E., Mross, E. F., & Kintsch, W. (1988). Time course of priming for associate and inference words in a discourse context. *Memory & Cognition, 16,* 283–298.

Torrance, E. P. (1968). Examples and rationales of test tasks for assessing creative abilities. *Journal of Creative Behavior, 2* (3).

Tranel, E., & Damasio, A. R. (1985). Knowledge without awareness: An autonomic index of facial recognition by prosopagnosics. *Science,* 228, 1453–1454.

Treisman, A. M. (1960). Contextual cues in selective listening. *Quarterly Journal of Experimental Psychology, 12,* 242–248.

Treisman, A. M. (1964). Selective attention in man. *British Medical Bulletin, 20,* 12–16.

Treisman, A. M., & Geffen, G. (1967). Selective attention: Perception or response? *Quarterly Journal of Experimental Psychology, 19,* 1–17.

Treisman, A. (1996). The binding problem. *Current Opinion in Neurobiology, 6,* 171–178.

Treisman, A., & Gelade, G. (1980). A feature integration theory of attention. *Cognitive Psychology, 12,* 97–136.

Treisman, A., & Gormican, S. (1988). Feature analysis in early vision: Evidence from search asymmetries. *Psychological Review, 95,* 15–48.

Treisman, A., & Sato, S. (1990). Conjunction search revisited. *Journal of Experimental Psychology: Human Perception and Performance, 16,* 459–478.

Trueswell, J. C. (1996). The role of lexical frequency in syntactic ambiguity resolution. *Journal of Memory and Language, 35,* 566–585.

Tulving, E. (1962). Subjective organization in free recall of "unrelated" words. *Psychological Review, 69,* 344–354.

Tulving, E. (1972). Episodic and semantic memory. In E. Tulving & W. Donaldson (Eds.), *Organization of memory.* New York: Academic Press.

Tulving, E. (1974). Cue-dependent forgetting. *American Scientist, 62,* 74–82.

Tulving, E. (1983). *Elements of episodic memory.* New York: Oxford University Press.

Tulving, E. (1985). Memory and consciousness. *Canadian Psychology, 26,* 1–12.

Tulving, E. (1986). What kind of hypothesis is the distinction between episodic and semantic memory? *Journal of Experimental Psychology: Learning, Memory, and Cognition, 12,* 307–311.

Tulving, E., & Psotka, J. (1971). Retroactive inhibition in free recall: Inaccessibility of information available in the memory store. *Journal of Experimental Psychology, 87,* 1–8.

Tulving, E., Schacter, D. L., & Stark, H. A. (1982). Priming effects in word fragment completion are independent of recognition memory. *Journal of Experimental Psychology: Learning, Memory, and Cognition, 8,* 336–342.

Tulving, E., & Thomson, D. M. (1971). Retrieval processes in recognition memory: Effects of associative context. *Journal of Experimental Psychology, 87,* 116–124.

Tulving, E., & Thomson, D. M. (1973). Encoding specificity and retrieval processes in episodic memory. *Psychological Review, 80,* 352–373.

Turner, M. L., & Engle, R. W. (1989). Is working memory capacity task dependent? *Journal of Memory and Language, 28,* 127–154.

Turner, M. L., LaPointe, L. B., Cantor, J., Reeves, C. H., Griffeth, R. H., & Engle, R. W. (1987). Recency and suffix effects found with auditory presentation and with mouthed visual presentation: They're not the same thing. *Journal of Memory and Language, 26,* 138–164.

Tversky, A., & Kahneman, D. (1973). Availability: A heuristic for judging frequency and probability. *Cognitive Psychology, 5,* 207–232.

Tyler, L. K., & Marslen-Wilson, W. (1986). The effects of context on the recognition of polymorphemic words. *Journal of Memory and Language, 25,* 741–752.

Tyler, S. W., Hertel, P. T., McCallum, M. C., & Ellis, H. C. (1979). Cognitive effort and memory. *Journal of Experimental Psychology: Human Learning and Memory, 5,* 607–617.

Underwood, B. J. (1965). False recognition produced by implicit verbal responses. *Journal of Experimental Psychology, 70,* 122–129.

Ungerleider, L. G. (1995). Functional brain imaging studies of cortical mechanisms of memory. *Science, 270,* 760–775.

Ungerleider, L. G., & Haxby, J. V. (1994). Network analysis of cortical visual pathways mapped with PET. *Journal of Neuroscience, 14,* 655–666.

Vallar, G., & Baddeley, A. D. (1984). Fractionations of working memory: Neuropsychological evidence for a phonological short-term store. *Journal of Verbal Learning and Verbal Behavior, 23,* 151–161.

van Dijk, T. A., & Kintsch, W. (1983). *Strategies of discourse comprehension.* New York: Academic Press.

Varner, J. L., & Ellis, H. C. (1998). Cognitive activity and physiological arousal: Processes that mediate mood-congruent memory. *Memory & Cognition, 26,* 939–950.

Velten, E. (1968). A laboratory task for induction of mood states. *Behavior Research and Therapy, 6,* 473–482.

Vogel, E. K., Luck, S. J., & Shapiro, K. L. (1998). Electrophysiological evidence for a postperceptual locus of suppression during the attentional blink. *Journal of Experimental Psychology: Human Perception and Performance, 24,* 1656–1674.

von Restorff, H. (1933). Uber die Wirkung von Bereichsbildungen im Spurnenfeld [On the influence of the segregation in the trace field]. *Psychologische Forschung, 18,* 299–342.

von Wright, J. M. (1968). Selection in visual immediate memory. *Quarterly Journal of Experimental Psychology, 20,* 62–68.

Viney, W. (1993). *A history of psychology: Ideas and context.* Needham Heights, MA: Allyn and Bacon.

Vu, H., Kellas, G., & Paul, S. T. (1998). Sources of sentence constraint on lexical ambiguity resolution. *Memory & Cognition, 26,* 979–1001.

Wagenaar, W. A. (1986). My memory : A study of autobiographical memory over six years. *Cognitive Psychology, 18,* 225–252.

Wallace, W. T., & Rubin, D. C. (1988). Memory of a ballad singer. In M. M. Grunesberg, P. E. Morris, & R. E. Sykes (Eds.), *Practical aspects of memory: Current research and issues: Vol 1. Memory in everyday life* (pp. 257–262). New York: Wiley.

Warren, R. M., & Obusek, C. J. (1971). Speech perception and phonemic restorations. *Perception and Psychophysics, 9* (3B), 358–362.

Warrington, E. K., Logue, V., & Pratt, R. T. C. (1971). The anatomical localization of selective impairment of auditory verbal short-term memory. *Neuropsychologia, 9,* 377–387.

Warrington, E. K., & Shallice, T. (1984). Category specific semantic impairments. *Brain, 107,* 829–854.

Warrington, E. K., & Weiskrantz, L. (1968). New method of testing long-term retention with special reference to amnesic patients. *Nature, 217,* 972–974.

Wason, P. C., & Johnson-Laird, P. N. (1972). *Psychology of reasoning.* Cambridge, MA: Harvard University Press.

Watkins, O. C., & Watkins, M. J. (1980). The modality effect and echoic persistence. *Journal of Experimental Psychology: General, 109,* 251–278.

Watson, J. B. (1919). *Psychology from the standpoint of a behaviorist.* Philadelphia: Lippincott.

Watson, J. B. (1925). *Behaviorism.* New York: Norton.

Weaver, C. A. III. (1990). Constraining factors in calibration of comprehension. *Journal of Experimental Psychology: Learning, Memory, and Cognition, 16,* 214–222.

Weingartner, H., Cohen, R. M., Murphy, D. L., Martello, J., & Gerdt, C. (1981). Cognitive processes in depression. *Archives of General Psychiatry, 38,* 42–47.

Weingartner, H., Miller, H., & Murphy, D. L. (1977). Mood state-dependent retrieval of verbal associations. *Journal of Abnormal Psychology, 86,* 276–284.

Weisberg, R. W. (1986). *Creativity: Genius and other myths.* New York: W. H. Freeman.

Weldon, M. S. (2000). Remembering as a social process. In D. L. Medin (Ed.), *The psychology of learning and motivation* (Vol. 40). San Diego: Academic Press.

Weldon, M. S., & Coyote, K. C. (1996). Failure to find the picture superiority effect in implicit conceptual memory tests. *Journal of Experimental Psychology: Learning, Memory, and Cognition, 22,* 670–686.

Wells, G. L., & Murray, D. M. (1984). Eyewitness confidence. In G. L. Wells & E. F. Loftus (Eds.), *Eyewitness testimony: Psychological perspectives.* New York: Cambridge University Press.

Wertheimer, M. (1959). *Productive thinking.* New York: Harper & Row.

Whorf, B. L. (1956). Science and linguistics. In J. B. Carroll (Ed.), *Language, thought and reality: Selected writings of Benjamin Lee Whorf.* Cambridge, MA: MIT Press.

Wickelgren, W. A. (1974). *How to solve problems.* San Francisco: Freeman Press.

Williams, J. M. G., Mathews, A., & MacLeod, C. (1996). The emotional Stroop task and psychopathology. *Psychological Bulletin, 120,* 3–24.

Williams, J. M. G., Watts, F. N., MacLeod, C., & Mathews, A. (1988). *Cognitive psychology and emotional disorders.* New York: Wiley.

Williams, J. M. G., Watts, F. N., MacLeod, C., & Mathews, A. (1997). *Cognitive psychology and emotional disorders* (2nd ed.). Chichester: John Wiley and Sons.

Wilson, F. A., Scalaidhe, S. P., & Goldman-Rakic, P. S. (1993). Dissociation of object and spatial processing domains in primate prefrontal cortex. *Science, 260,* 1955–1958.

Winne, P. H., & Hadwin, A. F. (1998). Studying as self-regulated learning. In Hacker, D. J., Dunlosky, J., & Graesser, A. C. (Eds.), *Metacognition in educational theory and practice.* Hillsdale, NJ: Lawrence Erlbaum Associates.

Winograd, E., & Killinger, W. A., Jr. (1983). Relating age at encoding in early childhood to adult recall: Development of flashbulb memories. *Journal of Experimental Psychology: General, 112,* 413–422.

Winograd, E., & Neisser, U. (1993). *Affect and accuracy in recall: The case of "flashbulb" memories.* New York: Cambridge University Press.

Wisniewski, E. J. (2002). Concepts and categorization. In D. L. Medin (Ed.), *The Stevens' handbook of experimental psychology.* New York: John Wiley and Sons.

Young, R. K. (1959). A comparison of two methods of learning serial associations. *American Journal of Psychology, 72,* 554–559.

Young, R. K. (1961). Paired associate learning when the same items occur as stimuli and responses. *Journal of Experimental Psycholgy, 61,* 315–318.

Zadah, L. A., Fu, K. S., Tanaka, K., & Shimura, M. (1975). *Fuzzy sets and their applications to cognitive and decision processes.* New York: Academic Press.

Zajonc, R. B. (1984). On the primacy of affect. American-Psychologist, 39, 117–123.

Zarogoza, M. S., McCloskey, M., & Jamis, M. (1987). Misleading postevent information and recall of the original event: Further evidence against the memory impairment hypothesis. *Journal of Experimental Psychology: Learning, Memory, and Cognition, 13,* 36–44.

Zaragoza, M. S., & Mitchell, K. J. (1996). Repeated exposure to suggestion and the creation of false memories. *Psychological Science, 7,* 294–300.

Zimmerman, B. J., & Schunk, D. H. (2001). *Self-regulated learning and academic achievement* (2nd ed.). Hillsdale, NJ: Lawrence Erlbaum Associates.

Zwaan, R. A., & Radvansky, G. A. (1998). Situation models in language comprehension and memory. *Psychological Bulletin, 123,* 162–185.

NAME INDEX

SUBJECT INDEX